Few army officers of King Charles I shone as bright as George Lisle during the English Civil Wars, yet have drawn so little attention from subsequent historians. Born in London in 1615, Lisle's father was a well-connected publisher and monopolist, and his mother a kinswoman of the Duke of Buckingham. Raised in the City of Westminster in a landscape of court intrigue, royal favouritism and ill-advised royal financial experiments, Lisle took to soldiering and was commissioned as a lieutenant colonel at the outbreak of war in 1642. He fought at Edgehill; then at Chalgrove and the First Battle of Newbury in 1643 – latterly where his courage in leading a forlorn hope against a wall of musketeers and artillery first drew him to public attention.

Commissioned shortly afterwards as a full colonel, in 1644 he took charge of a veteran regiment and was noticed again for his diligence and efficiency at the Battle of Cheriton, despite the battle being lost. Weeks later, he was promoted to tercio command and accompanied Charles on his critical 'night march' from Oxford. At the Second Battle of Newbury in October, to prevent his position being overwhelmed, he famously tore off his coat and led three charges in his shirt-sleeves – driving off the enemy and preventing disaster.

Reputedly refusing a knighthood, he wintered as a garrison commander before leading the principal assault on the city of Leicester in May 1645 and then being badly wounded at Naseby. Knighted in December, he remained at Oxford until its surrender in June 1646 – returning to London in 1647. In 1648, he took up arms again during the Kent rebellion before enduring a three-month siege inside the town of Colchester. Infamously (and controversially), he was executed after the starving town surrendered – and this catapulted him to the status of 'Royalist martyr'.

In this first ever biography of Lisle, the author has scoured dozens of primary sources for fragmentary references – painstakingly piecing together his personal background and re-examining every known detail of his career. The accuracy of existing stories and long-held assumptions about him is investigated minutely, and the first well-informed assessments made of his character and motives. Finally, the persistent memory of his execution is traced forwards through later writers and painters into the 20th century to complete the first cohesive picture of one of King Charles' most loyal, effective and respected military officers.

Serena Jones spent many years as an English Civil War re-enactor before earning a BA Honours in History as a mature student, and then starting her own publishing company to make primary 17th century texts available for modern researchers.

She is currently transcribing and annotating the Civil War newsbooks, and researching the lesser-known officers of Charles I's 'Oxford Army'. *No Armour But Courage* is the first of her works to be published outside her own company.

No Armour But Courage

Colonel Sir George Lisle, 1615-1648

Serena Jones

 **Helion & Company Limited**

Helion & Company Limited
26 Willow Road
Solihull
West Midlands
B91 1UE
England
Tel. 0121 705 3393
Fax 0121 711 4075
Email: info@helion.co.uk
Website: www.helion.co.uk
Twitter: @helionbooks
Visit our blog at http://blog.helion.co.uk/

Published by Helion & Company 2016
Designed and typeset by Mach 3 Solutions Ltd (www.mach3solutions.co.uk)
Cover designed by Paul Hewitt, Battlefield Design (www.battlefield-design.co.uk)
Printed by Short Run Press Ltd, Exeter, Devon

Text © Serena Jones 2016
Images © as individually credited
Maps drawn by George Anderson © Helion & Company 2016

Cover: George Lisle, leading his tercio at a critical moment in the fight for Shaw House, at the Second Battle of Newbury on 27th October 1644. In the dusk of the autumn day, Lisle is said to have removed his doublet to let his soldiers see him in his shirt. In 1648 the newsletter *The Kingdomes Weekly Intelligencer* notes that Lisle was "the same Gentleman, who the more to encourage his men, did lay by his Armes, and fling off his doublet, and in his shirt did bring up his Regiment …" An eyewitness to the event, *Mercurius Aulicus*, commented on the action "In which service the Colonell had no Armour on, besides courage and a good cause, and a good Holland shirt; for as he seldome wears defensive Armes, so now he put off his very Buffe Doublet, perhaps to animate his men …" Painting by Peter Dennis © Helion & Company 2016.

ISBN 978-1-911096-47-4

British Library Cataloguing-in-Publication Data.
A catalogue record for this book is available from the British Library.

For details of other military history titles published by Helion & Company Limited, contact the above address, or visit our website: http://www.helion.co.uk

We always welcome receiving book proposals from prospective authors.

For Laurence, Dorothy, George, Francis and Mary

and

My ancestor, Major Henry Leigh of Thelwall's regiment, Lisle's tercio, who saw it all unfold.

Contents

Appendices

List of Illustrations

List of Maps

Abbreviations

BL   British Library
CCC   Calendar of the Committee for Compounding
CSP   Calendar of State Papers
CTB   Calendar of Treasury Books
EHR   English Historical Review
ODNB   Oxford Dictionary of National Biography
HMC   Historical Manuscripts Commission
JHC   Journal of the House of Commons
JHL   Journal of the House of Lords
NA   National Archives, Kew
ROP   Royalist Ordnance Papers (ed. Ian Roy)
STC   (Pollard & Redgrave's) Short Title Catalogue
TT   Thomason Tracts (at the British Library)
WSL   William Salt Library, Stafford
'Wing'   Donald Wing's continuation of the Short Title Catalogue

Preface

> ... he gave the rebels three most gallant charges ... in which service the colonel had no armour on besides courage, and a good cause, and a good holland shirt ...
>
> *Mercurius Aulicus*, 28th October 1644

This book has been a very long time in the writing, not least because many aspects of George Lisle's life remain uncertain, and the pieces of the puzzle have taken a long time to fall into place. The research is now substantial enough to publish coherently, but gaps still exist. Frustratingly some sources remain unavailable or unseen and some potential research avenues unexplored, and it is my intent to produce an updated edition of the book if enough new material subsequently comes to light.

My aim is to offer the first explicit survey of what we know, and what we do not know, about Colonel Lisle. Popular history is usually content to condense it down to 'Son of a lowly bookseller, fought in Holland, took off his buffcoat at Newbury, and was shot at Colchester after some famous last words.' Only a very few people have troubled to question if Lisle's father was indeed a lowly bookseller, if Lisle did actually fight in Holland, why he took off his buffcoat at Newbury, and what he really said just before his death. People with a little more knowledge of the Civil Wars might add that 'He turned down a knighthood in 1644'; or, 'He fought at Cropredy and Naseby'. Yet even these statements are frustratingly vague. Noone has questioned *why* he (reportedly) turned down a knighthood, or explicitly what his role was at Cropredy and Naseby. Detailed source study reveals that at several actions he was indeed present with the army but cannot have been much involved; conversely, during at least one other engagement his role appears to have been far greater than anyone has previously realised.

Some 'facts' perpetuated about Lisle seem to be spurious hearsay from curious and well-intentioned, but never source-oriented, early commentators. Some nineteenth-century writers in particular were more interested in heroic narrative than strict factual detail, freely blending fact with supposition and giving source references intermittently or not at all. Their shaky biographies have then become accepted as fact when re-hashed by later writers who borrowed the story but did not care to verify the details first. Lisle's story has not escaped this. With twenty-first century communications at my disposal, and increasingly easy access to source material that was previously buried, I have gone back to the start and scoured primary sources for the facts. The book that follows is grounded on these, using later sources only to help analysis; hence the copious notes, included to allow readers to follow my trail, and perhaps pursue loose ends themselves. Where the facts have provided a narrative I have painted the resulting picture as coherently as they allow; where gaps appear or the details are still uncertain, I have drawn attention to this.

Following this process, one thing has become clear: whilst a lot more information has come to light about Lisle's personal background, and some parts of his military itinerary, there is still little direct information available about the character and motivations of the man himself. No diaries exist; no personal letters have come to light other than a few operational ones to Prince Rupert, and the rumoured stack of letters written to Sir Marmaduke Rawdon has not been found. Although Lisle's recorded military activities during the wars, the few words we have of his, and those offered about him by his contemporaries, help draw a good outline of his character and disposition, this is no better portrait than a blurry snapshot taken at a distance. With the information presently at my disposal I can only take what can be gleaned or surmised from those words and actions, and offer my own initial conclusions as to his character and motives.

It is not my purpose here to include wider analysis of the Wars of the Three Kingdoms or of the English Civil War(s) in particular, only to discuss Lisle's place in them and to examine him within his immediate context. Therefore I have made little reference to certain military aspects of the wars, for example the Northern, Welsh, Scottish, and Irish theatres, as he was never there; and I have avoided wading into Parliamentarian politics, or into the vexed question of religion, unless absolutely necessary. Occasionally evidence for Lisle's activities is scarce: where this occurs, for example in the Cornish campaign in 1644, or the period between the battle of Naseby and Oxford's surrender in 1645-1646, I have bridged the gap by continuing with a summary of the action around him, advancing my own suggestions as to what he may have been doing meanwhile. Whilst this approach may be criticised as potentially giving more history of the war than a history of Lisle, it continues the timeline and keeps his context intact, and helps winnow out the places he could *not* have been, and the actions in which he could *not* have participated: allowing for the better focus of future research.

I have assumed that the reader already has a basic knowledge of the period 1638-48, or has access to essential sources. Where it is necessary to discuss or outline battles and campaigns I have accounted for modern analyses but primarily made use of original sources in order to assess with a fresh eye what Lisle's part may have been. I am not by trade a military historian, and have not sought to reassess accepted battle narratives, except where Lisle's part in them raises an unexpected issue. It is difficult, perhaps impossible, to be expert in the fine details of all the campaigns and engagements in which he was involved, and whilst I have used every source available to me, questioned other writers and historians for their views and strived for accuracy of detail I ask allowance for any errors or misunderstandings of mine that may, nevertheless, have crept into the text. Where my interpretations deliberately differ from others, however, or where I challenge sacred cows, I respectfully ask the reader to give due consideration.

For completeness, and because it is indivisible from Lisle's story, I have included a chapter on the early history of Colonel Richard Bolle's regiment, up to and including the skirmish at Alton in December 1643 where Bolle was killed, leaving the gap in command into which Lisle was placed by some high-level order from Oxford. Thereafter, what we know of them is bound up with him.

If an individual is ennobled or retitled during the course of the book, I have noted this but continued to use the names or titles under which they were originally introduced to the reader. This is against convention, but prevents confusion.

I frequently use the term 'kinsman', in relation to other officers around Lisle: I use it in its loosest sense, meaning someone who is to some degree a relative, being connected via extended family. In Lisle's case, all these connections came via the Villiers family. George Lisle's character and early life would have been heavily shaped by his family ties, and the commercial and court-related activities of his father, Laurence: hence the inclusion of Part I, *A Bookseller's Tale*. I urge readers not to skip this section of the book, as besides offering insights into his son's upbringing, Laurence's activities in publishing, court politics and governmental administration, and his family's suffering during the Civil Wars, collided head-on with some of the most notable persons and events in the first half of the seventeenth century. His story is an incredible tale in itself.

My list of acknowledgements is rather long, but having begun the book over a decade ago, the assistance I have received has been considerable. Firstly I must mention the support and enthusiasm of the Freemasons at the former St Giles's Church in Colchester, where Sir George Lisle is interred. Of fellow researchers, I owe a great debt to Tony Rowland: for sharing his own initial summary of Lisle's career, which provided the inspiration for the biography proper, and for continuing to locate references and discuss possible scenarios long after I had taken up the challenge of writing a full biography myself. I must also thank David Hopkins, for relentlessly harvesting Lisle references on my behalf whilst conducting his own research. Andy Robertshaw generously gave his time to discuss the potential links between Lisle and Sir Marmaduke Rawdon, and Richard Dace pointed me towards Rawdon's family documents in Hertfordshire. Vic Judge sent me many snippets of military detail discovered during his exhaustive compilation of a new Royalist officer list, and Ivor Carr provided me with invaluable new information about the Dudley Castle skirmish of 1644. Stephen Ede-Borrett sent me copies of his own published research articles that I was unable to locate otherwise, and Gary Ashby provided details from a vital Edgehill account that I was hitherto unaware of. Jon Day, author of *Gloucester & Newbury 1643*, kindly shared his conclusions regarding the question of Lisle's participation at Aldbourne Chase, for which I am extremely grateful. Similarly, Chris Scott, author of *The Battles of Newbury*, offered his insights into the possible defences at Shaw House. David Appleby, author of *Our Fall Our Fame*, kindly answered my many questions about Sir Charles Lucas. Ian Dicker, Sue Sampson and Caroline Vincent gave me the benefit of their expertise in period clothing, to date one of the several portraits of Lisle. The use of Chris Jones's extensive library of ECW reference books, long before I had my own, was also a godsend during the early years of my research. Over the years a great many other people in the military reenactment and historical research communities have contributed research leads here and there, whose names time and lack of a notebook at the vital moment have unfortunately obscured; I put on record here also, my gratitude to all those individuals.

Finally I must acknowledge the assistance of the staff of the National Archives, the British Library, the Guildhall Library, and the William Salt Library; Berkshire, Staffordshire, and Worcester record offices; Sotheby's, and the Heinz Archive & Library at the National Portrait Gallery; Madresfield Court, Castle Howard, and Shaw House; Stephen Yates at Colchester and Ipswich Museum Service, and curator Annie Kemkaran-Smith at Leeds Castle. Also everyone at Helion & Company for their support, and their assistance in getting the book ready for publication.

Dates correspond to our modern calendar, the year beginning on January 1st, although where any doubt may exist I have dated events with both years, e.g. '1644/45', to indicate which winter they span.

Serena Jones, 2016

Part I

Laurence Lisle: A Bookseller's Tale

1

Opportunities

By the early 1600s St Paul's Cathedral – *Paul's*, as the locals knew it – had long since fallen into disrepair; but the great square tower still looked out across the City of London, and beyond to the buildings of Whitehall and Westminster, the seat of monarchy and government. To the literate, London had become synonymous with printed works of every sort, and in the confined space within its city walls Church and commerce were forced into coexistence. The north-eastern perimeter of St Paul's Churchyard was tightly lined with bookshops; a number of premises, including two binderies, were built against the walls of the cathedral itself. The open area in between was a traditional meeting place for Londoners, and contained the famous Paul's Cross, an open-air pulpit.

One of the bookshops crammed against the Churchyard wall was a four-storey building comprising both bookshop and living quarters, known as the *Black Bear*. In 1599 it gained a new occupant: a young Londoner, an apprentice stationer (bookseller) in his early or mid-teens by the name of Laurence Lisle. Probably born around 1583, he was the son of William Lyle, a Paddington yeoman;[1] a Restoration source links him with the well-to-do Surrey Lisleys from Tandridge, who held land in Cambridgeshire and whose members included William, the notable Anglo-Saxon scholar, and his younger brother Edmund,[2] a sewer (server) of the chamber first to Queen Elizabeth and then to King James. The Lord Chamberlain's Accounts of 1604 mention amongst the Royal Household staff not only Edmund, but also a William Lisley (one of the 'Gromes carriage men and muliters'), and Lawrence Lisley (a groom of the Pitcher House).[3] The latter would appear to be 'our' Laurence, yet by this time he was a stationer's apprentice, bound to Paul

---

1   The minimum age at which a man could gain the freedom of the City was twenty-four. Laurence gained his freedom in 1607, so his birth date may be estimated at 1583 at the earliest. It is also the Stationers' Company records that tell us his father's name and status.

2   Heath, p.136. Heath states that George – and thus by blood relationship, Laurence – was 'extracted from a Gentile [Gentle] Family in Surrey'. The Lisleys of Tandridge are the only known candidates.

3   Malone Society Collections, II.3, 322-3. The names are mentioned in a list of household staff to be given four yards of scarlet cloth for a coat, for the occasion of the entrance of James I into London.

Linley at the *Black Bear*.[4] It is not clear how an apprentice might also have held an active position in the Royal Household in 1604; perhaps the 1604 man was not the Laurence in question, but then the London civic and church records would be expected to provide details for two separate men, and they offer nothing besides a few references to a man from Kingston upon Thames with a similar name who died in 1612.[5] Furthermore, the listing of our Laurence beside Edmund Lisley from the Surrey family to whom George (and thus his father) was said to be related, is unlikely to be coincidence. The most practical explanation is that the Pitcher House office was a favour wrangled by Edmund or William for their young relative, so he could be part of the procession which greeted the new King's entrance into the City. It stood Laurence in good stead: in the 1630s he seems to have been working for or alongside the Board of Green Cloth in the Lord Steward's department, the same section of the Household as in 1604.

Not two miles from the Churchyard, at Whitehall, the court was ever turbulent but rarely more so than towards the end of Queen Elizabeth's reign. During the mid-1590s a power struggle had developed between Robert Cecil, Lord Burghley's son, and Robert Devereux, the second Earl of Essex. Devereux felt constantly frustrated by his rival's successes at court. In 1599, briefly forgetting his wits after his own failure to crush a rebellion in Ireland, he unthinkingly burst into the Queen's bedchamber unannounced. He was arrested and banished from the court. In 1601 he raised a short-lived rebellion of his own and was promptly executed, leaving a ten-year-old son, also named Robert, now shorn of titles and inheritance through his father's treason. The widowed Lady Essex struggled to raise Robert and his siblings and the boy grew up reserved and emotionally unresponsive, recently being described as 'a morose and incommunicative adult'.[6] He would later oppose his sovereign and help lead his country into civil war, facing Laurence Lisle's son on the battlefield; in the meantime his own family fortunes would become entwined with those of Laurence himself.

But although civil war was several decades away, already the old order was dissolving. On 24th March 1603 the aged Queen Elizabeth died, and was succeeded by her cousin James VI of Scotland, now also James I of England. James made genuine conciliatory efforts towards the young Robert Devereux, and quickly restored his lands and titles. By November 1605 Robert Cecil, doubtless mindful of useful political connections, had helped arrange the marriage of young Devereux to Frances Howard, the daughter of his (Cecil's) closest ally.

---

4   Mini biographies of Paul Linley and Laurence Lisle can be found in McKerrow. Linley died in March 1600 and Laurence's apprenticeship was transferred to his partner, John Flasket.

5   A gentleman named Laurence Lyndley/Lynlay, who confusingly also appears to have had a position in one of the Royal Households, last being recorded there in 1611.

6   Somerset, p.37. This book describes with great clarity the events leading up to, and culminating in the infamous murder of Sir Thomas Overbury in 1613, and offers a valuable grounding in the earliest workings of King James's court.

Meanwhile, beyond the self-interested confines of the court, events had taken a sinister turn. The Gunpowder Plot had been discovered in the early hours of 5th November and late in January 1606, a few weeks after the Devereux/Howard marriage, four of the Gunpowder Plotters were hung, drawn and quartered on a scaffold in Paul's Churchyard. As Laurence lived there, undoubtedly he would have witnessed the grisly event; perhaps his employers caught the popular mood and offered publications of suitable interest for the crowds. Certainly another business in the Churchyard may have capitalised on the fiercely anti-Catholic atmosphere: the *Tygers Head,* a tiny shop built against the wall of the cathedral's north transept, had been founded in the 1560s, originally selling Bibles. In the 1580s it was taken over by Toby Cooke, and in 1606 his son Matthew was co-proprietor with a bookseller named Samuel Macham. The business was highly successful, and Macham held the rights to the popular works of Joseph Hall, the Bishop of Norwich.

On 19th January 1607, a year after the executions, Laurence's apprenticeship at the *Black Bear* concluded. He was granted his freedom, and admitted to the Honourable Company of Stationers.[7] Yet traditionally the career path ahead was still difficult: he could be expected to spend the next eight to twelve years working as a 'journeyman' until he had saved enough money to start a business of his own. He may have stayed on briefly at the *Black Bear*; possibly he was unemployed. But whatever his new routine, City gossip – and possibly his own connections at court – may have made Laurence aware of the King's strong interest in a junior member of his household, who had broken his leg during a Royal pageant. By all accounts King James had forgotten the rest of the pageant in his concern for the young Scot, one Robert Carr.[8] The gossip may have taken a seedier turn as people reminded each other of the King's rumoured preference for the company of young men, and that Robert Carr was already a Groom of the Bedchamber.

James's infatuations did not prevent him regularly addressing Parliament. The latest political hot potato concerned his long-cherished vision of complete union between Scotland and England, to be known as 'Great Britain'. The Scots were more-or-less considered a different race, and the bi-national make-up of the King's household had already caused much faction within it. His Majesty's desire for the union of his two kingdoms was strongly opposed by the Commons, who feared it would result in the Scots pouring into England and securing all the Royal patronage for themselves.[9] James also desired free trade between the countries, but

---

7   Arber, ii.241, and iii.683.
8   The proper spelling was Kerr, but – apparently to ease Anglo-Scottish relations – he had taken to using the English version.
9   Smith, p.105.

the London merchants perceived that the Scots would take every benefit from it, then avoid paying their taxes.[10]

But whilst England's future was unclear, the future of one of its citizens was about to be secured, albeit due to another man's tragedy. In June 1607 Matthew Cooke died; he left a widow and young daughter,[11] and his partnership with Macham was only two years old. Both these details imply that he was still a young man. Early death was a commonplace, but this fact would not have lessened the impact of his demise, either on his family or his business partner. Macham moved into smaller premises next door, a shop named the *Bull Head*, and was publishing prolifically on his own account before the summer was out. He took his new apprentice with him, leaving Henry Seile, Matthew's new thirteen-year-old apprentice, at the *Tygers Head*.[12] Naturally it was Matthew's widow who came off worst materially, left with at least one young child and no immediate financial support besides what she may have been left by her husband. Yet she still had the shop itself, or the lease of it, and its established reputation; and stationers' widows could certainly continue in their late husband's business. Indeed, when Macham himself died in 1615 his wife continued to reprint his major titles for another five years.

The Stationers' Company was not blind to Joan's plight. On 5th October they judged:

> … that shee shall have [half] of the booke wch Sam: Macham hathe prynted, shee payinge halfe the Charge of the ympression. And likewyse that shee shall have halfe of the Booke wch is in hand to prynte shee bear- inge halfe the Charge of the ympression. And like[wise] for all the reste of the Copies that were entred to were entred to him and her husband that shee shall have the halfe of everye ympression [hereafter] bearinge halfe the Charge thereof.[13]

Macham and Cooke had jointly registered the copyrights on several books; Joan was now entitled to Matthew's half share of those particular books each time a new edition was printed, as long as she paid her half of the printing costs. But there was another proviso: in the same judgement, the Company decided that:

> … yf she Marrye in the Companye then here intereste to contynue still accordinge to like proporcon in all the said booke, but yf shee Marrye out

---

10 Fraser, p.114.
11 Matthew's burial is recorded on 19th June, in the parish registers of St. Gregory by St Paul. His daughter Margerie had been baptised on 8th Feb 1606.
12 McKenzie (p.58) states that Henry Seile, son of Humfrey, came from Oslaston in Derby and was bound to Matthew Cooke on 3rd April 1607. He was baptised at Sutton on the Hill on 2nd February 1594.
13 Jackson, pp.27-28.

of the Companye then her said intereste to Cease. And he from thence-
forth to enjoy all the said Copies to his own use.

It is likely that Joan and Laurence were already acquainted when Matthew died, given that they lived in the same tiny community around St Paul's. We cannot know what they thought of each other, but after Matthew's death each was faced with a situation that the other could redress. Aged twenty-four or thereabouts, Laurence needed a head start in his trade, or face a long slog to make his living in an age where a man's life-expectancy at birth averaged just twenty-nine;[14] and Joan needed a breadwinner, preferably someone in the same trade as her late husband. They were married at St. Gregory's on 14th December. From our modern stand-point it is difficult not to raise an eyebrow at such an arrangement; however, in an age where many marriages were thus organised, usually by the parents of young adults, the Company's requirement may not have seemed unreasonable. Besides, Joan and her family were now provided for, and by default Laurence had acquired an established and successful London business, despite as yet having no copyrights of his own. Other journeymen around St Paul's must have envied his good fortune.

At around the same time, Laurence finally published his first book: *The Wynninges of Worldelinges*.[15] The author's identity is unclear, although possibly it was a forerunner to *A Warning For Worldlings*, 'a short dialogue against atheisme' written by an Oxford student and published by Laurence in 1608.[16] The dedication, to the Lord Chancellor of England, no less, asserted that:

> … it cannot be, that he which is fully perswaded that there is a God who will punish those that do evill, and rewarde those that do well, should be careles how they live … Most necessarie therefore it is, to plant this Doctrine in the hearts of men, that there is a God who as hee made all things, so continually hee governeth all thinges, unto whome all men must give account of their doings.

Back at court, it did not appear that Robert Carr felt bound by the critical eye of God; certainly he found no moral difficulty in material gain, and in December 1607 was granted an annuity of £600 by the King. By Christmas he had been knighted and promoted from mere Groom, to Gentleman of the Bedchamber. He did not advance alone. Aware that his nationality grated on the English courtiers, Carr had been careful to distance himself from his roots and surround himself with English men. By 1608 his closest friend and ally was Thomas Overbury, the

14   Thomas, p.6. In fact, this figure applies to the third quarter of the seventeenth century, i.e. 1650-1675, thus someone born a century earlier – such as Laurence Lisle – might expect even less.
15   Listed by Arber, but otherwise untraceable.
16   Author Jeremy Corderoy.

son of a Gloucestershire lawyer. The pair had met first in Scotland seven or eight years previously, and when James moved his court to England in 1603 Carr and Overbury were reunited. Clearly Carr made many efforts on his friend's behalf: in September 1607 Overbury had received the lease of some property taken from a man attainted for treason, and in June 1608 he, like Carr, was also knighted. Like Edmund Lisley from Surrey, he was also made a sewer to the King.[17] Amidst this advancement, Overbury gave much time to writing. Perhaps by 1608 he had already written *A Wife*, a lengthy poem outlining the nature of man's relationship to woman, and what he considered to be the necessary virtues in a spouse; although as yet it had not been published.

In terms of the volume of material produced, it appears that Laurence's business got off to a good start, publishing at least six works in 1608, including one of Ben Jonson's. In June, a bequest to Joan from Matthew's late mother would have eased finances; and Laurence had been chosen as an executor of the will. In July he registered (well in advance) *A Ravens Almanack – foretelling of a Plague, Famine, and Civille Warre that shall happen this present yeare 1609…* perhaps a prophetic title, given what England was to suffer within thirty years. Officially the work's author was anonymous, although some authorities attributed it to the well-known writer and dramatist, Thomas Dekker. However we cannot be sure that Laurence exercised his right to publish: although the almanac went through three editions, the only copies still extant seem to have been published by another stationer.[18]

On 15th January 1609 the St Gregory's church registers duly noted the baptism of Laurence and Joan's daughter, Elizabeth; Laurence passed the rest of the year quietly, producing nothing until summer the year following, when he published *The Funeral Pompe and Obsequies of … King Henry IV of France*, who had been assassinated in May by a Catholic extremist.[19]

The reason for this sudden slow-down at the *Tygers Head* is a mystery, although Samuel Macham's prolific output at the Bull Head during this period affirms that there was no downturn in the book trade. Given the lack of material produced, we may wonder about Laurence's financial position: at some point during 1610 he would have benefited from Macham's reprint of two Bishop Hall works, originally part-copyrighted by Matthew Cooke; and certainly in May he took advantage of a bequest fund held by the Stationers' Company, and borrowed £10, to be repaid after three years (in fact, it was not repaid for five).[20] However, when considering his sources of income we cannot overlook family connections, and it is more than possible that he was being supported from some closer source of which we are

17   Somerset, p.63.
18   Thomas Archer.
19   Author Claude Morrillon; a translation from French.
20   Ferguson, p.25.

currently unaware. If he was indeed the Laurence Lisley listed at court in 1604, perhaps he yet retained his position there and enjoyed a salary from it.

If Laurence's business was in flux, his domestic situation soon fared worse: Joan died in September, and was buried at St Gregory's on the 30th. New publishing at the *Tygers Head* appears to have ceased completely, although the shop probably remained open to sell existing books. Laurence's subsequent 'none appearance on the qter day' (that is, 25th December) earned him a shilling fine from the Stationers' Company in January 1611;[21] thereafter his activities remain a mystery until April 1613.

Within Whitehall, meanwhile, the seeds of a very different intrigue were being sown.

---

21   Jackson, p.446.

2

Overbury

At the time of their marriage both Robert Devereux and Frances Howard were only fourteen years old: it was yet considered unwise that the couple should live together so early, or consummate the marriage, and for the time being they continued to live separately. Whilst Frances – much admired for her looks – took her place at court, chaperoned by her mother, in the summer of 1607 Essex embarked on a tour of Europe, visiting various countries and being grandly entertained by their leaders.

He returned to England in the summer of 1609. So did Sir Thomas Overbury; although his tour had covered similar territory, it was not an official visit, merely curious tourism which he took as an opportunity to pursue his writing, composing observations about his travels.[1]

He had also cultivated a blatant arrogance that earned him the dislike of many, including Queen Anne, who detested the influence Overbury and Carr exerted over the King. In May 1611 she complained tearfully to James of some unspecified insolence Overbury had shown her in the palace gardens at Greenwich, and succeeded in having him banished from the court. Carr's own influence was still increasing: he had recently been created Viscount Rochester and Knight of the Garter, and it was through his efforts that by September 1611 Overbury was partially restored to favour. By November he was back at court officially, albeit with instructions to avoid the Queen.

In parallel, Essex's fortunes were not bright either: on his return from the Continent it quickly became clear that there were vast differences of character between him and his wife, the situation doubtless worsened by the natural immaturity of their personalities, and the many months of separation which immediately followed the wedding. As their estrangement grew, it became apparent that the couple had never consummated the marriage; the tension was intensified by drifting rumours that Frances had planned to poison her husband, or even that

---

1   *Sir Thomas Overbury his observations in his travailes upon the state of the Xvii. Provinces as they stood anno Dom. 1609.*

she had been involved, in some manner, with Prince Henry, the heir to the throne. The mid-seventeenth century diarist, Sir Simonds D'Ewes, recounted that it was sometime early in 1612 that Frances began an affair with Robert Carr: they met often at the London house of Mrs Anne Turner, a close friend of Frances's. Perhaps Sir Thomas Overbury became jealous of his old friend's new obsession, or perhaps he feared it, owing to his own differences with the Howard family: he frequently begged Carr to end the relationship with Frances, finally telling him that:

> ... he would have no longer entireness [confidence] with him, knowing that his unlawful accompanying with her, being another man's wife, would be the means to ruin him and his fortunes.[2]

Carr was outraged. As his friend confronted him:

> ... [he] fell into hot tremors, telling Sir Thomas Overbury that he could stand on his own legs, and would be even with him; and not long after, revealing Overbury's words to the Countess of Essex, she was much enraged with it, and took up, doubtless thereupon that instant, a resolution of revenge, which should be prosecuted with the loss of his life, that had in such broad terms branded her honour.[3]

Frances's subsequent actions reveal the depth of her fury. Having decided that her lover's friend must be done away with, she first suggested the murder to a male servant of Queen Anne's whom she knew to have a particular quarrel with Sir Thomas; the man agreed that Overbury might be roughed up, but refused to pursue the matter to the death, saying he was '... loath to be carried to Tyburn for any Lady's pleasure.'[4] For the meantime Frances could do nothing.

In November 1612, to the nation's overwhelming sorrow, Prince Henry died from 'the pestilential fever of the season';[5] amidst wild tales of poison, a post-mortem was held, and the cause 'proved to be from the hand of God.'[6] D'Ewes was another to mourn for the Prince, saying in 1639:

> England's joy, that inestimable Prince Henry ... the lamentation made for him was so general that even women and children partook of it.[7]

2   D'Ewes, vol. I, pp.70-71.
3   *Ibid.*, p.71
4   *Ibid.*
5   Sir William Fleetwood to Sir Dudley Carleton,18th December (*CSP Domestic Series,* 1611-1618, p.162). Modern studies of Henry's autopsy notes confirm beyond doubt that the fever was typhoid.
6   Sir Thomas Luke to Sir Dudley Carleton, 12th November (*ibid.*, p.155).
7   D'Ewes, vol. I, p.46.

King James, paranoid as ever, ordered that his surviving son be closely watched. It was reported that:

> Prince Charles [is] kept as strictly as when he was Duke of York, and will not have the reins loose as early as his brother … To keep the Prince from Popery, 'two sober divines, Dr Hacknell and another, are placed with him, and ordered never to leave him.'[8]

Rumoured adultery with Henry aside, there were probably several causes for the failure of Frances Howard's marriage to Essex. D'Ewes states baldly that:

> '… the Earl of Essex was unfit to pay the rites of marriage for many years after she was ready to receive them.[9]

By December it was clear enough that the marriage was beyond salvage. In the spring of 1613 Frances's father, the Earl of Suffolk, approached the King to seek an annulment on the grounds of non-consummation.

For some, 1613 began on a happier note: at Whitehall on 14th February, after a postponement due to the devastating death of his principal son and heir, King James finally saw his daughter Princess Elizabeth married to Frederick, the Prince Elector of the Palatinate. The couple left the country soon after, bound for Frederick's homeland on the Continent; they were to raise a large family, two of their sons returning to England in the 1640s to fight for their uncle Charles, who upon Henry's death had become heir to the throne.

The Royal marriage festivities over, Londoners wanting to remain in the festival spirit could have picked up the new quarto printing of Francis Beaumont's anarchic play *The Knight of the Burning Pestle*; a satirical comedy first performed a few years before, it had not been particularly well received at the time, although it became very popular in the 1660s.[10] George Lisle claimed kinship to Beaumont: the precise connection is unclear, but Beaumont's uncle was one Thomas Ashby from Leicestershire, which suggests the connection came via Lisle's mother.

Meanwhile, Frances Howard still sought a way to be rid of Overbury. It was probably during the early weeks of 1613 that the then Earl of Northampton – her great-uncle, and no supporter of Sir Thomas – proposed that Carr should be

8   Isaac Wake to Sir Dudley Carleton, 2nd December (*ibid.*, p.160). The quotation indicates Wake's precise words in the letter.
9   D'Ewes, vol. I, p.88.
10 The play's content and structure – a fourth-wall-breaking satire of the knightly virtues espoused in works such as Spenser's *Faery Queen* – made it virtually 'alternative comedy', and perhaps just too far ahead of its time to be enjoyed by early Jacobeans.

reconciled with Overbury, yet should find some way to have him sent to the Tower; after which '… they might at leisure advise what further course to take.'[11]

Early in April King James – probably moved by Carr – decided that Overbury should be sent to Russia as Royal ambassador. According to D'Ewes, Overbury agreed after consulting with friends; yet Carr, now apparently reconciled to him, advised against it:

> promising better preferment at home within a short space; and that if he were committed to prison for his refusal, he would speedily procure his enlargement.[12]

Although initially reluctant to disobey the King, Overbury was at last persuaded, and stuck to his refusal. On 21st April instructions were sent to Sir William Wade (or Waad), the Lieutenant of the Tower, the Tower, ordering him:

> … to receive and keep close prisoner Sir Thomas Overbury, against whom the King is displeased for a matter of high contempt.[13]

News of the arrest would have spread quickly, but Laurence Lisle was not there to hear it: on 20th April, the day before Overbury's contrived imprisonment, Laurence was twenty miles away in Doddinghurst, Essex, marrying for the second time. Nothing is known about Dorothy Ashby, his new wife, besides her apparent kinship to Francis Beaumont and to a then little-known Leicestershire gentry family named Villiers. Neither do we know how she and Laurence met, although the marriage register states that she was 'attendinge in howse on Mrs Fage'.[14] Mary Fage of Doddinghurst was a writer, whose 1637 book *Fames Roule* (a book of acrostic verses and anagrams) demonstrates a familiarity with the court. Although, as Fage's entry in the ODNB notes, there is no direct evidence to place her or her husband at court, if she was there in 1613 she would undoubtedly have been in or around the household and circle of Queen Anne, who was a prominent patron of the written and visual arts.[15] It is highly likely that Laurence and Dorothy met somewhere within the sprawling precincts of Whitehall Palace.

Shortly after the wedding Laurence and his new wife returned to London, doubtless to discover the events escalating around Overbury. D'Ewes continues Sir Thomas's sorry tale, stating that, once he was safely in the Tower, Frances Howard pursued her ambition to see him dead. Wade had held his position as the Tower's

---

11   *Ibid.*, p.72
12   *Ibid.*
13   *CSP Domestic Series*, 1611-1618, p.181.
14   Held at Essex Record Office; also available to view online through their SEAX website (subscription required to view images of original documents).
15   Betty S. Travitski, ODNB.

Lieutenant for a number of years and was considered virtually incorruptible; however he was not a popular man, and Frances used 'means at Court' to remove him, probably engaging Northampton's help.[16] On this matter the Calendar of State Papers reports that Wade was:

> …discharged from the lieutenancy of the Tower, on complaint of having embezzled jewels from the Lady Arabella.[17]

On 6th May Sir Gervase Elwes (or sometimes Elvis, or Helwys) was appointed in Wade's place. Elwes was an unknown, a gambler, and of low status at court; he was also willing to pay Northampton £2,000 for the privilege of becoming the Tower's new Lieutenant, a profitable position, and at Northampton's behest he kept Overbury strictly isolated. On 8th May Richard Weston – a regular messenger between Frances and Robert Carr – was appointed directly as Sir Thomas's keeper. Thus Overbury was kept close by the instruments of his enemies; and at around 7 a.m. on 15th September 1613, he was found dead.

In his last weeks it was apparent that Sir Thomas was appallingly ill, and showing symptoms variously attributable to poison; he had also received various medical treatments which – when considered with the benefit of modern medical knowledge – would at best be ineffective and at worst capable of hastening death, if only by secondary causes. Towards the end it had been obvious even to contemporary minds that Overbury's worsening condition was the result of foul play, although the trails of possible guilt were tortuous and bare of hard evidence. When inspected later on the day of death, his body appeared to be deteriorating unusually rapidly, and was strangely marked and badly discoloured; yet a coroner's inquest – consisting partly of a viewing by other Tower prisoners – returned a verdict of natural causes.[18] Shortly afterwards, Sir Thomas Overbury was hastily buried in the chapel attached to the Tower. Northampton wrote gleefully to Carr regarding the death; Carr's reaction seems ambivalent, which, as Anne Somerset points out, is not surprising given the previous depth of his friendship with Sir Thomas.[19] Frances's reaction is not recorded, but nearly two weeks later, on 25th September, she would have been delighted to hear that her marriage to Essex been pronounced void, and the way was clear for her to marry Robert Carr. Yet he was merely a Viscount and her former husband an Earl: that Frances might not suffer any loss in status, Carr was created Earl of Somerset on 4th November.

16   D'Ewes, vol. I, p.73.
17   John Chamberlain to Sir Dudley Carleton, 13th May (*CSP Domestic Series*, 1611-1618, p.183). 'Lady Arabella' was Arabella Stuart, a cousin of King James. A rival claimant to the throne, she had been imprisoned in the Tower since 1611.
18   D'Ewes, vol. I, p.73.
19   Somerset, pp.200-201.

Meanwhile, Laurence's business at St Paul's had sparked back into life. In October he finally published another book: *The Dove and the Serpent*, a treatise detailing the finer techniques of conversation and verbal negotiation.[20] A shame, perhaps, that Overbury would never read it: chapter 5 offered advice on:

> How to converse in Court, and of the meanes whereby to purchase favour, and stand secure from the many dangers, which are there incident to all.

But Laurence's master stroke was yet in the making. It is unclear how he heard of, or obtained the rights to publish, a lengthy poem by the late Overbury; although Overbury's entry in the ODNB suggests that it had been written some time previously, and manuscript copies circulated around the court.[21] However it was obtained, *A Wife – Now the Widdow of Sir Thomas Overbury* was in publication by December 1613 at the *Tygers Head*.

It must have been galling for Frances Howard, that when she finally married Robert Carr on 26th December, the work of the man whose death she had so carefully procured had become an instant best-seller, bringing Overbury and his fate to the forefront of popular imagination and making him a posthumous celebrity overnight. The even heavier irony must have been, that Overbury had written of a female creature who surely Frances Howard – almost certainly an adulteress and at least an accessory to murder – could not now possibly hope to emulate. The wedding was celebrated at Whitehall in the Chapel Royal, as Frances's marriage to Essex had been; as before, it was celebrated by a masque, the details of which Laurence promptly published, entitling it *The Description of a Maske: presented in the Banqueting Roome at Whitehall … at the Mariage of the … Earle of Somerset and … the Lady Frances Howard.*[22] As if the description alone were not engaging enough for the reader, the work also included *divers choyse Ayres composed for this Maske that may be sung with a single voyce to the Lute or Base-Viall …*

The marriage celebrations stretched well into January 1614, a further three masques being performed in the couple's honour. Various poems were composed, some kinder than others. One pro-Frances piece in particular, *Andromeda Liberata*, appeared to condemn the webs of gossip at court by beginning:

> Away ungodly Vulgars, far away,
> Flie ye prophane, that dare not view the day,
> Nor speake to men but Shadowes, nor would heare
> Of any news, but what seditious were,

---

20   Author Daniel Tuvill.
21   John Considine, ODNB.
22   Author Thomas Campion.

Hatefull and harmefull ever to the best,
Whispering their scandals, glorifying the rest …'[23]

Written by the well-known poet and dramatist George Chapman, the poem
utilised the classical tale of Perseus and Andromeda to illustrate Frances's personal
story; in March her father, the Earl of Suffolk, was one of several prominent figures
who licensed the poem for publication. As before, Laurence was the bookseller
involved: it seems he was becoming a trusted contact of the Cecils and Howards,
supporting the possibility that he had previously held some position at court, or
had dealt with one or other of the families on a prior occasion.

Andromeda itself caused an uproar, being taken to insult, amongst others, the
Earl of Essex: commentators have since supposed that the references in question might be those referring to the 'barren rock' to which Andromeda was
previously chained. Chapman was forced to write a defence of his work, also
published by Laurence, the title page insisting that the poem had been 'maliciously
misinterpreted'.[24]

Meanwhile King James, short of money as ever, called Parliament on 6th April.
The MPs were also concerned about money: the problems lay chiefly in James's
astronomical court and household expenses, but higher on the Parliamentary
agenda was the issue of 'impositions', or customs duties, where a lessee, also known
as a 'customs farmer' collected the duties on the King's behalf and took a small cut,
duly passing on the remainder to the Crown. Had he known what lay ahead for
himself, Laurence might have done well to take note. By long-established right,
the Crown levied these duties on imported commodities, the specifics having first
been outlined in the *Book of Rates* in the 1550s. The book had been revised and
reissued in 1608, and now covered 1,400 items. Just previous to the reissue, one
merchant had refused to pay the duties demanded on his imports, but had lost his
legal case; crucially, the judge concerned then asserted that the King had two types
of Royal prerogative, the first being that defined by statute, and the second being
an 'absolute' prerogative that could not be guided by rules 'which direct only at the
common law'.[25] Unfortunately James had been advised by Robert Cecil, his Lord
Treasurer, that this judgement confirmed his absolute right to levy such impositions, and by 1608 the issue had condensed into a Parliamentary paranoia that its
liberties were under threat from this overriding privilege of the King's. The boil
finally burst in 1610, and James addressed Parliament himself, defending his right
to levy arbitrary impositions. Eventually he agreed to an Act which prevented

---

23   Author George Chapman.
24   *A Free And Offenceless Justification, Of A Lately Publisht and most maliciously misinterpreted Poeme:
     Entituled Andromeda liberata.*
25   Coward, p.140; quoting J P Kenyon's *Stuart Constitution*, p.55. See Coward's full text for a good analysis
     of James's financial difficulties at the time.

him levying any further duties without Parliament's consent, but existing duties continued; however in 1614 the issue arose in Parliament again, and a bill was presented declaring the taxes illegal. The Crown protested, and as the session wore on, the legal arguments between monarch and parliament intensified.

On 8th May 1614 Laurence and Dorothy baptised their first son, William, at St. Gregory's; on the 16th Laurence wrote a note to the readers of the fourth impression of *A Wife,* a measure of just how popular the work had become since Christmas.[26] Laurence himself said of the poem:

> Had such a volume beene extant among the ancient Romanes, though they wanted our easie conservations of wit, by printing; yet they would rather, & more easily, have committed the sense hereof to brasse, and Cedar leaves, then let such an Author, have lost his due eternitie.

In addition to the poem, and sold with it, Laurence now published Overbury's 'Characters': a collection of character sketches in prose, presumably drawn from Overbury's own perceptions of Jacobean society and the court where he had spent the last years of his life. The sketches were shrewd, even insightful, but frequently unkind. The titles speak for themselves: for example, *A Dissembler*; *A Courtier*; *A Flatterer*; *An ignorant Glorie Hunter*. By this fourth imprint there were nearly thirty such characters; in the very late editions there would be over seventy. Of course, only the first few were written by Overbury himself; as the popularity of this new genre spread, admirers and emulators submitted their own efforts, and to this day the authorship of many of the later Characters remains a mystery.

Where Laurence's fortunes were improving rapidly, Robert Carr's quickly began to wane. Much was expected of a court favourite, chiefly by those with petitions or suits of their own to promote; yet Carr neglected to attend these small matters of favour, often promising to make good a petition but then failing to follow it up at court. Northampton had written frequently to Carr on this subject, chiding him for forgetting this suit, or that favour, and advising him on the best course to take; and in fact it was Overbury who had taken care of many of these matters on Carr's behalf. Overbury was gone; and when Northampton died also, in June 1614, Carr was on his own. He quickly gained a reputation for not keeping his word, and his name was further sullied by his direct involvement in a bribery scandal. To make matters worse, Frances was also in the habit of making rash promises of promotion, even accepting payments in return; there were no refunds when the promises came to nothing.

The endgame for Carr approached. On 3rd June, exasperated by the Parliament's constant opposition, the King warned the House of Commons that he was

---

26 As it appears that no first or second impressions are extant, perhaps these were the manuscript copies apparently circulated by Overbury; perhaps Laurence's initial edition was in fact the third overall.

contemplating dismissing it; and on 7th June – after someone publicly told him to send the Scots back to Scotland – he made good his threat and dissolved the session. The House would not meet again for another seven years. By August James had left London for Northamptonshire, and the hospitality of Sir Francis Mildmay at Apthorpe Hall; and whilst walking the gardens there his eye fell upon another good-looking young man. His name was George Villiers.

3

Favourites

There is proof enough of the strength of King James's attraction to George Villiers, in that Villiers was installed at court before September was a week old and was shortly afterwards appointed as the King's Cupbearer. Moreover, in November 1614 James was preparing to make him a Groom of the Bedchamber.

Naturally alarmed at the King's sudden affections for the newcomer, Carr moved to block Villiers' appointment, insisting the post go to a relative of his own. It seems that he succeeded in his endeavour,[1] yet thereafter he appeared to lose all control, violently reproaching James for his attention to Villiers and suggesting that the young man's presence undermined his (Carr's) own influence. The King responded patiently at first, insisting that Carr would always be pre-eminent, but as the reproaches continued it became clear that he was losing patience. And Carr did not neglect bestowing his own attention on the new favourite. The courtier Sir Anthony Weldon noted that Carr told Villiers he would break his neck if he could; and a Victorian biographer of Villiers recounts that an attendant of Somerset's deliberately spilled soup over him during a meal at the court.[2] Villiers responded with his fist, which was regarded as treason – the incident occurring in the King's presence – the statutory punishment being loss of the hand. Yet James considered that Villiers had been provoked, and the matter was dropped. Against such favouritism, Carr could not win, and his supporters began to drift across the divide. Villiers already had strong support; Carr had made many enemies, and now they came together to seize their opportunity, giving their *protégé* money for new clothes, that he might make every possible good impression on the King. Against the odds they even persuaded the Queen to give Villiers her support, to the extent that on St George's day 1615 it was she who contrived to have Villiers knighted, kneeling with a sword before her husband and begging him:

---

1   A few months later, as the King was about to appoint Villiers a Gentleman of the Bedchamber, Carr sent James a message beseeching him to make Villiers *only* a Groom (Cammell, p.65).
2   Thomson; quoted by Cammell, p.72.

… to knight this noble gentleman, whose name was George, for the honour of St. George, whose feast he now kept.[3]

It is hard to believe that, working around the Royal Households and being related by marriage to Villiers, Laurence would not have been one of those who worked to promote the new favourite; Lisle's first, arranged, marriage and his printing of *A Wife* show him as a man quick to spot a profitable opportunity. Use of his own position to assist Villiers would also help explain certain financial favours bestowed on him by the new favourite once he was established at court.

As if a knighthood were not enough, James – even in the face of spiralling royal debt – then conferred upon Villiers the right to sell a barony to the highest bidder,[4] and gave him a yearly pension of £1,000.

Laurence's fortunes were yet on the rise. The popularity of *A Wife* continued, and would reach its fifth impression by the end of the year; the Characters still multiplied, and now the poem itself was to be emulated. On 1st July 1615 Laurence published Patrick Henny's *The Husbande. A Poeme expressed In a Compleat Man.* It seems Henny faced some ridicule when seeking to publish, as he explains in a note to the reader:

And yet (Reader) I must say something to thee, though against my will: For the Printer admonishes with much caution, & a conditionall If – that jeasts and noted Laughter will banish mee … from places which I never hope to be guilty of, Publicke invitations, and all Ordinaryes …[5]

Clearly Laurence had not held back in telling Henny what he thought of the work; and presumably in response to those who made the obvious comparisons to *A Wife*, Henny continued:

Neither condemne me of imitation, (though indeed the worke precedent, and worke-master, were both alike excellent): for … My own fewell therfore warmes my closet, though I kindle stuffe combustible with a borrowed Coale …

Perhaps the piece was given some credence, however, by the several commendatory verses which accompanied it – the first written by Ben Jonson.

3   Goodman (ed. Brewer), vol. I, p.224.
4   Baronetcies had been established in 1611, with worthy aims; but the cash-starved Crown rapidly began selling the honours to anyone who could afford them, the King occasionally allowing favoured servants and courtiers to sell them also, for their own profit.
5   An ordinary was an eating house; effectively a public restaurant that provided fixed-price meals.

It was in mid-1615, at around the time of George Lisle's birth, that rumours began to circulate about the circumstances of Sir Thomas Overbury's death. Privately, murder had long since been whispered of; Frances Howard's powerful family connections had caused a general reluctance to act, but now the vague whisperings began to solidify. Many years later Simonds D'Ewes was shrewdly to note that:

> Had Sir Thomas Overbury accepted and undertaken the embassy into Russia, he had perhaps been poisoned before his return, and the matter might have been more secretly carried.[6]

As the gossip intensified, the principle characters took fright. Anne Turner – Frances Howard's confidant – met Richard Weston, Overbury's gaoler, to discuss which story he should give if he was questioned. Weston then met Sir Gervase Elwes who was still Lieutenant of the Tower. For his part, Robert Carr made sure to recover as much of his correspondence with Overbury as Overbury's former servant would give him;[7] but he did not help his case by presently asking King James for a pardon against any crime he may have unwittingly committed in the past. Though the King agreed, the Lord Chancellor refused to authorise the document. Where before James would surely have backed his favourite, this time he seems not to have argued.

It is also D'Ewes who brings to us the fullest account of how the real truth beyond the rumours may finally have escaped: the occasion of a meeting between Sir Ralph Winwood (Secretary of State) and Elwes himself. Elwes had been commended to Winwood by a 'great man', at whose table it was arranged they should meet over dinner; Winwood was keen to meet the Tower's latest Lieutenant, but told him that:

> …he could first wish he had cleared himself of a foul suspicion the world generally conceived of him [Elwes], touching the death of Sir Thomas Overbury.[8]

Perhaps Elwes thought he might use acquaintance with Winwood to safely extract himself from the Overbury affair. For, D'Ewes continues:

> As soon as Sir Jervis heard that, being very ambitious of the Secretary's friendship, he took occasion to enter into private conference with him, and therein to excuse himself to have been enforced to connive at the said

---

6   D'Ewes, vol. I, p.78.
7   Somerset, pp.232-233.
8   D'Ewes, vol. I, p.69.

murder, with much abhorring of it. He confessed the whole circumstance of the execution of it in general, and the instruments to have been set on work by Robert Earl of Somerset and his wife.

Winwood's utter astonishment at this abrupt confession can be imagined, but with great presence of mind:

> … having gained the true discovery of this bloody practice from one of the actors, even beyond his expectation, parted from the Lieutenant of the Tower in a very familiar and friendly manner, as if he had received good satisfaction by the excuse he had framed for himself; but soon after acquainted the King's Majesty with it …

Elwes was summoned by King James to commit his account to paper, which obediently he did; however any remaining hope of escaping punishment was crushed as he was then promptly arrested, along with his co-conspirators. They were swiftly brought to trial, Weston first, being condemned on 23rd October; then Anne Turner on 9th November; and Elwes on 16th November. As each trial was concluded, the defendants were hanged at Tyburn. The trials of Frances Howard, who was then pregnant, and that of her husband, were postponed until the following year; meanwhile Carr was imprisoned.

Finally, on 24th May 1616, delivered of her child, Francis Howard was put on trial at Westminster Hall:

> … before Sir Thomas Egerton, Knt., then Lord Chancellor of England, and for that day created Lord High Steward. She was by her peers found guilty of Sir Thomas Overbury's murder, and so condemned, and in her return to the Tower, the axe-head was carried before her with the edge towards her, which in her coming forth was carried before her with the edge from her. The day following, being the 25th day of the same month, was Robert Earl of Somerset, her husband, arraigned at the same bar, before the same Lord High Steward, found guilty by his peers, and condemned, and from thence was remanded prisoner back again to the Tower.[9]

The scandalised but ever-fascinated English public had nearly a year to wait between Elwes's confession in July 1615, and the trials of the Earl and Countess of Somerset in May 1616; public interest meantime may be measured by noting that *A Wife* went through five more impressions before the end of 1616. In the eighth edition the title was amended to *Thomas Overbury – his Wife. With new elegies upon his (now knowne) untimely death*. Having also published several other minor

---

9   *Ibid.*, p.85.

pieces relating to Overbury, Laurence was clearly profiting from the scandal, even managing to pay back the ten pounds he had borrowed from the Stationers' Company in 1610.[10] But anyone expecting a grand finale to the Overbury affair was to be disappointed. D'Ewes explains that:

> … when all men's expectations were ready to anticipate the day of their execution, the Earl of Suffolk, continuing still in his place of Lord Treasurer, being father of the said Countess, so wrought the matter with Queen Anne and the new favourite, that they, with his other friends and alliance, by their earnest and daily intercession with the King, at last got the pardon of their lives …[11]

His predecessor safely beyond redemption, perhaps Villiers could more than afford to support the call for clemency. Their sentences commuted, Robert Carr and his wife would remain in the Tower until 1622; the new favourite could continue his rise unhindered.

10   Ferguson, p.25.
11   D'Ewes, vol. I, pp.85-86.

4

Patronage

Whilst 1616 saw Robert Carr's final tumble from grace, it saw also the incredible rise of his successor. During that year George Villiers was installed as Knight of the Garter; Viscount Villiers; Baron Whaddon of Whaddon, Buckinghamshire; Keeper of Whaddon Park and Chase; Chief Justice in Eyre, North of the Trent; Master of the King's bench office; Joint Commissioner for the Office of Earl Marshall; Lord Lieutenant of the County of Buckingham; and High Steward of Hampton Court. By this time he was also Master of the Horse, a coveted position which even Carr had failed to obtain. He became Earl of Buckingham in 1617, Marquess of Buckingham in 1618, and in 1623 took the title by which history infamously remembers him: Duke of Buckingham.

In parallel, Laurence Lisle's own fortunes were buoyant. Besides a steady income from continuing sales of *A Wife* (in its ninth impression by the end of 1616), he would doubtless have profited in many small ways from his wife's family's new connection to the court; although the grandest gestures from Buckingham were yet to come. With debts paid, enviable contacts, a steady business and a growing family, those uncertain, early days at St Paul's must have seemed as distant as the moon.

For the time being he continued to run the *Tygers Head*, but by 1617 he was preparing a change of command. In January he bound another apprentice, Christofer Sayer, then in April freed Henry Seile. Whilst there is no record of Christofer completing his apprenticeship, and his fate is unknown, Henry stayed on at the shop.[1] From 1619 he took over all the publishing and put his name on the books in place of Laurence's, although the usual phrase 'to be sold at his shop', which implies sole proprietorship, does not appear on the covers of his publications until 1625, when Laurence signed over his major copyrights to other

---

1 A lecture on Freemasonry given in 1975 (Beck, p.7), concerned with the origins of London Grand Master Anthony Sayer, also a bookseller, mentions finding details in the Stationers' Company records for Christopher Sayer, and states that 'Christopher was living in 1623'. Presumably this detail came from the said records, but unfortunately the lecture offers no specific source.

publishers and effectively left the trade. Notably, however, during the 1620s he did publish two works whose authors were related to Laurence: William Lisle's *A Saxon Treatise* in 1623, and in 1629 *Bosworth-field*, a compilation of poems by the recently deceased poet Sir John Beaumont, Francis Beaumont's brother. At some point during the 1630s the *Tygers Head* premises, along with many others around St Paul's, were condemned as part of a plan to clean up the precincts of the neglected cathedral, and in 1637 Henry moved the business to Fleet Street.[2] After changing the shop name to the *Black Boy* in the 1650s – perhaps revealing Royalist sympathies, as this was a popular nickname for Charles II – Henry died in December 1660, having ended a prolific publishing career as 'stationer to the Kings most Excellent Majesty'.

With Henry managing the shop between 1619 and 1625, Laurence probably took on the role of silent partner; however, precisely when he and his family physically left St Paul's is not clear. A third son, Francis, was baptised at St Gregory's in October 1617, but there is no sign anywhere in those parish registers of Laurence's second daughter, Mary. After Francis's arrival the family's domestic whereabouts remain a mystery until 1624, when a fourth son, Anthony, was baptised in the upmarket parish of St Martin-in-the-Fields at the western end of the Strand. Laurence had evidently become a rich man – whether through *A Wife*, or Buckingham's patronage, or both – and it is also possible that he had, like many well-off citizens keen to avoid London's dirt and regular epidemics, bought or rented a property outside the capital. Possibly he spent time in Warwickshire, as a 1628 record survives regarding the transfer of a manor in Warmington, for which Laurence releases 'all his interest in the said property';[3] as this paperwork exists amongst the papers of the Child-Villiers family – ultimately descendants of Buckingham's wider family – it seems likely that this interest was obtained through him. Alternatively Laurence and his family could have briefly moved out to Surrey: tax certificates from 1640 and 1641 declare him 'to be liable for taxation in Middlesex, and not in the hundred of Godley, Surrey, the previous area of tax liability',[4] although when the family might have lived there has not been established.

The tax certificates also reveal what was to become the Lisles' London address, on and off, for around twenty years: St Martin's Lane west side. That side of the lane had been developed from green fields during James's reign by William Cecil, son of Robert Cecil the royal minister, for lease by people of quality who desired

---

2   The condemned properties seem to have been pulled down shortly after: in 1644 a newsbook reporting Laud's trial noted that severall witnesses were examined, 'concerning his causing the houses about Pauls Church, being in all 65. to be pul'd downe and demolished, for the repaire thereof, and the defacing of Saint Gregories Church, by which meanes there was neither preaching nor prayer there for many weekes together nor ever since.' (*Mercurius Civicus*, Numb. 43, p.439).

3   Warwickshire County Record Office. Deeds concerning the manor and advowson of Warmington, ref. L5/281a, b and L5/286. 1628.

4   Exchequer: King's Remembrancer: Certificates of Residence. E115/241/12, E115/241/100, E115/250/84.

a smart residence near the Palace of Westminster. At that time the auxiliary buildings of the sprawling palace complex spread up from Whitehall almost to St Martin's, and Cecil's fashionable houses were rapidly populated by courtiers, creatives, and government officials. The Calendars of State Papers for the late Jacobean and early Caroline period contain numerous letters from secretaries, peers, and other notables who had penned their communications from St Martin's Lane. Inigo Jones was a resident, as was Abraham van der Doort, keeper of the King's pictures; William Dobson, Charles I's court painter, lived there both in the 1630s and at his death in 1646.

At some point between 1607 and 1633 a grant of arms was made to 'Lile of St Martins in the Feildes': *erminois, on a chief azure, three lions rampant, or*; as no first name is given the arms cannot be confirmed as Laurence's, but it would be in keeping with his continuing rise up the social ladder and given the conjunction of name, place, and time period, the attribution seems highly likely.[5]

The year 1621 began with a freeze. Diarist Simonds D'Ewes noted on 3rd February:

> The season of the year was now so sharp as that the river Thames was hard frozen all over on the hither side of the bridge towards Westminster, so as divers passed upon it this day and divers ensuing, very safely on foot.[6]

King James had dissolved the last Parliament, in 1614, after only eight weeks, as he and it had reached an impasse over the settlement of Royal finances. Late in January 1621, in dire need of money for a foreign military expedition, he finally called the Houses together, and they convened on 30th January. Both Buckingham and Prince Charles were urging James to threaten the Habsburg Emperor Ferdinand with force unless he withdrew his troops from the Rheinish Palatinate, the captured territory of James's son-in-law, the Prince Elector Frederick. Forced also to flee Bohemia – where he had been crowned King in 1619 – Frederick had taken temporary refuge under the protection of the Elector of Brandenburg. He was accompanied by his English wife, the popular Princess Elizabeth, and two of their sons, the princes Rupert and Maurice. Rupert was a year old and Maurice just a few weeks.

Nineteen-year-old D'Ewes found a convenient place somewhere near Westminster to observe the state procession to Parliament: the King was accompanied by several peers, and also his surviving son, Prince Charles, who:

5   BL, Harley MS 6140/78. 'A book in folio, containing Arms & Quarterings in Trick, being Grants by Seager …'; Seager was Garter King of Arms between 1607 and his death in 1633.

6   D'Ewes, vol. I, p.174.

rode with a rich coronet upon his head between the Serjeants at Arms carrying maces, and the pensioners carrying their pole-axes, both on foot ...[7]

The Lisles, now living close by at St Martin-in-the-Fields, might also have turned out to see the procession; George would have been a little over five years old. Laurence's interest in the new Parliament would have been deeper than mere curiosity, as six months previously he and a syndicate of several companions had been granted:

> ... the sole privilege of dressing arms, and repairing all manner of arms and armour, at the rates set down by Lord Sheffield for the county of York. All arms to be brought for view or repair yearly.[8]

Such privileges, or monopolies, had been in use in England since at least Elizabeth's time for the purpose of raising money for the Crown. However, like the tax impositions James fought Parliament over in 1614, they had long been considered a grievance. In a legal case of 1602, the judges declared that:

> The end of all these monopolies is for the private gain of the patentees', and although provisions and cautions are added to moderate them, yet ... it is mere folly to think that there is any measure in mischief or wickedness.[9]

They asserted also, firstly, that monopolies raised prices, because the patentee could make the price what he pleased; secondly, after a monopoly was granted, the commodity in question was 'not so good and merchantable' as previously, as the patentee had only his own interests at heart; and thirdly, that the monopoly impoverished those who were now unable to continue in the monopolised trade. In 1610 James had agreed not to grant them himself, and instructed that all proposals were to be examined prior to any grant being made.[10] However, as his finances worsened, necessitating more monopolies, bad feeling increased, and by 1620 this particular financial bubble was ready to burst. His pressing financial needs in mind, however, James was prepared to compromise with Parliament, and promised:

---

7   *Ibid.*, vol. I, pp.169-170.
8   Grant, July 11th 1620; printed, STC (2nd ed.) 8638. Mentioned also *CSP Domestic Series*, 1619-1623, p.163.
9   Lockyer, p.130. Quoting from *The Reports of Sir Edward Coke, Kt.*, (1738), Part XI, p.86v.
10 *Ibid.*, pp.130-131.

the removal of monopolies, of which there were at this time seven hundred in the kingdom, granted by letters patent under the broad seal, to the enriching of some few projectors, and the impoverishing of all the kingdom aside.[11]

Doubtless Laurence would have feared for his recently awarded twenty-one-year monopoly on arms repair. He might well be described, at least in a political sense, as one of Buckingham's dependents: writing after the Restoration, the Earl of Clarendon said Villiers had:

> … entirely disposed of all the graces of the King, in conferring all the honours and all the offices of the three kingdoms, without rival; in dispensing whereof he was guided more by the rules of appetite than of judgement; and so exalted almost all of his own numerous family and dependents, who had no other virtue or merit than their alliance to him …[12]

Perhaps it is hypocritical of Clarendon to throw stones at people receiving largesse from the Crown and court, when he enjoyed closeness to Charles I and II, and his daughter married the future James II; and indeed the entire era, particularly under James I, was marked by increasing social mobility and the snapping up of commercial and social opportunities wherever and however they fell. Good contacts in high places were essential, and as Overbury demonstrated (albeit ultimately to his cost) there was no shame attached to hitching a lift on someone's coat-tails in order to get ahead. After Buckingham's death Laurence successfully found his own way into several lucrative offices, yet Villiers' distribution of largesse to his personal circle is undeniable, as is the fact that besides the profits from shrewd publishing decisions, Laurence's access to major sources of income after 1616 sprang purely from a timely family connection to the rising political faction.

What may have stung even more to jealous onlookers than the Favourite's building up of his family, was his parallel knocking down of anyone who actively challenged him doing it. In 1620 it was the turn of Attorney General Sir Henry Yelverton, who had already crossed metaphorical swords with Buckingham and had made it clear that he would not bend his knee to the favourite. Suddenly in June he was accused of introducing clauses into the City of London's new charter which were not in the King's warrant. Despite Yelverton's desperate protestations that any such errors were unintentional, he was suspended, prosecuted, and in November sent to the Tower. D'Ewes says:

11   D'Ewes, vol. I, p.171.
12   Book I, 1840 vol. I, p.16.

Those, therefore, who searched more narrowly into the casual influence of his sudden fall, found that it proceeded from some displeasure conceived against him by the Marquis of Buckingham, the King's favourite, who having been denied by his Majesty the customs of Ireland, and finding that denial to have proceeded from the Attorney-General's advice, that it was too great a gift for a subject, he took this opportunity to make him sensible of his revenge.[13]

Shortly afterwards, on 8th February 1621, it was announced in Dublin that Laurence had been granted a lease of 'the new imposition of 18d per lb on tobacco and 2s on every gross of tobacco pipes imported into Ireland.'[14] Clearly Buckingham had gained control of the Irish customs as he desired, and distributed them to those whom he saw fit. Yelverton's loss was Laurence's gain, although gaining a customs farm at the expense of such a high-profile political casualty – albeit indirectly – would hardly have endeared him to Buckingham's detractors. However, the impost grant may have saved Laurence's financial bacon: on 10th July, according to his promise to Parliament, the King issued a proclamation revoking eighteen monopolies with immediate effect, including Laurence's, and allowing seventeen more to be reviewed by Parliament.[15] Some years later, in January 1628, three of the original arms monopoly syndicate – plus some new members, but minus Laurence – petitioned for its renewal. The then Attorney General, Sir Robert Heath, refused, saying it was 'inconvenient' to renew it as Parliament had already determined it to be a grievance.[16] Laurence's reason for leaving the syndicate is unknown; perhaps by 1628 he already saw which way the political breeze was blowing.

In March 1625 King James died, and was succeeded by his very different son. Whilst James's court was renowned for excess, Charles preferred decorum to the point of obsession; where James had enough political intelligence to make concessions to Parliament, Charles believed that, as King, he need not, which (as is all too evident in hindsight) set the scene for a politically troubled reign and ultimately civil war. A companionship with Charles as close as that with James kept Villiers in power throughout the transition period, despite some disastrous political misjudgements such as the attempt at securing the then-heir's marriage to the Spanish Infanta, and the abortive naval expeditions to Cadiz and the Isle of Rhé. Parliament attempted to impeach the Duke in 1626, and might have succeeded had Charles not dissolved the session to prevent it. How much longer Buckingham

---

13 D'Ewes, vol. I, p.156.
14 *CSP Ireland*, 1615-25, p.316.
15 *By the King. A Proclamation declaring His Majesties grace to his Subjects, touching matters complained of, as publique greevances.*
16 *CSP Domestic Series*, 1627-1628, p.519.

might have clung to power can only be speculated, for on 23rd August 1628, while in Portsmouth preparing for a second expedition across the Channel, he was fatally stabbed in the chest by a disgruntled soldier in the crowded hall of an inn.

As with any patron-client relationship, in any society, in any era, the sudden loss of the patron, particularly in violent circumstances, is a devastating blow to those relying on his or her goodwill and protection. To the Lisles, Buckingham was not just a patron but a kinsman: the family's reaction would undoubtedly have been one of profound grief and shock. In practical terms, without the Duke's protection his circle would have had to swiftly close ranks, call in favours and shift for themselves in the face of high-level political enemies. Possibly there is evidence of this in July 1629, when the Privy Council ordered that:

> Thomas Shelden, gentleman, now Prysoner in the Counter in Wood Street, in regard of the great danger he is in by reason of diverse hurts shall be removed from thence to the house of Mr. Lawrence Lisle, esquire, where he may be more conveniently attended. Provided that the saide Lawrence Lisle give sufficient Bayle for his forthcoming whensoever he shalbe called for or that he be lawfully discharged.[17]

Undoubtedly he is the Thomas Shelton mentioned two years later in March 1631, whom the Privy Council sent back to Norfolk with a letter for the local Treasurer for Maimed Soldiers, telling them Shelden had been:

> imprested out of that County and employed in his Majesties service both at Cadez and the Isle of Retz, in which service he hath received so many hurtes and maymes that he is thereby altogether unfit for further service and unable to get his living, in regarde whereof he is according to the statute … to be provided for in the County out of which he was imprested. [We] hereby will and require you to see him relieved with a convenient yearly Pension during his life …[18]

To bail this sick individual out of prison and allow him to stay in his private house for an unspecified period, Laurence must have felt either great compassion for him or deep obligation to him, which implies Shelden was a close friend or kinsman or a political ally. This in turn suggests he was a fellow client of Buckingham's, probably unable to service his debts after his wounding, and lacking the late Duke's protection, ending up in one of the London compters. There is no other information by which to fully identify him, however the Sheldons were a prominent family in Norfolk, and the surname was also known in the Favourite's circle: the main

---

17 *Acts of the Privy Council 1629-1630*, vol. 45, p.84.
18 *Acts of the Privy Council 1630-1631*, vol. 46, p.261.

petitioner for the arms monopoly was Edward Sheldon, one of King James's Pages of Honour, and Buckingham's brother, Christopher 'Kit' Villiers, had married an Elizabeth Sheldon, daughter of a Thomas Sheldon from Hoby in Leicestershire – Hoby fell within the same few square miles of the county that was home to the Villiers, Ashby and Beaumont families.

What support or favours Laurence himself may have received from friends and colleagues during the aftermath of Buckingham's murder is not known, however after the Deputy and Council for Ireland stopped Laurence collecting the tobacco impost in December 1636, he used his connection to Buckingham to petition Archbishop Laud for assistance. Laud had been a close friend of Buckingham; in April 1637 he wrote to Lord Viscount Wentworth – shortly to become Earl of Strafford – enclosing Laurence's petition:

> My very good Lord. I have been earnestly entreated to trouble your Lordship with these few lines, and in them to recommend unto your honourable favour this inclosed petition. And I do it the rather, because his request seems to me very reasonable; and he tells me he will be content with any indifferent composition. I doubt not but your Lordship knows the business already much better than I; and if for his sake to whom he had relation, and mine, you shall be pleased to show him kindness, at least such as hath been extended to others in the like case, I shall give your Lordship humble thanks …[19]

A few months later he continues:

> I writ to you last spring about a business of Mr. Lisle's … and I received your answer concerning it and him, very clear and satisfactory to me. But suitors in this age are not satisfied with any just denials. I write not this as if I meant to trouble you any more with that suit of his. But only to advertise you that he means to petition the King, and then, if it be referred to the Irish Committee, he will gain little by it; for I shall not fail to acquaint the Lords what you have written to me …[20]

A footnote below the first letter, in the nineteenth-century printed volume of Laud's *Works*, notes that in his petition Laurence 'represents that he had married a near kinswoman of the late Duke of Buckingham.' Evidently Laurence was marshalling every shred of influence he could call on, to have the tobacco farm restored. However despite taking his case to the Irish Committee in 1638, as he had

19   Laud vol. VII, p.341, Letter CCCXLVI (i.e. 146); 19th April 1637.
20   *Ibid.*, p.400, Letter CCCLXXII (i.e. 372); 19th Dec 1637.

told Laud he would, and the matter being referred to the King,[21] the impost was never reinstated; in 1660 Mary Lisle, petitioning Charles II for a pension, stated that the loss of the impost cost her father £20,000 (over £3m in today's money), although it is not clear if that was potential income or money already laid out.[22] Either way, this figure is astonishing for a non-landed, non-aristocratic individual in the 1640s, and illustrates the financial sphere into which Laurence had risen. Loss of the impost did not prevent him continuing in those circles, however: in 1638, with others including the Earl of Warwick, he was granted a commission:

> for discovery of offenders in buying and selling cards and dice, unsealed, contrary to proclamation. You are to repair to the dwelling-houses of such offenders, or such as refuse to appear to be examined before the commissioners, first having warrant from the commissioners certifying the offenders, and to take them into custody and bring them before us, and all mayors and other officers and subjects to assist you therein.[23]

In 1640 he was listed, again with several knights and peers, as a person considered suitable to sign off the accounts of the Company of Beavermakers, a short-lived monopoly set up by Charles I.[24] A 1647 reference suggests that Laurence worked on or alongside the Board of Green Cloth, which was part of the Lord Steward's department and oversaw the accounts of the Royal Household; during Charles's 'Personal Rule' the Board's remit would probably have stretched to involvement with his numerous schemes to bring in money, in the absence of Parliamentary grants. Certainly his departure from London in 1642, along with the court and attendant machinery, caused Laurence much trouble. On 2nd January 1643, the King being at Oxford, the House of Lords ordered that:

> Sir Edward Warder Knight, Jo. Castle Esquire, John Chichley Esquire, Laurance Lisle Gentleman, Richard Dukeson Doctor in Divinity, Tho. Fuller Batchelor in Divinity, with Two Coaches, with Four Horses or Six Horses for each Coach, and Saddles for Eight or Ten Servants, shall have a Pass, to go to Oxford, to present a Petition to His Majesty.[25]

---

21 *CSP Ireland*, 1633-1647, p.186.
22 *CSP Domestic Series*, 1661-1662, p.259; Measuring Worth (online), Relative Values/Real Price calculation, 1642 vs. 2013. These figures are only offered to give an approximate sense of scale, as the difference in social and financial factors between the two time periods makes it impossible to draw precise comparisons.
23 *CSP Domestic Series*, 1637-1638, p.295. A tax was payable on packs of playing cards; the role of Laurence and his colleagues was to apprehend those who evaded payment and avoided their court summons.
24 *CSP Domestic Series*, 1640-1641, p.365.
25 JHL, 5, 1642-1643, p.523.

However on the 5th the Journal reported a message received from the Commons:

> That they have received Information of Two Coaches and Twelve Horses, with Men, which are stayed at Uxbridge, going towards Oxford; and, upon their Staying, they produced a Warrant for their Passage, under the Clerk's Hand of this House; and being searched, there is found amongst them one Dr. Dukes, and some Clerks of the Privy Signet; and there is found about them Two scandalous Books, arraigning the Proceedings of Parliament, and Letters with Cyphers to Lord Viscount Falkland and the Lord Spencer: The House of Commons think it fit that they should be stayed; but, in regard they have their Lordships Pass, they thought good to acquaint their Lordships first with it.[26]

In the Commons, meanwhile, it was reported that:

> some Gentlemen had been examined, that were going to Oxon; and with them was found a scandalous Book, intituled, 'A Complaint to the Commons,' and other Letters and Matters concerning the Signet: That they had been stayed, had they not produced their Lordships Warrant: The Lords did own the Warrant; but, in regard they had abused it, they were willing to withdraw it, and that they might be sent for back.[27]

The Commons ordered the party's detention anyway, and Wardour, Duckson and Chichely were thrown into prison. The rest of the party were perhaps released without charge, as none are mentioned further by the Lords or Commons. Someone brought the offending *Complaint* to Oxford, however, as *Mercurius Aulicus* reports that at Oxford on 4th January:

> came a Booke from London, being the Complaint of London, Westminster, and the parts adjoyning, which the King caused to be read unto him as He sate at supper: His Majestie not rising from the Table till the whole was finished.[28]

The timing of the book's arrival is so close to Wardour's aborted mission that it might have been one of the rump of his party who brought it, perhaps someone allowed to continue after the interception at Uxbridge, but *Aulicus* does not

---

26   JHL, 5, 1642-1643, pp.529-530.
27   JHC, 2, 1640-1643, p.916.
28   Week 1 (1643), p.5. The document's full title was *A Complaint To The House of Commons, And Resolution taken up by the free Protestant Subjects of the Cities of London and Westminster, and the Counties adjacent* (Wing C5621).

record the carrier. Nor does it note the nature of the King's response, although his approval can be safely presumed, as the *Complaint* was subsequently published at Oxford and York.

Although Laurence may have got away lightly after the arrest of his colleagues, the incident may have caused other trouble for him: perhaps harassment from the Parliamentarian authorities or those in his community who had sided against the King. In an undated petition to the Earl of Salisbury, written in 1644, Laurence asked the Earl for help in recovering goods from a house in St Martin's Lane which he had had to leave in a hurry around April 1643.[29] The petition was apparently delivered on his behalf by his former apprentice Henry Seile, whose St Dunstan's address appears on the back. It reveals much about the worsening situation of the Lisles and of London early in the Civil War:

> Sheweth,
> That your peticioner took a Lease of a House in St Martins Lane belonging to one Mr Culpepper dureing his terme, which was expired at Michas last was two yeares and after bought of the said Mr Culpepper d[ivers?] goods and wainscott nr and about the house, and after the end of his terme your peticionor dwelte in it after it carrie to your Lor:pps hands, a little above halfe a yeare, but by the troublesomnesse of the tymes your peticonor left the house and the key att one Corbetts (where other keyes have been usually lefte,) and put a bill upon the dore, for letting the house with directions to the said Corbett to Shew it …[30]

He asks for an independent third party to value the purchased goods, to receive an agreed price on what could not be removed and to be allowed to collect everything else. He goes on:

> And forasmuch as your peticonors charges, about the house have been Great, his sufferinge (by reason of the distractions of the time) many, and the benefitt of his employment (ever since the beginning of this Parliament) taken away; whereof hee is deprived of the principall meanes of ordinary subsistence. And for that the house is not Letten but for fifteen pounds p[er] Ann hee further prayeth your Lor:pp that hee may pay onely after the same rate it is now letten for, for the short terme hee was in it, and in the Interim that there bee noe Proceedings in law against your peticoner …

---

29   A contemporary hand, different to Laurence's, has written '1642' above the reference to the end of Culpepper's term.

30   CP Petitions 1833; Hatfield House Archives.

An annex attached to the document detailing the total value of the items left in the house comes to £47 11s, around £7,100 today.[31] The lower rental rate of £15 equates to around £2,200 per month, and Laurence infers that the true rental value was far higher. The plea to pay the lower rate is stark evidence of how his circumstances had changed: the departure of the King's Household to York had robbed him of his income. With this in mind, another spur to leave London may have been the forced contributions being levied by Parliament: in April 1643, at around the time the Lisles fled, the Royalist newsbook *Mercurius Aulicus* reported that compliance rates were so low in Westminster in particular that the House of Commons ordered the collectors to take six musketeers with them to enforce payment.[32]

Given his connections to royal finance and the Green Cloth, his erstwhile landlord 'Mr Culpepper' is very likely to have been Sir John, who had been created Chancellor of the Exchequer in January 1642 and then also fled with the King to York. If the house was indeed his – or rather, he was the leaseholder subletting to the Lisles – this may have been when Laurence took on the remainder of his term. Laurence says he has done a lot 'for the bettering of the house' including installing lead piping to bring in water, so certainly this house would not have been the same one the family was leasing in 1624, as such improvements would have been carried out long since. Moreover Laurence's tax certificates state that he was recently living in Surrey. That 'Mr Culpepper' was indeed Sir John has yet to be proved, but the facts as currently known point strongly in that direction.

In 1647 Laurence was summoned to appear in front of the House of Lords: they having information that he possessed some paperwork regarding a deceased tax collector who had not passed on the money to the customs farmers who had employed him.[33] The debt was extraordinary: £945 (around £117,000 today), in arrears since 1634. Laurence was ordered to resolve the situation, obtain the money and pay it to the men who were owed it. He was granted an unspecified fee for his service, although it was unlikely to have been enough to relieve his own financial situation: although he is not mentioned in the Calendar of the Committee for Compounding and Sequestration, in 1660 Mary Lisle stated in her petition to Charles II:

> That your petitioner's father Lawrence Lisle deced was servant to your late royall father and for his constant loyalty had the value of 12 thousand pounds seized and taken neerely from him.[34]

---

31 Measuring Worth (online), Relative Values/Real Price calculation, 1642 vs. 2013.
32 Week 14 (1643), pp.175-176
33 The dead man was William Leachland; the unpaid monies dated back to at least 1641. References to the case are peppered throughout the Commons and Lords journals in 1647 and 1648.
34 State Papers Domestic, Charles II. SP 29/22, f. 244. National Archives, Kew.

When this money seizure occurred or in what circumstances is not known – possibly they occurred when the authorities probed George's activities in the wake of his death – but evidently like a great many Royalists Laurence was severely punished financially for his allegiance.

The last sighting of him is in 1652, when the State Papers record that he presented a petition to the Committee for Newfoundland; the contents are unknown, but given his previous employments it probably concerned another financial scheme.[35] His date of death and place of burial, and that of Dorothy, are unknown, but they were both deceased by 1660, when Mary stated in her petition that after George's death they had died 'overwhelmed with greefe' for the loss of their sons.

---

35   *CSP Colonial Series*, 1574-1660, p.377.

Part II

George Lisle:
A Worthy Commander in the Warres

He knowes the hazards of battels … and strives to gain reputation not by multitude, but by the greatnes of his actions. He is the first in giving the charge, and the last in retiring his foot. Equall toile he endures with the Common Souldier, from his example they all take fire, as one Torch lights many.

A Worthy Commander in the Warres – from Sir Thomas Overbury's *A Wife*, published by Laurence Lisle

5

Early Glimpses

Nothing is known of George Lisle's pre-soldiering life, other than the date and place of his baptism: 10th July 1615 at St Gregory by St Paul's, the little parish church built against the south-west side of the cathedral. In line with Laurence's frequent spelling of the name as 'L'Isle' the baptism register renders it 'Leyslie', not 'Lisle', possibly why it has not come to light before. As Elizabeth's and Francis's baptisms were spelled 'Lislie', and George is mentioned by numerous wartime sources as Colonel 'Lisley' or 'Lesley' – including the Parliamentarian newsbook *Mercurius Britanicus*, and Royalist William Sanderson in his 1658 history of Charles I[1] – it seems overwhelmingly that 'Lisley' was the usual pronunciation of the family name, not 'Lyle'.

Of George's wider family life, much is of course known via his father's story. Until he was two or three years old, the family almost certainly lived in St Paul's Churchyard in rooms above the *Tygers Head*;[2] of siblings there would have been Laurence's daughter Elizabeth from his first marriage, older brother William, and younger brother Francis, joined sometime between 1618 and 1624 by Mary, and then Anthony after the family had moved to St Martin's. Possibly Joan Cooke's daughter Margerie may also have remained in Laurence's care. With five or possibly six young children, two adults and an apprentice living above the shop, the living quarters would have been desperately cramped, and the move out to St Martin's must have been extremely welcome. Yet commonly enough for that period, it seems only some of the children survived to adulthood. Elizabeth married William Holman at St Martin's in 1632; Francis, like George, fought for the King during the Civil War; Mary survived, unmarried, at least into the 1670s. Of William and Anthony, however, there is no record of them joining their father and brothers

---

1   Numb. 6, p.44; Sanderson p.38.
2   A list of businesses around the churchyard in 1635 makes it clear that despite the shop premises being small, there were upper rooms: '8. Is the sign of the Tigers Head, a booksellers shop, over which 2 shops of number 7 and 8 dwelleth Henry Seile.' (State Papers Charles I., vol. 310, No. 35 (calendared as *CSP Domestic Series*, 1635-1636, p.67)).

in the Royalist cause, and in her 1660 petition Mary stated that she was 'the only person of her family surviving the oppression of the late government's'. Possibly her brothers died young, although William is not found in the burial registers of St Gregory's or St Martin's, and neither is Anthony at St Martin's, suggesting that either they died very soon after birth and were baptised and buried on the same day, or at death they were older children or young adults who had left the family home. Alternatively, if the Lisles did move out to Warwickshire or Surrey for a period, it is possible one or both of the boys died there. There are at least two records of William Lisleys dying in London before the Civil War – one of plague in 1636[3] – although there is no way of knowing if either of them was George's brother. The only trace of Anthony's existence is his baptism.

The most significant figure in George's early life beyond his immediate family would have been George Villiers, whose star Laurence followed until it was extinguished in 1628. Villiers was knighted on St George's Day in 1615, two months or so before George Lisle was born; given the timing, and Villiers' importance to the family, both politically and due to him being Dorothy's relative, it is tempting to speculate whether Lisle was named after the rising royal favourite. Almost certainly he must have met him, whether at an official function or in a family setting. He was thirteen when Buckingham was assassinated, and again we can only speculate about the effect the murder might have had on a boy whose entire life had been influenced by the Duke's presence and patronage. The Lisle-Villiers connection also brings up the question of potential childhood friends and acquaintances of George and Francis, who would later play their part alongside them in the Civil War. In this respect two of Villiers' nephews, William and Edward ('Ned') Villiers, particularly stand out. Their father was Buckingham's older half-brother; William inherited the Grandison viscountcy from a great-uncle in 1630 and went on to become a prominent supporter of King Charles. Prior to that, in 1640, George was one of Grandison's captains during the second Bishops' War, while Edward Villiers was an ensign alongside Francis in the regiment of George Goring. George's commission under Grandison suggests a link to earlier family ties, and Edward and Francis would have become well acquainted during the 1640 expedition, if too young to have done so through family connections before. The Lisle brothers would also have known Grandison's younger brother John, who succeeded William as viscount in 1643, and in February 1644/45 was quartered with his regiment at Faringdon, where George was governor of the Royalist garrison.[4]

The Villiers family tentacles stretched much further, however. Also connected to the family, in the Civil War context, were dragoon colonel Henry Washington, another of Buckingham's nephews, and – after the marriage of Henry's sister

---

3   St Mary Magdalen, Bermondsey, 3rd September.
4   Letter from John, Lord Grandison, to Prince Rupert, dated 7th February 1645; BL Add MS 62083, f.67.

Elizabeth in March 1642 – his brother-in-law William Legge, a senior Royalist in Rupert's circle with whom George Lisle would often have had contact. The Feilding brothers were also nephews of Buckingham: Basil, a Parliamentarian who succeeded as Earl of Denbigh in 1643, and Richard, a Royalist who infamously surrendered Reading to the Earl of Essex in the same year and narrowly avoided being shot for treason. All these men were roughly Lisle's age, and given their equally close connection to Buckingham, it is entirely possible that Lisle had met some or all of them during his youth.

Besides the dates of his baptism and death, and several portraits and engravings, the only other close personal detail known about Lisle is that he had a stammer: it is mentioned in two sources, one Parliamentarian and one Royalist, and was possibly alluded to at the time of his death. The first mention is found in the Parliamentarian newsbook *Mercurius Britanicus*, regarding his conduct at Leicester in 1645:

> … the young man being a stammering Royalist, uses [oathes] at every Pause to lispe out God dammee, to fill up his Oratory:[5]

The second comes from an elegy printed a month after his death:

> No need of swords to have the Rebels sped; He had soul enough to Lispe whole squadrons dead.[6]

Although the stammer was evidently prominent enough that both friend and enemy were aware of it, he must have had enough control over it that it did not greatly affect his communications on the battlefield. A significant quantity of his speech at Colchester was recorded by William Clarke, Secretary to the Council of the [Parliamentarian] Army: although there is no indication in Clarke's verbatim notes that Lisle had a stammer, a newsbook reference to him 'redoubling' his words in the closing minutes of his life might well suggest it re-emerged then. Notably, when his speaking style is compared to the flowery and often convoluted speech of the day, he appears concise and straightforward, saying just enough to make himself precisely understood. Although this may have come from having a publisher father who was an effective, even blunt, communicator himself, it may also have been a style he developed to mitigate the involuntary interruptions of his stammer.

When the war began in 1642 Lisle was immediately commissioned as a lieutenant colonel, which strongly suggests that he was one of the many early Royalist officers who had prior military experience. However, the documentary evidence

---

5   No. 87, p.789.
6   *An Elegie On the Death of Sir Charles Lucas and Sir George Lisle*, 1648.

for a previous soldiering career is sketchy: besides his captaincy under Grandison in 1640 there is no incontestable written evidence for him fighting anywhere else beforehand, although in both known portraits from the late 1630s he wears a gorget and scarf, and in one of them a buffcoat. In 1668 David Lloyd, a compiler of Royalist biographies, said of Lisle that he 'trailed a pike in the Low Countries'; he is the earliest known contemporary source to mention Lisle fighting on the Continent, and where he found this information is not known. It does not appear in the November 1648 pamphlet *The Loyall Sacrifice*, from which Lloyd para- phrases most of his piece on Lisle. It may simply be an assumption of Lloyd's however: his study of Royalist officers was lengthy, and as many began their careers abroad, naturally he would have turned to accounts of Continental actions in the 1620s and 30s. Undoubtedly would have mined Henry Hexham's famous account of the siege of Breda in 1637, at which a great many future Royalists were present. Hexham makes a single mention of a 'Mr Lyle' in a list of officers and volunteers who attacked a hornwork, and it may be this reference which informed Lloyd's biography in 1668.[7] Certainly, subsequent historians have uncritically taken the Breda reference to mean George Lisle, but as Hexham does not give a first name there is no way to tell; quite apart from his man being 'Lyle', when it has been demonstrated here that in fact George's surname was generally taken to be 'Lisley', and was usually spelled to sound so. Furthermore, Francis Lisle reportedly also served in the Low Countries, and spelling notwithstanding the Breda man could have been him.[8] On the other hand, Hexham lists Lord Grandison in the same company, which might tip the balance in favour of 'Mr Lyle' being George, but ultimately unless personnel records of that company can be unearthed, it is impossible to know for sure.

Where *The Loyall Sacrifice* suggests Lisle always sought to improve himself, Lloyd interprets this as gaining military skills 'by observation in the modern and ancient Militia', and adds that Lisle was 'admitted into inferior commands in England', both of which suggest that if he was not merely making creative assump- tions, that he may have had some minor source of information now lost.[9] Although 'inferior commands' may have referred in part to Lisle's Bishops' War captaincy, it could also conceivably refer to militia service as Lloyd suggests. As Lisle was a Londoner this would most likely have meant a local company of the London Trained Bands, but despite good sources being available for their membership, he is not listed.[10] Another possibility is membership of the Society of the Artillery

---

7   *A True and Briefe Relation* …, 1637, p.28.

8   *The London Post*, Numb. 1, pp.2-3.

9   *Memoires of the Lives, Actions, Sufferings & Deaths* …, 1668, p.478.

10 [Author: I am grateful to two separate researchers in that field, Andy Robertshaw and Steve King, who have confirmed to me that Lisle does not appear to have been a Trained Bands man.]

Garden, which met in the City, although it appears that few records for that period are extant.

The next military record of Lisle is absolutely certain: he was a Captain in Lord Grandison's regiment, in the English army sent north to repel the Scots in the summer of 1640. His contemporary, the journalist and later military secretary John Rushworth, offers two muster rolls for the army: one apparently taken when it arrived in Yorkshire and the other after it had retreated following the disastrous skirmish at Newburn, near Newcastle upon Tyne (Rushworth was at the battle himself).[11] The one usually quoted by modern commentators is the post-skirmish roll, which was reprinted by Edmund Peacock in 1874, and therefore readily available to researchers. Whilst that roll lists 'George Lisle' under Grandison, the previous roll (which Peacock omits) calls him 'Captain Lesley' and credits his company with 96 men. The soldiers for this second war against the Scottish Covenanters had been levied from the English counties, and Lisle's company came from Gloucestershire: a local record from 1640 notes '130 men levied from the City and its County, and delivered to Captain George Lisle'.[12] The loss of 34 men between there and Yorkshire is perhaps only to be expected, given the rawness of the recruits and the frequency of desertion and mutiny across the 1640 army as a whole. There is no record of Lisle's specific actions or experiences during the campaign, although both he and his brother returned safely and were recorded at the post-skirmish muster.

Lisle's whereabouts and activities between September 1640 and October 1642 can only be speculatively deduced, but it seems likely that he remained in the north until late 1641. That Grandison's regiment remained in Yorkshire over the winter of 1640/41 is clear from records of financial transactions extant in the State Papers. On 23rd October his quartermaster paid £4 for a regimental bread delivery from 'Trinity House',[13] which must have been the premises of the Trinity House mariners' guild in Hull, as Hull was where Commissary Leonard Pinkney, whose deputy received the quartermaster's money, was stationed during both Bishops' Wars. Furthermore, a letter from army treasurer Sir William Uvedale to his deputy reveals that Grandison received pay warrants up to 8th December from Sir Jacob Astley, Sergeant Major General of the English Army in the north, who was stationed at York.[14] Almost a year later, in September 1641, Grandison was sent into Scotland to monitor the Scottish side of the agreed mutual disbandment of

11 Rushworth, 1686, pp.1241-1252. Lisle is mentioned on pages 1241 and 1245 respectively. Peacock only reprints the second muster list (pp.73-91). Some officers present on the first are absent on the second, and vice versa, and it appears that between the two musters a few were promoted.
12 Gloucestershire Archives: Gloucester Lieutenancy Order & Letter Book, ref. GBR H/2/3, pp.20-21. According to a list printed at the time, Lord Grandison recruited in Leicestershire, Worcestershire and Gloucestershire (STC 19616).
13 *CSP Domestic Series*, 1640-1641, p.194.
14 *Ibid.*, p.517.

Bishops' War forces,[15] and this seems the most likely point at which Lisle would finally have returned to London. His absence from the capital over the previous winter and spring of 1640/41 clears him from any direct involvement in the 'Army Plots' fomented by a number of high-profile proto-Royalists in London, mostly those clustered around the Queen, although it is entirely possible that he was one of those officers in the north who signed the letter of complaint about the army's neglect that kicked the business off.

The King's precarious political position, which led to his dissolving the 'Short Parliament' of April-May 1640 after only three weeks, meant that the second Bishops' War was plagued by bad planning and chronic lack of funds. Post-Newburn, as the remnants of the English army lingered in the north well into 1641 as a buffer against the Scots occupying the northern counties, political and financial obstacles delayed the promised payment of Bishops' War arrears. Most significantly, the humiliating Treaty of Ripon which had formally ended the war in 1640 mandated that England would pay the Scottish army £850 per day, to maintain its occupying armies in the north: this was unaffordable even in the short term, and as early as 1641 Parliament was forced to divert funds raised for the English army to pay the Scots. The English officers were owed not just their own pay, but the costs of maintaining their soldiers from their own pockets in an effort to stave off mutiny and desertion. As late as July 1642, two years after the fighting concluded, the House of Commons Journal recorded that a number of officers, from colonels down to captains, were still owed 'their Arrears for their personal Entertainment for their Service in the late Northern Expedition'.[16] The Journal specifically records that:

> One hundred and Ten Pounds of the Arrears due to Colonel Goring, be paid out of the same Arrears that is due to Colonel Goring for his personal Entertainment in the North, as soon as the same is paid to Capt. Geo. Lisle, according to Colonel Goring's assignment.[17]

Goring's £110 in 1642 was equivalent to over £16,000 today; the above reference is ambiguous about whether George Lisle was owed the same amount, or just owed the same type of monies. Contemporary reports of Lisle's actions during the Civil War indicate that he was a diligent commander, determined to do whatever it took to get a job done: it is entirely in character that in the lowering atmosphere surrounding the army stuck in Yorkshire, although just a captain, he might have funded his company himself. If he did, and was owed anything like Goring, he can only have funded it with Laurence's support as he did not – as far as is presently

---

15   JHL, 4, 1629-1642, p.388; JHC, 2, 1640-1643, p.280.
16   JHC, 2, 1640-1643, p.688.
17   *Ibid.*

known – have an independent source of income. If two years later George was still waiting for Parliament to repay him, and thus his father, this would only have added to Laurence's money problems in 1642.

To add to the King's domestic troubles in England, and the financially-draining rift with the Scots, in October 1641 Catholic insurgents revolted in Ulster, and attempted to seize Dublin Castle. The State Papers and Commons Journal contain numerous Parliamentary discussions concerning the raising of troops to send over the water in response, however the timeline of what forces were raised, and when, and of whom they consisted is not particularly clear. A muster list for what historian Andrew Hopper calls 'Lord Wharton's projected expedition' was printed in June 1642;[18] Lisle is not mentioned, but the author of a London pamphlet published the following December, unable to account for Lisle's whereabouts post-Edgehill, noted that he 'had his Commission for a company in Ireland, but never came over'.[19] This suggests he was the Captain George Lisle commissioned under Colonel William Cromwell in the Marquess of Ormonde's new Leinster army, as per an undated list found amongst Ormonde's papers.[20] As the list is described as 'foote sent out of England', it would suggest Lisle had already gone over, but as 'Deserter' asserts that he never did – and whatever that pamphlet's faults, it is an odd piece of information to be mistaken about – it is fair to conclude that he must have had his paperwork but not yet crossed to Ireland when the King-Parliament split came to a head in late summer 1642. Hopper notes that when this occurred, men still in England who had recently signed up for the Irish army were shifted into Essex's army without consultation: to a fervent Royalist such as Lisle this would have been unacceptable, and would explain why he and numerous others either reneged on their 'Irish' commissions before Edgehill, or found opportunity to turn their coats early in the war.[21] A second list published in June 1642 a few days after the first, of reformado officers to be retained on half-pay for Irish service 'untill opportunity be offered',[22] was in Brigadier Peter Young's opinion a fig-leaf to cover Parliament's guileful attempt to secure experienced officers for the brewing English war.[23]

---

18 Hopper, Appendix 3 fn. 2; *A List of the Field Officers chosen and appointed for the Irish Expedition …* British Library, 669.f.6.31. The Wharton list largely tallies with a muster list in Ormonde's paperwork, however (Ormonde, vol. I, 1895, p.124), which would make it not 'projected' as Hopper suggests, but an actual register of officers.

19 *A Most True Relation of the Present State of His Majesties Army …*, 3rd December 1642. Usually referred to by modern historians as 'Deserter'.

20 Ormonde, vol. I, 1895, p.124.

21 Hopper, p.160. He also includes an appendix of men who defected from Essex's Army, 1642-1645. Deserter mentions a couple of others who reneged on their Irish commissions.

22 *A List of the Names of Such Persons Who are thought fit for their Accommodation, and the furtherance of the Service in Ireland …* BL, 669.f.6.32. Young's assertion is in *Edgehill 1642*, p.4.

23 *Edgehill 1642*, p.4.

If George Lisle, like his brother, had gone to Ireland, it seems likely given his royalism that he would have abandoned that commission later to fight in England for the King, as many of his later colleagues did: men such as Charles Lloyd, John Boys (who had served with George in 1640), and kinsman Henry Washington. All these men had signed up for the Lord Lieutenant General's regiment; coincidentally Francis went to Ireland with the same regiment and stayed there until the 'Cessation' in late 1643, when he returned as its major.[24] Why he did not do as George in 1642 and throw down his Irish commission, is not known; perhaps he was already in Leinster and so could not be duplicitously diverted to fight for Parliament.

So in summary, all that can be ascertained for certain about Lisle between the second Bishops' War and Edgehill is that he was owed money from the former and dropped an Irish commission between the two, probably to avoid being drafted into the Parliamentarian army. However, he was then commissioned in 1642 as a senior field officer. Two or three months spent largely in a Dutch trench in 1637 or attacking defensive works (if he was indeed Hexham's man), an abortive two-month expedition into the North to face the Scots for one morning's fighting in 1640, and an idle year stationed in Yorkshire placating mutinous men, would hardly give Lisle sufficient military education and experience to equip him in a colonel's role, at which he proved extremely capable. Whilst from a well-connected family who were not short of money, he was not born at the elevated social level where he might automatically expect a commission: his must have been earned. Furthermore, the type of fighting which he was frequently trusted to command, and clearly excelled at – dragoon work, fast and dirty scouting and skirmishing ahead of the body of the army – was a recent development in Europe, and as yet not used in England due to the long peace. The only sensible conclusion is that at some point during the early- or mid-1630s Lisle underwent military service abroad of which no record survives or has yet been unearthed. If it was in the Netherlands, as David Lloyd maintained, it must have extended far further than Breda. A fragmentary clue, perhaps, lies elsewhere in Lloyd's *Memoires*: in a footnote to a paragraph listing the names of a number of Royalists, Lloyd adds, 'Sir George Lisle bred them up and his Brother Major Lisle …' This would seem to mean that he trained or commanded some or all of these men at some point, although the confusing placement of the footnote callout makes it impossible to ascertain to whom Lloyd refers.[25]

24 Henry Warren was colonel by the time the regiment returned, and Francis was promoted to lieutenant colonel shortly afterwards when the previous incumbent was killed at Nantwich.
25 *Memoires* …, 1668, p.698.

Before this account moves on to the Civil War, a curious interlude from 1638 bears mention. On 18th June the Middlesex Sessions Rolls recorded 'the indictment &c. of George Lyle for the slaying of Robert Wood [? Wade]'. The roll notes that:

> [At] St. Martin's-in-the-Fields co. Midd. on the said day, George Lyle late of the said parish gentleman assaulted Robert Wade, and with a sword gave him in the right part of his body a mortal wound, of which he languished from the said 9th of May to the 24th of the same month at the said parish, on which last-named day he died at St. Martin's-in-the-Fields of the said wound. On his trial at the Old Bailey, George Lyle was acquitted of felonious slaying, 'sed cul se defendend' = but Guilty of defending himself.

The roll adds:

> He put himself Not Guilty on a jury of the country, and the jury says he is not Guilty of felonious slaying, but guilty of defending himself, that is to say, that the aforesaid Robert assaulted the aforesaid George, and pursued him even to the rails of the New Exchange, beyond which the said George could not escape without danger of life, and because the same Robert ran in furiously on the same George, the same George drew sword in self-defence, and thus slew the same Robert.[26]

Arrest and imprisonment records from the period are scarce, so a more precise identification of this acquitted defendant is unlikely. However his name (albeit Lyle and not Lisle), parish of residence, and description as 'gentleman' narrow the field enough to raise the significant possibility that he was the George Lisle of this biography, therefore the incident should be borne in mind when considering Lisle's whereabouts in 1638.

---

26 'Middlesex Sessions Rolls: 1638', Middlesex county records: Volume 3: 1625-67.

6

Proving Grounds: Edgehill to Newbury I

Powick Bridge

The detailed specifics of the slide towards war, in the twelve months between the Irish rebellion and the battle of Edgehill, can be studied in any good commentary on the period, and need not be covered here. Suffice to say, after the King's failed attempt to arrest the 'Five Members' in January 1642 and the subsequent uproar in London, in March Charles left for York with his supporters, where recruitment for a 'Royalist' army began in earnest. After Colonel George Goring, governor of Portsmouth, declared for the King on 2nd August, Parliament sent a force to reduce the town and Charles marched to Nottingham and raised the Royal Standard on the 22nd. Thus the moment when war, a possibility for months should the King manage to raise an army, became a genuine prospect. Thereafter Charles and his army travelled to Shrewsbury via Derby, Tutbury, Uttoxeter, Stafford and Wellington; they were shadowed by the Parliament's main force under the command of the Earl of Essex, who had occupied Northampton but now headed for Worcester.

It is unclear whose command Lisle served under prior to and during the battle of Edgehill, but there is evidence for a good working relationship with Rupert later on which may have been fostered on the Continent in the late 1630s, or by serving under him during the first few months of the war. Whilst Lisle's whereabouts before that first major battle are unknown, given his particular skill set it is most likely that he was travelling somewhere in the Prince's orbit: so it is the movement of his forces which this account will follow for the present. As the Royalist army paused at Stafford on 17th September, news came of Essex's intention to seize Worcester, and in response Rupert was ordered to take eight troops of horse and ten of dragoons to the city.[1] On the 20th he set up headquarters at Bridgnorth, midway between Worcester and Shrewsbury, where he firstly received orders to advance immediately on Worcester to protect Sir John Byron and a convoy of plate and money

---

1   Warburton, vol. I, p.396.

he was bringing from Oxford, and then secondly further orders containing the King's permission to engage the enemy as he saw fit.[2] Accordingly Rupert headed for Worcester. On the 23rd, as he and Sir John skirted the south of the city near Powick with 700 of the Prince's force,[3] which intended to cover Byron's retreat to the north, the party encountered 500 to 1,000 of Essex's cavalry and dragoons. Rupert led an immediate charge across the river Teme at Powick Bridge, and after some close combat routed the enemy; dozens of Essex's men drowned, and around 50 were taken prisoners. None of the surviving accounts specifically mention the involvement of Royalist dragoons or commanded men, but there were certainly dragoons in the vicinity: Nehemiah Wharton, a Parliamentarian sergeant who wrote an account of the skirmish for his employer in London, stated that 'Towards even[ing] Prince Robert entered the city at a bye passage with eighteen troops of horse …', which tallies perfectly with the troop numbers given in the Stafford order of the 17th. Moreover, Wharton adds that Rupert refused the mayor's offer of hospitality in favour of attacking the enemy, and 'immediately set some to lye in ambush, and with the rest sallied out upon our forces …'[4] As strategic ambushes were typical work for dragoons, it seems likely that it was they whom Rupert left in the city, perhaps to prevent an enemy encroachment from the rear via the other 'passages over the Severne' which Wharton said were kept by his side's troops to prevent the Royalists leaving. Although Lisle is not mentioned in the accounts of that engagement, given the fast-moving nature of Rupert's expedition to Worcester and the involvement of dragoons, it is very likely he was present in some capacity, probably with the force left behind to secure the city.

Edgehill

The Royalist cavalry were the first to arrive on the high ridge overlooking the Warwickshire village of Kineton on 23rd October. It was a Sunday, and the weather had been wet and extremely cold. For the Prince's troops, assembling at dawn on such exposed terrain must have proved miserable, many feeling the effects of inadequate rations and the accumulated fatigue of an eleven day progress from Shrewsbury. Even those men allocated billets the previous night would not have snatched much sleep: Clarendon states that it was around midnight when

2   *Ibid.*, p.398.
3   This figure was given by Lord Falkland, writing from Shrewsbury a few days later.
4   Wharton's account is reproduced by Peachey, *The Battle of Powick Bridge 1642*, p.18. Wharton was not present at the skirmish, but arrived with the rest of the Parliamentarian infantry a few days later. Eighteen troops, if substantially complete, would contain considerably more men than the 700 mentioned by Falkland – over 1,000 in total – but Falkland may not be including the troops Rupert left in the city. The Parliamentarian Edmund Ludlow, who was present, contradicts Falkland, saying 'Ours consisted of about a thousand Horse and Dragoons, the Enemy being more in number …' (*Memoirs* vol. I, p.44).

the Prince's quartermasters stumbled on their enemy counterparts in Kineton, confirmation of the Parliamentarian presence did not arrive until 3 a.m., and the King advised Rupert at four that he had given orders for the army to reassemble at Edgehill.[5] Peter Young offers a vivid description of the army's hasty muster: 'Drums beating in the dark of a frosty dawn, drowsy, breakfastless soldiers emerging from barn and cottage, buckling on their equipment, and stamping about to keep warm.'[6]

The only surviving Royalist account which mentions Lisle at Edgehill is that of Richard Bulstrode, a trooper in the Prince of Wales's regiment of horse:

> ... Colonel George Lisle, with Lieutenant Collonel Ennis were in the left
> Wing, with a regiment of Dragoons, to defend the Briars on that Side ...[7]

This is our first definite Civil War sighting of Lisle. At first it appears flawed, as Bulstrode calls him a colonel when in fact he was a lieutenant colonel like Innes, but this is explained by Bulstrode writing up his memoirs many decades later at the age of ninety-four, and using the men's later ranks, rather than those they carried at the time of the battle.[8]

Contemporary sources are clear that Innes commanded Prince Rupert's dragoons, but Lisle could not have been his deputy as he held the same rank; more-over, Bulstrode was outlining the cavalry and dragoon dispositions on that wing, and the other men he mentions were what he termed 'principal officers', that is, those with commands. It seems odd that he should mention Lisle alongside them if he did not also have a command. The most fitting conclusion must be that Lisle was a key player in his own right. Yet what was his role? Because of his positioning with Innes he is generally assumed to have been a dragoon officer, but none of the units known to be stationed at that end of the Royalist line had positions available.

Much ink has been spilled regarding the dragoon dispositions at Edgehill, and none of our modern commentators agree in their assessments. Of contemporary sources, we have at least sixteen Royalist accounts or partial accounts of Edgehill, but only four offer any insight into which regiments were placed where,[9] none

---

5   Book VI, 1840 vol. III, p.255; Rushworth, 1691, vol. II, pp.33-35 (viewed via British History Online); The King's brief letter containing his orders is reprinted in Warburton, vol. II, p.12.

6   *Edgehill 1642*, p.77.

7   Bulstrode, *Memoirs And Reflections ...*, p.81. Young also quotes Bulstrode's account in full (*Edgehill 1642*, pp.254-261).

8   In the seventeenth century this was a widespread practice when referring to someone in a historical account, but it causes much confusion for historians now; particularly when a particular title was carried by an earlier incumbent at the time the account is referring back to.

9   Those of Bulstrode, the Duke of York, Colonel John Belasyse and the Earl of Clarendon. The first three accounts are reprinted in Young's *Edgehill 1642*; Belasyse's account is also reprinted in the Marquess of Ormonde's MSS (vol. II, 1903), and Clarendon's account can be found in book six of his *History of the Rebellion*.

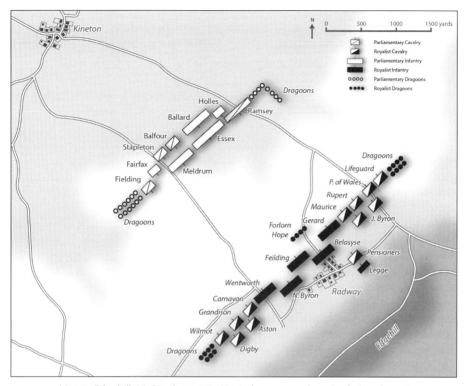

Map 1 Edgehill, 23 October 1642. Was Lisle commanding the forlorn hope?

of them offer a complete picture (though Bulstrode's account is probably the best in that respect), and two contradict each other regarding the position of Sir Arthur Aston, appointed Sergeant Major General of Dragoons three days earlier.[10] However, it is clear that there were at least two groups of dragoons on the left wing: those under Innes, and a party under Colonel Edward Grey which included his own regiment and possibly some additions. Stuart Reid believes Lisle must have fought under Grey,[11] however this does not fit the known battlefield positioning, as Lisle was on the front line with Innes, and Gray was stationed with the reserve: if Lisle was to assist Grey, he would have been stationed with him. James Ussher's dragoon regiment is out of the question as it was led by Lisle's kinsman Lieutenant

10   Basil Morgan, ODNB. Clarendon places Aston on the left, whereas the Duke of York says he was on the right. Both accounts were written many years after the event. However, it is perfectly possible that Aston as Sergeant Major General responsible for troops on both wings, made his way back and forth across the battlefield as his command required.

11   *All The King's Armies*, p.18.

Colonel Henry Washington, and all sources agree that that regiment was on the right wing, together with another, unnamed dragoon unit frequently suggested to have been Sir Edward Duncombe's.[12]

There is one final possibility. Colonel Belasyse's account observes that:

> … before every body of foot were placed two pieces of cannon, and before them the dragoons, and 1,200 commanded musqueteers as Enfants Perdu.

The first consideration must be whether Belasyse was correct about the presence of these commanded men, but at least one other account mentions them.[13] Few modern historians have picked up on their existence, and none raise the question of who commanded these troops.[14] If Lisle's subsequent career is taken into account, he becomes the prime candidate: he led commanded dragoons in the van at Chalgrove in June 1643; led 1,200 commanded men during the Gloucester/Newbury campaign in the late summer; led what *Mercurius Aulicus* described as 'the forlorn hope' at Newbury;[15] and in early 1644, after gaining full colonelcy, he took charge of the commanded Reading garrison force in Hampshire, previously led by Colonel Richard Bolle.[16] Three months later, even having become a tercio commander, he led a commanded force of 1,000 men in Lord Wilmot's whirlwind expedition to relieve Dudley Castle; in November he took a commanded force to Donnington Castle to recover its artillery after the second battle at Newbury, and then accompanied Rupert on at least one lightning raid on enemy-held Abingdon. Leading skirmishing forces was unquestionably Lisle's specialty. As this specialist officer with no known command was stationed at Edgehill near 1,200 commanded men whose commander is unknown, the obvious conclusion is that he was the officer who led them.

It is difficult to see where in the Royalist line-up these commanded men could have fought after the start of the battle, as at some point they must have moved out of the way to allow the infantry proper to march forward.[17] They cannot

---

12   A marginal note in 'Prince Rupert's Diary' (a set of notes made by an anonymous officer under his command) notes that when Rupert raided Essex's baggage train he took with him two regiments of dragoons. It would even out the known Royalist dispositions at the start of the battle, as it would mean there were two dragoon regiments on each wing (diary extract in Young, *Edgehill 1642*, p.274).

13   The account exists in a collection being readied for publication, therefore details cannot be given here at present.

14   [Author To my present knowledge, the only historians who have discussed them are Keith Roberts and John Tincey in their *Edgehill 1642* campaign book published by Osprey (pp.52-53, and map pp.62-63), and Stuart Reid, in *All the King's Armies* (p.19).]

15   Week 38 (1644), pp.528-529.

16   Bolle had been killed at Alton in December.

17   Roberts and Tincey assume the commanded men fought alongside the regular dragoons on the left wing; Reid (p.19) believes they and the dragoons must have 'formed a rudimentary skirmish line ahead of the infantry brigades.' However, Belasyse places the artillery line between the dragoons/commanded

have cleared off to one side, as such a large body would have been noted; possibly they scattered in small groups to either end of the line, or made towards the rear between the oncoming files. However as they are not mentioned again in any other account, it seems most likely that they dispersed completely within a short time, their task complete, and melted back into their usual regiments. What Lisle's role would have been during the remainder of the battle is unknown, but he may have joined Innes to assist the dragoons on the left flank or lead other, smaller bodies in the hedges – and in that position was recorded by Bulstrode.

In all probability, after an early start and a long wait in the cold – there being no recorded action until past noon – Lisle's Edgehill would have been brief and relatively uneventful. After soundly routing the Parliament cavalry at Powick Bridge, Prince Rupert had already gained a reputation as a commander to be feared. Hence at Edgehill, when the Parliamentarian commanders realised that the Prince was stationed on the Royalist right wing, they threw most of their best cavalry onto their own left to oppose him. The Duke of York continues:

> … as for their right wing of horse, which were not all come up, they drew that part of them which was present behind their foot, seeing they were not strong enough to encounter with the King's left wing, and lin'd the bushes with some dragoons to make a shew.

If we take this account as accurate, it appears that the Parliamentarians temporarily parked their incomplete right-wing cavalry, placing it safely out of the way behind the infantry, and merely leaving some dragoons in the hedges there. Once the battle was in progress, Rupert's right wing quickly broke the Parliamentarian left, and famously pursued it all the way to Kineton. Meanwhile, says the Duke:

> While this past, the left wing had not much to do, as having only some dragoons, and two or three regiments of foot before them, of which they made a quick dispatch …

And Prince Rupert's Diary states that:

> In ye meantime Lord Wilmott fell upon the Dragoons; and they ran away.[18]

men and those brigades, which would put Reid's skirmish line in a precarious position during the initial cannonade. Possibly the slope at Edgehill enabled them to keep well below any Royalist gun trajectory, or alternatively Belasyse may have meant that they were ahead of the gun line, but to the sides; thus negating Reid's theory.

18   Extract in Young, *Edgehill 1642*, p.274.

Henry Wilmot was Rupert's lieutenant general of horse, and besides commanding a regiment of his own, was in overall charge of the cavalry on the left wing; one would presume that the Duke of York, when referring to Wilmot falling on the (Parliamentarian) dragoons, is more precisely referring to the action of the left wing Royalist dragoon units who ultimately fell under his direction. Both the front and reserve lines of left wing horse then emulated Rupert and chased the enemy towards Kineton; what the dragoons did is unrecorded, but given that they would be either dismounted in the hedges or on slow ponies rather than horses fit for a chase, probably they would have stayed behind to secure the territory they had claimed, and to mop up enemy stragglers. Certainly there is no further mention of them in the battle accounts.

The fighting had not started until two or three o'clock in the afternoon, and it being late in the year, darkness quickly closed in. The official Royalist account recalls that:

> By this time it was grown so dark, that our chief commanders durst not charge for fear of mistaking friends for foes … whereupon both armies retreated … we retiring to the top of the hill from whence we came; because of the advantage of the place, and theirs to the village where they had been quartr'd the night before.

Once again the night was bitterly cold. As dawn broke on the 24th, any thought to resume fighting was quickly put aside. King Charles, observing various pieces of enemy artillery left on the battlefield, proposed to march down and retrieve them; but, as the Duke of York later reported:

> … the King finding his foot much decreased in number, the greatest part of them being stragled into the neighbouring villages to get victuals, thought it not adviseable to take that action, and therefore about evening return'd to his former quarters at Edgecott; the enemy at the same time retreating towards Warwick.

On 27th October Banbury Castle surrendered to the Royalists, apparently after just a single cannon volley; on the 28th Rupert took and spoiled Broughton Castle, the nearby home of Lord Saye. The composition of the Prince's force there is unclear, but given the assorted nature of his troops during later actions, it is likely that there were dragoons present. On the 29th, the King was militarily unopposed as his forces marched into Oxford and made it his headquarters. At around the same time, Rupert was investigating the town of Abingdon seven miles to the south;[19] it was later garrisoned for the King. Rupert had certainly moved

---

19   Nugent, vol. 2, p.320.

into Buckinghamshire by the 31st, for he spent at least one night of 'free quarter' at Aylesbury,[20] briefly leaving a garrison there before clashing with Parliament forces at a ford north of the town on 1st November. Rapid deployment and redeployment was to become his trademark. At Holman's Ford, the waiting Parliamentarian force gained the upper hand and for once Rupert and his men were forced to flee. With his forces temporarily in disarray, and his Aylesbury troops dislodged, the Prince regrouped his men at Thame and then headed for Maidenhead. Thereafter he unsuccessfully summoned Windsor Castle on 7th November and made his famous assault on Brentford on the 12th. But was George Lisle with him?

Winter 1642

Post-Edgehill, Lisle's whereabouts sink once more into a period of obscurity: the next time he is mentioned in action is in June 1643 at Chalgrove, near Oxford, where he led dragoons under Rupert's command. Where had he been since the autumn of 1642? The Prince was highly active over the winter and following spring, his breakneck itinerary including taking Cirencester, attacking Birmingham, and removing the Parliamentarian garrison from Lichfield after sieging the cathedral close. Barely a day after his Lichfield victory he was summoned south at a forced march to help break the Earl of Essex's siege of Reading. He failed, not due to any military shortcomings of his own but to the poor decisions of Reading's Royalist governor, Lisle's kinsman Richard Feilding. All these actions were recorded well enough in newsbooks and pamphlets, and many officers in Rupert's regular corps in the developing Oxford Army were frequent actors in those accounts. Yet Lisle is absent. Why, as a senior officer with European experience and Edgehill to his credit, was he apparently not given any further commands, or even mentioned in passing during the Prince's many expeditions or those performed elsewhere in the Oxford Army? As a lieutenant colonel he would have been at the forefront of the action, particularly so given that he customarily led dragoons or commanded men in the van, and also – when his entire career is considered – that he was an officer who led conspicuously from the front.

The most obvious explanation for Lisle's absence in contemporary accounts is that he simply wasn't there: that after Edgehill he had gone home, to London. At this stage in the war it was not yet a closed city: post-battle a flood of men returned to the capital, and for a few days it was awash with a mass of contradictory news. Clarendon notes:

> … by this time, so many persons, who were present at the action, came to the town of both sides, (for there was yet a free intercourse with all quarters,) and some discourses were published, how little either of these

---

20   *Ibid.*, p.323.

two had seen themselves of that day's business, that the city seemed not so much exalted at their relations, as the houses had [been] …[21]

'These two', to whom Clarendon alludes, must have been two accounts published in one pamphlet as early as 27th October: that of MP William Strode and Lord Wharton, who had been present at Edgehill and rushed back to give news of a Parliament victory; and 'A Letter sent from a Worthy Divine', written from Warwick Castle on the 24th.[22] The Houses took both at their word, but if Clarendon is to be believed, their versions were relentlessly questioned, probably in the main by London Royalists who had also returned. Other written accounts appeared in the following days and weeks, undoubtedly heating the subject further. Parliament loudly denounced much of the gossip as inaccurate, and the newsbooks mention numerous arrests for the spreading of 'false and scandalous reports'.[23] However, Parliament had no choice but to propagate whatever suited its cause, regardless of accuracy, and to crush dissenting voices. One unfortunate Edgehill survivor, a Captain Fleming, was:

> brought before the Parliament, and committed to prison, for raising false reports of the Lord Generalls Army, and the fight at Kynton, he being also a Captaine of the Kings party.[24]

Others, who went a step further by openly accusing Parliament of picking and choosing the most favourable news, were also hauled in front of the House:

> There was one Master Jo. Wentworth a Lawyer of Lincolnes Inne appre-hended and brought to the Parliament for divulging of false and scan-dalous untruthes, concerning the fight at Kinton and casting aspersions upon the Parliament as if they should go about to hinder the discoverie of

21   Book VI, 1840 vol. III, p.283.
22   Included in *A True Relation Of a Great and Happy Victory* … Wharton and Strode's account was described as 'a Message from his Excellencie the Earle of Essex, Being a Relation of the Battaile', but the pamphlet includes only a brief list of prisoners and some casualty figures. The number of Royalist dead is grossly exaggerated at 3,000: at time of writing (2015) the Battlefields Trust estimates total battle casualties at around only 1,000.
23   Naturally the London newsbooks focused on Royalist arrests, which might distort the perception of who was being arrested, and why. They did publicise at least one arrest of Parliamentarians, but the soldiers' inaccurate reportage was dismissed as mere ignorant scaremongering, their greater crime being that they had run away from the army before the battle. One had said he would 'take the Parliaments pay but would never fight for them against any of the Kings partie.' (*A Continuation Of certain Speciall and Remarkable Passages*, Number 16, no page numbers). Tellingly, whereas Royalists were brought before Parliament for their actions, these Parliamentarian defendants were merely imprisoned.
24   *A Continuation Of certain Speciall and Remarkable Passages*, Number 17, no page numbers.

the truth of things concerning that businesse, which matter was brought to the Parliament, for which by Order of the House he was committed to prison.[25]

Why Lisle would have gone home to this maelstrom, rather than continuing with the army, can only be guessed at, but two things besides his absence in the accounts support the suggestion that he did. The first is that it seems to have been in his nature to not stray too far from London. After the fall of Oxford in 1646 he did not go abroad like so many of his surviving fellow officers, but went back to London; he stayed there until forced to leave in mid-1648, when after a new wave of fighting the Parliament lost all patience and effectively ejected all Royalist sympathisers from the capital. It would be perfectly in character for Lisle to have earlier followed the same track: to have gone home after Edgehill, and stayed there unless he was obliged for his own liberty and/or safety to leave. With this in mind, the timing of his reappearance with the Royalist army is significant. Firstly, he and his family had fled their rented London home around April, taking only their most personal possessions and leaving the fittings to be recovered later; it seems natural that this exile would force George back to the army, possibly due to the limits of the family's new accommodation, but much more likely due to anger and defiance, and a determination to restore the King. Secondly, the political situation in London at that time was fevered. In May a number of conspirators were arrested in connection with a high-level plot to betray the capital to the King: the plot, subsequently dubbed 'Waller's Plot' after the MP who was primarily involved, coincided with an ongoing step-change in the character of Civil War London, after which it became increasingly enclosed and the penalties for displaying Royalism within its boundaries increasingly harsh. Just days before, an order of both Houses had declared that anyone coming from Oxford:

> … or any part of the Kings Army to London, or the parts adjacent, or to any part of the Armie under the command of the Earle of Essex, or to any fort or court of Guard, kept by the authority of both houses of Parliament, without the Warrant of both houses of Parliament, or the Lord Generall the Earle of Essex, shall be apprehended as Spies and Intelligencers, and be proceeded against according to the Rules and Grounds of Warre …[26]

London was already becoming dangerous for Royalists, and Waller's Plot was the final straw. The Lisles left Westminster at around this time; Waller and his

---

25   *Ibid.*

26   *An Order of the Commons Assembled in Parliament to prevent Spies and Intelligencers*, 10th April 1643. Reprinted in October as *An Order Of The Lords and Commons For the Restraint of Passage from Oxford*, 18th October 1643. Included in *A collection of all the publicke orders …*, pp.29-30.

known co-conspirators were arrested on 31st May, and George Lisle is recorded at the Chalgrove skirmish two weeks after that, on 17th June, the first time he appears in the Royalist record since Edgehill. The timing is perfect. Whether Laurence or George, in their desperation, might have had a hand in the wider strands of that plot is another unknown, although Waller and his companions did allegedly have 'the aide of the Malevolents in and about London'.[27] Yet George was certainly involved in something subversive in 1647-48: evidence uncovered by Parliament after his death revealed that after returning to the city early in 1647 he had spent eighteen months successfully raising money and horses for the King, without detection, under the Parliament's nose, and was involved in something later referred to as 'George Lyle's attempt'. This intriguing allusion remains obscure, but given the recent Royalist defeat and the King's captivity, it is highly suggestive of conspiracy.[28] If he was prepared to engage in such activities in 1647-48, it is reasonable to believe that he might have done so in 1642-43, when the paranoid Parliamentarian press regularly reported the detection of supposed Royalist plots. Furthermore, it appears that he may have been on good terms with Colonel Marmaduke Rawdon, who had remained a London Trained Bands officer during the early months of the war but was suspected of involvement with another plot, to seize the Tower armoury; certainly there is evidence to suggest covert preparatory activity in the capital before he fled, some of which can only be interpreted as being prejudicial to Parliament.[29] He fled to Oxford in March 1643, a few weeks ahead of Lisle.[30] The activities of Lisle's acquaintances do not prove his whereabouts, or what he was doing, but if his personal network in London was involved at that time in defying Parliament's authority, the odds are high that he participated at some level, particularly given his undeviating support for the King, and his own 'attempt' – whatever it was – in 1647-48.

Chalgrove

The Chalgrove raid, which occurred south-east of Oxford on 17th-18th June 1643, was led by Rupert. The primary account we have of the skirmish, written anonymously but generally believed to have been authored by the Prince's Flemish

27 *Certain Informations*, Numb. 21, p.166.

28 See chapter 15.

29 Dace, 'Who Lieth Here?' Sir Marmaduke Rawdon (1582-1646); http://richarddace.website/pdf/rawdon. pdf, (accessed 2nd January 2016). My thanks also to Andy Robertshaw for offering much useful information about Rawdon's possible activities.

30 A personal communication from a colleague some years ago suggested that Lisle and Rawdon wrote frequently to each other, and that a number of letters were still extant and were studied by the late Civil War historian Wilfrid Emberton. If the letters do still exist, their whereabouts remain frustratingly elusive.

engineer, Bernard de Gomme, gives a full list of the participating elements. Of dragoons it says:

> [There] marcht some 350. under my L. Wentworth, their Sergeant-major Generall, drawne altogether out of his Lordships owne Troop, Prince Ruperts Regiment, commanded by Colonell Innes, Sr Robert Howards, and Colonell Washingtons Regiments … The Van of this greater Partee, was a lesser Partee commanded by Sergeant-major Legg: made up of the Prince of Wales his Regiment, with 100. other commanded Horse; and some 50. Dragooners, under Lieutenant Colonell Lisle. These marcht like a forlorne-hope, a distance before the greater Partee.[31]

On the evening of 17th June the force had embarked on a successful night raid of some enemy quarters in the villages of Postcombe and Chinnor; the next morning it failed to catch the expected highlight of the expedition, a Parliamentarian pay convoy, which hid in a wood, and a skirmish developed in a nearby corn-field between the convoy's accompanying troops and Rupert's raiding force. The account describes a pure cavalry action, yet besides Lisle's 50 dragoons in the van, and the 350 in the main force, Rupert's forces included 'betwixt 400 and 500. commanded men without Colours'. As at Powick, the non-cavalry elements were kept on hand as part of Rupert's security strategy:

> His Highnesse perceiving this great Body, took care first of all how to secure the passe over Chesel-hampton bridge, for making good the Retreat to us; least other enemies as yet undiscovered, might cut it off from us. For this purpose Colonell Lunsford, & Colonell Washington being sent with all the Foot to lye on both ends [of] the bridg, the Princes next design was to line the hedges along the Lanes that led thither. For this purpose, my L. Wentworth and his Lieutenant-Colonell Mr John Russell were sent before hand with their Dragooners: for his Highnesse well hoped the Rebells might be trayned into that Ambush.[32]

The ambush failed, enemy troops almost getting between it and the Prince, but Rupert salvaged the situation by charging across a hedgerow, and ultimately the Parliamentarians were routed and Rupert returned in triumph to Oxford the next morning. Parliament's principal casualty was the MP John Hampden, who was wounded in the shoulder and died a few days later.

---

31   *His Highnesse Prince Ruperts Late Beating Up The Rebels Quarters …*, pp.2-3.
32   *Ibid.*, p.6.

Summer 1643

The late summer of 1643 in south-west England was dominated by two army actions: at the end of July the Oxford Army and other elements of the King's forces stormed and captured Bristol, and then in early August they besieged Gloucester. There is no mention of Lisle during the Bristol campaign, but as an *ad hoc* forlorn hope or dragoon officer with Continental and Edgehill experience to his credit, his skills would have been invaluable and it seems unlikely he would have stayed at Oxford. Given that he was active around Gloucester in September, it is most likely that he accompanied Rupert westward and had some role in the fighting at Bristol, but is simply not mentioned in the surviving accounts. Historians are divided as to whether Rupert participated in efforts to prevent Essex advancing on Gloucester as the Royalists began to lift their siege of the city. On 3rd September Rupert left Gloucester for Northleach, and the next day faced Essex at Stow-on-the-Wold, where a substantial skirmish occurred. Stuart Reid asserts that Rupert's force must have included Lisle and 1,200 commanded musketeers noted by the Royalist Ordnance Papers as being under his command on 7th September,[33] but author Jon Day questions this, noting that there is no record of Lisle's commanded force earlier than the 7th, by which time the army was regrouping around Winchcombe and nearby Sudeley Castle. There are also no references to any infantry in the detailed account of Stow given by London Trained Bands officer, Sergeant Henry Foster.[34] Day's preferred scenario is that Lisle's command was created subsequent to Stow, as a response to the failure to stop Essex's advance, and from a wider need for more dragoons (although the contemporary evidence suggests that Lisle's men remained standard foot musketeers). Day also addresses the question of where Lisle's soldiers came from, and suggests they were reinforcements sent from Bristol by Sir Ralph Hopton.[35]

Sergeant Foster stated that after Rupert's delaying tactics failed, Essex arrived on Prestbury Hill the next day, 5th September. Wary of being attacked, however, his forces approached the city slowly and did not enter it until the 8th. By this time the Royalists were at Sudeley, fifteen miles to the north-east on the far side of

---

33 Roy, ROP part 2, p.287 (WO 55/1661/283).

34 *A true and exact Relation of the Marchings of the Two Regiments of the Trained Bands of the City of London* …

35 Prince Rupert's Diary (EHR), p.734; Reid, *All The King's Armies*, p.60; Day, *Gloucester & Newbury 1643*, p.117, and p.231 fn. 13; Hopton's *Bellum Civile*, pp.60-61. Hopton had sent two batches of reinforcements to Gloucester, from Bristol. The first, described by Hopton as 'commanded men' are probably those mentioned in the Ordnance Papers on 22nd August as '[of] Prince Morris Regimt which came from Bristoll' (Roy, ROP part 2, p.278 (NA, WO 55/1661 [6])). Day notes that the second group of 'neere upon 2000 foote' vanishes from the record, other than Hopton claiming it arrived at Gloucester in time to follow the army to Newbury, where it did 'good service', and is therefore the perfect source for Lisle's 1,200 man commanded force in that engagement.

Prestbury. The armies must have passed within five miles of each other, avoiding a head-on clash only because the Royalists effectively swerved to avoid Essex by regrouping first at Birdlip. In any case, it is doubtful whether at that moment either army was in any position to seek full-on confrontation.

On 9th September, as the army continued at Sudeley, Lisle was issued with four 6lb cannon and four barrels of powder, match, and cannon shot. The Ordnance Papers add that:

> Montgarnier is to goe along with them and take such officers as he shall think necessary for that service ...[36]

Frenchman Nicholas Mountgarnier was one of three Comptrollers of the Ordnance listed in the Royalist artillery train in June 1643.[37] Comptrollers were essentially administrators who organised supplies and repairs for the artillery in their charge; there would be no need for Mountgarnier on a single 'hit-and-run' attempt on enemy quarters, which suggests the cannon and its crew and comptroller were allotted to Lisle for longer-term use to complement the commanded men, probably as part of wider housekeeping of the King's forces after Gloucester. Certainly there does not seem to have been a particular target in mind for Lisle, and no events are recorded in the few days before the army moved off, that would have required his infantry and artillery.

Meanwhile Essex had rested briefly at Gloucester, but finding the city stripped of food and supplies post-siege he moved his army north to find better pickings at Tewkesbury, arriving on 10th September. What followed next can only be described as a military mind-game. It seems Essex was undecided on his next move, and that his shift northwards was partly practical, and partly gave him the option of escaping north if he was cut off, and threatening Royalist Worcester. His biographer, Robert Codrington, seems to have believed the Earl was fearful of his lines of retreat being cut, and that 'the maine intent of the Enemy was to cut off all provision from his Army.'[38] If Essex's activities around Tewkesbury were designed to trick the Royalists into thinking he might head north, the plan worked: a Parliamentarian known only as 'T. V.' wrote in a letter home:

> We caused a Bridge to be made over the Severne, and sent some forces to Upton Bridge, in policy, as if we intended to march for Worcester, which caused the Enemy to draw all his forces together for the defence of that place, planted their Ordnance, and thought to tickle us by the way; but the fooles were cosen'd, for on Friday morning we went cleane another way

---

36 Roy, ROP part 2, p.287 (NA, WO 55/459, ff. 453-4).

37 *Ibid.*, p.360 (Rawl. MS. D. 395, ff. 208-9).

38 *The Life and Death, of the Illustrious Robert Earle of Essex, &c*, p.30.

marcht all day the greatest part of the night from Teuxbury to Cirencester 18 miles ...[39]

Both Codrington and Foster explicitly agreed with 'T. V.' that the bridge of boats was a deliberate feint. Having taken the bait and moved north in pursuit, the King lingered at Evesham for another twenty-four hours, his scouts apparently having failed to apprise him of the enemy's departure southwards again. Foster notes:

One that was present at Esum, where the King with his Army lay, affirmed that when tydings came to the King that wee were marched from Tewksbury, they did stamp and swear and curse their Scouts exceedingly, that they gave them no better intelligence of our departure.

Clarendon later blamed the King's lack of information on lethargic cavalry:

The king's horse ... were always less patient of duty and ill accommodation than they should be; and at this time, partly with weariness, and partly with the indisposition that possessed the whole army upon this relief of the town, were less vigilant towards the motion of the enemy ...[40]

Cavalry commander Sir John Byron, however, claimed that he had certainly informed Rupert of Essex's movements, and that:

had Prince Rupert been pleased to credit my intelligence, the advantage which Essex gained might have been prevented; which neglect obliged the army to go so hasty and painful a march, that before he reached Newbury there was about 2,000 horse and as many foot lost by the way.[41]

In turn Rupert, or at least his anonymous diarist, also passed the blame upwards. Warburton says that:

Rupert had sent notice of [Essex's] movements, but his Majesty believed himself better informed, and allowed Essex twenty-four hours advantage before he moved after him.[42]

Regardless of fault, the King was critically, as Warburton observes, 'out-manoeuvred ... for want of intelligence.' When it eventually arrived on the evening of

39   *A True Relation of the Late Battell Neere Newbury*, p.2.
40   Book VII, 1840 vol. IV, p.217.
41   Quoted by Money, p.15.
42   Warburton, vol. II, p.288.

Friday 15th the army prepared to move south-east after Essex, but a day later, by the evening of Saturday 16th, it had only gone six miles; Rupert's Diary notes that 'The King rested some howers at Broadway'.[43] As darkness fell on the Cotswolds and no more marching orders were issued, Rupert's patience gave out. Anxious to over-take Essex and cut him off from London, he finally sought out the King and found him playing a leisurely game of cards with Lord Percy in a nearby house. Rupert impressed upon him the situation's urgency, and Charles eventually agreed to let him undertake a fast pursuit, ordering 'George Lisle and one thousand musket-eers to follow the Prince as soon as they could be got under arms'.[44] Clearly Rupert did not intend to take Lisle: the cavalry had been waiting idly for some hours on Broadway Down, saddled-up and expecting orders, and if he had planned to take a body of infantry then they would have been ready and waiting at the same time. Lisle's inclusion appears to be an afterthought, perhaps suggested by Percy or the Earl of Forth, who was also present at the house. Given his natural dynamism, it is also unlikely that the Prince would have wasted yet more time at Broadway arguing with them and his uncle over the logistics of his planned interception. He had come for the King's permission to give chase; he obtained it, and according to Warburton and the Diary, left again at breakneck speed; musketeers be damned.

He must have reached Stanford-in-the-Vale in West Berkshire at around noon on Sunday as a letter he penned to the King there reached Charles and the rest of the army, now finally on the move and forty miles away at Arlescote, at 5 p.m.[45] Rupert's force had covered the thirty miles from Broadway in twelve to fifteen hours, not tardy considering the size of his force (Digby says 3,000; Clarendon 'near five thousand'[46]), that it was riding unfamiliar roads at night, with a new moon,[47] and as Sergeant Foster noted in his account, it had been raining: wors-ening autumn weather would be decaying the roads.[48]

43 EHR, p.734.
44 Warburton notes of the story: 'This sounds very strangely, perhaps, but it is told with all these circumstances in the note to 'Prince Rupert's Diary'; and these notes betray no signs whatever of imaginativeness.' (vol. II, pp.288-289, fn. 1). Rupert's 1899 biographer, Eva Scott, repeats the tale in less detail (E. Scott, pp.120-121). She does not offer a source, but a nearby footnote citing Warburton for something else suggests she probably used him for this part also. On 7th September Lisle's force had numbered 1,200; as it seems unlikely that he had lost two hundred men in the previous nine days – such a loss would have had to occur in a significant skirmish, and would not have been overlooked in either newsbooks or personal documents – we can put the 1,000 figure down to a simple inaccuracy in reporting.
45 Warburton, vol. II., p.290. Prince Rupert's Diary confirms he was at Stanford (EHR, p.734); Digby's account of the Aldbourne and Newbury campaign (TT E.69[10]) states Faringdon, although it is only three miles away, and he may simply have meant that the rest of the force was quartered there.
46 Book VII, 1840 vol. IV, p.218.
47 Clarendon notes that when slipping away from Tewkesbury, Essex 'took the advantage of a dark night' (Book VII, 1840 vol. IV, p.217); historical moon phase data confirms that the moon became 'new' on 13th September.
48 An anonymous pamphlet reprinted in Washbourne's *Bibliotheca Gloucestrensis*, which Parliament had sanctioned as its official account of the campaign, describes 'tempestuousnesse of weather' on Tuesday

Lisle's men would have spent Sunday cross-country on foot after the Prince; a particularly risky task given that with Rupert gone on ahead and the main Royalist army some miles east and to the rear, moving on a more direct trajectory towards Newbury, there was no prospect of rescue or reinforcement should Lisle's force encounter a significant party of the enemy. Keeping to an average human walking pace of 3-4 mph, perhaps faster if marching at speed, including a stop to rest and notwithstanding boggy roads, certainly Lisle's force could have completed the thirty mile trek and reached Stanford on Sunday afternoon, albeit some hours after Rupert. However it is not known how long after Rupert Lisle left Broadway; if he could not assemble his musketeers from their quarters and get underway until early Sunday morning, he may not have arrived until after dark on Sunday night.[49]

On Monday morning Rupert's forces set out after Essex, Rupert seeking the body of the army whilst recent Parliamentarian turncoat John Hurry and a large party of cavalry sought the rearguard. They discovered their quarry fifteen miles away in a valley by Aldbourne Chase, a few miles north-west of Hungerford. The Prince immediately shadowed it with his own cavalry whilst '[Colonel] Gerrard fell back, to wait for their loitering musketeers.'[50] *Mercurius Aulicus* says this was 'about three of the clocke in the afternoone';[51] assuming the entire force had set out together in the morning, Lisle cannot have been that far behind, as roads permitting it would only take four or five hours to cover the distance on foot; it is likely that he only just missed the opening moves in the skirmish that followed. Certainly his absence at the start tallies with the ongoing account of Sergeant Foster, who noted that:

5th September (*A True Relation of the Late Expedition … for the Relief of Gloucester*); Foster describes it as 'a most terrible tempestuous night of winde and raine, as ever men lay out in …' On the 16th he notes that 'this day we had a wet march'; the night of Sunday 17th was 'a very cold frosty night', and that Monday 18th was 'a night of much raine.'

49   The timings strongly suggest that Lisle commanded standard foot musketeers and not dragoons. Admittedly dragoon horses were of notoriously poor quality and Lisle's could have been slow or even lame; but regardless, nowhere in the sources are Lisle's commanded men spoken of as dragoons. When Hopton detailed the reinforcements sent from Bristol he only mentioned foot and cavalry, and described the second batch of men from whom Day believes Lisle's force was drawn as 'fower foote regiments' (Hopton, *Bellum Civile*, p.60). Moreover, the Royalist Ordnance Papers make no reference to them being dragoons, nor does Digby's account of Newbury I, nor Byron's (Money, p.44), and they appear to have fought their way up Round Hill in a coherent operation with other infantry units, not as independent dismounted skirmishers. The 1,000 men whom Clarendon says accompanied Rupert after the battle as he harried the Parliamentarian rear, and who some commentators believe were Lisle's men, were also only described by Clarendon as 'musketeers' (Book VII, 1840 vol. IV, p.223). Essex's biographer Robert Codrington specifically mentions Royalist dragoons at Aldbourne, but it is not clear if these were in fact Lisle's men.

50   Warburton, vol. II, p.291. Again, this delay can only have occurred if Lisle's force was on foot.

51   Week 38 (1644), p.525.

… we drew up all our Army into a body to the top of the hill, where we had a full view of the enemy over against us: there appeared a great body of their horse; it was conceived there was 7 or 8000 but no foot that we could discerne …

Certainly Foster would not have missed a formation of 1,200 musketeers. Initially the Parliamentarian army was strung out along the valley bottom, and Hurry's detachment routed a group of 200 rearguard cavalry that had become detached from the main body. Digby reported Rupert to be so encouraged at 'such evident symptoms of feare and distraction' amongst the men they encountered that he was tempted to attack the entire army; but:

newes arriving at the instant that our Foot was, beyond expectation, advanced within 6. or 7. miles of us, it imposed upon his Highnesse prudence this caution, not to adventure upon halfe our strength that rest, which the next day he might be sure to fight for with double power: upon which consideration he made a stand, resolving that night only to attend them and hinder their march.[52]

Day believes Digby and Rupert thought the musketeers to be Lisle's, however it would not be 'beyond expectation' for Lisle's foot to be close, and if only six miles away they would arrive within a couple of hours, not the next day; rather, they must have genuinely believed the sighting to be the King's main force. However, Day rightly points out that the main army was too far away, and this suggests a confusion on the ground: Lisle's approaching foot being mistaken for the main body. Poor though the Royalist scouts had recently proved, Rupert's intelligencers must have been aware of Lisle's imminent arrival, which suggests Rupert acted on local information rather than that from his own staff.

Meanwhile Essex began withdrawing his force up the steep south side of the valley where the Royalist cavalry could not rapidly follow, hastily ditching some of his baggage train as he went (presumably this was the point where Foster noted the absence of Royalist foot); his forces strung out even further, leaving the bulk of the cavalry some way behind. Rupert's aim being to prevent Essex moving nearer Newbury, he tempted the cavalry rearguard back to the valley floor and attacked.

At least a couple of hours had passed since he found Essex, and another early autumn night was drawing on: it is inconceivable that Lisle's party had not now arrived, particularly if they were indeed the force spotted earlier. However, sources conflict as to whether Royalist foot were involved in the skirmish that followed. Digby's account gives the impression that the skirmish was purely a cavalry engagement, although admittedly he was in the thick of the cavalry fight, being wounded and captured at one point, and simply may not have registered the infantry's activities. Essex certainly sent some dragoons and musketeers back to the valley to support his horse, but it is not clear if they shot purely at the Royalist cavalry or engaged Royalist foot as well. 'T. V.' wrote:

> My Lord Generall fell on with his Foot, and gave them a gallant charge, which accompanied with a Volley of our Dragooners ratled for the space of an houre without any cessation.[53]

Whether dragoons could have had an hour-long firefight with moving cavalry is debatable; it is more likely they were exchanging fire with another stationary body, and that obviously means musketeers or other dragoons. Codrington explicitly says that was the case, stating that:

> In the meane time the Dragoones on both sides gave fire in full Bodies on one another on the side of the Hill …[54]

Codrington is the only source to mention Royalist musketeers returning fire at Aldbourne; the accuracy of his detail is unclear, however, as he wrote in 1646 and it is not known if he was actually present at the skirmish or used other people's information. Given that Lisle would certainly have caught up with Rupert by dusk and the engagement's second phase, it is very possible that at least some of the 'dragoons' mentioned by Codrington were in fact from the 1,200 commanded men. Rupert did have a dragoon regiment amongst his regular forces, that commanded by Colonel John Innes at Edgehill; possibly at Aldbourne it fought alongside Lisle, but if so its presence was overlooked by all the other sources, including the Royalist ones.

The decision to send foot musketeers with Rupert was demonstrably a last minute one imposed on him by the King. It was incompatible with the need for extremely swift action across a long distance, the Royalists having already lost twenty-four hours of precious operational time. Rupert may not have planned what he would do when he found Essex – that would depend on as yet unknown factors – but he knew it was imperative that a rapid intercept was made, and 1,200 foot soldiers would merely act as a drogue holding back the cavalry. Certainly in regular circumstances some infantry would be vital in a strategy to delay the enemy or pin it down, but notwithstanding, on this occasion their presence was simply not practical. Whoever sent them overlooked the fact that given the distance, the

53 *From our Quarters at Reading Sept. 23. 1643.*, printed in *A True Relation of the Late Battell Neere Newbury*, p.4).
54 *The Life and Death, of the Illustrious Robert Earle of Essex, &c.*, p.31.

weather, and the state of the roads, they were not physically fast enough to make the intercept alongside the cavalry and would inevitably fall behind; and given the criticality of the intercept, the cavalry did not have time to hang back and wait for them, and indeed Rupert did not. This would leave the musketeers unsupported in country where Essex's entire army, and its intelligencers and hangers on, was somewhere on the loose; it was a significant risk to the lives, or at least the freedom, of a highly valuable commander and his men, who could have encountered any number of hazards en route with no back-up from cavalry or artillery.[55] It is easy to criticise hasty military decisions after the fact, but the factors to be considered were all apparent enough at the time to Rupert, at least, and should also have been obvious to the King and any military advisors present – in this case Lord Percy and Forth. If Lisle's musketeers did engage during the latter part of the Aldbourne skirmish then at least their slog from Broadway was not completely wasted, but the balance of potential benefit versus potential cost hung heavily towards the latter.

The skirmish ended with Rupert tacitly acknowledging that he could not cause much damage to Essex, and withdrawing his forces back to the north. It had been near dusk when the engagement started, and the rapidly gathering darkness in the valley would have meant the cavalry portion of the fight did not continue for long, perhaps leaving the musketeers to exchange parting shots into the night. During the fight, of which Digby, Byron, Foster, Codrington and Rupert's Diary collectively give good account, Lord Jermyn and Digby himself suffered minor injuries in the close-quarter entanglement and Rupert's horse was shot in the head, but there were no losses amongst the Royalist officers besides a missing lieutenant and a French noble (a volunteer) killed after allegedly trying to pistol his captor. The Parliamentarians admitted to losing a couple of captains, and figures tossed around at the time suggested an overall total of between one to two hundred dead and wounded of all ranks. Numerous prisoners were taken on both sides.

Newbury I

On the night of 18th September Rupert's force spent a wet night in the fields around Lambourn. Much like Foster in Gloucestershire a fortnight earlier, Royalist John Gwyn, a captain in Sir Thomas Salusbury's regiment, noted that:

> it proved to be a most miserable, tempestuous, rainy weather, that few or none could take little or no rest on the hills where they were; and the ceasing winds next morning soon dried up our through-wet clothes we lay pickled in all night …[56]

---

55 There is no evidence that Lisle's force still had the four cannon it was issued with on 9th September.
56 *Military Memoirs of John Gwyn*, p.36 (1822 edition).

Essex, having retreated safely into Aldbourne after Rupert withdrew, used the poor weather as a cover and slipped away south-east over the river Kennet to Hungerford, securing the bridge and capturing a stray party of Royalists into the bargain.

Throughout the next day the King's forces began to converge on Newbury. Besides the main force that had been at Gloucester, reinforcements summoned from various garrisons were also on the march, and, of course, Rupert's own force from Lambourn. A crucial race was on between Rupert and Essex to reach Newbury first; there was perhaps two to three miles difference in the length of their march, and Essex's covert night move to Hungerford had given him the advantage. The two armies moved almost in parallel towards the town, Rupert north of the Kennet on a south-east track along the Lambourn Valley, and Essex south of the Kennet, heading due east. His intention was to march through the village of Enborne and then on into Newbury, securing the town and the bridge and then crossing north of the river again and once more picking up the Great West Road towards London. Yet for some reason – and the offered explanations and analyses are many – Essex was too slow, and did not send soldiers ahead to secure his route, but a party of quartermasters, to prepare billets. Rupert rode into town sometime during the morning of the 19th and found it empty of the expected enemy, besides the quartermasters, some of whom escaped back to Essex to deliver the news of his failure.

The sequence of events on the 19th is fairly clear, although the timings and accuracy of the observations made by the various sources are not. *Mercurius Aulicus* reported Rupert's initial efforts to secure the town from Essex:

> All the Horse and some commanded Muskettiers were then immediately drawne out beyond the water towards the Rebels …[57]

Parliamentarian Bulstrode Whitelocke described the situation with better detail:

> The whole body of the King's Army had possessed themselves of the Town of Newbury, on their right hand they had the advantage of the River, and a hill half a mile from the Town where they had planted their Ordnance, so that there was no passage to them, but with great disadvantage, and by a narrow lane.[58]

---

57   Week 38 (1644), p.526.
58   *Memorials of the English Affairs*, p.70. Whitelocke's report is not completely reliable: more a politician than a soldier, he almost certainly hadn't marched west with Essex and so did not witness the battle first hand.

The 'narrow lane' was the road from Enborne on the south side of the Kennet, which Essex needed to pass along to reach the town; the hill must have been the rising ground to the south, towards the centre of what was shortly to become a battlefield. Rupert must have used Lisle and his commanded men to block the lane. As well as keeping Essex from Newbury, it also helped give the impression that the entire Royalist army had arrived, dissuading him from making an attempt on the as yet barely-secured town. However, regarding Whitelocke's observation of ordnance on the hill (one shared by the author of a 'certified', probably eye-witness, report seen by *Mercurius Britanicus*),[59] the King's artillery had not yet arrived, and there is no evidence that Rupert had brought guns with him from Broadway, indeed given the speed that he travelled it seems impossible. The four sakers issued to Lisle at Sudeley might account for the sighting, but as already footnoted, there is no evidence that he brought these south either, and it is implausible that he could have hauled them and their crews and equipment with him overnight from Broadway to Stanford and still only have been a few hours behind Rupert's cavalry. No ordnance could have been sent from nearby Donnington Castle, as Byron tells us that it was only secured for the King during that day, and London newsbook *Mercurius Civicus* that it was not properly garrisoned until a couple of weeks later.[60] Possibly some cannon could have arrived early at Newbury from another Royalist quarter, but if so this was not recorded. Moreover at dawn the next morning when (as will be seen) Essex secured Round Hill, although his biographer claimed that he 'beat [the Royalists] from the hill', both Digby and Byron claimed it was empty at the time: Digby admitted that the hill was 'not suspected nor observed by us the night before', a situation that Byron furiously called 'a gross and absurd error'.[61] *Mercurius Aulicus* also later denied that the King's cannon had ever been there.[62] The mistaken reports of ordnance probably stemmed from the overnight presence on the hill of some Royalist cavalry commanded by an anonymous officer, who reported being posted there by Rupert and sending out parties 'all night, which gave His Highness satisfactory intelligence'.[63] Evidently he used the rising ground as a vantage point rather than a strategic position and probably withdrew down the east face the next morning at around the same time Essex's men stormed up the west, giving the impression that the hill was being abandoned.

Rupert having kept Essex from Newbury, on the night of the 19th the Earl was forced to camp around Enborne, the rest of the Royalist forces having trickled into

---

59   No. 5, p.38.
60   Byron, quoted in Money, p.41; *Mercurius Civicus* noted in October that the Royalists were fortifying the castle, 'having turned out the inhabitants thereof' (Numb. 20, p.156).
61   Quoted by Money, p.42.
62   Week 41 (1644), p.581.
63   BL Add MS 18980, quoted by Money, p.49. Day theorises that the officer was the disgraced Richard Feilding (Day, p.147).

Newbury throughout the day and assembled south of the town. The weather and the forced marches had exhausted both Essex's soldiers and the King's; both were wet through and short of food, but the Royalists were succoured by a large amount of provisions prepared for Essex by the town's pro-Parliament inhabitants. That night there was no calm before the storm. Of the horse and commanded men on the Enborne Road, *Mercurius Aulicus* says:

> their whole Body being within two miles and a halfe at most, so as the parties fell to skirmish one with the other, but without effect, till night did separate them.[64]

Money notes Lords Percy and Jermyn being injured in a cavalry skirmish, Jermyn for the second time in two days. Overnight the King issued a formal challenge to fight.

The territory which contained the battle and its environs was an almost-square strip of ground stretching approximately two miles east-west between Enborne and Newbury, and roughly the same distance north-south between the river Kennet and the river Enborne, both of which at that point flowed east-west in parallel. The road Essex needed (the modern A4) also ran east-west but along the north bank of the Kennet, across the river from the battle site, meaning that after getting around the Royalists he needed to find a crossing point. There were at least two in the locality: the bridge at Newbury, and one at Thatcham; there was also a ford nine miles east at Padworth.[65] Obviously Newbury was no longer an option for him.

No definitive order of battle has been discovered for the Royalists, nor any contemporary map of the armies' dispositions, and our understanding of the event is shaped by the oft-conflicting work of subsequent commentators trying to reconcile contemporary letters, newsbooks and participants' accounts with much later maps.[66] Suffice to say that each army was drawn up on mixed terrain to the south-west of Newbury, the Parliamentarians in the west and the Royalists in the east blocking Essex's escape route. To proceed, the Earl needed to punch

---

64 Week 38 (1644), p.526.

65 In November 1644 *Mercurius Aulicus* reported that before the second battle at Newbury the Parliamentarians 'came privately over the water at a ford neare Padworth …' (Week 44 (1644), p.1232). Two London newsbooks mention 'Thatcham Bridge' (which was in fact nearer Newbury than Thatcham) being pulled up by the Royalists at the same time, to hinder their enemy's movements; the fords nearby were impassable due to heavy rain (*Perfect Passages* numb. 2, p.17; *A Diary, or an Exact Journall*, p.184).

66 The battle is so complex in respect of phases, movements and presumed dispositions around three battlefield sectors – much of which is still under debate – that there is no scope to coherently tackle the wider battle here. Readers are urged to study the original sources and consider the numerous secondary analyses available. I particularly recommend the recent highly detailed and well-sourced analysis of Jon Day.

past his enemy and cross the piece of land they presently occupied, known as either Wash or Newbury Common; to do that he also needed to control a crucial piece of adjacent rising ground to its north-west, in the centre of the battlefield, described as a 'round hill' (a description that subsequently stuck). Fortunately for him, as already noted, on the morning of the 20th his forces quickly marched up to occupy it. Rupert's anonymous officer makes it clear, however, that not only had the Royalists failed to secure the hill, but they had not seen the Parliamentarians subsequently take it:

> His Highness went with his own troops, a party of mosqueteers and my horse to take possession of a Hill, I drew ye party into a close that contained a considerable part of the Hil, then we discovered the enemy and there began the service.[67]

Thus Lisle and his musketeers, along with the cavalry, were immediately plunged into a firefight with the enemy on the slope above them, while Rupert left, presumably to report this unexpected engagement to the King and council of war. After an unspecified period Sir John Byron arrived near Lisle as back-up with two horse regiments and his uncle Nicholas's foot brigade. Meanwhile, says the anonymous officer's account:

> before relief could come to the mosqueteers, they retreated, and I drew ye horse into the next close though not without losse both with great and small shot where wee stood, untill in which time my horse received a shott in his neere shoulder. But ye foot crying out for ye horse, I returned into ye first mentioned close and was very slowly followed by reason of the straitness of the passage, but when I thought I had men enough to doe ye service, I went to ye furthest part of ye said close wheere were neere about 1,000 of ye enemies foot drawne up in order and one piece of artillery, and as I was charging my horse was shott againe into ye breast and faltered with mee.[68]

When the officer returned with a new horse he found his cavalry had been withdrawn in his absence, and he received orders to relocate elsewhere. Byron's account picks up the thread:

> The commanded foot not being able to make good the place, my uncle Byron, who commanded the first tertia, instantly came up with part of the regiment of guards and Sir Michael Woodhouse's and my Lord

67 Quoted by Money, pp.49-50.
68 *Ibid.*

Gerard's regiments of foot, commanded by his Lieut.-Col. Ned Villiers, but the service grew so hot, that in a very short time, of twelve ensigns that marched up with my Lord Gerard's regiment, eleven were brought off the field hurt, and Ned Villiers shot through the shoulder.[69]

What is unclear at this point is whether, after their initial repulse, Lisle's commanded musketeers had been withdrawn along with the anonymous officer's cavalry, or were still fighting with the support of the Byrons. Lisle was not the only commander on hand: Byron noted that his cavalry had been ordered to support 'the commanded foot led by Lord Wentworth and Col. George Lisle.'[70] Byron's account is the only one that mentions Wentworth, who at that time was sergeant-major general of dragoons. His role on Round Hill is unclear, although he and Lisle had fought together a few months before at Chalgrove and may have operated in a similar manner at Newbury, with Wentworth leading the primary body of commanded men or dragoons, and Lisle advancing ahead with a smaller party. *Mercurius Aulicus* specifically states that it was Lisle who 'bravely led up the forlorne hope'.[71] Both Wentworth and Lisle were later listed as wounded, Lisle specifically during this action, and the absence of any further mention of either officer anywhere else on the field during the battle might well be due to them being forced to retire during this early musket and artillery firestorm – Byron later wrote that the cannon were loaded with lethal case shot.[72]

The Byrons continued to fight amongst the hedges for Round Hill throughout the day, the ferocity of the action not abating. At one point, *Aulicus* says, Rupert himself came to their rescue with 'a fresh reliefe of Foot',[73] but despite some minor successes in holding, and even slightly pushing back the London Trained Bands, ultimately the Royalists could not push them off the hill. Whether Lisle continued to fight through any part of this is unknown. Certainly Royalist infantry continued to fight on the high ground throughout the day, and some or all of it may have been Lisle's commanded men, or the remnants of them. However, unless new evidence comes to light it seems unlikely that Lisle's presence there, or lack of it, subsequent to the initial skirmish and the wound he received during it, can be confirmed.

In his account of Aldbourne and Newbury, addressed to an anonymous 'Noble Lord', Digby noted of Round Hill:

69   Quoted by Money, pp.51-52.
70   Quoted by Money, p.44. Thomas Wentworth the eldest son of the Earl of Cleveland.
71   Week 38 (1644), pp.528-529.
72   Case (or 'canister') shot was shrapnel material packed into a two-part tin or wooden 'case', which flew open when ejected from the cannon muzzle and released its lethal payload. Byron wrote up his account much later, in a letter to the Earl of Clarendon.
73   Week 41 (1644), p.582.

The action of the hill was carried with as much bravery both by our Horse and Foot as on the Heath by the Horse alone, the Foot Commanded by Sir Nicholas Byron, the Horse by Sir John Byron … Officers of note hurt there, were Colonell Darcy, George Lisle, and Ned Villiers, and the Lord Viscount Falkland (volunteering it with too much bravery) unfortunately killed. I may have omitted many persons as eminent in their actions that day, as some of these I have named, but it being so endlesse a task to nominate all, I have only particularized such as I conceive to be of your Lordships acquaintance.[74]

Wentworth may well have been one of the officers omitted by Digby for lack of space in his letter. The mention of Lisle is perhaps notable, as it demonstrates that a year into the war he was well known enough, and his conduct thought worthy enough, to be noted by a figure as senior (or indeed as notorious) as Digby; and that the noble recipient was, according to Digby, likely to know who Lisle was. However, assuming that the letter was genuine, and not merely a propaganda piece, it is possible that the recipient was in fact the ailing Lord Grandison, who had missed the entire Cotswolds/Aldbourne/Newbury campaign due to the wound he had received at Bristol. An active and experienced commander of horse and foot, he fits the profile of a senior figure with close ties to the army but recently absent from it, and who Digby might have felt would want to be kept apprised of the military situation. The men 'of your Lordships acquaintance' named by Digby would indeed include Ned Villiers, Grandison's brother, and George Lisle. In fact to have known Lisle, who only seems to have returned to the army in June and had not yet accrued his later army-wide military reputation, the lord in question must have known him as a friend or relative, or been in the Oxford Army over the summer and fought with him, or been in the same political circle, which would imply he was in Rupert's orbit. Grandison fits all these criteria, and beyond him it is difficult to find another candidate.

As the day drew to a close, fighting in all sectors of the Newbury battlefield eventually dissolved into a bloody stalemate. Some time after dark it tailed off completely and the armies disengaged. Essex's troops stayed at their posts, expecting the fight to continue at daybreak, but the Royalists – critically short of powder and match – elected not to defend the ground they had fought so hard for, and could only watch as their enemy crossed the common late the next morning and headed east.

Characteristically, Rupert did not let the situation rest there: Clarendon wrote that:

---

74 *A True and Impartiall Relation of the Battaile Betwixt, His Maiesties Army, and that of the Rebells neare Newbery in Berkshire, Sept. 20. 1643.*

The earl of Essex finding his way open, pursued his main design of returning to London, and took that way by Newbury, which led towards Reading; which prince Rupert observing, suffered him, without interruption or disturbance, to pass, till his whole army was entered into the narrow lanes; and then with a strong party of horse, and one thousand musketeers, followed his rear with so good effect, that he put them into great disorder, and killed many, and took many prisoners.[75]

The 'official' Parliamentarian account admitted that:

the enemy fell upon us with eight hundred commanded musquetiers and most of their horse, who caused our horse then in the rere to make a very disorderly and confused retreat.[76]

The commanded musketeers are generally believed to have been Lisle's, although no account specifically identifies them. Foster agrees that the Parliamentarian cavalry retreated, but where the official account euphemistically talks of the horse being 'disorderly and confused', Foster states bluntly that they fled, leaving the London Brigade and a forlorn hope of 600 musketeers to face Rupert's attack. First, however, the terrified cavalry rode over their own foot:

running into the narrow lane … trampling many of them under their horse feet, crying out to them, *Away, away, every man shift for his life, you are all dead men*; which caused a most strange confusion amongst us.

Fellow soldier 'T. V.' was as blunt as Foster, describing the cavalry's retreat as 'base cowardise.'[77] Foster went on to describe a scene of chaos and terror:

We fired 10 or 12 Drakes at the enemy, but they came upon us very feircely, having their foot on the other side of the hedges; many of our waggons were overthrowne and broken: others cut their traces and horse harnesse, and run away with their horses, leaving their waggons & carriages behind them: our foot fired upon the enemies horse very bravely, and slew many of them; some report above 100 and not 10 of ours: some that we took prisoners our men were so inraged at them that they knockt out their braines with the butt-end of their muskets: in this great distraction and rout a wagon of powder lying in the way overthrowne some spark of fire

---

75   Book VII, 1840 vol. IV, p.223.
76   *A True Relation of the Late Expedition … for the Relief of Gloucester* (in *Bibliotheca Gloucestrensis*, p.248).
77   *A True Relation of the Late Battell Neere Newbury*, p.5.

or match fell among it, which did much hurt; 7 men burnt and 2 kild: the
enemy had got 2 of our drakes in the reer, had not our foot played the men
and recovered them again: this was about 4 or 5 aclock at night; many
of our men lost their horses, and other things which they threw away in
haste …

Before the attack Essex's troops were already exhausted, short of provisions, and
probably still highly agitated after the bloody and extended battle the previous day.
Codrington agrees that they were 'expecting no enemy so neere at hand.'[78] Rupert's
sudden charge from the rear after their unmolested march from Newbury caught
them completely unawares, just as they must have thought they were finally safe:
the shock of the new assault drove some of the infantry over the edge, frenziedly
beating out the brains of any Royalists who surrendered. Royalist tempers also
snapped after the loss of men and horses to Parliamentarian cannonballs scything
down the lane: Codrington wrote:

> The lane on our Reare was so crouded with the Enemy, that the Execution
> which the Drakes performed was very violent, for it did beare downe both
> Horse and Man, and in the middle of the lane made a new lane amongst
> them. The fall of these men was Rise of the Courage of their Companions,
> and thereupon adding fury to their valour, and desperatenesse to their
> fury, they adventured on the mouth of our Ordnance and on the Jawes of
> death, and became Masters of two of our Drakes.[79]

The exploding powder cart would have added to the mayhem, not to mention
the panic-inducing cries of the fleeing Parliamentarian cavalry that everyone was
doomed. To their credit some of Essex's officers held their nerve and managed to
muster what Codrington called 'a selected party of our Foote' and form them up
against their attackers, eventually driving them off and forcing them to leave the
captured cannons and (allegedly) 100 dead behind them.

Rupert's Diary states that Rupert struck the rear of Essex's force 'at the heath's
end, 3 miles from Newberrye';[80] this would put them between Greenham and
Crookham, although modern commentators believe the engagement occurred
another three to six miles further, around Brimpton or Aldermaston. Rupert's Diary
offers no composition of the Prince's force, and does not mention the musketeers,[81]
although 'T. V.' believes Colonel Hurry led the attack, and Codrington that besides

---

78   *The Life and Death, of the Illustrious Robert Earle of Essex, &c.*, pp.36-37.
79   *Ibid.*
80   EHR, p.735.
81   At least, there is no mention in the abridged version in 1898. The omitted footnotes of the original may
     be more forthcoming.

Rupert the force's commanders included the Earl of Northampton and Lord Wilmot. *Mercurius Aulicus* agrees with the Diary that the engagement was three miles from Newbury, and agrees with the Parliamentarian accounts that it did not happen until the afternoon of the 21st, the Parliamentarians 'forced to rise' around midday by 'hunger and scarcity of ammunition'. *Aulicus* does not mention musketeers either, only that the party consisted of 'such forces [besides the Horse] as His Majestie thought fit to send in the Reare of them'.[82] In regard to Clarendon's 'one thousand musketeers', this ties in with the 'official' Parliamentarian account which spoke of 800, and specifically noted that they were commanded men rather than dragoons.

As stated, however, none of the accounts of this post-Newbury action mention Lisle, and Warburton's dramatic portrayal of him and his musketeers 'pour[ing] a deadly volley into the dense columns [of Essex's men] struggling desperately, but resolutely onward', must be taken as flowery conjecture. Yet subsequent historians have tended to uncritically agree with him. Whilst Lisle may have been present, there is no specific evidence that he was, or that the men were those he had led the day before; or that, even if they were, that Lisle continued to lead them. He had been wounded early during the battle, and was possibly out of action for the rest of it; as an outnumbered forlorn hope in the teeth of a Parliamentarian onslaught, his commanded force would undoubtedly have suffered a large number of casualties. A significant wound sustained within the last twenty-four hours would be at the very least a major obstacle to participation in a further sortie, particularly if significant enough to have forced him from the battlefield at the time, or if the site of the wound made moving around awkward. Whilst the wound would not rule Lisle out of accompanying Rupert, and he was certainly obstinate enough to have fought while injured, he was not superhuman and the injury is a major factor which weighs against the suggestion of his involvement. Possibly the infantry Rupert took in pursuit of Essex were commanded by Wentworth, whose wounding was not widely reported and therefore may have been less severe than Lisle's, but again there is no specific evidence to confirm or discount it.

In any case, Rupert's action was little more than a pointless gesture of frustration. Essex and his men reached Theale the same evening and then Reading the next day, before moving on to London and a heroes' welcome.

Post-Newbury, presumably Lisle returned to Oxford with the rest of the army; it is to be hoped that he managed to visit Lord Grandison's sickbed in Jesus College before his death on 29th September.[83] In October the Parliamentarians abandoned

82   Week 38 (1644), pp.529-530
83   Sir William Dugdale records that 'The Lord Grandison dyed in Oxford at Jesus Colledge, of the Fever, and was buryed in Christ's Church, at ye foote of Sr Wm Pennyman, ye Munday following, viz. 2d Oct.' (*Diary*, p.55). Grandison's tomb is still extant at Christ Church, along with the monument put up later by his daughter Barbara.

Reading, which the Royalists snapped up for a second time and garrisoned under Sir Jacob Astley. The onset of a wet and snowy winter in November did not bring any lull in hostilities: in Hampshire Sir William Waller attempted to capture Basing House, and Sir Ralph Hopton attempted to dislodge Waller from Farnham Castle. Into this local scenario, in late November, marched a Royalist detachment of commanded men from the recently reinstalled Reading garrison, led by Lincolnshire colonel Richard Bolle.

7

A Staffordshire Regiment

Lord Paget

As King and government drifted apart there was little reason to think that William, 5th Baron Paget, would not support the Parliament. He had been one of the twelve peers who petitioned the King to summon the House in 1640, and had supported the proceedings against Strafford and Laud. Though his was a Staffordshire family it held estates in Buckinghamshire, a county with strong Parliamentarian leanings, and in 1641 Paget was appointed its Lord Lieutenant. However, shortly after the King published his Commission of Array in Buckinghamshire early in 1642 Paget seems to have panicked. Clarendon later wrote that Paget, and others who had 'passionately and peevishly (to say no worse) concurred in all the most violent votes and actions, which had been done from the beginning', were 'recovered to a right understanding' and returned to the royal fold. Of Paget himself, Clarendon continues:

> Paget … had contributed all his faculties to their service, and to the preju-
> dice of the king's, from before the beginning of the parliament; … and
> had been, as a man most worthy to be confided in, chosen lord lieutenant
> of one of the most confiding counties, the county of Buckingham, (where
> he had, with great solemnity and pomp, execute their ordinance, in defi-
> ance of the king's proclamation,) and had subscribed a greater number
> of horses for their service, upon their propositions, than any other of the
> same quality; convinced in his conscience, fled from them, and besought
> the king's pardon: and, for the better manifesting of the tenderness of
> his compunction, and the horror he had of his former guilt, he lustily
> discovered [i.e. revealed] whatsoever he had known of their counsels; and
> aggravated all the ill they had done, with declaring it to be done to worse
> and more horrid ends, than many good men believed to be possible for
> them to entertain.[1]

---

1   Book V, 1840 vol. III, pp.64-65.

Clarendon's description of Paget shows a man prepared to go to great lengths to prove his loyalty to whichever side he was presently courting. However there were many practical reasons for changing sides, and without full consideration of Paget's he should not be judged too hastily; particularly as his family, whose Catholicism during Queen Elizabeth's time had resulted in loss of title and estates, would have understood only too well what it cost to be out of tune with the prevailing political climate. Yet his surrendering himself to Parliament again in September 1644, and then managing to ingratiate himself with Charles II at the Restoration, puts Paget in an elite group of Civil War multiple turncoats whose actions still attract debate and criticism.[2] After his return to the King in May 1642, Parliament dismissed Paget from his Lieutenancy. His name appears in a Royalist list of lords in mid June,[3] and by August the King had commissioned him to raise men.

Recruits

Paget, although only thirty-three, had no intention of doing any fighting himself. He confined himself to funding and recruiting, and turned over his regiment's physical command to fifty-one-year-old Richard Bolle, a career soldier from Lincolnshire. In the Bishops' War of 1640 Bolle had fought as a lieutenant colonel, first under Colonel Feilding and then Sir Arthur Aston,[4] and later went to Ireland as lieutenant colonel to Sir John Clotworthy.[5] Clotworthy was still there in July 1642:[6] given that Bolle was in Staffordshire by August, it is fair to assume that he had left Clotworthy's service some time previously.

Bolle selected Richard D'Ewes as his own deputy. At twenty-six, D'Ewes was the younger and only brother of the Suffolk MP Sir Simonds D'Ewes; his recruitment as a lieutenant colonel implies that he had some military experience, and it is likely that in 1640 he was either the captain 'Richard Dowse' of the Earl of Northumberland's regiment, or lieutenant 'Richard Dowes' of Colonel Goring's, the same unit as Francis Lisle.[7] In 1642 Richard's letters to Simonds make it clear that he was an enthusiastic supporter of the King, and on several occasions he begged his brother to leave the Parliament and join him amidst the Royalist

2 Andrew Hopper's *Turncoats & Renegades* offers an excellent study of turncoats of both sides, and the phenomenon of side-changing in general.

3 *His Majesties Declaration To all His loving subjects, occasioned by a False and Scandalous Imputation laid upon his Majestie of an Intention of Raysing or Leavying War against His Parliament: and of having raised Force to that end.* Oxford, 1642; Wing C2548. The declaration was dated 15th June 1642. His name is omitted from a London version of the pamphlet printed at around the same time (Wing C2239).

4 Rushworth, 1686, p.1243 (pre-Newburn muster list), and p.1246 (post-Newburn muster list).

5 *A Most True Relation of the Present State of His Majesties Army* … London, December 1642.

6 As evidenced by *A True Relation Of the taking of Mountjoy in the County of Tyrone, by Collonell Clotworthy* …, published in London on 4th August.

7 Rushworth, 1686, p.1244 and 1245 respectively.

supporters gathering at York.[8] Simonds refused but remained only a moderate Parliamentarian, and was expelled from the House of Commons during Pride's Purge in December 1648.

On 15th August 1642 Richard wrote to Henry Hastings, High Sheriff of Leicestershire and the man who was quickly to become the King's key commander in the Midlands:

> Prince Rupert is dayley expected and 'tis given out by our best intelli-gencers, he has been chased by the Earl of Warwick, but what is become of it, is not yet known certainly. Sir, I am now going to Litchfeild, and cannot give myselfe more time then the assurance that I am yr faithfull servant …[9]

Paget did not receive his commission to raise men until around the time of Richard's letter, which suggests Paget and Bolle were recruiting officers well in advance of the official paperwork. Until recently Hastings had also been at York with the King, and his corresponding with the lieutenant colonel of a neighbouring Staffordshire regiment implies that some degree of regional planning had taken place while everyone was gathered in the north. A few days after D'Ewes wrote to Hastings, Paget was reportedly at Warwick with the King, which again suggests he had wholly left Bolle and D'Ewes to deal with regimental matters.[10]

Many of the King's officers had met before, whether on the Continent, during the Bishops' Wars or in Ireland. Bolle and his senior officers were no exception. Nathaniel Moyle, who 'Deserter' says was Bolle's major at Edgehill and was missing after the battle, had served with the Lincolnshire colonel in 1640.[11] Moyle's place in the regiment is highly dubious, however: as major of Sir Thomas Lunsford's regiment he was a coffin-bearer at D'Ewes's funeral at Reading in April 1643, and when killed at the storming of Bristol in July he had risen to lieutenant colonel.[12] 'Deserter' is riddled with inaccuracies, for example listing Lisle as Colonel Blague's second-in-command, and unless Moyle had transferred to Lunsford's regiment almost immediately after Edgehill, it is fair to accept that what 'Deserter' says about

8   The letters are preserved in vol. II of Sir Simonds' autobiography.

9   D'Ewes, vol. II p.300. Rupert arrived five days later, on 20th August.

10   *An exact and True Diurnall of the Proceedings in Parliament,* 8th-15th and 22nd-29th August (TT E.202[38], TT E.202[39]).

11   'Deserter' being the 1642 London pamphlet which mentioned Lisle (see chapter 5); presumably it gained that name for listing men who had deserted Parliament for the King. In 1640 Moyle is listed as a lieutenant in Aston's regiment, on Rushworth's post-Newburn list (Rushworth, 1686, p.1246); as previously noted, Bolle was Aston's lieutenant colonel.

12   W. Slingsby, *Colonel Slingsby's relation …,* in Hopton's *Bellum Civile,* p.91; Bernard de Gomme's account of Bristol adds that Moyle was shot through the bladder and died shortly afterwards (de Gomme, ed. Ede-Borrett, p.20).

him is similarly flawed. Both Bolle's and Lunsford's regiments were in Feilding's brigade at the time, which may be the source of the confusion.

How Bolle selected Richard D'Ewes as his deputy is unknown, but it may have been D'Ewes who introduced another 1640 officer to the nascent regiment: Captain Thomas Throckmorton (or Throgmorton), a lieutenant from Goring's. Throckmorton was a Catholic, and in December 1640 his faith had led to his expulsion from the army. Sharing this fate were sixty or so other officers,[13] including the Catholic ensign Robert Skerrow, then serving in the ill-disciplined unit of Sir Thomas Lunsford.[14] Only Skerrow's post-Edgehill commission as Throckmorton's lieutenant confirms the latter's presence in Paget's regiment at all.[15] The two probably knew each other through Catholic networks in 1640, and doubtless in 1642 Throckmorton was only too happy to accept a fellow Catholic amongst his closest comrades. When George Lisle spoke of the 'suspect religion' to be found in the regiment after he took command in January 1644,he must have been referring to men such as Skerrow, who by that time was a captain in his own right.[16] Why the regiment had enough Catholic bias to be irritating to its later colonel is not known, but as noted earlier Paget's family had been prominent Catholics during Elizabeth's reign: his grandfather and great uncle were involved in the Babington conspiracy, and although Paget himself was a Protestant, his personal history perhaps made him more likely than most to be tolerant.

Skerrow must have succeeded to Throckmorton's captaincy; Peter Young states that the latter had gone from the regiment by 23rd May 1643, as he does not appear on an arms delivery docket on that date, but the docket does not name the lieutenant colonel or major, and it is entirely possible that Throckmorton had been promoted and was the unnamed major, however briefly.[17] Skerrow's 1640 service under Lunsford was seen out in the presence of fellow ensign Edward Fowles (or

---

13 Throckmorton expulsion, Young, *Edgehill 1642*, p.166; other officers, *CSP Domestic Series*, 1640-1641, p.311.

14 Rushworth, 1686, p.1249. This was an earlier regiment than the one Lunsford raised for the King in 1642, and of which Nathaniel Moyle was major. Lunsford's 1640 troops had been in the thick of the action at Newburn in 1640, most of them fleeing their sconce under heavy bombardment from the Scots. Fissel (p.56) notes that the unit had brawled and argued its way north, disputing everything from religion to pay, and even attacking each other. Several men died at the hands of their own comrades, allegedly in self-defence. A proclamation issued in July states that 'Souldiers under the Regiment of Colonel Lunsford, were fallen into such Mutiny against their Officers, and disorder otherwayes, in the Countie of Warwick, in their passage thorow that County, as that a great part of them are run away, and the rest persisting in so much disobedience, as that they are ready all to disband.' (*A Proclamation for apprehending and punishing of Souldiers*).

15 The commission is dated 30th October 1642. Harl MSS 6804, f.221.

16 [Author: In one of the missing letters of Lisle's quoted to me by a colleague; see chapter 6.]

17 Roy, ROP part 2, p.238 (NA, WO 55/1661 [3]). The officers listed were as follows: unnamed captain of colonel's company; unnamed lieutenant colonel; unnamed major; Captain Lloyd; Captain Fowler; Captain Walden; Captain Skerroe; Captain Hawkred.

Fowler),[18] whom we find as a captain of Bolle's in 1643, and therefore probably one at Edgehill; he had made it to major by the time he was captured at Naseby in 1645.

It is possible to perceive a recruitment trail from D'Ewes to Throckmorton, Throckmorton to Skerrow, Skerrow to Fowles, amongst men who had previously met in arms. Perhaps D'Ewes had also found some raw recruits during his stay in York: John Hanmer was commissioned there as a Captain on 8th August,[19] and the 1663 list of indigent officers from York reveals a Lieutenant Edward Norbury.[20] D'Ewes's recruits would probably have travelled south to Lichfield with him in mid-August.

Meanwhile Paget recruited extensively around his native Staffordshire. His lands lay chiefly in the east of the county around Cannock and Lichfield, but he also made attempts to recruit further south. Lieutenant John Roane was arrested in Walsall in September 1642 while trying to drum up volunteers, and claimed Richard D'Ewes as his authority.[21]

At least three of the Littleton family enlisted as officers, although the familial relationship between Edward, James and Rugely Littleton remains unclear. Possibly Edward and James were the brothers who appear in the parish records of Seighford, near Stafford, both born around 1595. Of Rugely Littleton, the only records trace is the birth of a son, Edward, at Marchington near Uttoxeter in 1648. Regarding military careers, James and Rugely were both listed as prisoners of war after Naseby in 1645, James as an ensign and Rugely a captain. Both claimed bounty from Charles II in 1663, although James claimed as a member of Bolle's regiment, and Rugely as a member of Lisle's. Perhaps the difference lay in timing: Rugely may not have joined up until after Lisle took over.

Edward Littleton rose rapidly through the ranks during Bolle's tenure. Probably captain or major at Edgehill, he was lieutenant colonel by July 1643, when his actions at the storming of Bristol were praised in print.[22] Almost certainly he was the unnamed lieutenant colonel mentioned two months earlier on the May delivery docket: the anonymous incumbent would have been newly-promoted following the death of D'Ewes at Reading in April, and as the regiment was not in action between May and July it is unlikely that it would have lost another half

---

18   Rushworth, 1686, p.1249 (post-Newburn muster list).

19   Young, *Edgehill 1642*, p.214; Young does not specify his source.

20   Probably the Lieutenant Edward Norbury serving under Thomas Ballard in Leinster, in 1640 (Ormonde, vol. I, 1895, p.123).

21   Peter Young uncovered this reference (*Edgehill 1642*, pp.48-49; quoting from HMC Portland, vol. I p.63). Roane was examined at Northampton on 19th September, where it was found that 'he was employed by Lt. Colonel d'Ewes in a regiment assigned by Lord Paget to Colonel Bolls with a commission … to raise volunteers, which he showed to the Mayor of Walsall, who refused to let him beat up his drum and apprehended him.'

22   *Bristoll taken, by Prince Rupert: Julye 26, 1643…* (edited and reprinted in 1988 by Stephen Ede-Borrett as *The Storm of Bristol – De Gomme's Account*; p.42).

colonel in the intervening eight weeks without any record or at least a comment from the Royalist press. Whilst several of Littleton's fellow officers had soldiering experience in Ireland or the north of England, his early career is altogether more interesting: after his capture at Naseby in 1645, a Parliamentarian newsbook described him as:

> Lieuetenant Colonell Littleton, who was a Captaine at Cales voyage, and since lived in Staffordshire, a mad fellow, that hath his Religion to chuse.[23]

'Cales' was the old English name for Cadiz: unless Littleton was in his sixties and participated in the expedition led by the previous Earl of Essex in 1596, the reference must relate to Buckingham's ill-fated expedition in 1625, although there is no Captain Littleton mentioned in the list included with Glanville's journal.[24] The compiler of the Naseby list offers snippets of information about a number of captured senior officers, in a tone that can only be described as one of disparaging gossip (he tells readers that Colonel Boncle 'was formerly the Queenes Pastrey Cooke', and Colonel Slaughter 'A notorious Papist'): this does not lend credibility to his claim that Littleton was mad. The reference to Littleton's religion sounds suspiciously like an accusation of atheism, a common enough slur at the time.

The regiment was completed by the end of August 1642. In a letter printed on 1st September a supporter of Parliament noted,

> The Lord Paget and his followers have gathered 3. or 400. of the scum and refuge of the Countrey, and billeted them in Lichfield … where the Cavaliers and their scums have disarmed every man in the town, and seized upon the Magazine of the City, and exercise their souldiers with their Armes.[25]

After then surprising Tamworth, ejecting a minister from the town and having some prominent citizens arrested, the regiment travelled north-east to meet up with the King on 13th September, as the army marched from Nottingham to Derby. Paget remained Royalist for another two years, but the extent of his involvement with the regiment, besides the fact that he may have continued to fund it where necessary, is not clear. In November the Staffordshire gentry of both sides agreed that their county should remain neutral, and that further troops would be raised only for its defence.

---

23   *Perfect Occurrences Of Parliament,* The 25th Week (1645), no page numbers.
24   Glanville was present during the expedition; his journal was published by the Camden Society in 1883.
25   *Remarkable Passages from Nottingham Lichfield, Leicester, and Cambridge …*

Edgehill

By 12th October the King's army was quartered in Shropshire and Herefordshire. Paget's regiment, already generally referred to as Colonel Bolle's, was quartered with Richard Feilding's regiment at Wornhill near Hereford.[26] At Edgehill on 23rd October they faced the enemy for the first time, as one of five regiments in Feilding's brigade, at the centre of the line. Shortly after the action commenced, Prince Rupert, to their right, led the Royalist cavalry in a dramatic charge which smashed the Parliamentarian left wing. As the right wing cavalry also crumbled, its commander Sir William Balfour gathered a body of horse behind the centre of the Parliament infantry line in an attempt to salvage something from the disorder. Positioned behind a rise, his force would not have been seen by the Royalist foot. As the infantry of both sides advanced, Balfour took his opportunity. His charge smashed into Feilding's unwitting brigade, which quickly collapsed. Balfour chased the remnants back as far as their cannon, capturing three of the brigade's colonels (including Feilding), killing a lieutenant colonel and capturing a colour. Bolle and his senior officers evaded capture, although the effect of the devastating charge on such a novice regiment would have left a lasting impression.

Reading: first garrison and siege

That Edgehill had occurred at all was a rude shock to a country that had not seen internal strife for two centuries. Afterwards the armies backed off, and propositions for peace were discussed. Minor manoeuvring continued, and in early November the King and his army walked unchallenged into the strategically vital town of Reading when the Parliamentarian commander fled. Although the church bells rang dutifully to celebrate the King's arrival and brief sojourn, the town council and the local landowning families were divided in their loyalties. When the King and his army moved on towards London, Bolle's regiment and several others were left behind as a garrison under the unpopular Catholic commander, Sir Arthur Aston.[27] Bolle's men would have been forcibly billeted on unwelcoming people in an unwelcoming town, which sat unfortified on the front line between London and Oxford: for the Staffordshire soldiers, far from home and still smarting from

---

26   BL, Harley MS 6851, f.211.

27   The regiments present were Bolle's, Feilding's, Lunsford's and Fitton's, four of the five regiments in Feilding's Edgehill brigade; also those of Welshman Sir Thomas Salusbury, and Colonel Charles Gerard – as evidenced by the presence at the siege of Gerard's lieutenant colonel, Edward Villiers, Lisle's kinsman. Two cavalry regiments were also present: those of Sir Arthur Aston, and that of his kinsman Sir Thomas Aston. The latter had gone by the time of Essex's siege, but the foot regiment of John Belasyse had arrived (he who had noted the 1,200 commanded men at Edgehill). M. C. Barrès-Baker notes that Parliamentarian sources spoke of Royalist dragoons at the siege, and that this is highly likely given Sir Arthur's expertise in that arm (Barrès-Baker, p.28).

their Edgehill losses, the stay would have been far from comfortable. The execution of 'three of the Kings Souldiers' on 12th December, noted in one of the town's parish registers, evidences some degree of ill-discipline in the garrison at best, perhaps mutiny at the worst,[28] although Aston was well known as a harsh disciplinarian whose punishments did not always, perhaps, fit the crime.[29]

There was worse to come. On 15th April 1643 *Mercurius Aulicus*, the principal Royalist newsbook, reported that:

> … it was advertised this day from Reading, the Earl of Essex having drawne together all his Forces and caused the bridges over the river of Lodon (which he had formerly broke downe) to be set up again, was marched with all his Army towards that towne, intending to assault the same, and that he was already come within the sight of their workes, to the great joy of all the Garrison, who have long desired to see his Excellency, and try the mettaile of his Souldiers: whose brave exploits are so much talked of in the weekly Pamphlets, though not heard of otherwise.[30]

Like most newsbooks, *Aulicus's* role was principally vehement cheerleader for its own side, and its assertion that the Reading garrison of 3,000 foot actually looked forward to being vastly outnumbered by Essex's army of 15,000, despite now possessing some earthworks, can only have been political bravado.[31] Safe at Oxford, the King was certainly alarmed at the prospect of such an attack: on the same day Essex that arrived at Reading, Charles wrote to Rupert, who was up north in Paget's territory attempting to oust the enemy garrison at Lichfield.

> Nephew – I thought it most necessary to advise you, that the rebels have attacked Reading; not to recall you, though I could be content ye were here … I write this not to make you raise your siege, but that you lose no more time in it than you must needs.[32]

---

28 The registers of St Laurence, the only Reading church to keep up its register at this time. A new incumbent at St Mary's, in mid-1643, noted that 'neither in time of warr could any Regezter be well kept', and was forced to backfill two years of information for that church himself, by questioning the townspeople.

29 In December 1642 Aston arrested and hanged a visiting London merchant, claiming he was a spy; naturally the London press denied Aston's accusation, but as no evidence of Aston's has survived we are left only with his word against theirs (reported in *A Perfect Diurnall*, Numb. 29, and in various newsbooks thereafter).

30 Week 15 (1643), p.191.

31 The London newsbook *A Perfect Diurnall*, Numb. 45, puts the numbers at 16,000 foot and 3,000 horse, but M. C. Barres-Baker (p.56) argues that surviving pay warrants support no more than around 12,000 foot.

32 Warburton includes the full letter (vol. II, pp.165-166).

The next day, the extent of the crisis becoming clear, he changed his tone and ordered Rupert to Reading. Whilst those inside the town waited for resolution one way or the other, the garrison was forced to fend for itself. Over the preceding months great earthworks had been thrown up around the town, and now proved their worth. On 17th April *Aulicus* reported that the defenders 'couragiously beat off' a sortie against the town, and that the King had sent 700 musketeers and six cart loads of match and ammunition to assist it.[33] He followed in person a few days later, with all the men he could safely withdraw from Oxford and its surrounding garrisons. At the tilers' town of Nettlebed, in the Chilterns eight miles north of Reading, he was at last joined by Rupert who had dashed the hundred or so miles from Lichfield in just two days. The Prince had left a new governor there, a local man named Richard Bagot who had originally been recruited as a captain by Paget the previous August. It is not known when Bagot left the regiment, but he had stayed at least until early November when he signed another regimental arms docket.[34] Neither he nor his brother were greatly liked by Henry Hastings, D'Ewes's early contact, by then the King's colonel general of four midland counties and the man to whom Bagot would theoretically have had to defer on a local basis. Hastings was a volatile spirit, and P. R. Newman describes him and his Tamworth garrison as coming 'very close to a localised war' with the Bagots at Lichfield.[35] In 1645, this local argument would touch George Lisle's career.

Meanwhile on 18th April 1643 Bolle's regiment took its first significant casualty. Clarendon reports:

> they [the besiegers] had many batteries, from whence they shot their cannon into the town and upon their line at a near distance, but without any considerable execution; there being fewer lost by that service than will be believed, and but one man of note, lieutenant colonel D'Ews, a young man of notable courage and vivacity, who had his leg shot off by a cannon bullet, of which he speedily and very cheerfully died.[36]

At this time 'cheerfull' meant not 'happy' but something akin to 'bearing up in the face of difficulty.' D'Ewes did not in fact lose his leg, but was injured inside his left thigh; despite this, he managed to hobble away and was carried to a surgeon. However, although the bone was unbroken the wound was not properly cleaned and he contracted a fever and died three days later. M. C. Barrès-Baker writes a good analysis of his care, mostly based on the detail of a report from Sir Simonds

---

33   Week 15 (1643), pp.197-198.
34   On 5th November Bagot signed for the regiment's issue of powder, match and shot (Roy, ROP part 1, p.159 (NA, WO 55/423, f.14-15, 54, 194, 198)).
35   Newman, p.95.
36   Book VII, 1840 vol. IV, p.26.

D'Ewes, and concludes that Richard died of septicaemia.[37] The young, popular lieutenant colonel was buried at St Mary's. For Edward Littleton, the regiment's major by this point, D'Ewes's death meant immediate promotion to lieutenant colonel, although in the worst possible circumstances. For the garrison as a whole, misfortune piled upon misfortune, as *Aulicus* reported on 21st April:

> This day came Letters from Sir Arthur Aston from Reading wherein he sayes that he got a blow on his head by the fall of a tyle from the top of an house, but not dangerous neither disabling him from performance of the present service.[38]

The story is confirmed by Captain John Gwyn, who reported that Aston had gone outside to read a confidential letter in private, and:

> as his hasty fate would have it, for he had scarce a minute's time to look it over, but a cannon-shot came through the guard-house, and drives the tyles about, that one fell upon his head and sunk him almost to the ground before Colonel Lunsford and another officer catcht him by both arms … [he] faintly said 'My head's whole, I thank God'; and spoke no more there at that time, but immediately was carried away to his house in the town, where, during the rest of the siege, he was speechless …[39]

Being speechless would certainly render Aston incapable of any effective command, contrary to the report in *Aulicus*, which Barrès-Baker observes to be a blatant lie; he suggests Aston must have had a haematoma, as his doctors opened his skull to relieve pressure on his brain, after which he began to recover.[40] Unlike the popular and lamented Richard d'Ewes, Aston probably received little sympathy: despite having a long-standing military reputation – Clarendon noted that 'there was not in his army an officer of greater reputation, and of whom the enemy had a greater dread'[41] – he was also known for being harsh in his commands and unpleasant to deal with. Additionally he was openly Catholic. Clarendon was among his detractors, adding that he 'had the fortune to be very much esteemed,

---

37 Barrès-Baker, *The Siege of Reading, April 1643*, pp.87-89; D'Ewes, *Journal of the House of Commons*, vol. III (BL, Harley MS 164 f. 376 ff.)

38 Week 16 (1643), p.204.

39 Gwyn, pp.26-27.

40 Aston's operation is revealed in Secretary Sir Edward Nicholas's letter to Prince Rupert on 20th April, urging him to hurry from Staffordshire. He says Aston was delirious until trepanned, and 'It were much better the County of Stafford, then the Towne of Redding were lost as things now stand.' (WSL, S. MS. 564). This letter, written from Oxford, may in fact have crossed with Rupert's arrival in Reading, which seems to have happened a couple of days earlier.

41 Book VII, 1840 vol. IV, p.27.

where he was not known; and very much detested, where he was' and that when later appointed governor of Oxford, 'he was by this time too well known ... to be beloved by any.'[42] The Earl was habitually blunt about people he did not personally like, but the truth of Aston's unpopularity was demonstrated some time after his Oxford appointment, when he was attacked while doing his rounds. He subsequently adopted a personal bodyguard. Clarendon was dubious also about his Reading injury:

> The truth of it is, sir Arthur Aston was believed by many, not to be in so incompetent a condition to command as he pretended; and that albeit his head was so much swoln, that he might not in person venture upon any execution, yet that his understanding, or senses, were not much distempered, or discomposed; and that he only positively waved meddling, out of dislike of the condition they were in. And it is true, that, when he came to Oxford, he could speak as reasonably of any matter, as ever I knew him before, or after.[43]

Meanwhile, command of the garrison had fallen to Lisle's kinsman Colonel Richard Feilding who, Gwyn states, was the deputy-governor. He apparently perceived that no help would come, or if it did, that it would not be enough to negate Essex's huge advantage in numbers. Four days later, on 25th April, he asked Essex for terms. Several pamphleteers mention the garrison hanging out a white flag; it is to be hoped they used the word 'flag' figuratively, and that whatever was ignominiously draped over the defences that day did not belong to Bolle's regiment, who possessed white colours. Gwyn noted that the garrison was not in immediate peril through shortage of powder or provisions, and that the garrison's scoutmaster and several officers left the town and went to the King – who had left Oxford for Reading the day before – to tell him of Feilding's unfathomable decision to surrender. The King sent a letter to Feilding by return, telling him relief was imminent, even giving him the estimated hour of its arrival, and ordering him to break off negotiations. Feilding ignored him, exchanged hostages and began a parley, as a London newsbook explained:

> They sent to parley, Colonell Bolles, Lieutenant-Colonell Thelwell, Serjeant Major Gilby; and we sent to them, according to their demands, as Hostages, the Lord Rotchford, Lieutenant-Colonel Russell, and Serjeant Major Long ...[44]

42 *Ibid.*, p.516.
43 *Ibid.*, p.44.
44 *The third Intelligence From Reading*, p.6.

A three hour parley was agreed, but just as negotiations appeared to have been concluded, the King's forces appeared on the hill above Caversham on the north side of the river. Feilding messaged Essex and extended the parley so he could obtain the King's agreement to the surrender; however he appeared not to expect the full scale relief attempt that then ensued, under the torrential rain of a heavy thunderstorm. When the situation became clear, most of his fellow colonels all but mutinied, readying their men to break the truce and sally out of the town to assist the King. Barrès-Baker gives a comprehensive account of the skirmish, and the strenuous efforts of the Royalist relief force to dislodge enemy troops from the southern end of Caversham Bridge. Feilding refused to help or allow any of the garrison regiments to do so, even after a messenger from the King advised that Charles himself was present; allegedly Feilding answered that he would not break the truce, and forfeit his honour, even if the King himself should come personally and command him. Eventually, after several hours of heavy losses, the relief force was withdrawn.

That evening Feilding resumed communications with Essex he would agree on the previously discussed terms if the King did; accordingly Bolle and the Parliamentarian Colonel Russell were appointed to be sent over the river. They reached the King at his Caversham lodging and he finally agreed to surrender the town, though claiming later that he had never seen the paperwork in detail. Some dangerously close musket shots from nervous Parliamentarian pickets in Caversham made Bolle and Russell delay their return until the morning, when they delivered the news to Essex, and then the Reading council of war ratified the articles of surrender. Bolle was one of the signatories.[45] At ten o'clock the next morning, Thursday 27th April, the Royalist garrison began to evacuate. Sir Arthur Aston was brought out first, on a horse litter. Although Essex had agreed the garrison could leave unmolested, his men were apparently so unruly that neither he nor his officers could prevent the agreement being flouted.

> ... at their [the Royalists'] coming out of the town, and passing through the enemy's guards, the soldiers were not only reviled, and reproachfully used, but many of them disarmed, and most of the waggons plundered ...[46]

The Royalists did not forget this flagrant breach of the surrender terms and returned the favour later in the year, pillaging the Parliamentarian garrison retreating by agreement from Bristol. For surrendering the garrison Feilding

---

45   The full list of Royalist signatories ran as follows: Feilding; Belasyse; Bolle; Anthony Thelwall (Fitton's regiment); Theophilus Gilby (Belasyse's regiment, and later a battalion commander under Lisle); George Boncle (Salusbury's regiment). *The Kingdomes Weekly Intelligencer* adds Edward Villiers to this list (Numb. 17, p.132).

46   Clarendon, Book VII, 1840 vol. IV, p.38.

was 'largely condemned by a Council of war held at Oxford, to bee shot dead at a post',[47] but eventually reprieved; Stuart Reid, Lord Forth's ODNB biographer, suggests the reprieve was granted, when it was realised that by sticking to the surrender terms he preserved the soldiers to fight elsewhere for the King. His disgrace lingered, however, and he was removed from regimental command. A year later he commanded the artillery at Cheriton, but it is difficult to say whether this was a sign of his disgrace, or a sign of renewed trust and rehabilitation.[48]

In May the 3,000 evicted Reading men were put up in a temporary camp at Culham, near Abingdon; quartering this many soldiers at once on already saturated communities around Oxford would have been well-nigh impossible. As the Oxford Army began to assemble for the new season, other regiments were moved in alongside them. The men endured basic conditions in rickety huts and shelters, and it is no surprise that by midsummer an epidemic had broken out. The illness was most likely typhus or typhoid, the former spread by lice and fleas and the latter by contaminated food or drinking water. Given the cramped and unsanitary conditions at Culham, perhaps this epidemic was a combination of both. Certainly the 'camp fever', as it was generally known, took a huge toll on the assembled army. An undated ordnance receipt from mid-June 1643 gives details of the arms returned to the Oxford stores by the commanders of sick and deceased soldiers, and the figures speak for themselves: on this receipt alone (there may well have been others) a total of 466 muskets and 566 pike were returned.[49] To put it in context, these figures represent approximately three regiments' worth of men.[50] Bolle's regiment alone, having been issued with 20 muskets and 20 pikes as recently as 23rd May,[51] now turned in 53 muskets and 66 pikes; only one other regiment returned more. In May the village of Yarnton, north-west of Oxford, had been set aside as a hospital; the burial registers reveal that eleven soldiers from Bolle's regiment died in Yarnton between mid-June and mid-August, probably casualties of the outbreak.[52] It may have been a small consolation to the Royalists that Essex's troops, now cooped up in Reading and crowded into the surrounding villages, were enduring a similar epidemic, which plagued the Earl's army right into the summer.

---

47   William Lithgow, *The Present Surveigh Of London And England's State*, 1643.
48   Three months after Cheriton, however, in June 1644, the King sent him as a messenger to Oxford: which suggests he had at least to some extent regained Charles's trust (Walker, p.25).
49   Roy, ROP part 1, p.104 (NA, WO 55/459, ff. 386-7).
50   Based purely on average figures during the period. Technically a foot regiment was supposed to contain at least 1,000 men, but most Civil War regiments averaged 300 to 400.
51   Roy, ROP part 2, p.238 (precise source reference is unclear).
52   Yarnton parish registers, as quoted by Peter Young, *Edgehill 1642*, p.231.

From Bristol to Newbury

To put it mildly, July 1643 was not a good month for Parliament's cause in the West Country. Sir Ralph Hopton's army narrowly forced Sir William Waller's from Lansdowne Hill near Bath on the 5th, and on the 13th Lord Wilmot and a cavalry force from Oxford relieved Hopton's recovering force at Devizes, by drawing Waller away onto nearby Roundway Down. In a spectacular and unexpected defeat, Waller's army was split up and destroyed by the smaller relief force and some reinforcing Royalist infantry from the town. By removing him from the picture, albeit temporarily, the battle changed the direction of the war in the West.

In response to these victories Prince Rupert left Oxford and headed west with fourteen foot regiments, to take advantage of the sudden hole in the Parliament's campaign. Bolle's regiment was brigaded under the command of Colonel Henry Wentworth, and Edward Littleton was appointed his major. After some indecision as to whether Gloucester or Bristol was the better target, the Prince decided to force the latter. On the 23rd and 24th July his army and Prince Maurice's Cornish army converged on the city from the west and south. Despite both forces openly displaying their military strength to those inside the city, governor Nathaniel Fiennes refused to surrender; the Royalists responded by selecting likely breach points along the extensive ditch and bank defences that ran around medieval-walled Bristol as an outer defence, and building gun batteries to deal with the numerous forts placed along the line. A sporadic musket and artillery firefight ensued that lasted through the 24th and into the 25th; the Royalist command decided upon a joint attack by both armies at dawn on the 26th.

The next morning, at 'something before three in the morning',[53] the Cornish duly attacked in the south with a select part of their forces, but before the arranged signal. The Parliamentarian defenders gave everything they had, even throwing stones by hand, and this initial assault cost Maurice's force six senior officers: two lieutenant colonels were wounded, a colonel and a major were killed in the fight and two colonels died shortly afterwards of their wounds. Caught out by his brother's premature attack, Rupert immediately ordered the Oxford Army to fall on. Lisle's kinsman Lord Grandison, the Prince's colonel general, rallied the King's forces three times, trying in various places to break down or get over the earth bank, but the defence was just as fierce as in the south, and due to the mistiming of the attack, no scaling ladders were in position.

---

53   De Gomme, ed. Ede-Borrett, p.12. De Gomme gives 'an hower & halfe' from the start of the assault until the wall was breached; he adds that the securing of the breach and rout of the defenders took 'halfe an hower, & by 4: in the morning.' This totals two hours, which means the premature Cornish assault must have occurred at around two o'clock, in the dark, as supported by de Gomme's statement that 'Theyr fyrings wee sawe': both muskets and cannon emit jets of flame from their muzzles which is particularly noticeable in the dark.

A party comprising Wentworth's tercio, and dragoons under Colonels Henry Washington and Robert Howard, had been appointed to attack the defences at a point called St Michael's Hill, where the hill and a barn shielded them from attack on either side. Bernard de Gomme notes that:

> this Tertia of colonell Wentworths were the men, that had the honor and happynesse of the daye, first of all to beatte the Enemye out of theyr strengths; first of all to get over the Line, & to make waye for the rest of the Armyes.[54]

After a dirty ninety-minute fight along the western defences, during which Grandison was shot in the leg by a defender who came over the bank, Wentworth's party eventually secured their safe spot by the hill, and managed to clear the defenders beyond the bank by hurling grenades over the top and clambering over after them. A Parliamentarian officer attempted a counter-attack but was mortally wounded, and the remnants of his men ran away. The incomers began demolishing the bank to admit the rest of the army.

Meanwhile, Bolle's regiment had brought up the rear of the breaching party. De Gomme says:

> Leift. Col. Littleton ryding along the inside of the Line with a fire-pike, quite cleerd the place of the defendants: some of them crying out Wyld fire. Thus was the line cleared, for a greate waye together.[55]

After a counter attack from the defenders and some more skirmishing the defenders were seen off, and Wentworth's tercio was relieved by another which secured the breach, while the attack group pushed on towards the city proper. They fought their way up lanes and past houses, skirmishing for possession of defended buildings. Nathaniel Moyle, de Gomme tells us:

> allso commanded a Leiftenant of Col. Bowles with 30 Muskettiers into another howse, which much annoyed the Enemyes. So that hereabouts the fights was like skolding at one another, out of windows.[56]

This was one of Moyle's final actions: shortly afterwards, during heated fighting by the city's Frome Gate, he was mortally wounded by a shot through the bladder.

Inside the besieged city, men on the Parliament's side were beginning to desert: powder and ammunition were low, provisions short, and the defenders had no

---

54   *Ibid.*, p.15.
55   De Gomme, ed. Ede-Borrett, p.16.
56   *Ibid.*, p.18.

hope of relief. Retreat into the castle was not an option, as it was too small; this would also require the defenders to burn the city behind them. To top it all, governor Fiennes noted later in his published account of the events, low tide had allowed many of his men to desert across the quay to the Royalists:

> which not onely shewed the enemy that our men were disheartened, and that they should find but slender opposition, but it also shewed the enemy how they might with ease come over the water into the towne …[57]

Fiennes called for a parley, terms were accordingly agreed, and Bristol was delivered to the King. Prince Rupert was nominally appointed governor, although direct command fell to Sir Ralph Hopton as his deputy. The King arrived from Oxford during the first few days of August – perhaps, as Jon Day suggests, to settle squabbles amongst his commanders over the Bristol appointments – and held a council of war to decide where his campaign should march next. Amidst the conflicting interests of the various court and military factions, all of which had their own ideas about the best strategy to serve both their own and the King's aims, Charles was persuaded to agree to Gloucester as the next target; although not as a continuation of Rupert's existing plan to subdue the region but as an interim measure before attempting to starve London into revolt. What George Lisle, a native of the City and a former resident of Westminster, thought of the strategy, is not recorded.

By 6th August skirmishing was already occurring in the Gloucester area, involving Royalists already in the locality; in response Lieutenant Colonel Edward Massey, governor of the Gloucester garrison, conducted his own sporadic raids. The greater part of the King's recent Bristol attack force arrived on the 10th. However, it had not come expecting to fight, but to walk into the city: Gloucester's mixture of natural and man-made defences were adequate, but not unassailable, it had less powder than defeated Bristol had possessed, morale amongst the garrison and inhabitants was reportedly weak, and most importantly Massey had recently intimated to Major William Legge – an old military acquaintance of his, now serving under Rupert – that he might surrender it. But the Royalists were rudely disappointed. The city's resolve had recently stiffened, and its preparedness for a siege had been improved, and when the King's terms were read to an assembly of the city notables they were quickly rejected.

The siege began immediately: as the negotiations ended the city's defenders began burning the suburbs, and that same evening the Royalists moved in to secure their positions and dig trenches for a siege that was estimated as likely to last ten days, but in fact turned into a four-week grind of skirmish, bombardment, raid, counter-raid, mine, counter-mine, and attempts to fire the town with incendiary mortars. The defenders were not idle: civilians put out fires, and the

---

57   *A Relation Made in the House of Commons, by Col: Nathaniel Fiennes …*, pp.8-11.

garrison conducted numerous daring sallies to attack the siege trenches. Had the Royalists had another week or two it is conceivable that one of their mines might have succeeded, but rain, an abundance of underground springs and a high tally of desertions amongst their civilian miners had made the work painfully slow; the underground efforts petered out in early September along with the siege, when the King was forced to quit the place in the face of the imminent arrival of the Earl of Essex.

There is only one known mention of Bolle's regiment during the siege – an entry in the Royalist Ordnance Papers – but helpfully it reveals where the regiment was stationed:

Guards.   dd to Colonell Boules at the Trenches by the generalls Ring
Match   one bundle[58]

The general mentioned can only be the Earl of Forth (Lord General Patrick Ruthven), who had set up a leaguer or fortified siege camp (the 'Ring') by Llanthony priory on the south-west side of the city, in front of the South Gate. The docket was made out only four days before the end of the siege, so it is difficult to say whether the regiment had been in that position throughout, or repositioned as needed. The extent of the casualties it may have taken or of its losses due to sickness and desertion, these being prevalent in the army during the campaign, is unknown. It is also not clear to whose brigade the regiment was attached. Of the three Bristol brigade commanders – Grandison, Belasyse and Wentworth – Grandison and Belasyse were injured and absent;[59] Grandison's brigade was present but referred to in the Ordnance Papers as the Lord General's, presumably meaning it had been taken over by Forth,[60] and Belasyse's had been dispersed amongst other commanders as he and his regiment were still in Bristol. Two new brigades had been created under Sir Ralph Dutton and Colonel Darcy.[61] Wentworth's had apparently remained intact, so it seems likely that Bolle's men remained with him. The reference to the regiment being at Forth's leaguer is misleading, as the Lord General oversaw all the forces sieging that side of the city.

58 Roy, ROP part 2, p.285 (NA, WO 55/1661 [12]); 2nd-3rd September 1643.
59 Belasyse had been shot in the head, part of the musket ball remaining there permanently (Ormonde vol. II, 1903, p.383); he took a month to heal, then joined the army at Gloucester. His secretary later noted that 'the same day [Belasyse] arrived at the army the siege of Gloucester was raised by the approach of the Earl of Essex.' (*Ibid.*). Grandison never returned: the bullet wound in his thigh presumably became infected, as he died from it at the end of September.
60 Roy, ROP part 2, p.267 (NA, WO 55/1661 [19]).
61 Roy, ROP part 2, p.484, endnote 191. It is not clear whether 'Colonel Darcy' was Conyers Darcy or his younger brother Marmaduke. Newman (pp.94-95) states that Conyers was crippled at Burton in July and that command passed to Marmaduke at this point, but other historians seem to assume the Gloucester man was Conyers.

On 6th September the King's forces withdrew, first gathering to the south-east of Gloucester, then heading north-east towards Winchcombe, raiding Parliamentarian quarters and skirmishing as they went. From Winchcombe the army moved north to Evesham, taken in by the Earl of Essex's feint at Tewkesbury, and then in mid-September followed in the wake of Rupert and Lisle and marched south-east, for Newbury.

The location and layout of the First Newbury battle site, and Essex's desired route across it, has been described in the previous chapter. Although there is no mention of Bolle's regiment or any of its officers in the surviving accounts of the action, most of the Royalist infantry fought in the Wash Common area, the flatter southern part of the battlefield to the left of George Lisle's position, in two brigades. As at Gloucester, it is not certain which brigade the regiment fought in; no definitive Royalist order of battle has been discovered for Newbury, although it is known that there were two infantry brigades in the south, that of John Belasyse and that of Sir Gilbert Gerard. Through deduction from source clues, however, modern historians place Bolle's regiment with Belasyse.

However, unlike Lisle's intense involvement in the fighting on Round Hill, there is far less to be said about the involvement of Bolle's regiment in the south, or indeed of the Royalist foot in general. Although the cavalry fought a prolonged battle in that part of the battlefield throughout the day, the infantry in the south seem to have been far less involved, both Belasyse's and Gilbert Gerard's brigades remaining for the most part behind a large tumulus in the north-west corner of the common that protected them from enemy artillery fire. The rapid march from Broadway in appalling weather over the previous four days meant they were certainly not fresh troops, however Byron later put their recalcitrance down to cowardice rather than fatigue, laying the primary cause of the Royalist failure at Newbury at their door:

> … had not our foot play'd the poultroons extremely that day, we in all probability had set a period to the war … the advantage was extremely on our side, and had been more apparent had it not been lost by another very great error then committed, which was, that when we had beaten the enemy wholly from the ground we fought upon, so that not one of them appeared, and had possest ourselves of it and drawne off a piece of their cannon … our foot play'd the jades, and that intelligence was brought us of the great fright they were in, many of them stealing from their arms in the darkness of the night …[62]

---

62   Quoted by Money, p.56.

Lord Digby, in his letter to the anonymous Royalist lord, concurred:

> This action was done meerely by our horse, for (to say truth) our foot having found a hillocke in the Heath that sheltered them from the Enemies Cannon, would not be drawne a foot from thence.[63]

Evidently the recent stalemate and military failure at Gloucester, and perhaps lingering humiliation after the ejection and plunder at Reading, had left the Royalist infantry mutinous and dispirited. By mid-afternoon they had still not shifted from behind the tumulus, although at one point they had to fight for possession of it with the Red and Blue regiments of the London Trained Bands, who like them were seeking shelter from a mutual close-range artillery barrage; Sergeant Foster of the Trained Bands wrote that 'mens bowels and brains flew in our faces'. In response the Parliamentarians had brought up their own artillery and battered the Royalist cavalry and the gun battery behind it, killing the Earl of Sunderland and several other officers in the process and once again nearly taking out Belasyse.[64] Byron may have accused the Royalist infantry of cowardice, but the continual bombardment and resulting carnage would have created perfect conditions for at least mild shellshock, and made the subsequent desertions that night perfectly understandable. Of the fight for the tumulus Foster notes:

> … our red Regiment joyned to the Blew which stood a little distance from us upon our left Flank, where we gained the advantage of a little hill, which we maintained against the enemy halfe an hour: two Regiments of the enemies foot fought against us all this while to gain the hill, but could not: Then two regiments of the enemies horse, which stood upon our right Flank came fiercely upon us, and so surrounded us, that wee were forced to charge upon them in the front and reere …[65]

The Royalist cavalry were under Rupert's command; after overrunning the enemy artillery battery they made straight for the Trained Bands now sheltering behind the tumulus. The Bands responded with a defensive formation that saw off the horse and forced Rupert to retreat and regroup, turning the captured cannon on them. Meanwhile, Foster continues:

---

63   *A True and Impartiall Relation of the Battaile betwixt, His Maiesties Army, and that of the Rebells neare Newbery in Berkshire, Sept. 20. 1643.*

64   His secretary notes that Belasyse's horse was killed by a cannon ball, which also tore his breeches (Ormonde vol. II, 1903, p.383).

65   *A true and exact Relation of the Marchings of the Two Regiments of the Trained Bands of the City of London …*

the two regiments of the enemies foot in this time gained the hill, and came upon us before wee could well recover ourselves, that we were glad to retreat a little way into the field …

As the regiments retreated Essex rallied his men by going personally among them, making such an impression that they regained their spirits and charged the Royalists for a final time. The Earl's intervention at that point, by preventing the collapse of the right wing infantry, probably saved the battle for Parliament. This seems to have been the last major action on the common, although fighting continued elsewhere. At around four o'clock, the officially sanctioned Parliamentarian account notes:

> the enemy drew away from their pikes … five or six hundred musquetiers, besides dragoons, to encompasse our men on the right hand among the hedges; just at which time his Excellency sent to have two hundred of the three hundred musquetiers of the forlorn-hope to go to the relief of Colonell Barcley and Colonel Holborn's souldiers. But then the enemy falling upon our right hand diverted them, who with other of our musquetiers thereabouts beat the enemy off, who else had done us great mischief …[66]

Essex's forlorn hope was stationed at the extreme northern edge of the battle-field by the Enborne road, and had spent the day facing the third Royalist infantry brigade belonging to Sir William Vavasour. The brigades that the detachment was sent south to support, those of Barclay and Holburn, were those stationed on Round Hill that had earlier seen off George Lisle and his commanded musket-eers. By this time Barclay's brigade were at the southern edge of Round Hill near the top end of the common where the Royalist foot were stationed, which would explain how it met the Royalist musketeers and dragoons 'upon our right hand', 'among the hedges'. Whether Belasyse and Gilbert Gerard had seen the detach-ment approach and sent out their party to counter it, or their party was in fact intended to reinforce the Royalist infantry still fighting on Round Hill, is not clear. Nevertheless, clearly some of the foot had finally been persuaded to leave the shelter of the tumulus, by this time perhaps under the threat of dire consequences if they did not. The identity of the dragoons who accompanied them is not known, although Rupert was presently the driving force in that part of the battlefield, so possibly they were his. Regimental identity aside, it is possible they were led by Lord Wentworth, the King's sergeant-major general of dragoons who had begun

---

66   *A True Relation of the Late Expedition … for the Relief of Gloucester* (in *Bibliotheca Gloucestrensis*, p.247).

the day on Round Hill with George Lisle, but seems to have left that sector and ended the day wounded.

Byron says that after the fighting petered out, and many men amongst the Royalist infantry deserted:

> … we then upon a foolish and Knavish suggestion of want of powder quitted all our advantages, and about 12 o'clock at night drew off all our men as if we had been the beaten party, leaving to the enemy the field which from 6 o'clock in the morning till that time we had fought for and gained with the expense of so much good blood.[67]

Whilst Byron evidently did not believe powder was short enough to throw the entire battle away, Digby pleaded that:

> [We had not] Powder enough left for halfe such another day, having spent fourscore barrells in it, threescore more than had served the turne at Edgehill, nor could we be assured that the supply from Oxford of 100. Barrells more could come to us till the next day at noone.

Once the powder shortage had been discerned late on Wednesday 20th, an urgent message was dispatched the nearly thirty miles to Oxford, but as Digby had feared, by the time the messenger arrived there and fresh supplies were frantically packed up overnight and dispatched towards Newbury, the engagement was over and Essex was on his way to London. A document presumably written on the day which notes the numbers of Royalist infantry wounded – a miraculous survivor in itself – states that twenty-three of Bolle's 'common souldiers' were hurt, along with 866 other casualties. The battered Oxford-based infantry made its way back to its headquarters.[68]

Reading: second garrison; Basing and Alton

In early October the Parliament withdrew its garrison at Reading. London news-book *Mercurius Civicus* was initially sceptical about reports that the Royalists had moved in and re-taken it:

> For the taking of Reading by the Kings Forces, and their fortifying of it (of which many fictious reports were this and last weeke raised about this City and severall other parts;) it is neither certaine nor probable, that

---

67 Quoted by Money, pp.56-57.

68 *Hurt souldiers of Newberry* …; BL Harl. MSS, 6804, f.92. The document includes no figures for the cavalry, and as the Royalist order of battle is not definitively known, may not include all of the foot.

Towne being so impoverished, and destitute of any provisions, that it is neither fit nor of any consequence to be fortified by either party, onely for the present many Troops of Horse of both Armies make use of it for refreshment as they shall see occasion or conveniency.[69]

Presumably a dearth of local resources was one of the reasons the Parliamentarians had left. In any case *Civicus* was wrong, as a new garrison of a dozen Royalist regiments had been installed under Sir Jacob Astley, including Colonel Bolle's, and had begun securing the town. Astley immediately started putting a handhold on the local area, in particular raiding the nearby settlement of Wokingham: the Royalist Ordnance Papers confirm a mid-month report by London's *Mercurius Civicus* that:

The Cavaliers have lately plundered [W]okingham in Berkshire, and some other small Townes neere it, taking all things from those Townes which they conceived were worth their exportation …[70]

Fortunately for the local people around Reading, the garrison's focus quickly fell elsewhere: by the end of the month it was all but emptied as 1,500 men under Denbighshire colonel Anthony Thelwall were sent into Buckinghamshire to assist at Newport Pagnell,[71] while Bolle was drawn south under Astley with a party of commanded men to join Sir Ralph Hopton, ennobled a month prior to Newbury as Baron Hopton of Stratton. Just before the engagement the King commanded Hopton to bring more reinforcements from Bristol. Having duly reached Marlborough he was brought news that the battle had already been concluded; he was summoned to Oxford, and there given orders to clear Dorset, Wiltshire and Hampshire of the enemy. His detailed plans to begin the required work in Dorset were scuppered, he explained wearily in his memoir *Bellum Civile*, because Sir William Ogle had recently captured Winchester Castle – owned by Sir William Waller – without his knowledge, belatedly procured a commission to govern it, then pestered the King to send him Hopton and a relief force to help him keep it.[72] However, Hopton had a major shortage of infantry, nowhere near enough to face Waller's estimated 5,000 which had arrived at Alresford a few miles away. Relying on 'the reputation that he had there, rather than his strength', Hopton put together a small force of horse and artillery and faked a fast advance towards Winchester.

---

69   No. 19, p.146.
70   No. 20, p.158.
71   The mission was fruitless, the town falling to Parliament before the Reading party arrived. Meanwhile Thelwall's lieutenant colonel Urian Leigh took part in Astley's and Bolle's expedition and was captured at Alton in December (BL Harl. MSS. 6802, f. 94). Whether Thelwall's party returned before Astley's departed is unclear.
72   *Bellum Civile*, p.63.

The ruse worked: Waller believed Hopton still had a significant army and moved away to siege Basing House instead, arriving on 6th November. After an initial show of force he summoned the house, but Basing's owner, the Marquess of Winchester, refused to surrender. Waller began attacking in earnest; the Marquess quickly called on Hopton for help, who in turn:

> writt to Oxford to desire what assistance might be spar'd out of Reding for that service, which was granted and very well executed by Sr. Jacob Ashley … who, upon signification from the Lord Hopton, mett him at Kingsclere with 900. excellent foote, Lord Percyes Regiment of horse, and two field pieces.[73]

The size of the Reading force indicates that it must have been a mixture of men from across the garrison. Bolle had come with Astley, presumably as his deputy. Although the force's exact composition is unknown, probably his own regiment was well represented.

After Astley's contingent arrived at Kingsclere, it went directly with Hopton and some other horse and foot Sir Ralph had assembled, to assist Basing. Arriving on Tuesday 14th November, however, the Royalists found that Waller had retreated to Farnham. Lieutenant Elias Archer of the Yellow Auxiliaries explains:

> it was by divers Scouts and Troopers reported, that Sir Ralph Hopton was within two miles of Basingstoke with all his Forces, intending to give us Battell, which much encouraged our men, for then they hoped they should fight with men face to face; whereas before, for the most part, they fought against stone-walls. And to that end, all our Forces in generall were drawne into the field, but no Hoptonians appeared, and newes was brought that they were retreated: whereupon Sir William marched presently away towards Farnham, but that night quartered in the field, about two miles from Basing, expecting (as I conceive) that Hopton would have come thither … but he coming not in the morning, we marched away towards Farnham … where Sir William took up his quarters for a time, and began to fortifie the Towne …[74]

Hopton stayed at Basing overnight and then quartered his force around Odiham. Waller continued with his troops at Farnham; over the following ten days, Hopton recorded in *Bellum Civile*, 'scarce a day passed without some action or other.' When, Archer reported, a rumour arose on the 24th that Hopton had been brought extra troops by the King and intended to storm the town, the garrison 'were drawne

---

73   *Ibid.*, p.66.
74   Elias Archer, *A True Relation of the Marchings of the Red Trained Bands of Westminster*, p.7.

into the [castle] Park, wher we stood upon our guard al that day, and the night following …' but Hopton did not appear, and the men stood down. At dawn on the 28th, however, Hopton drew all his forces towards Farnham, tempting Waller to draw out his full force. Waller took the bait, drawing his men out into the castle park and setting up ambushes and a forlorn hope, but he did not advance towards Hopton, nor did Hopton attack him; after a minor firefight between advance parties from either side, Hopton retreated. A London pamphlet spoke of Waller heroically seeing off Hopton with a single cannon shot and then pursuing him with only six troops of horse, killing 'many hundreds of the Cavalliers',[75] but this was absurd rumour; Hopton admitted being 'smartly entertain'd by the Enemy', but 'retreated without disorder, or any considerable losse'. It seems likely that he forced the event purely to allow him to gauge Waller's strength and position:

> … upon consultation with his Officers, it appearing that those quarters grew bare, and that there was little good to be done upon the enemy, being so sheltered under the Castle of Farnham, he remov'd his own Tertio to Alsford, Sir Jo: Berkely with his horse, and foote to Petersfield, and left Sir Jacob Ashleys foote, and the Lo: Craford's horse and dragoones at Alton, intending speedily to remove them from thence to Midhurst, and Cowdrey-house …[76]

The plan was for Berkely, Crawford and Astley to possess and secure nearby Cowdray House at Midhurst with dragoons, then reassemble the whole force there, but Waller heard of the plan and possessed the house first, robbing Hopton's men of their intended safe headquarters. Astley departed for Reading; Bolle and his men settled into the small market town of Alton alongside the Earl of Crawford's cavalry.

Meanwhile Hopton occupied himself with surprising and seizing Arundel Castle, but remained mindful of Bolle's situation. He:

> retyr'd to Petersfield where having the dangerous quarter of Alton contin-nually in his care, he went thither the next day to visit it, and there to conferr with the E. of Craford, and Coll: Bolles. There the Lo: Hopton, viewing the large extent and unsecurity of that quarter, left expresse order with the E. of Craford, and Coll. Bowles, to keep as good guards and intel-ligence upon the Enemy as possibly they could, and that, if ever he found that the Enemy had moved out of Farnham with a body, they should pres-ently quitt that quarter, and retreat to him.[77]

75   *A Great Over-throw: Given to Sir Ralph Hopton's whole Army …*
76   *Bellum Civile*, p.68.
77   *Ibid.* p.69.

On the evening of 12th December, called west to Winchester to deal with a defeat at Romsey, Hopton was shown a letter by a local commander that revealed Waller had just received some leather guns from London. Immediately suspecting an attack on Alton, Hopton:

> forthwith writt, and dispatc'd a messenger on horse-back thither to the E. of Craford, with a letter wherein he sent him a transcript of that intelligence, and desir'd him instantly to send out scouts and partyes every way, and that, if he found but the least suspition, that the Enemy marched with a body, he should presently draw off from those quarters, and retire to him, with all that he had with him.[78]

The distance from Winchester to Alton is approximately seventeen miles, which a fast and fit horse could cover in perhaps two to three hours. The time of night that Hopton saw the officer's letter is unknown, but Crawford received his instructions before eleven o'clock and immediately sent out his scouts. Hopton also attempted to gather a force to assist, but he was too far away and Waller's plans too far advanced. The memoirs of Lieutenant Colonel John Birch, then commanding Sir Arthur Haselrig's foot regiment, reveal that he had been responsible for sending out spies who had thoroughly investigated the layout of the town.[79] Waller meanwhile, according to Archer;

> marched all that night, pretending at the first setting forth to goe towards Basing; but having marcht that way about two miles, we returned to the left, and (in a remote way between the wood, and hills) marched beyond Alton, and about 9 a clock on Wednesday morning Decemb. 13. Came upon the West side of the Towne, where we had both the winde and hill to friend …[80]

The surprise was not quite total. A little earlier Birch had encountered six of Crawford's spies; although, as an anonymous Trained Bands member reported, he managed to capture their leader and have him confirm that Crawford himself was in the town 'with about five hundred horse', the other men escaped.[81]

Alerted, Crawford 'finding horse to be of little use in that case' managed to evacuate most of his cavalry from the town via a southerly route, despite a brief skirmish where (the anonymous Trained Bands man reported), three or four of his

78   *Ibid.*, p.70.
79   *Military Memoir of Colonel John Birch*, p.4.
80   Archer, *A True Relation*, p.11.
81   *A Narration of The Great Victory … At Alton in Surrey …*', p.4.

troopers were killed.[82] After a half mile pursuit thirty horse and a number of other troopers were captured. The remainder of the regiment got away to join Hopton in Winchester, Crawford delivering 'the sadd news of the little possibility of the relieving of the rest.'[83]

Meanwhile, trapped in Alton as Waller's forces closed in around the town, Bolle and his detachment valiantly attempted to make a stand. As the first three enemy regiments approached from the north:

> they bent all their force against those three Regiments, and lined divers houses with musketeers, especially one great brick house neere the Church was full, out of which windowes they fired very fast, and might have done great prejudice to those men, but that when our Traine of Artillery came towards the foote of the hill, they made certaine shot which tooke place upon that house and so forced them to forsake it …[84]

Evidently Bolle had spent the previous two weeks doing his best to make the town defensible: Archer reported that as the London regiments now entered the town from the west, they:

> set upon a halfe moone and a brest-worke, which the Enemy had managed, and from whence they fired very hot and desperately till the Greene Auxiliaries marched on the other side of a little river into the Towne with their Collours flying and (being in the wind of the enemy) fired a little thatcht house and so blinded them, that this Regiment marched forwards and comming in part behinde the works, fired upon them, so that they were forced to forsake the said halfe moone and brest-worke …

The anonymous Trained Bands man describes the works as being 'neere the Church',[85] and an adjacent barn. It was the only place left to go.[86]

---

82 *Bellum Civile*, p.71. Crawford's departure without helping Bolle's infantry was not an act of cowardice but a necessity of war: throughout the period there are numerous reports of surrounded cavalry breaking free from constraint, for example Essex's horse at Fowey in 1644, and some Royalist horse at Colchester in 1648. Horses were no use in a siege situation as they could not be deployed, fed, or exercised, and were too valuable an asset to risk losing unnecessarily. Understandably, however, this was rarely appreciated by the infantry they had deserted. On this occasion, according to G. N. Godwin (*The Civil War in Hampshire*, p.143), Crawford had promised that he would return with reinforcements, although Godwin does not give a source for this assertion.

83 *Ibid.*

84 Archer, *A True Relation,* p.11.

85 *A Narration of The Great Victory* …, p.5.

86 Archer only mentions the barn later, which he says was 'joyned to the Church-yard'. The anonymous Trained Bands man says that it was fired by its Royalist owner, along with several houses, which allowed the defenders to hold out in their earthworks for a couple of hours before being driven into

Now was the enemy constrained to betake himselfe and all his forces to the Church, Churchyard, and one great worke on the North side of the Church; all which they kept nere upon two houres very stoutly and (having made scaffolds in the Church to fire out at the windowes) fired very thick from every place till divers souldiers of our Regiment and the Red Regiment … fired very thick upon the South-east of the Churchyard, and so forced them to forsake that part of the wall …[87]

A Royalist ruse of leaving unattended muskets propped against the wall to make it appear defended was quickly seen through by the London Trained Bands, who poured into the churchyard. Archer's detailed description of the fatal melee that followed bears inclusion in full:

… the enemies forces [betook] themselves towards the Church for safe-guard, but our men followed them so close with their Halberts, Swords, and Musquet-stocks that they drove them beyond the Church doore, and slew about 10. or 12. of them, and forced the rest to a very distracted retreat, which when the others saw who were in the great worke on the North side of the Church-yard, they left the worke and came thinking to help their fellowes, and comming in a disorderly manner to the South-west corner of the Church, with their Pikes in the Reare, (who furiously charged on, in as disorderly a maner as the rest led them) their front was forced back upon their owne Pikes; which hurt and wounded many of the men, and brake the pikes in peeces. By this time the Church-yard was full of our men, laying about them stoutly, with Halberts, Swords, and Musquet-stocks, while some threw hand granadoes in at the Church windowes, others attempting to enter the Church being led on by Seriant Maior Shambrooke, (a man whose worth and valour Envy cannot staine) who in the entrance received a shot in the thigh (whereof he is very ill). Neverthelesse our men vigorously entred, and slew Colonell Bowles their chiefe Commander at the present; who not long before swore, *God damne his Soule* if he did not run his Sword through the heart of him, which first called for quarter. He being slaine, they generally yeelded and desired quarter, except some desperate Villaines which refused quarter, who were

the church and churchyard; this is clearly connected to Archer's torched 'little thatcht house', although he states that it was fired by the Green Auxiliaries to flush out the Royalists. An anonymous report in *Mercurius Civicus* speaks of Bolle's men being 'smoked out of Aulton Church', but whether this is a general descriptive statement or describes a specific detail of the engagement is not clear (No. 31, p.343). Presumably the barn was not completely destroyed, as Archer records prisoners being held there briefly before being moved to the church.

87   Archer, *A True Relation,* p.11.

slaine in the Church, and some others of them wounded, who afterwards were granted quarter upon their request.[88]

Clarendon states that Bolle hoped to hold out in the church:

for several hours, that relief might be sent to him; but he had not time to barricado the doors; so that the enemy entered almost as soon …[89]

The *Memoir* of Lieutenant Colonel Birch, who had joined the Trained Bands in the churchyard fight, recorded that:

at the entring of that church, dreadful to see the enemy opening the doore when ready to receve you with their pikes and muskets, the horses slaine in the allies, of which the enimy made brestworks, the churchyard as well as the church being covered with dead and wounded …[90]

Mercurius Aulicus states that Bolle was slain:

defending the Church-porch with exceeding valour, but at length oppressed with their great numbers and Cannon was slaine with the butt end of a Musket choosing rather to dye honourably then to yeild himselfe a prisoner to those inhumane Rebells …[91]

Birch escaped with 'a few dry blowes with the musket stockes'. Archer put Royalist losses at 50-60, most killed in the church and churchyard after the Trained Bands had stormed it; and that Parliamentarian losses were 'not above 8. or 9. men at the most', besides wounded. *Aulicus* disagreed, putting the total Royalist dead at 27 and Waller's at 'above 200'. Archer reported 875 prisoners, including 'about 50. Commanders', presumably meaning senior officers, besides Crawford's captured troopers. Not surprisingly, *Aulicus* only conceded 300 infantry prisoners, scoffing at 'the great numbers of 7 or 800 which the London Pamphlets vaunt of'.[92] Archer's tallies from the scene look watertight, however: 60 dead, 875 prisoners and 32 wounded men taken to Farnham (this last figure added by *Civicus*, who concurred

88   *Ibid.*, pp.13-14.
89   Book VIII, 1840 vol. IV, p.426. It is not known whether Clarendon had been told of Bolle's intentions by someone who was present, or if that was simply the way he interpreted the facts. His statement may explain why Rev. Godwin said Crawford had promised to fetch help.
90   Birch, p.5.
91   Week 50 (1643), pp.713-714.
92   *Aulicus* seems only to have been aware of the approximately 300 prisoners *Civicus* reported as reaching London, and not the remaining 500 or so who had remained in Hampshire and (*Civicus* adds) changed sides.

almost exactly with Archer)[93] gives a total of 967, which allowing for small inaccuracies is acceptably close to the 900 that Hopton himself reported as coming from Reading. Bolle's commanded contingent, and probably a large part of his own regiment, had been annihilated.

The anonymous Trained Bands man reports much the same figures as Archer and *Civicus* but in more detail, claiming the presence of 'divers Irish men and women', and:

> neer 200. Horse, 1000. Arms, one Colonell, one Major, one Lieutenant Colonell, thirteene Captaines, three Coronets, one of which with the Princes Armes, another the Earl of Straffords, with divers other Colours hid in the Church; there were slaine of the Enemie neere 40. amongst which was Colonell Richard Bolles: the Enemies word was (Charls) Ours (Truth and Victory).[94]

Despite the report, there was no significant Irish presence amongst Bolle's men, or at least any that is presently known about; however the Reading garrison included four Welsh regiments, and it seems likely that the anonymous Londoner mistook the Welsh-speakers accompanying Bolle as Irish. In the seventeenth century most people would never have met a man from either place, let alone have heard one speak, and could not be expected to know the difference. That difference was critical, as Parliamentarian paranoia about Catholics and violent Irish soldiery was high, and non-English speakers were immediately regarded with suspicion. London newsbook *The Weekly Account* confirmed the force's composition as being commanded men with no colours, and to a great extent Welsh; and as Welsh soldiers were generally described as being shabbily dressed, the correspondent thought it 'very strange' that:

> they were all very well habited, which put our souldiers presently upon exchange for Hatts, Coats, Cloaks, Dublets, &c. which the enemy (by reason of the present danger they were in) told our men, *That they would exchange with all their hearts*.[95]

He was clearly unaware that in July all Oxford Army regiments had been given a suit of new clothes in red or blue.[96] Another newsbook, *The Parliament Scout*, reveals why the men were so agreeable to swapping clothes:

---

93   *Mercurius Civicus* No. 30, p.339.
94   *A Narration of The Great Victory* …, pp.6-7.
95   *The Weekly Account*, No. 16 (1643), p.2.
96   *The Life and Times of Anthony Wood* … vol. I, p.103. Wood also states that since January local tailors had been tasked with cutting out 4,000-5,000 soldiers' coats (pp.83-84).

… we came in upon them, and might have put them all to the sword, and much adoe there was to keepe our men from cutting them in pieces, could they have knowne the Irish and they that came out of Ireland, they had a great mind to have cut them in peeces as turn-coats …[97]

Evidently the prisoners were not only mistaken for Irish by some of their enemy, but recognised correctly as Welsh by others and suspected as traitors, presumably because at that time the King's English soldiers from Ireland were returning through North Welsh ports, or through nearby Chester. Perhaps some bought their safety: despite *The Weekly Account*'s report that 'there was not above 15. Pieces found in the pocket of Colonell Bolles' and 'but little money found' on the rest of the dead, *The Parliament Scout* asserted that 'Our souldiers had good bootie' and 'divers of our souldiers strouted along with their hands full of gold and silver …'

In addition to the misidentification of the Welsh, a minor possibility is that some of the prisoners were in fact English Catholics. As discussed, there seem to have been a significant number in Bolle's regiment, and if seen crossing themselves in a Catholic fashion or found carrying Catholic items, they would also have been afforded little mercy.

The prisoners were roped together in pairs and marched to Farnham, and those well enough to travel – 330 common soldiers, 37 'commanders and officers', and four officers' servants, according to *Civicus* – were marched on to London. Prayers of thanks were said there, and on 20th December the prisoners arrived and were distributed amongst various gaols. In April 1644 Captain Bevis Lloyd sought exchange together with Lieutenant Colonel Urian Leigh of Thelwall's regiment. Although his exchange paperwork states that Bolle was his colonel, Lloyd came from Denbighshire and was a cousin of Thelwall, which together with his partnering Urian Leigh for an exchange strongly suggests he may, in fact, have been in Thelwall's regiment.[98] Although both Lloyd and Leigh escaped to fight another day, many of their fellow prisoners were not so lucky: ten inmates from London House, used as a temporary prison for Royalists, were buried at nearby St Gregory by St Paul's between 12th January and 30th March.[99]

On 16th December Hopton wrote to Waller, a close friend before the war:

---

97   No. 25, p.217.
98   The King sent Lloyd to Rupert with a letter (BL Harley MS 6802/94) saying that the officer had arrived at Oxford seeking exchange, but as there were no suitable prisoners there he had passed him on to the Prince. That Bolle is listed as Lloyd's colonel is perfectly normal, as he had indeed been serving under him when he was captured. The argument against his regimental reidentification is that there was in fact a 'Captain Lloyd' listed in Bolle's regiment at Culham a year previously, although the same surname does not necessarily infer the same man (Roy, ROP part 2, p.238 (NA, WO 55/1661/3)). It is not certain whether he would fit into Fitton's regimental structure at Culham (Fitton died in August 1643 and the regiment passed to Thelwall). Nevertheless, Bevis Lloyd's links to Thelwall are compelling.
99   St Gregory's parish registers, London Metropolitan Archives.

Sir, This is the first evident ill success I have had: I must acknowledge that I have lost many brave and gallant men: I desire you, if Colonel Boles be alive, to propound a fit exchange; if dead, that you will send me his Corps: I pray you send me a List, of such prisoners as you have, that such choice men as they are may not continue long unredeemed: God give a sudden stop to this issue of English blood, which is the desire, Sir, of your faithfull friend to serve you, Ralph Hopton.[100]

Waller's response is not recorded, but it seems he was moved by his old friend's letter to have Bolle interred at Winchester Cathedral. In 1696 a kinsman of Bolle's put up a somewhat factually inaccurate brass plaque, inscribed as follows:

A Memoriall
For this Renowned Martialist Richard Boles, of the Right Worshipful Family
of the Bolses in Linckhorne Sheire, Collonell of a Ridgment of Foot of 1300,
who for his gracious King Charles the First did Wounders at the Battle of
Edge-hill. His last Action, to omit all others, was at

Alton, in this County of Southampton, was surprized by five or six thou-
sand of the Rebells; which caused him, there quartered, to fly to the Church
with near fourscore of his Men, who there fought them six or seaven Hours;
And then the Rebells breaking in upon him, He slew with his Sword six or
seaven of them, And then was slain himself with sixty of his Men about
him, 1641.

His gracious Sovereign hearing of his Death gave him as high Commendation
in that passionate Expression,
Bring me a Moorning Scarf, I have lost
One of the best Commanders in the Kingdome.

Alton will tell you of that famous Fight
Which this man Made, and bade the World good Night,
His vertuous Life fear'd not Mortalyty;
His Body must, his Vertues cannot die.
Because his Blood was there so nobly spent,
This is his Tombe, that Church his Monument.
Ricardus Boles Wiltoniensis: in Art. Mag.
Composuit posuitq Dolens
An. Dni. 1689.[101]

---

100 *The Kingdomes Weekly Intelligencer*, Numb. 36, p.281.
101 'Richard Boles of Wilton, M.A., composed and placed this epitaph to express his sorrow, A.D. 1689.'

8

A Rising Star: Cheriton to Cropredy

Commission; Command of Bolle's Regiment

In late November 1643, as the Royalists digested their military losses at Newbury, George Lisle was commissioned as a full colonel. The details survive in a modern transcription of a calendar of government documents:

> A Commission for George Lisle Esqr. to raise and ent'tayne a Regiment of 1200 foote volunteers to be employed in his Mats service. Issued between 15-25.11. Cha.xix.[1]

The circumstances around his receiving the commission are not known, but it was probably a mere formality, as Lisle had already proved himself a capable independent commander; presumably he was now fully recovered from the wound or wounds he had taken at Newbury eight weeks previously. However, if he thought that the onset of winter would give him time to plan the direction of his new command, he was not to see that plan through: less than a month after his promotion came the disaster at Alton, and sometime between then and March 1644 he was appointed colonel of the remnants of Bolle's regiment. Whether he applied for the job of his own volition or was persuaded, even appointed without choice, is not known; it is unlikely he had already managed to raise many, if any men for himself, as he was a Londoner without his own estates and therefore no sphere of influence in which to raise them. Unless members of his wider family were able to assist him with recruitment, taking on someone else's soldiers was his only option.

The date of his departure for Reading is not precisely known, but he was still in Oxford on 23rd January when a local census recorded him as billeted at the house of yeoman Richard Miles in St Aldates (in fact next door to Lord Forth, who

---

1   Black, *Docquets of Letters Patent … p.99.*

lodged with Oxford mayor Thomas Smith around the corner in Brewer Street);[2] on 2nd February Sir Samuel Luke reported that Sir Jacob Astley was made governor of Oxford and Lisle of Reading, but the report was incorrect.[3] Possibly Aston's unpopular governorship of Oxford was rumoured to be in question – in December he had been attacked in the city – and putting this together with talk of Lisle's departure to Reading, Luke's spies had put two and two together and made six. He must have left in February or early March, as an Oxford docket of 13th March states that 'Gilbert Crouch Ensigne to Collonell Lyle' received at Oxford, 'for the use of the said Coll his owne Company':

> Six Musquets fixed, with six payre of Bandeleeres which the said Collonell uppon returne to this Garrison againe, he doth promise to returne into the Magazine in ye same state they are delivered now delivered or otherwise to make satisfaction for them.[4]

Risking an ensign's life and liberty by sending him to Reading for six muskets seems excessive, and Crouch was probably also engaged on other business for Lisle, and perhaps for garrison governor Sir Jacob Astley.

Astley's new garrison appears to have seen out the winter with minimal defences: in February and March, as spring approached and the new fighting season loomed, a flurry of withdrawals were made from the Oxford ordnance stores to strengthen its neighbour's defensive capability. On 12th February a single cart ferried three small iron guns and some shot to Reading; on the 27th, fifty barrels of gunpowder were sent by water, 'with Match and ball proporconable', along with round shot for minions (cannons firing a 4lb ball); on 2nd March a much larger request was submitted to the stores, comprising five more minions and a falcon, their crews and requisite shot, 500 muskets, 500 bandoleers, and 200 brown bills.[5] The bills, simple polearms, were generally used for defensive purposes and were almost certainly intended for Reading's security rather than for use in the field. Astley himself signed for that delivery; concerns for the town's security would have grown in the wake of the ongoing trouble at nearby Basing House and Hopton's poor winter performance in Hampshire. Lisle's departure for Reading was probably part and parcel of this sudden burst of springtime garrison activity.

2   Toynbee & Young, *Strangers in Oxford*, pp.129-132. Miles's house still exists: it lies, with a small side garden, on the corner of Brewer Street and St Aldates, opposite the south-west corner of Christ Church College. At time of writing it houses Christ Church Cathedral School.
3   Luke, *Journal*, vol. 2, p.43.
4   NA, WO 55/1661/87
5   Roy, ROP part 2, pp.330-331 (NA, WO 55/458/66, f.119); pp.332-333 (WO 55/458, ff. 122-123); pp.333-334 (WO 55/459, ff. 12, 14, 15, 18).

Although Clarendon later said of Lisle that 'no man was ever better followed; his soldiers never forsaking him',[6] his first meeting with his new regiment may not have been a comfortable one. These veteran Staffordshire soldiers had lost the colonel who had recruited them, trained them, gone through Edgehill, Bristol, Gloucester and Newbury with them, a man of great military experience, initiative and courage; and undoubtedly Alton had also cost them a great many comrades and friends. What Bolle's men made of Lisle – of no less initiative or courage but newly-promoted, only twenty-eight, probably well-spoken with a London accent and a noticeable stammer – is not difficult to imagine. The brief mentions of his Newbury service in *Mercurius Aulicus* and Digby's published account of the battle might have raised his profile somewhat, assuming someone in the regiment had seen copies or had heard post-battle chatter about the situation on Round Hill; nevertheless, this could not have entirely mitigated their uncertainty. More difficult to resolve would be the fact that he had been inserted as colonel over the head of Edward Littleton, the lieutenant colonel who must have been at least ten years his senior, a survivor of Buckingham's disaster at Cadiz who since Edgehill had worked his way up the ranks from captain and distinguished himself at Bristol. Having been torn from its original commander the regiment was being asked to shift its tried and tested trust in Littleton to Lisle, an outsider and an unknown quantity; it is hard to believe that Littleton would not take Lisle's appointment, at least to some extent, as an affront. Conversely, Lisle's opinion of the regiment is hinted at in a lost letter to Sir Marmaduke Rawdon, where he allegedly described his men as 'A bunch of scruffy ne'er-do-wells with suspect religion.' If this was his genuine assessment and not just a humorous aside, and the regiment was indeed equally as suspicious of him, his first few weeks in charge must have been extremely taxing.[7]

What connection Lord Paget still had with the regiment at this stage, if any, is not clear; he did not defect to the Parliament until November 1644 and at the time of the Alton incident would probably still have been at Oxford. It was he who had selected Bolle as his first colonel, and if still nominally the regiment's patron he may have had to approve, or at least rubber-stamp, Lisle's appointment as his replacement.

6   Book XI, 1840 vol. VI, p.99.
7   [Author: As this is a reported quote the wording may not be exact, and as the quote has no context it is not known whether Lisle was serious or writing in jest. For my comment on these reputed letters, see footnote in chapter 6. The quote is given some validation in that by 'suspect religion' he obviously meant Catholics, and as discussed in the previous chapter there had been a Catholic presence in the regiment since the time of its formation.]

Hopton, Hampshire and the battle at Cheriton

Since Alton, Hopton had done his best to keep his Hampshire campaign on course, but it was not going well. Waller had retaken Arundel Castle; the King, besides declining to send new soldiers to replace those lost at Alton, had recalled some of his best cavalry, leaving Hopton an army of just 1,100 horse and 1,100 foot. Ever the optimist, Hopton sent west for new recruits as heavy new year snows fell, preventing Waller from troubling him. At last the King paid attention to his plight and ordered him to retreat to Marlborough, where he promised to 'take care to recrewte him';[8] however as the snows also hindered Waller's movement, Charles granted Sir Ralph's request to retreat at a time of his own choosing, which allowed the western recruits time to arrive, raising his numbers to 2,000 each of horse and foot, and even allowing him to recover his lost quarters at Romsey. Presumably the King was satisfied, as he seems to have rescinded his order to retreat, and sent the Earl of Forth to Hopton with 'a very hansome body, to the number of about 1200 foote, about 800. horse, and fower pieces of cannon'. Forth's contingent was composed of two commanded detachments: one from Oxford and its garrisons, led by Sir Henry Bard, and one from Reading led by Lisle, which must have been the larger of the two as he had eleven regiments to draw from at Reading whereas Bard had perhaps half a dozen. Lisle and his commanded garrison force had stepped directly into the shoes of Bolle and the ill-fated Alton men; they must have prayed that lightning did not strike twice. Hopton met the force at Newbury and escorted it to Winchester, where:

> By what time they had reasonably settled their quarters, and had once drawen out all theire troopes, and seene them joyn'd, they had notice that Sir Wm. Waller had gotten a recrewte of about 1800 horse and dragoons, under the command of Sir Wm. Belfore joyn'd to him, and therewith advanced out of Sussex towards Winchester and was come as farr as Warneford and Westmaine.

The incoming soldiers at West Meon ('Westmaine') were the London Brigade; ubiquitous Yellow Auxiliaries chronicler Lieutenant Archer reports that upon arrival they found some Royalist horse, 'which occasioned some action', and a Royalist quartermaster was captured.[9] The conjunction of Parliamentarian forces brought Waller's strength to around 3,000 horse and 7,000 foot, compared to

---

8   Hopton's account of Cheriton in *Bellum Civile* can be found on pages 77-84 of the Somerset Record Society publication.
9   *A Fuller Relation*, p.4.

Hopton's self-reported 2,800 horse and 3,200 foot.[10] Waller was not necessarily sure of Hopton's numbers, however, and so in turn was wary of his old friend's new reinforcements: he had apprised Essex of Forth's arrival and approach to Winchester, asking that the Earl either strengthen the Hampshire force or distract the Royalists by making some move against Oxford. Essex, who had positioned himself as no friend of Waller's despite their shared adherence to Parliament, sent a vague response and did not do either.[11]

News of their enemy's swelling army brought the Royalist commanders together at a council of war in Winchester on 26th March. 'All the field officers' attended, according to a later account by Ogle's secretary; therefore Lisle would have witnessed what must have been a heated discussion between Ogle and Hopton, Ogle insisting that the Royalists should use Winchester as a base and let Waller come to them, rather than seek out the enemy with 'raw men, new raised horse and foot'. Having invited Ogle to the meeting to give his opinion, Hopton promptly ignored it and continued with his preferred plan to face Waller in the field.[12]

Hopton claimed that he had surrendered military command to Forth, but the Earl 'was so extraordinarily civill to him' that he could barely be persuaded to take it. As Malcolm Wanklyn points out, however, Clarendon explicitly states that Forth refused to take command, and would only offer advice.[13] Forth's reluctance or refusal may partly have been personal necessity, as he was suffering badly from gout and could only move about with great pain, although that did not later keep him from the Cheriton battlefield. Mid-afternoon, after the council of war, he ordered the army to quietly draw up towards Warnford, Waller's headquarters, in preparation for a surprise attack the next morning. Their plan was discovered, however: Elias Archer reports a cavalry skirmish that day, and that the next morning Hopton's force appeared 'in a great body upon the hill on the left hand [of] the Town ...' Hopton confirms that early on the 27th the enemy were found to have left Warnford after the skirmish the previous evening, presumably the scuffle reported by Archer, and that they were now 'embattaild upon a hill about 2. English miles behinde their quarters in a woodland countrey.'[14] Archer adds that the London Brigade in West Meon a mile and a half to the east also 'drew our men into a body neer the town'. Presumably this body was what Royalist lieutenant colonel Walter Slingsby caught sight of from the Warnford direction when

10   According to John Adair's analysis of Waller's force (*Cheriton 1644. The Campaign and the Battle*, p.113). These figures vary in other narratives: for example John Dixon allows Waller only 4,500 (*The Unfortunate Battaile of Alresford*, p.58)
11   *CSP Domestic Series,* 1644, p.49.
12   *A true Relation of my Lord Ogle's Engagements before the battle of Edgehill and after*, BL Add MS 27402, f.82.Quoted by Adair, pp.117-118. Ogle was created Viscount Ogle of Catherlough (Irish peerage) in 1645.
13   *Decisive Battles of the English Civil War*, p.85; Clarendon Book VIII, 1840 vol. IV, p.429.
14   Hopton, p.78.

he reported 'a full Regiment with white collours stand in order facing us … about a mile and a halfe from us'. This sighting is generally accepted as being the White Regiment of the Trained Bands.[15]

For 'a while', Hopton says, the armies faced each other; he sent Major General Sir John Smith with some cavalry to try to tempt Waller out of the woods, but to no avail. Suspecting that Waller would send Balfour and some cavalry to secure the town of Alresford seven or so miles to the north, and his scouts confirming that was the case – although Archer says the London Brigade infantry were also 'in the Forlorn-Hope' – Hopton urged his army north 'with as much speede as they could to possesse Alsford before Sir William Belfore'. Alresford also sat just north of the Winchester-London road, and Royalist command of that would hinder Waller's supplies and any fast retreat towards Farnham.[16]

A race developed, as desperate as Rupert and Essex's dash for Newbury the previous autumn. According to Hopton:

> the busines was so hard prest on both sides, as the Lo: Hopton, a mile and a halfe before he came to Alsford, marching himselfe with Sir Edw. Stowell in the head of his brigade, did plainely discover Sir William Belfore's troopes marching in the lane levell with them, and they were not a mile a sunder …

Three days earlier Ogle had called the weather 'extream hot' and warned Hopton against wearying his men by marching them with a full load of equipment and provisions. Perhaps the weather was taking its toll on the infantry's speed; regardless, Hopton realised the current pace of march might not be enough and ordered his horse and dragoons, already half a mile ahead of him, to sprint for the town and hold it until the infantry arrived. They just made it; Balfour's advance party, which had cut across some upland in an attempt to cut off the Royalists, was forced to fall back. Archer says that during the march the London Brigade:

> [were] expecting the Enemy every hour to fall upon us, so that we were forced to make a stand a mile or so from the town in extream danger, till Sir William Waller's forces came up from Eastmean to joyn with us …[17]

Once the main body of Waller's force had caught up, the army as a whole moved off to lower ground to the south-west and quartered around the nearby

---

15   W. Slingsby, *Colonel Slingsby's Relation of the Battle of Alresford*. Bodleian Library, Clarendon MSS., vol. 23, No. 1738 (7). Reprinted at the back of Hopton's *Bellum Civile*, Somerset Record Society, 1903 (pp.99-103). Slingsby was a Yorkshireman who commanded Lord Mohun's former foot regiment, a Cornish unit serving under Hopton.

16   The modern A31.

17   *A Fuller Relation*, pp.4-5.

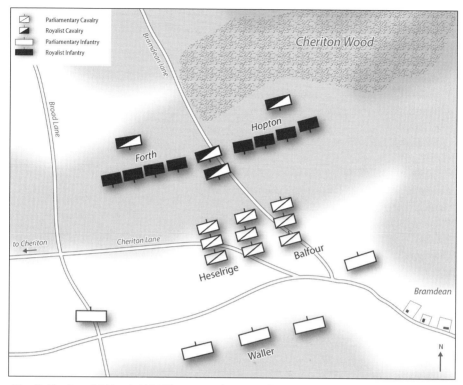

Map 2 Cheriton, 29 March 1644. The precise location of Lisle's forward position on the night of 28/29 March is uncertain.

village of Cheriton. The rest of Hopton's force stopped two miles north of them at Tichbourne Down, on the south side of Alresford, and spent the night of the 27th in formation, every man resting with his arms beside him. Gout-struck Forth, however, was persuaded to take proper lodgings.

The battle that took place thirty-six hours later on the high ground east of Cheriton was a highly confused affair, not least because the Royalists were the victims of a military 'unknown': in this case uncontrolled advances by their own men which blew any existing battle plan to pieces, and lost them the day although they started with nearly all the strategic advantages. The fight quickly descended into tactical anarchy, and although a number of accounts exist from both sides, all are fragmentary. The wildly varying newsbook reports printed afterwards also bear witness to the fact that not even the Parliamentarian participants, who had won, could agree on what had actually transpired. The main problem with interpreting Cheriton is the topography. The battle occurred on that upland Waller's men had crossed to make their attempt on Alresford: an area approximately two miles square, composed of a sequence of shallow depressions punctuated by ridges of higher ground, which makes it difficult to ascertain which ridge or depression a contemporary account refers to. English Heritage's 1995 battlefield report gives the clearest description:

> the higher ground … runs in a series of spurs or ridges from Cheriton Wood towards Cheriton. The ridges are separated by sloping valleys and each ridge, to a greater or lesser degree, represents a military crest … An army starting in the north, below Tichborne Down, and moving south towards Hinton Ampner would encounter three identifiable ridges. From the first, or northern ridge, the ground falls away onto Cowdown, then rises again to form the central ridge on East Down, before falling and then rising once more to reach the southern ridge overlooking Hinton Ampner.[18]

East Down was criss-crossed with lanes and flanked at the eastern end by Cheriton Wood, and at the western end by a descent into Cheriton village. The edge of the southern ridge fell away in a gentle slope towards Hinton Ampner and the lanes that came up from Warnford and the Meons.

The 28th was marked by skirmishes but, Hopton reports, by nightfall the Royalists had secured one of the ridges and were able to observe the movements of Waller's army to the south:

> they encamped … in a low field enclosed with a very thick hedge and ditch and theire ordnance planted upon the rysing of the hill behind them. Both the Generalls viewing the advantage of the ground they had gotten, and that there was a little wood on the top of that hill with a fense about it, plac'd Sir George Lisle therein with 1000 Muskettiers, and a guard of 500 horse upon the way by him …

Mercurius Aulicus adds:

> Colonell George Lisle with his commanded men was sent to keepe posses-sion, which (according to his wonted manner) he did like a Souldier, lying there all night.[19]

Meanwhile Hopton and the body of the army rested overnight on Tichborne Down where they had been the night before, again remaining in formation with their arms at the ready. Forth again lodged in the town.

---

18   *English Heritage Battlefield Report: Cheriton 1644.* © English Heritage.
19   Week 13 (1644), p.910.

It is at this point that modern narratives of the battle diverge. Traditionally, Lisle's ability to see Waller at Hinton Ampner overnight has meant historians placing him in or just to the west of Cheriton Wood, at the eastern end of the south-ernmost ridge overlooking the village; this is the view of all the classic modern narratives, including Alfred Burne and Peter Young (1959), Dr. John Adair (1973), and Peter Young and Richard Holmes (1974). The sketch maps in these narratives, where they show Lisle, place him near Bramdean Lane, which runs just to the west of Cheriton Wood between Bramdean and Alresford, and effectively splits the battle area in half. However, Wanklyn (2006) believes he could have been in some long-vanished copse on Broad Lane, a parallel lane further west, depending on the size of Cheriton Wood at the time.[20] Today the latter densely covers the entire portion of the southern ridge to the east of Bramdean Lane, but repeated references to hedges in the 1644 sources suggest that at that time the ground was much more open, the woodland perhaps interspersed with hedged enclosures. The remains of a Roman field system have been discovered in what is now Cheriton Wood, although whether that field layout was still clear of trees and in use in 1644 is unknown. John Dixon's reassessment of the battle (2012) places Lisle not near Cheriton Wood but further back, in Scrubbs Copse on the central ridge. He reasons that if Lisle was by Cheriton Wood, on the southern ridge, he would be too close to Waller's lines and too far forward from the rest of the Royalist army; and that – as he illustrates with a photograph – the central ridge is higher than the southern one, and it is still possible to see down towards Waller's quarters at Hinton Ampner and the ridge behind them where the artillery was placed. Dixon also believes that the size of the Parliamentarian army meant that they could not all camp in and around Cheriton: that they probably spilled eastwards into the other villages along the Hinton Ampner valley and northwards over the southern ridge, both to secure that ridge and because the fields below were at that time of year too waterlogged to camp on.[21] By this arrangement, Lisle would still see the northern edge of the opposing army from a position at Scrubbs Copse.[22] As historians of the battle broadly agree on the layout of each army at the start of the day, only significantly differing on the matter of where those armies were placed, and because there is no scope here to examine the many arguments, the battle and Lisle's part in it will be described here with as little specific locational reference as possible, so readers may apply it to their own preferred scenario.

Of Lisle's night vigil on the 28th, Hopton continues:

---

20 Wanklyn, p.93.
21 This is supported by *Aulicus* Week 13 (1644), which says Hopton 'forced Waller for that night's lodging to two or three small villages.'
22 Dixon, pp.94-107, 115-118.

That night Sir Geo. Lisle being verie watchfull upon the Enemyes motions, and giveing of them severall alarums, and being so neare as he heard them span and drive theire waggons, conceived they had bin drawing off, and so advertized the Lo Hopton, who presently sent the intelligence to the E. of Brainford,[23] and he forthwith directed his orders to command Sir Jo: Smyth to drawe out a party of 1000 horse to be ready to wayte upon the reare of the Enemy, which was presently prepared, and, as the day began to breake, the Lo: Hopton went up to Sir Geo. Lisle's guards to take the more certaine information of the Enemy's proceedings.

Lisle's assessment that the enemy was 'drawing off' is understandable. The Royalists held a strategically advantageous position, and as news was filtering through to the armies of Prince Rupert's relief of Newark, which would not help the morale of temperamental London soldiers a long way from home, he might have half-expected Waller to cut his losses and withdraw, and so interpreted the noises thus. He may well have been correct, however: Colonel Birch reveals that at a council of war the previous evening it was determined that Waller's army would retreat, but as captain of the watch Birch – believing that the opportunity to fight had been sent by God – argued hard for a battle, and even deliberately engaged his sentries with Lisle's so that it was impossible for either army to easily withdraw.[24] London newsbook *A Perfect Diurnall* appears to claim that Lisle's men were beaten from their hedges, but the report confuses and conflates several parts of the overall engagement, and in any case, if the Royalist sentries had been routed then Lisle would have known about it: and nothing of this nature is reported to have happened.[25] Whilst the noises Lisle heard that night may have been those of the aborted retreat below, they may also have been those of an enemy forlorn hope taking up position in Cheriton Wood, as Hopton discovered one had done the next morning:

> The morning was very misty, so as he could not make a cleere discovery till the sun was neere his two howers up, and then he found that the Enemy was not drawing off, but that they had in the darke of the night possest themselves of a high woody ground that was on the right hand of theire owne quarters, and plac'd men and cannon in it, that commanded the hill where Sir Geo: Lisle was; Of this he presently advertized the E. of Brainford …

23   Forth; he was created Earl of Brentford in May 1644, and Hopton uses this latter title in *Bellum Civile*.
24   Birch's account of Cheriton can be found in his *Military Memoir of Colonel John Birch*, pp.9-11.
25   No. 35, p.280.

Captain Robert Harley of Waller's own horse regiment reported that the men were:

> a partee of a thousand musquettiers, Colonel Pattle's regiment and the Londoners white regiment, sent thither, and three hundred horse to second them.[26]

Realising Lisle had been outflanked, Forth ordered the rest of the army brought forward. How far depends on the modern interpretation followed: Adair believes it came forward to the southern ridge, and Burne, Young and Holmes to the central one, where Dixon believes Lisle spent the night. A related question is whether Lisle, having been outflanked, was withdrawn back to the safety of the army or whether it drew up to his position. Adair argues that there is no reference to him being withdrawn, and believes that the army came forward to him on the southern ridge (a view with which Wanklyn concurs); Burne, Young and Holmes believe it drew up to the central ridge and he must have been pulled back. Dixon's assertion is that he was already on the central ridge, and the army was drawn up to him there. Whether he did move backwards at that point or not, later events suggest that by mid-morning he had certainly moved sideways, to the other end of the infantry line, at the left (eastern) end of Forth's army on the right wing.

Meanwhile, bringing the army forward on Forth's orders, Hopton positioned the left wing 'to the left, which was over against that woody ground that the Enemy had newly possest', placing cannon to his left to fire into the wood and on the enemy in the nearby hedges. Royalist sources barely mention their own artillery but they are noted by Lieutenant Archer, who says they 'discharged upon our men so thick, that the place was not tenible'. Both he and anonymous London officer 'H. T.' note that Colonel George Thompson who commanded the Parliamentarian forlorn hope was (Archer says) 'shot with a Drake, and his Leg is cut off', which injury presumably occurred when occupying the wood.[27] The 1810 Ordnance Survey map of the area shows two buildings and an unidentified oblong feature called 'Gunner's Castle' on the north-east edge of Cheriton Wood – today the site of a property named 'Common Farm' – which could corroborate Archer and 'H. T.'; however what was on the site originally is not clear from the 1810 map, and the origin of the name 'Gunner's Castle' – apparently first noticed by Godwin in 1904 – though on balance likely to be connected to the Civil War in local legend, has not been proven to be so in fact.

---

26 A letter from Harley to his brother, dated 12th April; HMC, Portland MSS., vol. 3, pp.106-10. John Adair includes a lengthy passage from it in *Cheriton 1644. The Campaign and the Battle* (pp.127, 130-131).
27 *A Fuller Relation*, pp.5-7; 'H. T.', p.5.

After bringing up the army to the reverse slope of Lisle's ridge, out of sight of the enemy's forlorn hope in the wood, Hopton sent Colonel Matthew Appleyard over the crest towards them with 1,000 commanded musketeers, who immediately came under fire. While they fired back, Hopton recalled some of Appleyard's party and sent them at full speed into the occupied wood with another commander, under the cover of a hedge. They completely surprised the outflanking soldiers who fled, according to Hopton, after a single volley. Appleyard pursued the remaining soldiers vigorously and swept the area clean of the enemy, taking a few prisoners and capturing a cavalry cornet. London newsbook *A Continuation of certain Speciall and Remarkable Passages* asserts that as the Royalists in the wood were recalled to their main body, the forlorn hope cavalry chased them all the way, that the wood was retaken and two of the Royalist cannon captured; it describes the men in the wood as:

> an Irish Regiment of Redcoats like unto ours, which at first were taken to be friends, but when we drew neare together, they fired on us ...[28]

A Perfect Diurnall claims not that these men were already retreating, but that they were properly routed, and that:

> ... the first that ran away is said to be his Majesties good Catholique Subjects that came from Ireland, whereof there were two Regiments ...[29]

The identity of the 'Irish' men in these reports will be examined later. Meanwhile, after Appleyard's pursuit, Colonel Slingsby reported eighty dead amongst the Parliamentarian contingent, 'and three times as many armes taken', adding that:

> This defeite putt the Rebells into such a fright as wee could discerne severall companys of thirty, of forty and more in some, running over the feilds in the reare of theire Army half a mile and as well discerne their horses span'd in theire carriages and to theire artillerye.

Evidently the panic was spreading into the rest of the army; how the officers there prevented a full scale flight we are not told, but if Slingsby's description is accurate they were lucky to contain it, particularly as the army had been minded to retreat the night before. Captain Harley did not hide his disgust:

> The citisens [i.e. Trained Bands] in the woode ... noe sooner did they see that the bullets would come otherwise then they would have them but

28   No. 14, p.3.
29   No. 35, p.280.

they made a foule retreat – I am confident that I smelt them – with a fair paire of heeles, which did soe discourage the rest, that they all left their charge with a shamefull retreat.

Hopton reports that he then sent two officers to Forth with the news of Appleyard's action, and the request that he might now charge the flank of Waller's force; Forth courteously declined to allow it, convinced that Waller's only option was to charge 'upon theire disadvantage' or retire. Hopton did not publicly demur, but 'settled all guards and orders upon the left whing' and rode towards the right wing to speak with Forth himself.

A similar scenario was unfolding on that wing, at the foot of the western slope near a 'little village' variously believed to be either Hinton Ampner, Hinton Marsh or Cheriton itself, where in symmetry to their right wing, a second party of Londoners and 300 horse had been sent to hold the hedges. Harley noted that the Royalists had sent down 1,500 commanded men – in symmetry to Appleyard's attack on the Royalist left – and chased off Waller's Londoners, despite 1,200 commanded reinforcements. They then fired the village. Harley was gloomy: 'the day beganne to looke blacke on our side, and if God had not wonderfully shewed himselfe, wee had lost the field …' Essentially he thought the Parliamentarians needed a miracle; one was about to come their way. The wind changed to their advantage just as the village was torched, presumably blowing the smoke straight into the Royalist commanded body: Waller's men seized their opportunity, sending several cavalry charges into the Royalist ranks and putting them into 'a disordered retreat', killing 'about a hundred and fifty' according to Harley, and capturing 'a hundred and twenty prisoners with divers commanders of quality.'

Hopton saw the carnage as he rode across to the Royalist right wing:

> … being neere the midd-way upon the brow of the hill he saw troopes of the right whing too farr advanced, and hotly engaged with the Enemy in the foote of the hill, and so hard prest, as when he came to the Lo: Brainford, he found him much troubled with it, for, it seemes the engagement was by the forwardnes of some particular officers, without order.

Unlike Hopton, Slingsby evidently felt no need for discretion:

> Sir Henry Bard, leading on his Regiment further then hee had orders for, and indeede with more youthfull courage then souldierlike discretion, was observ'd by the Enemy to bee a greate space before the rest, and out of his ground, who incontinently thrusts Sir Arthur Hassellrigs Regiment of horse, well arm'd, betwixt him and home, and theire in the view of our whole Army (much to our discouragement) kills and takes every every man.

Bard is habitually entirely blamed for making an unauthorised advance on his own initiative, but Slingsby's description of the incident makes it clear that he did have orders to advance, but for some reason he simply exceeded them. Rescue or reinforcement was out of the question. Bard was captured and taken to London, but exchanged shortly afterwards. Slingsby was critical of the decision to engage on the wings at all: the success in the wood, he says:

> encourag'd us soe muche that wee made too muche hast to finishe the businesse (for had wee but stood still and make signes of falling on, they had probably melted away without fighting a stroake more), but wee were order'd to fall on from both wings, which was the only cause of theire standing to fight; for then the Enemy finds most of our strength drawne of[f] the hill into a bottome, where hee had his desir'd advantage …

Harley's heat-of-battle estimate of 1,500 commanded men coming down from the Royalist right wing is close enough to the 1,200 given for Forth's Oxford/Reading contingent, that it seems likely it *was* that entire contingent, including Lisle. Slingsby remarked that Bard had gone too far forward 'with his regiment', which implies he took a smaller body of men, perhaps only the Oxford part of Forth's force; Wanklyn suggests that Bard may in fact have been guarding the artillery in the Royalist centre and only charged in to assist Lisle when the advancing right wing infantry came under attack. Evidently Lisle was able to complete the task of clearing the hedges in the Cheriton/Hinton Ampner area without losing control of his own soldiers, although as both sides were now committed to the fight he was unable to retreat back up the slope, remaining locked in that standoff for the rest of the day. At some point they seem to have been reinforced by other infantry, as Colonel Appleyard, who had started the day on the left wing, was later wounded on the right during the retreat.

The next action was an attack by a body of Parliamentarian horse on the Royalist left wing infantry – which, one Parliamentarian captain says, 'came downe with furie on the right wing along the hedges, which wee had lined'[30] – but all the charges were repulsed by the Royalist foot, or a significant part of them, whom Forth had placed under Slingsby's command. How those foot had also come to advance is not clear, although Dixon cites Parliamentarian comments to argue that the initial attack by Appleyard had not ended after the wood was regained – contrary to Hopton's account – but like the right wing action had pushed on imprudently, sucking in more infantry and horse.

Modern solar calculators indicate that sunrise on that day came just after half past five; Hopton states that the outflanking movement on the left was not discovered for a couple of hours after sunrise, which is almost exactly corroborated by

---

30   Captain John Jones, *A Letter from Captain Jones* …

Captain Jones who says the fighting started at eight; thus after the bringing up of the Royalist army, Appleyard's engagement on the left, Bard's engagement on the right, the burning of at least some houses in Cheriton/the Hintons and the skirmishing on the Royalist left wing, it must have been at least midday or early afternoon when Forth ordered Hopton to send 1,000 horse down the slope to charge the Parliamentarian cavalry, who had assembled 'in nine faire bodys' (Slingsby says) in the centre of the battle line, on a flat piece of ground between the armies. Hopton's cavalry advance was an abject failure: after a half hour the brigade was, according to Hopton, 'broken and rowted' and its commander Sir Edward Stowell wounded and captured. This was, as Slingsby attests, down to the Royalist horse being forced to enter the common via a narrow lane and not being able to deploy until they emerged onto the open ground: this made them vulnerable to immediate attack.[31]

Meanwhile the rest of Hopton's foot were sucked into the fight: Captain Jones states that after Slingsby's action the Royalists 'fell downe with a great bodie of horse and foot in those fields', the foot fending off all comers for three hours before being driven back. This would support Dixon's theory that the fight on the Royalist left wing had not ended earlier, as per Hopton's account.

Slingsby records that while Hopton was dealing with Stawell's ill-fated cavalry charge the rest of the horse, besides a small reserve, were also 'wholy engaged' and charged the enemy. It resulted in the death or mortal wounding of many officers, including prominent figures such as Lord John Stuart and his deputy, Major General Sir John Smith, who had been knighted for his retrieval of the Royal Standard at Edgehill. Many others were seriously wounded. Slingsby also says that several horse regiments were put out of action due to reduced numbers and the loss of so many officers, although *Aulicus* reports that one staged a successful intervention to prevent capture of the Royalist artillery. Faced with losing his entire force, Hopton eventually managed to get 300 horse to stand 'at the entrance into the Common' – presumably the narrow entry point from the lane. With Forth's help he managed to protect the escape route, and allow cavalry and stray infantry to escape back up the lane and through the hedges to the top of the ridge. Archer reports a lull of about an hour, after which a final charge from some Parliamentarian infantry forced the remainder of the Royalist horse to retreat. The rout was on. Slingsby, Hopton and Birch all offer their perspective. Slingsby says:

> … before wee could theire reduce our selves to order, the Enemys left wing advances up to the end of the hill where our right should have bin in readynesse to resist them, but after some strugling to repulse them,

---

31   Adair (p.133) believes this must have been Bramdean Lane, which runs right through the battle area and away towards Bramdean village to the south-east, but like many other aspects of the battle, identification of this lane is disputed.

in which Collonell Appleyard was shott, wee were Compeld to draw of in such disorder as wee were forced backe to the ground where wee had hutted the 6 daies before …

Hopton:

> … by this time the disorder was so generall, and the Enemy pressed in that part so hard (espetially with theire muskett shott) that it was with great difficulty that we gott off all our cannon; and making our reare as good as we could with some of the best of our horse and dragoons, we recovered our first ground upon the ridge of the hill by Alsford-towne, with all our Army, cannon and carriages; from whence we shewed so good a counte-nance towards the Enemy, that they gave us some respitt, unwilling (as it seem'd) to hazard theire whole army upon us.

Colonel Birch's *Memoir* describes the pursuit from the Parliamentarian angle; as usual it credits him with performing the most critical actions of the hour, in this case requesting the drawing out of 2,000 musketeers:

> one thousand whereof on the left wing were comanded by Collonel Rea, whoe did very gallantly, the rest by your selfe on the right wing; all the rest of the army being to second them. Those twoe great parties went on with such success, that in one houre the enimies army was between them, all our horse and foote comeing on in the front of them. The first thing that I could perceive, they puld of their collours, thrust them in their breeches, threw downe their arms, and fled confused. Your selfe and others hot in pursute had not followed them above 100 paces into their owne ground, before one, whome I shall not name, overtooke you, comanded you to stand: but for what end I never yet could tell, except it was to give the enimy leave to runn away, and carry away there cannon; sure I am you stood there 3 quarters of an houre, untill the enimy was far enough.

It is possible that the high-level officer who overtook Birch and ordered him to let Hopton go was Waller himself; we will never know, but nobody else would have the authority to stop such a close pursuit with the possibility of capturing so many senior Royalists. It is unlikely that Waller's long friendship with Sir Ralph would be a prime reason to cease pursuit, however: night was coming on and the army was already exhausted.

Cheriton: Lisle, the 'Redcoat Irish' and the Royalist rearguard

According to Slingsby, when the Royalist army drew up at Tichborne Down only 800 horse remained, although there were 'a reasonable number' of foot. They waited for over an hour, which tallies with Birch's report of another pause, during which Parliamentarian cannon were brought up and fired three salvos;[32] meanwhile, in that breathing space, Forth and Hopton conferred. Winchester was indefensible and unfit to host an army, so they settled on a retreat to Basing House, splitting the artillery, foot and horse across three different routes to avoid further trouble. First the artillery, under Colonel Richard Feilding, was dispatched to safety, initially towards Winchester to confuse any pursuers. The army then retreated through Alresford, leaving some soldiers behind to secure it as a temporary rearguard. According to Harley and Sir Arthur Haselrig these men were Irish, and many were killed by their pursuers (Harley says 'very many Irish men' and Haselrig 100[33]), however as R. N. Dore explains, most of the troops returning through Wales or Chester at that time were English: only later was it the King's policy to attempt to bring over Confederate soldiers rather than recall English ones, in order to chip away at the troublesome native Irish forces.[34] Moreover John Barrett's 1998 analysis of the role of Irish in the English armies uncovers only one report of native Irish coming ashore in the North West before Cheriton occurred: a group of 500 which landed at Neston or Chester in March, just days before the battle.[35] There is no report of them joining Hopton – without question spymaster Sir Samuel Luke or someone in Waller's army would have commented on the arrival of 500 native Irish – and in any case it is incredible to imagine they would have landed and then of their own volition immediately marched the approximately 180 miles to Alresford in time to fight. Dixon's recent reassessment of Cheriton was unable to offer any identification for the Alresford 'Irish' troops, and discounts a quote from London newsbook *Britaines Remembrancer*, that describes them as 'most of them being Red-coats of my Lord Inchiquires Regiment, led on by his Lordships brother',[36] as that 300-strong regiment – which unlike the majority

---

32 *Mercurius Aulicus* Week 14 (1644), p.917. A Parliamentarian newsbook offers a different story, saying that some of the Royalist artillery was seized and turned on Hopton's men as they withdrew (*A Perfect Diurnall*, No. 35, p.280).

33 Harley; Haselrig's speech to the House of Commons, BL Add MS 18779, f.87.

34 Dore, 'Dee and Mersey in the Civil War', p.10.

35 Barrett, 'A Cure for the Scots', *English Civil War Times* no. 54, January 1998, pp.19-23.

36 Numb. 3, p.22. 'Inchiquire' is probably a contemporary typo for 'Inchiquine'. The quote is included by Godwin (p.183), although he does not word it precisely as it appears in the newsbook. The newsbook author does not make it clear whether he already knew that Inchiquin's regiment wore red coats, or whether he was assuming that the redcoats who had been identified as Irish must be Inchiquin's; this ambiguity seems to have given rise to numerous assumptions amongst later historians that 'Inchiquin's

of other arrivals from Ireland had landed at Weymouth, in January[37] – almost certainly remained in the West Country. *Mercurius Civicus* supports Dixon's assertion: in early March the newsbook reports that Inchiquin's men, presumably still residing in Weymouth under the command of his brother Henry O'Brien, had been attacked and 'totally routed' by garrison forces from Lyme Regis and Poole.[38] In April they stormed Wareham, eighteen miles away, and the likelihood of them marching to Hampshire and back between February and April is small to say the least.[39] Moreover if recovering from a brutal defeat in late February, it is unlikely in any case that they would be in any condition to march nearly 80 miles into Hampshire in significant numbers to gatecrash Hopton's campaign in March. Bulstrode Whitelocke records the killing of an 'Irish Rebel' in a skirmish near Winchester in late March, but this does not of itself mean that there were large numbers of Irish with the Royalists; if indeed the man's origin was correctly ascertained, and Whitelocke does not give his source.[40]

The contention made here is that the slain Alresford men were in fact from Lisle's Reading contingent. However, before explaining that identification it is important to clarify that *Britaines Remembrancer* does not say the routed redcoat 'Irish' were those later killed in Alresford, nor is the coat colour of the slain Alresford 'Irish' known, therefore the two sightings could be of different groups; regardless, it is clear that the Royalists had amongst them a large group of redcoat soldiers who were almost certainly not Irish yet habitually spoke a language other than English, and who were chased firstly out of Cheriton Wood in the morning, and secondly off the battlefield at the end of the day.

As noted at Alton, most English people would never have specifically heard an Irishman speak and would be unlikely to pick out his accent or language in a crowd of other British languages or dialects, opening the way for panicked misidentification in the heat of battle. Thus it appears highly likely that Harley and Haselrig made the same error as their colleagues at Alton, and the men killed at Alresford after the battle were in fact Welsh. Lisle's commanded party from the Reading garrison, like Bolle's previously, would almost certainly have included soldiers from the five Welsh regiments there; there is an outside chance that the slain men were Slingsby's Cornishmen, but the Cornish tongue was rapidly dying out by the

men wore red', although that may not in fact be true. Moreover, as the Irish had only landed in Dorset in January and the newsbook was published in late March, one must ask how and why a London newsbook author had come to know what colour a few hundred troublesome native Irish on the Dorset coast were wearing, or indeed, that they had been issued with coats at all.

37 Whitelocke, p.76. Godwin mentions this entry, but incorrectly states that 800 men landed, when Whitelocke clearly says 300.

38 No. 41, p.428.

39 The same argument can be applied to Lord Broghill's Irish foot, who arrived in England with Inchiquin's and in April were at the siege of Lyme Regis.

40 Whitelocke, p.81.

seventeenth century and it is unlikely that there would have been enough Cornish speakers there to match the numbers of 'Irish' suggested by Harley and Haselrig. Hopton's army did include regiments recently returned from Ireland – those of Sir John Paulet and Matthew Appleyard – but these were English units who had gone out to suppress the Irish Rebellion before the start of the Civil War, and they would certainly not have started speaking Irish. During their lengthy stay in Ireland they would have recruited native men, but these would in the main be English-speakers of recent English or Scottish descent. Neither Harley nor Haselrig mention coat colour, but in any case both the ex-Irish regiments wore yellow, which does not match the *Remembrancer*'s report. Of Forth's forces, Bard's Oxford contingent reportedly comprised men from Bard's own regiment and Charles Gerard's, neither of which were Welsh, Irish, or redcoats, and in any case most of that force had been annihilated early in the battle.[41] Hopton brought no Welsh with him, and the only known redcoats amongst his infantry were Apsley's regiment, who were from Devon. Reading is the only possible source for Welshmen at Cheriton, and the regiments there would have been recipients of the new red or blue coats issued at Oxford in July 1643. Indeed, the 'well habited' Welsh from Reading garrison who were captured at Alton three months earlier, have already been noted.

However, as noted, Alresford was not the only place where 'Irish redcoats' were reported on the day of the battle. The account in *A Continuation of certain Speciall and Remarkable Passages* appears to be an anonymous but detailed eyewitness account of the day's early events. As the Londoners mistook the redcoats as their own, there cannot have been any appreciable difference in style or quality of clothing, therefore again, the only thing to mark out the Royalists as 'Irish' can have been their speech. Furthermore, as Lisle's men were at that point on hand in the immediate vicinity of the wood, it is entirely possible that one or more of the commanded divisions Hopton sent forward with Appleyard, and then into the wood, were his. The second account, in *A Perfect Diurnall*, states that there were two regiments of 'Irish'; although the report telescopes the morning action in the wood and that below it the night before, and therefore its reliability may be suspect, the conflation of the two actions does not detract from its statement that there were two *regiments* of 'Irish': which suggests a large number of men, and which does not fit anything we presently know about the King's forces at Cheriton or indeed in the south-east of England. If he had had two substantial bodies, perhaps regiments, of Irish quartered in the region then without any doubt we would have some indication in surviving records; yet there is not a trace.

After the battle Lisle and his men must have retreated through Alresford with the rest of the army, and the 'Irish' slain in the town were, as demonstrated, probably redcoat Welshmen from his Reading contingent. Three of the primary Parliamentarian eyewitness accounts (Harley, Archer and officer 'H. T.') state that

---

41 Luke, *Journal*, vol. 2, 13th March 1644.

the town was set alight by the Royalists as they fled, but extinguished by their pursuers; the existence of these multiple reports indicates that the fire itself was genuine, although who started it is another matter. Although both Harley and Haselrig suggest that the 'Irish' were the only remaining Royalists in the town when the Parliamentarians arrived – Haselrig asserts that they were deliberately 'lieft to mayntayne that towne' – there is no proof or explicit suggestion by Harley, Archer or 'H.T.' that these men set the fire, only that the Royalist army as a body was assumed to have caused it, and the remaining rearguard 'Irish' were the ones who received, in Harley's words, 'their reward' for it. Unlike more bellicose commanders such as Sir John Byron (who had burned the village of Swanbourne), and occasionally Rupert (whose forces had burned Birmingham), torching towns is not known to have been part of Lisle's modus operandi, although that does not definitively exonerate him, if indeed the slain men were his and it was he who oversaw the Royalists' final rearguard action of the engagement.

Cheriton: the consequences

The Royalists arrived at Basing House in the early hours of Saturday 30th March, not, Slingsby asserts, 'loosing a gunn or a coullor, nor a man of that body with which wee made our retreat.' A few days later a deserter told the authorities in London that:

> he fled with Hopton and some others to Basing house, and that Hopton went into Basing House, and he conceives is there still, but the rest lay in the Churchyard and thereabouts all night, and the next morning marched some of them towards Oxford. He said that moreover himselfe and some others went from thence to Redding, where there is but a small strength, be believes not above three or foure hundred, and from thence, with some others, he hath disserted the enemy to come to the Parliament ...[42]

Evidently the Hampshire force split up after its arrival at Basing, Hopton's men and the remnants of Forth's contingent departing for Oxford and Lisle's commanded force continuing to Reading, where the deserter made his getaway. A London pamphlet suggests that its commanders still had business to conclude, however:

> Generall Fourth and Sir Ralph Hopton came to Redding on Satterday morning with about thirty men (though I deny not that a greater party of Horse came thither afterwards) and are since gone to Oxford.[43]

42   *Mercurius Veridicus*, No. 10 (1644), p.4.
43   *A Continuation of certain Speciall and Remarkable Passages ...* No. 14, pp.5-6.

A second newsbook confirms the story, asserting that Hopton arrived with 'a very small Retinew' at noon on Saturday, stayed for only an hour and a half and then departed.[44] Possibly he sought to apprise governor Sir Jacob Astley on the size and composition of Waller's army. Where Lisle's commanded Reading infantry was at this point is unclear, as the newsbooks agree that Hopton arrived at Reading with just a few men; probably it was simply lagging behind with baggage, casualties and perhaps some of the artillery. Neither do we know if Lisle had left it to go ahead with the advance retinue, but as Hopton and Forth apparently required only the briefest conference with Astley, it seems unlikely that he would have been needed.

The contemporary fog of confusion over the battle's details has already been noted, but additionally nobody thought to immediately apprise the King, as his secretary Sir Edward Nicholas complained sharply to Forth in a letter two days later:

> The King hath no perfect relation from your Excellency or Lord Hopton of the fight at Alresford, nor any certainty how many of the rebels or of his Majesty's forces were there lost; only we hear the King lost neither colours nor cannon, and that Sir William Waller came late on Friday night into Winchester, but whether he continues there or goes westward or what he doth or intends to do we hear nothing. Nor doth his Majesty hear where Lord Hopton is, or where his foot or horse are; whereof your Excellency may be pleased to send advertisement by the first express.[45]

The public fallout from the battle was as messy as the fight itself, *Mercurius Aulicus* and nearly a dozen London newsbooks publicly haggling for weeks over the number and identities of the dead (Forth was widely reported slain),[46] and what spoils were captured during the pursuit or recovered from the battlefield. The only fact agreed on was that the battle's death toll was relatively low: the total loss of life across both armies was reported to be somewhere between 300 to 500 men. Rumours abounded that Prince Rupert was bringing his forces south, to link up with Hopton and reinforce his army, but in fact Cheriton marked the end of Hopton's independent command and he reverted to being a regimental or subordinate commander. The rumours were not unfounded as the King had expected

---

44 *The Weekly Account*, No. 31 (1644). In fact the newsbook states that they arrived at Basing at noon, not Reading, but this appears to be an error as both Hopton and other sources are clear that the army had reached Basing he night before and made the fifteen mile trip to Reading the next morning.

45 Dated 31st March. *CSP Domestic Series*, 1644, p.85.

46 David Lloyd states that Forth was shot in the head at 'Brandean Heath fight', which would explain the reports of his death (*Memoires ...*, 1668, p.674), although it seems that no surviving newsbook of either side specifies how he was shot. *Aulicus* scorns a report of 'General Forth shot all to pieces', but does not say where it originates (Week 14 (1644), p.916).

Rupert's return, but a series of crises in the north had demanded the Prince remain there. At the start of the year Charles's intent had been to go on the offensive and threaten Parliament's strongholds in London and the south-east, but with the failures in Hampshire and Rupert's and Maurice's armies being unavailable to support him – Maurice was sieging Lyme Regis in Dorset – he was forced to rationalise his military assets and focus instead on protecting Oxford.

Aldbourne muster; royal retreat to Worcester; skirmish at Dudley Castle

A few days after his return to Reading Lisle was on the march again, this time with his own regiment, to the scene of Rupert's pre-Newbury skirmish with the Earl of Essex at Aldbourne Chase. Here, on 10th April, in response to Waller's westward motion, the King held a general rendezvous of the Oxford Army. Richard Symonds, a trooper in the King's Lifeguard of Horse, made detailed notebook sketches of the sets of regimental colours present, a row of boxes representing each flag in the sequence and the device upon it. For Lisle he gives seven boxes, the first containing an 'A' (heraldic notation for 'Argent', or white), the second has the customary canton in one quarter containing the cross of St George, and the rest are blank. The sketch must be incomplete: the remaining flags must have borne a device of some sort or there would have been no way to tell the companies apart, or indeed to tell those flags from the first white colour in the sequence, which was presumably the 'colonel's colour'. Unfortunately, however, no record has survived elsewhere of what the devices on Lisle's colours were. Separate to the sketches, Symonds drew a grid in the back of his notebook detailing the compositions of the Reading garrison regiments present at the muster. Lisle's regiment had 6 captains (Lisle would nominally have been a seventh), 7 lieutenants, 8 ensigns, 7 gentlemen (of arms; responsible for maintenance of the company weapons), 17 sergeants, 22 corporals, 14 drummers and 189 soldiers, a total of 270 men.[47]

Clarendon says the army remained in the field 'for some weeks, to watch and intend Waller's motion',[48] and describes how the Parliament's relentless levying of troops from around London was waking Charles to the danger he and his cause faced; the London press made no secret of Parliament's intentions, *The Kingdomes Weekly Intelligencer* in its 10th-16th April issue describing in detail the intended composition of Essex's, Waller's and the Earl of Manchester's armies, and concluding that:

---

47   Symonds, untitled notebook, BL Harley MS 986, f. 81 and 98.
48   Book VIII, 1840 vol. IV, p.437.

the Forces intended to waite upon his Majestie at Oxford, will be in all at least 28000. (if some faile) besides the Forces that are to come from Northampton, Coventry, and Newport Pannell.[49]

Sir Edward Walker, the King's secretary-at-war, relates that Charles thought it best to put his men in the field as quickly as possible, and to this end the Oxford parliament was prorogued on 16th April and on the 17th the heavily pregnant Queen departed for Exeter.[50] Meanwhile the safety of Reading continued to be a difficult issue: the Council of War, sitting at Marlborough at around that time:

> proposed the quitting of that place, in regard the Men left there were not enough to defend it, and if any more were put in, it would weaken the Army; his Majesty then approved of that advice, only differing in point of time, as conceiving the Rebels could not so suddenly draw before it, as not to allow us time to withdraw, or to put in more Men as there should be occasion; and therefore as yet, Reading was to be looked upon … as well as Oxford; that if they should attack either of those places, some Forces might be drawn out of the one to add to our Army, for the other's relief …[51]

Thus the King's desire was to hold the garrison for as long as practicable; accordingly the army quickly left Aldbourne and shifted fifteen miles south-east to Newbury, so as to better reinforce Oxford, Wallingford, or Reading as the need arose. Yet the existence of the latter's garrison hindered the army's movements: the still doubtful Council of War believed that if the town was retained and then besieged after the army moved away, 'we could not probably have timely relieved [it]'. It is not clear how many soldiers remained in Reading for the duration of the muster. All twelve garrison regiments were recorded by Symonds as being at Aldbourne, yet Walker makes it clear that while the town was poorly manned it was not empty; if it had been, undoubtedly Essex would have contrived to snatch it earlier, irrespective of the King's optimism that he could not do so quickly. The skeleton force there may have been that of Colonel Richard Neville, who was recruiting an auxiliary regiment for the town's defence; he would have had at his disposal the cannon and gunners sent to strengthen the defences prior to Cheriton, but without serious manpower they would not keep off the enemy for long. Possibly each of the departing regiments had left men behind, but this seems

49 No. 50, pp.402-403.
50 'His Majesty's Happy Progress and Success from the 30th March to the 23rd November 1644', printed in *Historical Discourses, Upon Several Occasions* … pp.5-121 (April movements and the Queen's departure, pp.9-10). Walker's account, written up Charles's request, was presented to the King in April 1645. *Discourses* was printed in 1705, and dedicated to Queen Anne. His chronicling efforts perhaps contributed to him being knighted in February 1645.
51 *Ibid*, pp.11-12.

unlikely, as given the small size of most Royalist regiments at the time it would – as the Council of War acknowledged – have reduced their capacity for active service and weakened the army.

On 9th May Parliament publicly confirmed its plans by issuing an ordinance authorising the raising of more troops in London to enable Essex to 'proceed for the Recovering of the City of Oxford'.[52] The King had not been idle, and besides the Reading auxiliaries he had begun raising similar regiments within Oxford that would allow him to withdraw more of the existing garrison to bolster the army in the field. Yet in the face of a wave of new London troops the Reading garrison's demise was inevitable, and rapid. As early as 12th May Sir Jacob Astley was ordered to begin slighting the works, the local populace being ordered to bring in tools for this purpose; by the 15th the magazine had been removed to Oxford, and Forth reported that as the garrison was at the end of its provisions, it would finish the demolition on Thursday 16th, and finally march out on Friday 17th.[53] This was accordingly done; the King marched the rest of the army to join the departing garrison, and the entire force paused for a rendezvous near Wantage before dispersing, the foot being put into a leaguer at Culham, near Abingdon. Although the final date of departure is confirmed by Forth and Nicholas's correspondence in the State Papers and by Walker,[54] it seems that rumours of the move were rife from early April, as *Aulicus* felt obliged to deny abandonment of the garrison in its first two April issues.[55] The trigger for these stories was probably the garrison's departure for Aldbourne. Reading was immediately taken by a party of the Earl of Essex's forces from Windsor; it was the town's fourth garrison of the war, each side having now held it twice.

Walker records that the Royalists had determined to either keep or abandon Abingdon depending on the direction from which the enemy approached. If they approached from the east, which put the Thames between them and the town, the garrison would remain and defend itself; if from the open countryside to the west, it would withdraw to Oxford with the rest of the local forces. As Essex's men approached from the east on 25th May, however, the forces there were withdrawn, contrary to agreement; dismayed, the King frantically sent back the messenger who had brought the news, with orders that the men should return, but too late: the force was already within sight of Oxford and the soldiers dispersing to billets. Essex took the empty town with a small party that night and moved in himself the next day with his entire force, and Waller quickly diverted to join him. Although the final decision about Abingdon's fate had been left to Lord Forth, Walker and

52   *A collection of all the publicke orders …*, pp.487-488.
53   *CSP Domestic Series*, 1644, p.161, 163.
54   *CSP Domestic Series*, 1644, p.163; Walker, p.12.
55   Weeks 14 and 15, 31st March-6th April and 7th-13th April 1644. London's *The True Informer* reported demolition of the works as early as its 30th March-6th April issue (p.198).

Clarendon both make it clear that he was believed to have been influenced by Lord Wilmot; Clarendon adds that Wilmot had contempt for the old general, although how true that was we cannot know.[56]

While the King withdrew his foot to the north of Oxford, Essex and Waller settled in to their preferred positions from which to threaten the city, Essex to the east and Waller to the west, to divide the garrison's attention and prevent it withdrawing to Worcester.[57] A week of local manoeuvring and skirmishing followed: the Earl of Cleveland attempted to recover Abingdon but failed, Essex tried several times to cross the Cherwell at Islip, Enslow and Tackley to the north of Oxford but initially failed, and Waller attempted to cross the Thames at Newbridge, to the south-west, and failed. To some degree the Parliamentarian failures may be put down to 'this great fall of rain, [which] hath much hindered them from attempting any thing of moment as yet.'[58] The Royalist foot were much engaged to the north and east along the line of the Cherwell, repulsing Essex: it is likely that Lisle and his regiment were engaged in the defence at some point, or that Lisle at least was dispatched somewhere with a body of commanded men to do what he did best, but no evidence of such details has survived.

On 1st June Waller forced his way over the river at Newbridge on his second attempt: Oxford was now almost encircled, the only break in the circuit being a rapidly narrowing corridor of land to the north-west. After news of Waller's success arrived on 2nd June the King held a council of war at Woodstock in the afternoon, only three miles from where Essex was at that very moment finally taking the bridge at Enslow;[59] later that evening Charles was still vacillating between fight or flight when news arrived of Waller's entire army mustering at Newbridge.[60] Presumably news of Essex's nearby success must also have reached him, as he ordered the Cherwell defenders to withdraw while he returned to Oxford to organise his escape. The next night, 3rd June, having put his wartime capital in the hands of the ten-year-old Duke of York, governor Sir Arthur Aston and others, he slipped out from the north of the city with the Prince of Wales and a personal retinue and met the army nearby. Walker recounts that he:

> gave Order for a Party of 2500 Musqueteers to be drawn out of the whole Body without any Colours, commanded in chief under the Earl of Brainford and Forth Lieutenant General, by Sir Jacob Astley Sergeant Major General, Collonel Blagge [Blague], Collonel Lisle, Sir Bernard

---

56   Walker, pp.14-15; Clarendon Book VIII, 1840 vol. IV, pp.441-442.
57   A full outline of the movements of Essex and Waller in the month preceding the battle at Cropredy is given by John Adair in chapter XII of *Roundhead General*, pp.152-156.
58   *The Spie*, no. 19, p.152. The wet weather persisted throughout June.
59   *Mercurius Civicus* Numb. 54, p.526.
60   Symonds, *Diarye*, p.8.

Asteley Collonels of Tertias, Collonel Lloyd Quarter Master General, and divers other Officers of the best Repute and Esteem in the Army.[61]

Lisle's star had soared: in six months he had risen from a low-profile lieutenant colonel leading occasional forlorn hopes, to a commander trusted enough to be part of the King's personal military escort in a crisis. Notably the men in charge of Charles's escape were Astley and Forth, with whom Lisle had worked closely at Reading and in Hampshire; Perhaps, ironically, the debacle at Cheriton brought him favourably to their notice.

This is the first occasion on which Lisle is mentioned as a tercio commander. Until very recently Bernard Astley, too, had only been a colonel. Walker was writing retrospectively towards the end of 1644, so we must consider whether he was employing the common practice of titling the men with the ranks they held at the time he wrote, rather than those they held at the time he was writing about. However, Symonds states that all the tercios existed during the Cornwall campaign in July/August and gives their compositions then, and they almost exactly reflect the parts of the army as they stood at Aldbourne Chase in April: Blague's tercio comprised Oxford-based regiments, Lisle's the late-demised Reading garrison, and Bernard Astley's the regiments which had formed Hopton's foot during the Hampshire campaign and latterly at Cheriton. Therefore, almost certainly Lisle's tercio had come into existence by the time of the King's 'night march' from Oxford in early June, although it had not yet seen battle. One Reading regiment, that of Stephen Hawkins, had recently been sent elsewhere, but the remaining eleven were put under Lisle's command. Besides his own, these were the regiments of Anthony Thelwall; John Owen; Sir James Pennyman; Charles Lloyd; Theophilus Gilby; John Stradling; Sir Jacob Astley; Sir Thomas Blackwell; William Eure; and Sir Henry Vaughan. Three of these colonels – Owen, Lloyd, and Gilby – would be knighted in the course of events, before Lisle received the honour himself.

Whether any of Lisle's own regiment were included amongst the commanded men accompanying him on the march from Oxford is not known. During Lisle's numerous absences in higher command the regiment must have been managed day-to-day by Lieutenant Colonel Littleton, which may have eased resentment, if any existed, about Lisle's appointment as colonel over Littleton's head. At Naseby in 1645 Littleton acted as Lisle's major in the tercio, that is, his deputy, and given Lisle's frequent absences it is highly likely that he had performed this role since the tercio was formed.

Walker describes how the King's overnight march via Long Hanborough passed directly between a detachment of Essex's forces, now at Woodstock, and a detachment of Waller's at Eynsham, a space of only five or six miles. Historian Frederick Varley notes that the procession 'seems to have had some sixty or

---

61   Walker, pp.19-20.

seventy carriages';[62] even if an exaggeration – the Committee of Both Kingdoms only reported thirty[63] – given the rain-soaked roads, it makes the success of the army's escape even more remarkable. Lord Digby describes how a parade through Oxford by the rest of the army the next day:

> drew Waller back over Newbridge, and Essex also thitherward on the other side, and so gave us the opportunity of gaining Burford ere they would be ready to move after us …[64]

The escape was quickly discovered and pursuit made, but the Royalists had a head start and safely reached Worcester on Thursday 6th, having eschewed Burford for Evesham, withdrawn the garrison there and slighted the bridges there and at Pershore. At Worcester the King dug in, strengthening the defences and increasing the city garrison while, Walker says, he and his councillors debated endlessly about their next move.

His escorting force was not idle, however. On 12th June, Walker says:

> Opportunity was taken of relieving Dudley Castle, at that time besieged by the Earl of Denbigh. The Lord Wilmot being sent thither with the Earl of Northampton's, and the Earl of Cleveland's Brigades of Horse, and Collonel George Lisle with 1000 Foot, whereof above 500 were of the Garrison of Evesham … Upon the Approach of the Lord Wilmot, Denbigh retreated; and ours advancing somewhat disorderly, gave him Opportunity to draw off his Cannon …[65]

Symonds is even briefer:

> Munday the 10 of June, the Lord Wilmott with his horse went from Worcester on that side of Severne next Hereford, so to Bewdley, and relieved the Castle of Dudley, which was besieged by the Earle of Denbighe: took some prisoners.[66]

Mercurius Aulicus offers an equally terse summary from an account apparently received by letter, but the details are minimal and it may not have been an

---

62 Varley, *The Siege of Oxford*, p.124.
63 *CSP Domestic Series, 1644*, p.212. The Committee, which sat at Derby House in London, had been set up in February to direct the war, and comprised members of both Houses plus some Scottish 'commissioners'.
64 Digby to Prince Rupert, from Worcester, 8th June 1644. Reproduced in Warburton, vol. II pp.416-417.
65 Walker, p.23. He gives the wrong date, as Denbigh states it was the 11th and the anonymous eyewitness account was written afterwards at Walsall on the 12th.
66 *Diarye*, p.13.

eyewitness account.[67] Indeed no Royalist eyewitness account exists, so once again Lisle's role during the proceedings is not explicitly stated. For the Parliament's part Denbigh submitted a lengthy and detailed report to London, and an anonymously authored printed pamphlet and a manuscript (MS) account are also extant; although of course these do not mention Lisle by name either.[68] Contrary to the impression given by Walker, Symonds and *Aulicus* that Wilmot forced Denbigh to retreat, Denbigh cogently explains in his report to the Committee of Both Kingdoms that he was already effecting an overnight withdrawal from the area due to lack of military support from the local county committee, and the receipt of pragmatic advice from his council of war advising he lift the siege; as proof, he encloses the Council's advice to him. The MS account adds that he had been benefiting from the support of Welshman Sir Thomas Myddelton, but Myddelton had for several days been 'pressing his Lordship to have his horse and foote away to do service in his own associacon.'[69] Whilst Denbigh does give the King's movement in his general direction as another reason for leaving, Wilmot's coincident arrival on the morning of 11th June was not the specific trigger, and he cannot be credited with relieving the castle: already, Denbigh could do no more at Dudley. At two o'clock in the morning, the anonymous pamphlet author tells us, as Denbigh began withdrawing his ordnance from the siege batteries, news of the approaching Royalist force triggered an alert; although as Wilmot's force did not actually appear for another seven hours, the men discovered or sighted were probably only scouts. Parliamentarian cavalry were summoned from their local quarters to support the Earl nevertheless, but – probably owing to the local dispute – did not arrive until eight, when he was also informed of 2,000 approaching Royalist horse.[70] Denbigh pressed on with his task, hoping to finish it and outrun them, but the road was 'almost with this rain made impassable' and the withdrawal of the artillery a struggle.[71] He was determined not to leave without it – according to the anonymous author he swore 'he had rather lose 10 lives had he them to lose than one piece of Artillery' – and despite at least two broken carriages the cannon were eventually, many hours later, dragged three quarters of a mile north up a narrow lane onto Tipton Green. He described it as:

---

67   Week 24 (1644), p.1026.
68   Denbigh's report in *CSP Domestic Series,* 1644, pp.235-237; *A happy defeat given to the King's forces neere Tipton Green in Staffordshire …*; *A true relacon of the Earle of Denbigh his proceedings …*, Warwick Record Office ref. CR 2017/R8. [Author: I am indebted to Ivor Carr for pointing me to the MS account, which does not seem to have previously come to light.]
69   Myddelton's ODNB biographer, J. Gwynn Williams, notes that in early June he was on his way back from London to attend an army muster in Cheshire; this would explain his eagerness to move on quickly from Dudley.
70   *A happy defeat …*
71   *Ibid.*

circular and set round with hedges except some avenues that led from [Dudley] Castle and other parts. The Place was hardly large enough to set our small forces in Battalia …

Lord Wilmot and his force were now almost on top of him, formed up to his rear on the high ground around the castle, the Royalist cavalry facing Denbigh's. Taken together, the various accounts of the action suggest a hiatus between Wilmot's arrival and the start of the fighting at the green; the anonymous pamphlet author specifically gives the timings as nine o'clock and two o'clock respectively, and says the fighting continued until five. Denbigh says the Royalists arrived at the castle as he was still attempting to retrieve one of the broken guns stuck near the walls, yet he managed to complete his problematic task apparently unmolested even by the garrison, inch the gun away through the quagmire, regroup briefly when he eventually reached Tipton and then begin a planned onward march towards Wednesbury, all before he was finally attacked. Walker offers no explanation for the delay, other than attributing the Earl's getaway to the Royalist advance being 'disorderly'. Yet despite this assertion that the hiatus was an error or failure, it makes much sense: to reach Denbigh directly from the castle or follow him towards Tipton the Royalists would also have to use the lane, and it would be folly to attempt a cavalry fight on a narrow, churned up road blocked by the enemy, where horse could not properly deploy. The 'unknown' of this situation is what may have been discussed meanwhile between Wilmot and castle governor Colonel Thomas Leveson: we might surmise the delay was in part due to one of them, perhaps both, being sceptical about expending men and resources on an attack in such atrocious weather, when the enemy was plainly already intent on leaving the scene without further confrontation.

Yet despite the castle no longer requiring relief, having an enemy earl literally stuck in the mud half a mile away was probably too much of an opportunity for Wilmot to pass up, and eventually he sent the cavalry and commanded musketeers forward. Denbigh, meanwhile, assured by a captured Royalist colonel that the scouts' earlier report of 2,000 Royalist cavalry was half the true number and that reserve forces were also on their way, had determined to expedite his north-easterly bid for Wednesbury, and then Walsall.[72] Although he could not know that his prisoner was lying – Wilmot's force did indeed only number 2,000 horse and there was no reserve, the remainder of the King's force still being at Worcester – Denbigh knew even on his scout's estimates that he was outnumbered at least two

72 Denbigh says of the prisoner that he was 'by his commission called Captain Keile, but since thought to be a Colonel': tentatively this might be Colonel Robert Kyrle, formerly a Parliamentarian officer. He defected back to the Parliament in November 1644, betraying Monmouth in the process; if him, his capture so early during the Tipton event appears extremely suspect, even if he did mislead Denbigh about the enemy's numbers.

to one, a figure echoed by the anonymous pamphlet author. The MS account puts Denbigh's force at 'not above 1500 horse & foot at the most (his forces being much disbanded for want of pay)'; it is not clear if this included Myddelton's own horse and foot or the local cavalry that had grudgingly joined Denbigh that morning.[73]

It was Myddelton who hurried the vanguard off the green towards Wednesbury, with Denbigh and the main body behind him and a forlorn hope at Denbigh's rear; 'to amuse the enemy', says the MS account. Then, it continues:

> the enemy with about 1500 horse marched down into a narrow lane, leading towards the greene and theire foot flanked theire horse upon either side of the hedges, at the same time intelligence was brought that the enemy with 500 other horse were marched upon the other side of Dudley and had taken a long circuit with intencon to fall upon the other side of the lane that leads to Wedgbury …

The anonymous pamphlet corroborates the report of Royalist cavalry creeping around the leading edge of Denbigh's force, noting that after the vanguard left the green, 'We had not marched half a mile but the enemy had ambushcadoed the hedges.' As Denbigh ordered Myddelton to halt, and hastily set up sentries, his rearguard was still a wet and exhausted sitting duck on the open ground behind. The MS continues:

> … some of the foote on both sides now began to be engaged upon the Greene which drew his Lordship back & that was seasonably for he mett a greate part of his foot leaveing theire cullers (many of them haveing never seen an enemy in the feild before).

Half of Lisle's musketeers had occupied a house on the eastern edge of the green and waited for the choicest moment to open fire on the Earl's inexperienced rear-guard. Pressured by Lisle's men on their flank and seeing the Royalist cavalry stream towards them from the castle, these novices began to flee; however, as Denbigh describes, one officer's initiative saved the day with devastating effect:

> Major Fraser, Major to my regiment of horse, suffering their horse to enter and rank themselves upon the green to the number of 300, after one of our drakes had been very successfully discharged upon them, surrounded them with the horse, making a large front, and then my regi-ment of foot came up and gave very good fire. The Major with the horse

---

73   The Royalist prisoner's misleading figure of 4,000 horse somehow reached the London press, as *Mercurius Aulicus* later mentions it in his weekly refutation of Parliamentarian reports (Week 26 (1644), p.1062).

charged them so bravely that they were presently routed and driven back with such violence into the lane upon their own horse that they all retired in great disorder, and were pursued and execution done upon them by my horse above half a mile to the bottom of Castle hill. Upon the flight of the enemy's horse, their foot cast away their arms and ran, so that in that lane there were no less than 1,500 horse routed and the ditches on both sides were filled with their men and horses, but most of them got away, some through the hedges, although many mangled and cut.

The MS account concurs that Denbigh's cavalry pursued Wilmot's men to the foot of the castle hill, where they gave up the chase as:

his Lordship thought it not convenient to continue further having so smale a number, but was contented to get back to the greene and there to regard the motions of the Enemy …

Denbigh recounts how his infantry, meanwhile, had turned on Lisle's musketeers and were later assisted by soldiers returning from the rout:

On the other side of the green the Staffordshire foot fell upon Mr Dudley's house on the one side, and part of mine in their return from the execution with the horse fell upon the other side killed 16 of the enemy and drove the rest from the house, and took 40 arms.

He adds that this part of the engagement 'continued two hours, and for three quarters of an hour was very hot'. It is not known whether Lisle was there, or with the other half of the commanded musketeers on the western side of the green – in which case he would have been routed back along the lane with everyone else. By the time the musketeers were finally ejected from the house, the soggy fight was substantially over; Denbigh had beaten off his attackers and secured his opportunity to escape. He was fortunate: although the rain had severely hampered his initial night retreat, and may have persisted throughout the day, had the weather been fairer and the ground not already sodden – the exceptionally wet weather that had protected Oxford continued throughout most of the month – the Royalists may not even have allowed him to get as far as Tipton Green. After the fight he waited two hours for Wilmot's force to retire, then marched on to Walsall, and a few days later gratefully joined his force with Waller's at Stourbridge, at Waller's request. Wilmot had retreated to Stourbridge first, and then rejoined the King at Worcester.

In terms of casualties the Parliamentarian reports, all eyewitness accounts, broadly concur on numbers. Even when author bias and lack of balancing Royalist reportage is considered, there is little doubt that Denbigh's side came off best, perhaps a dozen men being killed and a few more captured, whereas 60-100

Royalist troopers and soldiers were killed in the lane and a dozen or so more in the house, with the specific report of '40 arms' taken there. While he gives only a summary of the action, *Mercurius Aulicus's* author John Berkenhead approximately agrees on casualty numbers; yet curiously he seems to have misread the letters he received and reported the entire situation in reverse, claiming that it was Denbigh who was given a 'plaine and downe-right routing' and lost 'an hundred at least' and '50 common souldiers' captured. He even includes an implausible report that the entire Warwick Castle garrison was withdrawn to go to Denbigh's aid, 'but meeting on the way with the newes of his routing, they returned back again this morning.' Berkenhead was no fool, however, and had a good intelligence network at his disposal; so it is difficult to know whether such a significant mistake was a genuine failure, or a blatant lie on the part of Berkenhead or his informant, designed to boost the reputation of the King and his army during an acute Royalist crisis.

Cropredy

Although the Royalists did not know it at the time, the result of the cat and mouse chase around the south Midlands was effectively decided as early as the 6th June by the Earl of Essex. On this date, after meeting with Waller and Sir Arthur Haselrig at Chipping Norton, he decided to withdraw his army from the present situation, move south to relieve Lyme Regis and other ports and leave Waller to pursue the King alone. He headed south the next day, in one stroke removing any danger of the King being caught between two great armies: all Charles had to do was to stay out of Waller's way and make it back to Oxford to rejoin the rest of the Oxford Army. When the parting of Essex and Waller was discovered some time between the 9th and 14th, Charles – then at Bewdley – was persuaded by the advice of some of his Council of War to do just that, and accordingly retraced his steps. On the 18th, arriving at Witney, he sent an apparently rehabilitated Richard Feilding with some other officers to Oxford with his instructions that the troops there were to draw into the field and combine once more with his smaller force; Symonds states that this was achieved the next day, 'Wednesday, 3910, besides officers, which are at least 1000.'[74]

Essex's withdrawal from the Oxford theatre had left Abingdon vacant once again; around 8th June, *Mercurius Aulicus* reports, someone in the Royalist command had seen fit to station there 'a strong Garrison of 1000 Foot (which went thither upon Saturday last with five Peeces of Ordnance)'.[75] The garrison was short-lived, however, as barely a fortnight later on 18th June, when the King reached Witney:

---

74   *Diarye*, p.18. Toynbee and Young state that that part of the King's infantry which had remained in Oxford was 'computed at 3,500 foot' (*Cropredy Bridge, 1644*, p.40).
75   Week 24 (1644), p.1025.

the Garrison, which the other week was put into Abingdon, with their Armes and Ordinance ... came unto him also, and were embodied with the rest of His Forces ...[76]

The garrison's brief existence not passed without notice, however: a Parliamentarian report dated 19th June noted 'There is Sir Lewis Dyve's regiment at Abingdon, with Col. Vaughan's and Col. Lisle's'.[77] It seems that the regiments' parting act was to fire the suburbs as they left for Witney, as London's *Perfect Occurrences of Parliament* noted with disgust:

But the horrid Act of the Kings Forces appeared extreame cruell this day at Abbington, who sate the Towne on fire in foure severall places, and burned downe 50 houses, besides the like act done by other Cavaliers at Worcester, and shall we still be perswaded, that this is for the priviledges of Parliament, and liberty of the Subject.[78]

Both *Mercurius Civicus* and *A Perfect Diurnall* repeated the accusation, although predictably *Aulicus* denied it.[79] In July Abingdon was secured by Waller, and by August Major General Richard Browne was installed as governor: the King never regained it.

Meanwhile Waller, initially missing the King's doubling back from Worcestershire and then being unable to catch up, despaired and informed London that he would head back to the West Country. The Committee of Both Kingdoms had other ideas, and after pulling together reinforcements for him from numerous garrisons, ordered him to follow the King wherever necessary and be ready to accept battle if opportunity offered.

Also ready for battle but without an opponent in view, the reconstituted Oxford Army had passed to the north of Oxford and now hovered around Buckingham while the King and his advisors yet again dithered about how and where to force a fight; Walker states that even a 'strange and desperate' plan to march on London was proposed.[80] However on 25th June the Royalists became aware of Waller's

---

76 *Mercurius Aulicus*, Week 25 (1644), pp.1038-1039.

77 *The Letter Books of Sir Samuel Luke*, p.667, scout report no. 165.

78 Numb. 26 (1644), no page numbers.

79 *Mercurius Civicus*, Numb. 56, p.547 (Worcester) and p.548 (Abingdon); *A Perfect Diurnall*, Numb. 47, p.373; *Mercurius Aulicus*, Week 26 (1644), p.1061. Burning suburbs to deny them to an enemy, either when under siege in a town or retreating from one, was an established military tactic. Civil War examples include Alresford, Hampshire (by Royalists after the battle of Cheriton, March 1644), Gloucester (by Parliamentarian defenders, August 1643), Bridgnorth (by Royalist defenders, March 1646) and Colchester (by Royalist defenders, August 1648).

80 Adair states that the King marched east in order to threaten the Eastern Association and spare Oxfordshire the burden of provisioning his army (*Roundhead General*, p.157). Of the London plan, Walker (pp.28-29) says it was almost put into motion: the King and his advisors debated the possible

orders to pursue them, and accordingly headed north-west via Brackley to Culworth, intending to then move north to Daventry. They changed their plans again when news came that Waller had approached nearby Banbury from the north-west, and as Walker relates:

> It was thought best to march thither, and to lay hold of a fit Opportunity there to give the Rebels Battel. Wherefore early the next Morning, being Friday the 28th of June, the Army advanced in good order towards Banbury, and about ten of the Clock had a Rendezvous on Leigh-grounds about a Mile on the East side of that Town.[81]

Toynbee and Young believe 'Leigh-grounds' may be Bandon or Bandy Leys in Chacombe parish, just north-east of Banbury.[82] If so, the Royalists were two miles east of the river Cherwell, directly opposite the village of Hanwell two miles away on the other side; near which, when the morning mist and rain cleared on 28th June, they discovered Waller was encamped. Immediately the King made to secure Crouch Hill, a strategic vantage point across the river a mile south-west of Banbury, but Waller was closer and ascended it first, his men remaining there in battalia for the rest of the day.[83] The Royalists must have used the thirteenth-century bridge which crossed the Cherwell by Banbury Castle, as after they failed to capture the hill they immediately fell back across the river: the next available crossing was Slat Mill and its adjacent ford, three miles to the north, or Cropredy Bridge a mile beyond that, which are too far away to fit the circumstances.[84] However Colonel Thelwall, one of Lisle's tercio colonels, was left with a thousand commanded men at the village of Neithrop on the Banbury side, a mile north of Waller's position on the hill: *Mercurius Aulicus* says, 'to defend that side of Banbury towards the Rebels, together with Nethorpe',[85] but also presumably to observe Waller. The area is now built up and the original landscape difficult to envisage, but in 1644 Thelwall's

route, and which towns might be garrisoned along the way, and even composed the message they would send into London when the army was positioned outside it.

81   *Ibid.*, p.30.
82   *Cropredy Bridge, 1644. The Campaign & the Battle*, p.73.
83   Symonds (*Diarye*, p.22) states that only part of Waller's force ascended Crouch Hill; it is not clear whether he was correct, but he was an eyewitness to the events.
84   Apparently Slat Mill was still standing as late as 1927, as W. G. Bond includes a photograph in *The Wanderings of Charles I* (the photograph itself is undated but its good quality suggests it is contemporary to the book). The mill has now disappeared, although the ford remains. Banbury Bridge, also called 'East Bridge' or 'Millstream Bridge', located at what is now Bridge Street, was largely destroyed by the building of a nineteenth-century railway bridge. The remains are Grade II listed. Originally the seven-arched bridge spanned both the main channel of the Cherwell and a mill stream, which could explain the presence of 'Preston Mills' to which (Parliamentarian soldier Richard Coe tells us) the Royalists fell back.
85   Week 26 (1644), p.1055.

position must have been highly defensible: Walker reports that during the day he repelled numerous attacks, on one occasion killing eight of Waller's soldiers and a lieutenant colonel (although *Aulicus* states that the man was only shot through the thigh); Symonds records that a body of enemy horse 'endeavoured to passe the river on the right hand of Banbury, but were repulsed', losing a captain in the process.[86] Although snipers or the Oxford Army artillery could have accounted for the casualty, the attempt may have been foiled by the Royalist garrison in Banbury Castle, which as stated previously lay in town next to the Cherwell. Strangely only one account – that of Trained Bands soldier Richard Coe – mentions the castle, and then only in passing, so it is easy to overlook its presence.[87] *Mercurius Aulicus* also mentions it, but only after the fact, claiming Waller had bribed local Parliamentarian garrisons to turn out and assist him in return for his helping them capture the castle later.[88] A substantial double-bailey site, it was a Royalist stronghold throughout the war, governed by Sir William Compton, a younger son of the late 2nd Earl of Northampton and a committed Royalist.[89] Just days later the garrison was strong enough to withstand what became a four month siege, yet its absence in all but Coe's account would suggest that it played little part in the proceedings of 28th-29th June. It would be astonishing if this was the case, and its absence from the record on this occasion must surely be due to an accidental deficiency in the accounts that have come down to us.

On the night of the 28th Waller's army 'quartered within the inclosures' on Crouch Hill;[90] evidently Thelwall was withdrawn across the Cherwell, as the next morning he and his men reappeared as part of the Royalist rearguard. Symonds states that the King quartered 'at a howse on the bottome of the hill neare Banbury'; Walker relates that overnight Charles concluded:

> That it was not likely he should get Waller to quit his Strength, and that it was more dangerous to attempt to force him thence, [and] resolved to march to Daventree, and thence to observe Waller's Motion, and to expect a fitter Opportunity and Place to give him battle.[91]

86   *Diarye*, p.22.
87   Coe, *An Exact Dyarie, or a briefe Relation Of the progresse of Sir William Wallers Army* …; Coe states that 'our Horse and they face one the other, the water lying between them and us, we not willing to venture betweene them and the Castle, they not daring to come over to us …' On Monday as the Oxford Army moved off towards Oxford, Coe adds that Banbury was partially on fire and blames the Castle 'for giving some small entertainment to our souldiers.' Toynbee and Young include several quotes from Coe, and reproduce his account of the battle.
88   Week 26 (1644), p.1060. The pages in this edition are misnumbered, so in fact it should be p.1058.
89   Compton kept the garrison until May 1646; he took up arms again in 1648, and was present at the siege of Colchester with George Lisle.
90   *CSP Domestic Series,* 1644, p.290.
91   Walker, p.30.

In the morning, however, while the Royalists organised their north-westerly march, Waller penned a hasty letter to the Committee of Both Kingdoms:

> The King's army is drawing up the hill, most of his horse are fallen down towards Cropredy, whether it be to secure their retreat or to make their passage that way to fight upon more equal ground, is yet not certain, but we shall quickly know.[92]

The 'hill' was the high ground carrying the Banbury-Daventry road (the modern A361). In a subsequent, more leisurely letter he told the Committee that from Crouch Hill early on the 29th he had observed the Royalists 'going with bag and baggage to Northampton';[93] the King's leaving unintentionally achieved what he had previously failed at, for Waller shifted three miles north, telling the Committee that the high ground at Great Bourton, approximately a mile west of the ford at Slat Mill, 'brought me full in upon the flank of the enemy and gave me a very great advantage.'

John Berkenhead, the author of *Mercurius Aulicus*, had evidently attached himself to the army at some point, perhaps to make up for the inaccuracy of his report about Dudley: he included his own account of the Cropredy action in the next edition, observing that:

> Assoone as it was light, this morning Waller drew off from the place where he stood embattelled, and advanced to an hill called Burton hill, some-what nearer Banbury; and there drew up againe in Battalia, having the advantage of springs and boggs before his front, and both on his flanks and back strong hedges (you know his conditions of old, hils, boggs, hedges, ditches, these you must grant him, hee'll not fight else). Here the Rebell was couchant all the forenoone.[94]

Walker reports similarly:

> We were no sooner on our March, but the Rebels drew off from their Ground, and coasted us on the other side of the River, but at such a distance that we did not at all believe they would have attempted us; yet to be sure they could not have any advantage, a Party of Dragooners was sent to keep Cropredy Bridge, until the Army was pas'd beyond it.

92   *CSP, op. cit.*
93   *CSP, op. cit.*, p.293.
94   *Op. cit..*

Charles seems to have made one last attempt to engage Waller in his new position: *Aulicus* continues:

> His Majestie endeavoured, but could not invite him downe (where was now the game of King-catching?) till His Majestie drew off and marched towards Daintry, leaving a guard of Dragoons at Cropredy Bridge, which was the passe over Charwell betwixt the two Armies.

The two-phase battle which followed – a roaming, cavalry-dominated engagement followed by a static bid for control of the bridge – stemmed from mistakes made on both sides: by the Royalists, for not keeping their army together as one body, and by Waller, for misjudging the positioning of his attack. Walker gives the order of the King's march as:

> the Van of his army being led by the Earl of Brainford Lieutenant General, in the Body was His Majesty and the Prince, and the Rear consisted of 1000 commanded Men under Collonel Thelwel, and the Earls of Northampton and Cleveland's Brigades of Horse.

This rear portion also contained, as *Aulicus* noted, Sir Bernard Astley's tercio of foot.[95] Lisle's location is not precisely known at any point. He cannot have been leading the dragoon detachment on Cropredy Bridge, despite such a task being his area of expertise, as his elevation to tercio commander would have made him prominent in the army and either Walker or Berkenhead would have mentioned his presence there; certainly later that summer his role as the army's regular forlorn hope commander was assumed by Colonel Matthew Appleyard, while Lisle seems to have stood on the sidelines. Moreover, Walker was writing up his account of Cropredy in later 1644 or early 1645, after Lisle had become something of a celebrity due to his actions at the second battle of Newbury being recounted in *Aulicus*, and had he done anything else outstanding, the secretary would undoubtedly have included it. Toynbee and Young suppose that Lisle was in the van at Cropredy, but do not explain that conclusion; they may have simply made an assumption based on his previous activities.[96] *Aulicus* mentions a man in Pennyman's regiment, Blague's tercio, taking prisoners at Hays Bridge two miles further around a westward bend in the Cherwell, where the body of the army stood: possibly Toynbee and Young deduce therefore that Blague must have marched with the body and Lisle with the van, but on such thin evidence that conclusion is also flimsy at best. In any case, it is unlikely that Lisle participated in the early part of the fighting: the

95 Astley had been knighted at Burford on 18th June.
96 *Cropredy Bridge, 1644*, plate 17.

weight of the battle fell on the rear portion of the army, and with a few defenders at the rear of the main body who secured Hays Bridge.

Waller's attack was one of opportunity, made when a gap of at least a mile and a half opened up between the Royalist centre and rear.[97] The gap was such, that he believed the entire army had passed, and planned to attack its rear. Unfortunately, as trooper Thomas Ellis of Haselrig's regiment recounts:

> they had placed a Guard to secure Cropready-bridge, which wee readily beat off, and made the bridge our owne … being over the River, through mis-information, wee too speedily pursued the enemy, (being enformed that their whole bodie was marched away, when as a third part of them were left behinde unknowne to us.)[98]

Whilst Lord Digby later attributed the extensive gap in the army to 'supine negligence',[99] Walker offers a reason, if not an excuse:

> Our Army marching in this Order, certain Intelligence was brought that a Body of 300 Rebels Horse were within two miles of our Van, intending to join with Waller; by which it was judged that they might be easily cut off by our quick advancing. Whereupon our formost Horse upon Order hastened their March (our Van and Battel having the same Directions) without any Apprehension of the Rebels intentions; who perceiving an Interval of a considerable Distance … advanced with 1500 Horse, 1000 Foot and 11 pieces of Cannon to Croprady, and forced that Pass, our Dragoons quitting it without much Resistance.[100]

Where the information about an approaching enemy came from is unclear, but presumably it was inaccurate, as no new cavalry is recorded as having entered the fray on the Parliament's side. However we can assume that if Lisle and his tercio were indeed in the van, he and his men were concerned not with what might be happening behind them, but hastily preparing themselves to intercept and neutralise a new enemy at their front.

Intending to hit the perceived Royalist rearguard in the side and rear, Waller launched a two-pronged attack across the Cherwell: his cavalry and dragoons dislodging the Royalists from Cropredy Bridge, and Waller himself commanding

---

97   As estimated by John Adair (*Roundhead General* , p.160).

98   *An Exact and Full Relation of the last fight between the Kings Forces and Sir William Waller* …

99   In a letter to Prince Rupert, written at Evesham on 12th July; reproduced by Warburton, vol. II, p.472. An anonymous eyewitness report in the Parliamentarian *Perfect Occurrences of Parliament* claims that Digby was in the Royalist van; if true, he was well forward of the action and therefore could easily have misjudged how far behind the rest of the army was (Numb. 28 (1644), 2nd July entry).

100 Walker, p.31.

a thousand foot across the ford at Slat Mill.[101] Once across the river part of the cavalry, comprising Haselrig's and Vandruske's regiments, split off into a third arm and took up a north-easterly pursuit of the Royalists towards Hays Bridge, believing they were at the rear of their enemy's column; they were rudely checked at the bridge by an overturned carriage and musketeers from the Royalist main body. The rest of Waller's cavalry, streaming east across Cropredy Bridge towards their quarry, were charged proactively by the Earl of Cleveland, who broke them and drove them back towards it. Meanwhile at the extreme southern end of the Royalist column, opposite Slat Mill ford, the Earl of Northampton saw that Waller's infantry intended to attack him directly, faced about and routed the enemy foot back towards the river. Back up at Hays Bridge, Haselrig's and Vandruske's rebuffed regiments turned back to find the rest of their own army in disarray behind them: it would now have been painfully apparent that they had hit the King's force in the wrong place. As they prepared to charge the preoccupied Cleveland in the flank, Charles ordered Lord Bernard Stuart and the King's Lifeguard to cross back over Hays Bridge and they quickly put the rogue arm of Parliamentarian cavalry to flight, leaving Cleveland unhindered to complete his initial charge. The Earl then made an emphatic second one against 'a great Body of the Rebels Horse of 16 Colours (and as many Colours of Foot placed within Hedges) all within Musquet Shot of him',[102] and routed them so effectively that he captured their artillery park and a large amount of ordnance.[103] Colonel John Birch blames the rout on a lack of musketeers, stating that 1,500 had been drawn out for an intended action two days previously but through haste and 'pollicies in warr far beyond my reason' were still positioned at the rear, leaving not 1,200 to face Cleveland's charge; Birch credits Tower Hamlets Trained Bands for making a stand on the bridge with a couple of drakes, and preventing the King from taking it.[104] Waller also secured Slat Mill ford as he withdrew his army to Bourton but it was quickly overrun, leaving him only with the bridge. By now – Walker says it was 3 p.m. – Charles and the forward part of his army had returned from their position north of Hays Bridge and stood at Williamscote, just to the south-east of Cropredy and opposite Waller's position

---

101 Toynbee and Young (p.90) and Adair (p.160) conflict over which commander led at which crossing, but it is not important in respect of Lisle's part in the battle, and this biography has followed Toynbee and Young.

102 Walker, p.32.

103 Walker states that eleven cannon were taken, as well as 'two Barricades of Wood drawn with Wheels, in each seven small brass and leathern Guns, charged with case shot.' *Aulicus* describes the eleven cannon as brass, '5 Sakers, 1 Twelve pound Peece, 1 Demiculverin, 2 Mynions, 2 Three pound Peeces,' and the barricades as 'Two blinders for Muskets and Leather Guns invented by Col. Weems a Scot …' Despite this disaster Waller evidently still had some ordnance, as it continued to play upon the Royalists during the second phase of the battle. Some shot fell near the King, and *Aulicus* claimed it was a deliberate attempt to kill him.

104 Birch, pp.12-13.

at Bourton on the other side of the river. Meanwhile, Waller says, there was 'hot service at Cropredy Bridge' which continued until the end of the day.[105]

Unfortunately, despite giving good details of the earlier cavalry action, the Royalist accounts give no detail about the final, static infantry tussle for the bridge, or state who on their side was involved. As Lisle's and Blague's tercios were fresh it is possible that they were drafted in to attempt dislodging the Trained Bands, perhaps with Lisle or Blague in a position of command, but the lack of reportage means this must remain an untested suggestion.

At around 8 p.m., Symonds says, the Oxford Army drew down towards the ford, and the Parliamentarians:

> ranged their Foot on the top of the opposite Hill, and drew three great Bodies of their Horse within the reach of our Cannon; which being discharged amongst them, made them retire in great disorder.[106]

Symonds reports that Waller's artillery fired 'ten or more great pieces' into the Oxford Army's midst, and that 'some of them fell neare the King';[107] Walker claims it was twenty. This is where Berkenhead in *Aulicus* makes his claim that it was an attempt on Charles's life, asserting that prisoners had confirmed the gunners had been shown through telescopes where the King was. Toynbee and Young read Waller's salvo as retaliation for the Royalists', but in fact none of the contemporary accounts confirm which side fired first in this exchange. Haselrig's trooper Ellis claims there were 'fourty shot apiece', and that his side's contribution forced at least part of the King's force to retreat: presumably to Williamscote, and not surprisingly, if there was a perception that the guns were targeting the King. Some credit must be given to Charles for having remained in the field so late, so close to the enemy; that night, after Waller had refused to even grant safe passage for delivery of a 'Message of Grace and Pardon', offering amnesty to all who laid down their arms, he retired to a 'very poor man's house at Williamscote.'[108]

The night passed in stalemate, the Royalists massed at Williamscote and holding Slat Mill and its ford, and the Parliamentarians opposite at Bourton, and holding Cropredy Bridge a mile to the north. The standoff continued in relative quiet throughout the next day, Sunday, although Symonds reports thirty cannon shots being fired harmlessly towards some of the Royalist horse; Birch states that the King's force threatened to cross the ford 'sundry times' throughout the day, but as Symonds adds, there was 'Nothing of any moment done all this day.'

105 *CSP Domestic Series,* 1644, p.293.
106 Walker, p.33.
107 *Diarye,* p.24.
108 Toynbee and Young (p.103) from the *Iter Carolinum,* which recorded the King's whereabouts throughout the war.

That night, Walker tells us:

> His Majesty having intelligence that Brown was about Buckingham, with a Force of near 4000 Foot and 500 Horse, and that probably he would speedily advance and join with Waller; and finding that Victuals were scant in the Army, and that our Souldiers were oppressed with too great Duty, His Majesty took Resolutions answerable to those necessities.

Accordingly, after a brief false alarm and exchange of fire during Sunday night, caused by a stray shot from a careless Parliamentarian musketeer,[109] the Oxford Army foot left the field overnight and the horse and artillery at around 4 a.m. on Monday. Waller did not follow, perhaps understandably: his army, having already served a long campaign in the field and propped up with a hotch-potch of local garrison troops, had taken a beating and was probably in no fit state to risk a second major encounter so soon and before any significant reinforcement had arrived. Moreover at least one large group of soldiers was reported to have deserted,[110] and Waller cannot have remained unshaken by a near-fatal accident on the Sunday whereby the floor of his lodging collapsed, sending him and two of his senior officers crashing into the cellar.[111]

Mindful that Major General Browne might join with Waller and attack the Royalist rear, the King crossed the Cherwell south-east of Banbury and headed west, fetching up at Evesham again on 3rd July. Walker explains why this was the destination, saying that provisions were still a problem in Oxfordshire, particularly with the armies of both sides in the vicinity, and that the risk of Oxford being besieged had not abated. Most importantly, it was not believed that Waller would be able to drag his temperamental London troops westward again.[112] It was during the ten day sojourn at Evesham that conflicting reports began to arrive about a large battle near York; after weighing up whether to march north to support Prince Rupert or westward to pursue the Earl of Essex, Charles chose the latter, not least because Essex was threatening Exeter and thus the Queen.[113] Lisle and his tercio were to see out the summer in Cornwall.

---

109 As reported by Trained Bands man Richard Coe.

110 According to Berkenhead, whose report of the battle in *Aulicus* noted '240 were met towards Warwickshire, labouring to find out a better Master then Sir William.' (Week 26 (1644), p.1060 (correctly, p.1058)).

111 *Perfect Occurrences of Parliament*, Numb. 28 (1644), 2nd July entry.

112 Walker, pp.34-35. The latter assumption was correct: a few days later most of the London regiments deserted Waller and Browne and returned to the capital.

113 Immediately following the birth of her daughter, a severely weakened Henrietta Maria had twice requested safe conduct from the Earl of Essex, ostensibly that she might travel eastwards to Bath to take the waters there but presumably, in truth, that she might be reunited with the King; the Earl refused on both occasions, offering her only a pass to London (Whitelocke, p.88 and 89).

9

A Waiting Game: The Cornish Campaign

In pursuit of Essex

On Friday 12th July, having dispatched Ned Villiers to inform the Queen and Prince Maurice of the intention to join them in the west, the King and the Oxford Army began their march.[1] Late that night as the King quartered at a 'poore howse' south of Cheltenham,[2] firm news finally arrived from Prince Rupert himself of the disaster at Marston Moor on 2nd July.

George Lisle would not yet have been aware that his younger brother Francis had been killed at the battle, while commanding Henry Warren's regiment.[3] Peter Young states that Major Daniel Moore was 'probably acting as its commanding officer',[4] but Francis is recorded as the major in February,[5] so if Moore had taken his position by July, then Francis also must have been promoted by that time and must have led the regiment to Yorkshire as part of the 'Shrewsbury Foot' under Rupert. No personal correspondence between Francis and George survives, so it is not possible to know if George had been aware of his whereabouts. Perhaps in the following days and weeks, as details of the decimated and destroyed regiments trickled south, he was able to guess his brother's fate, if no personal message had already come to him by letter or word of mouth. Some weeks later he may have seen or been told about the first edition of the new *London Post*, dated 6th August, which in a list of casualties announced the death of:

---

1 Maurice had raised his siege of Lyme Regis on 15th June, and then joined his aunt at Exeter. Unknown to the King, the Queen had been gone from Exeter nearly two weeks by the time he dispatched Villiers in July.
2 Symonds' *Diarye*, p.28.
3 The regiment which had been decapitated at Nantwich in January, where Warren was captured and his then deputy killed. He was still a prisoner in October, when his exchange was refused (JHC, 3, 1643-1644, p.658).
4 *Marston Moor 1644*, p.88.
5 In a letter from Lord Byron to the Earl of Ormonde, 6th February 1644; Bodleian Library, Carte MSS. vol. 9.

Lieutenant Col. Lisle, who heretofore had done good service in Holland.[6]

As Laurence and Dorothy were no longer in London they may not have seen this newsbook, and it is impossible to know when they found out about their younger son's death. Possibly George had to break the news. Francis's place of burial is unknown, but unless he was wounded and carried elsewhere to die, his grave would have been one of the mass burial pits on or near the battlefield. Sadly there is nothing more that can be said about Francis or his death, unless new personal or military sources come to light.

According to Symonds the Oxford Army arrived at Exeter on 26th July;[7] Walker says it was met by Prince Maurice and other supporters,[8] but was too late to see the desperately weakened Henrietta Maria, who with Maurice's aid had given Essex's patrols the slip and boarded a ship to France.[9] That afternoon, Walker continues:

> His Majesty held a Council of his own Officers, with Prince Maurice and the chief Officers of his Army, and then took into Debate what Course they should steer in the Pursuit of Essex …

Whether Lisle attended any of the King's councils of war at this time is not known. Charles's regular council at this period, Walker tells us, comprised the Duke of Richmond, the Earl of Lindsey, Lords Forth, Digby, Hopton, Percy, and Wilmot, Sir John Culpepper and Sir Jacob Astley.[10] Other peers and officers were brought in as needed, however, and Walker's explicit references to meetings including 'senior officers of the army' suggests that this continued in Cornwall. Whilst the minutes of many council meetings have been preserved, unfortunately none of the few which date from 1644 mention Lisle.[11] The great pity of this incomplete documentation is that it has potentially robbed us of Lisle's contributions to such meetings, along with any insights into his character and military abilities. Like so many of the soldiers in the opposing army, he was also a Londoner more than 250 miles from home. They, it seems, were perpetually homesick, often to the point of mutiny as both Essex and Sir William Waller had repeatedly discovered; whilst Lisle had at least learned something of the outside world by travelling abroad and to the north of Britain, unlike the majority of the rank and file Trained

---

6   Numb. 1, pp.2-3. The mention of Holland should be considered with caution, as it is possible that the newsbook confused Francis with his better known brother.

7   *Ibid.*, p.38.

8   Walker, p.47

9   Clarendon notes that the baby princess had been left at Exeter with Lady Dalkeith, who got her safely to France after the city's surrender in 1646 (Book VIII, 1840 vol. IV, p.493).

10 Walker, p.14.

11 Many rough copies of council minutes are extant in Harl. MS 6852, at the British Library.

Bands – some of whom, one of their officers noted, had never even seen cows[12] – he cannot have been immune to thinking wistfully of his home city, particularly as it seems he preferred to remain there whenever he could and it was impossible to know when he would be able to return. Concerns for his family were probably also uppermost in his mind: besides being in temporary accommodation somewhere they were – as Laurence had recently told the Earl of Salisbury – desperately short of money, and now also dealing with Francis's death.

By the time the Oxford Army arrived at Exeter Essex was, as Walker puts it, 'endeavouring to make his way into Cornwall'; Maurice and other commanders were sent to hinder his movements while food for the Oxford Army was stock-piled at Exeter and in Somerset. Essex's recent decision to continue west, rather than turn back and face the Royalists closing on his rear, was based partly on the urging of Cornishmen such as Lord Robartes, and also the Earl of Warwick, who rashly promised that the county would rise up to support him;[13] and partly on the assumption that Sir William Waller had the King within his grasp and would deal with him while the London army relieved Plymouth and recovered the West. However when Essex informed the Committee of Both Kingdoms of his decision on 18th July he had not heard about Waller's defeat at Cropredy Bridge, therefore his ill-informed expectation of swift assistance at his rear was a major compo-nent of what proved to be a catastrophic decision.[14] Professor E. A. Andriette succinctly describes how, when Sir Richard Grenville lifted his siege of Plymouth and retreated as Essex approached, the Earl – whose campaign so far had been very successful – ill-advisedly:

> followed the Royalists further into Cornwall. Instead of keeping open his supply lines with Plymouth, the lord general led his army further west until he found himself caught between the combined forces of Charles and Maurice (by now grouping at Exeter), and the royalist forces of

12   Captain Robert Harley, the officer who was also present at Cheriton and wrote an account of that action in a letter to his brother (see chapter 8). Of the townies, he says: 'Here you should have seen the Londoners runne to see what manner of thinges cowes were. Some of them would say they had all of them hoornes, and would doe great mischiefe with them …' (quoted by Adair, *Cheriton 1644*, p.121).

13   Clarendon claims Robartes 'had much greater credit in the parliament than the earl of Essex' , and promised the Earl a popular uprising if he marched into Cornwall (Clarendon Book VIII, 1840 vol. IV, p.492). However in an undated letter in mid-June, Essex himself told the House of Lords that it was 'the Lord High Admiral' (i.e. Warwick) who had assured him of this (JHL, 6, 1643, p.603). Perhaps he thought Warwick's name would carry more weight in the House than Robartes'.

14   Essex's letter to the Committee of Both Kingdoms, 18th July, from Tiverton; *CSP Domestic Series*, 1644, pp.358-359. This letter also crossed with two from the Committee, dated 16th and 17th July, advising him that Waller's forces were weak – only 2,500 horse and 1,500 foot – although they had asked him to send some dragoons into Dorset (*ibid.*, p.354, 358). Stephen Ede-Borrett suggests that the fault lay partly with Waller, who had misled everyone as to the extent of his defeat at Cropredy Bridge (*Lostwithiel 1644*, pp.13-14).

Cornwall under Grenville. Essex's intention was to 'clear that country [i.e. Cornwall] and to settle the same in peace.' It does not appear that the general actually gave much thought as to just how he would accomplish this major task. Instead, he walked into the trap of the narrow Cornish peninsula, where he found a hostile countryside, limited supplies, and meagre contributions.[15]

Clarendon agrees, saying that:

The Earl of Essex's good fortune now began to decline: and he had not proceeded with his accustomed wariness and skill, but ran into labyrinths, from whence he could not disentangle himself …[16]

On Monday 29th July the King continued his own march west from Exeter, arriving the next day at Okehampton, through which Essex had passed eight days previously. However, whereas Essex had at this point turned south towards Tavistock, skirting the western edge of Dartmoor and heading towards Plymouth as planned, the Royalists continued south-west towards Launceston. They reached the river Tamar, dividing Devon and Cornwall, on 31st July and quartered on the eastern side at Liston; the next day, after assembling the army and forbidding plunder – the Cornish being 'exceedingly affectionate to His Majesty and His Cause', and plentiful lines of supply already organised[17] – Charles crossed into Cornwall with his forces. At Launceston they heard that Essex, who had left Plymouth and passed the Royalists some fourteen miles south at Liskeard, had now moved west to Bodmin; the next day, Friday 2nd August, the Oxford Army was joined by Maurice and his army at nearby Coryton Down. Symonds states that the two forces together numbered 10,000 foot, 5,000 horse, and 28 cannon.[18] Shortly afterwards Sir Richard Grenville exhorted them to join him and his army at an unspecified rendezvous,[19] but for the present no meeting occurred, despite the King ordering him to quarter nearby to prevent Essex being resupplied overland.[20]

However at Coryton, Symonds reports, news came that Essex had secured the port of Fowey, south-west of Liskeard, through which he presumably hoped to

15 *Devon and Exeter in the Civil War*, pp.116-117.
16 Book VIII, 1840 vol. IV, pp.490-491.
17 Walker, p.49.
18 The army's size is more-or-less confirmed by the Duke of Richmond, writing to Rupert around 8th August, who believed it was 9,000 foot and 4,000 horse (Warburton, vol. III, fn. p.8).
19 *Diarye*, p.45. The size of Grenville's force is disputed. Although Symonds states that Grenville claimed a force of 8,000, when Sir Richard finally met up with the King at Boconnoc on 8th August he had, so Walker says, 'really not above 1800 Foot and 600 Horse' (Walker, p.62)
20 Walker, p.51. The King wrote to Grenville 'again' from Liskeard, suggesting heightened concern in the Royalist camp not to squander the golden opportunity to sew Essex firmly into a trap.

receive resupply by sea; his army was mostly still at Bodmin. Early on Saturday 3rd the King followed the Earl's trail down to Liskeard, where locals flocked to complain that the Parliamentarians were plundering the country. Walker says that:

> we had hourly Notice of the Rebels Actions, and the Country People (nay the very Women) were so incensed against them, as being of the Militia (for under that Notion the Gentlemen had made them odious) as that they could not straggle out of their Quarters, but they were presently either slain or taken; so that during our stay at Liskerd His Majesty had daily Presents made him of the Rebels Prisoners.[21]

The Liskeard plundering was not an isolated occurrence: a few days previously Symonds had recorded numerous acts of theft and vandalism perpetrated by Essex's army in and around Crediton.[22] Evidently Essex had not taken anything like the same care as Charles to get or keep the inhabitants on his side. In fact the Earl was discovering that the Cornish, far from greeting him with the acclamation that Warwick and Lord Robartes had promised, were very much *not* on his side. In a plaintive letter to the Committee of Both Kingdoms from Lostwithiel on 4th August, which displays a perceptible note of panic but absolutely no sign of carrying any responsibility for the situation himself, he says:

> We now hear that three armies are marching against us from the east ... and the country rising unanimously against us, with the exception of a few gentlemen, we must expect another army upon our backs from the west.[23]

He blames his position on 'the persuasions of the western men', and pleads that he and the army were 'induced to march to Bodmin' by their assurances and promises of welcome and succour. He adds that his soldiers 'want bread' and that the army cannot move until it receives supplies from Plymouth, and rounds off the letter with the rather petulant comment that, as the Committee had not sent Waller's force to him entire but had 'appointed him to send only a party' (and therefore there was no real threat at the King's rear to check any attack on Essex), 'this makes us trust at present in nothing but God's blessing, the courage of our officers and soldiers, and our faithfulness to the cause.' The Committee responded by arranging food and money to be sent by ship, but the winds were westerly and

---

21   *Ibid.*, pp.50-51.
22   *Diarye*, p.41.
23   *CSP Domestic Series*, 1644, pp.398-399.

prevented any supplies reaching Fowey from the east.[24] As this chapter will later describe, it seems an arrangement was subsequently made between Plymouth and the coastal town of St Austell, near Essex's position, to ship supplies around to the Earl; this was probably the only source of provision for his army once any existing supplies ran out and local hamlets had been stripped of anything edible. As later events would prove, it was not nearly enough.

Two days later Essex refused to respond formally to a letter from the King suggesting the Earl go over to his side for the sake of peace, reportedly saying 'he durst make no Answer to it without Leave from the Parliament, unto whom he would send it.'[25] Verbally to the bearer, however, he advised that the King 'go to His Parliament.' Charles's letter was persuasively written, and the bearer sent with explicit instructions about how to win over the Earl, but Essex was either firm in his political convictions and had not given up on the hope of relief, or did not trust the King to fulfil his promise of bestowing 'Marks of my confidence and Value'. This is no surprise, as even before the war he and Charles had never been on agreeable terms. There was also the question of whether his officers would have followed him to the King anyway, not to mention what the Parliament might do to him if he himself was to submit to Charles and later get caught by its agents or soldiers.

Symonds says that on 7th August the King and his army moved to Braddock Down, 'within three myles of Essex his head quarters, being at Listithell'.[26] first contact was made when scouts of both sides clashed. The next day Colonel Matthew Appleyard was sent off with a 1,000-strong forlorn hope in search of the enemy. In the past, such tasks were frequently allotted to Lisle; Appleyard was equally as capable, perhaps even slightly senior in colonelcy terms, but it is noteworthy that from this time Lisle rarely performed such tasks again.

The arrest of Lord Wilmot; the Royalist officers' letter to Essex

During the second week of August growing tension between Lord Wilmot, Lord Digby and the King exploded into a scandal that rocked the combined Oxford-Maurice army at the precise time that it should have been placing its entire focus on nailing down its enemy. It is difficult to coherently piece together the sequence of events, as the three main sources – Walker, Clarendon and a printed pamphlet – offer slightly different perspectives, and both Walker and Clarendon's narratives

24 According to the Earl of Warwick, writing from Plymouth on 18th August (*ibid.*, p.436).
25 Walker, pp.52-57.
26 *Diarye*, p.49.

jump back and forth in time.[27] However, the affair appears to have proceeded approximately as follows.

Clarendon claims that Lord Wilmot, General of the Horse, was dissatisfied with his prospects and for some time had been actively agitating for peace. Furthermore he detested the presence on the Council of War of Lord Digby and Sir John Culpepper, who were politicians rather than soldiers, which caused 'implacable animosity' to them in the army. Wilmot attempted to raise a petition to have them removed; his colleagues prevented its delivery to Charles, who heard of it in any case and was incensed. As Clarendon is not known for political impartiality his account should be regarded with caution, but it is evident from the sources overall that Wilmot had been making waves for some time and had not helped his own case.

Meanwhile, when the King had sent his letter to Essex suggesting the Earl join him, Wilmot allegedly gave the bearer a private message for Essex, reminding him of their good personal relations pre-war and advising that if he did decide to come over to the Royalists, none nobody around the King or at court could stop it. Essex, as described earlier, refused any advances. Yet despite that refusal, Walker says, 'some busie spirit' now:

> prepared a Letter to Essex, to be subscribed by the Principal Officers of His Majesty's and Prince Maurice's Armys. This was formed as some Hands got unto it before His Majesty knew of it … But His Majesty to satisfie all the World of His real Desires for Peace, was pleased to give way that it should be subscribed and sent.[28]

The letter claimed that the officers undersigned had taken up arms for the same reason as Essex: to defend the King's known rights, to defend the liberty of the subject and to protect 'the true Protestant religion' against popery. As per the King's letter, it suggested the Earl and the King come to terms. It is not clear whether Wilmot was Walker's 'busie spirit', but the secretary comments:

---

27   Walker, pp.52-61; Clarendon, Book VIII, 1840 vol. IV, pp.492-501; *The Accusation Given by His Maiestie Against the Lord Wilmot* … Walker would have been on the spot but his account was approved and in some places even edited by the King, who for the sake of public appearances is unlikely to have permitted inclusion of every unpalatable detail. Clarendon, who as one of Charles's close political advisors (although not on his council of war) was probably also in Cornwall, wrote up his version in the 1660s; however he was more concerned with the motives of the primary political movers involved, and in the main used Walker's earlier work to flesh out the timings and primary details. The pamphlet was printed in London, probably a copy of some lost Royalist version.

28   Walker, pp.59-60.

> I shall only observe and leave it to your Judgment, Whether His Majesty could any longer delay, by the Example of one, to terrifie all mutinous Spirits …

The King did not delay: when the army formed up at Coryton Down on 8th August, the same date as that borne by the letter, Wilmot was arrested and sent to Exeter under guard. Unsurprisingly, the combined Royalist armies were stunned at the arrest of one of their generals. Evidently the King was, as Walker suggests, fearful of an outright mutiny: immediately after Wilmot's removal he personally rode out in front of the assembled cavalry and told them that with Rupert's agreement George Goring, previously a commander under the Marquess of Newcastle, had been made a general of the horse. For the time being, however, Wilmot had not been deprived of his office. The latter assurance seems to have been crucial in preventing trouble, as Wilmot was well-liked. Walker states that Charles was accompanied by 'the Principal Officers of his Army', but whether that included senior infantry officers such as Lisle, is not known. Richard Symonds, a trooper himself, was tight-lipped about the affair, remarking only that:

> This morning the Lord Willmott, Leift.-General of the horse, was comitted … Goring was made generall of the King's horse this morning.[29]

Both Clarendon and the Irish cavalry officer Daniel O'Neill suggest that Digby and Wilmot had fallen out – presumably over Wilmot's petition to have Digby removed from the Council of War – and that Digby had turned the King against him;[30] Richard Bulstrode, Wilmot's Adjutant, also mentions Digby in connection with the affair (despite placing the blame on Goring).[31] Certainly the plan had been in motion since at least late July, when Digby explicitly spoke of it in a letter to Rupert (then at Chester), noting that Goring was already on his way via Bristol;[32] Rupert's biographer Frank Kitson goes further, stating that the Prince had known of the King's uneasiness about Wilmot since June, which coincides with Wilmot's involvement in the initial loss of Abingdon in the last days of May;[33] Ronald Hutton, in the ODNB, believes that the King's animosity went back as far as 1641, when Wilmot voted for the Earl of Strafford's execution.

Thus Goring had arrived at Boconnoc the evening before the arrest. Lisle and his fellow officers at the headquarters cannot have remained unaware, although

---

29   *Diarye*, p.49.
30   Digby's 1924 biographer cites part of a letter from O'Neill to the Earl of Ormond, written at Boconnoc in August, in which he tells of his despair that despite his best efforts his two friends are irreconcilable (D. Townsend, p.58).
31   Bulstrode, *Memoirs And Reflections …*, p.114.
32   Digby's letter was dated 27th July; Warburton, vol. III, pp.2-3, fn.
33   *Prince Rupert. Portrait of a Soldier*, p.210.

Bulstrode is clear that nobody had guessed the true reason for his coming.[34] The atmosphere in the army's upper ranks on the night of 7th August must have been febrile, particularly if the 'busie spirit' behind the Essex letter was already touting for signatures. The letter was dated the next day, the same as Wilmot's arrest, but was not sent until the evening of the 9th;[35] it is not clear whether Charles knew of it before the arrest or why he gave his assent to its subsequent delivery. It was published twice, once in Walker's account, and also as a pamphlet at Oxford: on both occasions it was accompanied by a full list of signatories, although they appear in a slightly different order and it is difficult to ascertain who signed earliest.[36] As Stephen Ede-Borrett notes, the Journal of the House of Lords contains yet a third version of the list, where the names are not only in a different order but are accompanied by a further eight names omitted by Walker and the Oxford pamphlet.[37] The seventy-eight signatures in Walker's version – which given his role as the King's chief chronicler is probably the most reliable – appear in three columns: if they accurately reflect the order of signing, Lisle was the fifty-first officer out of the seventy-eight to add his name (fifty-eighth in the Oxford version). This would suggest his was not one of the early 'hands' that Walker says were added to the letter before the King knew about it; in fact Goring himself was the forty-sixth (or fifty-fourth) officer to sign, and as he had only just arrived and was at that moment being publicly illuminated by the King's approval, it is inconceivable that he would have added his name to a decidedly murky enterprise of which the King was unaware. Whilst the precise order of names cannot be confirmed, signing only after the King had indicated consent was almost certainly the majority position amongst Charles's officers; for Lisle in particular it fits entirely with what in the long view appears to be a very clear trait of his: utter obedience to the King and his legitimately appointed officers, in their particular order, and to no-one else.

On 9th August, the same day the Essex letter was sent, Wilmot's officers presented a petition to the King: styling themselves 'your Maiesties old Officers of Horse', they declared that they had followed Wilmot's orders in good faith, and requesting he explain the reasoning for their former commander's arrest 'that they may not have reason to suspect themselves partakers of his crimes'.[38] The King responded, giving a full account of the charges, which were summed up in a long first sentence as Wilmot having:

---

34   The Duke of Richmond, in a letter to Rupert written just after the event, says, 'That which has lately happened, that was here least expected, was the making my Lord Wilmot prisoner and giving Goring the command of the horse …' (Warburton, vol. III, p.7).

35   Symonds, *Diarye*, p.53.

36   *The Letters From His Maiesty* … It carries some minor differences in name order, but substantially it uses the same format as Walker. Notably, in the pamphlet Lisle's name is spelled 'Lisley'.

37   'The Signatories to the Letter to the Earl of Essex', *Arquebusier* vol. XXIII, no. 5.

38   Warburton includes a full list of the forty-four officers who signed the letter (vol. III, p.17).

endevoured principally these three months last past to possesse the officers of his Majesties Army with disvalue and contempt of his Maiesties person, and with prejudice against the sincerity of his intentions for the good of his people, and endevoured (as far as in him lay) to draw men to revolt from their alleagance.

A more specific list of the charges followed. The 'Old Horse' letter, the King's response and Wilmot's answer to the charges were published in London on 30th August. How printer Francis Leach obtained them is not known.[39] A few weeks later the King permitted Wilmot to retire to France, pending a trial. None was ever held, the monarch being overtaken by events.[40]

According to Symonds, Essex responded promptly to the Royalist officers' letter the next morning, 10th August, 'about ten of the clock'; as before he made no attempt to address the content in detail, stating merely that:

In the beginning of your Letter you express by what Authority you send it. I having no Power from the Parliament (who have employed me) to Treat, cannot give way to it without breach of Trust.[41]

Walker comments that:

This short and unexpected Answer produced this Good, that it gave His Majesty and Army assurance that there was no other way but by Force to reduce these Rebels.[42]

The response of Lisle and the other signatories to Essex's dismissal of their extended hand is not known; perhaps a mixture of anger and dismay that the fighting and destruction must continue, and hot anticipation that with the inevitable destruction of Essex's army, Parliament would finally be put in its place. Certainly Sir Ralph Hopton, in a contemporary letter to Rupert, speaks of Essex's responses 'inflaming Our Army'.[43] It is not so incredible that the officers could have expected Essex to give way: as experienced soldiers they would not have offered

39 *The Accusation Given by His Maiestie Against the Lord Wilmot* …Walker mentions the three documents in the same breath, which confirms that the London pamphlet was no clever fake; however he does not state whether a Royalist version was printed at Oxford.

40 Bulstrode reports that Wilmot was later instrumental in spiriting Charles II to France after the battle of Worcester, and his disgrace under Charles I was put down to Goring's influence on the King (Bulstrode, *Memoirs And Reflections* …, p.115).

41 *The Letters From His Maiesty* …, p.9.

42 Walker, p.61.

43 Manuscript letter, Cornwall Records Office, Truro; R(S) 1/1-58. Included in full by Stephen Ede-Borrett, *Lostwithiel 1644*, pp.77-79.

their signatures unless they really thought that the Earl was strategically in such dire straits that his only sensible option was to honourably surrender or join his forces with the King. Essex had already proved that tactical foresight was not his strong point, however. His increasingly desperate situation was largely of his own making, which by now he must have understood; unless he benefited from a rapid change of fortune in events he could *not* control, such as the adverse winds presently preventing his full resupply, the most likely outcomes for his army now were surrender or a messy and probably fruitless defence. A third option, going over to the King, was (as stated) tactically highly risky if not personally suicidal; seemingly incapable of the flashes of military brilliance that Rupert or Waller might have brought to bear on the situation, Essex's choice was to sit tight and brazen things out, although he later claimed – not unreasonably – that the local topography prevented serious fighting and reduced the standoff to a game of 'he who can subsist longest'.[44] Lieutenant General John Middleton was gradually heading west though Dorset with some cavalry, ostensibly to provide relief, but realistically he was unlikely to provide the Earl with a lifeline.

Lostwithiel

A week or so previously the Royalist cavalry had raided a nearby great house at Boconnoc and captured a number of senior Parliamentarians as they dined. It is appropriate to note the principal officer in this design, an Italian professional soldier named Bernard Gascoyne: he was almost certainly unacquainted with Lisle at the time, but four years later their paths were to cross in the most desperate of circumstances. The King subsequently took over the house at Boconnoc as his headquarters. On 11th August he was visited by Sir Richard Grenville, who had just taken Bodmin, and the same day took possession of Lord Robartes' house three miles south of the town, at Lanhydrock. That night Essex's forces bowed to the inevitable and abandoned nearby Respryn bridge, which crossed the river Fowey between Grenville and the King; Grenville secured it, completing the line of communication between Lanhydrock and Boconnoc. The Royalist position now consisted of a north-west to south-east line between the two; their enemy lay a mile and half to the south-west around Lostwithiel, at Restormel Castle to its north, and some rising ground across the river to the east. Their cavalry had secured the road to the vital outpost at Fowey port, two to three miles due south, at the base of a deep coastal canyon on the river Fowey's west bank. Walker states that the King had secured several vital positions along the Fowey's east bank, opposite and to the north of the town, notably including Polruan Castle at the mouth of the river: which, once manned with guns, effectively prevented Essex's forces on the other side receiving resupply even if the winds became favourable. They

44   *A Perfect Diurnall …*, p.458.

also secured the eastern ends of both local ferry crossings on that stretch of the river, preventing the Earl potentially using these to evacuate his troops or bring in provisions. Essex was trapped. Walker thought it 'miraculously strange' that the Earl had not secured such positions himself and preserved his line of supply, and observed that 'we had little to do but to expect the Event', that being the enemy's starvation and disintegration.

Meanwhile the King was still restructuring the head of his army. On 14th August, Walker says:

> His Majesty ordered the Lord Percy to resign his Commission of General of the Ordnance, and then conferred that Place on the Lord Hopton.[45]

Contemporary sources do not specify the reason for Percy's fall, but most historians take it to be his closeness to Wilmot. Clarendon says that Percy was 'as much inclined to mutiny as the lord Wilmot', but this oft-quoted statement is usually dismissed as personal spite. For a final reshuffle, Charles was also inclined to replace Lord Forth, his aged lord general, with Prince Rupert, but for the moment this did not occur.[46]

Apart from this incident, in mid-August Walker can record 'no account of any memorable Action, for at least eight days together.' The army was not idle, however, Grenville pushing his forces 'nearer the enemy on the west side of the river', and the Royalists standing to arms throughout a wet and blustery night on the 14th;[47] a pity they could not know, and be cheered by, the news that during that day Middleton had suffered a setback at Bridgwater, when 500 of his cavalry – attempting to disrupt the King's supply lines – were lured into a trap by local Royalists, routed, and the force destroyed. Middleton subsequently retreated, finally putting to flight any serious chance of Essex being rescued overland.

The weather continued very wet. On Saturday 17th August, after the King had inspected the east bank positions and narrowly missed becoming a casualty of enemy musketeers across the river, Walker reports that:

> His Majesty came back to Boconnock, and the next Day advised with His Council what was now to be done, for as yet we saw little Fruit of the posture we were in, and less Prejudice done to the Rebels …[48]

---

45   Walker, p.65.
46   For Clarendon's comments on Percy, see Book VIII, 1840 vol. IV, p.497. A letter of Digby's to Rupert, dated 15th August, stated that Percy was voluntarily 'withdrawing himself, upon good advice'; this letter is also that which reveals Charles' intentions to remove Forth, 'as soon as he shall find means to satisfy the old general, that it may be no disgrace to him.' (Warburton, vol. III, p.12).
47   Symonds, *Diarye*, p.55.
48   Walker, p.66.

It is reasonable to suppose that the feelings of Charles's senior officers arriving at the council of war may well have been those of mounting frustration: besides being on constant alert and enduring the continual discomfort of inclement coastal weather, their enemy was a sitting duck who refused to treat, and Royalist intelligence must been bringing in tales of the Londoners' growing supply short-ages – Symonds mentions two deserters bringing such news on Friday 16th – yet the King's armies had made no major move on Essex for a week, despite repeated alarms including one on Boconnoc itself. Possibly the rain was a delaying factor, swelling streams and blocking roads; Stuart Reid suggests the delay was due to Forth methodically bringing together the strands of the three armies' advance;[49] yet it is difficult to ignore the habit of Charles and his closest strategists to procras-tinate whenever an important military movement needed to be made, as had occurred at Worcester and Buckingham in June. Now, however, whether due to the culmination of Forth's preparations, upward pressure from wearied officers to nail the business, to military advisors suddenly seeing the possibility of an immi-nent victory, or – as *Mercurius Aulicus* suggests – to the worsening weather, there was suddenly action.[50] Walker reports that:

> it was unanimously concluded that we should draw all our Horse and Foot out of our Quarters, and Sir Richard Greenvile should do the like from Lanhetherock, and then march nearer to the Rebels on every side, and either engage them to fight, or place our Quarters so near theirs, as to keep them to greater Duties, or to take other Opportunities when we should see the Place on which they lay.

After three more days' delay, calling straggling infantry to their colours on Tuesday and awaiting outlying cavalry from Liskeard, the King's combined forces finally made their move at 5 a.m. on Wednesday 21st. The weather was foggy, allowing the Royalists to attack with complete surprise. In a coordinated single advance, all parts of the King's line moved together: Grenville quickly forced a novice regiment on Essex's left wing to abandon Restormel, and took possession of a ford over the adjacent river Fowey. Meanwhile, Walker says, over to the east Maurice's forces and the Oxford Army 'marched in Battalia' up onto a hill between Boconnoc and Lostwithiel: a long, high outcrop which gave way to a broad plain that dropped westwards towards the river and the town. Along the river's eastern edge were several smaller hills, along which Essex had ranged his infantry. At the northern end of the Royalist outcrop was an area nowadays called 'Druid's Hill', 'the lower part of which were less than Musquet Shot of the Rebels',[51] and

49   Reid, p.179.
50   Week 36 (1644), p.1150.
51   Walker, p.67.

at the southern end another summit referred to by both Essex and Walker as '[The] Beacon Hill'. Two commanded parties of 1,000 foot, one led by a colonel of Maurice's and the other by Matthew Appleyard, took possession of these respective points and were the focus of the enemy's half-hearted response throughout that day, which mostly seems to have been badly-aimed cannon shot; there were few casualties. Meanwhile the rest of the Royalist infantry formed up between them on the ridge, flanked with cavalry and supported by the Earl of Cleveland's cavalry brigade to the rear, as a reserve. No action of the main body is recorded, if any occurred; in the evening the Oxford Army withdrew back down to Boconnoc, while Maurice's forces held the high ground; they used the darkness to plant artillery '[in] the closes on the hills of the left and right side of the playne that goes down to Listithiel'.[52]

Low-level fighting continued throughout 22nd and 23rd of August, both at Grenville's position and on the plain. Overnight on the 22nd some part of the force, perhaps Appleyard's or men from the artillery train, had 'made a worke twenty yards square' on or just to the west of the summit of Beacon Hill, which Essex's men fired at on the morning of the 23rd, tricked by the mist into thinking it was a body of cavalry.[53] The weather was still variable, as Symonds reports 'This halfe of the day fine, four in the morning till twelve'; and 'mornings and evenings very misty; through the night starlight.' Walker describes the enemy positions that day, as seen from the hill:

> The most of their Foot being placed on two rising Grounds, the one opposite to our new Fort, and the other to Prince Maurice's Quarter, and within little more than Musquet Shot from either. All or the greatest part of their Horse were quartered beyond Listithiel to the West …

It seems that the King was present on the hill that afternoon, as this survey of Essex's positions, and the distance observed between his cavalry and infantry, gave rise to the idea that Prince Maurice should attack the nearest enemy positions to Druid's Hill; besides, Walker adds:

> His Majesty had good Reason to endeavour to bring it to a speedy Issue; for his Army (especially the Cornish) was much diminished, Provisions grew short, and Middleton was then coming on our Backs, to the Relief of Essex.[54]

---

52 Symonds, *Diarye*, p.57.
53 *Ibid*. Symonds makes it clear that the fortification was on Appleyard's hill, as he states that it was 'on the top of the hill aforesaid next to the said chappel' where he previously places Appleyard's commanded men.
54 Walker, p.67. This is one of the few examples of the Royalists admitting they, too, were short on provisions; in his letter to Rupert in early or mid August, the Duke of Richmond outlines the standoff

Middleton, of course, had retreated, but the King was apparently still unaware. There and then he held an impromptu 'Council of War in the Field; of the Principal Officers of both Armys', where it was decided that Maurice and Grenville would attack early on Saturday morning, with the Oxford Army ready to second them if necessary. When Charles arrived on the hill at dawn, however, he found the plan on hold for reasons Walker either did not remember or chose not to specify. The King approved a secondary plan to send Goring westward to St Blazey, around the back of the enemy; yet he still favoured the former scheme and ordered that Maurice's attempt should be repeated the next morning.

While the armies endured yet another slow day on the hill, Symonds records a sudden intensive effort from the enemy artillery to remove the Beacon Hill fortification, but 'No harme: wee gott many of their bullets.' Walker, clearly still struck by Essex's lack of strategic initiative, comments that:

> … if the Rebels had but made a Work, or kept the Beacon Hill, which was easie for them to have done for at least ten Days before, we could not have held the Ground we had got.

Back in the reign of King James the young Laurence Lisle, familiar with the court and Households and carving out a lucrative niche for himself there, would have been very familiar with Essex's character and reputation; not to mention that he was also publishing items for Essex's ex-wife, and may have gleaned all kinds of subtle information not known to us now. We can only guess at whether Laurence had ever talked of this with George, and whether George, waiting out August on a rainswept hill above Lostwithiel in 1644, remembered his father's opinions of the man and formed a few of his own.

Hopes of a quick resolution must have been raised when on Saturday afternoon, Symonds notes, the King was informed that the enemy appeared to have gone. However the planned Royalist advance on Sunday dawn was delayed by many hours, again for unspecified reasons, and by the time Maurice signalled his readiness to the waiting King at noon, it was clear that the Parliamentarians had not gone but merely 'hid from the danger of our battery', had discovered the planned raid and readied a response.[55] The raid was abandoned and the secondary design involving Goring put into action: he was sent round to St Blazey with all but 500 of the horse, and 1,500 foot under Sir Thomas Basset. An anonymous Parliamentarian officer reported that:

> … that partee marched towards a place called Blazey Bridge, about three miles from Lestithiel, which they did, to stop the passage of Provision

with Essex and admits 'it is likely we may want victuals before him.' (Warburton, vol. III, p.8).
55   Symonds, *Diarye*, p.58.

from Milly-Billy Bay, if they could, from comming to my Lord General: for by taking it, my Lord could not have provisions, but by breaking through them.[56]

'Milly-Billy' was Menabilly, on the same headland as Fowey, but a couple of miles west. The large bay to *its* west is home to both St Austell and the tiny port of Par, the latter of which, Walker adds, Goring took possession of, 'whereby he took from them the chief place of Landing any Provisions from the Sea …'[57] The seizure is explained by a letter which arrived in London around 6th September and was read in the House of Commons. It speaks of St Austell being well-provisioned, and supplies being bought there with Parliamentarian money from Plymouth; the supplies must have then been ferried eastward around what is now known as Carlyon Bay to Par, close to Essex's position, hence the Royalist intent to cut it off.[58]

Essex sent reinforcements to St Blazey, his first positive military action; the skirmishing there lasted several days, but neither side made much headway. Now even Walker voiced the army's frustration:

Five days were now past before we had any Assurance that this dividing of our Force would produce any good Effect; besides the season of the Year, and illness of the Weather in that narrow Country, made us impatient, and wearied our Expectations.

Yet Essex's campaign was now indisputably in its death throes. With no sign of relief by sea he finally conceded, although with what pressure from his officers we do not know, that it was finally time to effect his own withdrawal and save what he could of the army. On 30th August, Walker reports, two deserters gave notice that Balfour intended to break out of the closing Royalist net with the army's 2,000 or more cavalry. The King's military machine acted quickly, sending its own horse to intercept them and sending messages eastward that the Tamar bridges were to be broken; it took time to assemble the army from its scattered quarters, however.[59] Balfour's force roared through Sir Ralph Hopton's helpless pickets on the Liskeard road at dawn, and despite a few hopeful volleys of shot, and a belated hard pursuit by the Earl of Cleveland's brigade against his rearguard, Balfour brought his troopers safely to Plymouth with minimal casualties. The Royalist message to destroy the bridges arrived too late.[60]

---

56 *The Copie of A Letter From The Lord Generall his Quarters …*
57 Walker, p.69.
58 *A Perfect Diurnall*, Numb. 58, p.263.
59 Clarendon insinuates that Goring was too busy carousing to organise a proper pursuit (Book VIII, 1840 vol. IV, p.512).
60 Cleveland's detailed account of the pursuit is included by Walker, pp.70-73.

Meanwhile, after kicking their heels for several weeks on the Boconnoc estate or in local billets, Lisle and the Oxford foot finally had the promise of action. Symonds says that after the deserters gave the alarm:

> General notice was given thereof at one of the clock in the night. His troop and the Queen's troop came to Bocconnoc, whither came newes that the enemyes horse were then upon the downe and coming up betweene the hills where our whole army's leaguer was, but most of our foote were stragling, 3 parts of 4 …[61]

The next morning, as Cleveland rushed to pursue the fleeing horse, Walker – who had presumably accompanied the King to the fort at Beacon Hill – describes viewing the enemy across the valley below:

> … their Foot [was] drawn through the Town of Listithiel into some high fields towards Foy. Here His Majesty stayed until His Army could be drawn out of their Quarters and ready to march; a Party being sent down to possess the Bridge of Listithiel, which the Rebels were breaking: but they were quickly forced thence, making little Opposition.[62]

As Grenville's forces approached from the other side of town, he and some cavalry who had ridden down with the King forced Essex's foot to withdraw further towards Fowey, where the Earl was perhaps still vainly hoping for a miracle evacuation by sea. After 2 p.m. the rest of the Royalist foot finally arrived; by now Essex had been pushed back almost to the river, in an east-west line centring on Castle Dore and the vital Fowey road. Intense skirmishing continued throughout the day, the Parliamentarians literally fighting for their lives but gradually being compacted into an ever smaller area of ground. Undoubtedly the Oxford foot must have played some part, but it is not mentioned specifically by Symonds or Walker. By early evening, however, Symonds says:

> Now was our foot in great bodyes gott upon the high hill just in the narrowest passage of land between Trewardreth parish church and the passage over the river which run by Listithiel.

'Great bodyes' suggests the greater part of the Royalist foot, and may offer a clue as to where Lisle spent the latter half of the day. Symonds continues:

61 *Diarye*, p.62.
62 Walker, p.74.

Just at 6 of the clock the enemy made a very bold charge both of cannon, muskets, and horse, to gaine this hill … but were valliantly beat off, and our men not onely keeping both but gott some ground also: this heate lasted about an howre …

At the end of the short encounter at the hill, which may have been Lisle's only hot service in the Cornwall campaign, the Parliamentarians were driven back by fresh Royalist cavalry: as his men routed and the line crumbled to the left and right of him, Essex found himself isolated and moved those men under his command eastward across the road to close up the line, and join the artillery train on some high ground. In the early hours of 1st September he gave orders to move the army and artillery train further towards the coast, but was soon advised by his General of the Ordnance that the army was too fragile to reposition, and that in any case, complete encirclement was now inevitable. Other advisors told him that the only way to save the army now was to treat with the King, and it would be easier to do that if Essex was not present.[63] To his credit, Essex took that advice and accepted that his part in the game was over: with Lord Robartes and one other officer he immediately found himself a boat and escaped towards Plymouth.[64]

No source states precisely when it was that the Royalists discovered his departure, but when the news eventually broke the mood must, again, have been mixed: elation that his departure surely meant the end of his army, and perhaps a permanent upswing in the King's fortunes; yet also raw frustration that such an eminent prey had been so close to the snare, yet had managed to evade it. Certainly nobody would have known about the Earl's leaving by early the next morning, Sunday 1st September, when the King held another council of war which decided to rest the army and prepare for an assault on the penned-up enemy foot on Monday. The assault was not to be, however: later on Sunday Essex's own lieutenant colonel came to the King and asked for a parley. Walker confirms that the request was granted and a ceasefire called; overall responsibility for the Parliamentarian surrender fell to Skippon. His first set of terms were rejected, probably because they demanded that the army should march away with all its baggage, arms and artillery;[65] after

63 *Attestation of the Officers of the Army concerning their Disaster in Cornwall* …; presumably intended for the Parliament's eyes, the *Attestation* relates events at Lostwithiel from the officers; point of view. It is supportive of Essex. Letter dated September 3rd 1644; printed in Rushworth's *Historical Collections*, 1691, part III, vol. II, pp.708-709 (viewed via British History Online; original page number not given).

64 Essex's biographer Robert Codrington, he who gives so much detail about the Earl's relief of Gloucester the previous year, understandably skates over most of the Cornish campaign, giving it no more than a couple of broad-brush pages and emphasising how the Earl was let down by the lack of supplies and men. Of the escape to Plymouth he says that Essex took a boat from Fowey, 'and the Seas danced to receive him whom our land was not worthy of.' (Codrington, p.47).

65 Interestingly these initial terms (included by Walker, pp.76-77) also demanded that Essex should have forty-eight hours to ratify them; this was impossible, because he was then on a boat on his way to Plymouth. When examined later, Skippon told Parliament that 'his Excellencies absence was no

further negotiations it was agreed that the force should march away only with its officers' personal weapons, their own servants, horses and belongings, and any money and provisions Plymouth cared to send them. They would then march towards Poole and Wareham with a protective convoy, and could then pass on to Southampton or Portsmouth. There is no evidence that the opportunity to wait for supplies was taken up, and the best explanation for this is that the local Cornish would no longer tolerate the army's presence: for despite its cavalry escort, the retreating army was looted not only by Royalist soldiers,[66] but by the inhabitants it had itself so freely looted over the previous weeks. Richard Symonds had predicted as much, saying beforehand, ' 'tis conceived very few will gett safe to London, for the country people whome they have in all the march so plundered and robd, that they will have their pennyworths out of them.'[67] By the time it reached Poole, attacked also by the twin military terrors of disease and desertion, its numbers had reportedly dwindled by perhaps two thirds to around a couple of thousand. The King's triumphant forces also headed eastwards again, to squeeze what advantage they could from the greatest, yet most easily won, Royalist victory of the civil wars.

disadvantage to the Treaty' but this is understandable if his absence was still not known to the Royalists. As Essex had previously refused to respond to even personal overtures from the King, it is easy to believe that the Royalist negotiators would not expect him to be involved in the surrender, and so perhaps never asked where he was.

66   Walker (p.80) insists that 'all the chief Officers of the Army used their utmost endeavours to prevent it'; Symonds (*Diarye*, p.66) says that the King gave strict orders against plunder, 'Yet notwithstanding our officers with their swords drawne did perpetually beate off our foot, many of them lost their hatts, &c.' He adds that 'The rebells told us as they passt that our officers and gentlemen carried themselves honourably, but they were hard dealt withall by the common soldjers.' Essex himself acknowledges the officers' efforts to prevent plunder, in a letter to the Committee of Both Kingdoms on 14th September (*CSP Domestic Series*, 1644, p.502).

67   *Ibid.*, p.67.

10

A Good Holland Shirt: Newbury II

The overwhelming impression of the Cornwall campaign, in terms of how it must have been experienced by the majority of the Oxford Army infantry, is one of tedium: an endless march west, and then rain-soaked inaction for another month while only a tiny portion of the combined foot was involved in minor skirmishing with a dispirited enemy, and internecine politics saturated the court at Boconnoc. Lisle may have been particularly frustrated: having to watch Colonel Appleyard fulfilling the military role Lisle had performed in so well since Chalgrove, while he remained on hand near Boconnoc waiting for orders, his proximity exposing him to the political hurricane thrown up by Wilmot and Digby.

Lisle: politics and ambition

George Lisle does not seem to have engaged in politics: at least, there is no surviving evidence that he deliberately tried to engage with the political set around the King, or worked to improve his own social and material position through opportune contact with the foremost men in the kingdom. In that period it was certainly possible to do so, as his father had proved, but unlike Laurence – a shrewd businessman and seizer of opportunities – it does not seem to have been George's driving motivation, at least during the war. A pamphlet published three months after his death describes him as 'an excellent distinguisher of Societies; using ever to consort with those most, where he hoped to be improved best', but whilst this does hold echoes of Laurence's ability to keep 'in' with the most useful people – Buckingham being the prime example – the pamphlet in George's case seems to suggest a desire for self-improvement in practical skills, rather than social or financial advancement.[1] His rapid ascent from colonel to tercio commander and then, albeit briefly, lieutenant general, suggests not only great military skill but a willingness to advance and to accept greater challenges. Whilst this could be framed as 'military ambition' it is as well to remember that, demonstrably, Lisle

---

1 *The Loyall Sacrifice*, November 1648, p.62.

was primarily focused on doing the best job he could, to preserve his King, not lining himself up for a future career.

A popular assumption about Lisle, which seems to float around his name without obvious historical basis, is that he was in Rupert's political circle. Indeed, politically Lisle and Prince Rupert seem to have been agreeable in that neither appreciated politicians such as Culpepper, who supported negotiation; both intently pursued whatever military goal was set in front of them, Rupert with his seemingly limitless natural energy, and Lisle with his obdurate determination to see even the most challenging tasks through to completion. Rupert would have greatly appreciated Lisle's abilities, particularly as his forte lay in the sort of dynamic skirmishing at which the Prince himself excelled, and it is possible that Lisle had encountered him in some military context abroad. Yet there is scant evidence of him being close to the Prince. Of his brief service as a garrison governor under Rupert in 1644/45, there is no suggestion that it stemmed from political proximity; in fact there is nothing at all to suggest that his appointment was awarded for any reason other than merit. If he actively 'followed' Rupert at all, it was almost certainly because he saw him as an ideal military commander from whom he could – as the 1648 pamphlet puts it – 'consort with those most, where he hoped to be improved best'.[2]

Although no correspondence sent to him is known to survive, if Lisle had made any concerted bid for social or political preferment then his own letters would have left some trace in the numerous surviving archives of knights, lords and senior royal servants. Yet besides a few operational letters to Rupert, nothing has been noted. In 1648 he was recorded by a third party as saying that the King was his 'Prince and Master' and that he was happy to die 'for the service of my country':[3] he comes across as conservative, an adherent of 'divine right' and absolute monarchy, fighting for his sovereign's preservation, and driven by irreconcilable disagreement with those intent on altering the King's role or removing him altogether. This is merely well-informed supposition, however: as far as is presently known, he left no personal written confirmation of his motives. By the end of 1645 Charles had bestowed several honours on him, but he initially turned down the first, the second was probably a compensatory sop for loss of position, and the bestowal of the third appears to be related to Laurence's pre-war employment in the Royal Household.

The long march home; Parliament gathers its forces

In Cornwall, the eventual chasing of Essex's army to Fowey and the resolving action in the dying moments of August were brief and intense, and probably particularly bloody as the King's wet, hungry and under-employed soldiers finally

---

2   Rupert's 'clique', as far as it relates to Lisle, is examined in chapter 11.
3   *The Clarke Papers*, vol. II, p.33.

met their enemy *en masse* and at close quarters. Yet despite their proverbial victory on a plate, Essex had escaped and now there was the prospect of an exhausting march home. The victory was won and the fighting season's natural end in sight, but the campaigning was far from finished. Despite the arrival of the devastating news that York had surrendered, and also that Oxford's encircling garrisons badly needed the return of the King's southern armies – Basing and Banbury were under siege, and Donnington Castle was threatened – Charles's return march from Cornwall, though constant, was by necessity not hasty. Although he personally rested at Exeter from around the 17th-23rd September,[4] after which he moved to Chard, the armies marched throughout and took no break until they joined him at Chard at around the same time. Both he and they paused there until the 30th, which Walker insists was essential, as the armies were physically in a bad way and haemorrhaging men. His insistence that this 'growing Evil' needed urgent attention seems genuine: in a letter to Rupert written as the army left Cornwall, Goring had told the Prince that

> This is the most mutinous army that ever I saw; not only horse, but foot: though I believe it is rather their poverty and fear than any general dislike of the remove of officers.[5]

Discipline was breaking down, as evidenced by both Walker's and Essex's later statements that the King's officers had strenuously tried, but failed, to prevent plunder of Essex's defeated army.[6] At Chard the King and his council ordered the men reclothed for the winter, without which, Walker adds, 'the Army would not have been well pleased to have gone away.' Unlike Goring he only hints at the extent of their discontent, and perhaps the hope that new clothes might go some way to preventing more of the homesick and unpaid in the ranks from deserting in the face of a gathering enemy. Walker reports the diminishing force as only 5,500 foot and 4,000 horse across the two armies; the infantry numbers now well below the 8,500 he himself quoted at their conjunction at Crediton on 27th July, and the 10,000 the King believed he had at Launceston on 1st August.[7] The numbers

---

4   Walker, p.88; Warburton, vol. III, p.4; Symonds, *Diarye*, p.97. Symonds states that the move to Chard was on the 24th.

5   Warburton, vol. III, p.16.

6   See end of chapter 9.

7   Walker, p.98 and p.87 respectively. His July figures are corroborated by a correspondent Warburton believes to be the Duke of Richmond, who in early August told Rupert that the King had 9,000 infantry (Warburton, vol. III, p.8, fn.). The King's reckoning of 10,000 foot is given by Symonds (*Diarye*, p.45); Digby agrees with the King's figure in a letter to Rupert on 15th August (Warburton, vol. III, p.11). Sir Richard Grenville reportedly had around 3,000 men during the campaign (see Digby, same letter), but they had mostly disbanded after its conclusion and Grenville was left behind with a small force to blockade Plymouth.

given for Lisle's shrunken tercio at Newbury a few weeks later support Walker's assertion.

Meanwhile, Richard Symonds reports, Sir William Waller had moved into Dorset and was raising cavalry just fourteen miles away at Bridport.[8] Walker insists that Charles's slow march was due to practical reasons rather than fear of the enemy, and that if his army had not been forced to rest, he would instead have 'put the Issue of His Majesty's Affairs to the Uncertainty of a Battel'.[9] He believed that in any case Waller appeared only to be observing the Royalists' movements, 'dislodging' as they advanced; Waller offers a different perspective, telling the Committee of Both Kingdoms on 14th September how Dorset was bare of recruits, and on the 15th that:

> Truly, my Lords, I am in a very weak condition, having nothing with me but my Lieut.-General's party, which is about 1,500 horse and 800 dragoons, besides those poor troops which I brought with me. I have not one horse come to me, either out of Wilts, or this county [Dorset], to mount a musketeer, so that if the King advance all that I can do is but to retire, before I be forced to run.[10]

The previous day Essex had remarked to the Committee about the arrival in Southampton of the destitute dregs of his army from Fowey, declared that he would not send yet more money and food to Plymouth, and reminded Westminster of 'the bleeding condition of the army';[11] a flurry of Committee letters in the State Papers at this time reveals frantic redistribution of clothes, victuals and reinforcements between garrisons. Evidently both sides were primarily occupied with keeping their exhausted armies together and not being caught off guard; it seems neither was satisfactorily informed about the other's size, position or condition. Captain John Gwyn, who we last saw at Newbury I, speaks of 'great want of intelligence'.[12] Battle between them at one location or another was already inevitable, however, as the Parliament's southern forces were rapidly coalescing: the Earl of Manchester,

8   *Diarye*, p.97. Walker adds that Middleton was with him (Walker, p.88). Christopher Scott, in his recent Newbury battlefield guide, notes that since June Waller's infantry had been gradually peeled away and put into garrison, so that by September he commanded only horse (C. Scott, *The Battles of Newbury*, p.69).
9   Walker, p.89.
10 *CSP Domestic Series*, 1644, p.506.
11 *Ibid.*, pp.502-503. His letter of explanation would have crossed with a noticeably uptight one written in London the same day, advising that it was aware he had stopped the provisions and ordering him to give way and send them on. The exchange developed into a bureaucratic standoff which lasted until Plymouth was relieved.
12 Gwyn, p.48. Just prior to Newbury I Gwyn's commander Sir Thomas Salusbury had died, and his new colonel was Charles Lloyd. Lloyd's regiment (as it now was) being part of the former Reading garrison, was now part of Lisle's tercio.

having brought his forces south after York's surrender, was presently at Reading with 4,000 foot and 2,000 horse and dragoons;[13] another 5,000 comprising five Trained Band units were preparing to leave London;[14] additionally the re-equipped remnants of Essex's tattered army were expected to join them from Portsmouth, as were Middleton's forces from the west.

During his stay at Chard the King met with Rupert, who had made his way down through the Welsh Marches with the remnants of the Northern Horse. While he quartered at Bristol Sir Marmaduke Langdale and 2,000 cavalry waited in Monmouthshire, and Charles Gerard with 2,000-3,000 foot waited in South Wales. Rupert and the King decided to combine all these forces with the Oxford-Maurice army.[15]

On 30th September, the day he and his force finally continued eastward, the King issued a proclamation declaring that he intended to march for London with the aim of obtaining a peace treaty, and summoning his subjects to rise up and support him.[16] He complained that he had not received a reply to an offer of negotiation sent to the Parliament from Evesham on 4th July; London's *Mercurius Civicus* reports the arrival of the July document during the second week of September – suspiciously late, even during a wet summer in wartime, for an official document on a five or six day journey from the King – and dismisses it as 'specious pretences of affection to peace'.[17]

On 5th October Rupert left his uncle and returned to Bristol to summon Langdale and Charles Gerard. The King was presently in Dorset, where after Rupert's departure he was informed that Banbury, Basing and Donnington were on the cusp of being lost; he summoned Rupert to meet him again at Salisbury the following week with 'what strength of horse and foot you can',[18] and also sent Sir Bernard Astley with 600 foot and the Earl of Cleveland and his cavalry to relieve

13 As of 22nd September; letter from the Committee of Both Kingdoms to the Earl of Essex, *CSP Domestic Series,* 1644, p.521.

14 Walter Money gives both Manchester's and the Trained Bands' strengths as 5,000 each, although he does not specify his sources (*The First and Second Battles of Newbury* …, p.140). The imminent departure of the Trained Bands was noted on 26th September (*CSP Domestic Series,* 1644, p.535); they were ordered to leave for Colnbrook on 11th October, and on the 16th to join the Earl of Manchester (*CSP Domestic Series,* 1644-1645, p.30, 48).

15 Gerard had been lieutenant general of Wales since May, and had secured it sufficiently that the King was able to call him eastward again now, to assist him.

16 *By the King. A Proclamation declaring His Majesties Resolution for settling a speedy Peace* …; Wing C25577. Walker also reproduces it (pp.96-98).

17 Numb. 69, p.651. The distance from Evesham to London is roughly 115 miles. A mounted messenger and escort could easily manage this in under a week.

18 Warburton, vol. III, pp.26-27.

the Royalist garrison at Portland.[19] *Mercurius Aulicus* reports their success on 12th October.[20]

The King finally reached Salisbury on what Symonds says was a 'wett, cold, and wyndy' 15th October and was given details of the rapid assembling of Parliament's forces around Reading and Basing. He also received word that Rupert's reinforcements could not reach him in time for such a sudden advance against the enemy; with hopes of facing his outnumbering enemies presently dashed, Charles abandoned his plan to march on London and determined to relieve his garrisons and then go into winter quarters. Already, in early September, Colonel Henry Gage had miraculously managed to deliver vital supplies to the beleaguered Basing House garrison, but Basing remained under tight siege well into November. General Goring offered a solution: attack Sir William Waller, who had reportedly retreated to Andover, seventeen miles north-east of the King, and prevent him joining Essex and Manchester. This Royalist advance would draw the Parliamentarian forces together, away from their respective sieges, and then the King could withdraw and wait for Rupert's reinforcements. The attack, on Friday 18th October, was a complete success: although Waller withdrew most of his army when he saw the strength of the attackers, the cavalry and dragoons left as a rearguard were chased through Andover and utterly routed. This successful pursuit was not all good news, as Walker points out, as retreat and rout rather than destruction meant that Waller's army was not rendered incapable of fighting later.[21]

Buoyed by the success at Andover, the King abandoned Goring's plan to retreat and wait for Rupert: after advancing to Andover he continued eastwards to Whitchurch, halfway between Andover and Basing, and decided to bring his entire force forward with him to await the enemy response. Walker admits this was widely considered unwise:

> for now we were engaged and could not in Honour retreat; neither could we give any Relief to Basing, the Rebels then lying about it. As for Banbury, we might as well have endeavoured to raise that Siege by Forces sent from Andover; and Dennington then needed not any Assistance, the Rebels being drawn thence the Friday before (the Notice of which came to His Majesty whilst he lay at Whitchurch) yet nothing but the Consequence made this an Oversight.[22]

In regard to the reasoning behind it, he adds:

---

19 Richard Symonds says Astley took 3,000 foot, but this must be a mistake as it would represent more than half the King's available force (Symonds, *Diarye*, p.127).

20 Week 42 (1644), p.1202. Walker gives a few more details in his account, but confesses that he does not have the full story of the action (p.104).

21 Walker gives a full account of the action, pp.105-106.

22 Walker, p.107.

We then concluding our selves not much overpowered by their Forces united; so as although we would not voluntarily attempt them, yet we would not avoid them if they sought us out.

As noted, however, the Royalists *were* significantly outnumbered. Besides the forces already named, Lieutenant General Oliver Cromwell, who had been at the siege of Banbury, had since brought his cavalry brigade to join Manchester at Reading; in turn, Manchester's entire force now moved to join Essex and Waller at Basing. In total, Cromwell stated later, the army numbered 'neare 11,000 foote and about 8,000 horse and dragoones.'[23] Unaware, the King continued his pursuit throughout Saturday the 19th, although he paused on Sunday to wait for Lord Forth, who for some reason lagged behind, and to await the return of the Portland force. Symonds notes that it was still raining. A party of horse was sent to relieve Donnington Castle, but discovered that the siege had been lifted; Walker claims that in nineteen days the attackers had 'spent 1000 great Shot, and done very little hurt to the defendants.' The castle was in a bad way, however, the attackers having 'overthrown three Towers and a part of the Wall.'[24]

On Monday 21st the armies moved seven or eight miles north to Sydmonton, where they held a general rendezvous. The King quartered at nearby Kingsclere, his intention being to attempt the relief of Basing House the next day; Essex, Manchester and Waller had now converged on the house, however, and after a party of Waller's horse captured sixty prisoners in or near Kingsclere in an overnight raid, Charles considered his position too exposed. The next day he moved north towards Newbury, for the present leaving Basing to its fate.[25] The next day the Royalist armies held a general rendezvous at Red Heath, south-west of the previous year's battle site at Wash Common; the Earl of Northampton, with a large party of horse, was sent relieve his brother at Banbury, while the King knighted John Boys for his defence of Donnington.[26]

---

23   Quoted by Money, p.142, fn.; Professor Malcolm Wanklyn believes Cromwell overestimated (*Decisive Battles*, p.145). Despite the appearance of cooperation, there were at the time numerous rifts amongst the Parliament's military commanders and their supporters in the Commons. Cromwell and Manchester were at odds, for example, as were Commissary-General Behr and Lieutenant General Middleton, and of course Waller and Essex. It was also widely known that there were designs afoot against Essex in the Commons, which may or may not have contributed to his failure in Cornwall. There is no scope to examine these politics in this book, but readers should bear them in mind, and consider reading the CSP for September and October 1644 to gain an understanding of the frustration expressed by the Committee of Both Kingdoms as it tried to mediate between all the parties involved.

24   Walker, pp.107-108.

25   Symonds (p.142) explicitly says the three commanders 'made assault' on Basing, but nothing about this is reported in the State Papers. A letter to the Committee of Both Kingdoms, written by one of its members the next day, confirms the details of the raid on Kingsclere (*CSP Domestic Series,* 1644-1645, p.65).

26   Northampton was successful, albeit with help from Langdale and Gerard (Warburton, vol. III, p.28; Warburton does not give his source for their involvement).

Lisle does not seem to have been involved with any of the foregoing activity: he was not on the expedition to Portland, and although some infantry did join the Earl of Northampton in relieving Banbury, it came directly from Oxford under the command of hero-of-the-hour Colonel Gage. By all accounts both the Andover attack force and the Donnington party consisted purely of cavalry. It was Symonds who reported that Lord Forth had trailed behind the army; possibly some minor military action had occurred of which we are not aware and with which, potentially, Lisle could have been involved. Unfortunately Forth's delay is more likely to be related to an entry Symonds had made two weeks previously, on 9th October, when he records that '[the] Lord Generall broke his shoulder.'[27] However, Lisle's summer of inaction was shortly to come to a dramatic conclusion.

Newbury II: topography and battle dispositions

For several days the King quartered at Newbury while the army waited near the site of the battle the previous year. His next move was uncertain: he still intended to relieve Basing but could not while Northampton's force was still at Banbury and Rupert had not arrived with reinforcements. Charles had promised not to fight until Rupert arrived, but keeping that promise would now be tricky. Charles did not believe his enemies would attack him at Newbury, perhaps because he was mistaken about the size of their forces, but also because Newbury was reasonably defensible due to local topography, including the river Kennet. However he could not have accounted for the actions of Sir John Hurry, the regular turncoat who on 30th July had been officially discharged from Royalist employ by Rupert at Chester; it appears that he was still hanging around the army while waiting for a secondary pass, and having then been captured in Hampshire he reportedly informed the Parliament of everything he knew about the King's strength. Walker says that:

> Here though it concern a private Person, I cannot but mention that from hence Collonel Hurry had his Pass to go beyond the Seas; but he made use of it no farther than to the Rebels Army, to whose Service he again returned; of whom I shall say no more but that a Turncoat Souldier can hardly prove an honest man.[28]

---

27 *Diarye*, p.124 and p.142 respectively. Forth was around seventy and had existing health problems: transporting him on churned up autumn roads with a broken shoulder would have been a slow and painful process.

28 Walker, p.104. For a transcription of Hurry's pass see Macray, *Letters and Papers of Patrick Ruthven …*, p.162. London newsbook *Mercurius Civicus* reports that his quarters were captured by Waller on 7th October, and he was taken to London (*Civicus* Numb. 72, p.673); Waller discusses his fate with the Committee of Both Kingdoms at around this time (see *CSP Domestic* 1644-45), and it seems he was paroled on condition that he once again work for Parliament.

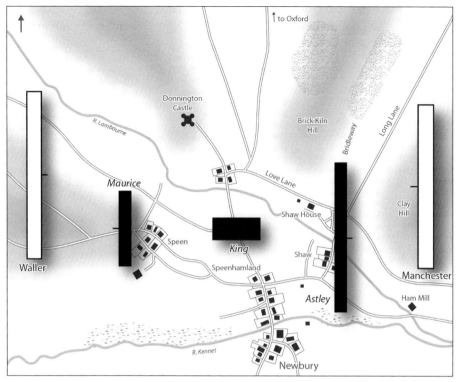

Map 3 The Second Battle of Newbury, 27 October 1644. Lisle was stationed at Shaw House, on the Royalist right wing.

Realising that the King was outnumbered and not in a position to attack, his enemies 'quickly apprehended this Opportunity', and on Tuesday 22nd withdrew from Basing and moved twelve miles north to Aldermaston Manor (or 'Aldermaston Park'),[29] adjacent to Padworth ford on the river Kennet just east of Newbury. Symonds reports that in response the Royalists marched north overnight, across the river towards Donnington, but backtracked in the morning when the Parliamentarians appeared to retreat.[30] The 'retreat' was probably a report that Essex and the Earl of Manchester, with the bulk of the foot, had not followed their horse to Aldermaston but struck east to Swallowfield, south of Reading; the army spent the night there, one of many delays on Manchester's part that prompted

---

29 Richard Bulstrode, *Memoirs and Reflections …*, p.117

30 *Diarye*, pp.143-144. A London newsbook asserts that in fact the King was unable to reach Oxford 'by reason of the great flouds', and indeed this might also have been a factor (*The True Informer*, Numb. 51 (1644), p.384).

Cromwell to lay charges against him in 1645.[31] However Vernon F. Snow, Essex's 1970 biographer, asserts that in fact the Earl had instructions from the Council of War to travel via Reading and attack Newbury from the north-east, although he gives no source reference for these instructions and they do not fit with Cromwell's understanding of the plan to intercept the King. In the event, Essex, who had been unwell for over a week, set out again from Reading with his forces on the 25th but could not continue and had to be persuaded to return to the town.[32] The Parliamentarian cavalry waiting near Newbury were not deterred, however. *Mercurius Aulicus* reports that 'On Thursday night they came privately over the water at a ford neare Padworth …'[33] Moving five miles north-west the combined forces held a rendezvous at Bucklebury, but 'severall parties' making an attempt on the quarters of the Royalist horse further west were repulsed.

By way of setting the scene, we may recall from the previous battle at Newbury that the town straddles the river Kennet, flanked north and south by rising ground; Donnington Castle lies a mile and a half away, on that rising ground to the north. Symonds confirms these southern and northern boundaries of the Royalist quarters, noting that on the 25th 'The King's army was drawne out upon the bottome between Newbury and Denington Castle'; he omits to add that in the west-east direction the Royalists commanded a two-mile stretch between the villages of Speen and Shaw – Newbury lay between them and slightly south – and that to the east and north-east of Shaw lay more steeply rising ground and a summit called Clay Hill (known at the time as Highdike).[34] Explaining the roundabout approach from Bucklebury, Parliamentarian cavalry colonel Edmund Ludlow reports:

> The River that ran through the Town defended the Enemy on the South-side of it, so that we could not come at them: And on the North-west part of it, within Cannon-shot, lay Dennington-Castle, in which they had

---

31   Money reproduces an extract from 'Cromwell. The Information against the Earl of Manchester', much of which can be found in the *CSP Domestic Series* 1644-1645, pp.146-161. The particular extract Money provides is not to be found there, however: whilst he wrote it in 1884, the CSP was not printed until 1890, therefore he must have looked at an original paper that was abridged or not included in the later publication. Manchester's decision to divert was not unsupported, however: both the author of *The Parliament Scout* (Numb. 71) and Sir Archibald Johnstone, the representative from the Committee of Both Kingdoms (*CSP op. cit.*, p.62, pp.66-67), were with the foot and speak of foul weather and lack of supplies.

32   From Portsmouth on 15th October Essex wrote to the Committee of Both Kingdoms, to say he had 'suffered from indisposition' since Friday 11th (*CSP Domestic Series* 1644-1645, p.44). Snow quotes a fragment of a report that says he had 'excessive flux and vomiting' (*Essex the Rebel*, p.461). *The Parliament Scout* states that he was 'ill of a Boyl, and some other distemper, [and] was perswaded at last to return to Redding.' (Numb. 71, p.567).

33   Week 44 (1644), p.1232. Christopher Scott, in his 2008 battlefield guide to the Newbury battles, says that the ford was at Lodge Farm (C. Scott, p.75).

34   Examination of Captain John Hooper; *CSP Domestic Series,* 1644-1645, p.149.

placed a Garison; so that we had not other way to the Town, but on the North-East of it …

It is not clear whether the King's forces had crossed back to the southern bank of the Kennet, to Red Heath, after the curtailed night march on the 23rd, but if so they were back on the north side by the morning of Friday 25th.[35] Sporadic skirmishing occurred between the 25th and 27th, the principal day of battle, but it is not clear when the various elements of the Royalist forces took up their final positions.

The Royalist account of Newbury II preferred here is primarily that of *Aulicus*, as it is so detailed, and reads so much like a primary eyewitness account from a non-combatant – particularly when it describes the action around Mr Dolman's house ('Shaw House') – that one wonders if once again Berkenhead was present at the action.[36] If he was not, then certainly a very observant agent was. Walker also gives a good report, but was writing a few months later and clearly based his text on the newsbook, whereby he omits some useful detail, although he is good in summary. John Gwyn, of Colonel Lloyd's regiment in Lisle's tercio, gives a brief, disordered account that cannot be used as narrative but gives several eyewitness details that are essential to understanding how the battle at Shaw unfolded. Of secondary sources, the earliest comprehensive study was Walter Money's *The First and Second Battles of Newbury*, written in 1881 and revised in 1884. Whilst Money had access to vital information about local topography which is now lost to us due to development of the town, and uncovered some fascinating fragments of local history pertinent to the battle in 1644, he includes several errors that make a diligent reader wary of his overall analysis; although the value of his work presently outweighs the queries. The text of his second edition is referred to here, so as to account for any corrections he inserted in the revision.[37] Modern analyses have come from Professor Malcolm Wanklyn (2006), Christopher Scott (2008), and John Barratt (2010). Scott's work is primarily a battlefield guide, but is very helpful in understanding the basics of the battle and the much changed locality where it took place.[38]

Of the contemporary Royalist sources Walker certainly gives the most concise breakdown of the final Royalist dispositions: the King was in Newbury, with

---

35   It was also risky for the army to remain south of the town: as Wanklyn points out, the open land around Greenham was tempting to enemy cavalry and the bridge at Newbury too narrow to accommodate a fast retreat over the Kennet (Wanklyn, pp.145-146).

36   Week 44 (1644); the account occupies most of this issue of the newsbook.

37   Readers should also be cautious of Money's foldout battle plan, which places Lisle on the wrong side of the Lambourn, and includes a positioning for 'Lucas', presumably Sir Charles, who was at that time in the Tower.

38   Wanklyn, *Decisive Battles of the English Civil War*; C. Scott, *The Battles of Newbury. Crossroads of the English Civil War*.

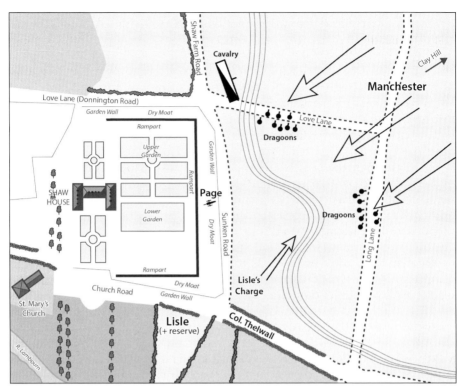

Map 4 Lisle's position at Shaw House during the Second Battle of Newbury, 27 October 1644.

'strong guards on the south part of town'; and a 'work' had been cast up at a mill on the Kennet to the east.[39] On the King's left hand lay all of Prince Maurice's infantry at Speen, with some of the Western horse; and on his right hand, directly north of Shaw, lay the artillery and the rest of the horse.[40] Walker names three other points of defence at the eastern end of the line:

> the greatest part of his Army was placed towards the Rebels Quarters, as Mr. Doleman's House at Shaw, in the Village near it, defended by the River that runs under Dennington Castle, [and] in a House between that Village and Newbery …

39 Ham Mill; nearby was a major bridge which the Royalists broke down to hinder their enemy's movements.
40 These cavalry fields are now the site of a multinational telecomms company, the modern buildings of which are clearly visible on aerial photographs, and therefore very useful in pinpointing the adjacent Shaw House.

This second river was the tiny Lambourn, a shallow chalk stream flowing south-east to its nearby junction with the Kennet. It flowed south-east, just a couple of hundred yards south of Dolman's house, and whilst a newsbook that week said it was swollen with rain, so would have given good protection on that side, it was no defence against the enemy massing on Clay hill to the north-east.[41] Shaw village was a few hundred yards south-east of the house, and is as Walker describes immediately adjacent to the Lambourn: the river runs directly through the centre of the village. The 'House between that Village and Newbery', which Gwyn's editor calls 'a castellated and moated mansion, called Stone-House', appears to have been somewhere nearby, south of the river but fairly close to it and not far from the centuries-old mill;[42] Money notes that 'This entrenched house formerly stood at the south-east angle of Shaw Park', which would indeed put it near to where Shaw Road crosses the Lambourn on its way to Newbury.[43] Malcolm Wanklyn believes there was a second crossing at the mill, but probably no more than a footbridge.[44]

Shaw House is a large 'H' shape Elizabethan mansion built in 1581. Known at the time only as 'Mr Dolman's house', it faces very slightly to the south-west: the King's cavalry and artillery lay in the fields behind it and the greater part of the Parliamentarian army, on the high ground to the east and north-east, faced the end of its east wing, and its north-eastern corner to the rear. George Lisle was in charge of the house and the north bank of the Lambourn, between the house and the village; in turn he was under the wider command of Sir Jacob Astley, Sergeant Major General of all the foot. Ludlow states that the house had 'a Rampart of Earth about it';[45] Money says it was built by the Royalists, but they would barely have had forty-eight hours to build it, and while the contemporary accounts suggest filling in of hedge gaps and building barricades, they do not mention a massive earth-moving project around the three sides of the garden for which much of the infantry would have been required.[46] Almost certainly the rampart was constructed when the house was built: as by the 1580s there was no need for a private English house to be genuinely fortified, the rampart must have been a decorative feature or a practical measure to keep roaming livestock from the gardens. The original three-sided rampart still exists, perhaps eight to ten feet high in most places, and

41 *Perfect Passages*, Numb. 2, p.17. The author states that the Royalists having pulled up Thatcham Bridge, near Ham Mill on the Kennet, 'our Pioners are laying the Bridge againe, because the waters are too high to passe over the Fords.'

42 Gwyn, p.55, fn.; Gwyn's 1822 editor says Page was posted here, but is contradicted by the numerous contemporary references that place him at Shaw House.

43 Money, p.153. 'The Old Mill' which is found in Shaw today is not the original building, but a replacement from 1760. The entrenchments around the long-vanished Stone House were still visible in Money's time.

44 Wanklyn, p.139.

45 *Memoirs* vol. I, p.111.

46 Money, p.152.

encompasses the entire eastern garden.[47] In 1644 the garden area was probably laid out formally, intended to be admired from the grand first floor window in the stairwell at the end of the east wing; today it is simply a large open lawn. Nowadays the encompassing rampart is topped by trees, but as in 1644 the house was only sixty-four years old, there would be nothing ancient there; perhaps some smaller or middling trees as a decorative screen, or a hedge, or a combination of both.

The rampart was not the garden boundary, however: parallel to it on the northern, eastern and southern sides lay what Gwyn called a 'dry moate', bounded on its outer side by a brick wall. The moat is still visible today: the northern side has been built on, the 80 foot wide eastern side is a car park, and the southern side is now a wide lawn that runs parallel with the road on that side. Compared to the rampart the moat is fairly shallow, but was probably deeper in 1644. The encircling wall was banked, at least on its outer side: Money says that 'a sunken road … with a raised bank on each side' ran down the eastern portion. He recounts that when the eastern wall was taken down early in the nineteenth century, 'several human skeletons were met with; and a 6lb cannon-ball was found firmly imbedded in the brickwork.' The fact that a ball could be lodged without being discovered for 200 years, or indeed knocking down the wall in the first instance, confirms that the brickwork must have been protected by grass and earth.[48] As Gwyn states that artillery and musketeers defended the moat, the wall must have been of significant width along the top, or nobody would have been able to lodge there, to fire from it, or indeed set up cannon there. He also states that Lieutenant Colonel Richard Page, stationed in the moat, fired through 'pailes', meaning there was either a fence along the top of the wall, or fixed into the bank. This may have been a last-minute addition by the Royalists, to give the defenders some cover.

Only the northern stretch of wall survives today, six to seven feet high, although whether it was that height originally is unknown. It looks to have been extensively patched up or possibly even rebuilt; it borders a lane (today called 'Love Lane'; then known only as the Donnington road), beyond which were more fields, mostly now built on. The road surface may have been slightly lower in 1644, and perhaps banked like its now-vanished counterpart on the eastern side. The field immediately to the east of the sunken road, down which Manchester's infantry advanced, is now a modern housing estate. It is small, only 200 yards in length; to reach it the attackers had to descend Clay Hill, then get across Long Lane (the modern B4009) on its eastern side, or Love Lane on the northern. This square field was set diagonally across a slope, meaning the north-eastern corner at the Love

---

47   Scott, p.82. Money says the rampart was 'still well defined' at the time he wrote in 1884 (fn., p.171), confirming (in case there were any doubt) that the rampart existing today is not merely a feature thrown up in the last century. However, owners of the house subsequent to the Dolmans may have substantially repaired or reinforced the original.

48   Money, p.172.

Lane-Long Lane junction was higher than the south-west, down by the junction of Church Road and the sunken road at the corner of the garden wall. Towards its centre the field abruptly bulged upwards towards the north-eastern corner, into what Money calls 'a hillock', and he believes the Royalists erected a barricade here. However this would put the defenders immediately in the path of Page's short-range guns on the eastern garden wall only a hundred yards away. Money provides no diagram or photograph to explain his supposition, and can only say that the feature '*has the appearance* of having been artificially raised for defence'.[49] A water tower was built on this rise in the later seventeenth century or early eighteenth, and it seems more likely that any earth-moving in this area to build up the hillock was connected to this construction.

Both Godson's 1730 map and the 1817 Ordnance Survey indicate a second track or lane running north-south down from the high ground (today called Shaw Farm Road; in earlier centuries the property was 'Red Farm'), intersecting with Love Lane at the corner of the garden wall and passing down the house's eastern boundary – Money's 'sunken road' – before meeting another, west-east, lane and taking a sharp easterly turn towards Shaw village. This lane, known today as Church Road, ran along the garden's southern boundary from the ancient Saxon church of St Mary at its western end, to Shaw village at its eastern end.[50] The line of the sunken road still exists, but only as a tiny footpath between the Shaw House boundary and the new housing.

Although we have much fragmentary information about the location of particular officers and regiments around Shaw, we have no formal plan of battle. Page's position at the house is plain enough; it is Gwyn who tells us he had 400 men and some leather guns 'loaden with key-shot' (probably 'case shot') in the dry moat.[51] Page would have to use them judiciously, however: leather guns had a short firing life, as they quickly overheated and became too dangerous to load. Adjacent to Page, starting at the sunken road and extending the defensive line into Shaw village, was Colonel Thelwall. He commanded a long hedge that ran along the southern edge of the small field: Gwyn says 'Colonel Thelwell was making up of the gaps in the quickset-hedge, which he was to maintaine, and making of the ditch under it deeper and wider'. He had been ordered 'not to give fire upon the enemy until they came within a pike's length of him', although it is not clear if

---

49 *Ibid.*, p.171, fn.; emphasis added.
50 The Saxon church was pulled down in 1840 and replaced. The original building had a round tower, which given the church's proximity to the house might well have been manned for lookout or defence in 1644. According to the old maps, 'Church Road' used to terminate at St Mary's, but in modern times has been extended to access a school built to the west of the house.
51 These may well have been the leather guns captured at Cropredy in June, when the Royalist cavalry overran Waller's artillery park and took 'two Barricades of Wood drawn with Wheels, in each seven small brass and leathern Guns, charged with case shot' (see chapter 8).

there were actually pikemen in the hedge with his musketeers.[52] His men must also have held Shaw village, and may have sent out small parties among the lanes and hedges to the north of the house. As noted, although in overall command, Lisle also seems to have taken charge of some men behind Thelwall, on the north bank of the Lambourn; it was a relatively confined area with the house wall just across the lane to the north, the church to the west, and only a hundred yards of sloping ground to the south, between Lisle and the swollen river. Gwyn also speaks of 'two hundred horse, commanded by Sir George Lysle, in the interval between Dolman's House and the field Thelwall was in.' The cavalry action occurred largely to the north of the house, but perhaps Gwyn means it also covered the sunken road along the house's eastern boundary; the horse regiment was Prince Charles's, commanded by Sir John Browne. Extending the line further, Sir Bernard Astley's tercio covered the area across the river south of Shaw, and the road between Shaw and Newbury. *Aulicus* states that he had 400 men at the fortified Stone House; his task was to prevent incursions into Speenhamland behind him, a large area of open land to the west where the King was stationed. *Aulicus* also says that besides the cavalry, Lisle had at his disposal Sir Thomas Hooper and Prince Rupert's dragoons, who were 'to keep the hedges and lane', presumably meaning Long Lane and Love Lane, and the hedges that separated them from Clay Hill.

Manchester's men, if they pushed over the lanes, would not easily be able to assault the garden wall directly due to Page's guns and musketeers. As it seems there were no breaks in it, the only way to reach the house would be either to head westwards along Love Lane and face the cavalry, dragoons, and Page's men manning the northern wall and rampart; or head for the south-western corner of the small field, where Page's and Thelwall's commands joined, and break through there into what is now Church Road. Latterly some men did, and an intrepid minority got into the gardens; some may have survived the artillery on the eastern side and made an attempt on the wall. Gwyn's account confirms that the above positioning of Page, Thelwall and Lisle must be correct, as he later states that Manchester's men:

> could [not] come to charge Sir George Lysle but through the enemy's fire, for Sir Richard Page, with his leather guns, loaden with key-shot, and his four hundred musketters in the dry moate, plaid between the pailes upon the flanks of them; and Thelwell, with his body of musketters, likewise played through the quickset-hedge in their teeth, that made a heavy slaughter among them, maymed and so disabled them, that they came in disorder to charge Sir George Lysle, which made him the better able to defend himself against so powerful an opposition.[53]

52 Gwyn, p.55.
53 *Ibid.*

Lisle held back some reserves. Gwyn states that Thelwall commanded 800 men, but *Aulicus* that 300 only came forward later, indicating that at the outset Thelwall had only 500 in the hedgerow and the village. Combined with Page's 400, the 1,200 total under Lisle made up just under half of what his tercio had been in April. At Newbury it comprised nine regiments, which from the rounded total of 1,200 given at the time gives a theoretical average of 133 men per regiment. If we apply this average to Astley's tercio (11 regiments × 133 = 1463) and Blague's, at that time westward in the centre of the line with the King (7 regiments × 133 = 931), the total number of Oxford army foot present would be a little under 3,600, and 3,500 is the presumably rounded figure Walker gives for the Oxford army a few weeks earlier at Chard. Moreover, the ratio of Lisle's available foot at Newbury (the approximate 1,200), to the Earl of Manchester's reputed 7,000-strong infantry would be a little under seven to one, which tallies nicely with Gwyn's observation of Parliament 'having on their side more than six to one the odds of it'.[54]

Whilst the figures are not precise, as we have no muster rolls and contemporary commentators rounded larger numbers up or down, the general direction of the sum cannot be disputed: Lisle's tercio in October was half the size it had been in April, when Symonds' figures put it at over 2,700. In part the shrinkage was due to Sir Jacob Astley's and Page's regiments (approximately 700 men, on April numbers) transferring to fight under Blagge at Newbury;[55] but that still leaves a deficit of nearly 900 men whose absence can only be accounted for by battle, desertion and sickness. In the hedge ahead of Lisle, when the battle began, Thelwall stood with his initial 500; in the gardens was his 300-strong reserve, and Page's 400 manning the house, rampart, garden walls and undoubtedly anywhere else where they could easily get off a shot at the enemy. Gwyn does not say whether Lisle specifically led his own party or attended to the fight himself as needed, in his capacity as the local commander, but there is no room in the above calculations to extract another command of usable size. He does say that Lisle had a reserve, however: Lord Hopton, whose men must have come from Sir Bernard Astley's tercio, of which his regiment was part. It is logical that these were the men waiting in the riverside enclosures, behind Thelwall. However, as there was no fat to spare on army numbers they cannot have been many, perhaps a couple of hundred.

Lisle's own regiment is virtually absent from surviving records in 1644: besides its fleeting stay at Abingdon in June we have no sight of it during the summer campaign, although it must have been in Cornwall with the rest of his tercio. Lisle had become a tercio commander soon after taking over from Bolle, and it is not clear how much time he had spent with his own men. At Cheriton and Dudley he

---

54 *Ibid.*, p.56.
55 Page was Pennyman's lieutenant colonel: why he remained with Lisle at Shaw is not known, but it was probably down to logistical necessity on the day. Pennyman retired shortly afterwards and Page took over the regiment.

led commanded men not necessarily from his own regiment, so unless he and they fought a significant action together at Cropredy or in Cornwall of which we are presently unaware, Newbury may have been the first occasion on which the entire regiment fought with its colonel at close quarters.

Newbury II: the battle on the Royalist right

The battle that took place at Newbury on 27th October was hard fought all along the Royalist line, but this account will focus on the eastern end of it, where Lisle was stationed.

Aulicus records that the first tentative clash of arms occurred at around noon on Friday 25th, whereby the enemy:

> drew down their whole Army between Thatcham and Shaw; whence by diverse strong parties they attempted to have forced the Horse quarters at Shaw, but were met by part of Prince Maurice his Regiment of Horse, which skirmished with them, kill'd some of them, and then drew back to a field before Shaw, leaving some Foot and Dragoones to dispute the Hill, which (according to Order) was done till Midnight.

Walker clarifies that the enemy had attempted to gain Clay Hill, and that despite preventing them from doing so, the Royalists were withdrawn down to Shaw 'in the Night … by order'.[56] The identity of the foot who assisted Maurice's horse in this action is not known, so there is every possibility that Lisle may have been involved. As Maurice was later stationed on the King's left wing, it may be that the armies had not yet taken up their final positions at this early stage. Symonds adds:

> Toward night both sides fired upon one another from the hedges on their side of the river. Wee at night retired to the passe and kept it all night; by that meanes there was shooting all night.[57]

If Symonds was still referring to the exploratory action between Thatcham and Shaw, 'The passe' must mean the narrow corridor of low-lying land between the Kennet and the rising ground to its north that overlooks Shaw. Thatcham lies further to the east along this corridor, which tallies with *Aulicus*; the adjacent rivers were in spate, and the Royalists' pulling up of the bridge there would have hindered Parliamentarian movements.[58]

---

56   Walker, p.110.
57   *Diarye*, p.145.
58   *Perfect Passages*, Numb. 2, p.17; *A Diary, or an Exact Journall*, Numb. 25, p.184.

Mercurius Aulicus reveals that 'the greater part of the [Parliamentarian] Army seeing it impossible to engage them without much hazzard' decided to split the force and make joint attacks on the King's west and east;[59] they were also concerned about Prince Rupert being able to approach from the west with his reinforcements, and the Earl of Northampton being able to rejoin the King's force from Banbury. On the morning of Saturday 26th the Parliamentarians took cannon and infantry up the now vacant hill, and according to *Aulicus* 'shot with their great Ordnance all afternoon, but effected nothing.' It was a not a one-sided firefight: Symonds says that 'Cannon on both sides played very much.' Scott notes that this high ground also overlooked the Oxford Road which ran north out of Donnington to the west, effectively preventing the King's use of it and cutting him off from his headquarters.[60] During the artillery exchange, which was undoubtedly partly diversionary, Sir William Waller took Balfour, Skippon and around half of the combined forces on a long march around the high ground north of Newbury, to the north-west of the King – *Aulicus* says, via Winterborne and Boxford – with the intention of falling on Charles from that direction and attacking his left wing at Speen. From Boxford the Lambourn valley runs south-east towards Donnington and Newbury, presenting Waller with an easy advance towards his target. Money says the Royalists had sent horse detachments north-west to Boxford and Bagnor, to guard fords over the Lambourn, but does not give his sources.[61]

The action began in earnest in the early morning of Sunday 27th October. *Aulicus* says that 'above Eleven hundred' men, which he names as 'the Earle of Manchesters Army & London Trainedbands', descended Clay Hill, crossed the Lambourn, and surprised a party of Royalists at Shaw mill;[62] Symonds states that it was a tercio, who '[came] over a bridge they made in the night, intending to surprize one of our guards.' He adds that the surprised Royalists retreated to Astley at Stone House, and under his command the attackers were seen off.[63] Astley then routed two more bodies of attackers who, *Aulicus* reports, reportedly fled back across the river 'in such distraction and confusion, that abundance of them were drown'd …' Normally it would be difficult to drown in a chalk stream, but the Lambourn was

---

59   Numb. 75, pp.528-529.
60   Scott, p.75.
61   Mills existed at both locations, therefore probably crossing points (Boxford Mill is still extant; the mill building at Bagnor is a later replacement that is now a theatre).
62   Most likely they crossed somewhere on the stretch of the Lambourn which nowadays lies between Kiln Road and London Road: this would put them within perhaps 400 or 500 yards of the mill. Although *Aulicus* says that they crossed the Kennet, this does not make sense (as argued elsewhere), as Manchester's men would be too far from Astley at his position at Shaw Mill, and they would have to cross the flooded Kennet twice: firstly to the extreme south-east of Clay Hill, approximately where the railway line now crosses it; and then, having moved north-west again, cross back to the north side, perhaps near where the modern A4 bends south-east as it heads towards Thatcham.
63   Money notes that the house was long gone by the time he wrote (1881, in his first edition), but that the remains of earthworks around it were still visible (p.153).

in spate, and *Aulicus* hints at a fatal stampede that would have killed men on dry land, let alone in several feet of water. Symonds mentions Astley taking 'about 40 prisoners and a 100 armes', and that 'then they lay quiet till 3 afternoone, onely our cannon and theirs playd.'[64]

By 1 p.m. the forces under Waller which had circled around to the north-west of Newbury had brought up all their stragglers and artillery west of Speen, and at around 3 p.m. made their attack on the western end of the Royalist positions. Despite defensive works thrown up there, they pushed the King's forces into a series of retreats which *Aulicus* describes in great detail, and which as Walker describes were eventually halted by:

> two Troops of the Queen's Regiment of Horse, commanded by Sir John Cansfield, with so much Gallantry and Courage, as that the Rebels seeing the King's Guards coming to fall on their Flank, this great Body of their presently fled; we having the Execution of them from thence near half a Mile, wherein we slew most of their Musquetiers and some of their Horse, and put so great a Terror into them, as that they durst not advance again that Night.[65]

This, he adds:

> proved the Safeguard of His Majesty's Person and Army, there being on that side no other Force but His Majesty's Guards to defend them.

Gwyn maintains that 'His Majesty was engaged in his royal person', although how literally he was 'engaged' is not clear:[66] Charles certainly remained in the centre of the line with the Prince of Wales, however, encouraging his men on and intervening to rally men in flight. However, the fight was so intense that not even the sight of their King could stop a whole brigade of horse fleeing from Speen: Walker says they:

> very basely forsook Him and ran into Newbery; out of which they were speedily forced by our Guards placed at the Bridge.

At the same time as the action on the left, more Parliamentarian foot had been deployed in 'certaine Inclosures and ditches' in the fields to the north of Shaw House; they were seconded by the advance of the left wing cavalry, but were

---

64   *Diarye*, p.145.
65   Walker, p.112.
66   Gwyn, p.52.

repulsed by the King's horse in two head-to-head encounters led by General Goring, in which:

> the couragious Earl of Cleveland engaged himself so far, and by the illness of his Horse which fell with him, was taken Prisoner. This Charge was the more gallant, because this Brigade of Horse, not only went over the Ditch to meet the Rebels, but passed by three Bodied of the Rebels Foot, who shot at them both when they pursued the Rebels as they came back.

Cleveland remained a prisoner for the rest of the First Civil War, but was involved in various strands of plotting from the Tower during the second war in 1648. Unlike several other Royalist lords who had been involved, Cleveland was fortunate to escape with his life, fleeing to the Continent in December a few weeks before the beheading of the King.[67]

At around 4 p.m., an hour after the western and northern attacks had got underway, the Earl of Manchester's forces finally descended Clay Hill.[68] By this time, on a late October day probably as dull and damp as the rest of the autumn had been, the daylight would have been receding fast. *Aulicus* says:

> The Rebells (to the number of 1200 Horse and 3000 Foot of the Earle of Manchesters and London Trained-bands) came singing psalms down the hill, and advanced hastily upon Colonell Lisle's guards; at first they fell on a hedge where fourty Musketeers were placed, these Musketeers were easily overpowered by the Rebells, who upon their quitting the hedge gave a great showt.

The advance was challenged by Sir John Browne and Prince Charles's regiment of horse, who 'did very good execution' before retreating from a 1000-strong cavalry charge and instead attacking the enemy foot who had been settled in the hedges beforehand. Manchester's cavalry retreating, Browne attacked them in the rear 'and bravely kept that ground all day.'

At the same time as Browne's action, *Aulicus* continues:

> the Reserve of Foot came on (which was 300 of Colonell Lisle's Tertia commanded by that experienced Souldier Colonell Thelwall) where-unto were joined those Musketeers in the lane and those other fourty

---

67   David L. Smith, Cleveland's ODNB biographer, states that he was at Colchester in 1648, but this is incorrect: he was nearly exchanged for two Parliamentarian prisoners inside the town, but the swap was never completed.

68   Manchester was accused of beginning his attack late; the alleged delay is seen by some commentators, both contemporary and modern, as part of his increasing reluctance to prosecute the war against the King and for which Cromwell later pressed charges.

which were driven from the hedge; and this Body of Foot came up so couragiously and gave such excellent Fire, that the Rebells had small comfort in their new gotten hedge; shot flew extreme thick on both sides, but these gallant Musketeers were resolved to win all or dye in the place; and therefore after they had sufficiently gauled the Rebells with severall brave Volleys, they fell off with butt ends of their Muskets, and beat the Rebells not onely back from the hedge, but quite out of that field (then His Majesties Forces gave a good lowd showt) the Rebells running off in great confusion, leaving both their Colours and Canon behind them …

Meanwhile, at the house:

another great Body of the Rebells Foot fell upon those in Mr Dolmans house, and Garden; upon their approach, a notable Officer of the Rebells came daringly up, and commanded those in the House and garden *not to shoot*; Lieutenant Colonel Page bid his men give fire upon him, who instantly shot this fine Rebell in the belly, so as he never gave more orders; which done, they powred out shot so fast upon the Rebells whole Body, that they begun to runne, His Majesties Forces pursued with exceeding great execution, which was the greater, because the Rebells race was up the Hill. Then His Majesties Souldiers showted again, for the Rebells never gave showt but once, and were now so farre from it, that they left 500 of their brethren dead within a small compasse of ground, where His Majesties Souldiers had much and good pillage, divers Prisoners and some Colours, and then they drew off those two peeces of Canon which they tooke from the Rebells.

Aulicus seems to suggest a lull in the engagement after these two repulses; if so, perhaps the defenders took the chance to ferry the many wounded of both sides into the house. The alleged fate of these injured men later, would affect Lisle directly.

Half an hour after Manchester's men retreated, a body of his horse dared approach the house to attempt recovery of their artillery, but were seen off by musket vollies and retreated back up the hill behind the shelter of their remaining guns. During this incident Colonel Page was 'shot through both his thighes, besides a shot through his arme', although apparently these wounds were not life-threatening. *Aulicus* adds 'indeed, none could doe more gallantly then he did in that place which Colonell Lysle put under his Command.'

It must have been at around this point that, Gwyn notes:

… the King was hotly ingaged in close fight with the other two armies, which were so severe upon him, that he was forst to send for my Lord

Hopton to come to his assistance, who was a reserve to Sir George Lysle; and he could as ill spare him at that time, that it was thought impossible for him to be without him or some other reserve: But that Sir George did wonders to maintain his post with that party of his own men, without a reserve, and so bravely incouraged them to stick close to him (the King being ingaged in the next field in his royal person,) that he threw off his upper garments to charge in his shirt, whereupon they all unanimously, as one man of one mind, resolved to live and die with him upon the spot, fought it courageously, and came off victoriously …[69]

That Lisle had no further reserve, and the very fact that he needed men from outside his own tercio to second his position, is more proof of the reduced size of his forces. *Aulicus* seconds Gwyn's story with a lengthy account of Lisle's personal conduct during the battle, which has become famous:

As for Colonell Lysle himselfe, we professe it troubles us we want language to express his carriage; for he did all things with so much judgement, cheerfulnesse, and present dispatch, as had speciall influence on every common Souldier; taking particular care of all, except himselfe. The truth is, he gave the Rebels three most gallant Charges; In the first his Field word was FOR THE CROWNE, and then he beat them back, and knocked them downe both with Bullet and Musket-stock; In the second, his word was FOR PRINCE CHARLES, and then he cut them off as they came on, and hewed them downe sufficiently as they ran away; In the third, 'twas FOR THE DUKE OF YORK, and then he slasht them so home, that they troubled him no more, for had they come againe, he resolved to have gone over all the Kings Children, till he had not left one Rebell to fight against the Crowne or the Royall Progeny. In which service the Colonell had no Armour on, besides courage and a good cause, and a good Holland shirt; for as he seldome wears defensive Armes, so now he put off his very Buffe Doublet, perhaps to animate his men, that the meanest Souldier might see himselfe better Arm'd then his Colonell, or because 'twas darke they might better discerne him from whom they were to receive both direction and Courage. However, it gave occasion to a Londoner this week in Print to say, *The Irish Papists in the Kings Army at Newbury, had diverse Witches among them, which many of Colonell Cromwells Souldiers did plainly perceive to fly swiftly from one side of the Kings Army to another,* which hath thus much truth in it, that this Spirit, Ghost, (call it what they please) frighted all those guilty Rebells quite out of the field, and made them run for protection to their Canon and main body which got away to

69 Gwyn, p.56.

the hill where they quartered, above a mile from the place of fight, leaving the whole pillage of the field to His Majesties Souldiers without shooting one Musket to disturbe them.

It is fair to say that when Hopton's men were called away, the outcome of the battle depended on George Lisle: he could not single-handedly have won it for the King, but he could certainly have lost it. Thelwall was now the last line of defence, and if his line crumbled with no reserve to plug the gaps, Colonel Page and his contingent at Mr Dolman's would be overwhelmed in minutes by several thousand of Manchester's infantry and the day would be lost. Moreover, Page had just been severely wounded and was probably incapacitated. Lisle *had* to prevail. On the face of it, throwing off his buffcoat and charging into the enemy appears to be a reckless action unsuited to the disciplined persistence he displayed at Cheriton, and his dogged attempts to dislodge the London regiments and their artillery at Newbury I. He was no hothead, but there are possible explanations: spotting some sudden opportunity for advantage; losing his temper; encouraging everyone else (as *Aulicus* suggests); or simply making sure he could be seen. The last two seem most plausible, given Gwyn's statement that Lisle encouraged everyone to stay close. Sunset that day fell at around 4:20 p.m., shortly after Manchester attacked, and the heavy autumn twilight would have quickly descended: dark-clothed men would melt away in the dusk, brighter colours would become indistinct, the fiery discharge from massed muskets and artillery would become visible in the growing gloom and debilitate night vision, besides distracting and confusing. The new danger now, was losing men in the darkness and formations falling apart. The colour white glows eerily bright at dusk: perhaps, as Lisle came up to join Thelwall and surveyed his situation, something white caught his eye and in a flash of inspiration and intense focus on the moment's need he saw the only way to keep his beleaguered soldiers together, and tore off his coat. After charging in his shirt sleeves through the loose formations of tired and outnumbered men, shouting at them to keep together, and drawing their focus towards an unmissable beacon in the dusk – himself – he then bellowed a battle cry and led them personally, three times, uphill, into the opposing infantry. If *Aulicus's* report is accurate, the first charge involved firing whatever ammunition remained, then going in with guns reversed; the second and third charges were straight hand-to-hand attacks, with swords drawn also. That Lisle, in his shirt, was not killed or even seriously wounded in this desperate melee, is nothing short of miraculous. He later spoke of having a 'genius' or guardian spirit: perhaps this was partly due to his survival at Newbury.

Even Symonds, in the cavalry, acknowledges the events at Shaw:

> At the same instant they made as hott an aproach on the other side upon
> Mr. Dolman's howse, which Colonel Lisle kept with a 1000 musqueteeres,

but were beate off, with the losse of their cannon and ground, and ___ prisoners.[70]

Walker omits any description of Lisle's actions, but admits that:

truly very much of our Happiness and Preservation is to be ascribed to the singular Courage and Conduct of Our Forces at Shaw, especially to Collonel Lisle who commanded in chief there, and to Collonel Thelwel, Lieutenant Collonel Page, and the Officers and Souldiers under their Command …[71]

The last word had not quite been had, however: Walker notes that 'it was a fair and Moonshine Night', which elicited one final cavalry charge from the Earl of Manchester's quarters on the house at Shaw. The raid was quickly seen off; and then all was quiet.[72]

Aulicus freely admits that:

The exact number of the slaine is not certainly knowne, for very many of the Rebels dyed that night and the next morning after the Battaile was ended.

The London newsbooks speak of a couple of hundred Royalist dead, and perhaps 300 captured; Sir Archibald Johnstone informed the Committee that 'Skippon guesses the number slain on both sides at between two and three hundred';[73] *Aulicus* admitted to 100 common soldiers and three senior officers on the Royalist side, but insisted 500 of the enemy were killed at the Shaw end of the line alone. If *Aulicus* is not being coy about the facts, the Royalists need not admit to a long list of slain officers, although plenty were badly wounded, including Lord Forth once again in the head. Despite Norman Tucker claiming that Lisle's indispensible officer Anthony Thelwall 'Met death heroically at 2nd Newbury', and P. R. Newman suggesting that if not dead he may have been mortally wounded, in fact it seems he was sent back to Wales with Sir John Owen to help deal with the situation there.[74]

70 *Diarye*, p.145.
71 Walker, p.114.
72 Modern moon-phase datasets agree that on 27th October there was a near-full moon.
73 *CSP Domestic Series,* 1644-1645, p.77.
74 Tucker, *Royalist Officers of North Wales 1642-1660*, p.58; Newman, *Royalist Officers in England and Wales*, p.369. Letters from Rupert to Sir John Owen on 2nd April and 25th June both mention 'Colonel Thelwell' (Warburton, vol. III, p.74, 119). He was arrested in London in September 1648, a few days after Lisle's death, which suggests he may have been in the same circle of Royalist activists; his father then mentions him in his will in 1649 later, proving that Thelwall, at least, avoided Lisle's fate and escaped the war alive (will of John Thelwall senior, written 13th September 1649 and proved in 1652,

One of the regiments in Lisle's tercio, that of Colonel William Eure, also disappears after Newbury. Eure himself had been killed at Marston Moor after returning to the north with his cavalry, and leaving his foot at Oxford; Symonds records the regiment as only 91-strong at Aldbourne in April, and presumably either the long summer campaign or the fury of the season's closing fight at Newbury finished it off.

While Lisle had succeeded in holding his end of the King's line at Shaw, the west end at Speen had taken a severe battering, losing its ground and its artillery. Money suggests that Charles was not aware of Lisle's success at Speen, although it must have been obvious by the fact that the entire army had not been swept away from that direction and the King captured or pursued. Despite Gwyn describing him as 'in the next field' from Lisle, he was in fact some distance away in Speenhamland, and could not have witnessed what occurred; if he had, he may well – as was his habit – have knighted his officer on the spot, rather than waiting another week to offer the honour. On Sunday night the monarch's personal security was the important issue at hand: Walker describes at length how after darkness fell Charles went to Donnington Castle, was apprised of his entire situation, and decided it was too much of a risk to continue the engagement. Before the battle he had planned a march to Wallingford, for which purpose the baggage was already assembled at the castle; he now ordered the army on to Wallingford, but decided he would go to Bath and rendezvous with Rupert. If the army at Newbury was able to retreat intact, he would bring Rupert's forces to join it. As he left, with various servants and a retinue of around 300 horse, the army began to withdraw.

Of course this included Lisle, who now had to leave the house and grounds he and Thelwall had overtly risked their lives to maintain, for which Page was severely wounded, and for which undoubtedly a number of men in the tercio had lost their lives. It must have been a very bitter blow. Walker hints that he understands how they felt, saying that Lisle, Page and Thelwall:

> … likewise made their Retreat, as well as they kept their Ground. For in order to [obey] His Majesty's Commands, about ten of the Clock that Night, all the Army, both Horse, Foot and Cannon was drawn from their several Guards to the Heath about Dennington Castle, wherein they first left most of their wounded Officers, with all the Ordnance, Ammunition and Carriages; and then Prince Maurice, the Lord Goring, the Lord Hopton, and Sir Jacob Astley marched away in good order to Wallingford,

The National Archives; Kew, Prerogative Court of Canterbury and Related Probate Jurisdictions: Will Registers; Class: PROB 11; Piece: 222; arrest, *CSP Domestic Series*, 1648-1649, p.260, 273 'for raising arms against the Parliament' (thanks to Tony Rowland for bringing the arrest to my attention). Tucker and Newman probably took their cue from David Lloyd, who claimed Thelwall was killed at Newbury after not accepting quarter, despite none of the battle sources mentioning his fate (*Memoires … p.661*).

leaving Sir Humphry Bennet (who had behaved himself very well that Day) with his Brigade of Horse to bring up the Rear …[75]

Only the higher-ranking Royalist wounded were removed to Donnington, however. As noted, it seems that many men of both sides wounded at Shaw had been taken into Mr Dolman's house: probably into the main hall, as it is the largest space inside the building. In its 10th November edition a fortnight later *Aulicus* denounces a Parliamentary order to imprison maimed soldiers begging for aid, in case they are Royalists, adding:

And to evince this to the world (the Rebells bloudy disposition as well to their owne creatures as His Majesties good Subjects) we have this day received a most pregnant instance from their friends at Newbury; whence we have it most certainly advertised, that the day after the last Newbury fight, when his Majesties Armey was drawne off, the good Earle of Manchester went into M. Dolemans house in Shaw (near Newbury) where he found some wounded Souldiers: Colonell George Lesle (who so gallantly commanded those Guards the day before) left a note in the house, wherein he certified, *that certaine hurt men (some whereof were His Majesties Souldiers, the rest were Prisoners whom the Colonell tooke in the late fight, which could not at present be removed from that place, without hazzard of the poore mens lives. Therefore he desired all Gentlemen, Officers and Souldiers whom it might concerne, to afford them protection and assistance as he had done, for as much as the poore men were unable to help themselves.* But the Lord Kimbolton and his Rebells, no sooner entred that house, but most barbarously they knockt those poor wretches braines out, not onely his Majesties Souldiers, but their owne men also (for the bloudy fit was now upon them) lifting up boards, breaking down Wainscot, and pulling out the very barres of the windowes, pretending *that His Majesty was concealed in that house, else* (said they) *the Popish Malignants would never have fought so desperately to maintaine it, therefore they vowed to find Him* (the poor mens bloud being not yet dry upon their hands) *else they would put the Maister of the House to death.* In conclusion (ere they left the house) they did all mischiefe imaginable to the owner of it (M. Doleman) leaving him not so much as clothes to put on, nor any thing else either in or about his house.[76]

---

75   Walker, p.115.
76   Week 46 (1644), pp.1254-1256.

Given that Parliamentarian soldiers had reportedly also destroyed the house in Newbury where the King had been staying, and torn up his bed,[77] the above report of the aftermath at Shaw House does not seem far-fetched, although both accounts should be treated with caution as they come from Royalist *Aulicus* and there is no balancing reportage. Author Berkenhead is unlikely to have completely made up either incident, but certainly the seed stories he received would have been spun to suit Royalist sympathies. We also have no secondary or independent corroboration of Lisle's note, although it is entirely in keeping with an officer reportedly always concerned for men's welfare, and who later claimed 'I have given many hundred men quarter'.[78] His feelings about the slaughter of unarmed men he had been forced to leave behind, can only be imagined.

Whilst Lisle was not an overt political player, it is clear that he had strong opinions about the politics going on around him. On 6th November the King's forces gathered to rendezvous south-east of Oxford; Essex's scoutmaster general, Sir Samuel Luke, reporting on the 10th, revealed that the King had knighted two officers at the rendezvous,

> ... and would have knighted Col. Lisle for the good he did at Newbury but he swore he would not be knighted or receive any honour till he was sure to keep it and then he doubted not but he should as well deserve to be a Lord as many that were near his Majesty.[79]

The veracity of this astonishing report will probably never be confirmed, but there was no plausible reason for Luke's man to lie to his master; if someone at Oxford had deliberately fed the agent a lie, it seems odd to attach it to such an uncontroversial officer, one whom Parliament and the London press did not at that time have in their sights. On balance the report was probably true, and assuming the wording was more or less accurate, Lisle's reason for refusal appears twofold. Firstly, regarding the keeping of honours, he was commenting on either the fickleness of royal favour, or the loss of the King's favour due to the hostile actions of political rivals. Secondly he alluded to the behaviour of particular unnamed peers. In the first part he must have been referring to Lord Wilmot's recent removal and the political intrigues in Cornwall which he would have observed at close quarters: certainly Wilmot had not helped his own case, but all contemporary fingers point to Digby as the prime mover in his colleague's eventual downfall, with the King's consent and some level of acquiescence from Rupert. That Lisle would criticise the King's decisions in this matter, or indeed any other, is unlikely in the extreme; most likely he was disgusted by the quarrels and backstabbing that had engulfed

77   *Mercurius Aulicus* Week 44 (1644), p.1241; the 'battle' issue quoted extensively here.
78   *The Loyall Sacrifice*, p.63; *The Clarke Papers*, vol. II, p.38.
79   Luke, *Letter Books*, pp.71-72, letter no. 113.

Boconnoc and endangered the army's stability at a critical moment, and he could not be sure that he himself would not become another target for such behaviour if he accepted an elevation in his own status. The second part of his refusal undoubtedly concerned Sir John Culpepper, he of Charles's council who may have been the Lisle family's erstwhile landlord, and who had been created 'Baron Colepeper of Thoresway' a week or two before the Newbury battle. As David L. Smith, the author of Culpepper's biography in the ODNB explains:

> Colepeper sat in the Oxford parliament and soon found himself at odds with more hardline royalists over whether to pursue further talks with the houses. In the king's council he likewise urged that propositions be sent to Westminster. This did not endear him to more hawkish figures such as Digby and Prince Rupert, and there was considerable resentment at his creation as Baron Colepeper of Thoresway on 21 October 1644.

Lisle could absolutely be described as a hardline Royalist, and to him the idea of compromising with Parliament would have been abhorrent. His clear reference to the unsuitability of certain men to become peers, immediately after the contentious appointment of one in particular, would have been immediately understood. Additionally if Lisle did know Culpepper from London, the slight would have been deeply personal. Knotting the issue further, Culpepper was one of the non-military men the ousted Wilmot had been agitating to remove from the King's council, and in this matter Lisle may well have agreed with the exiled lord, if not in the matter of his treasonably corresponding with the enemy.

Whether Lisle offered his refusal directly to the King or to one of his secretaries is not known, but it must have raised many eyebrows and been widely talked about in public if the details reached enemy ears. Culpepper's response, if he deigned to give one, is not recorded; neither is the King's, which is unfortunate, as refusing to accept a knighthood was virtually unheard of and ritual-loving Charles was not accustomed to his officers spurning favour.

'Newbury III'; closing manoeuvres of 1644

The second battle at Newbury did not quite mark the end of the fighting season. The day after, following a bout of infighting, the Earl of Manchester and the other Parliamentarian commanders eventually agreed that the combined armies would push on in pursuit of the King. Finding that his forces had already crossed the Thames at Wallingford they returned to Newbury and summoned Donnington Castle again, but Sir John Boys refused point blank to surrender. The King, meanwhile, had returned to Oxford on 1st November, having left Rupert, Gerard and Langdale at Burford. Assured by Sir Jacob Astley – now made a baron – that the army at Oxford was once again fit to give the enemy battle, on 6th November the King assembled all his forces at Bullingdon Green, where Lisle reportedly turned down his own knighthood, and the next day Rupert was officially promoted to replace the ailing Lord Forth. He was nominally under the command of the Prince of Wales, however, which was probably a conciliatory move amidst growing political splits in the Royalist command.

The army advancing, on the 9th it crossed the Lambourn and encountered the combined enemy forces in the now all-too-familiar landscape between Newbury and Donnington: whilst emergency provisions were put into the castle, the Parliamentarians loosed a cannonade and there was some cavalry skirmishing, all of which reportedly passed with the loss of only fourteen Royalist infantry soldiers and a trooper. Walker claimed 'the Rebels lost twice that number',[80] although London's *Perfect Passages* would only admit to three.[81] Bernard de Gomme drew up a map of the army dispositions of both sides at the engagement: whilst it confirms that all of Parliament's forces were in Newbury, with a line of dragoons strung out along some hedges to the north, unfortunately it only includes the Royalist cavalry and dragoons, so there is no way of knowing how or where Lisle might have been involved.[82] At a council of war the King decided to withdraw, Parliament's forces in Newbury 'having the Advantages of Breastworks and Batteries and a Town at their Backs', but he nonetheless believed he had won the honours by relieving Donnington and successfully crossing the river. Rupert's Diary dubbed the standoff, which could so easily have developed into a highly significant battle in the course of the English Civil Wars, 'the third battle of Newberrye'.[83] *Perfect Passages* very reasonably queried why the Parliamentarian commanders made no concerted attempt to attack the King or to stop him leaving, particularly as he was outnumbered. An explanation was given on 10th November in a letter from Manchester, Waller and Balfour to the Committee of Both Kingdoms: it pleaded that worsening weather, dead horses, 'much diminished' infantry and mass desertion of troopers, not to mention the King's 'advantages of ground', had turned them against it.[84]

The King retreated north-west to Lambourn and then on Tuesday 12th south-west to Marlborough – yet another 'miserable wett windy day', according to Symonds[85] – to rest and reprovision the army, which camped nearby. Meanwhile news arrived that Parliament's forces had left Newbury for Basing, then had decided to continue into winter quarters rather than renew their siege of the house. Accordingly the Royalists moved directly east again towards Hungerford, having completed a triangular movement and almost come back to Newbury.

80   Walker, p.118.
81   Numb. 4, p.32.
82   BL, Add MS 16370, f.61.
83   EHR, p.737.
84   *CSP Domestic Series,* 1644-1645, p.110.
85   *Diarye,* p.151.

At Hungerford Colonel Gage was once again appointed to deliver provisions to Basing; meanwhile on 19th November, Walker says,

> The Army was drawn out to a Rendezvouz, and Colonel Lisle sent with 1000 commanded Men, with Provisions to relieve Dennington, and to bring thence the rest of the Artillery and Ammunition, which he perform'd that day …[86]

It was fortunate that the King had delayed this task, as Manchester had anticipated removal of the train as early as 6th November, and a few days later *Perfect Passages* had offered a list of important and valuable items it believed the King intended to retrieve besides the artillery, including one of the King's crowns and the Great Seal.[87] How accurate this list was, is unknown, but the newsbook also reports:

> about 18 small pieces, of Artillery, carried into the Castle, besides 5. or 6. great pieces of Ordnance that were planted on the Works below, and good store of Ammunition, some say 60. cart-loads … and the great pieces lie still upon their Works.[88]

With that sort of ordnance and ammunition at stake even a crown paled into insignificance. Like Gage's, Lisle's expedition was of critical importance, both in delivering provisions and retrieving vital artillery, but with the enemy gone his task was straightforward. Hungerford and Newbury are only nine miles apart on the Bath Road (the modern A4), and for Lisle, sent out independently once again with a commanded party to do what he did best, it must have felt like old times. Rupert's biographer Kitson states that when approaching the castle the party 'met some feeble resistance, which they easily brushed aside', but does not give his source; Money, however, offers an unattributed quote saying Lisle's task was achieved 'without let or hindrance'. All that is certain is that he completed the job with minimal loss, if any.[89] The next day the Ordnance Papers recorded a saker, four six-pounders and some ammunition being received at Oxford 'from Dennington Castle &c.',[90] but given the noises made on both sides about the amount and importance of the Donnington ordnance this seems a very small train for such a large recovery expedition, and it is doubtful that this particular delivery was Lisle's. Moreover, Abingdon lay directly between him and Oxford,

---

86   Walker, p.120.
87   *CSP Domestic Series,* 1644-1645, p.100.
88   *Perfect Passages, op. cit.*, pp.28, 32.
89   Kitson, p.218; Money, p.196.
90   Roy, ROP part 1, p.143 (NA, WO 55/1661 [14]).

and despite a guard of 1,000 men his train would have been too great a target for governor Richard Browne's garrison to ignore.

In fact as Lisle was in action with Rupert two days later, he must have gone straight back to the army at Hungerford. The movements of both he and it can be pieced together from Rupert's and Symonds' respective diaries, along with Walker's account. On the night of the 19th – presumably after Lisle had returned with the ordnance – the army moved north from Hungerford to Great Shefford, and then on the 20th to Wantage. While the King moved on to Faringdon during Thursday 21st, Rupert's Diary says that:

> The Prince drew out to surprise Abingdon: but the night was so sharpe, the soldjers could not marche. So the Prince came home after midnight.[91]

Walker's note of Rupert's expedition reveals that Lisle was with him:

> the Foot under the Command of Colonel Lisle, and some of our Horse drew towards Abingdon, with a design on that Place; but they were prevented, and so they came to the Army the next day.[92]

Lisle's foot may well have been the same 1,000 commanded men he had taken to Donnington. It seems unlikely he and Rupert would have succeeded against Abingdon, however: despite their outstanding skirmishing abilities in foot and horse respectively, the town was well-situated for defence, and London's *Mercurius Civicus* reported that week that the garrison had been reinforced by some horse from Northampton.[93] Walker hints that the delay in attempting to recover Abingdon since its abandonment, meant the enemy had 'gained time and made it strong.' The occupied town was to remain a concern of Lisle's: a few days later Faringdon, fifteen miles away, was chosen to host a new Royalist garrison and he was appointed governor. Though supposedly an honour and a mark of trust, the position would rapidly turn out to be a poisoned chalice.

91   EHR, p.738.
92   Walker, p.120.
93   Numb. 79, p.730.

11

'May It Please Your Highness':
Faringdon Garrison

'I sooner feare a famine then an Enemy'

On Monday 23rd November, after forty-eight hours at Faringdon, the King left the army there and returned to Oxford; Rupert went with him, and according to his Diary, 'faced Abingdon, till the King marcht by,' presumably to prevent Browne offering any trouble. It was now up to Rupert, in his new role as lord general, to organise the army's quartering and supplies. Control of Oxford's protective garrisons also fell under his remit and he created several new ones including that at Faringdon. Lisle himself said that his governorship there came directly from Rupert (see letter following), and given that they had just been on the aborted Abingdon raid together, it is perhaps possible that the subject was discussed during this expedition. Even if not, their brief collaboration would have put Lisle directly in the Prince's sights during the next fortnight, when he was formalising the garrison.

Historian Cyril Hartmann explains that Faringdon:

> was situated at the crossing of one of the main roads from London to Gloucester with another minor but important highway from south to north which crossed the river Isis, or Upper Thames, at Radcot Bridge about 21/2 miles distant from the town. With its excellent inns and it weekly market Faringdon was at all times a convenient halting-place for travellers, and still more do for troops on the move.[1]

---

1   Hartmann, *Faringdon in the Civil War*, p.1. Until the county boundary changes of 1974, Faringdon was in Berkshire.

Letter from Lisle to Prince Rupert, 6 December 1644.
(With kind permission from the Trustees of the Leeds Castle Foundation)

Letter from Lisle to Prince Rupert, 13 December 1644. (Worcestershire Public Record Office)

Indeed the Royalists had used Faringdon to station soldiers and troopers, as occasion required, since December 1642,[2] and during the next two years various commanders of both sides had passed through the town or quartered in it, yet surprisingly no formal garrison was installed by either side. Now, with Abingdon taken, Faringdon suddenly assumed more strategic importance for the King. The obvious location for a garrison was a large Elizabethan brick building on the north side of the town, where the King had spent the previous two nights. Since 1622 the house – which Symonds referred to as 'the manor howse called the Place, neare the Church, a faire habitacion' – had been owned by Sir Robert Pye, formerly one of Buckingham's circle, who when the war broke out passed himself off as a Parliamentarian but secretly donated money to the King.[3] His son and namesake, on the other hand, was John Hampden's son-in-law and a genuine supporter of the Parliament. Yet despite surviving until 1770, when it was demolished following a fire, only one image of The Place exists: a contemporary sketch, in which it appears to be similar in style to Mr Dolman's house at Shaw.[4] We know its successor as 'Faringdon House', but other than Symonds' reference to the original building as 'The Place', contemporary documents do not usually name it.[5] It is not clear how the King commandeered such a significant building without a fight, but given Pye senior's Royalist sympathies, it was probably with his discreet agreement. Most likely it was possessed only when the King arrived on the 21st, as Lisle had to start his garrison from scratch, according to his letter to Rupert on 6th December:

> May it please yo[r] Highness,
> According to yo[r] commands I am arrived to Farringdon, but finde soe many discouragem[ts] that were it not in obedience to yo[r] Highness, I should be very unwillinge to undergoe soe many troubles, and difficultyes that of necessity I must here finde. Sir, the Cattell and all sorte of provisions in the Towne and five or sixe miles about it are all destroyed and eaten upp. Soe that I sooner feare a famine then an Enemy; Therefore I shall humbly Entreate yo[r] Highness That you wilbe graciously pleased to allowe me that halfe of Heyworth Hundred in Wiltshire, wh[ch] lyeth on this side Cricklade conteyneing the Markett Towne of Heyworth, wh[ch] lyeth soe convenient for mee as for many more reasons I shall hereafter give your Highness. Sir I am confident yo[r] Higness will not dispose eyther of the Governem[t] of Heyworth (it being so neare a bordere to me) nor any place about me,

2   Prince Maurice's regiment and two regiments of dragoons wintered there after Edgehill (BL Harley MS 6851; transcription in Young's *Edgehill*, pp.181-182).

3   Symonds, *Diarye*, p.159; Hartmann, p.2.

4   The sketch appears in a book, *Great Faringdon Past And Present* (Rev. P. J. Goodrich, 1928); unfortunately the image is unsourced.

5   The only example found by this author is an issue of the newsbook *Mercurius Veridicus* from April 1645, which calls it 'Farinton House' (No. 3 (1645), p.20).

although I am assured there are some att this p[r]sent are sueing for it; But where there shalbe necessity of Secureing such places, yo[r] Highness wilbe pleased to leave it to my owne disposing. S[r] although my Lord Astley hath received moneyes wth materialls and all other Encouragements to begin his worke, I shall humbly submitt my selfe to what only yo[r] Highness shall please to comaund me to rest satisfyed withall; And shall allwayes pray for that life and and happiness that hath soe much obliged

yr highness most humble and ffaythfull affectionatt servant
and poor disconsolatte soonne,
George Lisle
Farringdon
6. December 1644

S[r] here is nothinge yet donn concerneing o[r] fortificacon; Therefore I shall humbly Entreate yo[r] highnes to give yo[r] comande for Colonell Lloyde or some other Engineeres suddeyne repayre hither.[6]

'Heyworth' was Highworth, eight miles south-west of Faringdon, and Lloyd's letters to Rupert at this time reveal that he was based there while surveying possible new garrison sites for the Prince.[7] Evidently Rupert heeded at least Lisle's postscript, on 8th December Lloyd wrote to Rupert from Faringdon, complaining that:

the horse of the Prince of Wales are taken away from mee by your order to Col. Lisle, all my munition duringe my absence by my Lord Astleys order, for that it wilbe impossible for me to remaine there unlesse I be supplyed with both.[8]

Lisle's letter reveals that someone unnamed was attempting to have Highworth split off as a separate garrison, presumably for their own benefit; the obvious candidate was Lloyd, but later in December in a further letter to Rupert, Lloyd mentions that:

---

6   Fairfax Papers, Leeds Castle. C1, unnumbered folio. Astley was now based at Cirencester, as confirmed by his sending several letters to Rupert from there during this period, and also a letter of Sir Samuel Luke's on 24th February, which lists the town amongst other Royalist garrisons (Luke, *Letter Books*, p.161, letter no.315).

7   BL Add MS 18981, f.272 (8th December); on 22nd December Lloyd headed for Devizes, where apparently he had an outstanding commission as governor (f.336).

8   *Ibid.*, f.330.

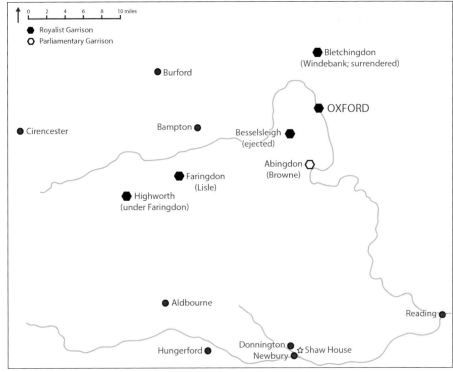

Map 5 Regional map showing garrison locations around Faringdon in early 1645.

Sr John Browne assuring mee that by yor Highness order he is to have the place and the Hundreds Contribucion, wch as my livelyhood, thus I was lost …[9]

Browne commanded the Prince of Wales's regiment of horse, which was quartered at Highworth, and although attached to Lisle's command at Faringdon he may well have been bidding for his own governorship.

On 13th December Lisle wrote to Rupert again:

May it please yor Highnes
I am much ashamed to trouble you soe often wth the many discouragements I doe here soe Dayly receave; But that wch I am chiefly concerned

---

9   BL Add MS 18981, f.272 (8th December). Richard Symonds records Lloyd as being knighted at Oxford on this date (Stephen Porter, ODNB): this may account for the 'absence' he mentions in his letter. In his 1657 'New Catalogue', Thomas Walkley records it as 1st November (p.165).

in, and wch dothe moste trouble me, is in the little regard that is had to yor highnes Commaunds, in that they Doe still persever to send for contribution, and to q^rter in those hundreds yor highnes hath allotted me, wch if they were entire, and w^thout interruption, would fall much shorte of the mayntenance of my Garison (having such an Innumerable Company of Officers) I shall therefore humbly desire, that yor Highnes will once more be pleased to give yor Comaunds unto the Governors of Donnington Castell, & Wallingford to desiste Intermedlinge att all in any of those hundreds Assigned me by yor Highnes. I am obliged to Informe your Highnes, that the Governo^r of Donnington Castell gives out, that I have nothinge to doe wth Lambourne, or Kintbury hundreds, because (as he Reports) they were assigned him by his Ma^ty, and heele therefore keepe them. I am confident that w^thout theise hundreds he hath contribucon from Newberry and backwards, twice sufficient to paye his Garison. I have alsoe this daye had a conference with the High Constables, and Inhabitants of the Hundreds assigned me, and doe finde them to be soe muche Impoverisht, That I must Expect noe other (from them that are able to paye) but three pts provision, and one pte money, of their proporcons, allowing them alsoe for all such provisions as his Ma^ts wholle Army have received from them since the date of my Comission; And howe to give the Officers content, wth Bread, and Cheese (whoe expect money) I know not. Soe humbly begging yor Highnes pardon for this trouble, and praying for yor Highnes longe prosperity, and healthe, I Rest

> yor highness most faythfull and obleiged humble servant
> and obedient sonne
> George Lisle
> Farrington
> 13th December 1644[10]

Such letters set the tone for the winter: the army faced a constant shortage of resources over which garrison commanders were forced to squabble, haggle, and obtain underhandedly in order to maintain their own commands. Some even resorted to violence: a fortnight before Lisle wrote to Rupert, Colonel Leveson at Dudley had complained to the Prince that Richard Bagot at Lichfield in Staffordshire was taking his Warwickshire contributions and had ordered his men to fight Leveson's for them.[11] Admittedly this took place in the context of existing inter-garrison hostilities; fortunately Lisle, Blague and Boys at Faringdon, Wallingford and Donnington respectively did not descend to that level. George

10 Worcester Record Office, 899:749/8782/68/46. There is another word above 'obedient' but it is partially obscured; possibly it is 'happy'.
11 WSL, 1st December 1644 (S. MS. 546).

Lisle fought alongside Boys in 1640 and Francis Lisle had embarked with him for Ireland; whether either brother had any specific friendship with him is not known, but even if so it cut no ice with George when it came to telling Rupert that Boys was a thorn in Faringdon's side. Neither was Lisle backward in disrupting the enemy's supply lines: on 30th December Major General Browne at Abingdon wrote to the Committee of Both Kingdoms, complaining that:

> I pray you to consider the prejudice we suffer by the new garrison at Farringdon, which stops all cattle and other provisions usually coming hither by that way, and which might yet be removed by an indifferent party, if I had soldiers to spare.[12]

Evidently Browne was no more able to rid himself of the King's presence at Faringdon, than Rupert was able to rid the King of Browne at Abingdon; despite both sides persisting with raid after raid and alarm after alarm, the frustrating stalemate endured into 1645.

Relations with Rupert: 'the cult of the Prince'

Rupert was forced to mediate between his garrison commanders, while enduring his own problems. In a letter to William Legge on 16th October he told his friend that:

> Great factions are breeding against Rupert, under a pretence of peace: he being, as they report, the only cause of war in this kingdom.[13]

Undoubtedly the persons he primarily intended were Digby and Goring, although on the surface at least he and Digby had allegedly made up;[14] David Appleby, Sir Charles Lucas's biographer, believes this was a pragmatic move on Rupert's part, his influence having declined after the King's losses in the north.[15] In early March 1645 the King set up a separate council at Bristol for the Prince of Wales, partly because it prevented monarch and heir being captured together, and partly because he wished to remove the more troublesome of his political opponents from Oxford. Rupert saw it as another faction that would damage the Royalist high command, somewhat hypocritically as he still had his own: his many adherents and admirers amongst the King's officers whom biographer Eva Scott calls,

12   *CSP Domestic Series*, 1644-1645, p.204.
13   Warburton, vol. III, p.28.
14   Letter from Rupert to William Legge, 10th Oct 1644 (WSL, D(W)1778/I/i/39). Shortly after this, Goring specifically demanded his own independent command in the West so that he would not have to serve under Rupert.
15   Appleby, *Our Fall Our Fame …*, p.117.

with some hyperbole, 'the cult of the Prince'.[16] His employment in late 1644 and early 1645 of a variety of useful officers in new roles, however, simply reflected the demands of his new position as lord general and his recognition of the large pool of talent and experience available to him. It was only sensible that he employed focused and relatively apolitical officers such as Lisle, Lloyd, and Sir Charles Lucas: men agreeable to his appointment and intent on the task of defeating the enemy, not on undermining Rupert or each other for personal political gain. It was war which concerned Rupert first and foremost, not politics. For men like Lisle, with military ambition and the desire to prove themselves, this round of appointments was a golden opportunity.

For Rupert's part, also, picking out able men at this time was not enhancement of his clique, but a military necessity when the possibility of victory was edging away. That is not to say he did not favour people whom he considered friends: he appointed William Legge governor of Oxford after Gage's death at Abingdon, and in May made Legge's brother governor of Evesham against the advice of a council of war. Evesham was taken two weeks later, and Walker acidly remarked that 'Prince Rupert's Pleasure was not to be contradicted'.[17]

Although Hartmann unaccountably states that Rupert was also Lisle's 'close friend',[18] there is no evidence of this, or that Lisle was actively part of Rupert's personal or political circles, as has already been touched upon. The three letters we have from Lisle to Rupert are frank and informative but absolutely professional, showing no trace of the avuncular tone taken by Legge, or the informality that, for example, Daniel O'Neill had shown in 1642 when he bluntly informed Rupert that his cavalry were unruly and he would rather be the Prince's groom than command them.[19] Perhaps letters which do suggest friendship or at least informality have been lost, but given the amount of the Prince's correspondence that has survived, and the tiny number of Lisle's letters extant there, it seems unlikely. Late in 1645 Rupert asked William Legge to:

> tell Sir Chas. Lucas that I would have written to him before this and to G. Lisle, but [was kept close] here … if I can but get [permission] I hope to see you and the rest of my friends once more …[20]

16   Scott, p.75
17   Walker, p.126. The council of war preferred Colonel Henry Washington 'by Priority of Commission'; his sister was, coincidentally, married to William Legge.
18   Hartmann, p.3. [Author: I have also heard this asserted verbally on a number of occasions, so possibly the suggestion of a friendship has been made elsewhere, in a source of which I am presently unaware.]
19   Warburton, vol. II, p.82 (fn.).
20   *CSP Domestic Series*, 1645-1647, p.215. See also chapter 14 of this book, for further discussion of the letter.

The broad reference to friends does not necessarily relate to his mention of Lisle and Lucas, although it may be that his definition of 'friends' was a wide-ranging one; moreover given the seniority of these men in the King's service by that point in the war, it would have been natural and necessary for the Prince to keep in touch with them.

Eva Scott believed Lisle was not a friend but one of Rupert's admirers in the 'cult', remarking specifically of his December letters that:

> … the gallant George Lisle carried his devotion to such a pitch as to sign himself always, 'your Highness's most faithful affectionate servant, and obedient sonne.'[21]

Whilst Lisle did style himself 'your son' in both letters, Scott's specific quote is a fabrication, merging the sign-offs. Although she is correct that some officers do appear, to our modern taste, overly servile – Sir Lewis Dyve, for example, informs Rupert of 'the fervent desire I have to sacrifice my life at your feet'[22] – Lisle's styling sounds more like a formal nod to seventeenth-century notions of divine order and 'the Great Chain of Being', which he seems to have firmly espoused: from top to bottom, God, King, Parents, Children. Signing off as 'your son' – bizarre at first glance, particularly as Rupert was four years younger than Lisle – in fact implied loyalty, obedience and the acknowledgement of the writer's and the recipient's respective social stations. Herein is a further reason why Lisle, though he 'loved all' and was 'beloved of all',[23] would probably not have considered himself Prince Rupert's friend: he may not have thought it socially appropriate.

Whereas most surviving letters to Rupert are written in the author's own individual hand, and thus with varying degrees of legibility, both Lisle's December letters appear to be in two different hands: the main body in a very fair and formal one, presumably a clerk's, and the sign-off and signature added by Lisle. Lisle's hand is perfectly legible – far more so, in fact, than certain other individuals writing to Rupert at the time – so there was no need to employ a clerk unless as a formality. Lisle's doing so could boost Scott's case that he was some eager disciple wanting to impress the Prince, but as nobody else around Rupert felt it necessary to do this – even recently knighted fellow colonel Charles Lloyd – it would appear to be more evidence of Lisle's insistence on correct form. It is also another factor weighing against the 'friend' suggestion, as no formality would be necessary if writing to a familiar. Finally it is as well to note that the clerk may not have received a word for word dictation of the letters but merely the heads of what to write: some or all of

21   Scott, p.75.
22   8th April 1644; BL Add MS 18981, f.138.
23   According to Clarendon, Book XI, 1840 volume VI, p.99.

the phrasing could be his own, written up in the first person as if Lisle had said it himself, and then signed by Lisle when he had read and approved it.

Lisle, then, at least on the evidence presently available, cannot be defined as a 'follower' of Rupert. Although it seems they had a good working relationship while Lisle was at Faringdon, Lisle assiduously observed social protocol, and they were not 'friends'. Whilst accepting that the Prince had been placed into his immediate chain of command, and doing his best to follow his orders under the most trying circumstances, Lisle had not tied himself to his political fortunes; the only preferment he took an interest in was military, and when he found himself advanced he channelled that advancement to help him further serve the King. His inclusion in the Prince's orbit was incidental: a conjunction of time, place, and Rupert acknowledging his worth by preferring him for a garrison command.

Yet for all that, it may be that after his post-Newbury outburst against royal advisors Lisle was unsure of his own position, or expected hindrance from those he had criticised. In April, Rupert rescued Sir Charles Lucas from detainment in Oxford after he fell victim to a political squabble nurtured by Digby;[24] Lisle may have been wary of being sucked into something similar, perhaps concerning Culpepper, and welcomed the opportunity to shelter in the Prince's shadow from the increasingly destructive squalls within the Royalist command.

Besselsleigh and Abingdon

In the dying hours of December Rupert called on Lisle to provide support for another raid: in his response of 1st January Lisle's exasperation is barely hidden:

> Fearing that the messenger sent last night may not have arrived safely, the writer has despatched another trusty agent with information, that it was 10 O'clock last night before he received his Highness' orders, when he had just come in from observing the enemys horse quartered at Steneton, Deaton and the adjacent villages three hours before his Highness' letter came, the Kings horse marched back to their quarters at Hyworth having been out 2 days and 1 night. In obedience to the Princes orders however, the writer has recalled the horse who are expected to be with him at 2 O'clock. With 200 additional musketeers he will await commands in the march towards Bissing Leigh. I shall not be able to march with above 100 horses, in regard all the best as I am informed are tired and lame.
>
> Sir, I beseech your highness to take it into your consideration in what hazard I shall leave this place behind me, being not as yet ye third part fortified and not able to leave so many able men behind as I carry, by

24   Appleby, pp.118-120.

reason of great sickness and want of arms and the rest which I left at Hyworth being hourly threatened by the enemy.[25]

'Bissing Leigh' (Besselsleigh) lies just west of Oxford and Abingdon, and the house there – an extensive property described in an 1851 gazetteer as an 'ancient manor-house' – was owned by the Commons Speaker William Lenthall.[26] On 30th December, in a letter to the Committee of Both Kingdoms, Richard Browne at Abingdon had reported that:

> Great part of the enemy's forces that lately went to hinder the relief of Taunton are returned, and last night possessed themselves of Mr. Speakers house at Besesly, which is 3 miles off us. Some say they are 100 foot and 60 horse, but their exact number I cannot learn. The house is very strong, and they will be very ill neighbours to us.[27]

The Royalist occupation of the house did not last long however. Late on 31st December Browne wrote again:

> By my last of the 30th inst. I gave you an account of our condition, and of our danger of annoyance by the enemy's possessing Mr. Speaker's house at Besselsleigh. I sent a party under Lieut.-Col. Bosvile, who this morning early summoned the house, and, to prevent bloodshed, suffered the garrison to march away with their arms, except Capt. Beckman, of the Queen's life-guard, and Lord Digby's incomparable engineer, who are made prisoners. Not being able to spare a party to garrison the house, I gave order to preserve it from further violence than was necessary to prevent the enemy from repossessing himself of it, by breaking down the walls and doors …[28]

Presumably Rupert required Lisle's immediate support to retake the house, hence his demand sometime late on the 31st. Evidently the attempt was unsuccessful, as on 6th January Browne wrote to the Committee again, reminding them that:

25 HMC 9th report. The publisher appears to have modernised the letter's punctuation; unfortunately the location of the original letter is not known, so it is not possible to check the details, or whether the HMC included all the contents.

26 *The Parliamentary Gazetteer of England and Wales*, vol. I, p.168. Like the house at Faringdon, Besselsleigh Hall was damaged by fire in the 1770s, and torn down in 1784 (Neal Zaslaw, *An 'English Orpheus and Euridice' of 1697*, Musical Times vol. 118 no. 1616, p.805).

27 *CSP Domestic Series*, 1644-1645, p.204.

28 *Ibid.*, p.205.

I desire to know your pleasure touching Mr. Speaker house at Besselsleigh, in danger of being again taken possession of by the enemy, as I acquainted you in my last. In order to prevent the ruin of this garrison by the soldiers deserting it, I wish you to give order for the exemplary punishing of such officers, undernamed, as have not only run away themselves, but taken with them many soldiers, some being at the time on guard.[29]

Browne seemed to be having as many challenges maintaining Abingdon as Lisle was Faringdon. Perhaps Rupert knew this, and was hoping that if he continued to apply pressure, Browne or his garrison might break. Certainly Abingdon's recovery was one of his key objectives at this time: its abandonment in June 1644 had arguably been one of the worst strategic moves for the King in the First Civil War. Just seven miles south of Oxford, it lies on the north side of a bow in the Thames; on the south side is Andersey Island, one of the largest Thames islands, bounded on its southern edge by 'Swift Ditch', an ancient navigation channel that creates Andersey by cutting across the bow of the main river. In the mid-seventeenth century the road to Dorchester crossed the Thames to Andersey via Abingdon Bridge, then continued across the island via a causeway, then passed across Swift Ditch to the mainland by way of the medieval Culham Bridge. Four days after his rather agitated letter to the Committee – which, it appears, did not reply – Browne wrote yet again, reporting that:

The enemy at Oxford, with a party of 800 horse and 1,000 foot, drawn together from Wallingford, Farringdon, and their horse quarters round Oxford, marched forth on Friday night, commanded by Prince Rupert, and accompanied by Prince Maurice, Sir Henry Gage, the Governor, and most of the gentry of Oxford, who came to see the event. Their intention, as appears by a letter of Prince Rupert to Major Farmer, was to storm Abingdon on Culham side of the town, whilst a body of horse from Farringdon should fall on our horse quarters on the other side, to prevent their coming to our assistance ...[30]

Colonel Samuel Harsnet of the Red Auxiliaries, who wrote an account of the skirmish to a fellow officer in London, believed that Rupert had also brought two cannon.[31] If so, they were of no use to the Prince as this attempt on Abingdon ended in disaster for the Royalists. On Saturday morning, after lining an elevated

---

29 *Ibid.* p.233.
30 *Ibid.*, pp.245-246.
31 *A Full Relation Of The Defeat given, and Victory obtained upon Saturday last* ..., p.2. Harsnet's account contains a number of details worded almost identically to Browne's; Browne wrote to London on the 11th and Harsnet on the 12th, but who borrowed from whom is not clear. Harsnet's estimates of the Royalist numbers are higher than Browne's, however, at 'three thousand Horse and Foot'.

hedgerow behind Culham bridge with musketeers, they broke down much of the stonework leaving just a few planks for their own retreat. Advancing, they made it halfway across the island towards Abingdon Bridge before the town garrison was alerted by an escaped sentry and its men crossed to Andersey themselves from the other direction, also with a couple of cannon. The infantry then waded across the island's flooded meadows to surround the King's men on the causeway. After a three or four hour firefight, and despite the musketeers in the hedge being of 'great annoyance' to Browne's men,[32] the Royalists were forced back and the broken bridge retaken, with the significant loss of Colonel Gage, who had only recently replaced Sir Arthur Aston as governor of Oxford.[33] Meanwhile the Faringdon cavalry were beaten back from the village of Drayton a mile or so south-west, with the loss of the major of the Prince of Wales's horse regiment and a few other officers. Browne claimed the Royalists took away three cartloads of dead from Culham while he lost only a major and eight or ten common soldiers, and 50-60 men wounded; *Mercurius Aulicus* estimated Browne's losses at 'betwixt 30 and 40'.[34] Harsnet claimed that in the Drayton action no Parliamentarian men were lost, but that 'not twelve horses' made it back to Faringdon and five Irish troopers were captured and later hanged in Abingdon market place.[35] Rupert's repeated inability to retake the town was becoming a sore, both for the army as a whole and for Rupert personally: it was another blow to his reputation, already under scrutiny after the defeat at Marston Moor, and the London press made the most of it by claiming that on this occasion he slunk back into Oxford via a back way. It is not clear whether Lisle took part in this raid, or whether the 1,000 infantry came purely from Wallingford; as his garrison was already stretched thin, however, it was unlikely he could provide more than a couple of hundred men. He may have been involved in plans for yet another attempt a few weeks later, when on 7th March the King commanded Rupert to take 'this party of horse and foote now redy drawne forth and to endevor therewith to reduce the towne of Abingdon'.[36] On the same day, and so possibly related to the intended raid, Lisle was authorised to have '50 muskets 150 pike for arming of his regiment', and three days later 'the long pykes within mencioned were delivered by indenture to Mr Thomas Lisle servant to the Prince of Wales.'[37] Presumably Thomas was a member of the Prince of Wales's Highworth-based horse, but whether he was related to George is not known. Neither is it clear whether this final attempt on Abingdon ever took place; in any case it had been the last opportunity to recover the town, as by 11th March

32   Harsnet, p.2.
33   Gage had replaced Aston only two weeks earlier, on Christmas Day: Sir Arthur had broken his leg in a riding accident on 19th September and it was amputated on 7th December (Dugdale, p.73, 76).
34   Unnumbered, 5th-12th January 1645, p.1331.
35   Harsnet, *op. cit.*
36   Gloucestershire Archives, D7348/3.
37   Roy, ROP part 2, p.357 (NA, WO 55/423, f.287).

Rupert was in the Marches on his way to deal with the worsening situation in Shropshire and Wales.

Bletchingdon and Bampton

The dawn of the third year of the war had been grim for the Royalists: on 10th January Archbishop Laud was executed in London, and another round of nego-tiations at Uxbridge failed to deliver a peace; on 22nd February Shrewsbury was assaulted and fell to the Parliament. Moreover, Parliament was undertaking a drastic military reorganisation which would dramatically increase its military efficiency. To avoid a repeat of the corrosive internal squabbles between Waller, Manchester, Cromwell and other officers the previous year, in December the House of Commons had passed a 'self-denying' ordinance under which Lords and MPs gave up their military roles and freed the military from political interference. After some quibbling the House of Lords finally passed it also, on 3rd April, but in February had been quicker to approve another ordinance, which removed the regional army structure to create the single 'New Model Army'. The retirement of all the well-known commanders besides Sir Thomas Fairfax, neither a lord nor an MP, left him as the man deemed best to command the new single military force. Philip Skippon was appointed his deputy. Although an MP, Oliver Cromwell was considered too valuable to lose, and his command was extended every 40 days until in June it became permanent.

Perhaps Lisle's own pains over the winter had not gone unnoticed at Oxford, as on 16th April, along with William Legge, he was made an honorary Doctor of Civil Law (DCL) by Oxford University.[38] Such awards were not unusual: after Edgehill King Charles had prevailed upon the university to award 400 honorary degrees to his supporters, and by the end of the month DCLs had also been bestowed on Colonel William Leighton and Sir Thomas Glemham. What is more significant is that Lisle was now prepared to accept an honour, albeit only an academic one; perhaps he felt his point had been made, or perhaps friends had persuaded him that it might be unwise to refuse the King again. Either way, within a fortnight any sliver of satisfaction Lisle may have been savouring from the honour would have been swept away by more critical matters: on 27th April, 221 men from his garrison were surprised by Lieutenant General Cromwell's cavalry six miles away, cornered, and captured.

Lisle's men had been caught up in a week-long streak of military good fortune enjoyed by Cromwell. Oxford had been organising a rendezvous between the artil-lery train and the Princes' cavalry, then at Worcester. Rupert needed the ordnance to relieve the besieged city of Chester, and Maurice had already arrived at Oxford with 1,000 horse, to collect it. Learning of this design, on 20th April the Committee

38   Wood, *Athenae Oxonienis*, vol. II, p.733.

of Both Kingdoms had ordered Cromwell up from the West to disrupt the escort.[39] Accordingly with '1500 Horse and Dragoons', and:

> having intelligence that they intended to pass through Shotoverwood, drew towards Woodstock and so thereabouts towards Islip, to be ready to attend their motion, in case they came that way.[40]

According to *Six Severall Victories,* the officially sanctioned London account of the week's events, after a close but uneventful encounter on the evening of the 23rd, Cromwell mauled the assembled escort at Islip the next day, pursued some of the remnants to the small garrison of Bletchingdon, north of Oxford, and demanded its surrender.[41] Joshua Sprigge, Sir Thomas Fairfax's chaplain, records that Cromwell:

> faced the house with Horse and Dragoons, summoned the Governour with a sharp Message (our Souldiers casting out words for the Foot to fall on, as if there had been Foot in readines) the Answer was required to be instantly given, or else he must expect the greatest severity that the souldiers could use towards him ...[42]

Evidently the trick was effective: according to Symonds, Lisle's counterpart Francis Windebank:

> valiantly gave up the howse and all his armes, &c., besides 50 horse that came in thither for shelter; and this without a shott.[43]

Dugdale adds that Windebank made 'noe endeavours of resistance.'[44] Although *Six Severall Victories* states that the house was 'strong surrounded', Symonds tells us that the house was in no condition to withstand a siege, having '200 foot, sans workes, and provision for only two or three dayes'.[45] Parliamentarian intelligence

39   *CSP Domestic Series,* 1644-1645, p.419.

40   *Six Severall Victories Obtained* ..., p.2.

41   *Ibid.*; Dugdale, p.78. Dugdale says the Islip skirmish occurred on the 23rd, and Bletchingdon surrendered the following day; Symonds that Islip was on the 24th and the surrender on Friday 25th (*Diarye*, p.163). Symonds appears to be correct, as he is supported by a Parliamentarian newsbook which reports the Islip skirmish in detail and specifically states that it occurred on Thursday 24th (*The Kingdomes Weekly Intelligencer,* Numb. 97, p.780). Confusingly, however, the articles within the newsbook are incorrectly dated as the 24th.

42   Sprigge, *Anglia Rediviva*, p.11.

43   Symonds, *Diarye*, p.163.

44   Dugdale, p.78.

45   Symonds, *op. cit.*; S. R. Gardiner states the contrary, saying that the house was 'strongly defended' but given the contemporary evidence about Windebank's troubles at Bletchingdon, Symonds is more likely

suggests that the garrison's size varied wildly between February and April, reportedly as low as 50 and as high as 300, and that sometime in March Windebank fled to Oxford after being threatened by his men. On 27th March he was formally ordered back to Oxford, leaving the garrison under the care of Sir Thomas Coghill, who owned the house, and the circumstances of his return to Bletchingdon in April are unknown.[46] Evidently Parliamentarian spies were as busy thereabouts as the cavalry, as the day after Bletchingdon's surrender *Six Severall Victories* reports that:

> Colonell Windbank was brought before a Councell of War … and that divers great persons in Oxford were much inraged against him, taking it very ill, that a Garrison of so great consequence to them (as they value it) should be so soon lost; in so much, that it is beleeved Col. Windebank will be put to death for it.

The assumption about the death penalty was correct: Windebank's failure to even attempt a defence led to his being condemned the next day by an Oxford council of war, and shot a few days later, Sir William Dugdale tells us, 'in ye garden at Oxford Castle.'[47]

Undoubtedly news of Windebank's sentence would have sent a chill through other garrison commanders such as Lisle who faced a daily struggle to maintain and defend their own garrisons without satisfactory resources and with little practical support from Oxford. Lisle in particular might have sympathised with Windebank's predicament, as Faringdon's defences were barely any better although the occupying garrison was significantly larger. Whilst Lisle seems to have managed Faringdon far better than Windebank did Bletchingdon, and as far as we know Lisle did not suffer a mutiny, in fairness to Windebank we do not fully understand the circumstances at his garrison or how far he was responsible for them. Certainly he had been put in an impossible position: the garrison was in such a poor state that realistically he had no hope of retaining the house against even an initial attack, but if he refused Cromwell's summons then by the established customs of war Cromwell could, as indeed he had threatened, legitimately come in

---

to be correct (Gardiner, vol. 2, p.201). Gardiner seems to have misunderstood the London account: it says the house was 'strong surrounded', but this means by Cromwell's forces, not by fortifications.

46 Luke, *Letter Books,* p.687, scout report no. 232; p.688, scout report no. 237; p.689, scout report no. 241; p.466, document no. 1122; p.693, scout report nos. 252, 254.

47 Dugdale, p.79. Heath says that King Charles later greatly regretted the execution, 'when he understood the business, and for which he was highly displeased with Prince Rupert.' (*Chronicle*, p.75). Sir Henry Bard sent a desperate letter to Rupert on 28th April, asking the Prince 'Sir, pity him and reprieve him', and citing Windebank's courage at Cheriton, but despite a brief reprieve the execution went ahead on 3rd May (*CSP Domestic Series*, 1644-1645, p.438; Symonds, *Diarye*, p.164). Rupert's biographer Eva Scott believes Bard's letter was intercepted and that Rupert never received it (p.170).

and take it anyway with no regard for the lives of those inside. Perhaps, being only four miles from Oxford (as opposed to Faringdon's seventeen), Windebank could have at least played for time and hoped for rescue, but James Heath later asserted that:

> The governour over-ruled by his fair young Bride, and some Ladies that were come thither to visit, and frighted with the menace, delivered the House ...[48]

Windebank's wife was certainly in the house, as provision was given in the surrender articles for the safe departure of her, her servants, and a chaplain.[49] Evidently the colonel had not expected the arrival of the routed cavalry or the enemy on their tail, and had no time to evacuate civilians. However, Heath's source for his assertion that Windebank's wife was a factor in his decision to surrender is not known. In Faringdon's case, whilst there may have been a few civilians or women lodging at The Place, perhaps the wives of senior officers who were quartered at the house rather than in the town, there is no specific evidence for it. Indeed if Lisle really was as short of provisions as he suggested to Rupert, he may not have tolerated the presence of unnecessary civilians in any case.

The Islip attack and Bletchingdon surrender had plainly left Oxford in turmoil, calling in local support: Richard Symonds says that on the morning of Saturday 26th:

> Some horse and foot came from Farringdon from Colonel Lisle's garrison, and all the horse in Oxford were to be drawne out ...[50]

Hartmann believes that the Faringdon force was intended to help defend Woodstock from Cromwell.[51] Twice that day Abingdon's forces engaged Royalist parties on the move in the district; subsequently, Symonds recounts:

> When we had drawn out and marched, newes came that the enemy was gone. We returned to our severall quarters. At seven of the clock the Queenes troope of Life Guard was beate up, and 60 horses taken, but [only] 6 men ... On Sunday the enemy pursued Lisle's men, and took and killed neare 200 of them.

48   Heath, *Chronicle*, p.74.
49   *The Kingdomes Weekly Intelligencer*, Numb. 97, p.781.
50   *Diarye*, pp.163-164.
51   Hartmann, p.5.

Mercurius Aulicus recounts that Lisle's men, chased by Cromwell immediately afterwards:

> were forced to get into a Country house at Bampton, which [Cromwell] presently surrounded, but durst not have approached, if either that house had beene fit for souldiers, or those souldiers had Ammunition.[52]

Despite the assertion of *Six Severall Victories* that Cromwell's name so terrified them that they 'little courage to fight', they held out overnight and refused an initial summons. Eventually they decided that the odds were against them, however, and surrendered on mercy. The prisoners were taken to Abingdon and *Perfect Occurrences of Parliament* gives a full list, including the names of 148 common soldiers.[53] The most senior officers were Sir Henry Vaughan; Lieutenant Colonel Urian Leigh and his nephew Major Henry Leigh, both of Thelwall's regiment;[54] and Lieutenant Colonel Littleton from Lisle's.[55] Littleton and Urian Leigh were quickly exchanged – perhaps for prisoners taken at Faringdon shortly afterwards – but the others languished at Abingdon until late June, when they were sent to London at the same time as the prisoners from Naseby:

> Col. Sir Henry Vaughan (a Member of the House of Commons) who was some weeks since taken by Lieut. Gen. Cromwell, was brought to the Barre of the House of Commons, and thence committed to the Tower. Col. Conquest, Major Lee, Capt. Lee, Capt. Powell, and other Officers taken at the same time, who had ever since been prisoners in Abbington, came up likewise with him and were committed to severall prisons.[56]

52   Unnumbered, 20th-27th April 1645, p.1565.

53   Hartmann (p.6) gives a very detailed account of the proceedings, but does not give a source reference; *Perfect Occurrences of Parliament*, The 19th Week (1645). Prisoner lists of the time rarely named unranked soldiers, let alone so many.

54   Urian Leigh had only just returned from a prisoner exchange organised in late February (JHC, 4, 1644-1646, p.63). In April 1644 he had sought exchange after his capture at Alton (see chapter 7); evidently he was released soon after that, as he signed the Royalist officers' letter to Essex in Cornwall in August. Where he was captured on this latest occasion is not known, but if not Abingdon on 10th January then it must have been at Shaw House in October.

55   Not Sir William Vaughan, as Sprigge asserted in 1647, and James Heath in his 'Chronicle' in 1675. All the 1645 sources repeatedly state that it was Sir Henry, and in any case, Sir William operated in Shropshire and the Marches and was nowhere near Faringdon. Presumably following Sprigge or Heath, historian S. R. Gardiner repeated the mistake, and this misled later biographers including P. R. Newman, who consequently misunderstood Bampton's location and therefore the identification of 'Lieutenant Colonel Littleton'.

56   *The True Informer*, Numb. 9 (1645), pp.59-60.

Vaughan's position was precarious, as the previous year Parliament had excepted him from the ongoing peace propositions, as someone 'who shall expect no Pardon, either for Life or Estate.' When the Bampton captives arrived in London on 18th June, he was immediately sent to the Tower 'for High-Treason, for levying actual War against the King and Parliament.'[57] As Vaughan had been sitting at the Oxford Parliament in 1644, Peter Young assumes he had permanently turned courtier-politician, and suggests that the man taken at Bampton must in fact have been his son and namesake; this newsbook reference proves otherwise.[58]

Although the captured Littleton's first name is not given, given the context it *must* be Lisle's half colonel Edward Littleton. P. R. Newman disagrees, instead believing the captive to be the son of baronet Sir Edward Littleton of Pillaton, Staffs, 'regiment uncertain'; however Sir Edward's son was only thirteen at the time and thus even by contemporary standards very young to be attending the army, let alone be a half colonel. The House of Commons gave their final approval to Littleton's post-Naseby exchange on 18th June, four days after he was taken prisoner, mortally wounded;[59] post-Bampton he must have been back at Oxford before 7th May, when the army left Oxford for the north. Of other officers, *Perfect Occurrences* also lists a captain and an ensign known to be Thelwall's,[60] but besides Littleton there are no men known to have served under Lisle. There is no definitive list of Lisle's officers to check against, however, and some of the common men may have been his. Judging by the surnames, the majority of the prisoners appear to have been Welsh, which is consistent with Vaughan's and Leigh's commands as their regiments were raised in Wales. It is not clear if Lisle was with the party: Sprigge says that Vaughan commanded 350 foot that day, but as Sprigge's source is not known, that figure should be viewed with caution.[61] If true, however, it may mean that the party split when attacked, 221 men getting into Bampton and the rest escaping; perhaps Lisle was with them.

His reaction to Bampton is not recorded, but needless to say it was a very significant blow and the loss of 221 men, including three senior tercio officers besides his own lieutenant colonel, can only have greatly added to his problems at Faringdon. The tercio, 1,200-strong at Newbury, was not greatly diminished by the battle

---

57   Excepted 21st September 1644, JHC, 3, 1643-1644, p.636; sent to the Tower, JHC, 4, 1644-1646, p.178.

58   Young, *Naseby 1645*, p.106.

59   *Royalist Officers*, p.236; *The History of Parliament* online: 'LITTLETON, Sir Edward, 2nd Bt. (c.1632-1709), of Pillaton Hall and The Moat House, Tamworth, Staffs.'; JHC, 4, 1644-1646, p.176: 'Resolved, &c. That this House doth approve of the Exchange of Lieutenant-Colonel Littleton, Prisoner to the Parliament's Forces, for Captain Gouge, Prisoner to the King's Forces.'

60   'Captain Lee', who must have been Major Henry's brother Charles, as their other brother, Peter, stated later that he was captured at Naseby (CCC, vol. II, p.893); and Ensign Edward Davenport, who in 1663 claimed bounty as a former officer of Thelwall's. By April 1645 Urian Leigh is in charge of the regiment, subsequent to Thelwall's departure.

61   Sprigge, p.12.

there, but had halved in size again over the winter: presumably partly due to the 'great sickness' he spoke of in his letter to Rupert of 1st January, and to incremental losses in minor local skirmishes. The perpetual problem of desertion also probably played a part. Since December he had also lost Colonel Lloyd and his regiment to the Devizes garrison, and there is a question mark over whether Sir Edward Stradling's Glamorganshire regiment was still with him at Naseby; if not, it too must have been reassigned at some point over the winter.[62] Like Colonel Eure's, Sir Thomas Blackwell's tiny regiment may have also disappeared after Newbury. Indeed Lisle's January letter, in which Lisle says he is 'not able to leave so many able men behind as I carry', and that most of his men are away defending Highworth, suggests The Place was being held by a skeleton garrison as he juggled resources to secure it and other local strongholds in his territory from the enemy.

Whilst Lisle has left us no comment on the aftermath of Bampton, Lord Digby's correspondence suggests that Cromwell's activities had caused significant alarm at Oxford. On 27th April, as Littleton and his colleagues fled for the shelter of Bampton with Cromwell on their heels, Digby wrote to Rupert: advising him that if he wanted the artillery train he must now come and get it, and unless he did come with significant forces then the King was likely to be besieged at Oxford anyway, and Rupert 'be forced to march hither to relieve him upon worse terms than now.'[63] The next day, the 28th, as the Bampton men surrendered, he wrote to Goring in the King's name, ordering him up from the west with 3,000 horse.[64] In a further letter to Rupert on the 29th he reiterated a lack of available draught horses to move the artillery – Cromwell had taken every horse he found – and that unless the Prince brought some with him, and Goring's cavalry could 'entertain this field power of the rebels':

> the reputation of Cromwell's successes is already likely to draw such swarms out of London upon us, and the King will be in hazard of being suddenly besieged in this place.[65]

Whilst the atmosphere at Oxford should not be judged on Digby's excitable missives alone, the situation he describes was real enough, although as his letter to Goring was dispatched early on 29th April the King added a postscript countermanding previous orders and bidding Goring bring only 2,000 horse.[66] Perhaps by this time Lisle had arrived at Oxford to give a more precise account of his Bampton

---

62   Stuart Reid states that they were present at Leicester and Naseby (*Officers and Regiments of the Royalist Army*, vol. 4, p.166), but Peter Young suggests that by Naseby they may have been back in South Wales (*Naseby 1645*, p.107).

63   Warburton, vol. III, p.77.

64   *Calendar of the Clarendon State Papers*, vol. I, p.264. Rupert needed the artillery to relieve Chester.

65   BL Add MS 18982, f.46.

66   Goring still brought 3,000, meaning the letter must have reached him after his departure.

losses, to put in a word for Littleton's exchange, and to reassure the King that Faringdon was still secure and that despite Cromwell's good fortune there had been no general invasion of Lisle's territory in north-west Berkshire. That Lisle made such a trip to Oxford is pure supposition: however after an event such as Bampton he might well be expected to report to the King and his council immediately with an explanation, and he was certainly not at The Place later that day when Cromwell, flushed with his previous successes, arrived to summon it.

Toynbee and Young hint at another reason for Lisle's absence at Faringdon in the last few days of April: the burial of a Margaret Lisle at St Mary the Virgin in Oxford, on 1st May, whom they suggest 'was probably George's wife.'[67] This is unlikely, however. There is no record in London of him marrying before the war, and there is no evidence to suggest he was living anywhere but with his parents in St Martin's Lane, until they fled London in early 1643; also no wife is mentioned living with him in the St Aldates census of January 1644, whereas the wives and children of other officers are recorded alongside them.[68] It is perfectly possible that Lisle had married since then, but if so there is no record at Oxford despite the parish records for the period being extremely good in comparison to many other places. He could have been married somewhere else, perhaps during a campaign, but for many practical reasons this is also extremely unlikely. In any case there is no evidence at all to suggest a connection between Lisle and the deceased woman, and Toynbee and Young seem to have made their assumption purely on the basis of a shared surname. It remains most likely, then, that his absence from Faringdon when Cromwell arrived on 29th April was either a trip to Oxford to report on the Bampton debacle, or military business elsewhere.

'We feare not your storming': Cromwell's attempt on Faringdon

Lisle's deputy governor was Lieutenant Colonel Roger Burgess (or Burges), half colonel to Sir John Owen, who had recently been appointed major general of the King's forces in Wales but left his regiment with Lisle's tercio at Faringdon. It was Burgess who dealt with Cromwell during Lisle's unexplained absence on 29th April; the principal account of the action comes from *Mercurius Aulicus*. Cromwell, 'whose beating up a quarter is so heightened so at London as if he had not since paid for it at Faringdon', arrived at around 4 p.m. and according to

---

67   *Strangers in Oxford*, p.131. The register entry reads 'Lisle Margaret Mrs. buried in Ad. Brome's Chapel.' Elsewhere Young repeats the assertion, saying Lisle was 'apparently at Oxford' during Cromwell's attack, although he offers no further explanation (*Naseby 1645*, p.208 and p.225 (fn. 14)).

68   *Ibid.*, plates 2 and 3.

Hartmann probably stationed himself initially on a small hill east of the town.[69] Having already sent to Abingdon for some foot, he sent the garrison a summons.

> *Sir,*
> *I summon you to deliver into my hands the house wherein you are and your ammunition with all things else there, and persons to be disposed of as the Parliament shall appoint, which if you refuse to doe you are to expect the uttermost extremities of warre. I rest*
> *Your servant*
> *Oliver Cromwell*
> *April 29. 1645*[70]

However if Cromwell hoped to terrify Faringdon into submission as he had done Bletchingdon, he was to be disappointed. *Aulicus* continues:

> The brave men in Farringdon were only afraid that Cromwell would not come neare enough to assault (for they were all strangely resolved to welcome him) and therefore Lieutenant Colonel Burges ... laboured to invite him nearer by this calme civill answer, *That the King had entrusted them to keep that Garrison, and without speciall order from His Majesty Himselfe they could not deliver it.*

This was propagandist nonsense from *Aulicus*, of course, but probably made in response to the claim of *Six Severall Victories* that Lisle's Bampton men had been terrified of Cromwell. Moreover, Burgess had given the standard Royalist response to a garrison summons, and with Windebank's impending execution at the forefront of everyone's minds, he was not about to follow that colonel's example. *Aulicus* goes on:

> This faire answer gave Cromwell some encouragement, so as he presently drew into Farringdon town, and blustered high in a second Summons, which to shew his confidence he sent written in such a small shred of foule paper as if Captaine Phips had given it before it came to the paper mill, his words were these:

> *Sir, I understand by 40 or 50 poore men whom you forced into your house that you have many still there whom you cannot arme, and who are not serviceable to you: if these men should perish by your meanes it were great inhumanity, surely honour and honesty requires this, and though you*

---

69 Now known as 'Folly Hill', after the small tower built on its summit in the 1930s.
70 Unnumbered, 27th April-4th May 1645, pp.1570-1573.

be prodigall of your owne lives, yet be not of theirs, if God give you into my hands I will not spare a man of you if you put me to a storme. Oliver Cromwell.

This particular of forcing men into the Garrison was Cromwell's meer pretence whereon to ground another Summons, for he was willing (if possible) to word it onely; but the brave Lieutenant Governour did hope Cromwell was now engaged to fight, & therefore instantly dispatcht him this answer. *Sir, we have forced none into our Garrison, we would have you know you are not now at Bletchington: the guiltlesse bloud that shall be spilt God will require at your hands that have caused this unnaturall warre. We feare not your Storming, nor will have any more Parlies. Your servant, Roger Burges.*

The wording of Burgess's stinging second response might as well have come from Lisle himself: he had chosen his deputy well. The garrison made 'great acclamation' as Burgess read out his message; Cromwell's answer, he having now received 'about five or six hundred' foot from Abingdon, was to carry out his threat.[71] At around 3 a.m. on Tuesday 30th he 'fell upon the Sconce on the South-west side' with four troops of dragoons and the Abingdon foot, carrying ladders,[72] *Aulicus* reckoning 1,200 foot in total. Despite the pre-dawn darkness – sunrise was not until 4.30 a.m. – the garrison was waiting, and Burgess fended off the first oncomer himself with a pike, hurling him back into the ditch then duly taking the man prisoner when he begged for quarter. The mention of a 'sconce', an earth-work of some description, reveals that Lisle had managed to organise at least some defensive improvements to The Place over the previous four or five months. Unlike Windebank, he had had the significant advantage of having Charles Lloyd, one of the King's best engineers, in his own tercio.

Aulicus claims that after the capture of Cromwell's man, a captain, 'the Rebels never offered to scale, but left all their Ladders rear'd before the Workes'; meanwhile, however, they had also fallen on both the north and north-west sides of the defences. The heaviest assault came against the former, but:

it proved so fruitlesse, that they killed but two common Souldiers and hurt foure, not any Officer so much as toucht, though the storme lasted full three houres, wherein the Rebels lost 200 Officers and Souldiers kill'd in the place, and great numbers wounded, Captain Canon taken prisoner, with an Ensigne, and 8 common Souldiers, 100 Armes, besides some

71   Rushworth, 1722, vol. 6, Chapter II, pp.23-89 (viewed via British History Online; original page number not given).

72   Sir Edward Nicholas, writing to Prince Rupert the next morning, states that Cromwell has four dragoon troops (Warburton, vol. III, p.79); Rushworth that the dragoons took part in the assault.

clubs with spikes (called Roundheads) made for the New Modell; with all
the pillage of the Rebels bodies within musket shot of the Workes, most
whereof had ropes swaddled about their middles (you may guesse why) ...

The nature of the rest of the fortifications is not known, however given the
resources available to Lisle and Lloyd they may have been little more than temporary earth ramparts with palisades and ditches. Historian Richard Dace, writing
about Faringdon in relation to subsequent governor Sir Marmaduke Rawdon,
states that the house already had a dry moat, which again suggests its layout was
similar to the house at Shaw.[73] The fact that the attackers brought ropes, suggests
that either the moat was very deep, or as at Shaw it may have been surrounded by
a high wall.

For the first half of the assault, darkness would have precluded the use of
muskets by either side unless the scene was exceptionally well torchlit; to compen-
sate, however, every defender had beside him a heap of stones with which, *Aulicus*
says, 'the brave Garrison beat the Rebels out of the Trench'. The 'great numbers
wounded' must have been as much down to the impact of jagged lumps of local
limestone, as to musket balls. Presumably pikemen were also heavily employed
to keep the attackers at bay. Whilst full credit for the successful repulse must go
to the cool-headed Burgess, Lisle should be acknowledged for getting what he
had clearly considered a hopeless location for a garrison into a fit state to repel
Cromwell in the first place. It is also unlikely he would have left the house without
giving Burgess explicit orders and ensuring that some sort of emergency plan
was in place. Fortunately Cromwell had not come equipped for a full-on siege:
he had no artillery, and after his unexpected good fortune at Bletchingdon and
Bampton he was merely shaking the proverbial tree at Faringdon to see what fell
out.[74] *Aulicus* had massively exaggerated his losses, as according to Sprigge only
fourteen dead were reported at the time, although conversely it is possible that the
casualties were deliberately under-reported. Heath gives a 50 man loss, but does
not offer a source.[75] Whatever the actual size of Cromwell's attack force, it plainly
outnumbered Lisle's garrison, perhaps two to one: as taking into account Lisle's
known and possible losses since Newbury II, his tercio could have numbered only
around 600-700 men at most. Moreover only part of the tercio may have been at

---

73   Dace, *'Who Lieth Here?' Sir Marmaduke Rawdon (1582-1646)*; http://richarddace.website/pdf/rawdon.
     pdf, (accessed 2nd January 2016).
74   Cromwell acknowledged his run of good luck (which he attributed to God) in a letter to the Committee
     of Both Kingdoms concerning Bampton: 'I did much doubt the storming of the house, it being strong
     and well manned, and I having few dragoons, and this being not my business, and yet we got it.' Had
     Vaughan, Leigh and Littleton only known of Cromwell's doubts about the viability of his threat to storm
     their refuge, and held their nerve, the outcome for them might have been very different (letter dated
     25th April; quoted in Wing, *Annals of Bletchingdon*, p.40)
75   *Chronicle*, p.75.

The Place, or quartered near enough to get to it quickly, when Cromwell arrived. Despite his superior numbers Cromwell evidently agreed that this garrison was no second Bletchingdon, and his pragmatic acceptance of his repulse on the morning of 30th April, in a further letter to Burgess, was understandable:

> *Sir, There shall be no interruption of your viewing and gathering together the dead bodies, and I doe acknowledge it as a favour, your willingnesse to let me dispose of them. Captaine Cannon is but a Captaine, his major is Smith so farre as I know, but he is a stranger to me, I am confident he is but a Captaine, Master Elmes but an Ancient, I thanke you for your civility to them, you may credit me in this, I rest,*
>   *Your servant*
>   *Oliver Cromwell*
>   *April 30.*
> *If you accept of equall exchange I shall performe my part.*

Aulicus's assertion that Cromwell blamed Browne's foot, and that he said 'he could have taken Farrington if Abington Foot had not been the worst Foot in England', was almost certainly a fictitious barb intended to be seen by Browne and his men, who being quartered so close to Oxford would undoubtedly have been monitoring the Royalist newsbook for intelligence. Whether Cromwell intended to, or indeed did, make another attempt on the house is not clear. Symonds states that his men were 'twice repulsed by Farringdon men', suggesting that he did indeed try again, although there appears to be no contemporary account of a second assault.[76] To what extent Cromwell had isolated the garrison from outside support is not known, nor is whether Lisle managed to get back into the house after the first attack and direct any further defence himself. On the morning of the 30th there was genuine concern for the garrison's survival: Goring, writing to the Earl of Berkshire from Wells, said he was on his way but would 'favour his own retreat' if the enemy at Faringdon was too strong;[77] Digby, writing to Rupert, believed The Place would hold only for a short time until he or Goring arrived, although a postscript adds that

> Since the writing of this, there is one come from the Commander in Farringdon, to assure unto the King that they are strong enough to hold on five days, and that there is a hundred of George Lesley's men supposed to be lost – gone in to them with their arms.[78]

76   *Diarye*, p.164.
77   *Calendar of the Clarendon State Papers*, vol. I, p.264.
78   Warburton, vol. III, p.81.

Cornelius Johnson: Portrait of Sir George Lisle. Referred to in this biography as 'The Lace Portrait'. (Private collection. Author's photo, reproduced with kind permission of the painting's present owner)

Sir George Lisle. School of Sir Anthony Van Dyck.
(Castle Howard Collection. Reproduced by kind permission of the Howard family)

Sir George Lisle. Circle of John Michael Wright (1617-1694).
(Photograph courtesy of Sotheby's Picture Library)

The former home of Richard Miles in St. Aldates, Oxford, where Lisle was billeted in January 1644. (Photograph courtesy of R. Jones)

Shaw House east lawn, showing the eastern rampart.
(Author's photo, with permission of Shaw House, Newbury)

Shaw House from the east. (Author's photo, with permission of Shaw House, Newbury)

The eastern section of the old 'dry moat' at Shaw House, looking south. Note the earth rampart on the right; the fence on the left approximately marks the line of the eastern garden wall, where Colonel Page's leather guns were stationed. (Author's photo, with permission of Shaw House, Newbury)

The grass verge on Church Road, Shaw, which was originally the southern stretch of Shaw House's dry moat, and enclosed by the southern garden wall. The wall in view here is almost certainly a later addition. (Author's photo, with permission of Shaw House, Newbury)

The rear wall of Colchester Castle, taken from the monument. (Author's photo)

The monument at Colchester Castle, marking the reputed spot where Lisle and Lucas were shot. Erected for the public opening of the castle park in 1892. (Author's photo)

THIS STONE
MARKS THE SPOT
WHERE ON AUGUST 28. 1648,
AFTER THE SURRENDER
OF THE TOWN,
THE TWO ROYALIST CAPTAINS
Sir CHARLES LUCAS,
And Sir GEORGE LISLE,
WERE SHOT BY ORDER OF
Sir THOMAS FAIRFAX,
THE PARLIAMENTARIAN
GENERAL.

The Colchester Castle monument inscription. (Author's photo)

Oxford was in a high state of alarm, but almost certainly Digby was writing before he had heard about the failure of Cromwell's attack the previous night. The news in the postscript may well have been his first notification of it. However the correspondence of the Committee of Both Kingdoms at this time reveals that as Digby had feared, Parliament was withdrawing soldiers from numerous garrisons and from the City of London to strengthen its hand in the Oxford and Faringdon area, and Browne was to join Cromwell to take charge of the local foot.[79] The Committee was focused on Goring's approach to Oxford from the south-west and increasingly concerned about Rupert's from the north-west, and it seems that briefly Faringdon was the 'ground zero' of an accelerating build-up of forces on both sides. Despite Cromwell remaining in the area, Sir Edward Nicholas advised Rupert on the 30th that the lieutenant general was 'now lying at Stamford and other places next to Farrington', which suggests that after his first attempt on the house he had withdrawn at least some of his forces to a safe distance prior to Goring's arrival.[80] He was unable to take the garrison by force with the soldiers available to him, but others were on the way and he would have known that his mere presence in the vicinity and the threat of a further attack would have a deleterious effect on the men inside. The situation at The Place had become a waiting game: the garrison waiting for Goring to arrive or for Cromwell to leave, and Cromwell waiting for reinforcements or for the garrison's resolve to crumble, like Bletchingdon's, before help materialised.

It may have been around this time, when the garrison was on high alert for more activity from Cromwell, that it reportedly fell prey to a trick of Browne's. In an undated report from between 26th April and 3rd May, *Mercurius Veridicus* reports that:

> Major General Browne going out with a Partee to Farinton House, sent some of his Scouts before, but meeting with none of the Enemies till his whole partee drew near to the House where they kept a Garison, he pretended to be of the Kings party, and that he had discovered a partee of Collonel Cromwel Horse not farre off, wishing that what assistance could be spared should come out of the House, for they had an opportune advantage to fall on Collonel Cromwell, &c. At which, a Captain and twenty or thirty more that were most inveterate, came running out of the House, and were taken by Major Generall Brownes Forces, without the losse of one drop of bloud.[81]

79 *CSP Domestic Series*, 1644-1645, p.445; the Committee of Both Kingdoms to its representatives with Sir Thomas Fairfax's army, 29th April.
80 Stanford-in-the-Vale, approximately four miles south-east of Faringdon. Warburton, vol. III, p.79.
81 *Mercurius Veridicus*, no.3 (1645), pp.20-21.

The story is perfectly plausible, and there is no reason to disbelieve it. Browne may have been very pleased to personally score a point off Faringdon, Lisle having harassed Abingdon's supply lines since his appointment in early December.

What Lisle was doing during the attack and the subsequent flurry of military activity, however, is not known. As a highly diligent officer it is reasonable to suppose that during the siege he was in Faringdon town, monitoring the situation and perhaps trying to communicate with Burgess. No doubt he would have returned to the house as soon as he spotted an opportunity during the siege, or when Cromwell had withdrawn far enough afterwards. Ultimately Goring's arrival at Faringdon on 3rd May ended the standoff: Cromwell and his force retreated eastward, 'els if they had stayed,' Symonds says, 'Prince Rupert and General Goring had falne upon them'. In fact on arrival Goring had indeed 'fallen' on them, beating up some of Cromwell's troopers at Radcot Bridge near the garrison, and then falling into a skirmish with Cromwell himself at Newbridge. Yet Cromwell's brief campaign around Oxford had not only achieved its objective of ruining the King's artillery convoy, but had also successfully shaken up two local garrisons, cost one colonel his life, dragged Rupert back from the Marches and removed Goring from critical business in the West Country.

Sir Marmaduke Rawdon

In his 30th April letter to Rupert, Sir Edward Nicholas stated that Cromwell was 'expecting the coming of Colonel Royden's regiment hither'. He meant Sir Marmaduke Rawdon: military governor of Basing House until the owner, the Catholic Marquess of Winchester, had successfully appealed to the Privy Council to have the garrison designated as Catholic only and Protestant Rawdon and his 500 soldiers forced out. Basing historian Wilf Emberton calls Winchester's actions 'a monumental folly', and 'a major factor leading to the eventual destruction of the House.'[82]

It is well documented that when Rawdon arrived at Oxford he and his men were put into the Faringdon garrison, in place of Lisle and his tercio. The circumstances are ambiguous, however. The onset of spring meant the earnest resumption of hostilities, and at the start of May the Oxford Army was about to march away for the new fighting season. There is no doubt that Lisle was indispensible to the army, and would probably be recalled to it, leaving the garrison behind. However, a Rawdon family document preserved in the Hertfordshire county archives complicates the situation. It says that when Sir Marmaduke's departure from Basing was agreed, sometime around the end of 1644, the King first decided to make him governor of Weymouth and Melcombe Regis. In late February, however, news arrived that Weymouth had been captured:

---

82   Emberton, *Love Loyalty*, p.82.

At which the good King was troubled, not knowing how to dispose of Sir Marmaduke. But at last he sent for Sir George Lisle who was then Governour of Farringdon, who told him he had a request to him. Sir George desired to know what it was. The King told him he desired that Collenel might have his garrison at Farringdon. Sir George swore that with all his heart and that he would leave it to him as to any man in England because he was sure he would keep it. Soe the King sent for Sir Marmaduke and told him that he was to be Governour of Farringdon and that he should stay there till some better place offerd ...[83]

Hartmann disputes that Rawdon was ever officially Faringdon's governor, but this family document seems to confirm it;[84] it is unlikely that Lisle had any choice in the matter, despite the King's reported formal courtesy. Technically Lisle was immediately under Rupert's command, the Prince being lord general, it being he who had given him his commission and being he to whom Lisle had previously reported. Rupert was away in Herefordshire or Shropshire, however, and presumably the King felt he had no choice but to deal with the Rawdon issue personally. Whether he wrote to Rupert about the matter is not known.

The timing of Lisle's meeting with Charles is uncertain, but it must have occurred sometime during March or April. If it was early in that period, it may be that Lisle's honorary DCL, bestowed mid-April, was partly a modest gesture of compensation for his loss of military position; if later in April, the meeting may have been the reason for his absence during the siege. Whatever the chronology, the situation was a personal 'win' for Lisle: having yet again proved his military merit, this time by successfully keeping a difficult garrison from capture or mutiny through a turbulent winter, he was now able to leave the troublesome post to someone else with no loss to his own honour. The Rawdon document dispels any suggestion that Sir Marmaduke's tenure at Faringdon was Lisle's idea, due to an existing friendship; it does not *disprove* any such friendship, however, and indeed as Rawdon was firmly in Buckingham's orbit in the 1620s it is highly likely that he knew Laurence. Via Buckingham, Rawdon would almost certainly have been acquainted with Sir Robert Pye senior, of whose house he now took possession.

Walker, Symonds and *Mercurius Aulicus* all concur that the Oxford Army drew out from Oxford on 7th May.[85] Symonds confirms that 'Colonel Sir Marmaduke Royden is come to Farringdon with his foot to be governor there.' Lisle may have been very relieved to leave Faringdon's localised troubles behind, but by any measure those of the King's cause as a whole in 1645 were to prove far, far worse.

---

83   Biography of Sir Marmaduke Rawdon. Hertfordshire Archives and Local Studies, ref. DE/Gr/49/1/16.
84   *Faringdon in the Civil War*, p.12.
85   Walker, p.125; Symonds, *Diarye*, p.163; *Mercurius Aulicus*, Unnumbered, 4th-11th May 1645, p.1578.

12

Unto the Breach: The Storming of Leicester

The plan for the North: Walker's assessment

By the spring of 1645, the military landscape for both the King and the Parliament was very different to that at Newbury II. Parliament's organisational changes to its military have already been noted, as has the dramatic shrinking of the Oxford Army, the divisive personal quarrels amongst the King's closest personnel which had prompted Lisle to turn down a knighthood, and the growing scarcity of vital resources. The only comprehensive overview of the Royalist situation in May 1645 comes from Sir Edward Walker. The first part of his account, covering 1644 and presented to the King in April 1645, was evidently written up from detailed notes and was so well dated as to be virtually a daily diary of the Oxford Army. Titled *The happy Progress and Success of the Arms of King Charles I …*, it still carried the hope and belief that the King would prevail. The very title of the second part, however, *Memorials of His said Majesty's Unfortunate Success in the Year following*, sets a different tone. Its narrative begins on 7th May 1645; according to a note at the end of the piece, Walker completed it from the safety of Paris in February 1647. It is no detailed, hopeful diary but a broad narrative of a political and military disaster, written with bitter hindsight. Though a gloomy and accusative retrospective which displays personal biases, particularly against Prince Rupert, it clearly outlines the King's broader predicaments in May 1645 and how he chose to confront them.

Firstly Walker decries the King's decision to send numerous councillors into the West with the Prince of Wales, he being then 'solely left to the Council and Will of His Nephew'; his assessment of the army's intentions as it left Oxford on 7th May, reveals his despair:

> the Resolutions … were such as laid the Foundation of our future ruin. For although the whole Design of the Winter past was to march Northward for the Relief of those Parts, and particularly Pomfret Castle; yet this march was the more hastned under the Pretence of relieving Chester then besieged, and in danger to be lost; though the true cause was, the earnest

Desire of Prince Rupert to be revenged of the Scots for the Defeat he had received the Year before; and had he not made too great haste, he had come time enough to have done it …[1]

Meanwhile Sir Thomas Fairfax was preparing to take Newbury; Walker believed that success would have followed 'if the King's Army bent that way', dealing with Fairfax there and preventing him joining with Parliament's other forces in the West, before moving on to deal with them separately and assisting Goring with his vital siege of Taunton. Rupert, Walker claims, was influenced by the officers of the Northern Horse, who wished to return to their territories there; additionally, fearing Goring as a rival, the Prince preferred to have him go back to the West 'with the best Horse of the Army' while he headed north, 'Contrary to the sence of all about the King, except Prince Rupert and the Northern Officers.'[2]

Meanwhile Parliament was also creating problems for itself, although perhaps they were only apparent to Fairfax at the time, and then more widely in hindsight. Despite ostensibly being free to act without political interference, he was still taking orders from the Committee of Both Kingdoms in London; which despite being comprised of experienced former commanders such as Waller, Manchester, and Essex, seems to have been oblivious to, or at least it completely ignored, the practical issues of maintaining a large army and moving it around at any speed. On 25th April it told Fairfax to be ready to move west to assist Taunton; he left Reading on 1st May. However the Committee then feared that the King intended to attack East Anglia, and when Fairfax reached Blandford in Dorset a week later he received a recall order and instructions to move north to support Cromwell, after shaving off a relief force to send on to the original destination.[3] As Glenn Foard points out, besides this indecision physically tiring the soldiers – of which Fairfax made sure to apprise the Committee[4] – it split up the supposedly unified army into three pieces and left none large enough to take on the King, whose forces were rapidly coalescing.[5] The Scots had been ordered to march south, but this was to meet the King as he moved north, not to bolster Fairfax. Moreover, the Marquess of Montrose was having good success against the Covenanters in Scotland itself, which despite repeated orders from the Committee to hurry further into England,

1   Walker, p.125.

2   Warburton, the Victorian editor of Rupert's correspondence, notes Walker's inclination 'to attribute every subsequent misfortune to Prince Rupert's advice': seizing a comment in Sir Henry Slingsby's account of Naseby which Walker himself had borrowed (H. Slingsby, p.152), Warburton asks whether, had the left wing of horse at Naseby performed as well as the right where Rupert commanded, and the battle won, Walker and Clarendon would still have found some occasion to blame him (vol. III, p.85).

3   *CSP Domestic Series*, 1644-1645, p.443; recalled by instructions dated 5th May, p.459.

4   11th May; *ibid.*, p.488.

5   Foard, *Naseby: The Decisive Campaign*, p.94. Foard concisely explains how despite being reorganised over the winter, the Parliament's army was still dogged by 'management mistakes'.

was distracting the Scots army from its task. Cromwell was receiving similar start-stop orders, and was now told to hang back and not attack the King 'unless you see apparent advantage'.[6]

Northward march

Thus Walker sets the scene. Leaving William Legge behind as governor, the King's army left Oxford for Woodstock on 7th May with only a guard of 800 horse and 700 foot: 200 of the latter being the King's Lifeguard, the rest Lisle's tercio. The remainder of the infantry had assembled near Worcester with Astley. John Corbet, writing in 1647, recorded that the army had been swollen by:

> impressing the countrey, taking in lesser brigades, and draining the garrisons ... After a little stay to perfect the recrute the army drew thence, the infantry and artillery lay betweene Worcester and Beaudley commanded by Sir Jacob Astley, whilest Rupert and Maurice with the horse and some select foote fetch off the king from Oxford ...[7]

At Woodstock, says Slingsby, the King:

> had my Ld. Gorings horse to meet him, and keep a pass & prevent Cromwells horse from troubling our rear: & accordingly they did attempt, but were beaten & put to retreat.[8]

This encounter occurred at Burford early the next morning, where according to Symonds Goring took 40 troopers and two colonels, 'Which newes saluted us in Woodstocke Parke'. Doubtless such news was considered further payback for Islip, Bletchingdon and Faringdon, but besides raising spirits it may well have exacerbated the existing rivalries between Rupert, Goring and their respective factions.

That day the Oxford force met Rupert's at Stow-on-the-Wold, adding another 2,500 horse under Langdale and the Prince's 1,000 foot; and at Evesham on the 9th, picked up Sir Henry Bard's former Campden garrison of 300 – having at Rupert's order burned Campden House upon their withdrawal – and Sir Jacob Astley's 3,300 infantry.[9] Symonds notes that 'This day, Generall Goring marched

---

6   10th May; *CSP, op. cit.*, p.476.
7   *An Historical Relation of the Military Government of Gloucester*, John Corbet, 1647. Included in Washbourne's *Bibliotheca Gloucestrensis*, 1825 (p.146).
8   H. Slingsby, p.143.
9   It is Henry Slingsby who names Rupert as ordering the house burned, to deny it to the enemy: Slingsby admits to setting the fire himself. Clarendon, who evidently did not approve of Bard, later justified the destruction by asserting that that house 'had brought no other benefit to the Publick, than the enriching the licentious Governour thereof' (Book IX, 1840 vol. V, p.164).

into the West with 3,000 horse',[10] which Walker ascribes not to military need but to personal politics and Rupert 'in probability' being:

> jealous of having a rival in Command, and so feared Goring who had the Master Wit, and had by late Actions gotten much Reputation; and therefore was willing that General Goring should return for the West, and take with him the Horse under his Command, which were the best Horse in the Army …[11]

Walker ascribes too much power to Rupert in the making of that decision, however, besides being painfully over-keen to present him in the poorest light possible.

The entire force then marched up through Worcestershire, Sir Bernard Astley's tercio sieging and taking a small enemy garrison at King's Norton: according to Walker the successful two day action at Hawkesley Hall, which involved draining the moat, 'gave some Reputation to the Army';[12] the hall suffered the same fate as Campden House. After meeting with three local garrison commanders, the King moved on into Staffordshire and then up into Shropshire. Richard Symonds says that on Saturday 17th May Colonel Richard Bagot from the Lichfield garrison joined the proceedings with 300 foot and 200 horse, and four days later the army rested while Sir Marmaduke Langdale and his cavalry made a fruitless attempt to surprise the enemy garrison at Wem.[13]

On 22nd May, at Stone in Staffordshire, Lord Byron – the bellicose Sir John who had fought alongside Lisle at Newbury I, now a baron and governor of Chester – came south to meet the King. Byron:

> acquainted him, that the Rebels upon Notice of the Advance of the Army were drawn off, that he was not so pressed but that he could well enough defend the place (if they drew not a greater Strength about him) for many Months …[14]

The Scots army had withdrawn to Westmorland ahead of the advancing Oxford Army. Byron suggested that if the King stayed in Cheshire it would give him (Byron) an opportunity to take Nantwich and 'make Himself Master of that

---

10 *Diarye*, p.166.
11 Walker, p.126. Whilst Walker may have been correct about the politics, his tendency at this time to blame Rupert for everything should be borne in mind. Certainly the presence of Goring's horse may well have helped prevent the disaster at Naseby a month later.
12 *Ibid.*, p.127.
13 *Diarye*, p.175.
14 Walker, *op. cit.*

Country', but Charles's council saw more benefit to Byron personally than to the King in general, and declined. Walker adds:

> The Fear of the Loss of Chester, which had lost us so fair an Opportunity in the West being taken away, the Design of the North was then pursued …

The army rested again on the 23rd. Whilst this may not have been for the sake of rest alone, as logistical concerns and the intelligence situation may have played a large part, undoubtedly another pause would have been welcomed by the furthest-travelled elements of the infantry – that is, Lisle's tercio and the King's Lifeguard – who had marched approximately 115 miles in two weeks.[15] This was a not-too-arduous average of eight miles per day, but after two solid weeks of it with a personal pack and weapon and probably less-than-satisfactory food, the cumulative effect on the newly-recruited or generally less hardy would be starting to show. The King could not afford to repeat the scale of losses from sickness and desertion sustained on the Cornwall campaign the year before. A decisive fight at some point was also in the offing, and whilst time was of the essence he would not want to face a battle with exhausted men. Reportedly, however, Charles made at least a token effort to share his soldiers' hardships. Yorkshire infantry colonel Sir Henry Slingsby, present on the march, felt it appropriate to compare him to Julius Caesar, who had famously endured physical difficulties to inspire his men:

> for no weather how foul soever did ever fource him to take his coach, but would show ye like patience in enduring as any of ye rest.[16]

Whilst much is intimated about how Lisle inspired his men, or how Rupert's party was almost cult-like, there is only infrequently any discussion as to how Charles I in turn inspired such deep devotion in so many of his officers. It may simply have been his status as King and his place in the divine order, but Lisle later described him as 'so just, so good a man',[17] and despite history's often harsh pronouncements about Charles's personal character and behaviour, evidently much of it was positive enough to convince many of his subjects – like Lisle – to support him to the end, many at the cost of their own lives.

Perhaps the King's own travails alongside his men, whether genuinely made or done for effect, were the reason for yet another day of rest on the 26th. He had continued north and arrived at Tutbury Castle, near Burton upon Trent, on Sunday 25th, which was Whit Sunday. Here, however:

---

15   According to point-to-point mapping software, using Symonds' detailed report of the army's itinerary.
16   H. Slingsby, *The Diary of Sir Henry Slingsby*, p.146.
17   *The Clarke Papers*, vol. II, p.34.

… intelligence was brought that Fairfax had sent a Party to relieve Taunton, and that himself with his Army was sate down before Oxford. This staggered our design, yet not so as instantly to return thither, or solely to abandon it; but only so retarded it, as to put the Army in a Capacity to come to the timely Relief of that place if there should be occasion; and also to act somewhat to divert Fairfax's Designs, by attempting the taking of Leicester, which was set on Foot as feasible. Prince Rupert, whose Mastery and chiefest Delight is in Attempts of this kind, was easily induced to undertake it …[18]

What Walker did not appreciate, was that 'Fairfax's Designs' were nothing of the sort. His stop at Oxford was ordered by the Committee on the 15th, as part of its current plan for him, which was that he should block up the Royalist capital rather than pursue the King north, where other forces could now intercept him instead. On 10th May it had ordered Richard Browne to put a garrison into Bletchingdon, and on the 13th ordered him and Cromwell to 'lie in such other places as you conceive most convenient for straitening Oxford.'[19]

It was at the army's designated headquarters at Burton where the Royalist Council of War faced a choice: turn north, pick up new recruits promised in Yorkshire and face the Scots, or turn south and relieve Oxford. A compromise was reached: to draw Fairfax away from Oxford by attacking Leicester.

According to Symonds the King's forces were rested again on Monday 26th May; on Tuesday 27th, according to a later London report, they were 'quartered about Loughborrow and all the Towns about it'.[20] The local inhabitants were:

not yet knowing, whether they intended for Leicester or Newark, for those Towns where they quartered were just in the line of their march to either place: But upon Wednesday they put us out of all doubt, by surrounding us with their Horse, and firing three Wind-mills, and one Water-mill.[21]

The newly arrived cavalry were Langdale and the Northern Horse who, while the army was at Loughborough, had been ordered further south to patrol the area between Coventry and Leicester, and prevent the latter being resupplied or reinforced before the King's arrival. Evidently Sir Henry Slingsby marched with Langdale, for he recounts some skirmishing with local enemy horse near the town

18   Walker, p.127.
19   Fairfax's orders to siege the city, *CSP Domestic Series*, 1644-1645, p.493; Browne's and Cromwell's orders pp.486-487, 492.
20   *A Narration of the Siege and taking of The Town of Leicester* …, p.5.
21   *Ibid.* The burning of the mills was corroborated by a report to Sir Samuel Luke (*Letter Books*, p.548, letter no. 1316, from Sir John Norwich).

when the cavalry arrived on the 28th;[22] the London report, entitled *A Narration of the Siege and taking of The Town of Leicester*, also mentions skirmishing, and reports that Royalist foot began arriving that night and starting to build a battery to face the town's citadel. The garrison:

> played upon them all night abundantly from our works with our Musketeers, and Cannon shot from the south Centry, in the morning care was taken for the disposing all our Horse and Foot …

The overnight arrival of the Royalist construction party implies that they already had excellent information about the town's defences, and had already decided where they were going to strike. The next day, Thursday 29th, they were joined by the rest of the army. Leicester's 340 cavalry (240 local, and 100 from a nearby garrison[23]) and 1,500 infantry (450 'foot Souldiers in pay in the towne', 900 townsmen issued with weapons, and 150 reluctant county recruits[24]) prepared to face the King's combined army over just over 11,000.[25]

The storming of Leicester

In an 1839 lecture about Leicester's Civil War history, local historian John Hollings admitted that:

> With respect to the plan of operations against the Town during the Siege, the reader will hardly require to be informed, that the line of defence laid down in it, is in some degree conjectural; it being impossible at the present day to ascertain the precise situation of works which were demolished soon after their completion, the site of which moreover is now for the most part covered by buildings.[26]

Of defensive works, certainly Leicester's medieval defences had virtually disappeared by 1610, when map-maker John Speed depicted the town without any outer walls at all; only mounds and ditches remained. The remains of Leicester Castle had been demolished in 1633, and only an ancient citadel, 'The Newark', remained in a walled condition, situated on the southern corner of the town next to the south gate. After Lisle stormed it, Richard Symonds speaks of bodies 'in the graffe': that is, in the medieval moat surrounding the town, which at this point in its circuit

---

22 H. Slingsby, p.146.
23 *A Narration* … p.5.
24 *A perfect Relation of the taking of Leicester*, p.1; *A Narration* …, p.5.
25 Symonds gives a detailed breakdown of the cavalry at this time, numbering it at 5,520; the King's total infantry, after picking up the various units along the way, was at least 5,600 (*Diarye*, p.166, p.182),
26 Hollings, *The History of Leicester During the Great Civil War* …, p.iv.

ran along the citadel's southern wall. Although dry in the 1640s, it appears from a map included by Hollings to have originally been wet, fed by water diverted from the River Soar.[27] Its dimensions are not known, but during the storming Lisle and his men were reportedly pushed back into it, which suggests significant width or depth although, the *Narration* says, they had 'cut down many bushes and faggeted them', in order to fill up the ditches and effect a crossing from the south bank.[28] The citadel was packed with houses, mostly owned by the town's wealthiest citizens who, Colonel George Booth warned local MP Lord Grey of Groby six weeks previously:

> sensible of their danger, and careful of their own security, have all of them, got houses in a place of this Town called the Newark, where they are fortifying themselves, as strong as may be, which will prove, as I fear of most dangerous consequence, for I perceive the Townsmen much discontented, conceiving themselves destined by the Committee to the enemy's mercy …[29]

Booth was correct: whilst the Newark was walled, and the western edge of the town was protected well enough by the Soar, the rest of Leicester had remained exposed until Lord Grey had made start on a new line of fortifications the previous year. However as Dr Jeff Richards describes, this was as yet in no fit state to repel a determined attack force. The work:

> consisted of little more than a simple embankment, protected by a fosse or ditch, and strengthened at a few important points … with 'horn works' and some drawbridges, and was still in an unfinished condition.[30]

On Thursday 29th, *Mercurius Aulicus* says:

> His Highnesse Prince Rupert betimes in the morning faced the Towne with Horse, viewed it every way, and suddenly girt it round; in the afternoone the whole Army came up and sate downe before the Towne.[31]

---

27 'An Aspect of the town of Leicester during the Civil War 1642-5'; Hollings, *The History of Leicester*, 1840 (plate or map number unknown). Image accessed online via University of Leicester 'Special Collections Online'. That the moat was dry in 1645 is confirmed by *The Weekly Account*, which says the Royalists 'made entrance at the South Gate, where the water was dried up …' (The XXII Week (1645), no page numbers).

28 *A Narration …*, p.7.

29 *Ibid.*, pp.11-12

30 Richards, p.80.

31 Unnumbered, 25th May-8th June 1645, p.1601. This was to be the last *Aulicus* until 13th July; after that edition, only two more were ever printed.

With good timing the army was now joined by Richard Willys, governor of Newark, who arrived with Ned Villiers and around 1,000 horse.[32] They also brought an unspecified number of foot, probably no more than a couple of hundred: thereafter known as the 'Newark Foot' and placed under Lisle's command.

Increasingly, however, the wider military situation was darkening: news came on the same day that Evesham, governed by Rupert's appointee Robert Legge, had been lost to the enemy. Legge had not meekly surrendered the town but had told Colonel Edward Massey, who faced it, that he would defend it:

> so long as I can … being nothing terrified by your summons. I perceave you are a stranger to our strength and resolution, further treaties will be troublesome.[33]

Windebank cast a long shadow. Massey stormed and took the garrison within a few hours: as Richards points out, the loss of Evesham severed Royalist communications between Oxford, Worcester and South Wales.[34]

At noon on Thursday, according to both *Mercurius Aulicus* and the Parliamentarian *Narration*, Rupert summoned the town, offering quarter to all within it, and liberty to one Major Ennis who had been passing Leicester with his dragoons and stopped to assist. *Aulicus* adds that Rupert made sure to inform the townsmen that the King was present in person; Symonds adds that the Prince fired 'two great peices' into the town, presumably those two cannon which *Aulicus* says 'were taken from the Earle of Essex at Lestythiel in Cornwall',[35] and presumably using the battery built overnight by the advance party.

In response, and perhaps unwisely, the local committee in the town detained Rupert's trumpeter while they debated their answer. Rupert sent a drummer to demand a response within a quarter hour, but when one did not arrive, waited no longer for a resolution.

At this point the timeline becomes confused, as the primary accounts conflict over the precise order of events. *Aulicus* suggests a lull in the proceedings here whilst the second, six-piece battery was built overnight and the ensuing events continued on Friday morning; Symonds and *A more Exact Relation* that everything, including the building of the second battery, occurred on Friday; and the *Narration* begins with Rupert's arrival on Thursday and continues straight into Friday's events without indicating where in the proceedings Thursday night intervened. It is clear, however, that by Friday morning the six-piece battery was

---

32 A prisoner captured by Sir John Norwich on 30th May told him that Newark had sent 1,400 horse, although such an admission should be taken with caution (*Letter Books*, p.548, letter no. 1316).

33 Corbet, p.148.

34 Richards, pp.103-104.

35 Cannonballs found nearby in the nineteenth century weighed 7-12lb, which was correct for a demi-culverin. Bar shot was also found, which is usually used against ship's rigging (Hollings, p.51).

complete, set up on some ancient earthworks by the road that led up to the town's south gate. The battery's swift completion, whether performed overnight or during Friday, was all the more remarkable given that as on Thursday night the work parties had come under constant fire from muskets and artillery in the town;[36] even Walker, in a moment of praise quite unexpected given his recent criticism of the Prince, concedes that 'by the admirable Diligence and Command of Prince Rupert a Battery was raised.' The size of the construction party is not known, but as Lisle's tercio was stationed here on the south side, it is likely that if manpower was short they were roped in to help. This larger battery was sited to attack the same piece of flimsy southern wall of the medieval citadel, and Hollings puts the firing distance at just over 300 yards.[37] Hollings, having examined the artillery-damaged remains of the Newark wall in 1840, noted that two different faces of the wall had been struck and confirms the presence of two batteries: one near the river, that built on Wednesday night, and the six-piece structure built on the ancient earthworks on Thursday night or Friday. Yet despite staring down the barrels of eight substantial guns, throughout Friday the town continued to play for time.

At about 2 p.m. on Friday, Symonds says:

> one of the Leicester trumpets was sent to desire time to consider of it till the morrow morning, and to tell him that they wondered he would rayse any worke, &c. during this summons. His Hignes told the trumpet if he came agen with such another errand, he'de lay him by the heels.[38]

Half an hour later, however:

> [he] comes agen with this note directed thus: 'To the Commander in Cheife;' desiring time to consider till the morrow morning. The Prince commits the trumpet to his Marshall. Still the first trumpet they keepe. Then the Prince about three of the clock sent them an answer in lowder terms; six great peices from the fort on the south side of the towne playing upon a stone wall unlyned, and made ere six of the clock a breach of great space.

According to the *Narration*, Rupert's several-hour cannonade was accompanied by muskets, Slingsby says to prevent the defenders repairing the breach;[39] given the Royalist positions later in the evening this must have been Lisle's tercio. The

---

36   *A more Exact Relation* …, p.5.
37   'Plan of the Operations Against The Town of Leicester, during the Siege of 1645'; Hollings, *The History of Leicester*, 1840 (plate or map number unknown). Image accessed online via University of Leicester 'Special Collections Online'.
38   *Diarye*, pp.179-180.
39   Ibid., p.6.; Slingsby, p.147

defenders used firing loopholes cut in the walls; whether Lisle's men had any cover at all is not known, but the distance was short enough that they might have made use of Grey's half-finished defence line.

Aulicus continues:

> This afternoone the Cannon played upon the Newarke wall, and by seaven of the clock made a Breach, so as 10. might enter a breast. 'About 10. of the clock his Highness commanded the Souldiers to draw neare the Workes, and upon the signall given (which was the firing those 6 pieces of Canon all once) to fall on; within halfe an houre the souldiers were all ready to assault; therefore the Ordnance giving the word, they all cryed *On, On*, and assaulted with so much gallant wonted resolution, that in lesse then an houre and an halfe they tooke the Towne, which was before two of clocke this morning; … They stormed it in 5 severall places …

The Royalist field word was 'God and the Prince', presumably in honour of Prince Charles, whose birthday it had been the day before.[40] The first to get into the town, *Aulicus* says, were the men of Sir Bernard Astley in the north and Sir Henry Bard and Colonel Richard Page in the east, using scaling ladders; they were followed by Rupert's regiment of foot under Colonel John Russell. Slingsby says Bard and Page's attempt:

> was carry'd wth better success as it prov'd, some wth ladders get over their works, other break ye chain & letts down ye Drawbridge & fells down ye works in 20 or 3 several places yt our horse may enter, so yt by the time it was light, ye town was ours …[41]

The *Narration*, however, records that during the scaling Bard was 'beaten down' with a musket and badly bruised, along with his major, 16 men killed and 60 more 'mortally wounded'. His second attempt was successful, however, and entry gained by plentiful use of 'hand-granadoes'. The welcome midsummer sunrise which Slingsby recalls, came just before 4 a.m.; Rupert's colours were soon flying from a battery. Meanwhile, simultaneously, Lisle and his men had stormed the breach on the southern side. *A more Exact Relation* offers the fullest account of the action against the Newark; although from the defenders' perspective, it clearly describes Lisle's attempts to get his tercio through the breach. After the six-cannon signal from the Royalist artillery, the report says:

40   *A perfect Relation …*, p.2.
41   H. Slingsby, pp.147-148.

… they did draw the most of their strength to the breach which they had made in Newark wall; and not thinking of any Work made within that Breach, they with confidence entred …

They met with an unpleasant surprise: Symonds records that despite having being harried for several hours by Lisle's musketeers:

they in the towne had gotten up a handsome retrenchment with three flankers, (a great Spanish peice,) within four or five yards of the wall.

The *Narration* reveals that this inner wall at the Newark had been begun some time previously but never finished; now the women of the town, along with dismounted troopers, had laboured to complete it during the bombardment, despite being showered with debris from the disintegrating citadel wall.[42] Even in its unfinished state, its deficiencies hastily built up with 'Wool-packs, and other materials'[43] – when Lisle and his men entered the breach the inner wall would have prevented their immediate entrance into the Newark, confining them to a small area which the enemy controlled and had presumably covered with artillery and musketeers. Forced to halt, *A more Exact Relation* continues, they:

beat our Musketiers from the louphole of the stone wall: Major Ennis perceiving the Enemy to have entred the Breach, drew his Horse down towards them, and caused some troopers serve with carbines on foot, & with the rest of his Horse upon the footgang of the Line, beat the Enemy back with losse. The Enemy attempted again, and entred the Breach, and all the Musketiers there run away basely; so that Major Ennis was forced to maintain that Breach with his Horse, and some he caused quit their Horse and serve on foot, and with admirable resolution repulsed the Enemy five severall stormed, and caused them at last draw quite off; and did conceive no probability of entring there, for there was a peece of our best Canon drawn thither, and load with case-shot, did wonderfull execution upon the Enemy …

The *Narration*:

… at the Newarke breach was the fiercest assault, the enemy there comming to push of Pike, four times they attempted, and were as often repulst, our men taking two of their Colors from them, and pluck'd many of their Pikes out of their hands, and Captain Hacker, and Cap. Babington

42   *A Narration …*, p.6; *A more Exact Relation*, p.6.
43   *A perfect Relation …*, p.1.

with their horse, and the Cannon from a corner of the wall made a miserable slaughter of them …

This was the point at which the Royalists' most significant casualty occurred:

> … amongst the rest Colonell St George, in a bravery, came up to our Cannon, and was by it shotter'd into small parcels, and with him many more …

In a fit of extraordinarily poor taste, Parliament's *Mercurius Britanicus* crowed that:

> He was never truly a *Saint George* till now, by his death in the Catholique Cause; Now he may chance to be *Canonized* for his merits …[44]

Aulicus offers the assault from Lisle's perspective:

> … the hottest and most desperate service was at the Breach in the Newarke-wall, which the Rebels had within fortified, having cast up a worke against the breach, and bestowed there the most and best of their men; here Colonell George Lisle with his Tertia of tryed Souldiers forced his entrance in despight of all the Rebels Pikes, Canon, and Muskets, which poured thicke upon him; the Rebels advantage was here so great, that twice the Colonell was forced backe, the Colonell himselfe being knockt downe into the Ditch, but he and his brave men (sworne never to yeild) went on the third time, and with unexpressible valour beate downe the Rebels and entered the breach, (these were Edgehill Regiments.) Those that first entred opened the Ports and let in the Horse which instantly entered the Towne …

Britanicus – who as demonstrated, dealt chiefly in punning and cheap wit, and whose weekly output always began with an attack on *Aulicus* – was having none of it:

> He tells of Colonel Lisle's Regiment forcing his entrance at the strongest breach with his Souldiers; and with Oathes too, I warrant you, for the young man being a Stammering Royalist, uses at every Pause to lispe out *God dammee*, to fill up his Oratory: Nay *Aulicus* himselfe within three lines confesses, that when they had been repulst severall times, *and knockt down in the Ditch*, both he and his Souldiers swore never to yield; for,

---

44   Numb. 87, p.789.

sayes he, these were Edge-hill Regiments; which you may easily beleeve by their Swearing, and being knock't down so often.

Britanicus had mentioned the King's stammer on the first page of the issue, suggesting that perhaps when captured and brought to London he would be able to 'speak plaine' to the Parliament and not 'brand them any more with that S'tammering … slander of Rebels.' His subsequent mention of Lisle's stammer seems merely to be continuing a theme. It was not a fabrication, for (as noted previously) a later Royalist source also refers to it, and in any case *Britanicus* much enjoyed poking fun at people's physical attributes and deficiencies. Whether he had heard of the stammer beforehand is not known, but when it is taken together with the part about Lisle swearing as he tried to get his tercio through the breach, it seems most likely that he was seen and heard by someone very close by in the crush at the breach or positioned on the citadel walls. That they took the time to mention his conduct in their dispatch to London, implies that he stood out in the melee. As at Newbury, the fact that Lisle fought conspicuously from the front yet escaped such brutal close-quarter fighting apparently without significant injury, is remarkable – particularly if, as *Aulicus* had put it, he still seldom wore 'defensive Armes'.

Symonds records that when the tercio was initially repulsed from the breach, 'the King sent his foot regiment of lifeguards to assist, but they gott fully in before.'[45] The 200-strong Lifeguard, who had left Oxford alongside Lisle on 7th May, were presumably acting as his reserve. Later on, according to Slingsby, 'some men dismount'd wth Sword & pistol did second him',[46] and the Parliamentarian *A perfect Relation* recounts that 'their horse who were behind the foot did force them on again',[47] suggesting that every available man was called upon to add weight to the assault and help break the desperate resistance of the defenders in the Newark. Possibly, when officers are considered, the Lifeguard numbers were in fact higher than Symonds reported, and they may have been augmented by Bagot's men from Lichfield, whose position at Leicester is otherwise not clear.

Eventually Lisle succeeded, but it was a close-run thing: evidently the defenders in the citadel began to be attacked from behind by Royalists who had entered the city from the other side, and were eventually forced to give way. Walker says that Lisle and his men:

> had drawn off had not the Town been entred on the other side by Sir Henry Bard, Collonel Page and the Newark Horse, on Foot with their Swords and Pistols.[48]

---

45   *Diarye*, p.180.
46   H. Slingsby, p.147.
47   *A perfect Relation* …, p.2.
48   Walker, pp.127-128.

By coincidence, the man in charge of the portion of Leicester's defences attacked by Lisle was Sir Robert Pye junior, whose family owned The Place at Faringdon: he had been en route to a rendezvous with his regiment but was stranded in town by the Royalist advance and agreed to help with the town's defence. Captured, he was paroled shortly afterwards and allowed to leave as part of a prisoner exchange. Whether he ever discovered that the fiercely single-minded officer who had wrestled the town defences from him that night, was he who had occupied the Pyes' Berkshire home for the last six months, we will never know.

A 'Legion of Canibals'

As to casualties and prisoners, Sir Edward Walker notes that:

> By the Break of Day all ours were entred the Line, and presently Sir Robert Pye the Governour, and all the Officers, Souldiers and Townsmen in Arms, being about 1200, were made Prisoners … I am confident we lost three for one in the Assault; the number slain on both sides being about 300, amongst whom of ours Collonel St George and some Officers lay dead in the Breach.

Slingsby agrees that Lisle was repulsed 'leaving many dead bodies, both wthin & upon it';[49] Richard Symonds says that:

> More dead bodyes lay just within the lyne farre then without or in the graffe. I [was] told 30 and more at the breach, as many within as without. Every street had some. I believe 200 on both sides were not killed. We lost Colonel St. George. Major Bunnington, gentleman pensioner, shott in the eye just as he was on the top of the ladder. 28 or 30 officers. Major of the Prince Rupert's firelocks.[50]

Aulicus is strategically honest in its assessment of the number of Royalist casualties:

> The Pamphlets (the *Scottish Dove* for one) say His Majesty *took this Towne with the losse of 50 men*; we might say too, but the truth is we lost more, in all neare 80, many whereof were killed at the Breach; The cheife man of note was Colonell St. George, a gallant Gentleman, and of the Rebels were slaine about 120 (all agree 200 was the number killed on both sides) which

---

49   H. Slingsby, *op. cit.*
50   *Diarye*, p.180.

may fully stop their shamefull mouthes that offer to talke of cruelty in His Majesties Souldiers …

Despite *Aulicus*'s protests, there is no question that once the Royalists entered the town, it was thoroughly and bloodily sacked. If Berkenhead was attempting diversion or damage limitation by making an admission of larger Royalist losses than the enemy themselves had claimed, he was doomed to fail. Naturally the event was seized on greedily by the London press:

> The particulars of the taking of Leicester by the Kings forces, and their cruelty upon the inhabitants there are too sad to be reiterated, sure the end of the blood-thirsty cavaliers is neere, when they doe strive every day to excell in cruelty and inhumanity.

So spat *Mercurius Civicus*; *The Weekly Account* went as far as to label the Royalist forces 'a Legion of Canibals'. As to casualty figures, the London presses disgorged figures equally hysterical, compared to the modest numbers claimed by the Royalists: for example *The Weekly Account* claimed 1100 people were put to the sword; *The True Informer* that there were 500 dead on each side, plus 200 'Reformado Scots' put to the sword and 'many woman and children murthered', plus 1500 (military) prisoners taken along with 700 horses and 1000 'Country-people'. *Perfect Occurrences* claims that the Royalist soldiers were so drunk with wine and blood that they 'tumbled up and downe the streets like Swine, many lying along in the streets amongst the dead corps …'; a letter printed in *Perfect Passages* claimed that 'they ravish women and maids in a most barbarous manner', and at least one woman was 'ravished … in the open street'.[51] Most of the news-books carried similar stories. Surprisingly for a Parliamentarian report, however, *A Perfect Relation* plays down such stories:

> I finde some of the Pamphlets speaking of the horrid cruelty of the insulting enemy, putting man, woman, and child to the sword. I know their tender mercies are cruelties, but give the divell his due, there was indeed many slaine at the first entrance, and some that made little resist-ance, and some women and children amongst the multitude by the rabble of common souldiers; but I cannot learne of any such order given to destroy all, as is said by some, and it is the generall opinion of many that have since got out of the Towne that in the conflict and since there was not slaine of the Parliaments party, souldiers and others, above 100. and some

---

51 *Mercurius Civicus* Numb. 106, p.944; *The Weekly Account*, The XXII Week (1645), no page numbers; *The True Informer* Numb. 7 (1645), p.50; *Perfect Occurrences of Parliament*, The 23rd Week (1645), no page numbers; *Perfect Passages* numb. 32, p.252.

of those in their cold blood, after they had granted quarter of life, picking out some active men and setting common souldiers to quarrell with them and slay them, but of these not many. It is confidently believed that not above 300 are slaine on both sides …[52]

The estimate of 300 dead on each side chimes well with the *Narration*'s report that 'There was buried in Leicester 709. as hath been collected by the burials there …[53]

Whilst the wilder tales may indeed have been compounded exaggerations, carried far on a wave of word-of-mouth reporting which quickly rippled out across Leicestershire and beyond, unquestionably for the Royalists there were many uncomfortable, if not downright shameful grains of truth. To their credit they did not attempt to deny it: whilst *Aulicus* tried to mitigate the facts, Sir Edward Walker frankly admitted that 'the Town miserably sackt without regard to Church or Hospital',[54] while Richard Symonds conceded that a number of Scots were indeed killed after the Royalist cavalry were let into the town at about 1 a.m.:

> in the meane time the foot gott in and fell to plunder, so that ere day fully open scarse a cottage unplundered. There were many Scotts in this towne, and no quarter was given to any in the heat.

Where Europe's generally accepted 'rules of war' at this period were adhered to, the sacking of a city was to be expected if a surrender summons was not obeyed and the besiegers chose to take it by storm. A benevolent general might grant mercy or pardon to some or all of those inside, or order the city and inhabitants to be preserved, if he had some particular reason and if he could keep his plunder-hungry soldiers in check; more often than not, however, those inside the walls were subject to the whim of the enemy army. So it was at Leicester in the early morning of 31st May.

The sources conflict over whether on this occasion quarter was promised or not. As noted above, *A perfect Relation* records localised brawling 'after they had granted quarter of life'; *Mercurius Civicus*, however, prints an eyewitness claim that the Prince had threatened to kill any man who gave quarter to anyone (and that he had carried out his threat). Similarly *Perfect Occurrences of Parliament* claims that:

> Rupert himself commanded, that not a Country-man that came in to their assistance, should have quarter for their lives, but all be put to the sword both young and old.[55]

52   *A perfect Relation* …, p.3.
53   *A Narration* …, p.11.
54   Walker, p.127.
55   *Mercurius Civicus, op. cit.,* p.948; *Perfect Occurrences of Parliament, op. cit.*

Mercurius Veridicus, on the other hand, cites a claim from Leicester inhabitants who had fled to London, that Rupert declared 'he would not see a pennyworth of wrong by plunder', and that '[having] formerly forbidden quarter', he then granted it to prevent the slaughter of Protestants by Welsh and Irish Catholics.[56] Even Walker, who as the King's war secretary might be expected to know the full details, says that in fact 'It cannot be said whether for the time ours better attempted it, or they defended themselves': in other words whether the Royalists were in the first place the more aggressive, or whether the defenders put up such a fight that they were taken to be resisting and therefore under the 'rules' invited harsher treatment. *The Weekly Account* claims the latter, that:

> ... the Kings Forces ... swore, that when they came into the Town, they would give never a man quarter: which the Soldiers and Townesmen having notice of, and perceiving there was no quarter to be given, fell to it with much courage and valour, they were two houres fighting; at last upon the Enemies entrance they were so inraged, that they most inhumanely slew both women and children, all that they could come near ...[57]

Presumably it was fevered reports such as this which *A perfect Relation* had felt moved to contradict. *The Weekly Account* does confirm stiff resistance in the town, and that the defenders:

> disputed every street with them, till they came into the Market place; but at last being over-powred by the Enemies numbers, and a Bridge being let down by a perfidious Butcher, they were inforced to yeeld ...

A Perfect Diurnall corroborates the *Account* by recounting in great detail a street fight which ended up in the market place, and describes a showdown involving artillery, blood running in the streets, the defenders pelting the Royalists with missiles from upper windows, and the Royalists again accused of offering no quarter.[58] It is perfectly understandable that the 900 armed townsmen put up such a fight, as they were no stranger army which had been caught in the city and had attempted to hold it: this was their home, and their very lives and livelihoods were at stake, as was the safety of their families. Ultimately if they kept their lives that night they may have lost their fortunes: at least two sources state that the population around Leicester had sent their goods and valuables into the town – it being

---

56   No. 8 (1645), p.62.
57   The XXII Week (1645), no page numbers.
58   No. 97, p.768.

the most strongly defended place thereabouts – only to have them plundered by the Royalists when the town fell.[59]

The pertinent question here, is how or if Lisle was involved in the pillaging of the town, and in particular in any of the incidents mentioned by the Parliamentarian press that were in fact genuine. As we have come to expect with Lisle, his reactions to the overnight events at Leicester have not been preserved and after the initial storming he is not mentioned in any of the accounts. As an effective and experienced soldier he would have understood, and must have accepted, the 'rules of war' and all they entailed, including the plundering of captured enemy strongholds. Yet ever attendant on such matters were the human ideals of discretion and proportion, and the Christian ideals of compassion and mercy: 'rules of decency' which went hand-in-hand with the 'rules of war', to be properly considered and appropriately applied by the conquering soldier. Lisle's comments before his death at Colchester show that he had fully expected such 'rules of decency' to be applied there: so unless he was given to gross double standards, then we can take this to mean that he had routinely pursued their ideals himself. The storming of Leicester perfectly exemplifies an extreme situation requiring a temperative hand, so we can confidently expect that applying one where necessary was uppermost in Lisle's mind. His alleged note at Newbury displays a deep compassion, and Clarendon – who as one of the King's councillors would have known him well by repute, if not in person – says he had 'the most gentle nature imaginable', and was 'without a capacity to have an enemy'.[60] Quite apart from human or Christian ideals, these are not things to be said of a man who would relish gratuitously plundering private houses or randomly abusing civilians, and it is unlikely that he would have allowed his men to do so.

That is not to say none of his tercio were involved, particularly if the unit was split up during the subsequent street fighting and parts of it lost to his control. However, it is reasonable to assert that those men remaining under his hand were the least likely to have been those perpetrating the grosser crimes that night. Furthermore, other contemporary sources say 'no man was ever better followed; his soldiers never forsaking him', and he was 'Infinitely belov'd and observed by his Souldiers',[61] which means he commanded a high level of respect and was therefore unlikely to have lost that control at a critical moment. There is no suggestion, however slight, in any known contemporary source, that his soldiers – regimental, tercio or commanded – were ever blamed for poor behaviour when under his personal command, or that he ever faced a mutiny against it.[62] Certainly there

---

59   *The Scottish Dove*, Numb. 85, p.668; *A Diary or An Exact Journall*, Numb. 55, no page numbers.

60   Book XI, 1840 vol. VI, p.99. Notably, this seems to be a personal comment from Clarendon and not something lifted from an earlier source.

61   *The Loyall Sacrifice*, p.63; Clarendon, *op. cit.*.

62   The one exception of poor behaviour is the accusation that his regiment, along with two others, had burned the suburbs at Abingdon in June 1644 (see chapter 8), but notably on that occasion they were

was a mutiny at Colchester at the end of the siege, but this was not aimed specifically at his leadership, and in fact he is one of the officers credited with talking down the mutineers and reimposing order whilst avoiding bloodshed. There is one further point regarding the potential participation of his men in the worst of the violence reported inside Leicester: the fight at the breach was the stiffest and most prolonged action of the night, and having struggled there for several hours his tercio would be bloodied and exhausted, and less likely to be fit for subsequent skirmishing than men who had simply climbed a ladder into the city elsewhere or been let into the streets by the treacherous opening of a gate. Whilst some of Lisle's men may have vented their frustration and anger on the populace, particularly after witnessing the horrific death of Colonel St George, again it is likely they could only have done so if separated from their tercio and its commander.

There is one personal factor which may have weighed on Lisle's mind that night: his mother was from Leicester, or one of the large family estates which surrounded it. He may well have had relatives who lived in the city, or who had significant interests in it, or he may have been familiar with its streets from visits to family members. Whilst he had a job to do for his sovereign, such a family link could only have made him more determined to see that job done with as little destruction as possible; given what happened after the storming, it is a great pity that his thoughts on the night's events have not been preserved.

In the next few days, Walker says, the army rested while the city was secured and temporary repairs made to the breach in the wall; reportedly, cart loads of plundered goods were sent on to Newark. According to Symonds, Colonel Appleyard was appointed governor of the town, allegedly having been the first man to enter it; he and Colonel Page were knighted for their actions during the assault. Lisle was not, despite his efforts at the breach, but after the sting of his refusal to accept that honour for Newbury, perhaps it is understandable. Symonds says, however, that 'Colonel George Lisle was made Leiftenant General of this shire under the Lord Loughborough ...'[63] Whilst knighthoods were a mark of favour bestowed for a wide range of reasons, the rank of lieutenant general was firmly a recognition of high military esteem, and in that respect may have meant far more to Lisle. It was to be a very short-lived appointment, however.

---

not under Lisle's command: he had joined the King on his 'night march' when Oxford was threatened, and had not yet rejoined his tercio.

63   *Diarye*, p.184.

13

Naseby

The King's march south

The decisive but unexpected loss of Leicester shook the Parliament and its supporters to their core. In a letter to Sir Samuel Luke, Major Leonard Watson – formerly scoutmaster for the Earl of Manchester and now for the New Model Army – wrote that:

> The consequences of it will be very sad and prove very dangerous to the whole kingdom. The opportunity the King has of recruiting himself with men and horses is such as he has not a greater.[1]

Watson was correct, for as Sir Henry Slingsby noted:

> While his Majesty stay'd here, my Ld of Loubrough sends out his warrants to call in ye country to assist ye King wth their Arms, & in a short time I saw an appearance of near a 1000 men, & all taken out of one division.[2]

Evidently the Committee of Both Kingdoms was also in a high state of alarm, as on 1st June it wrote to the local committee at Coventry to warn them that:

> The sudden surprise of Leicester makes us very solicitous concerning the security of the adjacent garrisons, and particularly of yours. We desire you to be vigilant, and to use all the means in your power to strengthen your garrisons and to victual them.[3]

---

1   31st May; Luke, *Letter Books,* p.551, letter no. 1324.
2   H. Slingsby, p.148. Henry Hastings had been created Baron Loughborough in October 1643, and lieutenant general of the Midlands counties.
3   *CSP Domestic Series,* 1644-1645, p.554.

Similar warnings were sent to Newport Pagnell and Northampton; Lord Fairfax was told to 'look carefully to the security of York', and the Scots commander Alexander Leslie was desired to 'speedily advance southward to interpose between York and the enemy.' The Bedford committee was ordered to pay its overdue monies to Newport Pagnell, to enable it to defend itself. Two small garrisons within twenty miles of Leicester had been abandoned in a panic, Sir John Norwich of Rockingham Castle garrison informing Luke that he had sent a party of horse to one of them to retrieve 'ordnance and ammunition and other provisions … if it be not too late.' It would have been a dangerous mission: the next day Norwich recorded that the King's forces 'Straggle up and down the country, plundering, imprisoning and laying great impositions on the country.'[4]

Walker also recognised the opportunity now presented to the King, remarking that it was widely believed even Derby would now surrender if summoned; certainly Watson supposed it was the next Royalist target.[5] It did not happen: Walker blamed Rupert's refusal to do it – although Rupert quite reasonably pointed out that if it refused his summons he was obliged to storm it – and lamented what he saw as opportunities squandered:

> As the gaining of this place made the King and His Army terrible, so the use that was made of it, and the Consequence thereof, conduced to our Destruction; for now instead of either retiring towards Worcester to join with General Gerrard, which was in a few Days after by an order to come to us with 3000 Horse and Foot, whereby we might have secured our new Conquests; or else of marching Northward with the Terror of being Victorious, we turn our Faces towards Oxford …[6]

For Oxford was still threatened by Fairfax. Walker concedes that Rupert was against the army's return in that direction, but adds that he gave in to the desires of those who claimed to fear for 'the Duke of York, the Council, Magazine, and all the fair Ladies at Oxford'; the latter of whom, Walker claims, wrote to Rupert begging him to save them. Walker may have scoffed at such fears, in his eagerness to slight the Prince, but certainly many influential members of the army and council would have left their families in the city. The clamour of their concerns for Oxford's safety, and their reluctance to leave that to chance, can be well imagined. Whether the city was likely to fall to Fairfax and the New Model, is debatable: as Foard points out, Rupert was in close contact with William Legge, the governor,

---

4   1st June; Luke, *Letter Books*: p.552, report no. 1325. Norwich later informed Luke that his men had safely completed their task, partially firing the house to prevent the Royalists garrisoning it (p.556, letter no. 1334).
5   3rd June; Luke, *Letter Books*: p.555, letter no.1332.
6   Walker, p.128.

and if Legge believed the city was in serious trouble he would have let the Prince know. Furthermore, Legge was a natural military administrator who during the first Bishops War had been master of the armoury and inspector of the defences of Newcastle and Hull. If Oxford needed an effective minder, Legge was the perfect choice.[7]

Nevertheless, on the 4th or 5th of June, the Royalist forces left Leicester and headed south-east. Their march was observed anxiously by their enemy: the Northamptonshire Committee reported that 'we hear not which way they bend', and Sir John Norwich, a little way eastward at Rockingham and potentially in the King's path, informed Luke that he had been told they were heading due south for Northampton but other information led him to 'expect them before me ere morning.'[8] There still seemed to be an expectation that the Royalists might head into East Anglia, as Norwich notes the large bodies of Parliamentarian men at Stamford and Huntingdon who would 'protect those counties who are well prepared by their grievous oppressions to assist against the enemy.'

In fact, on the night of the 5th the Royalists quartered around Market Harborough, some twelve miles west of Rockingham, and held the first full rendezvous of the army since the action at Leicester. It was only now, Walker says, that:

> we found the Loss we had by the taking of that Place; for what with those that were slain and wounded, when we took the Town, those were left there in Garrison, and those that ran away afterwards with their Plunder, we were not 3500 Foot …

The infantry had numbered approximately 5,600 at Leicester, meaning that in one week it had lost more than a third of its strength. Presumably the men Hastings had recruited were only intended for local service. Meanwhile, says Symonds, Richard Willys had departed for Newark with 400 horse, leaving the rest to march with the King; the Northern Horse, says Walker, were discontented to the point that they also left the army – despite a promise from Charles that he would move north within fifteen days – and had to be persuaded to return.[9]

Leaving Harborough, the army veered south-west, avoiding Northampton, and headed for Daventry; either at Harborough (Walker), or at Daventry on 7th June (Symonds), news arrived which was both welcome and unwelcome: Sir Thomas Fairfax had quit the siege of Oxford and lay just south of Northampton. He left the siege, Walker explains:

7   Ian Roy, ODNB; Foard, p.140.
8   Luke, *Letter Books*: 5th June, p.557, letter no. 1338; 4th June, p.556, letter no. 1334.
9   Whitelocke, p.144.

without having made any Attempt or Approach, and without doing or suffering much; and that after he had likewise attempted Bostal House, where he was notably repulsed by Sir William Campion the Governour, with some Loss, that he was marched towards Buckingham. This was not welcome News, yet such as obliged us rather to make towards him and hazard a Battel, than to march Northwards and be met in the Face with the Scots, and have him in our Rear.

The decision to abandon the siege was made a week earlier by the Committee of Both Kingdoms, when on 1st June they wrote to Fairfax advising him that Leicester was taken,

> whereby those parts are much discouraged, besides there are no forces in the field to oppose them and protect the country. Upon consideration of the present state of affairs we conceive it very probable you will speedily receive orders to take the field.[10]

Sprigge relates that despite the besiegers having lain before Oxford for fifteen days, the 'requisites to a close siege' did not arrive until the 3rd, and too late: on the 4th Fairfax duly received his orders 'to march toward Buckingham and Brackley', the intention being for him to defend the Eastern Association.[11] In a letter to his father that day, Fairfax wearily suggests that the siege had been an unprofitable waste of time, but 'The Parliament is sensible of this now ...' He adds that the army has long been keen to follow the King, but – alluding to the Committee's constant interference – 'the endeavours of others to prevent it hath so much prevailed.'[12] He left Oxford on the 5th, and the army was joined near Newport Pagnell by the several cavalry regiments under Colonel Bartholomew Vermuyden, and then by those under Cromwell.[13]

The Royalist change of plan; the 'New Model' closes in

As Eliot Warburton points out, the raising of the siege removed any need for the King to move towards Oxford, and the northern plan so favoured by Rupert and

---

10   *CSP Domestic Series*, 1644-1645, p.554.
11   Sprigge, p.21, 27; *CSP, op. cit.*, p.557.
12   Bell, *Memorials of the Civil War: Comprising the Correspondence of the Fairfax Family* ..., vol. I, p.228.
13   On 9th May Vermuyden had been ordered north to assist the approaching Scots army with '2,500 horse and dragoons', but allowed, if the King did not go north, to act as he saw fit; on the 24th he was ordered to place himself so as to prevent Charles getting into East Anglia (*CSP Domestic Series*, 1644-1645, p.482, 518). Almost immediately after joining Fairfax he asked to resign his commission, officially because he had 'special business' to attend to abroad (Sprigge, p.29) but in truth due to religious differences with the 'ungodly' New Model Army (Luke; quoted in Marix Evans p.43).

the Northern Horse came back into play.[14] Meanwhile a convoy of provisions was sent to succour the city while the army was away: Rupert's Diary records its departure on the 8th, and it was reported to Luke on the 9th;[15] Dugdale records its arrival at Oxford on the 10th:

> Great store of Cattell, Sheepe, and other provisions, were brought to Oxford, out of Leic. and North'tonshire, by a convoy sent from his Maty for ye better victualling the same.[16]

According to Walker the army stayed at Daventry for five days, to monitor Fairfax's movements and wait for the convoy to return. Walker then mentions news of a significant defeat at Ludlow, and that:

> although when we had the first Intelligence we could not see the sad Effects of this Loss, yet after the Battel at Naseby, when we retreated into those Parts and had occasion to use them, we too soon felt it.

Unknown to the King's forces while they rested at Daventry, a decision was made in London which was arguably to prove fatal to their cause. On 9th May, shaken by the events at Leicester and with recriminations flying around Westminster, the Committee of Both Kingdoms agreed:

> To write to Sir Thos. Fairfax taking off all limitations or restrictions imposed upon his action in former letters; … That having considered his letter we leave it to him and his Council-of-War being upon the spot to do as they shall think most advantageous; … To report to the Commons that Sir Thomas may be empowered to impress men for a month where he shall come with his army …; Likewise that he may be empowered to take up horses within the enemy's quarters.[17]

Fairfax finally had the complete military freedom that the Self-Denying Ordinance had promised; at his own request, he was also allowed to appoint Cromwell as his lieutenant general of horse. After Naseby, Cromwell was allowed to keep that position at the pleasure of the House.

Sprigge reports that on Wednesday 11th it rained; on Thursday 12th, Symonds reports, when the King was hunting deer:

14 Warburton, vol. III, pp.99-100.
15 Marix Evans, *Naseby 1645. The triumph of the New Model Army*, p.45; Prince Rupert's Diary (EHR), p.739; Luke, *Letter Books*, p.563, letter no. 1357.
16 Dugdale, p.80.
17 *CSP Domestic Series,* 1644-1645, p.578.

two myle of Daventree there came a strong alarme, so that the whole army was drawne to the Beacon hill, and lay there that night.[18]

The 'beacon hill' was Borough Hill, a flat-topped piece of rising land east of Daventry, the site of an Iron Age fort. According to Sprigge the Parliamentarians thought the King had deliberately chosen it as a place of strength, and indeed John Rushworth reported 'ordnance planted on the hills', and that perhaps Charles sought to 'force us to fight on disadvantage.'[19] Slingsby describes it as:

so high as it overlooks a good part of ye Country between it & Northampton; & there upon yt Hill ye whole army of horse & foot stood in arms yt same night.[20]

The alarm had been the attack on some Royalist horse quarters in the village of Flore, three or four miles south-east of Borough Hill. Sprigge reveals the extent of the surprise:

A commanded party of horse gave the Enemy an alarm, and took some prisoners, by whom they understood the King was a hunting, the Souldiers in no order, and their horses all at grasse, having not the least knowledge of our advance …

The Royalists were quick to take up the alarm, however, and the Parliament's foot being 'somewhat behind', the commanded party was withdrawn. Symonds says that early the next morning, the Oxford provisions convoy having returned – 'that being the cause of this unhappy stay here so long' – the army left Daventry and marched back towards Harborough.[21] At about the time they departed, five or six a.m., Cromwell arrived from his earlier rendezvous near Newport Pagnell, joining Fairfax at Kislingbury, eight miles east of Daventry. Walker records that:

our Army retired back to Harborow with resolution to march the next Day to Melton Mowbray, and so to Newark there to strengthen our Foot by Additions out of that and other adjacent Garrisons …[22]

It was not to be, however. That night Henry Ireton surprised and beat up some Royalist horse quarters near Naseby; Sprigge remarks that:

18 *Diarye*, p.192.
19 Sprigge, p.30; Rushworth, 10th June, to Sir Samuel Luke; Luke, *Letter Books*, p.565, letter no. 1364.
20 H. Slingsby, p.150.
21 *Diarye*, pp.192-193.
22 Walker, p.129.

the confidence of the Enemy, in possessing these quarters, grounded upon their slight esteem of this Army, and want of intelligence, was very remarkable.[23]

This rings true: taken collectively, the impression from both sides is that the Royalist command was not focused on its enemy, and simply unappreciative of the immediate threat offered by Fairfax and the approaching New Model Army. The deciphered parts of a letter written by King Charles to Secretary Nicholas – then at Oxford – include the word 'Mowbray', indicating that the plan was still to head that way.[24] Presumably Rupert had also been oblivious, assuming that the diversionary tactics he had organised throughout the march to confuse Fairfax had been successful. Walker continues:

This altered our design, and a Council being presently called, resolutions were taken to fight; and rather to march back and seek him out, than to be sought or pursued, contrary (as 'tis said) to Prince Rupert's Opinion; it being our unhappiness, that the Faction of the Court, whereof the most powerful were the Lord Digby and Mr. Ashburnham, and that of the Army ever opposed and were jealous of others.'

Walker's mention of a council meeting contradicts Lord Digby, who later claimed in a letter to William Legge that none was never called.[25] It seems that political rifts once again dominated the military decision making. Rupert and the army still wanted to push north: the best option given that they now knew the New Model Army would be the stronger force, as Gerard had not yet brought reinforcements from Worcester, and news had arrived that Goring – apparently inextricably engaged around Taunton – could not provide cavalry support. Yet the politicians used whatever means they could to override the Prince, and the decision was made to turn and fight. Symonds records marching out of his quarters at about 2 a.m. on Saturday 14th; Rushworth reported that the King's army 'was in great confusion on the alarm and stood in arms all night.'[26] Sprigge noted that it was still raining. Early the next day Fairfax moved north, and assembled his force around Guilsborough, two miles south-west of the village of Naseby; a few miles to the north, at Market Harborough, the Royalists held a general rendezvous at 7 a.m.

23   Sprigge, p.32.
24   *The Private Correspondence Between King Charles I. and Sir Edward Nicholas*, William Bray (ed.); vol. 5, p.134.
25   Warburton, vol. III, p.127.
26   Rushworth to Samuel Luke, *Letter Books*, p.575, letter no. 1386.

Lisle's forces

By June 1645 Lisle's tercio looked very different to the one which had accompanied the King to Cornwall and seen off Manchester's forces at Newbury II. In fact, strictly speaking it was now barely large enough to qualify as a regiment, let alone a block of several, now numbering 500 men rather than the 2,783 recorded by Symonds at the Aldbourne muster in April 1644.[27] Certainly engineer Bernard de Gomme only remembered the once enormous Reading tercio as one unit: when he drew up his famous map of the Naseby battle order, he listed only 'Sr George Liesle', and none of the other Reading colonels.[28] By process of elimination, the only regiments remaining of the original eleven were Lisle's own, Gilby's, Thelwall's, and Vaughan's: it seems that by now they were so small that for practical reasons they were all fighting as one unit under Lisle's name. At Naseby Symonds names 'Major Fowler' amongst the tercio's leading officers, so evidently Fowles was minding Lisle's regiment while Lisle ran the tercio, and Lieutenant Colonel Littleton was his tercio major.[29] Alongside Lisle's regiment, and mentioned in its own right by de Gomme, was the late William St George's Newark Foot, whom Young suggests may have now been led by his major.[30]

Lisle also commanded five regiments – four English, one Irish – which were formerly in the Irish service and had returned after the 'Cessation' in late 1643 / early 1644: Broughton's, Tillier's, Hunk's, Gibson's, and Warren's. They had taken significant casualties at Nantwich and Marston Moor, Warren's being the regiment Lisle's brother Francis had died commanding. George must have known this, and most likely the men knew whose brother he was, or guessed from the surname. The 'Shrewsbury Foot', as these regiments were collectively known, had joined the army at Stow-on-the-Wold on 8th May, as part of Rupert's infantry. It would seem natural that at some point during the march north, or perhaps when they came under his immediate command prior to Naseby, George asked them for their recollections of Marston Moor, and what they remembered of Francis, whom he would not have seen since the younger brother embarked for Ireland in 1642.

Lisle's Naseby tercio was divided into two battalions: comprising firstly his combined regiment and the Newark Foot, under Theophilus Gilby, and secondly

---

27 See chapter 8; Symonds, untitled notebook, BL Harley MS 986, f. 98. Although Symonds also includes figures for Stephen Hawkins's regiment, who had also been members of the Reading garrison, I have omitted them: just after the Aldbourne rendezvous they were sent to garrison Greenland House near Henley, and did not become part of Lisle's tercio. Thus the 1644 figure given above is for the other eleven regiments only.

28 De Gomme, BL, Add MS 16370, f.62.

29 *Diarye*, p.194.

30 Young, *Naseby 1645*, p.92.

the Shrewsbury Foot under an officer de Gomme names only as 'Coll. Smith'.[31] Colonel Gilby's battalion command is explained by his being the most senior officer available: amongst the other Reading regiments Thelwall was gone, his remaining men presumably overseen as usual by Lieutenant Colonel Urian Leigh; Sir Henry Vaughan was still a prisoner at Abingdon, the rump of his regiment probably overseen by his son and namesake who had commanded as his half colonel during his absence in 1643 and 1644. Lisle's own regiment, as noted, was being commanded by his major. Of the Newark Foot, Colonel St George was dead, and his major's possible command at Naseby has been noted.[32] Gilby's command also confirms that Reading tercio colonel Sir Thomas Blackwell, senior to him by date of commission, must now have been absent; his regiment was probably either gone, or the remnants absorbed with another.[33] As noted earlier, the only regiment from the old tercio not accounted for by disbandment or deliberate departure, is Sir Edward Stradling's, commanded since July 1643 by his brother John: John was a half colonel and so theoretically could still have served under Gilby, but it seems more likely that the regiment had been called elsewhere, perhaps back to South Wales where John Stradling compounded for his estates in December 1646.

The battle

The King's army drew up at around 8 a.m. on a high piece of ground at East Farndon, a mile south of Market Harborough. Four and a half miles further south as the crow flies, behind another ridge, stood Naseby village; Fairfax's rendezvous took place near a windmill on the far side, out of the Royalists' sight. Of army numbers, de Gomme's map records the Royalists as '4000 foot and 3500 horse, with 12 pieces of Ordonance', and John Belasyse's account states the total was 'not exceeding 12,000 Horse and Foot'; secondary analyses of all available sources presently concur that the King's army was around 10,000 in total. Numbers for the New Model are less reliable, but seem to have been between 12,000 and 15,000 in total, and there is presently no dispute that the Royalists were outnumbered.[34] The presence of Goring's several thousand horse would have gone some way towards at least balancing out the numbers.

---

31   Peter Young believes him to be Ireland veteran Lieutenant Colonel George Smith (*Naseby 1645*, p.ix); P. R. Newman names him as Robert Smith, without explanation (*Royalist Officers*, p.349).
32   Young includes a breakdown of the Naseby tercio, *op. cit.*, pp.90-95.
33   Peter Young believes Blackwell was now serving in the Northern Horse (*Naseby 1645*, p.64).
34   De Gomme, *op. cit.*; Belasyse's secretary in Ormonde vol. II, 1903, p.38. Foard gives an exhaustive analysis of the figures (pp.198-209); Marix Evans *et al.* also include a good summary of all the calculations for both sides, in *Naseby; English Civil War – June 1645*, pp.63-64. In *Naseby 1645* (pp.58-59), using evidence from contemporary drill books, Marix Evans argues that the Parliament's numbers have been 'consistently overstated'.

As the Royalists waited on the hill for a sight of their enemy, Walker notes that 'it was a question whether the Intelligence were true'; a scoutmaster was sent out, but returned saying 'he had been two or three Miles forward, and could neither discover or hear the Rebels.'[35] Walker accuses him of lying, whilst he may simply have done a poor job. However a landscape study by Marix Evans *et al.* reveals that due to the topography between the armies, an observer who stood at a certain point in the valley ahead of the Royalist forces would not see the top of the ridge-line where Fairfax's army was placed. However, even if they were positioned to see it clearly, they would still not see Fairfax's men on the ridge if those men had not yet been deployed, which Glenn Foard suggests might be the case.[36] Unsatisfied with the scout's report, Rupert himself took a party forward:

> But he had not marched above a Mile before he had certain Intelligence of their Advance, and saw their Van. Whereupon he drew nearer with his Horse, and sent back to have the Army march up to him; and either supposing by their Motion, or being flatered into an Opinion they were upon a Retreat, he desired they should make haste. This made us quit our Ground of Advantage, and in reasonable order to advance.

Walker blames Rupert for moving forward too quickly in the arrogant belief that the enemy would not stand if they saw him, and complains that the forward march meant they could see the Royalist army in full array and had the opportunity of 'disposing themselves to the best advantage' before the King's army could even choose its ground. Sprigge agrees that the Royalists were in plain view, and it greatly concerned Rupert, who as he picked his own ground on the right wing – shifting west to avoid unsuitable terrain – urged the King to hurry with the rest of the army as everything they did was being observed. The Royalists, on the other hand, were still unable to observe the dispositions of the New Model: Sprigge reveals that:

> we retreated about an hundred paces from the ledge of the Hill, that so the Enemy might not perceive in what form our battell was drawn, nor see any confusion therein, and yet we so see the form of their battell …[37]

He adds, however – citing later information which presumably came from prisoners – that this step back made the King's army think that their enemy was retreating, and thus:

35   Walker, p.130. Francis Rouse, 'Scout-Master General', was knighted at Oxford on 4th April 1646 (Walkley, p.167), so presumably his Naseby error was eventually overlooked.
36   Marix Evans *et al., op. cit.*, p.66; Foard, *Naseby: The Decisive Campaign*, p.221.
37   Sprigge, p.34.

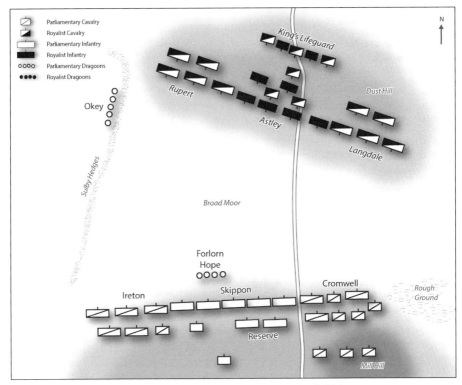

Map 6 Naseby, 14 June 1645. Lisle led two battalions onto the field, but at some point was carried off severely wounded, and taken to Leicester.

made them the more to precipitate; for they made so much haste, that they left many of their Ordnance behinde them.

Surprisingly, however, Sprigge is complimentary of the approaching army, noting that it 'marched up in good order, a swift march, with a great deal of gallantry and resolution …' Their field word that day, he says, was 'Queen Mary', and the New Model's 'God our strength'; *Perfect Occurrences of Parliament* says the Royalists' word was 'The Lord is our strength', *Mercurius Civicus* 'God and Queene Marie', and *A Diary, or an Exact Journall* claimed 'God and King Charles.' *Perfect Occurrences* adds that 'they had Beans in their hats, we Handkerchiefs, or something white'; *Mercurius Civicus* specifies 'white linnen or white paper in their hats.'[38]

---

38 *Mercurius Civicus*, Numb. 108, p.963; *Perfect Occurrences of Parliament*, The 25th Week (1645); *A Diary, or an Exact Journall*, Numb. 57.

Bulstrode Whitelocke describes this area in the valley bottom as 'a large Fallow field, on the North-west side of Naseby, about a Mile broad',[39] and known as Broadmoor. This open 'field', which would become part of the battlefield, was bounded to the east (the Royalist left) by an area of furze and by Lodge Hill, the site of a rabbit warren and therefore unsuitable for cavalry; and to the west by a parish boundary known as Sulby Hedges. To its north was a piece of rising ground called Dust Hill, where the Royalist front line began the battle; to its south was the ridge on which Fairfax's force was deployed. The ground was boggy in places, 'full of burts [gorse thorns] & Water' according to Slingsby. He records that the poor terrain forced Rupert to veer west (that is, to his right) before settling his final position:

> & by our guides were brought upon a fair peice of ground, partly corn & partly heath, under Nasby.

Symonds notes that the King's army later 'marched up … through a bottome full of furse bushes', and Sprigge that some of the Parliament's left wing cavalry was hindered by 'pits of water, and other pieces of ditches that they expected not.'[40] Fairfax also shifted westward, although there is much debate as to whether this was due to similar constrictions of the landscape, or because he was matching Rupert's move.

Compared to some battles, the basic deployment of the armies at Naseby is fairly easy to visualise, as they faced each other in classic parallel lines. From left to right (that is, east to west) the Royalist line comprised a left wing of horse, mostly the Northern Horse under Marmaduke Langdale; then the infantry, comprising Lisle's, Bard's, and Sir Bernard Astley's tercios; then the right wing of horse comprising the rest of the cavalry, commanded by Prince Maurice. Small bodies of commanded musketeers were attached to each wing of horse. De Gomme records 'tree Devision of Horse between the foot Comanded by Colonel Hawerd': a Continental practice which helped drive the infantry forward. The New Model line-up was, again from east to west, right wing cavalry commanded by Oliver Cromwell; infantry in the centre; and left wing horse commanded by Henry Ireton. A small forlorn hope stood out in the front centre ahead of the New Model infantry. Lisle, being at the extreme left end of the Royalist infantry, faced the extreme right end of the Parliamentarian foot: that is, Fairfax's own foot regiment, seconded by Colonel Thomas Rainsborough's. The Shrewsbury Foot waited behind Lisle as a second line.[41]

---

39 Whitelocke, p.145.
40 *Diarye*, p.193; Sprigge, p.38.
41 It seems that when the two lines of infantry actually met, the terrain altered the trajectory of Lisle's advance, and his tercio missed Fairfax's men and hit Colonel Edward Montagu's regiment beside him.

Perhaps more than any other battle, the finer details of that which followed on 14th June 1645, in a rain-soaked stretch of unenclosed land between Northampton and Leicester, have been the subject of numerous books and continue to be the subject of much debate. Understandably so, as it was the most significant action of the First Civil War, in that it effectively ended it; the King himself was on the field with his Lifeguard of horse and was nearly engaged in person. New archaeological evidence is also changing our traditional understanding of how the battle unfolded, and is creating more controversies. The following account does not seek to address these unless they materially affect Lisle; it is intended only as a context in which to place him, and to examine his particular role.

The battle opened somewhere between 10 a.m. and noon, when Prince Maurice made a charge with the right wing cavalry. However, at the last minute Cromwell had ordered some dragoons to line the substantial Sulby hedge to Maurice's right. Slingsby records that:

> they had possess'd an Hedge upon our right wing wch they had lin'd wth Musketeers to Gall our horse, (as indeed they did) before we could come up to charge theirs. It fell upon prince Ruport to charge at yt disadvantage, & many of ye Regiment [were] wound'd by shot from ye hedge before we could joyne wth theirs on yt wing …[42]

Presumably the commanded musketeers attached to the cavalry wing responded to the dragoons. Rupert himself now joined the cavalry charge, holding it together despite a brief hiatus as broken ground interrupted both sides, and as Slingsby famously added:

> had our success been ye like upon our left wing, in probability we might have had ye day.

Walker asserts that the right wing 'bore all down before them', reportedly taking six cannon – although a later pamphlet denies it[43] – and even Sprigge admits the Parliament's left wing was 'worsted'.[44]

Both infantry lines now advanced, the New Model coming up to the brow of the ridge to meet the Royalist infantry coming across Broadmoor from Dust Hill. Sir

---

42   H. Slingsby, pp.151-152.
43   *A True Relation Of a Victory obtained over the Kings Forces* … The author will only concede that the cavalry were 'almost masters of our Artillery'. Foard (p.262) believes the cannon were captured a little later, by the Royalist infantry.
44   Walker, p.114; Sprigge, p.38. Rupert was supposed to be staying on the sidelines as Lord General; Peter Young makes several suggestions as to why he abandoned this position and became engaged in the fight himself (*Naseby 1645. The Campaign and the Battle*, p.260).

Bernard Astley's tercio moved first and Lisle's last, so that the whole line wheeled slightly to the left. Walker says they:

> advanced up the Hill, the Rebels only discharging five Pieces at them, but over shot them, and so did their Musquetiers. The Foot on either side hardly saw each other until they were within Carabine Shot, and so only made one Volley; ours falling in with Sword and butt end of the Musquet did notable Execution; so much as I saw their Colours fall, and their Foot in great Disorder.

A letter printed in London three days later, and purportedly written by John Rushworth, claimed that both sides 'gave a little backe', which suggests that at this point there was a second charge.[45] Marix Evans notes the presence of a depression in the centre of the ridge which would have funnelled the King's advancing infantry into a wedge shape.[46] This would mean Bard's central tercio being forced to the front, with Lisle's trailing to its left and Astley's to its right, which would seem to be corroborated by Sprigge's remark that:

> The right hand of the Foot, being the Generals Regiment, stood, not being much pressed upon: Almost all the rest of the main Battail being over-pressed, gave ground and went off in some disorder, falling behinde the Reserves ...[47]

Foard believes that it was at this point Royalist infantry reserves such as the Shrewsbury Foot were brought forward; he also notes that as Fairfax's regiment was not engaged, it would now be able to wheel around and hit Lisle in the flank, and suggests that Rupert's regiment of foot was brought up from the rear to protect it.[48] Here Foard and Marix Evans differ, as the latter tends towards that regiment's famous last stand happening further back; Fairfax's foot never made the flanking move, but whether that was incidental, or due to the possible presence of Rupert's men, is not known.

Marix Evans notes musket ball survey evidence which suggests there was limited opportunity to fire in the depression, and that most of the action must have been hand-to-hand. A stiff fight ensued between the Royalist wedge and the disordered Parliament foot. Whitelocke reports that:

---

45 *The Copie of a Letter sent from a Gentleman of publike employment in the late service neere Knaseby*, pp.2-5. Included in *An Ordinance of the Lords and Commons ... For next Thursday to be a day of Thanksgiving ...* Although the letter is anonymous, a contemporary annotation on the British Library copy of the pamphlet suggests it was written by Rushworth.
46 Marix Evans, *Naseby 1645*, p.67.
47 Sprigge, p.36.
48 Foard, p.259.

the Main Bodies had charged one another with incredible fierceness, often retreating and rallying, falling in together with the But-ends of their Muskets, and coming to hand blows with their Swords.[49]

Whitelocke's precise source is unknown, but his description gives a good enough impression of a desperate fight, with the Parliament foot, Sprigge says, 'choosing rather there to fight and die, then to quit the ground they stood on.' The account of the recently ennobled Colonel John Belasyse, who at Naseby was attending on the King, recalls that:

All this time our old infantry fought it out gallantly (amongst which my Lord's old regiment which he had given to Sir Theophilus Gilby was) and beat those of the enemy's, making themselves masters of their cannon, till such time as finding no relief from our horse and being surrounded by the enemy's whole army overpowering them, they were at last forced to yield themselves prisoners upon quarter.[50]

In fact the time and place of the tercio's demise is not clear. A concentration of musket ball finds back on Dust Hill might suggest the tercio retreated back to it and the end came here, but the site of an even heavier further concentration much further back, at Wadborough, is also a possibility. Many of the senior officers of Lisle's tercio were listed as captured, which at first glance suggests it surrendered while still a cohesive, functioning body; yet it is equally possible that the officers were picked off or picked up one by one during the last phase of the battle, a wide-ranging retreat and pursuit with parties of men being rounded up for miles afterwards. As to the veracity of Belasyse's story: he and Theophilus Gilby met again at Newark later in the year – where Gilby was knighted – and Belasyse may well have heard it from Gilby first-hand.

The front rank of the New Model foot broken, Philip Skippon led up the reserves only to be wounded in the stomach in the melee; to his credit, he stayed on the field and saw out the rest of the battle. Meanwhile the right hand end of the King's line had been exposed both by its wheeling movement and the fast advance of Rupert and Maurice on the Royalist right wing, and Ireton turned his cavalry to attack it. Unexpectedly he was wounded and captured; meanwhile Maurice's troopers smashed through the rest of the Parliament's left wing. As at Edgehill they did not stay to consolidate the action but continued forwards towards Naseby village, to make an attempt on the Parliamentarian baggage. Marix Evans, citing Rupert's

---

49   Whitelocke, p.145.
50   Ormonde vol. II, 1903, p.386.

Diary, states that before the impact Rupert had gone back to the King, although Foard sticks with the premise that he had remained with the cavalry.[51]

On the basis of the heavy musket ball evidence in this area, Foard's analysis is that the two sides, having regrouped, engaged in a lengthy firefight; and that if Skippon's reserves had broken at this point, the battle would have been lost.[52] Meanwhile, Sprigge reports, Colonel Whaley's divisions on the New Model right wing charged part of Langdale's cavalry in front of them, driving them right back to the rear of the King's army and into the infantry regiments waiting in reserve. Whaley's reserves then charged the rest of the Royalist left wing and put it to flight. Walker describes it from the Royalist perspective:

> Our Foot and right Wing being thus engaged, our left Wing advanced, consisting of five Bodies of the Northern and Newark Horse; who were opposed by seven great Bodies drawn to their right Wing by Cromwell who commanded there, and who besides the Advantage of Number had that of the Ground, ours marching up the Hill to encounter them. Yet I must say ours did as well as the Place and their Numbers would admit; but being flanked and pressed back, they at last gave Ground and fled: Four of the Rebels Bodies close and in good Order followed them, the rest charged our Foot.

Instead of Skippon's men breaking at this point, Foard maintains, it was the King's: Sir Jacob Astley had pulled in his second line reserves as support but with the third line – Rupert's regiment of foot and the King's Lifeguard of foot – disrupted or destroyed by the cavalry action on his left wing, he now had nothing left. Rupert's regiment may not have yet been out of the picture, however.

The traditional view of Naseby has been, that the Royalist infantry was pushed back, overwhelmed and began to surrender; there was a straightforward rout, and the King and the remnants of his army fled north to Leicester. However, new archaeological techniques, musket ball surveys in particular, now indicate that in fact the Royalists did not simply flee: they staged a determined fighting retreat to the north for several miles, probably concluding on rising ground at Wadborough, east of Sibbertoft, where the heaviest concentrations of musket shot have been found. In a nearby field, the site of an abandoned village, many of the army's fleeing camp followers were reported assaulted or killed, women in particular, and a great number taken to be whores or 'Irish' and slashed in the face. The precise movements and timings of the retreat are open to conjecture, and it is extremely difficult to put the individual events related in the primary sources into a coherent timeline.

51   Marix Evans, *Naseby 1645*, p.66.
52   Foard, p.265.

It is impossible to say what happened to Lisle and his men after the infantry retreat began, and when it happened. Belasyse's account is the only specific evidence we have for the tercio's eventual fate, but there is one other possible sighting, tangled up with a frequently quoted 'last stand' by a body of blue-coats. The story given by most commentators is that the blue-coats were charged twice by Fairfax's own cavalry and went down fighting, but a re-examination of the primary sources reveals that two separate events have been conflated.

Firstly, from London newsbook *A Diary, or an Exact Journall*:

> The blew regiment of the Kings did fight most bravely, and held out to the last man.[53]

Then from *The Kingdomes Weekly Intelligencer*, issue 104:

> The Blue Regiment of the Kings stood to it very stoutly, and stir'd not, like to a wall of brasse, though incompassed by our Forces, so that our men were forced to knock them down with the But-end of their Musquets: It is conceived that a great part of them were Irish, and chose rather to die in the field, then be hanged.[54]

Thirdly, in the *Intelligencer's* next weekly issue, no. 105:

> Sir Thomas Fairfax commanded Colonel Fines to fall upon the Kings and Prince Ruperts two Regiments, of stout old Souldiers; which he accordingly performed with great resolution, breaking through this firme body, that stood like a wall of brasse to receive this Charge: the event of this businesse gave us a full Victory …[55]

Rupert's blue-coat foot had begun the battle with the King's Lifeguard of Foot at the rear of the army, as a reserve, which tends to corroborate the story. Where these regiments were at the time they were hit is not clear, as they may have moved forward to Dust Hill, or even further, to the Naseby ridge to closely support Lisle's tercio; or as the battle concluded they may have retreated even beyond their own starting point, and made their stand at Wadborough. The mention of Irish soldiers is probably genuine, as it is documented that Rupert had Irish officers in his regiment of firelocks, and possibly amongst his foot. Their last stand, wherever it occurred, is usually conflated with another, which is related both by Sprigge and

53   No. 57, no page numbers.
54   No. 104, p.838.
55   No. 105, p.842.

by Bulstrode Whitelocke. Sprigge says that the Royalist foot had all surrendered upon mercy:

> except one Tertia, which with the other part of the horse we endeavoured to break, but could not, they standing with incredible courage & resolution, although we attempted them in the Flanks, Front and Rear, untill such time as the General called up his own Regiment of foot ... which immediately fell in with them, with But-end of Muskets (the General charging them at the same time with horse) and so broke them.[56]

Bulstrode Whitelocke records a conversation between Fairfax and Charles D'Oyley, the colonel of his lifeguard of horse, concerning the same event. Fairfax:

> seeing a Body of the Kings foot stand, and not at all broken, he asked D'Oyley *if he had charged that Body*, who answered, *that he had twice charged them, but could not break them*. With that Fairfax bid him to charge them once again in the front, and that he would take a commanded party, and charge them in the Rere at the same time, and they might meet together in the middle ... D'Oyley pursuing his General's Orders, and both together charging that Body put them into a confusion, and broken them, and Fairfax and D'Oyley met indeed in the middle of them, where Fairfax killed the Ensign ...[57]

Notably, in this story, D'Oyley says it is *he* who has hit the tercio twice: there is no mention of Fiennes, who in fact had explicitly been sent to knock down two regiments, not 'a Tertia', which is a much larger body. Nor is there any mention of the prominent blue coats. The evidence is clear that there were two events: Rupert's blue-coat foot and the King's Lifeguard being hit by Fiennes, and presumably some New Model foot or dragoons, assuming the reference to musket butts is accurate; and a stubborn tercio being hit by D'Oyley with Fairfax's Lifeguard, by Fairfax himself with a commanded body, and by Fairfax's foot regiment.[58]

The identity of the tercio cannot be confirmed. Peter Young believes it was Lisle's, based on him starting the day opposite Fairfax's foot, which Fairfax called in when the multiple cavalry charges on the tercio failed to finish them off. However, since Young published his book in 1985 we have the new archaeological evidence of the fighting retreat: it means that retreating bodies of foot turned repeatedly to stand

56 Sprigge, pp.38-39.
57 Whitelocke, p.145. Italics as in the original.
58 It appears that to date, Foard's is the only work which makes any distinction between the two incidents. However whilst he does not conflate them, neither does he address the common confusion between them, or Young's assertion that the tercio involved was Lisle's.

their ground, therefore it is no longer by any means certain where Lisle's tercio might have been by this point in the proceedings and when, or to whom, they eventually surrendered. Belasyse's account tends to suggest it was early on in the retreat or even before it started, as he mentions a lack of cavalry support, which would fit with the routing of the Northern Horse to their left. Sprigge suggests otherwise, however: after describing the breaking of the tercio, he says that:

> The enemy had now nothing left in the Field, but his horse, (with whom was the King himself) which they had put again into as good order as the shortnesse of their time, and our near pressing upon them would permit.

Sprigge, therefore, would put the breaking of the tercio as one of the last actions involving a body of Royalist infantry. After that foot had gone, he says, the New Model also took the opportunity to reorder itself:

> endeavouring to put the Army again into as good order as they could receive, to the perfecting of the work that remained …

A *True Relation* continues:

> After this they rallied again, and put their Horse into a posture to Charge, which party wee are assured his Majesty led up, and charged with … But this body was also within lesse then half an houre dissipated and then they fled …

Famously, Walker relates a story about the King being ready to charge at the head of his horse, when the Earl of Carnwath forcibly grabbed his bridle and prevented him; this gesture coincided with a particular order being given, and the army thus finally turning to flee. It is not clear where or when this happened, although Marix Evans believes it was somewhere around Wadborough.[59]

Sprigge claims that on seeing the reinvigorated army:

> which the enemy perceiving, and that if they stood, they must expect a second Charge from our Horse, Foot, and Artillery (they having lost all their Foot and Guns before) and our Dragoons already begun to fire upon their horse, they not willing to abide a second shock upon so great disadvantage as this was like to be, ran away, both Fronts, and Reserves, without standing one stroke more …

59   Marix Evans, *Naseby 1645*, p.79.

This probably describes the end of any remaining pockets of resistance at Wadborough, and it appears that some of the King's horse, perhaps the King himself, may have been the last elements of his army to make a stand. A newsbook report a few days later claimed that Charles was wounded in the arm, or at least seen with blood on his arm, but this is not reported elsewhere.[60] As any concerted resistance finally died, the remaining cavalry scattered, some being chased nearly to Leicester by the Parliamentarian horse. Cromwell claimed to have:

> persued the enemy from three miles short of Harborough to nine beyond, even to sight of Leicester whether the King fled.[61]

Meanwhile Symonds describes an incident just four miles short of Leicester itself:

> The horse escaped to Leicester this afternoone, and were persued by a body of the enemyes horse and loose scowters, to Great Glyn, and there the Earle of Lichfield charged their loose men with halfe a score horse and beate them back.[62]

Besides Belasyse's account, the only information we have regarding the tercio's fate are the details of casualties and prisoners, the first casualty being Lisle himself. The nature of his injuries are, once again, not known, but on this occasion they seem to have been severe: Sprigge mentions him being found in Leicester four days later when the town surrendered, presumably too sick to be moved.[63] The extent of his injuries is also implicit in two letters from Henry Hastings to Prince Rupert which will be examined shortly. At some point during the tercio's retreat, or during its final surrender, wherever and whenever it occurred, Littleton, Fowles and Gilby were taken prisoner, as was Major Whitmore of the Newark Foot. Of Lisle's own regiment, four captains, a lieutenant, and two ensigns were also taken.[64] Daniel Moore of Warren's regiment in the Shrewsbury Foot, Francis Lisle's former major, was captured; Colonel Smith, however, got away, and if he was the man identified by Peter Young, was fighting again at Bridgnorth by the end of the year.[65] The tercio's most significant casualty was Edward Littleton: *Mercurius Civicus* records that:

---

60 *Perfect Occurrences of Parliament*, The 25th Week (1645), no page numbers.
61 Letter to William Lenthall, 14th June, from Market Harborough: *Three Letters, From the Right Honourable Sir Thomas Fairfax,* pp.2-3.
62 *Diarye*, p.193.
63 Sprigge, p.51.
64 *Three Letters … * p.7; *Mercurius Civicus*, Numb. 108, p.956; *Perfect Passages*, numb. 34, pp.270-271.
65 Symonds, *Diarye*, p.276.

There are about 500 souldiers of His Majesties that were wounded and taken in the late fight, in the Villages and Townes about Northampton, and in the Towne of Northampton, which in regard of the desperatenesse of their wounds were not brought up with the rest …[66]

Civicus reported that Littleton 'lyeth wounded at Navesby', but evidently he was then transported to St Sepulchre's church in Northampton, where Royalist prisoners were being kept, as he was buried there on 29th June.[67] Soberingly, the man listed next to him in the parish register was a trooper of Ireton's. The last laugh was on Littleton, however: he was entered in the parish register as 'Sr Edward Littleton, bt', the clerk confusing him with Sir Edward Littleton, baronet, Keeper of the Great Seal, who coincidentally died a couple of months later at Oxford. Lieutenant Colonel Littleton had lost his life for his king, but posthumously, if accidentally, had been made a baron for it.

Of the other officers around Lisle, fellow tercio commanders Sir Henry Bard and Sir Bernard Astley escaped capture or injury; however Sir Richard Page, and Lieutenant Colonel Burgess from Owen's regiment were taken.

'Foure Lords came to Harborough': a sighting of Lisle?

We cannot know when during the fighting Lisle's injuries were sustained, but the fact that he was safely evacuated without capture strongly suggests he had already been extracted before the fighting retreat began: that he was already with the baggage train around Sibbertoft, or was carried north before the fighting reached the village, and the army finally disintegrated. An early departure from the battlefield would mean he was probably wounded in the heavy fighting when the Royalist 'wedge' broke the New Model's front line infantry, and Belasyse's cannon were captured, but this can only be conjecture. Indisputably he left the field before the tercio's final surrender, or he would have been captured with everyone else and shipped off to Northampton with other badly wounded men such as Littleton. Peter Young suggests that Lisle 'escaped, presumably because he was on horseback', but this does not fit the evidence: to be wounded so badly that he could not accompany Hastings and the other gentlemen and officers when they left Leicester in the early hours of the 18th, suggests that he could not have escaped the field without significant help on the 14th, let alone have stayed on a horse and independently ridden nearly twenty miles to the town. Symonds records that the wounded were carried to Leicester that evening; Foard that 200 managed to make their way there.[68]

66   Numb. 109, p.970.
67   *Mercurius Civicus* Numb. 8, p.956; parish registers, Northampton St Sepulchre.
68   Foard, p.309.

Sprigge reported that later, after Leicester was surrendered:

> the Army entred the towne, where we found divers Commanders of note, *viz.* Serjeant-Major-Generall Eyres, Colonell Lisle, Lieutenant Colonell Mouldsworth, Lieutenant Colonel Pemberton, Major Naylor, Major Trollop, besides divers persons of quallity, all wounded in the battle.[69]

Eyre was commander of the Newark Horse; Guy Mouldsworth (or Molesworth) commanded Prince Maurice's regiment of horse; and Michael Pemberton was an officer with the Northern Horse. With this in mind, the latest *Perfect Occurrences of Parliament,* which hit London's streets a couple of days later, carried the following intriguing snippet of news:

> Four Lords wounded went at one time through a Countrey village in Lestershire towards Lester, all dangerously wounded.[70]

Were these four 'lords' in fact Lisle, Eyre, Mouldsworth, and Pemberton? Firstly, as to whether the report was true, it is like so many newsbook references, so mundane that it is unlikely someone would have made it up. *Mercurius Civicus* offers a second version of the story: 'foure Lords came to Harborough mortally wounded but durst not stay';[71] the existence of two distinct versions suggests it was a genuine sighting being circulated after Naseby. Fairfax and Cromwell were in Harborough that evening, according to the letters they wrote to London: no doubt many other letters were dispatched with them that night, and perhaps the story was sent back with one of them and made its way to a press. Assuming, then, that there was a grain of truth at its core, the tale must have come from someone in the 'Countrey village', or in Harborough, who had perhaps related what they had seen to the Parliamentarians who came along after: if it had come from the soldiers themselves, the 'lords' and their rescuers would have been arrested. As to whether the casualties *were* lords, the witness might have been told that, but it is more likely they would be keeping well clear of the torrent of fleeing soldiers, and had simply made a judgement about something significant they saw: four seriously injured men being given priority treatment, perhaps even a cavalry escort from the officers' own regiments as they were hurried along the rutted roads towards Leicester. High status casualties would have stood out: the *True Informer* reports that many of the Royalist wounded were simply 'lying in the adjacent villages'.[72]

69 Sprigge, pp.50-51.
70 The 25th Week (1645), no page numbers.
71 Numb. 108, p.956.
72 Numb. 9 (1645), p.67.

If the casualties were not Lisle and the three cavalry officers, and were indeed lords, then it is odd that there is no trace of such lords in any contemporary newsbook or battle account, and even in historical biographies written in the centuries since, no one peer stands out as being critically wounded at Naseby, let alone four. Sir Jacob (now Lord) Astley and the Duke of Richmond are repeatedly reported as seriously wounded or dead, but whilst Astley may have had a head wound, it was not reported by the Royalists, and the report of Richmond's injury or death seems to stem purely from him losing his distinctive cloak on the battlefield. Moreover, for the said four lords to be so badly injured, they must have been in the thick of the fighting, which means we should be able to trace them from the Royalist battle order, of which we have excellent knowledge. Yet with the exception of Astley, and the Earl of Northampton – who fought with the right wing cavalry and was not reported wounded – there is nobody who fits the bill. There were at least four lords accompanying the King, to the rear: Belasyse, Digby, Lindsey and Carnwath, but any major wound to them would have been reported. Symonds reports that Lord Lichfield fought off a pursuit near Leicester, but not that he was wounded.[73] What is more, any significant incident around the King would have featured in Belasyse's account of the battle, but again there is nothing.

The only alternative, then, is that the four men were simply dangerously wounded senior officers: and the only four we know of at the top of the Royalist command structure who were in that condition, are the four mentioned by Sprigge in Leicester, which is where the report from the 'Countrey village' said the casualties were going. All of this is conjecture, of course. Yet the original stories are highly plausible, and whilst Sprigge does also mention two majors and 'divers persons of quallity' being found on 18th June, the four men in question were clearly the highest ranking to be found: anyone ranking higher, socially or militarily, would – according to the social norms of the time – have been mentioned in the list before they were. Certainly the discovery of any wounded lord in Leicester would have been greeted with alacrity by the London press; yet no such discovery is mentioned. Even Hastings himself, when he later gave Rupert a detailed account about the surrender, made no reference to any wounded lords, and when he needed advice about keeping or surrendering the town, he went straight to Eyre and Lisle and made no reference to anyone higher.

The King flees; the second siege of Leicester

Richard Symonds records the King's last actions of the day, at Leicester:

> Towards night this dismall Satterday, his Majestie, after the wounded were taken care for in Leicester, and that the two Princes were come safe

---

73 *Diarye*, p.193.

to him, and had taken order with that garrison, and left two regiments of horse there, viz. the Queenes and Colonel Caryes, he marched that night (for now wee had left running) to Ashby-de-la-Zouch.[74]

Walker adds:

in the Evening the King and Prince Rupert with the broken Troops marched to Ashby de la Zouch, and from thence the next Day to Lichfield, and in two Days more to Bewdly in Worcestershire, where He rested one Day. And upon Advice His Majesty resolved for Hereford, and so for Wales …[75]

Walker concludes that Fairfax was left 'Master of all our Foot, Cannon, Baggage and Plunder taken at Leicester.' Indeed, in the following days, the London news-books were awash with reports of the vast amount of loot captured after the battle: arms, colours, horses, wagons, coaches, money, trunks, the Royalist boat train used for crossing rivers, the Great Seal which the Lord Keeper took with him to the King in 1642, and even a copy of Walker's recently written manuscript of the King's military affairs.[76] Most devastating, however was the capture of the King's correspondence, which revealed he had been seeking aid from France and peace with the Irish Catholics. The letters were published soon afterwards in London; the King of France's envoy claimed that Charles hanged the unfortunate servant who had been in charge of them. The newsbook *Perfect Occurrences* claimed that Rupert's correspondence was also taken.[77]

The many prisoners taken during the battle – Parliamentarian sources agree on around 5,000 – were marched to London and paraded publicly through the streets. *The Kingdomes Weekly Intelligencer* reports that:

The Standards, Ensignes, and Colours, being on all 55. which were brought to Westminster the day before, were carried before the Prisoners, 16 of the chief Commanders, *viz.* Sir Richard Page, Col. Sir George Barkley, and others, came on horse-back, the rest, and the common Souldiers on foot …[78]

---

74 *Diarye*, p.194.
75 Walker, p.116.
76 Boats, *Mercurius Civicus*, op. cit., p.963; *Three Letters* …, op. cit., p.4; the Great Seal, *Perfect Occurrences of Parliament*, The 25th Week (1645); Walker's manuscript, Sprigge, p.45.
77 Charles's correspondence, Warburton, vol. III, p.132, fn.; Rupert's, *Perfect Occurrences*, The 25th Weeke.
78 No. 105, p.840.

Reports of the number slain vary, but hover between 500-1000 for the Royalists, and perhaps half that for the New Model; many accounts speak of bodies being strewn across the countryside between Naseby and Leicester.

The King had been right to leave Leicester the same evening: as he fled to Ashby-de-la-Zouch, Fairfax and Cromwell were already turning their attentions on recovering the town. In two letters to Rupert, in late June and late July, Henry Hastings – whom the fleeing King had told to defend the town – describes the approach of the triumphant Parliament army:

> The Enemy quartered nere us upon Satterday night and the next day five and twentie hundred Horse Comanded by Gell drew on the west syde the Towne wch hindred the coming in of workmen and Hay both wch wee had much want of. They planted their Cannon fower Peices upon the place; and against St Sundayes Bridge and north Mill ye rest having drawne the water on that syde the Towne to a great lowness wch made those Guards unwilling to stay upon them …[79]

The next day, Monday 16th, Sir Thomas Fairfax sent a surrender summons:

> and putting it to them to consider how the King was routed, and shewing them what use they might make of that Clemency, with divers other very gallant expressions to the summons, to advertise them how much better it was for them to surrender then to force him to take it by storming.[80]

Hastings was a shrewd soldier, however, and was not inexperienced in the matter of storming or defending fortified positions: he had taken several garrisons himself, and Parliament forces had been trying to force him from his house at Ashby-de-la-Zouch since the start of the war. He returned an initial refusal to Fairfax, and while the latter held a council of war 'to consult about the Storming of it', Hastings rapidly assessed the town's situation, to see if holding it was viable. He later apprised Rupert in detail of the situation he faced:

> first for Amunicon as Collonel Ellis well knowes, I had left mee but sixteene Barrells of Powder and not a hundred weight of Match, the rest that was found in the Towne being taken for those of the Army: for the two small Regiments of Horse that remained, many would not stay, and for the rest provisions was very scant, very many hurt officers and souldiers I found

---

79   From Lichfield(?), late June 1645; WSL, S. MS. 520/21. Hastings' letter can be approximately dated by his mention of the Scots being 'now not farre from Nottingham': their army had arrived at Mansfield on 20th June.

80   *A Copie of a Letter of the taking of Leicester*, p.3.

in the Towne, contrary to my expectacon, but many fewer souldiers then I had before the battle, that misfortune striking such a terror into them, as they were either gone wth the Armye or home; of old souldiers wee had not many and the new raised either false or Cowardly; that what men wee had were forced to bee uppon perpetuall duty, and yett none upon some times, but att a good distance: to pacifie discontente, wee had noe moneye to give them, the Countrye people being all prisoners, or pillaged; there came not in a dayes pay while I was in the Towne, those wch were the late Masters of that place knewe the weaknesses when they appleyed their chiefest endeavors …[81]

The situation was bleak. Surrendering Leicester would cause an earthquake far stronger than the loss of Windebank's tiny Oxford garrison. Meanwhile Fairfax erected batteries with which to bombard the town, as the King's army had done less than three weeks before. On the morning of Tuesday 17th:

wee drew downe our Ordnance and playd with our Pieces against the Towne, we stormed it playing with our Ordnance very hot on the Newarke side, which we conceived was their greatest strength. And in short time we made a breach in their workes …

Despite his wealth of experience, Hastings was not arrogant enough or ill-advised enough to carry the decision about the garrison's viability on his own shoulders. Repeated political attacks had already battered his standing in Royalist circles over the previous year: if he was to give up the town, and like Feilding or Windebank be hauled in front of a council of war on trial for his life, then at the very least he wanted plenty of friendly faces onside as corroborating witnesses of the necessity of surrender. In a story related in full across the two letters, he told Rupert that:

on tewsday morning or men having beene all upon duty for three nights together began to grow very weary and call for reliefe some refusing to stand any longer to the walls without it …

seeing the state wee were in, I acquainted Maior generall Eyre and Coll Lisle wth it, whoe were of opinion the Towne could not be kept, then called a Councell of warre …

… wee mett with many Officers together att Collonell Lisles Chamber where after debate it was concluded by all that the Towne was not to bee kept and though wee might repulse the first storme yett wee should want Amunicon for the next and if the Towne were then lost all those Officers

---

81   From Lichfield, 30th July 1645; WSL, S. MS. 520/23.

wch came wounded from the Army would be Prisoners and all the rest
not wounded[,] wch number was conceaved to bee a hundred and fifty[,]
and that they and the souldiers might bee more serviceable to the King
another way then to bee Prisoners ...

... all the officers then presente delivered the same opinion, before I
expressed myne ...

The letters present a vivid, even extraordinary, window into the critical moment
of decision: an emergency council of war in the room of a severely wounded
commander unable to leave his bed, other officers – many wounded, but walking
– crowding into the chamber to give their opinions about the garrison's viability.
Outside the town, the enemy artillery pounded the already compromised wall of
the Newark. This would not be the last time Lisle had Fairfax beating down his
gates.

The decision amongst his officers unanimous, Hastings immediately asked
Fairfax for a parley. The London pamphlet reporting the events crowed that the
bombardment:

struck such a terror into the hearts of the Enemy, that the Governour sent
us to desire a Parley, and offered to surrender on very faire termes ...

The insight we have into the defenders' discussions reveals, of course, that the
surrender was anything but a timorous, terrified capitulation, but was a careful
consideration of all the options. The Civil War newsbooks offer many examples of
partisan bluster, but this one is particularly striking as the contradictory evidence
is available to throw it into relief.

Fairfax immediately sent two colonels into the town to discuss terms; one was
Colonel Thomas Rainsborough, whom Lisle would encounter three years later.
Whether they met Hastings alone or if there was another meeting somewhere with
other officers present, is not known: Hastings may have called on Eyre and Lisle
again for support, particularly as Lisle was his deputy in the county, although it
seems unlikely that such a public discussion would also have occurred in Lisle's
room.

A mystery which bears mention at this particular point, is the role of Colonel
Matthew Appleyard, whom the King had appointed governor of Leicester when
the town was taken on 31st May. His regiment, or part of it, was present at Naseby,
as evidenced by the number of his officers captured there;[82] traditionally historians
have concluded that he must have sent them to Naseby while he stayed behind at
Leicester, but if so then it is odd that as the King fled via Leicester after the battle
he specifically told *Hastings* to keep the town – 'the Kinge tould mee it was his

---

82   *Three Letters, From the Right Honourable Sir Thomas Fairfax*, p.6.

pleasure, I should stay there'[83] – and Hastings makes no mention of Appleyard when he consults Lisle and the other officers about whether to surrender. Clause eight of the surrender articles mentions 'the Governour of the Towne, and the Lord Loughborough', which suggests Appleyard *was* there, but the complete silence about him elsewhere in the business is peculiar to say the least.

At 2 p.m., Parliament's officers returned to Fairfax with a set of twelve surrender articles. The rapidity of the agreement is surprising, although a swift resolution was in the interest of both sides. The Royalists, accepting Leicester was lost, now simply wanted quarter and a safe departure for everyone inside; Fairfax, though fully prepared to storm the town if he had to, would prefer not to tie up the army for days, as he was needed in the West Country at the siege of Taunton. The agreed terms allowed the garrison to leave unarmed but with quarter granted for their lives, and given safe passage to Lichfield; Fairfax was to enter the town at 10 a.m. on Wednesday 18th, to take possession of the garrison and all cannon, arms, ammunition, horses, provisions, colours, and 'bag and baggage', apart from such horses and personal arms that belonged to the senior officers.[84] The terms were not adhered to, however. Hastings informed Rupert later, that:

> the condicons made by us were in noe kind kept but both Officers and souldiers miserably plundered against Articles.[85]

Sprigge concurs, reporting that on Tuesday night, after the Royalists withdrew their guards and disarmed, they complained of New Model soldiers subsequently entering the town before the given time and plundering it. To his credit, Fairfax responded by forbidding his men to plunder upon pain of death, telling Hastings to restore his guards, and to shoot any man who 'offered violently to enter the Towne before time'.[86] Hastings had had quite enough of the business, however: long before 10 a.m. he and a large party of officers and gentlemen quit the town, leaving only the inferior officers and common soldiery to move on to Lichfield as arranged by the articles, and the immovable wounded to hope they were adequately cared for until they were able to follow. Hastings must have made his decision during the night, as the garrison prepared to surrender, and those hours between his early departure and the official hour of handover must have been anxious ones for Lisle and the other wounded officers. Sprigge says that when Fairfax arrived at 10 a.m. he found 'all the towne in a confusion': the result of an unexpected hiatus

---

83   WSL, S. MS. 550 23.
84   The pamphlet misdates the negotiations, saying Rainsborough and his colleague went into the town of Monday, then returned with the articles on Wednesday afternoon: which is not possible, as Hastings says that he only asked for terms *after* his sentries grew discontented on Tuesday morning, and the articles specify that Fairfax was to enter the town at 10 a.m. on Wednesday morning.
85   WSL, S MS. 550 21.
86   Sprigge, pp.50-51.

in military control which, if pent up anger in the Royalist soldiery or amongst vengeful townsmen had been sparked off at any point, could have resulted in a riot or an armed military confrontation. Fairfax's soldiers had been warned on pain of death not to break the articles, but that does not mean none of them would be prepared to try it, or to slip into town and inflict a measure of revenge for the alleged excesses of violence against soldiers and civilians which they had heard about three weeks earlier. Arguably, during those few hours, Lisle was in similar danger to the men whose lives he had tried to preserve when ordered to abandon Shaw House: wounded, immobile, and at the mercy of whoever might decide to loot the building where he lay and violently dispatch everyone in it. It is unlikely that he had been left unarmed there, as the articles allowed him, as a senior officer, 'to keep [his] owne particular single horse and armes'; although as he had probably lost both when carried off Naseby battlefield, the most he might have expected was that Hastings had left him a pistol in case his room was invaded. The unmistakable sound of a disciplined army marching into the town centre at 10 a.m. may have been a huge relief, despite it being on the wrong side.

Upon reaching Lichfield, or at least within a few days of the King hearing about Leicester's surrender, Hastings was arrested.[87] No doubt he had expected it, although the detention would have been undertaken by Lichfield's wounded governor Richard Bagot, one of his political enemies, which must have particularly rankled. Hastings' two letters to Rupert seemed to have formed the basis of his defence and vindication; there may have been others in between, now lost, pleading his position. Having summed up the forces ranged against the town and explained the timeline of the surrender, he concluded,

> Sr none can censure mee more for the rash and foolish stay in that place nor wish mee more to a halter then I doe my selfe I have onely this to say that when it was concluded the place was not to be kept and the Newark lesse[,] I thought the sacrificing my reputacon the onely meanes to preserve soe many good officers for his Mats service wch I feare would have beene long in getting att libertie … Sr I am not more miserable in anye opinion then my owne and not soe deserving as to continue in yor highnes favour[,] only begg this that if it shall appear to you I could not keepe the Towne you will believe what I did was wth a faythfull Hart to his Mats service and looke upon mee as I esteeme my selfe
>   Yor hignes most unfortunate though obedient servant
>   Loughborough

---

87   Whitelocke, p.153. Whitelocke diaries this as 18th August, but is well behind with the news: Hastings had received the King's approbation for the surrender by 30th July. Whitelocke's original source for the information is not known.

Walker had pinned the original idea to take Leicester on Prince Rupert; evidently Hastings felt it appropriate to take on the blame himself, even if for effect, as part of a grovelling apology. It is not clear whether the testimonies of Eyre, Lisle and perhaps other officers were obtained during July to help clear Hastings of any imputation of treachery or cowardice; perhaps after Hastings' arrest Eyre and Lisle wrote proactively to Rupert or the King to defend him, much as Bard wrote to Rupert to beg clemency for Windebank. 'Governor' Appleyard is still missing from the scene, and if he was in town at the time, evidently escaped any implication in the affair.

The only good fortune for Lisle on 14th June, was that his rank made him a casualty of significance, and – however his rescue occurred, and whether or not it was he who was spotted in a village along the way – he was taken directly to Leicester for treatment, presumably to an excellent surgeon, and not to an 'adjacent village' where medical care would have been rudimentary or non-existent. As his survival at Newbury II demonstrated, Lisle was one of those officers who, despite frequently hazarding himself in 'forlorn' skirmishes or in the forefront of a major fight, seemed to have the proverbial nine lives. At Naseby, once again, luck alone had preserved him from either an immediately fatal wound, or from the lingering infection which two weeks later carried off Lieutenant Colonel Littleton, and after three killed Hastings' enemy Colonel Bagot. Lisle himself probably attributed his Leicester escape to the protective 'genius' he later spoke about at Colchester.

We may presume Lisle spent some days convalescing at Leicester under the watchful eye of Fairfax's men; if he did have relatives in or around the town, perhaps he was able to call on them for assistance. How long he stayed is not known, but undoubtedly he would have been evacuated to Lichfield at the earliest opportunity. At Bristol's surrender three months later, the following clause was inserted into the surrender articles:

> That such Officers and Souldiers as shall be left sick or wounded in the City, Castle or Forts, shall have liberty to stay till their recovery, and then have safe Conducts to goe to his Majesty, and in the interim to be protected.[88]

Nothing so explicit was included at Leicester, but there is no documentary trace of imprisonment or exchange, so presumably Lisle and the other officers were covered by the articles allowing all in the garrison to depart unmolested. The Articles did provide for this, stating that the officers would have 'protections for their own persons', and that the common men would be 'conveyed safely' to

---

88   *An Exact Relation of Prince Rupert His marching out of Bristoll.* A slightly differently worded version exists elsewhere (Wing P1505A: *A Perfect Relation of all the Proceedings Betwixt his Excellency Sir Thomas Fairfax and his Highnesse Prince Rupert*).

Lichfield, suggesting that Fairfax was prepared to provide an escort for the thirty-five mile westward march there.[89] It is in connection with Lichfield that Lisle next appears in the documentary record: in mid-July, when he was caught up in a political row over the town's governorship.

---

89   He also provided one to Oxford in September, for the retreating Bristol garrison.

14

Losing the War

From 19th June 1645, until the surrender of Oxford on 24th June 1646, Lisle's whereabouts are sketchy at best. What he did after being escorted across the Leicestershire-Staffordshire border to Lichfield with the other wounded Naseby officers, or how long he remained there, is a mystery: there was no longer any army to command in. In late June tiny timbered Lichfield, its grand cathedral – battered by the war – and the town's environs would still be crowded with stray soldiers and dispossessed officers coming to terms with what had occurred at Naseby. It would also have been awash with rumours and news, and by now probably copies of London newsbooks discussing the contents of the King's letters, and the public exhibition of the Royalist prisoners and their captured colours. The newsbooks were full of prisoner lists, and it may have been here that Lisle began to discover the fate of his tercio, his regiment, and his officers. What must primarily have caught Lisle's attention, however, was that by the time he arrived at Lichfield, Henry Hastings was under arrest there for the surrender of Leicester. Whether Lisle managed to see him is not known, but he may, as suggested earlier, have written to Rupert or the King, or both, to confirm the circumstances inside the town. Hastings seems to have been released by 21st July; whether he remained under suspicion is not clear, but a letter he wrote to Rupert on this date suggests he was continuing his role as chief of the Midland counties as normal. While this was going on another situation developed at Lichfield which became closely entwined with his.

Uncertain loyalties: the governorship of Lichfield

Confirmed details of this affair are few, and confined only to the dates and locations on letters and the verifiable whereabouts of Hastings, the King, Prince Rupert, and Rupert's adjutant general John Scrimgeour (or Skrimshaw).[1] From

---

1   Hastings was at Lichfield, the King's and Prince Rupert's movements are available in Rupert's Diary, and Scrimgeour's location is apparent by the letters involved. P. R. Newman confuses him with David

these it is possible to draw up a conjectural account of the sequence of events which followed.

On 7th July Colonel Richard Bagot died from the arm wound he had received at Naseby: this left the governorship of Lichfield officially vacant, although his brother Harvey (or Hervey) stepped in to replace him in the meantime. He must have had to inform the King, and his letter, which does not survive, would have found Charles advanced to Raglan Castle in Monmouthshire, perhaps around the 9th or 10th. At around this time, we may conjecture, Lisle left Lichfield and joined the King, the court, and the remaining Royalist colonels and commanders at Raglan; he had certainly left Lichfield by the end of the month, because Hastings was still there and says Lisle had written to him from somewhere else. On 13th July, Adjutant Scrimgeour arrived at Hereford with a letter from Rupert, then at Bristol, and informed Charles that he was now to be Lichfield's governor. Charles wrote a perplexed letter to Rupert, reminding him that:

> Rupert promised at Hereford to deal freely with him. Charles therefore was a little surprised when Adjutant Skrimshaw today told him, casually, that Rupert had given him a commission to be Governor of Lichfield; without advising with or even informing Charles. Knows this is just forgetfulness and thoughtlessness; for if he had considered Lord Loughborough's dispute with the late [Colonel Richard] Bagot, he would have considered more deeply and perhaps thought George Lisle fitter for it. Has spoken of this only to the bearer. Expects Rupert to reply equally frankly.[2]

As Hastings' deputy, it was obvious to the King that the position should have gone to Lisle; unfortunately we do not have Rupert's reply. Hastings was not merely surprised at Scrimgeour's appointment, but furious: on 21st July he advised Rupert that:

> I received yor letter by Adjutant Skrimshawe, whereby I understand yor intentions of giving him a Command here and therefore am bold to present my humble desyres and reasons against it. First, Collonell Lysle takes it as granted to him by yor Highnesse to have the next power to myne in these Garrisons, and hath writt to mee to that purpose not doubting of yor Highnes favor to hym and upon the expressions of some Gentlemen of this County to give mee their best assistance in his mats service if I

Scrimgeour, apparently no relation, who had been buried at Oxford in December 1644 (parish register of St Mary the Virgin, Oxford). John shared Rupert's disgrace after the fall of Bristol (Newman, pp.334-335). Lisle's whereabouts during the affair are completely conjectural, although Hastings' letter of 21st July makes it clear that he is no longer at Lichfield, meaning almost certainly he had joined the King in the Marches.

2   Summary from WSL calendar of letters, S. MS. 497.

should continue wth them. I have made them promise and hope you will sudainely heare this Garrison is in a better Condicon then ever, in the third place I beseech you Sr give me leave to tell you that I know Adjutant Skrimshawe was the chiefest assistant Collonell Bagott used in his opposition against mee, and our minds both too high to acknowledge a superioritie his present expressions declaring an impossibility of our agreemt wch must needs bee destructive to the King's Service; Sr now I have presumed to open my thoughts to you I shall withall humility submit to yor pleasure and not desyre to continue in this or any other Comand you have honored mee wth longer then I am happy in yor good opinion wch I have ever prised more then the greatest imployment[.] Sr however unfortunate soever I may be made by the reports of others yett my endeavours shall ever bee to approve my selfe

Yor highnesse Constant & faithfull servant
Loughborough[3]

Why the Prince overlooked Lisle for the position is unclear, but there are several possibilities. Firstly, Rupert may simply have believed that Lisle was of more value as a field officer. Secondly, he may have initially considered him for the post of governor, wanting to put someone he trusted into Lichfield as an antidote to the Bagots' bellicose bickering with Hastings and Leveson which had caused him so much trouble; Lisle being Hastings' deputy, however, Scrimgeour worked against him and won the position for himself, thus securing the Bagots' influence. Thirdly perhaps Rupert was, as Charles suggested, simply being thoughtless: perhaps he wanted to reward Scrimgeour for some service and offered him the Lichfield position, overlooking the fact that he was Hastings' enemy and would inflame existing local antipathies. Rupert also neglected to think who else might be 'fitter' for the post, or indeed be technically the next in line for it. If this was the case, then his not considering Lisle's position is another indication that Lisle was not an important element of the Prince's political clique. Lastly, Rupert may have deliberately acted against Hastings *and* Lisle, because of the surrender of Leicester: throughout July Hastings was still under suspicion of treachery, Lisle was his deputy and may even have written to Rupert supporting Hastings. Perhaps in a moment of paranoia, maybe encouraged by Scrimgeour or other of Hastings' enemies, Rupert did not want to put anyone in charge of the Lichfield garrison who might then act in Hastings' interest rather than the King's if the charges against Hastings were proven. To bathe Lisle in such a light is ridiculous, as anyone in the army would have attested, but again, if suspicion was Rupert's motive for overlooking him, it highlights a distance between them. Lisle, of course, told Hastings he believed he was in the Prince's favour, but that might simply mean that he wasn't aware that he

---

3   WSL, S. MS. 550/22; also quoted in Warburton, vol. III, p146.

had done anything to displease him. Ultimately Rupert came down on Hastings' side, Hastings' letters suggest, the Prince having presumably persuaded Charles that the loss of Leicester was inevitable and no fault of its keeper. It was too late to pull back from backing Scrimgeour as Lichfield's governor, however, whatever the reasons for doing so.

We do not know how the Lichfield dispute was resolved, but neither Lisle nor Scrimgeour took up the appointment, as Harvey Bagot was still the *de facto* governor of the town when it underwent its final siege in July 1646.[4] Understandably, given the unceasing political attacks on him, and the growing instability within the Royalist political structure generally, Hastings was becoming wearied of the whole business. In October he withdrew to his house and headquarters at Ashby-de-la-Zouch, and in February 1646 surrendered it to the Parliament.

If indeed Rupert did harbour concerns about the loyalties of such unswerving Royalists as Hastings and Lisle, however ridiculous those concerns were, it foreshadowed similar events a few months later: governors being suspected, arrested and removed due to their associations with someone who was themselves under suspicion for treachery. Ironically, the man under suspicion on those occasions was Rupert himself, having surrendered Bristol, and the governors were his friends. Undoubtedly the Lichfield issue remained a loose end because Rupert's disgrace meant that he could do nothing else about it.

Summer 1645: King Charles, and the plan for a new army

By 30th June three more Shropshire garrisons had fallen, and also Highworth near Faringdon: the thoughts of many Naseby survivors must have been turning towards the inevitable demise of the King's cause. Goring had finally abandoned the siege of Taunton, and was then decisively beaten by Fairfax and Massey at Langport on 10th July. Fairfax's *coup de grâce* had been swift and deliberate: he had ignored the King's person and instead taken out his only remaining fighting force. By the end of July eleven more Royalist garrisons had disappeared, including Carlisle, Pontefract Castle and Scarborough Castle. Even Rupert was now bereft of hope, and in a complete about-face from his previous 'no negotiation' stance he told the Duke of Richmond on the 28th that:

> If I were desired to deliver my opinion what other ways the King should take, this should be my opinion, which your Lordship may declare to the King. His Majesty hath now no way left to preserve his posterity,

---

4   In fact during the siege Harvey was outranked, and thus superseded by, Sir Thomas Tyldesley, at that time the commander of the Royalist horse in Staffordshire.

kingdom, and nobility, but by a treaty. I believe it a more prudent way to retain something, than to lose all ...[5]

Revealing the breathtaking extent of his denial of the situation, Charles responded:

I confess there is no probability of my ruin. If I had any other quarrel but the defence of my religion, crown, and friends, you had full reason for your advice ...

After fleeing from Naseby the King spent much of July at Raglan Castle, being hosted by the Marquess of Worcester; during his stay he flitted back and forth around Monmouthshire and Glamorgan, organising contribution money and attempting to raise levies. At Hereford sometime between the 19th and 26th June – the one week where both Charles and Rupert were present – a grand plan was hatched for raising a new army, which included a new regiment for Lisle, still with white colours: 500 men were to be garrisoned at Monmouth.[6] The plan quickly fell apart, however. Although in Rupert's initial draft of the army structure the force would total 8,300 men in seventeen regiments, a note under the list reveals that the counties did not provide the levies they had promised. A revised list follows, dated from Raglan on 4th July, after Rupert had departed: it totals only 3,700 men in ten regiments, and Lisle's men have been reallocated to Chepstow. He does not seem to have gone there, however: when the garrison was surrendered on 11th October, the governor was a Colonel Fitzmorris and the most senior officers taken with him were 'three Lieutenant-Colonels and Majors'.[7] It seems that this revised smaller army became a victim of 'mission creep': Belasyse's account records that the King:

[marched] to Hereford and Ragland Castle to recruit himself with a new foot army in South Wales, but those which were raised there were otherwise disposed of being sent over the Severn, some to supply the garrisons in the West, others to Prince Rupert at Bristol, who was gone thither to his Government to defend that place during His Majesty's residence in South Wales.[8]

Walker, typically, entirely blames Rupert for the shift of focus to Bristol, remarking that:

5   Warburton, vol. III, p.149.
6   BL Harl MSS 6852, f.275.
7   A Perfect Diurnall, Numb. 116, p.921; Mercurius Britanicus, Numb. 101, p.899.
8   Ormonde, vol. II, 1903, p.387.

At Hereford the manner and the number of the Levies upon the Counties of Worcester, Hereford, and the six Counties of South Wales (such as I remember should have been about 5000 Foot) was put in some method; but before any thing was executed Prince Rupert, having a design for the Preservation of Bristol, went thither, leaving the managery of this Affair confused and in disorder.[9]

Besides Lisle, the 4th July revised roster of colonels included Sir Bernard Astley, Sir Henry Bard, Sir Matthew Appleyard, William Pretty, Henry Tillier, and William Murray.[10] In an annotation that must have been added later, the list notes that Rupert's foot and firelocks and Sir Bernard Astley's foot, a total of 1,100 of the intended 3,700, were 'put over ye River' to shore up Bristol, as confirmed by Charles's 11th July letter to Rupert, where he hoped 'all the Foot with Sir Barnard Asheby will be gone over by to-morrow at furthest'.[11] Shortly afterwards Appleyard, Pretty, Tillier, and Murray also crossed to Bristol, although how many men they took is unclear. Bard seems not to have gone, but to have had some quasi-official position at Worcester. The assumption is still firmly that, having left Lichfield, Lisle had joined the King at Hereford or Raglan; where he went when the other colonels departed for Bristol, however, is not certain. A note beside his name on the 4th July list says '150 put over ye River': whether he accompanied those 150 men or stayed behind with the remaining 350 is not known. If he went with them then he would have been present at the siege and capitulation of Bristol, and would have accompanied Rupert back to Oxford in mid-September. Besides hinting that his relationship with Rupert was perhaps not as difficult as the evidence suggests, this would neatly place Lisle at Oxford in time for the next confirmed sighting of him in November. However, unlike all the other colonels he is not mentioned in any of the Bristol sources, which given his seniority is extremely odd; therefore until some other evidence surfaces to definitively locate him, his whereabouts in July and August must be considered as unknown.

At this time the Scots army had come as far as Hereford; which, Belasyse's account continues:

gave occasion to the King to suppose it seasonable to fall with those horse he had (being about 3,000) into the north, both to attempt the release of some garrisons of his which were besieged at Pontefract, Scarborough

---

9   Walker, p.116.

10   Pretty would have known Lisle, as he was also a captain in Lord Grandison's regiment in 1640. Tillier was newly released after his capture at Marston Moor, and his regiment had fought with the Shrewsbury Foot under Lisle at Naseby. A final colonel on the revised list of ten, 'Sir John Palott' is presently unidentified.

11   Petrie, p.11.

and others, as also to endeavour the recovery of those parts; and raising of forces.'

Walker frames it rather that the King's safety was now at stake: he had choice of crossing the Severn and joining Goring in the west, or heading north to take advantage of the continuing Scottish successes of the Marquess of Montrose. The latter option was taken, and in early August, with Rupert now ensconced at Bristol, the King and his army of mainly cavalry headed north via Ludlow and Bridgnorth. On Sunday 10th August they passed through Lichfield: here, according to Symonds, the King drew out 100 or 150 foot, but he makes no mention of Lisle, and there is no record of the officer who commanded these men.[12]

On the 16th the army reached Doncaster. Additions of foot and horse along the way had increased the army: Richard Symonds was present and gives a breakdown, which totalled 2,200 horse and 400 foot.[13] Pursued by the Scots horse from Hereford and finding Yorkshire closed off by local Parliamentarian forces, the procession headed south again via Nottingham and even dared to raid Huntingdon, Cromwell's birthplace and parliamentary constituency, overwhelming the garrison and taking the town after a heavy fight in the streets. According to Walker Charles believed that the local inhabitants 'for Fear or Love seemed very forward to His Service', and intended to stay for a while to take advantage of it. Hearing of the capture of Sherborne Castle, however, and guessing that Fairfax would now make an attempt on Bristol, he left two days later and headed into Buckinghamshire before reaching Oxford on 27th of August.[14] After just a day or two there, the locals fearing that his presence would cause another siege, he marched towards Hereford, intending to relieve it: the Scots, however – hearing of Montrose's victory at Kilsyth – raised the siege of their own accord and marched north.

Walker notes that:

> Our speedy march from Oxford caused the stay there of the Duke of Richmond and many other Gentlemen, tired with the Tediousness and Misfortune of the Summer.

The next time we can positively locate Lisle is in early November, at Oxford. If he did not go to Bristol with Rupert, and remained in the Marches and accompanied the King on his trip around the north in August, it is possible that he could be one of those 'gentlemen' whom Walker says remained at Oxford at the end of the

---

12 *Diarye*, p.223 and 225. Symonds first says 100 men, then 150.
13 *Ibid.*
14 Walker, p.136; Dugdale (p.81) says he reached Oxford on the 27th, but Symonds was actually with the King.

month, after the King finished his circuit and moved back to the Marches. Only ten weeks had passed since Lisle's critical wounding at Naseby, and if he did stop at Oxford it might imply that he had still not recovered his former strength.

Walker believes that Charles, meanwhile, had a workable plan to relieve Rupert which might have succeeded, had the timing come together. The King intended that Goring should come to Bristol out of the West, and that he (the King) would:

> draw a Force of at least 3000 Foot out of all His Garrisons of those parts, to pass them over Severn at Beachley, and at the same time our Horse, which were then above 3000, to ford the Severn not far from Gloucester and join with our Foot, and so on both sides to fall on Fairfax's Quarters.[15]

There was no time to bring the plan together, however, before Bristol surrendered on 11th September.

Summer 1645: Prince Rupert, and the surrender of Bristol

At Bewdley on 18th June, the day Leicester was surrendered, Rupert wrote to William Legge at Oxford, asking him:

> Pray let me know what is said among you concerning our last defeat. Doubtless the fault of it will be put upon [Rupert] … Since this business, I find Digby hath omitted nothing which might prejudice [Rupert], and hath this day drawn a letter for the King to Prince Charles, in which he crosses all things that befel here in Rupert's behalf. I have shewed this to the King, and in earnest; and if, thereupon, he should go on and send it, I shall be forced to quit generalship, and march into my … towards Prince Charles, where Rupert hath received more kindness than here.[16]

What passed between nephew and uncle over the next week is not clear, but although they do not appear to have fallen out, presumably Rupert was in some respects unsatisfied: for on the 26th June, having written a letter to Sir John Owen and Colonel Thelwall about some levies in North Wales,[17] he left the King at Hereford and took a boat from Cardiff to Barnstaple, where he joined the Prince of Wales. On 4th July he arrived in Bristol, and took up governorship of the city; perhaps he and the King had discussed this arrangement whilst at Hereford.[18]

15   Walker, p.129.
16   Warburton, vol. III, pp.119-121.
17   *Ibid.*
18   Prince Rupert's Diary (EHR), p.739.

Having relieved Taunton and destroyed Goring's army at Langport, Fairfax moved on to siege Bridgwater, which duly surrendered on the 23rd. All of this would have kept Rupert busy, and indeed he seems to have spent much of July and August beating up enemy quarters, while the King was processing around the north of England. Partway through July came the spat with Charles and Hastings about the governorship of Lichfield. Royalist strongholds were falling every few days; Bath had been taken on 30th July, and on 15th August Sherborne Castle, owned by the Digbys and which had been bombarded and then stormed, surrendered to Fairfax. Sir Lewis Dyve, the governor, was taken to London and sent to the Tower. Sprigge records that Fairfax now had to decide between taking Bristol or moving west to prevent Goring regrouping; the fear of Rupert using the Bristol garrison, with recruits from Wales, to field a new army, and the fact that Bristol was the only port the King had in the south, swung the decision towards it. On Thursday 21st Fairfax approached and viewed the city, and began placing the army so as to blockade it. The growing toll of destroyed garrisons must have been alarming William Legge: despite having Fairfax on his doorstep, Rupert wrote to Legge on 28th August reassuring him that:

> I wonder that Stevens should give you so many false alarms. We never were in better condition than now. All our officers and souldiers are paid and billeted in town. Fairfax engaged before Sherborne …[19]

The Prince was no longer convinced of the wellness of the wider war, however, and on the same day wrote the aforementioned letter to the King, advising him to seek a treaty. Evidently when he wrote to Legge on the 28th he had no idea of Sherborne's fall, and his letter was to prove disastrously over-confident of Bristol's chances.

Sprigge gives a full account of the siege.[20] Rupert had answered Fairfax's initial summons with a request to ask the King first, which Fairfax refused. Over the next few days the Prince and his garrison made numerous sallies, losing Sir Bernard Astley as a prisoner on the 26th; he had been wounded, and died at Bath a few days later. On 2nd September Fairfax's council of war agreed that the city should be stormed. Two days later his artillery began to batter the fortifications, and another summons was sent. Rupert again asked to send to the King but again Fairfax refused; finally, on the 7th, the Prince sent propositions. Fairfax, responding to them with some queries but not receiving an answer, stormed the city in the early hours of the 10th, and eventually the Royalists asked for a parley. This time articles were agreed, and on Thursday 11th Rupert and his garrison marched out with 'Colours, Pikes, and Drums, bag and baggage.' Common soldiers were allowed

19   Warburton, vol. III, p.151.
20   Sprigge, pp.90-112.

to leave with their swords, and the entire force escorted to a Royalist quarter of Rupert's choice: naturally he chose Oxford and arrived on the 15th, the Bristol foot three days behind him.[21]

Richard Symonds notes that five days later 'His Majestie dispatched letters of buisiness to Oxford':[22] presumably these included the following one to Rupert:

> Though the loss of Bristol be a great blow to me, yet your surrendering it as you did is of so much affliction to me … For what is to be done after one that is so near to me as you are, both in blood and friendship, submits himself to so mean an action? … My concllusion is, to desire you to seek your subsistence, until it shall please God to determine of my condition, somewhere beyond seas: to which end I send you herewith a pass …[23]

The further sting in the tail was that the pass sending Rupert overseas was signed by, of all people, Lord Digby. The King's Hereford dispatch evidently contained far more than just the letter to Rupert, as on the 17th the Prince's diary records:

> Wednesday, by letters from the King, the Lords dischargd the Prince of his Generallship : cashierd his Regiments of Horse and Foote, his troope and firelocks. That daye was Colonel Legg discharged of his goverment of Oxford, and confin'd to his howse.[24]

Sir Edward Nicholas, who was tasked with the dirty work of arresting Legge and presenting Rupert with his dismissal, advised the King that he would shortly hear from his nephew:

> who I believe will stay here till he hears again from you, for that he cannot, without leave from the rebels, go to embark himself, and without your Majesty's license I hear he will not demand a pass from the rebels.[25]

Rupert's letter, incredibly restrained and eloquently written considering the circumstances, requested a hearing, else he would 'publish to the world what I think will clear my erring …'[26]

By way of confirmation that Lisle may now have been at Oxford, surviving documents concerning the fall of Bristol suggest he was not there during its siege,

---

21 Dugdale, pp.81-82.
22 *Diarye*, p.240.
23 Warburton, vol. III, p.185.
24 Prince Rupert's Diary (EHR), p.740. Legge remained under house arrest until 9th November (Dugdale, p.83).
25 *CSP Domestic Series*, 1645-1647, p.144.
26 Undated; *op. cit.*, p.189.

storming and loss. A pamphlet was published in November, apparently by Rupert, containing a testimony of the state of the city when he arrived, the various correspondence between Fairfax and the Prince during the event, and a confirmation by the King that his nephew had been cleared of 'the least want of courage or fidelity'.[27] Notably, the documents include the names of Rupert's council of war – dominated, unlike the King's council, by military men – and those of eighteen senior officers in the garrison who assented during the negotiations to the laying down of the garrison's arms. Lisle is not mentioned, and given his rank and experience, if he had been in the city with Rupert his name would undoubtedly have been one of those two lists. It is possible that he simply escaped the record, but with his seniority this is unlikely.

The King's second march north: Chester and Newark

Rumours had been circulating since at least late July that Charles intended to head for Scotland, where the Marquess of Montrose was having success after success.[28] After dismissing Rupert from his service the King now planned exactly this, and headed north with what forces he had. Hearing that Chester was in danger of falling, he diverted to assist it, arriving on 23rd September: the battle of Rowton Heath ensued the next day, where Langdale's and Gerard's cavalry were broken. Granting Byron, the Mayor and the citizens permission to 'treat for their own Preservation' if there was no relief within eight days, the King left the city with just 500 horse. Fleeing westward to Denbigh Castle, he heard that Montrose's army had been destroyed at Philiphaugh by the returning Covenanter army, putting Scotland out of Charles's reach. His choice now was to head for Anglesey or Worcester. The latter being deemed more strategically suitable, he headed southeast to Chirk; on the 27th he met Maurice with his own troop and the remnants of Rupert's from Bristol, and at Bridgnorth on the 29th, Walker says:

> we had the News of the taking of Berkley Castle whereof Sir Charles Lucas was Governour, and of the Devizes where Sir Charles Lloyd our late Quarter-Master General and chief Enginier commanded. The first was well defended, but the Loss of the other, in regard of the natural Strength of the Place and Ability of the Governour in Matters of Fortification, was not as yet ever answered by him. But our Misfortunes gave us not Opportunities to reward, and so we did not punish the Loss of these Places.[29]

27 *A Declaration Of his Highnesse Prince Rupert.*
28 Rupert to the Duke of Richmond, 28th July (Warburton, vol. III, p.149). The Prince says 'it is now in everybody's mouth, that the King is going for Scotland.'
29 Walker, p.142.

Presumably Lloyd had brought the news of the loss of Devizes to Bridgnorth himself, as a month later Richard Symonds noted that he and his men were still quartered in the town.[30] Cromwell had arrived at Devizes on 15th September and overrun it, forcing Lloyd and his men to retreat to the castle gatehouse and new supporting fortifications added by Lloyd. Sprigge records that when Cromwell suggested that it was more fitting that Parliament kept such places, Lloyd merely retorted 'Win it and wear it'. Cromwell bombarded the place for several days, and the garrison surrendered on terms on the 23rd. Sir Charles Lucas had surrendered Berkeley on the 25th after a three day bombardment and then a storming; whilst he lost the garrison, he had had the foresight to send away the cavalry beforehand to preserve it for the King. Walker's comment about punishment being required for these losses seems incredible when Royalist garrisons were daily being overwhelmed by superior forces; many of these garrisons initially put up a spirited defence, and were not more 'Bletchingdons'. Yet when we consider Feilding's arrest after Reading and Hastings' arrest after Leicester, as well as Rupert's dismissal, it seems to have been a pattern, certainly post-Bletchingdon if not before: that the King would not admit any excuse for losing a garrison, even when the reasons were, militarily, perfectly understandable.

Walker's account was written for publication, and for the use of Clarendon, and his comments may simply have been propaganda, to ensure blame for the King's failures lay on individual commanders and not the monarch.[31] What is undoubtedly not mere propaganda, however, is Walker's claim that Digby was behind the King's decision to dismiss Rupert without a hearing. Walker also claims that Digby, realising that as Rupert was determined to have a hearing and that 'all the Odium of that Action likely to fall upon [Digby] himself', and 'to prevent the breaking of this Cloud which threatened his Ruin,' persuaded the King to meet his nephew at Newark; it was, Walker suggests, difficult for the Prince to get there, and Digby hoped that by the time he did, the storm might have abated.[32]

Having sent Sir Thomas Glemham to Oxford as the new governor, the King and his ragtag force made its way back into the Midlands, arriving at Lichfield on 2nd October and then heading for Newark. Once there, urged by Digby, Charles was briefly drawn north by a rumour that Montrose had managed to land a blow on the Covenanters; receiving news at nearby Welbeck that in fact the Marquess

---

30   *Diarye*, p.252.

31   At time of writing there is academic debate as to whether 'propaganda' is the correct term for the pamphleting activity which went on during the English Civil Wars. Throughout history mutual enemies have always sought to protect their own reputations and make each other look bad, but the Civil Wars provided the first opportunity for large scale direct distribution of what we might call 'propagandist material'. If this was not yet propaganda in the sophisticated form that we are now familiar with, it was at the very least propaganda *in utero*.

32   Walker notes that Digby was also at odds with Charles Gerard, having allegedly contrived to lose him his command in Wales. Gerard had received a barony from the King as recompense for his removal.

had retreated, he sent Langdale and Digby north in an attempt to join up with Montrose, and then returned to Newark. Meanwhile, bringing an entourage of 'about 120 Officers and Gentleman', and meeting Maurice *en route*, Rupert had fought his way up to Belvoir Castle, fifteen miles south of Newark. The next day, 15th October, he approached the town in defiance of a letter from the King telling him not to do so; in a show of support for the Prince, Charles Gerard – recently made a baron – and Sir Richard Willys risked Charles's anger and took a cavalry escort to meet him.

The account of John Belasyse, who was based at Newark and an eyewitness to the events, explains in some detail what transpired. He has a particular bias on the situation, however, being no friend of Willys, and his account should be treated with caution:

> the King ... called him before the Council of war and such officers who were in his train from Bristol to be witnesses for what had passed during the said siege. His Majesty charged him home upon the account of want of conduct, clearing his Highness of the two other Articles, vizt., treachery and want of courage, upon which the trial by martial law did pass, which was all could be obtained, tho' the allegations were that he surrendered that important place to Sir Thomas Fairfax to secure the men for His Majesty's service, there being no likelihood of release, the garrison consisting of 5,000 soldiers, who were dispersed into other garrisons; and this was all the Prince could obtain for his justification, the King telling him that the loss of that important place was a precedent to several other garrisons that without disputing did daily render themselves.[33]

Rupert's Diary is brief on the affair:

> Tuesday [21st], the Prince by 2 Courts of warre at Newark, cleerd from Bristoll. And by the King too.[34]

The timing of subsequent events is confused, and Walker gives a markedly different version to Belasyse, but in brief the King told Willys in private that he had to remove him; Willys discovered that despite this private meeting the matter was already public, however, and a row ensued. He, Gerard, the Princes, and some of their supporters confronted the King but were thrown out of his presence; they sent a petition demanding Willys now receive a court martial – presumably to clear him of any imputation concerning his dismissal – but the request was refused. The King agreed to give passes to all who wanted them, and after an armed standoff

33   Ormonde, vol. II, 1903, p.389.
34   Prince Rupert's Diary (EHR), p.740.

in the castle courtyard, Rupert and his entourage departed for Belvoir.[35] Richard Symonds, who knew Willys well in later years and presumably heard a full account from him then, states that Willys was ousted by Digby and Ashburnham, who wanted a more pliable governor.[36] The new governor was John Belasyse; a few days later Willys attempted to challenge him to a duel, using Gerard as an intermediary, but nothing came of it.

One eyewitness to these events who was already at Newark was Lisle's former tercio colonel and battalion commander Theophilus Gilby. Captured at Naseby, he had presumably been exchanged and then found his way to Newark. Unintentionally he benefited from Rupert's fall: formerly Belasyse's lieutenant colonel, on 27th November, after Belasyse was installed in Willys's place, Gilby was knighted, presumably at his command. Whilst Gilby may well have deserved a knighthood for his long military service to the King, it seems that in the end he received it as part of a bitter struggle to secure loyalties as the Royalist high command tore itself to pieces.

The Belvoir party wrote several letters to Oxford on the 2nd of November, including one from Ned Villiers to his brother George asking that he clear his house. 'I am much pleased with your selling of my horse, as I intend presently to go into France.'[37] Rupert, meanwhile, wrote to William Legge:

> Dear Will, I hope Goodwin has told you what reasons I had to quit his Majesty's service. I have sent Osborne to London for a pass for to go beyond seas; when I have an answer you shall know more. Pray tell Sir Chas. Lucas that I would have written to him before this and to G Lisle but [was kept close] here. [I consider the King's cause] totally [lost]. This by many circumstances I can make appear to you was his [Rupert's] intention. I will name but one. He entrusted me with his business under the highest secrecy. Pray let me know [what you hear, that I] loose not the occasion. If I can but get [permission] I hope to see you and the rest of my friends once more …[38]

He finished the letter with an ironic, and clearly highly satisfied remark about the comprehensive defeat of Digby's force in the north.[39] Although the letter is unsigned, the reference to sending Lieutenant Colonel Henry Osborne to London confirms that Rupert is the author, as several other sources confirm that he gave

---

35   Walker, pp.146-148; Belasyse in Ormonde, vol. II, 1903, pp.389-390.
36   *Diarye*, p.270.
37   *CSP Domestic Series*, 1645-1647, p.214.
38   *Ibid.*, p.215.
39   Digby and Langdale were defeated at Sherburn in Elmet on 15th October; they fled to Cumberland but were defeated again, subsequently fleeing to the Isle of Man, and then Ireland. By May 1646 they were in France.

Osborne this task.[40] Lisle and Lucas cannot have accompanied the Prince to Newark, or Rupert would not have needed to write to them; that he asks Legge to speak to them, means they must have been at Oxford when he left and perhaps they were expecting to hear from him. Why neither went to Newark to support him is not clear. David Appleby suggests Lucas had urgent family matters to attend to;[41] Lisle's absence is more difficult to explain, as we know nothing for certain about his whereabouts between June and November, what his present duties were, and what might have kept him from joining the Newark-bound party. Not that it is compulsory that he should have joined it, but the 120 men the Prince reportedly took with him to Newark must have included a significant chunk of the dwindling Oxford officer corps, and as a senior officer who had spent the previous winter under the Prince's command, and who had told Hastings in June that he did not doubt Rupert's favour towards him, Lisle's absence requires some attempt at explanation.

There are few practical reasons that would have kept him from Newark. As noted, his wounds would long since have healed, although it is possible that they had left some lingering issue that, for example, made it difficult for him to ride. If health was not the issue, then he had at this time no elevated appointment – as far as is known – that would tie him to Oxford; and if he had some position immediately around the King, then he should have been at Newark anyway, as that was where Charles presently was. Possibly, like Lucas, he had urgent personal matters to attend to, but whereas Lucas's family were lodged in Oxford, Lisle's must have been somewhere near London, perhaps in Surrey. He might have been planning to visit them, but besides the risk of being captured, it is unlikely that he would have sought leave to be away in the middle of a crisis, or that his ageing parents would have risked the journey to see him.

The most likely reason for him not accompanying Rupert, is that he simply declined to go. As established previously, there is no specific evidence that Lisle was part of the Prince's political circle, but perhaps he knew of his realignment towards a negotiated settlement, and opposed it. Alternatively, he may still have felt the sting of the Lichfield matter and felt too humiliated, or too aggrieved with Rupert to give him his support. A conscious refusal to go is easiest to explain, however, when considered alongside Lisle's habitual obedience to proper order: Rupert had been formally removed from his chain of command – indeed, from all Royalist appointments – and Lisle was no longer obliged to obey him, or to consider his demands. Critically, if he did obey him, or openly support him, he would be directly challenging the King, and the King's decision to remove him. Lisle may have been as indignant as anyone about Rupert's treatment, but nevertheless, his

---

40 For example, Belasyse in Ormonde, vol. II, p.390; a copy of Rupert's request to General Poyntz, that Osborne have a convoy to London (*Calendar of the Clarendon State Papers*, vol. I, p.284).
41 Appleby, p.129.

loyalty lay solidly with the King, and Rupert was not the King. In this scenario, which seems the best fit, Lisle made his choice, and stayed at Oxford.

David Appleby suggests that Lucas had also drifted from Rupert's orbit in recent months, having endured 'considerable friction' with the Prince over his governorship of the remote Berkeley Castle, and besides his own family affairs this may also have influenced his decision to cut loose from Rupert.[42] Rupert's letter does not suggest any ill-feeling towards either officer, however; whatever may have been said between him and them before he departed was evidently not acrimonious – at least, not from Rupert's perspective – and once at Belvoir he was anxious to keep them informed.

On 3rd November, the same night Rupert wrote his letter, the King began his march back to Oxford; he passed through Belvoir at 3 a.m., picking up a local escort from the governor, and within three or four days made it safely back to Oxford.

Walker gives a long description of the dismal situation discovered by the King on his return, including a long list of more lost garrisons, including Basing House. He also bewails the fact that Charles became distracted by the possibility of yet more peace propositions, ignoring:

> the thought of new Levies, of His Majesty's endeavouring to get into the West by His Presence to enjoy that Army, or of going to Worcester and gathering together the Forces in those Parts, and hastning Recruits from Ireland …[43]

Soldiers were becoming 'weary of their ill Fortune', he adds, and 'hoping for better Employments abroad.' Not everyone had gone abroad, however: Osborne's trip to London had come to nothing, Parliament refusing passes unless oaths were forthcoming, that the recipients would not fight again. Walker says many of Rupert's entourage 'swallowed the Oaths and went to London', but the Princes, and Charles Gerard, returned to Oxford on 9th December and were reconciled with the King by kissing his hand. Sir Richard Willys seems to have been with them, although he was not similarly reconciled until 3rd April.[44]

Honours

Meanwhile the King's army – what little there was – underwent another restructure. Sir Jacob Astley was appointed lord general in Rupert's place, and on 27th November Lucas was appointed lieutenant general of the horse: Goring had fled

---

42   *Ibid.*, pp.130-131.
43   Walker, p.149.
44   Dugdale, p.83, 84.

the country a week earlier. *The Kingdomes Weekly Post* provided its readers with a long list of the new appointments, ending with:

> Leiut. Gen. Lile Commander in chief of the Counties of Oxford, Berks, and Buckingham for the King.[45]

Despite his previous high energy and constant activity as a regional commander, Henry Hastings was now a spent force, his former territories rapidly slipping into Parliament's hands. It is reasonable to assume that Lisle's association with him was now over – perhaps the reason he was now back in Oxford – and his previous appointment as lieutenant general of Leicestershire was a redundant role. His precise remit in the three crucial territories surrounding and adjacent to Oxford is unclear, however Astley was made commander in chief over Staffordshire and the Marches, presumably a similar role, and Walker describes him as being given 'large Power and Instructions to raise Forces and settle Contributions'.[46] If Lisle thought managing Faringdon's small territory was troublesome, the size of his task now was colossal, particularly as the three counties were increasingly overrun by the enemy; unfortunately no paperwork survives to indicate how he went about it. Neither should the extent of the King's trust in him be underestimated: the wider security of Oxford itself was now in his hands. As if to underline this, he was finally knighted there on 21st December 1645.[47] How this honour was negotiated, he having previously refused it, is not known. Perhaps Charles absolutely insisted; or perhaps it was tentatively offered and Lisle accepted, finally feeling that the squabbling lords who had undermined the cause for so long were finally no threat to it, or him. At the same time he received the knighthood he was appointed 'Master of the Household', that is, Master of the Green Cloth, the Household department which looked after the King's finances. The job had been in abeyance since 1632; it was a peculiar position to revive for Lisle, even as a sinecure, but as discussed elsewhere, the Green Cloth had been the area of the household in which Laurence was working before the King's removal to York in 1642. His petition to the Earl of Salisbury in 1644 reveals the financial trouble he was in. Perhaps when offered the honour of a household position alongside his knighthood, George reminded the King that his father had served him and had suffered greatly by his removal from London, and was able to secure the Green Cloth appointment on Laurence's behalf, effectively getting him his old job back plus a promotion. Not that it would have paid anything at the time, but it may have been a promise for 'after the war'.

45   Unnumbered; week ending 28th November 1645, p.56. The list is incorrect in that it says Langdale was general of the horse, when in fact it was Lucas; and that Lord Mohun was 'Governor of the Horse' in the West, although in fact Mohun had been out of the picture since 1644. There is no reason to doubt Lisle's appointment, however.
46   Walker, p.150.
47   Walkely, p.167.

The end of the war

Despite his seniority, ability, and experience, Lisle is notably absent from reports of Royalist actions during 1646, and no longer seems to have had a field role. Whether this was simply lack of available roles in the King's dwindling forces, his being too busy with his three-county appointment, or because some lingering injury from Naseby still afflicted him, is not known. Perhaps his participation has simply escaped historical record. By March, however, the civil war in England was in any case little more than a weekly roll of collapsing Royalist garrisons. Hereford had surrendered on the 18th December; Belvoir Castle on 31st Jan, and the castle almost destroyed. Chester had surrendered on 3rd February; Sir William Brereton took the Cathedral Close at Lichfield on 6th March. Fairfax was rapidly gaining a foothold in the West, and Newark was now under siege.

'Spring coming on', Walker says,

> Sir Thomas Glemham Governour of Oxon had a Design upon Abingdon, and had carried it by Surprize had not the Cart with Materials been broken on the Way; many of our Foot and Captain Mead with some Horse being gotten over the Works, and those within running out of the Town on the other side; only some Horse made a stand, and drove ours out again … Prince Rupert attempted it two Days after, but then it was too late.[48]

Meanwhile on 14th March the King's beleaguered forces in the West, under Hopton, were finally defeated, and the army disbanded. The King had one last card: over the winter Astley and Lucas had against all the odds put together an army of around 3,000 foot and 500 horse. Charles decided to gather '1,500 Horse and Foot drawn out of Oxford and other garrisons', and meet Astley at Chipping Norton, with the aim of relieving Banbury or retiring to Worcester. Astley and Lucas, then at Bridgnorth, duly marched to Worcester. Walker records what followed on 21st March: the final battle of the First English Civil War.

> The Lord Asteley presently marches, and whether Letters failed or were mistaken, I know not, he was no sooner on his March but Brereton had Notice of it; and drawing off a Party from Lichfield, and joining with the Forces of Evesham and Warwick follows him, and lets him pass the Avon without Interruption that Evening. The Forces of Gloucester under the Command of their Governour Morgan join with Brereton, and follow the Lord Astley's Rear over Cotswold; but he makes his Passage good and marches all Night, imagining that they had not followed him any farther, and so early begins to draw into Quarters, when they appeared and fell

---

48   Walker, p.152.

upon him. His Foot behaved themselves gallantly, and repulsed them; but all the Horse the first Charge turned about and fled, and so was the good old man and all his Foot taken Prisoners. Sir Charles Lucas was taken not far off at his Brother's Sir William Walter's House.[49]

After blaming Rupert and Digby on so many occasions, the first largely unfairly and the second usually quite rightly, Walker now had noone left to blame but the King: whom, he says should have gone to Astley, rather than expecting Astley to go to him. He adds,

Thus we lost our last Game, which fixed His Majesty at Oxford. Nothing now but a Miracle, or the Victory of His Forces in the West being able to fetch him off …

In fact the Western forces had surrendered a week previously: writing this much later, in 1647, Walker must have mixed up his dates. With victory in sight, the Parliament did not rest on its laurels. On 30th March the Committee of Both Kingdoms wrote to Colonel Edward Whaley,

we have determined to employ Col. Rainsborough's foot with such other as we shall join with him, and all the four regiments of horse from [Fairfax's] army in such places about Oxford as we conceive will wholly block it up, and put those within presently to live at the expense of their stores.[50]

As the Committee drafted its letter to Whaley, Colonel Sir John Boys, who had been under siege at Donnington Castle since the previous November, was enduring two final days of siege and bombardment. He handed over the castle to Colonel Dalbier on 1st April, and the rest of the building was subsequently destroyed. With the last Royalist army gone from the field, the Prince of Wales and his advisors fled to Jersey five days later; garrisons continued to fall. Bridgnorth town on 31st March; Exeter on 13th April; Bridgnorth Castle on 18th April; Woodstock Manor on 26th April, after a stiff defence and bombardment which lasted at least eleven days. With Woodstock gone, and Fairfax on his way to Oxford after taking Exeter, the King decided that it was time for him to leave. For some time, Walker says, he had been negotiating with the Scots via 'Monsieur Montrell the French Agent', the Scots having promised 'protection and safety for Himself and Followers'.[51] When a planned rendezvous with a Scottish escort at Market Harborough fell through,

---

49 *Ibid.*
50 *CSP Domestic Series*, 1645-1647, p.390.
51 Dugdale notes that the French agent, Jean de Montreuil, 'went from Oxford toward Scotland' on 3rd April (p.85). He was in fact going to Newark.

314 NO ARMOUR BUT COURAGE

Charles took his life in his own hands and decided to leave Oxford anyway. On 27th April he left the city for the final time, making a feint through the East Gate with cropped hair, disguised as an attendant of John Ashburnam and a 'divine', Dr. Michael Hudson. With a faked pass bearing Fairfax's signature they headed some way towards London and then turned north. Charles had had no option but to leave the eleven-year-old Duke of York behind. On 5th May Charles went to Southwell, three miles from Newark – under siege since November – and gave himself up to the Scots army. After ordering Newark to surrender – which it did, on the 8th – he then marched with the Scots to Newcastle.

News of the King's escape reached the House of Commons on 29th April; the next day it ordered:

> That no Person be received, or admitted to come, out of Oxford, by Pass or otherwise, except it be upon Parley or Treaty, concerning the Surrendering of the Garison, or some Fort, or otherwise advantageous, for Reducing of the Garison …[52]

Meanwhile the entire town of Faringdon, and a small Royalist fort at Radcot, had been under siege since 10th April; the Faringdon siege was directed, appropriately, by Sir Robert Pye junior, who had faced Lisle's storming of the breach at Leicester, and whose family owned The Place. Pye bombarded the town, destroying the church steeple and also starting a fire which caused significant damage among the town's wooden buildings. Sir Marmaduke Rawdon, who was still governor, had been ill for some time; on 25th April he was struck down by pneumonia, and died three days later. He was buried in the shattered church, but the town continued to hold out.

On Friday 1st May, Dugdale records,

> Sr Tho. Fairfax his Horse appeared in the feilds on ye East of Oxford, and began to keep guards.

Dugdale adds that five days later the city stores was opened, to feed the army; 4,700 were fed from it. Five days after that, the first notable casualty of the siege was Prince Rupert, who was shot in the arm in the fields north of the city. Incredibly, it was the first time he had been wounded during the war. On the 13th, the first cannon shot landed within the city, in Christ Church meadow; two days later:

---

52   JHC, 4, 1644-1646, p.527.

All the Lords of ye Councell ... joyned in a command wch they signed to Sr Tho. Glemham, ye governor of Oxford, to send a Letter to Sr Th. Fairfax for nominating Commissioners to treate for ye delivery of Oxford.[53]

Walker explains that:

The Lords and others of the Council there, who had taken upon them all the Authority of Command (in regard Sir Thomas Glemham the Governour, at His Majesty's Departure had His Majesty's Orders to obey them) enforced him contrary to his Sense at that time to accept the Summons and to begin a Treaty ...[54]

The 'Council' was the King's Privy Council; that its members should disagree with Glemham, the soldier, disagreed, was of course a familiar story. Dugdale notes that after instructing Glemham to treat, the Council members immediately began burning all their books and papers. Presumably the capture of the King's letters at Naseby was still fresh enough in their minds. Doubtless many other Royalist officers and officials across the city did the same: although the King had not yet sent official word to all his remaining garisons to surrender, undeniably the Parliament had won, and very soon there would be a reckoning.

Glemham, however, challenged the Council's power to surrender the city, asking the members to prove they had the authority to do so; presumably they did, as on 17th May Glemham and 'all his principall Officers of the garrison' – twenty-four of them – signed a paper declaring that:

it is absolutely against or wills and opinions to treat at this present with Sr Thomas Farefax. Butt upon the Governour's intimation of order received by him from the King to observe what the body of the Privy Councell should determine in his absence, have in obedience to his Maty order bin inforced by the Lords of the Privy Councell to this treaty. And doe further declare to the world, that what inconvenience soever may arise to the King's cause or his freinds upon this Treaty, is nott in or hands to prevent.[55]

Frederick Varley, in his account of the siege, calls the declaration a 'bombastic disclaimer of responsibility on the part of the military',[56] but Glemham's caution about surrendering the city is perhaps understandable. He faced the now familiar

53 Dugdale, p.87.
54 Walker, p.153.
55 Dugdale, p.88.
56 Varley, p.139.

spectre of Windebank, of course. Yet he was not new to such matters, having been governor of York when it surrendered in 1644 and in command of Carlisle at its surrender in 1645. Accordingly he sent the propositions, naming fourteen commissioners besides himself, to handle the negotiations. Notably Lisle was not one of the twenty-four officers to sign Glemham's declaration, who included Colonels Henry Tillier and Stephen Hawkins; or one of the fourteen commissioners, who included Sir Richard Willys. Possibly Lisle – who had himself experienced the dilemmas of town surrender, at Leicester – also disagreed with negotiating so soon, and declined to be involved, but equally it may simply underline the fact that for some time he had not played any active military role.

The negotiations got underway at Marston, two miles north-east of the city, and went back and forth for a number of days. Initially Fairfax rejected the Royalists' propositions and sending others. On 10th June authorisation arrived from the King confirming to the council that it should surrender Oxford on the best terms possible; three days later another arrived, with his preferred instructions for the safety of Rupert, Maurice and the Duke of York.

Meanwhile Fairfax diverted the river Isis away from the city, and prevented a sally to fetch in more cattle, and at around this time the two sides freely exchanged cannon fire; Sprigge suggests the Royalists were doing little more than randomly expending shot and powder, although he commends their skill in landing a cannon ball high up on Headington Hill, killing an officer. The Parliamentarians retaliated:

> and much annoyed them in their Works and Colledges, till at last, a cessation of great shot was agreed to on both sides.[57]

Evidently feelings in the city were running high, as on the 17th, Dugdale says:

> the Lords forbore to meete at ye Audit house, as they had done, in regard of the mutinous souldiers, especially Reformadoes.[58]

Two days later the council felt it necessary to wear their swords in public. Meanwhile, suggesting a post-cessation mood in the city quite contrary to that which forced the council to go armed, Dugdale observed that 'Divers of the Enemyes souldiers came to ye Ports and dranke wth ours.'

Finally, on 20th June:

---

57   Sprigge, p.259.
58   Dugdale, p.90. Gardiner states that they were 'clamouring or pay which was not forthcoming', but does not specify his source (vol. 2, p.109).

This Evening late, divers of the Treaters for Sr Tho. Fairfax came wth the other from Marston into Oxford, and signed the Articles, in ye Audit house, on their p'te, as the Lords and Governor on their's, for delivery up of Oxford.[59]

A far as Parliament was concerned, the war was over. Lisle, however, had one more contribution to make. On 20th June, Sprigge says:

The same morning that the Treaty for Oxford was concluded, Farrington Garrison sent also to capitulate, the Governour thereof Sir George Lisle, being then in Oxford, and to be briefe, surrendred upon condition to have the benefit of Oxford Articles; and so they were included in the same Agreement.[60]

Where Sprigge heard that Lisle had been involved is not clear; however he cannot be correct that Lisle was once again Faringdon's governor, as when Rawdon died in April, he had recommended Sir William Courtney replace him, and Courtney appears to have done so.[61] How Lisle managed to intervene in the negotiations and have Faringdon included is not known, but his reasons for doing it were probably personal, given that he had spent so many months there; it may also have been a gesture made in Rawdon's honour.

Against the King's wishes, the articles specified that the Duke of York was to be conveyed to London, to join his brother and sister as a prisoner in Parliament hands. On Monday 22nd June, between the conclusion of the treaty and the official day of departure, Rupert and Maurice left Oxford. As the treaty was being concluded, Rupert had requested that he could go to Oatlands 'for a little time' as he had no money';[62] presumably he did not receive a reply in time, as he and Maurice went there anyway, which violated article III of the treaty which specified that they should keep at least twenty miles from London. Parliament demanded that they leave the country,[63] and accordingly they made their way to Dover. On 5th July Rupert took ship for Calais; on the 8th, Maurice for Holland.[64] We will never know whether Lisle spoke to Rupert one last time before the Prince's departure, and if so, what was said; they would not see each other again.

The Oxford articles permitted the Royalists to leave Oxford with honour: with horses, drums, colours, arms, powder, bag and baggage. Once out of Oxford,

59   *Ibid.*, p.92.
60   Sprigge, *op. cit.*
61   Dace, p.23.
62   *The Moderate Intelligencer*, Numb. 68, p.503.
63   *The Kingdomes Weekly Intelligencer*, Numb. 154, p.151
64   Prince Rupert's Diary (EHR), p.741.

however, they had to surrender their arms at prearranged locations within fifteen miles of the city, and then receive:

> the Generalls Passe and protection for their peaceable repaire to, and abode at the severall places they shall desire to goe unto …

Both Oxford's city gates were to be used, north and south, those using the north heading for 'Yorkshire and Gloucestershire and those parts …'

On 24th June, Sprigge says:

> The Enemy marched out about twelve of the clock; a Guard of our Foot was appointed for them to march through, which extended in length from Saint Clements neer Maudlin-Bridge, to Shotover-Hill: Our Horse were drawne up into severall Bodies in severall places in the Reare of the Foot: There marched out in a Body and well Armed, with Colours flying and Drums beating, about three thousand.

Lisle's former military rank and his final role as Commander in Chief of Oxfordshire probably afforded him a place at or near the head of the last Royalist column that would ever march out of Oxford. After leaving the city and obtaining a pass he would have headed south: towards London. After four years of fighting for his King, and on at least one occasion nearly dying for him, it was time to go home. However it was not time, at least in Lisle's mind, to give up the fight.

15

'A King and No King'

1647: Independents, Presbyterians, the Army and the King

> The King feares the Parliament, They the Army, And both the King: The Parliament is jealous of the King, his Majesty of the army, the City of them all. If the King joyne with the Parliament, the Army is in feare; if with the Army, the Parliament is in feare; If with neither, the Kingdome is in fear …[1]

Thus *Mercurius Morbicus* concisely summed up England's political situation at the end of 1647. The political manoeuvrings between the various English factions that year, and between England and the two rival factions in Scotland, are highly complicated and worth several books in themselves; only a simplified summary of some of the major details is required here, however, to explain the ongoing fate and whereabouts of the King, and the background to the outbreak of the Second Civil War in 1648, in which Lisle was a significant participant.

After giving himself up to the Scots in May 1646, the King remained in semi-imprisonment at Newcastle upon Tyne. On 13th July Parliament sent him its proposals for a settlement, which became known as the 'Newcastle Propositions'. The most important of the nineteen clauses required that the King sign the Covenant, agreeing to a Presbyterian church settlement in England, and the imposition of it on his English subjects; that episcopacy (bishops) would be abolished; that Catholic Mass would not be said at court; that Parliament was to control the militia for twenty years. As historian Robert Ashton explains, the King's religious views would not permit him to turn Presbyterian or to force his subjects to; preventing Catholic Mass would prevent the Queen coming to court, and it would also violate the marriage treaty with France; giving the militia to Parliament for

---

1   *Mercurius Morbicus*, Numb. 1,2,3, p.2.

twenty years was in the King's view far too long.[2] Charles had already written to Henrietta Maria, telling her his best option was to employ delaying tactics;[3] this he did, and in December, realising that the King was not interested in their demands, but only to use Scotland as a safe haven from which to intrigue against his English enemies, the Scots told him he must accept the Covenant and the propositions or he would be barred from Scotland and involvement in its government. At this time their army was withdrawing from England, having haggled for a £400,000 settlement of their expenses, the Commons having voted several months before to pay it off; as the Scots would not take Charles with them, and Parliament was fearful that if he should go, he would – as the Scots had realised – reside in safety while contriving against them, the Houses of Parliament voted that in the interim he should be taken from Newcastle to Holdenby House in Northamptonshire. The Scots agreed, and on 26th January 1647 he was handed over at Newcastle and they went home.[4]

In London that same day, on the first page of its seventh large volume of correspondence concerning the fining of Royalists, the Committee for Compounding recorded:

> Sr George Lisle, Knt: petitioned recd ordered to have a lycence.[5]

The 'lycence' can only have been a pass to enter London. Article XI of the Oxford Articles specified that all persons who:

> have Estates reall or personal under or liable to Sequestrations according to Ordinance of Parliament, and shal desire to compound for them (except persons by name excepted by Ordinance of Parliament from pardon) shal at any time within six moneths after rendring the Garrison of Oxford be admitted to compound for their Estates …[6]

Where Lisle had been since he left Oxford is not known, but almost certainly to begin with he would have returned home, which meant to his parents' house, wherever that now was. He had been away for over three years. January 1647 was a month beyond the six month deadline for applying to compound, however Lisle may have been in correspondence with the Committee beforehand. Presumably, after his licence arrived, he went to London, but there is no further mention of

2   *Counter Revolution. The Second Civil War and its Origins*, p.8. Ashton includes a detailed chapter about the failure of the King and his opponents to agree a negotiated settlement in 1647.
3   Camden Society, *Charles I in 1646. Letters of King Charles the First to Queen Henrietta Maria*, p.50.
4   This handover, when taken in tandem with the expenses payment, is generally perceived as the Scots 'selling' Charles to the Parliament.
5   Committee for Compounding with Delinquents. SP 23/172, f.1. National Archives, Kew.
6   Sprigge, p.265.

him in the Committee's paperwork. This may be an oversight, or perhaps the documents were lost before the indices were printed in the nineteenth century: his original petition is also missing, which tends to suggest that the entire file was lost somewhere. Yet 'compounding' entailed much more than simply paying a fine. It meant going to the Committee at Goldsmith's Hall and taking the Covenant, which meant agreeing to Presbyterian church government, and also taking the 'Negative Oath', which began:

> I, *A. B.*, do swear from my heart that I will not directly or indirectly adhere unto or willingly assist the King in this war, or in this cause against the Parliament, nor any forces raised without the consent of the two Houses of Parliament in this Cause or War ...[7]

That George Lisle would stand in front of a Parliamentarian committee and sincerely take an oath to not assist the King, is near impossible to believe, although his former colleague Sir John Owen – perhaps even more hardline than Lisle, if that is possible – took both the Covenant and the Oath, and then promptly led an uprising in North Wales in 1648. Lisle may have taken both with crossed fingers, but oaths at that period were a serious matter. Given that there is no more paperwork for his case, it is possible that in fact, rather than his paperwork simply being missing, he never actually compounded: that he used his licence to get into London, then simply went underground, or used it to enter and leave the city at will, on the excuse that he was attending to his case. Whether or not he did compound, and what his activities were during this time, we can only speculate, as once more nothing is known of him until he resurfaces a year later at the outbreak of the Second Civil War. Whilst adherents of the Royalist cause did not generally show themselves openly – although Ashton offers a number of contrary examples[8] – fines and fear of imprisonment would not stop determined people covertly supporting the King. Parliament could crush public dissent, but it could not step into every private home to prevent Royalist networks discussing how they might aid the King's cause, and undoubtedly the serious Royalist 'conversation' was still in full flow, though now confined to underground channels. Indeed this remained the case all the way through the Interregnum, the best known example being the secret Royalist organisation, 'The Sealed Knot'. The very nature of such secret support means there is scant evidence by which to identify those involved. All that can be confidently assumed with respect to Lisle between the fall of Oxford and the Second Civil War, is that as a prominent Royalist and highly-respected former officer of the King's, and particularly one with such visceral loyalty to him,

---

7   *A collection of all the publicke orders ...*, p.636.
8   Ashton, pp.199-205, re. the extreme types who drunk and fought their way around the city, and did little for the King's cause beyond confirming the 'Cavalier' stereotype.

inevitably where such discreet conversations were being had, he would have been a part of them. Whether he was exchanging information with any of the King's former officers or advisors in France, as other Royalists were, is not known, but it should not be ruled out.

There is one clue, however, about what he had been doing over the winter of 1646. In February 1647 stationer Humphrey Moseley published the first folio of playwright duo Beaumont and Fletcher's collected works. It was prefaced by thirty-three 'commendatory verses', including contributions from Lord Grandison (John Villiers), John Berkenhead, the poets Richard Lovelace and Robert Herrick, and also one from George Lisle:

> To the memory of my most honoured kinsman, Mr. Francis Beaumont.
>
> Ile not pronounce how strong and cleane thou writes,
> Nor by what new hard Rules thou took'st thy Flights,
> Nor how much Greek and Latin some refine
> Before they can make up six words of thine,
> But this I'le say, thou strik'st our sense so deep,
> At once thou mak'st us Blush, Rejoyce, and Weep.
> Great Father Iohnson bow'd himselfe when hee
> (Thou writ'st so nobly) vow'd he envy'd thee.
> Were thy Mardonius arm'd, there would be more
> Strife for his Sword then all Achilles wore,
> Such wise just Rage, had Hee been lately try'd
> My life on't Hee had been o'th' Better side,
> And where hee found false odds (through Gold or Sloath)
> There brave Mardonius would have beat them Both.
> Behold, here's FLETCHER too! the World ne're knew
> Two Potent Witts co-operate till You;
> For still your fancies are so wov'n and knit,
> 'Twas FRANCIS-FLETCHER, or IOHN BEAUMONT writ.
> Yet neither borrow'd, nor were so put to't
> To call poore Godds and Goddesses to do't;
> Nor made Nine Girles your Muses (you suppose
> Women ne're write, save Love-Letters in prose)
> But are your owne Inspirers, and have made
> Such pow'rfull Sceanes, as when they please, invade.
> Your Plot, Sence, Language, All's so pure and fit,
> Hee's Bold, not Valiant, dare dispute your Wit.
>   George Lisle Knight[9]

---

9   *Comedies and Tragedies. Written by Francis Beaumont And John Fletcher, Gentlemen.* London, 1647.

Lisle's reference to 'Mardonius' is telling. He was a captain in Beaumont and Fletcher's 1611 play, 'A King and No King': the story of Arbaces, a king who had 'ended the wars at a blow'. The play's title had become widely quoted in reference to Charles I.[10] Kept by Parliament from demonstrating his loyalty, and perhaps heavily fined for it, Lisle did not miss the opportunity to publicly reference his own monarch's situation. The verse is well-written, and sheds some light on the level of his education, of which we know nothing. Brought up around books, and then in a privileged atmosphere close to the court, we might naturally expect that he had been well-educated and exposed to plays, poetry, and literature: the verse confirms that he was well-read, dextrous with language and appreciative of other people's use of it. Ironic, then, that he had a stammer. The verse's tone and length echoes other clues we have about Lisle's style of communication, such as his letters to Rupert, his initial refusal of a knighthood, and his recorded speech at Colchester in 1648: clear, incisive, free of frills, and at times extremely cutting.

In Parliament at this time there were two principal factions: the Independents, who grew out of the 'war' party which had pressed for the total military defeat of the King, and had created the New Model Army; and the Presbyterians, who had emerged from the 'peace' party who during the war had pressed for a settlement. Whilst at that time the war party had dominated, now the successors to the peace party were the more influential. A third key player was the Army. The radicals within it were aligned with the Independents, and whilst it was fighting for arrears of pay and the addressing of grievances, the dominant Presbyterians were determined to see it dissolved regardless of its demands. Forced to stand up for itself, in 1647 it became increasingly politicised. The King, meanwhile, did his best to play off all the factions against each other.

Meanwhile Charles had arrived at Holdenby House. He had finally made a set of offers which might have been the basis for negotiation with Parliament, or rather with the dominant Presbyterians, but in May any chance of this bearing fruit was crushed on 4th June when a cornet from the Army abducted the King from Holdenby. On whose orders he did this has never been established, although Fairfax and his primary officers took full advantage of it. The reason for the abduction, the Army claimed, was to prevent a Scottish-Presbyterian plot to move the King to Scotland, but the Presbyterians derided this as fantasy. Meanwhile Cornet Joyce took Charles to the Army headquarters at Newmarket, where the New Model was creating its own 'Council of the Army' to represent its members in their quest for resolution of grievances. On 15th June Parliament demanded that Fairfax handed over the King, but he was not taken to Richmond Palace, as

<hr/>

10   For example, the Royalist newsbooks *Mercurius Pragmaticus*, Numb. 3: 'if we say the old Play proves true, King and no King ...' ; and *Mercurius Melancholicus* Numb. 8: 'The Parliament have strained hard ... and now they are very fairely, and in good time delivered of a King and no King, a Parliament and no Parliament ...'

planned, due to objections from the Army that he was far too near London; on 2nd July Parliament reluctantly agreed that he should not be lodged nearer than the Army, and when the army withdrew to Reading the next day, he was taken to nearby Caversham.

Throughout July London saw several 'counter-revolutionary' incidents. On 13th July the London apprentices had called for the restoration of the King, and the disbandment of the Army; on the 21st, numerous groups including the apprentices and the watermen signed the *Solemn Engagement of the City*, supporting the Covenant but also calling for Charles's restoration, on the basis of the terms he had offered for discussion in May, before his abduction.[11] The Houses denounced it, but on 26th July the demonstrators invaded Parliament and forced first the Lords, then the Commons, to rescind their denunciation. William Lenthall, the Speaker, was pinned in his chair and forced to call a vote on inviting the King to London. Overwhelmed, he complied and the Commons meekly passed the vote. The Army had recently presented charges of impeachment against eleven leading Presbyterians in the Commons, including former Civil War commanders Edward Massey and Sir William Waller, and forced them to quit the house; now, following the mob violence from Presbyterian supporters, it was a large number of Independent peers and MPs, including the Earl of Manchester, now fled the house and sought refuge with the Army, which moved its headquarters south to Uxbridge. It had also called for a march on London if Parliament did not answer its grievances and demands for pay; when only one regiment of the Trained Bands responded to an order to muster, Parliament created a new Presbyterian-led 'Committee of Safety', which attempted to raise a new army under the command of Massey, to defend London against the New Model. However there was no appetite to support the Presbyterian proposals, and the Common Council of London refused to back a levy.

The flight of the Independents left the Presbyterians in control, and in the face of the approaching Army they elected new speakers, recalled their 'Eleven Members', took charge of the militia once again, and ordered Fairfax not to bring the Army closer to London than 30 miles. Fairfax ignored this demand, and began to encircle the city. As S. R. Gardiner neatly summarises:

> It may well be believed that neither Fairfax nor Cromwell desired to enter London as conquerors. They were coming, they alleged, not as enemies, but as protectors of the true [Independent-led] Parliament, expelled by the violence of the mob. On their side was peace and order; on the side of their opponents was riot in the streets, and a New Civil War in the land.[12]

11 He had offered to accept Presbyterian church rule for a trial period of three years, and to give up control of the militia for ten.
12 Gardiner, vol. 3, p.340.

London was still troubled internally, and by 2nd August the Common Council had decided to permit the New Model to enter. Fairfax marched from Hounslow, and entered London through a gate opened by sympathisers in Southwark; the City surrendered, and by the 6th the handover was complete.

One wonders how Lisle, himself a native of the City, viewed these upheavals. He would have cared for neither party: to him they would all be rebels, fighting amongst themselves. There was presently little he could do for the King unless he was quietly biding his time amongst Royalist networks. Laurence, too, must have watched in despair: this was not the peaceful, prosperous, hopeful city where he had made his fortune, and raised his family.

Parliament's balance of power was about to change again. On 14th August, after some in the Army demanded a purge of Presbyterian MPs from Parliament, six of the Eleven Members, including Waller, fled to France; Massey was already in Holland. When Cromwell subsequently marched to the House on the 20th and forced through a nullification of all business transacted there during the absence of the Independent MPs, many Presbyterian MPs, fearful for their safety, withdrew from Parliament, leaving the Independents in a majority.

At the end of July, the Army had presented its own terms to the King, dubbed 'The Heads of the Proposals': they offered him more than the Newcastle Propositions, including the retention of episcopacy but in a limited form, and although it demanded the repeal of all acts demanding church attendance, the Covenant would be revoked. Charles rejected it out of hand, however, making more demands of his own; he also unthinkingly gave away the fact that he had been negotiating privately with the Scots, thus their representative was now intercepted by the Army and prevented from seeing him. On 12th August he was moved to Oatlands Palace, and on the 24th to Hampton Court, near the new Army headquarters at Putney. Even as a prisoner, the King's recent travels around the country had always attracted crowds, and it was no different at Hampton Court: besides well-wishers, or perhaps those seeking a touch from him to cure 'The King's Evil' – hundreds had sought it at Holdenby – 'The confluence of people to see his Majesty at Hampton Court is great, and increaseth daily' reported *The Kingdomes Weekly Intelligencer*. Observer William Corbet noted 'the comming of diverse Malignants hither', and Colonel Edward Whaley, in charge of the King's security, that 'there is great resort of all sorts of people to him, but not so many Cavaliers as is reported …'[13] Lord Capel was in touch with him there, however, and may well have visited, and the Italian officer Sir Bernard Gascoyne certainly did.[14] Sir Edward Ford, another First Civil War officer, dispatched intelligence to Hopton and Hyde (later Earl of

13   *The Kingdomes Weekly Intelligencer*, Numb. 227, p.669; Corbet, 29th August: *The Copy of a Letter from his Majesties Court at Hampton Court*; Whaley, same date: *A Letter Sent from Col: Whaley* …

14   As reported in both men's respective ODNB entries. After the First Civil War Gascoyne joined the exiled court at Paris, and acquired a knighthood, but had returned to England by September 1647.

Clarendon) in France. Given the assorted makeup of the Royalists now once more around the King, from peers, to intelligencers, to professional soldiers, it would be odd that a man as devoted to the King as Lisle was not there also.

Hampton Court, and the King's escape

September and October 1647 saw two months saw rival sets of propositions vying for the King's attention: the revised 'Newcastle Propositions' from Parliament, and the existing 'Heads of the Proposals' from the Army. Meanwhile the Council of the Army discussed terms for restoring him, but he refused to negotiate and the Council abandoned its efforts. On the 22nd the three Scots Commissioners, the Earls of Loudoun, Lauderdale, and Lanark, finally gave Charles written confirmation that he had Scotland's full support to restore him to his throne; they also offered to help him escape, but he refused to break his promise to Whaley, that he would not.

Under Whaley's benevolent regime, the King was allowed a number of comforts, including favourite paintings, a pet greyhound, and 'houshold stuffs and Moveables of all sorts'. He was also allowed to hunt in the park, and was permitted attendants and household servants of his own choosing, presumably providing they were not personally objectionable to the Parliament. In October, however, negotiations with the Army Council broke down; on 1st November two of Charles's closest attendants, John Ashburnham and Sir John Berkeley, were ordered by Whaley to leave his service. Charles was left only with Lisle's old acquaintance and distant kinsman William Legge, who was a groom of the bedchamber. On 11th November, fearing assassination, Charles fled Hampton Court for the south coast.[15]

There is no specific evidence to place Lisle at Hampton during the King's time there. However, Lisle was Master of the King's Household, and therefore as a royal servant had every legitimate reason to have gone to the palace when Charles was taken there. Moreover, if Lisle's parents had returned to Godley Hundred after fleeing London in 1643, this was only fifteen miles or so from Hampton, an easy ride that would allow Lisle to regularly attend to his duties even if he was unable to lodge nearby. Another possible clue is his appearance at Rochester in May 1648, at precisely the same time as Sir Bernard Gascoyne, who had certainly been at Hampton. If Lisle did spend time at the palace he would undoubtedly have encountered Colonel Whaley, who coincidentally would be one of the men involved in his death nine months later.

In early November 1647, using Legge as a go-between, the King planned his flight with Ashburnham and Berkeley. On the day of his escape, Charles took advantage of his habit of retiring early in the evening to write letters: he locked

---

15   Charles's fears were not unfounded: Cromwell had written to Whaley just that morning, to warn him of rumours about intended attempts on the King's life (Gardiner, vol. 4, p.16).

himself in his chamber, telling one of the Scots Commissioners who knocked that 'hee was busie, and desired to be private, and would not sup that night …'[16] Later, however, Whaley grew suspicious, and after some hours eventually gained entry to the King's chamber to find him gone. *The Kingdomes Weekly Intelligencer* reported that:

> information being given to the House, that many who had accesse to his Majesty were privy to the designe of his Removall; it was ordered that Sir Edward Ford, Sir John Berkly, Master Ashburnham, and Doctor Goffe should be sent for, in safe custody.[17]

Secondary commentaries deduce, although the primary sources are coy to suggest it directly, that Whaley was fobbed off by the King's household staff for as long as they could manage, until he eventually forced his way into Charles's room. His 1983 biographer, Charles Carlton, attributes the successful delay in discovery to a newly arrived servant named Patrick Maul, presumably because Maul was also brought up to London for questioning the day after. He arrived with another detainee named Murray, whom the King later mentioned as a groom of the bedchamber; presumably Maul was one also.[18] A Committee was appointed 'to examine the whole businesse' and send for 'parties, Witnesses, Papers', but it is not known whether they questioned anyone else.[19] If Lisle was at the palace, then given his position and reputation for loyalty undoubtedly he would have known of the King's plans; however if like Maul and Murrey he was directly involved in some way, then he was lucky to get away with it without any trouble.

Mindful of the King's abduction from Holdenby, Parliament considered that he might have been the victim of another at Hampton Court, and ordered:

> that such as shall detaine his Maj. & not make it known, shall have his estate confiscate, and lose his life. Ordered, the E. of Northumberland to be desired to take care that the Kings children be not stollen away.[20]

The King, of course, had left of his own volition. His adventure was soon ended, however. While he waited at Titchfield, near Portsmouth, Ashburnham and Berkeley crossed to the Isle of Wight to seek assistance from governor Robert Hammond: though a Parliamentarian, he was thought to be sympathetic or even

---

16   Edward Helaw, *A Letter from Hampton-Court, of the manner of His Majesties departure*, p.1.

17   Numb. 234, p.730.

18   Carlton, pp.320-321; *A Letter from Hampton-Court* states that Maul was 'newly come from London' (p.1); Maul's detention, *The Moderate Intelligencer*, Numb. 139, p.1371; Henry Murrey on list of servants requested by the King in 1648, *The Moderate Intelligencer*, Numb. 180, no page numbers.

19   *Perfect Occurrences of Every Daie Journall*, Numb. 46, p.315.

20   *Ibid.*, p.316.

ready to change sides, but after crossing to the mainland himself and bringing back the King, Hammond detained him at Carisbrooke Castle. Writing to Parliament on 13th November he claimed that he resolved:

> to use the utmost of my endeavours to preserve his person from any such horrid attempt [that, is attempted assassination] and to bring him to a place of safety ... Hereupon I went immediately with them, over the water ... and found the King neere the water side, and conceiving my self no way able to secure him there, I chose (he desiring it) to bring him over into this Island, where he now is.[21]

Whatever Hammond's motives, the King was now detained for what would be the final time; if Lisle had visited him or served him at Hampton Court, then that was the last time he would set eyes on him. The King's already faltering relations with Cromwell and the Army were finally crushed ten days later when Cromwell and Ireton reportedly intercepted a letter from the King to Henrietta Maria, saying that:

> 'he was now courted by both the factions, the Scotch Presbyterians and the army, and which bid fairest for him should have him, but he thought he should close with the Scots sooner than the others. Upon this we took horse and went to Windsor, and finding we were not likely to have any tolerable terms from the King, we immediately, from that time forward, resolved his ruin.[22]

The turbulent political year ended with one last flurry of activity before Christmas. On 28th November Sir John Berkeley proposed to the Army that it should put the King in command; unsurprisingly, Fairfax rejected the suggestion outright. Shortly afterwards, Berkeley was contacted by a disaffected Army officer who informed him that Cromwell had openly declared that he had given up on the King.

Meanwhile Charles was, as his intercepted letter had revealed, still courting the Scots: on 29th November he proposed new negotiations, in response to which they sent the Earl of Traquair to Carisbrooke to press for religious concessions in return for armed support; on 15th December Charles responded with a copy of the terms he would now accept. On the 24th the three Earls returned to negotiate with him, and a few days later they and he signed 'The Engagement', which promised that the Scots would provide him with an army. Meanwhile Parliament had drawn up its

21   *Ibid.*, p.317.
22   Gardiner, vol. 4, p.29; quoting from a biography of Roger Boyle, first Earl of Orrery. Orrery was allegedly told the story by Cromwell himself.

own 'Four Bills', which set out preconditions for negotiations; a committee took them to Carisbrooke but Charles was now intent on doing a deal with the Scots, and rejected the Bills the day after signing the Engagement.

That day, 28th December, was another fateful one. Hammond's regime at Carisbrooke was relaxed, and during a short period when he was absent from the castle, Charles had been planning to escape on a ship which had arrived for him. However the wind changed as he prepared to leave, and before he had decided what to do, Hammond returned and locked the gates. As Gardiner puts it:

> Hammond at least had no doubt that Charles's rejection of the Four Bills was tantamount to a declaration in favour of the Scots, and that it would now be his duty to become, in a real sense, the gaoler of the King.[23]

Conflict renewed: the Second Civil War

On 8th June 1647 the Parliament had passed an ordinance which would, six months later, come back to haunt it:

> Forasmuch as the Feasts of the Nativity of Christ, Easter and Whitsuntide, and other Festivals commonly called Holy-Dayes, have been heretofore superstitiously used and observed Be it Ordained, by the Lords and Commons in Parliament assembled, That the said Feast of the Nativity of Christ, Easter and Whitsuntide, and all other Festival dayes, commonly called Holy-dayes, be no longer observed as Festivals or Holy-dayes within this Kingdome …[24]

Essentially – and infamously – they had forbidden the celebration of Christmas. As the now banned holiday approached, the London authorities lost no time in attempting to enforce the prohibition. One newsbook observed that:

> The Ministers, and Magistrates of the City of London laboured this day to hinder the deckings of places with Rosemary, Bayes, Holly, and Ivy (as of ould was wont on Christmas day) and also to hinder Delinquent Ministers from preaching, The Lord Mayor found much opposition, and one of the Marshalls men had like to have been killed neere Leaden-Hall …[25]

Nor was it only London residents who were discontented with the new law. A letter from someone the Army, written on 29th December reported that:

23 Gardiner, vol. 4, p.49.
24 Firth and Rait, *Acts and Ordinances of the Interregnum*, p.954.
25 *Perfect Occurrences of Every Daie Journall*, Numb. 52, p.358.

… there was a great insurrection at Canterbury, it began Saturday last when they abused the Mayor of the place, broke his head, & dragged him up and down, till at last he got into a house. They broke into divers houses of the most honest and Religious in the Town, broke their windows, abused their persons, and threw their goods about the streetes: Munday their number increased to above 1000 2 or 300 kept together, they sent abroad for the Countrey to come in, blockt up passages, seized upon the Magazine and Armes in the Town-Hall, made use of the Arms for themselves and party: Kept Courts of Guard in 4. or 5. places, examined passengers, 2 Scouts were sent from Dover, to observe passages, and to inform the Major that Captain Temple would send him 50. horse for assistance, but the Major could not be met withall: the Tumult was so great: At last the Cry was FOR GOD, KING CHARLES, AND KENT …[26]

The trouble was quickly quelled, and the ringleaders imprisoned; the Lisles may have received their own personal report, as George's Holman niece and nephews now lived in Canterbury with their father and stepmother.[27] Similar disturbances occurred in Ipswich. The Christmas protests marked the start of an upswing in Royalist sentiment, which had been brewing for some months and boosted by the appearance of a number of new Royalist newsbooks: *Mercurius Melancholicus*, *Mercurius Elencticus*, and *Mercurius Pragmaticus* all appeared for the first time in the autumn of 1647. In what literary professor Joseph Frank calls 'an active game of cops and robbers' between the censoring authorities and the newsbook authors, Parliament had tried repeatedly, but unsuccessfully, to control the presses since the Triennial Act of 1641 had wiped away the Crown's censorship mechanisms.[28] In September 1647 the appearance of *Melancholicus* prompted Sir Thomas Fairfax to push for the appointment of a new censor, the previous incumbents having been dismissed in March, but the renewal of censorship proved ineffective: all three Royalist papers survived into 1649 and recorded vital details of the Second Civil War along the way. *Pragmaticus* is responsible for capturing much of the detail that has come down to us about Lisle's last final hours at Colchester. Ironically it was written by Marchamont Nedham, he who had written so caustically for the Parliament in the guise of *Mercurius Britanicus* and commented on Lisle's stammer at the storming of Leicester: he had now lent his pen to the King.

In the early months of 1647, the two Houses and the Army Council voted for the 'Vote of No Addresses' – that is, to refuse to engage in any further discussions with

26 *Ibid.*, p.362.
27 The youngest nephew, Laurence Holman (b.1636), was married at the city centre church of St Mary Bredin in 1662; the parish records show a William Holman marrying there in 1643, indicating Elizabeth's death some time before. Her burial is untraceable, so whether she died at the family's former home in Shere, Surrey, or at Canterbury, is not known.
28 Frank, *The Beginnings of the English Newspaper*, p.136.

the King – and this added fuel to the growing Royalist revival. One Colonel Poyer, the Parliament's governor of the key stronghold of Pembroke Castle, declared for Charles after his men were not paid their arrears; rioting apprentices in London shouted for the King and briefly took control of the City. In Norwich, the Mayor permitted the customary celebrations for Charles's accession day and was promptly taken before Parliament, prompting riots in Norwich itself. Meanwhile Charles tried and failed to escape from Carisbrooke, although the Duke of York was successfully rescued from London disguised as a girl, and spirited away to France.[29] In late April, the tentative flames of a new rebellion became a full-scale inferno. On the 24th, two thousand residents of Essex came to London bearing a petition signed by 30,000 more, demanding the disbanding of the Army and negotiations with Charles; four days later Sir Marmaduke Langdale seized Berwick upon Tweed and urged the North of England to rally to his cause.

It was, however, the Kent rebellion which finally drew George Lisle back into arms. Whilst the first stirrings of the rebellion can be traced back to Canterbury at Christmas, the next phase of it can be said to have begun in the town of Sandwich on the 17th May, when it was summoned by a certain Matthew Carter, and secured by the insurgents.[30] At Rochester on the 22nd, *The Moderate Intelligencer* reports:

> divers dis-affected to Parliament, about 600 in number, understanding somewhat like the Prince was come to Sandwich, had seised the City of Rochester ... possessed themselves of the Magazin, planted Ordnance upon the bridge, and make all that passe sign their Petitions, or secure their Persons ...[31]

'The Prince' intended was the Prince of Wales, although the youth who was delivered to Sandwich by fishing boat turned out, unsurprisingly, to be an imposter. The Rochester gathering was not as orderly as the *Intelligencer* suggested: another account reports that:

> Gunnes were shot off in the night, in the streets; which gave an Alarme to the town the watch not daring to oppose them. This morning early there were Drummes beaten, and horse and Foot gathered together, declaring that it was for the defence of the town against the Army, and they did in short time grow to a considerable number.[32]

---

29 Particular efforts were made to get Prince James away at this time, as it had become known that the Parliament intended to depose Charles in favour of his son.

30 Carter, *A Most True and Exact Relation of That as Honourable as unfortunate Expedition of Kent, Essex, and Colchester*, pp.38-39.

31 Numb. 166, p.1359.

32 *A Letter from Kent on the Rising at Rochester ...*, p.2.

The protestors were joined by numerous mariners from ships then nearby in the Medway, and the magazines were seized in several other local towns. In an 'engagement' or vindication of themselves, the Kentishmen revealed that the Parliamentarian 'county committee' had not only condemned their petition a fortnight since, which called for the King's restoration and the disbanding of the Army, but had also summoned horse and foot from London to deal with those who supported it. Although Parliament declared that the allegation of a request for military aid was 'rumours', this was disingenuous, as it was in fact precisely what had happened, the Derby House Committee ordering Fairfax into Kent 'for the speedy remedy and redress of those evils and risings'.[33] Instead, the Houses now sent three local MPs to the area with letters promising redress of grievances, but despite appeasing the gathering the Members could not make it disperse, and it continued to grow. The next day Parliament responded with a typical knee-jerk, and issued an ordinance ordering:

> That all Papists whatsoever, and all Officers and Souldiers of Fortune, and all other persons whatsoever that have borne Armes against the Parliament, or have adhered to, or willingly assisted the Enemy in this late Warre, not being under restraint, and hereafter excepted, shall at, or before the five and twentieth day of this instant May 1648. depart the Cities of London and Westminster, and the late Lines of Communication, and all other places within twenty Miles of the said late Lines of Communication …[34]

On 24th May insurgents in Kent, Essex, Middlesex and Surrey published a joint call to arms;[35] meanwhile, while Parliament attempted to negotiate with the three professed leaders of the Kent uprising, the disaffection in that county spread. On Friday 26th the Kentishmen caused trouble at Sandown, Deal, and Walmer Castles, and managed to seize Dover Castle; the navy's Vice Admiral Thomas Rainsborough came ashore to deal with the situation, but on returning to his flagship faced a mutiny and was told the crew would no longer obey him, 'but would have the King brought to London.'[36] The flagship's lieutenant was one Thomas Lisle, but whether he shared any lineage with George is not known. Eight other crews joined his in revolt: Parliament acquiesced to the crews' demands and replaced Rainsborough with the Earl of Warwick, who had been admiral during the First Civil War, but he was unable to return the nine ships to Parliamentary

33 Kent 'engagement': Carter, pp.27-30; *The humble Petition of the Knights, Gentry, Clergy, and Commonalty of the County of Kent* …, p.2; Parliament's declaration in, *A Narrative of the Great Victory Obtained by the Lord Generall in Kent* …, p.1.; Fairfax's orders, *CSP Domestic Series, 1648-1649*, pp.75-76.
34 *An Ordinance … For Putting Malignants and Papists out of the Cities of London, Westminster, late Lines of Communication, and twenty miles distant.*
35 *The joynt Declaration of the severall Counties of Kent, Essex, Middlesex, Surrey* … (single page).
36 *A Letter from Sandwich in Kent*, p.1.

obedience and gave them up as lost. Subsequently they sailed to the Netherlands to appoint the real Prince of Wales as their admiral. Meanwhile the Kentish forces were met at Rochester by representatives from Essex, where many inhabitants were also taking up the King's cause again.

On the 28th or 29th of May news arrived that, after some trouble at Deptford and Southwark, Parliament believed the Kentish protestors would be marching on London, and:

> they knew not the Intentions of it, and had therefore referred them to treat with the Generall the Lord Fairfax, and the Committee of Derby-house.[37]

In other words Fairfax and his New Model were being sent to deal with the situation: against whom the Kentish had no chance, being 'a new rais'd and unmodelled body of raw men.' *The Moderate Intelligencer* was disparaging about the force's makeup, calling it:

> the Army called Kentish but chiefly composed of Royalists, and disaffected to Parliament, living about London for such good ends …[38]

The *Intelligencer* was correct in that by the end of May, the top level of the Kentish force consisted not only of Edward Hales and Sir Thomas Peyton, two of the original leaders, but also a clutch of highly experienced Royalist military commanders: amongst others, Colonel Henry Washington, Sir William Compton, former Northern Horse officer Gamaliel Dudley, the former northern infantry commander Sir John Maney, the Florentine professional soldier Sir Bernard Gascoyne, and Sir George Lisle.[39] The Earl of Norwich, Goring's father, was also present, although the sixty-three-year-old diplomat had never been a soldier; he had recently returned from France and his reason for being in Kent at this time is not clear. Barbara Donagan, his ODNB biographer, presumes he had either been sent by Royalist leaders in London, or was on his way to deal with family matters in Sussex. Carter – who states that he heard Norwich himself speak of the circumstances – confirms the Sussex story, saying that the insurgents waylaid the Earl as he travelled through Kent to avoid the New Model, and he agreed to help them negotiate the leadership of the Duke of Richmond. Despite visiting him in Surrey, however, could not persuade the Duke to take on the mantle of leader, and eventually fell into the role himself.[40]

37   Carter, p.77.
38   Numb. 168, p.1374.
39   *Bloudy Newes from Kent*, cover page; *A Narrative of the Great Victory …*, p.6.
40   Carter, pp.83-85. The Duke had remained a close advisor to the King, even in the latter's captivity, and perhaps did not want to rile Parliament or the Army, and jeopardise his ability to negotiate for Charles.

The Kingdomes Weekly Intelligencer also gives a breakdown of the Royalist presence in Kent and notices Lisle in particular, reminding readers that he was:

> the same Gentleman, who the more to encourage his men, did lay by his Armes, and fling off his doublet, and in his shirt did bring up his Regiment against our Forces in the first great Battell at Newbury.[41]

The author had the wrong battle, of course, but it demonstrates just how far the story of Lisle's shirt-sleeved charge at Newbury had spread. A notable absentee from the Kent reunion was William Legge, who had been captured with John Ashburnham in Hampshire on 19th May and sent to Windsor Castle.[42]

Where all these veterans had sprung from in just a few days is not clear, but it must have been at least partly connected to the ordinance of the 23rd which forcibly ejected former Royalist officers from London. Whilst Parliament may have rested easy in believing its capital was secure, removing those it perceived to be a threat simply pushed them straight into the febrile military theatre developing beyond its boundaries. Throughout the First Civil War, both Parliament and the London authorities in general had always been paranoid about plotters in their midst; often they were proved right to be, and it was no different in 1648, particularly as the city was now filled with former Royalist officers and other supporters who were allowed to reside there upon licence, provided they compounded and took the Covenant and Negative Oath. The ordinance pushing them out again, however, revealed how flimsy Parliament believed that parole was, and how it knew that in reality there was no way to bind the actions of a man who took the oath in his mouth, but not in his heart. As discussed, it is not clear whether Lisle had compounded, but if so then he had taken the Covenant and Oath with no intention of keeping them, for there is specific evidence that a year after applying for his licence, he was actively pursuing Royalist activities in London. Firstly, on 13th September 1648, a man named Thomas Foster testified to the Committee for the Advance of Money that:

> last Christmas Sir George left with him 15*l*., with order to deliver it to the person who should bring him an indented piece of paper, one part of which Sir George left with Foster, and that he paid accordingly a few days after, but he never had any other money of Sir George's except 5*l*., which he repaid him.[43]

---

41 Numb. 263, p.963.
42 *The Moderate Intelligencer*, Numb. 166, p.1350.
43 *Calendar of the Proceedings of the Committee for the Advance of Money*, Part II, p.948.

Foster was lying, however: five years later, on 30th November 1653, the Committee recorded:

> Information that [Thomas] Foster, head drawer at the Fleece Covent Garden has '300*l*. in his hands, delivered him by Sir George Lisle, in keeping Cavaliers, executed at Colchester, to be repaid to Sir George, but hath it still in his keeping'.

The reference to 'last Christmas' proves that when Lisle arrived in Kent in May 1648, possibly alongside Gascoyne, he had been already been actively working towards Royalist ends in London for at least the previous six months, and was pursuing them at the time of the Christmas uprisings in Kent. How long, prior to that, he had been part of the Royalist underground – if we may loosely term it that – is not known, but clearly he was raising money for the cause. On 27th July 1649, one Jos. Simson testified that:

> he lent Sr Geo Lisle 100*l*. to buy horse and arms for the late King to maintain the war against Parliament. This charge was given against him to the Committee for Examinations, supported by two affidavits, whereupon order was granted for seizing his goods, and an inventory of them was given to the said Committee, and being appraised at 800*l*., and security given, he continued in possession; but the Committee being subsequently dissolved, he has ever since remained unquestioned.[44]

In a treasury document of 1679, Sir Lionel Walden:

> craves allowance … in respect of … two bonds, one entered into by his father for King Charles I at Oxford, and the other entered into by his father and himself for furthering Sir George Lyle's attempt …[45]

Walden is known to have been a Royalist officer, and given the connection to Lisle, is almost certainly the 'Captain Walden' mentioned under Richard Bolle on the Culham docket of 23rd May 1643.[46]

Presumably, when Parliament ejected all the Royalist officers in May 1648, Lisle left his money with Thomas Foster and rode out to Rochester.

In response to the news that Fairfax and the New Model were on their way from London, the Kentish commanders sent orders to Dartford to fetch up the main

---

44   *Calendar of the Proceedings of the Committee for the Advance of Money*, Part II, p.1118.
45   *Calendar of Treasury Books*, vol. V part II, p.1288.
46   *The History of Parliament* online: 'WALDEN, Lionel I (c.1620-98), of Huntingdon'; Roy, ROP part 2, p.238 (NA, WO 55/1661 [3]).

body of their force, and positioned a party at Stonebridge near Gravesend, to hold off the New Model as long as possible. They were right to be hasty, as Fairfax had been given his marching orders on the 25th, along with permission to use whatever force was necessary to suppress the uprising.[47] Matthew Carter had now been appointed Quarter-master Generall of the Kentish forces, and reported them as:

> Mustred in rank and file, compleatly arm'd, seven thousand of the Infantry, and as well accoutred, being most of them very sufficient men of ability, and not wanting of as Honourable resolutions.[48]

He adds that around 3,000 more had not attended the muster, but remained at Canterbury, Maidstone, Sittingbourne, Sandwich, and Dover. At a rendezvous at Burham Down the next day, halfway between Rochester and Maidstone, the Earl of Norwich was appointed general of the new army, and despite 'very faire weather' which could have kept it in the field and ready for action, he spread it out across various civilian quarters. He was later criticised for this decision: Fairfax arrived later that day and in the evening, despite suffering from a fit of gout, personally oversaw the storming of Maidstone, where a large portion of the Kentish army lay. The defenders fought hard in the streets, but were eventually routed and the entire force lost. The next day, presumably believing the town was simply besieged, Norwich marched his division towards Maidstone in an attempt to relieve it, but halted when he was informed that it was a total loss. Fairfax himself reported 'near three hundred' Royalist dead and 'about thirteen hundred prisoners'.[49] Colonel Dudley had been taken, and Maney and others killed; Peyton was captured not long after, at Bury St Edmunds in Suffolk.[50] Fairfax moved off and began to disperse the remaining Kentish insurgents.

The Engager Army

Meanwhile, on the England-Scotland border, Scots levies began to gather: the seeds of the 'Engager' army which the Scots had promised Charles back in December 1647. Six months in the organising, it was led by the Duke of Hamilton, a diplomat and long-time supporter of Charles who had shuttled between him and the Scots during the First Civil War. Scotland was divided over the Engagement issue, numerous lords opposing it, and the Kirk (church) declaring against it because Charles had not confirmed his support for Presbyterianism. The government was determined to proceed, however. In April the Scottish Parliament

---

47 *CSP Domestic Series*, 1648-1649, pp.78-79.
48 Carter, p.79.
49 Fairfax's gout, Bell, *Memorials of the Civil War*, vol. II, p.31; Maidstone casualties, p.32.
50 *The Moderate Intelligencer*, Numb. 76, p.335.

threatened its English counterpart with war unless it established Presbyterianism; in early May the Lords and Commons capitulated, declaring their support for the Covenant although they did not formally agree to reopen negotiations with the King until 24th August. Despite their capitulation, however, the Scots had already begun to recruit, and on 28th April Sir Marmaduke Langdale had surprised and seized Berwick for the King, in anticipation of their arrival. In a parallel move in the north-west, Sir Philip Musgrave had seized Carlisle, the two Royalists thus securing the north for a Scottish invasion.

Norwich's march on London; night march to Essex

As Lisle, Gascoyne and Compton subsequently ended up in Colchester with Norwich, evidently they were not quartered at Maidstone, unless they had managed to escape. What became of Washington is not clear, as he was not at Colchester; yet he must also have survived or avoided Maidstone, for a year later he was arrested at a Gravesend inn with Robert Legge.[51] Evidently the Evesham affair had not caused any bad blood between them.

Norwich marched back to Rochester in what Carter records as 'an extremity of Raine', and held a council of war. Fairfax estimated that he had:

> about three thousand horse and foot, most of which were cavaliers, apprentices, and watermen.

The decision in hand was, whether to march on London and present the original petition to the Parliament, as per the stated aim in the Kentish 'engagement'; or to remain in Kent and fight alongside the other pro-Royalist parties now active in the county. London was chosen. Whilst the infantry was strong enough to fight Fairfax, the horse was not; to retreat was to be cornered and cut off from support from Essex or Surrey, but to advance was to draw Fairfax after them:

> And by drawing nearer those two Counties be both an encouragement, and assistance to draw them together; who once joyning with them, would make so great a Body, as in all probability would be formidable to the Enemies; for now they were forc'd by that violence, into an absolute defensive War.[52]

At Dartford the army paused while Norwich sent a letter to the Mayor, Aldermen and Common Council of London, explaining their intentions and

---

51   Newman, *Royalist Officers*, p.227, 400.
52   Carter, pp.98-99.

requesting to march through Westminster unmolested. However the Council, as Carter explains:

> (like a Dogge to his Vomit) turned to their old course of Parliament Service; and no sooner received the Letter, but immediately instead of returning a civill Answer to the Generall, dispatch'd it away to the Speaker of the House unbroke up.

Knowing nothing of this, Norwich and his men marched on, arriving on Saturday 3rd June only to find London closed to them and no assistance waiting from the other counties. Whilst they waited at Greenwich, however, a man from Essex arrived with news of 2,000 armed men at Bow, and more at Chelmsford. Leaving Compton in charge, Norwich went to see for himself, but finding nothing at the first place, continued to the second. Meanwhile, exhausted and despairing of any success, his men at Greenwich began to panic, and desert *en masse*; Carter describes the disorder as:

> such a distraction amongst the whole Party, as every man was almost in an amazed confusion.[53]

Lisle, Gascoyne, Compton and the other seasoned officers present must have done their best to impose order on the situation, but they would have been hopelessly outnumbered; besides, these foot were not well-drilled infantry who would respond to a sharp order, but raw recruits and volunteers who responded principally to their own fears. After darkness had fallen, those who did not desert – perhaps five hundred, out of several thousand[54] – were spooked by a passing horseman in the park who informed them they were all in great danger: panic spreading amongst them, they commandeered the Greenwich ferry and began transporting themselves blindly across the Thames, believing the friendly county of Essex lay immediately opposite. All they found on the far side, however, was the Isle of Dogs and Tower Hamlets Trained Bands. With spectacularly quick-thinking which probably prevented a massacre, Compton kept the two sides apart while he single-handedly negotiated and signed a set of surrender terms with the Londoners. The accord did not last long, however: as soon as the Kentish men began straggling up the peninsular's single narrow track towards Poplar, three miles away, the treaty articles were broken and some men were plundered. Yet as they made their way across the former marsh, their route lined with jeering militia, the realisation of how faithless the Trained Bands had been, began to sink in:

53   *Ibid.*, p.104.
54   Gardiner, vol. 4, p.144.

and how these Gallants had broken conditions; we began to think of some other way then so lamely disband, and submit our selves by such worthlesse Boores, (who understood not so much Honour (I except the chiefest of them) as to know what was meant by drawing, and signing Articles of Conditions) and so began to sift out the disposition of the private Souldiers, who we soone found so resolute as to expresse ourselves rather desirous to die there, in the bed of Honour, than to survive such an infamous misfortune, and live slaves all the dayes of their lives after …[55]

The rest of Carter's extraordinary tale bears telling in full. Their morale returning:

> … all concluded to make a second dispute for Conditions, and Charge through them. And being now in the midst of them, every man provided himselfe accordingly, the Foot all lighting their Matches, and the Gentlemen drawing their Pistols, began to alter the constitution of our fleering Hamletteers, who left their vanity of jeering, and so we marched on from guard, to guard, through the midst of them, as moving to the place of disbanding, where we expected an opposition, and as much resolv'd to force through it; but that proved the last and utmost guard just at Bow Towne. But now they beholding us marching in this resolute manner, and still moulding our selves into better order, were absolutely dasht from a thought of opposition; so we marched on without the least affront till we came to Bow-bridge, where we supposed was the place for our disbanding: At the other end of which bridge was a turne-pike strongly guarded with Musketteers, and having entred upon the bridge, we made a stand to parly with them; but after a very short discourse being asked whether they were Friends, or Foes, we were answered from them, Friends; whereupon we replyed, if you are Friends let your turne-pike be opened; so they opened their turne-pike, with a very great shout let us in. And now we were in Essex.

The night march to Bow is a vivid testament to the abilities and experience of the experienced military officers such as Lisle and Compton who were present. Carter says that when the panicking recruits made landfall on the Isle of Dogs, they were:

> every man Marching according to his owne phancy, and comming up from the River sides at severall places and wayes; Yet all, as [if] it were by a strange sympathy, steering one and the same course.

---

55 *Ibid.*, p.109.

Carter gives the vivid impression of a herd of panicked sheep, all blindly following the individual in front. Yet three miles later at Bow Bridge, despite the darkness and the presence of hostile militia lining the route, the Royalist officers had turned their men's terror on its head to dispel panic, restore pride and morale, and turn the 'sheep' into a purposeful column of armed men with which the enemy no longer wanted to interfere.

The night's action was not yet over, however: a party of Colonel Whaley's horse and dragoons, having expected the Kentishmen to disarm at Bow, followed them through the turnpike to attack them but was chased back into Middlesex by a party of thirty horse.[56] The 'Hamletteeres' then attempted an attack, but in a reversal of their earlier fortunes were penned up in Bow Church, forced into a treaty, and sent home. The Kentish force then marched on to Stratford unmolested, where it was reunited with the Earl of Norwich, who ordered the army to rest before embarking on the twenty-eight-mile ride to Chelmsford to speak with the leaders of the Essex uprising. Despite opposition from three local justices of the peace, the exhausted army rested at Stratford until Wednesday 7th.

Carter records that Norwich found the situation in Essex 'strangely confused', and 'backward' as regards their previous association with the Kentishmen. Moreover the Parliament had sent down an Act of Indemnity – that is, pardon for previous 'illegal' acts – which under pressure from the county committee, most of the Essex men accepted. The atmosphere in Chelmsford was deteriorating, and local man Sir Charles Lucas:

> being there urgently tending upon the designe, and many other Gentlemen with carefull diligence for the advancement of the King, and Countries Liberty … though it the best course in that distraction to depart privately forth the Town …[57]

Some local supporters, however, bid him not to leave:

> but if he would be pleased to draw them into the Field, and stay with them, they would one and all engage with him, and live and die in that Engagement, according to the intention of their meeting together, having resolved not to returne till they had performed something.

Thus animated, Lucas and his men immediately seized the Committee. Long pent-up Royalist anger was unleashed, Carter noting that the Royalists were 'so

---

56 A turnpike was a gated toll collection point.

57 Carter, pp.121-122. David Appleby states that Lucas's command was not a spontaneous appointment, as he had already received a commission from Prince Charles to command the forces in Essex (Appleby, pp.182-183, n.10).

furiously incenst against them' that the committee men had to be rescued and put under guard. One committee member, Sir Thomas Honywood, was absent and escaped capture: *The Kingdomes Weekly Intelligencer* reported that the county had:

> raised a considerable body of fifteene hundred horse and foote under the Command of Sir Thomas Honywood, who were to joyne with Col. Whaley against Sir Charles Lucas and his adherents.[58]

Norwich and Lucas already saw Honywood as a threat: the Committee of Both Houses in London subsequently informed him that the Royalists had 'by violence and unsoldierlike ways' forced the county committee to write to him, 'under fear of violence to their persons', telling him not to attack them; and that he should realise it was done under duress. A similar letter was sent to Colonel Whaley, and asked him:

> to signify to Goring and Lucas that if they shall [in future] so depart from the rules of war and the customs and practice of all nations they must expect a retaliation, and that they shall not serve themselves by these practices to their advantage.[59]

Norwich now called up his force from Stratford, which had been augmented by the return of stragglers, and by the daily arrival of 'divers Prentices from London'. On the evening of Wednesday 7th the army rendezvoused with Norwich at Romford, harassed by their enemy but suffering no harm from it; the next day they met with Lucas and his followers at Brentwood.

Unless they had met up in London, where Lucas had been living until recently, Lisle and Lucas would not have seen each other for over two years, Lucas being captured at Stow-on-the-Wold in March 1646. The extent of their acquaintance in Oxford is not known, although they would have known each other by sight and reputation, and undoubtedly would have come to know each other better as the pool of senior Royalist officers dwindled dramatically towards the end of the First Civil War. Even more so after three months cooped up in Colchester in 1648, and the powerful propaganda value of a distraught man kissing his dead friend – with all the attendant connotations of that Royalist keyword, *loyalty* – was endlessly milked by the Royalist newsbooks, whether a long-standing friendship lay behind the scene or not.

Although the two men may not have known it at the time, genealogical records suggest they were distant kinsmen. As already noted, the playwright Francis Beaumont, to whom Lisle claimed kinship, had an uncle named Thomas Ashby,

---

58   8th June; Numb. 264, p.973.
59   *CSP Domestic Series*, 1648-1649, p.111, 112.

which undoubtedly identifies Thomas as a relative of Lisle and his mother, Dorothy Ashby. Thomas's daughter Frances, perhaps Dorothy's aunt or cousin, was married to one Robert Throckmorton, while Sir Charles Lucas's aunt, Ann Lucas, was married to Robert's brother Arthur: meaning that Lucas's aunt, and Lisle's Ashby relative, were in the broader sense sisters-in-law.

On 9th June the newly-combined Royalist force returned to Chelmsford, to be met by Hertfordshire peer Lord Capel – noted by the London press to be 'very active in the County of Hartford to draw the discontented and disaffected people to him'[60] – and Lisle's former Leicestershire commander Henry Hastings. Soon afterwards they were joined by a party of 'about fifty' gentlemen from London, who not without hazard had made their way from Hyde Park Corner to Chelmsford. By now Lisle would probably have discovered the presence of Robert Skerrow, his Catholic captain from the First Civil War, now serving as major to local Essex man William Ayliffe. Lisle would not have seen Skerrow since Naseby: after Lisle was carried from the field, the captain was captured along with Littleton, Fowles, and six other officers. When Skerrow was released, and what he had been doing since then, is not known.

On Saturday 10th June the force headed north, where Carter says it gained entry to 'Leeds House', belonging to the Earl of Warwick: he must have meant Easton Lodge near Great Dunmow, an Elizabethan edifice eight miles west of the town.[61] The Royalists raided its extensive armoury for arms, ammunition, saddles, and even 'two brasse field pieces', before marching east to Braintree. Meanwhile another large body of horse joined them, recruited in Hertfordshire and Bedfordshire, and at Braintree on Sunday morning a general rendezvous was held, to put the growing army into effective order. At some point Lieutenant Colonel Henry Farr of the Essex Trained Bands, he who had read out the Act of Indemnity to the Essex insurgents, had changed sides with a number of his soldiers, and joined Norwich and Lucas. The Royalist newsbook *Mercurius Pragmaticus* claims this occurs as soon as he read out the Indemnity at the head of every company:

> and when he had read it, demanded whether they would accept it? But they all with one voice and loud Shouts, cried it down, not so much as one person disputing it. Then the Colonel seeing their Resolutions, declared himself, and not before.[62]

60 *The Kingdomes Weekly Intelligencer*, Numb. 264, p.974.
61 Warwick's descendants owned the property into the twentieth century. The Elizabethan house was destroyed by fire in 1847 and replaced with a Victorian gothic mansion, which was itself demolished in the 1950s.
62 Numb. 23, no page numbers.

Despite his repulse at Bow, Whaley had not given up the chase, but dared not risk a fight. On the Saturday he advised Fairfax that:

> The enemy hath quitt Chelmesford, march't to Lees, where as soon as hee came he had 500 armes besides ordinance without resistance. Wee marched close in the reare of him, but he doth so overpower us with foote that wee cannot ingage in this close countrey, but with great disadvantage, to the hazard of the brigade. Wee are indeavouring a conjunction with Sir Thomas Honiwood's forces, who is reported to bee 1200 horse and foot. Itt behoves you to hasten all the foot up you can, and to come your selfe; other wayes the Enemie will be suddenly formed into a considerable army, and will engage us.

As a postscript he added:

> Our frendes repourt the Enemy to bee 3000 horse and foote, and like a snowball increasing.[63]

Whaley was so close that the Royalists could not but realise he was tailing them: Carter notes that while they were plundering the Leeds House armoury, his force were:

> very neer the other side [of the park]; but adventured not to appeare all that day in sight of our Army.[64]

While Norwich's men lay at Braintree on the Sunday, Whaley wrote again to Fairfax, this time from Witham to the south-east, where he had placed himself 'for the better interposing betwixt the rebells and London …' Presumably he or his scouts observed the details of the Royalist rendezvous and were further alarmed by their numbers, for he added:

> Wee desire your Excellency would expedite your march, for wee cannott engage them heere without more foote, and the longer they are suffer'd the more numerous they growe …[65]

While Whaley urged Fairfax to hurry, the *Kingdomes Weekly Intelligencer* was sure that Sir Thomas:

63 *The Clarke Papers*, vol. II, p.26.
64 Carter, p.128.
65 *The Clarke Papers*, vol. II, p.27.

who will lose no opportunitie is come from Kent to Gravesend, and in his owne person, though weake and full of pain, he is resolved to make haste to suppresse those whom he shall finde to be in Armes against him.[66]

Allegedly, Norwich's response on hearing this was that:

he thought Fairfax had been sick of the Gout in Kent; But now he knows he is come over thither, he will cure him before he goes out of Essex.[67]

The army marched throughout Sunday night, 'to amuse the Enemy that they might not sodainly follow us'; it rested briefly at daybreak on Monday 12th before marching onward until late afternoon. 'About which time', Carter says, 'we drew neere Colchester.'

66   Numb. 264, pp.974-975.
67   *Perfect Occurrences of Every Daie Journall*, Numb. 76, p.340.

16

Encircled: The Siege of Colchester

By the seventeenth century the ancient tribal settlement of *Camulodunum* had developed into a prosperous English wool town, famous for its cloth; its street plan and city walls bore witness to its extensive Romanisation, and its relatively remote position north-east of London had so far preserved it from the worst depredations of the English Civil Wars. The river Colne curved around the north and east sides of the city, passing Wivenhoe, Brightlingsea and Mersea Island before flowing out into the North Sea. The core of the town was its walled Roman heart, outside of which lay various suburbs. Inside the walls, in the north-east, lay its eleventh-century Norman castle, now used as a gaol.

Sir Charles Lucas was born in Colchester in 1613, in his family's large house on the estate of the old St John's Abbey, south of the town. The Lucases had long been part of the local fabric, being lawyers and MPs and holding local administrative posts; famously they had once played host to Queen Elizabeth. The Colcestrians considered the family aloof and high-handed, however, and even by the mid-1640s there were tensions between them and the town's other leading families. Part of this was due to religion: Colchester tended towards Puritanism, whereas the Lucases were 'high church' Laudians. Sir Charles was one of eight children and the youngest of three sons; Thomas, the eldest, had married Sir John Byron's sister. Of Lucas's five sisters the youngest, Margaret, had been a lady-in-waiting to Henrietta Maria, but whilst attending her in exile in France had met and married the Marquess of Newcastle.

According to Matthew Carter, Lucas had intended to do 'very much' recruiting in Colchester, but the town authorities would not admit his advance party on Monday 12th June, shutting the gates and guarding them with a troop of horse. While Lucas summoned up the army, a group of unnamed 'Gentlemen' charged a manned turnpike and forced its keepers to retreat to the City's 'Head Gate', towards the south-western corner of the Roman walls. After a scuffle at the gate, the rest of the army arrived and the townsmen offered to treat: after Lucas promised that the town would not be sacked, they agreed to let him enter, and the army quartered there that night.

Meanwhile Whaley dropped some way south-west, to finally meet up with Fairfax at Romford. At this stage it was thought that Norwich and Lucas intended to move north, to relieve Pontefract Castle – seized for the King on the 8th – or to join Sir Marmaduke Langdale.[1] What they actually intended to do is not anywhere clearly stated. If Lucas's commission from the Prince of Wales only applied to Essex then he may not have legitimately have been able to command forces anywhere else, but in the current chaotic circumstances of the counter-rebellion, such a technicality might have been quietly ignored. Norwich, it seems, had no formal commission to lead the Kentish part of the force, and did so only by its specific request.

13th June: first contact

Perhaps, safe in Colchester with their minds fixed on recruitment, Norwich and Lucas had let down their guard: for the next day at noon, Carter says:

> we received a very strong Alarum, and that the Enemy was advanced within a mile of the Town; and indeed by that time we could provide parties to send forth, their Forlornes were engaged with our Out-guards in the Suburbs ...[2]

The 'out-guards' were doubled, and horse and foot sent to reinforce them; Fairfax approached 'on all parts of the Town next Lexden', a village a mile or so west of Colchester. The fight was immediately a sharp one, the New Model firing:

> up to the very Hedges and Guards of our Foot, but were as furiously opposed, till at the last some of the Guards wanting Ammunition to maintain the heat of the Service, about the Almes houses, and the house called Grimstones house, were over-powred with the number of men that threw in their Shot like haile upon them, and so forc'd to retreat, and gave the Enemy the Liberty of all that ground ...

The house of Sir Harbottle Grimston, MP for Harwich, lay in the suburbs at the south-west corner of Colchester, between the town and Lexden, and in the path of Fairfax's advance. The Royalist retreat from there, says Carter, allowed the attackers to fall on Shere Gate, the next gate eastward of Head Gate in the town walls. In response, the out-guards were ordered to fall back into the town, but the fighting grew too hot for them to do so, 'the Enemy coming on so violently'. At this point, asserts a letter to London from eyewitness 'T. O.':

---

1   According to *The Kingdomes Weekly Intelligencer*, Numb. 264, p.976.
2   Carter, p.131.

[they] were pursued by our men to the very gate, where many of the enemy were cut off, and very few or none escaped either killing or being taken prisoners, for Col. Farr which commanded them, hastned into the gate, and shut it against his own men which followd after …[3]

Presumably this was Shere Gate, as Carter describes Lord Capel:

Charging at Head-gate (where the Enemy was most pressing) with a Pike, till the Gate could be shut, which at the last was but pind with his Cane.

The fight did not abate, however:

The Enemy still gallantly enough too, (to give them their due) endeavouring to force their entrance in upon us, adventured on so farre as to fire under the Gate, and oft times to throw stones over.

Carter claims that the fight lasted seven or eight hours, the new Royalist army proving fiercer than the New Model expected. He says the Royalists took 'above one hundred and thirty Prisoners', which is a reasonable claim for such a long and heated fight, but also claims that Fairfax lost seven hundred men, their bodies being strewn around the suburbs, and that many of his soldiers changed sides: both of these claims appear spurious, as a letter written to the Parliament that night, and therefore free from propaganda as it was not intended for public consumption, reported that:

The L. Gen. entred the Suburbs at Colchester, hath lost some 20. men, killed nigh 100, and taken some 400. prisoners. Most of which (the Enemy being persued) were shut out of the Towne, that they might have time to make fast the gates.[4]

Presumably these 400 were the stranded guards mentioned by Carter. A 'diary' of the siege – undated, but judging by the typeface, contemporary – reports the lost guards as numbering 500. Of casualties it says:

there were slain of the Enemies part, Sir William Campion, Colonel Cooke, and divers Officers of quality, and about 80 private souldiers; Colonel Panton, Capt. Brunkerd, Clifford, Worsop, and divers other Officers wounded. On the Lord Fairfax side, Col. Needham, Capt.

3   17th June, printed in *The Kingdomes Weekly Intelligencer*, Numb. 265, p.979.
4   *Perfect Occurrences of Every Daie Journall*, Numb. 76, p.340.

Lawrence of Horse, Capt. Cox of foot, and neer 100 private souldiers and inferrior Officers slaine …[5]

Carter confirms the deaths of Campion and Cook, 'both receiving mortall shouts upon the first charge in the suburbs', although he only admits to 'thirty or forty private souldiers.'[6] Nightfall finally ended the fight: sunset that day was at 8:20 p.m., so Carter's timings of Fairfax's approximate noon arrival and a battle of seven or eight hours must be accurate. The Royalists recovered a brass cannon of Fairfax's, 'which they had brought to force the gate', and 'about five hundred Armes'. Carter claims that Fairfax's men set fire to some buildings near Head Gate as they retreated, hoping it would spread and burn the town, but the Royalists quenched it.[7]

Lisle's part in the day's action – as indeed his specific part in much of the siege, until the town's surrender – is not known, but whilst the diary lists 'Sir George Lisles Regiment' amongst the ten Royalist regiments present, it is unlikely he commanded any of the remoter 'out-guards' or he would have been locked outside. As one of the most experienced infantry officers there, it is reasonable to suppose he was heavily involved in the organising of the town's subsequent defence.

Fairfax digs in

The next day, Carter says, the New Model Army

fell immediatly to work, and cast up a Fort just upon the high-way to secure the head-quarters, and barricado's crosse all the high-way …

The siege diary explains that these headquarters were strategically placed at Lexden, south-west of the town, and the road blocked to prevent aid reaching Colchester from London; slightly further north, horse were stationed on the Cambridge Road where it crossed the Colne, to prevent any attempt to escape northward to join Sir Marmaduke Langdale. Suffolk, to the east, was uncertain due to the unfriendliness of local forces there, so the Royalists had nowhere to go but south or south-east, into the sea. Mersea Island had also been secured, however, to prevent the revolted naval vessels from bringing help up from the river mouth.

5   *A Diary of the Siege of Colchester by the Forces under the Command of his Excellency the Lord Generall Fairfax*, BL 669.f.13[6], single sheet. The diary, or at least this copy of it, appears to be incomplete, extending only as far as Monday 26th June. Another copy exists, with the diary entries arranged around a plan of the siegeworks (Wing D1378A).

6   Carter, p.135. During the First Civil War, Campion had been governor of Boarstall House garrison, another of the ring of garrisons around Oxford of which Lisle's command at Faringdon had been part.

7   G. F. Townsend, p.23.

The blockading continued apace, Carter says: the besiegers:

> every night broke up fresh ground in severall places, which they thought
> most advantageous, running their lines by degrees from one Redoubt and
> Fort to another.[8]

Even after his surprise repulse from the town, it is unlikely that Fairfax believed,
at this stage, that Colchester's occupiers would stay there for as long as they did and
require the complete encirclement which followed. His flurry of activity, industri-
ously building the first forts and trenches, was probably just as much a straightforward demonstration to them, of his determination to have them out, as it was
a strategic endeavour. If he thought the sight of some blocked roads, trenches and
barricades would dent the determination of Norwich and his force, however, he
was mistaken, however, and besides, Carter says:

> To march away now we could not, for we had no way to march, but that we
> must within a day fall into a champian [open] country, where the enemy
> being so very strong, (as we were weak) in horse, would have cut us off at
> an instant; our Foot being no such experienced souldiers as to maintain a
> charge of themselves, both against Horse, and Foot, where there were no
> hedges to guard and shelter them from Horse …

Effectively the force was trapped, and whilst this was largely down to simple
misfortune, the apparent lack of a coherent military aim or a fixed plan of march
on the part of its leaders cannot be ignored as a factor. George Fyler Townsend is
dismissive of the Royalist leaders in his 1874 account of the siege, claiming that
the force was:

> Led by men ignorant for the most part of the rules and strategy of war,
> who had previously lived at home as magistrates and peaceful country
> gentlemen.[9]

This statement is untrue in every respect. Besides Norwich, all the principal
officers in the force were well-known, experienced military officers. Lucas and
Gascoyne had verifiable European experience, and although we lack the evidence,
Lisle is likely to have had a similar background. Compton was too young to have
fought abroad, but had been extremely active during the First Civil War and in
1644 spent three months successfully defending Banbury Castle before being
relieved by his brother. His negotiating skills, and the practical knowledge of Lisle

8   Carter, pp.138-139.
9   G. F. Townsend, *The Siege of Colchester*, p.9.

and others in marshalling an army, as demonstrated on the Isle of Dogs, were the primary reason Norwich's largely untrained force had made it as far as Colchester in the first place. Hastings' career in Leicestershire and the wider Midlands is worthy of a book in itself; Capel had fought in Shropshire and Cheshire and had as much experience, albeit with fewer successes and less flamboyance. The numerous other colonels, half colonels, majors and captains listed later in the prisoner of war list, a number of them being identifiable or possibly identifiable as participants in the First Civil War, would also have collectively possessed a large pool of military experience.

However, whilst inaccurate regarding the army's uppermost personnel, G. F. Townsend is probably correct in describing it as 'without plan, fixed purpose, commissariat, or materiel', and it was certainly not prepared in logistical terms for a three month siege in an unwelcoming town. Whereas on 13th June Parliament believed they intended to head for the Isle of Ely,[10] the claims of some Royalist prisoners captured early in the siege claimed that their intent had been to:

> go thorow Colchester into Suffolk, so into Norfolk, and back through Cambridgeshire, by which time, they shoud have a gallant Army, and then they would up to the very walls of London, where their own party would joyn with them in plundering that Rebellious City …[11]

This is more of a plan than Townsend gives the Royalists credit for, but it is hardly definite in purpose and left the army much at the mercy of unexpected events. The prisoners' claim makes sense in the light of Carter saying that the army did not intend to stay in Colchester more than a couple of days,[12] however a plan to sack London seems far-fetched; a plan to siege it in whole or in part, would be more likely, to force the Parliament to come to terms. Furthermore, the word of prisoners may not be the best to rely on.

Just as Fairfax had underestimated the occupiers' spirit until he tested them in a fight, so they had underestimated his determination until they saw his initial line of siegeworks: Carter admits that the sight of them:

> gave us just occasion to believe that they intended to plant themselves before us for a longer continuance then before we had imagined, and to block us up; by which were invited to consider of our own future security, which then consisted in the greatest care of victualling and fortifying; the only two things to be first thought on in such a case … no man, I think, that had surveyed it with the judicious eye of an experienced souldier,

---

10   *CSP Domestic Series*, 1648-1649, p.125.
11   *The Moderate Intelligencer*, Numb. 170, p.1407.
12   Carter, *op. cit.*

could be so weak as to suppose it a fitting place to be mantled, or maintained for a garrison; it was our intentions only to take it as a present quarter for a night or two. But this engagement having forc'd us to it, enlivened every man with an active and cheerfull diligence to forward an advancement of all requisites.[13]

Critically Lisle, Lucas, Hastings, and Compton all had experience of being besieged, although as Quartermaster Generall the responsibility for victualling would have fallen largely on Carter whilst they dealt with the defence. For the time being crisis was averted, when at a quay called The Hythe, on the river Colne to the south-east of the town, they found corn, wine, salt, and fish,

> and a good quantity of powder, the want whereof would have suddenly have thrown us into absolute ruine, having very much exhausted our magazine by the last days businesse.

The stores were ferried into the walled town with all speed, in anticipation that Fairfax would attempt to cut it off: and with good reason, for as 'T. O.' writes on the 17th:

> Wee have also sent a party on the other side of the water, neere the Heath, which is the harbour, or Key to which the shipping comes and is not halfe a musket shot over, or at least a mile from the town …

Eventually Fairfax did cut it off: the map of the completed siegeworks shows the line of circumvallation cutting straight past The Hythe on its western side, severing it from the town, and from the rest of the suburbs. The occupiers were fortunate to discover and retrieve its provisions so early.

While Carter focused on provisions, everyone else went to work on:

> strengthening the walls of the town, and fortifying where no wall was, by casting up rampires and counterscarfs, as a very great part of the town required …[14]

Fairfax, meanwhile, continued to entrench and to build forts and batteries. These were not yet fully operational, as he had ordered up large siege artillery which had not yet arrived. Royalists had already set up a battery in the south-west corner of the inner town, however, by the church of St Mary-at-the Walls, and sent

---

13   Carter, pp.138-139.
14   Ramparts and counterscarps, that is, defensive earthworks and ditches.

a stream of shot south-west, past Sir Harbottle Grimston's house towards Lexden. On 15th June, the siege diary reported:

> The Besieged Canon from the Royall Fort at St Maries, plaid very hard, killed severall of our men as they did the day before; some as they were raising the first Work called Fort Essex, others as they were stragling in the field.

The next day, the diary continues, three men were killed with one cannon ball, presumably fired from the same place. A London newsbook reports the funerals, inside Colchester, of Sir William Campion and Colonel Cook, attended by Norwich, Capel and Hastings, although who brought them this information is not revealed.[15]

Despite the resoluteness of both sides to see the situation through to a conclusion in their favour, there was no lack of communication between them. Firstly Fairfax did not neglect to summon the town, promising that:

> if they would lay downe Armes, he would mediate for them to the Parliament; the Lord Goring did move to send this answer, That if the Lord Fairfax would lay down his Commission, he would move on his behalfe unto the King, and did make no doubt but he should prevaile.[16]

Then Parliament wrote to Colonel Whaley with regard to the Essex county committee, which was still in Norwich's hands inside the town, desiring him to send a trumpet to obtain their release.[17] Whaley must have passed this straight to Fairfax, as on 17th June he sent a message requesting a prisoner change, and that the bearer be permitted to see the committee. Norwich responded with a request for a list of Royalist prisoners, but shortly after he received it, responded that:

> I have received the List your Lordship sent of some prisoners with you, but find them not to be listed under us, and therefore cannot take any notice that they were under our command, wherefore I wil not have to do with their exchange leaving then to your Lordship to hang, or dispose otherwise of them as you see good.

On the face of it this repudiation is astonishing, particularly as so many men were involved and he cannot have known they had fought for him on the 13th. At the very least, one would expect Colonel Farr to have reminded Norwich that they

---

15   *The Perfect Weekly Account*, Numb. 14, no page numbers.
16   *The Kingdomes Weekly Intelligencer*, Numb. 265, p.980.
17   *CSP Domestic Series*, 1648-1649, p.125.

were his men. However, repudiation may have been the only option: if Norwich took responsibility for them then Fairfax might have forced the prisoners back inside, which would mean another 500 mouths to feed.

The account continues:

> The General's trumpeter is returned, who left Sir Wm. Masham and the other gentlemen in a reasonable good condition. But when a list was sent to Goring of what prisoners we had taken, and in what condition they were, at present, he excepted against the Essex train-band men who were taken prisoners, and said that he had nothing to do with them, and bade his Excellency do with them as he thought good; by this it may plainly appear that the Cavaliers do use their seduced men but only for their own ends.[18]

Fairfax lost no time in disposing of the repudiated men. That same day:

> were … drawn out, every thirteenth man of the Essex batchelars are to die, every tenth of the married men, every fifth of the Londoners and Kentish-men, and the other batchelars to be sent beyond Sea, and the married to their families.[19]

During the First Civil War minor prisoners were usually freed after being disarmed, perhaps being required to take an oath not to fight again, or even being offered the opportunity to change sides. War-weariness and frustration at the Royalists' resilience had hardened attitudes, however. Freedom and an oath was now frequently replaced with deportation to the colonies or an appointment with a hangman. Colonel Farr's men from the Essex Trained Bands might not have expected much better at any time, however, having revolted from Parliament in the first place and therefore being deserters.

That same day, Saturday 17th, the siege diary records a Royalist sally eastward into Tendring hundred, where it gathered provisions 'which we could not prevent till ye Suffolk Forces march'd to our assistance.' This was reported in detail the next day, in another letter sent to London:

> A Party of horse and foot, consisting of 300 sallied out of Colchester the last night, towards Harwich their design not known; it was conceived at first that the Grandees were gone with them, to endeavour an escape, but it proved otherwise, for they all returned the next day with about 40 head

---

18   *The Perfect Weekly Account, op. cit.*; reprinted in *CSP Domestic Series, 1648-1649*, p.136.
19   *The Kingdomes Weekly Intelligencer*, Numb. 265, p.983.

of Cattle, and 100 Sheep: A Party of 400 horse and dragoons were sent after them, but met them not, the Enemy being gone a private way.[20]

Carter confirms the sortie, although he places it a few days later, and confirms the taking of 'about one hundred sheep, and sixty beeves.'[21] The London letter also noted that:

> The great Work upon the top of the Hill is finished, it holds 1000 men, the great Canons planted, and intend to play tomorrow upon the Town, being within Musquet shot thereof. The head quarters within half a mile, the Army lying at a nearer distance.[22]

The siege diary confirms this was 'Fort Essex' which lay between Lexden and Sir Harbottle Grimston's house. Just as it was completed, yet more men arrived to strengthen Fairfax's hand: Colonel Isaac Ewer came in from Chepstow in Monmouthshire, where he and six companies of foot had recently ended the Royalist occupation of Chepstow Castle. Ewer and his men were stationed to the north-west of Colchester by a bow in the river Colne and immediately began building another fort: another link in the chain of works and guards which was gradually encircling the town. The lines were not yet watertight, however: Carter reports that at around this time there was a local rising in favour of the King, and Lucas sent a party of horse and foot through the Suffolk lines to escort these supporters back into the town; a week later they returned safely with their supporters. A newsbook at around this time admits that despite the taking of Mersea Island:

> and the whole channell ours almost to the Heath dock, yet could not all passes other ways for present be made so good, but that it was held possible for a party of horse to get away, the League being of a very large circumference, and the Enemy strong in horse.[23]

Evidently this reporter, at least, believed that the Royalist cavalry were far stronger in numbers than they actually were.

Meanwhile *The Moderate Intelligencer* reported that the Earl of Norwich told his men that Langdale was at nearby Coggeshall with 10,000 horse and foot, and the *Kingdomes Weekly Intelligencer* said that the Royalists believed he was at Cambridge; how the Parliament's side heard such rumours is not known, but in

---

20 *The Moderate Intelligencer*, Numb. 170, p.1406.
21 Carter, pp.146-147.
22 These were not the great siege cannons which Fairfax had sent for: they did not arrive until early July.
23 *The Perfect Weekly Account*, Numb. 14, no page numbers.

any case, it was woefully incorrect as Langdale was very definitely still in the north of England.[24]

Matthew Carter endeavours to explain why Norwich, Lucas and their men did not simply march straight out of Colchester to face Fairfax. He suggests they might have done:

> had we had no hopes at all of relief, which we then had, both from the Scots, and divers other places, at the same time in action; besides it was conceived the greatest piece of policy, by keeping the enemy in a lingering action, to give a remora to their designes, and so ruine them by delaies; by which meanes especially we should give liberty, and all opportunity to others that intended any action, to work their designes without interruption … And it was a not a rash or fond supposition to think that we could hold what we had, till the rest of the Kingdome should rise, we should then do as good a service, as in the immediate victory …[25]

Carter's explanation is supported by an intercepted letter sent to Sir Marmaduke Langdale in July, by Lord Capel, who said:

> we here conceive, that our tying and obliging Fairfax to us, is the best way of proceeding for his Majesties service, for the rest of the Kingdom have the more scope to act their parts by it, and a disaster here would let him loose, which is the reason we hazard not more then needes must stand with our duty, and honour, considering also the advantage the enemy hath of us in numbers …[26]

19th June: Royalist endeavours

Monday 19th June was perhaps one of the busiest days of the siege. News of Colchester's situation was spreading, and other pockets of rebellion were indeed rising, but discretely, and at present all far too small to trigger the immediate release of the town as Carter says was hoped. On the 19th the siege diary reports a skirmish at Linton, some 30 miles north-east, where a number of Royalist officers were slain or captured, and 'about 500' dispersed. The most notable prisoner was Sir Barnabas (or Barnaby) Scudamore, the former Royalist governor of Hereford.

Meanwhile *The Moderate Intelligencer* reported that:

---

24 *The Moderate Intelligencer, ibid.*, p.1408; *The Kingdomes Weekly Intelligencer*, Numb. 265 p.983.
25 Carter, pp.142-143. A remora was a suckerfish which was anciently believed to prevent vessels from sailing.
26 18th July; *Perfect Occurrences of Every Daie Journall*, Numb. 82, p.402.

Lieutenant Colonell Gardner, once Vice-Governour of Farrington House, and others, were taken prisoners going to Colchester; he confessed to the Lord Gen. he went to take a command there.

'Gardner' may have been the Captain William Gardiner noted as serving at Faringdon under Sir Marmaduke Rawdon, or Sir William Courtney.[27] The newsbook also reported that:

Four Walloones, extraordinarily well-mounted, and as well armed with blunderbusse Pistols, each of which would carry seven Bullets, going towards Colchester, were intercepted by some of Captain Fisher's Troop (Suffolk Horse) they are sent prisoners to the Head Quarters.

Even a few weeks later, antiquarian Anthony Wood – then a student at Merton College – recorded that his elder brother fled to Ireland:

he being one of the prime plotters of the remaining cavaliers in Oxon to seize on the garrison, Visitors, and all the armes they could find, to the end that they might joyne themselves to others that had plotted in the same manner in other parliament garrisons, to relieve the distressed cavaliers that were besieg'd in Colchester, the plot was discovered by one or more of them when they were in their cups; which made every one shift for themselves as well as they could …[28]

If true, it seems that the Royalist spirit was alive and well even in locations firmly under Parliament's heel, but lacked cohesion and organisation to bring their dissent together.

Also on 19th June, the diary reports, Norwich sent a trumpeter to ask for a peace treaty. Fairfax responded with an offer that the Royalist Gentlemen and officers should go beyond sea, and the common soldiers given passes to go home, 'without prejudice'; perhaps expecting his offer to be accepted, he published a declaration to his own army ordering them not to affront or plunder any who might peaceably out of Colchester before the terms were agreed.[29] Lucas responded with a counter-offer, however, suggesting the exchange of townsmen for captive Royalist officers; it was quickly rejected. *The Moderate Intelligencer* wished that Lucas's trumpeter had not returned:

27   Numb. 170, p.1406; Dace, p.27.
28   *Life and Times*, vol. I, pp.145-146.
29   *The Perfect Weekly Account*, Numb. 15, pp.117-118.

till the Morter-piece and Granadoes come up and then accept of what the Gen offers, else Thunder-bolts and Granadoes.[30]

Fairfax now sent a letter into the town:

> to acquaint them that Sir Charles Lucas had ingaged his honour to him never more to take up Arms against the Parliament, which ingagement he had forfeited, being his Prisoner upon the reputation of his word, and therefore he was not capable of any command, or place of trust in the affaires of Warre.[31]

Lucas reportedly responded with an answer 'wherein he indeavoured to excuse himselfe.' Shortly afterwards, the imprisoned county committee was permitted to send a letter to Fairfax, desiring him to effect a treaty with Norwich and Lucas, who had countersigned the letter to show that they had approved it.[32] The letter being read, says *The Kingdomes Weekly Intelligencer*:

> his Excellence conceived that it was a busines of greater concernement, then what might require a suddaine answer, he therefore for the present did forbeare to returne the Trumpet, but not long after he sent him back with an answer to the Letter which is not yet thought fit to be made publicke.[33]

Royalist supporters were now trying to reach Colchester by sea. In yet another incident on the 19th, two ships from Harwich prevented two vessels moving up the Colne and landing supplies for the town. Dragoons from the Parliament's Mersea garrison went aboard the Harwich ships to assist in the fight, and eventually the Royalist ships were boarded and taken. By the end of the siege the 'two Tun of Match, 9. Barrels of powders, great store of Bullets' and numerous stores which the vessels had attempted to deliver, would be desperately missed.[34] *The Kingdomes Weekly Intelligencer* reported that additionally:

> In one of the Ships were found ten peices of Ordnance, in the other twelve. A party from Colchester were commanded to relieve the said Ships but they were incountered by a stronger party and forty of them taken Prisoners.[35]

---

30 Numb. 170, p.1408.
31 *The Kingdomes Weekly Intelligencer*, Numb. 266, pp.988-989.
32 *Perfect Occurrences of Every Daie Journall,* Numb. 77, p.563.
33 Numb. 266, p.989.
34 *A Great Victory Obtained … Neer the Island of Mersey …*, pp.1-2.
35 *Ibid.*, p.988.

This report of a Royalist relief party may have been incident reported in the same issue, in which the besieged:

> had made a sally forth, taking the advantage of a low Water when the Ebbe had left the sands uncovered, but they were discovered and incounterd: The fight was sharpe and gallantly maintained on both sides. In the end they were forced into the Towne, and (it is said) with losse, some of their Men being taken Prisoners by the Army, and some of them by Death.

Yet another report asserts four Royalists had died in the sortie, and that afterwards:

> stakes [were] driven in to prevent them from passing out that way, That the Line is compleated on the one side, and approaches, and brest-workes on the other, so that they are strong enough to maintain that Garison.[36]

Tightening lines

The completion of the line on the eastern side would have cut off the Royalists from the water mills on the other side of the Colne, which explains a report on the 22nd that they were reportedly constructing hand mills and horse mills to grind their corn.[37] Meanwhile Fairfax had ordered work begun by the town's north gate: the circle was edging nearer to completion. *The Moderate Intelligencer* reported that 'they have twice marched out with foot and long boats to regain Mersey Island but returned, without attempting it.' Carter confirms this last detail, saying that:

> About the twentieth day of the moneth, divers gentlemen were sent forth privately with Commissions to raise men in Norfolk, Suffolk, and Cambridgeshire: But the Country forces having broken up the bridges, and guarded the passes, and the enemy taken the Fort called Mersey Fort, that commanded the passage into the Island, so there was no passage left open for them, so they were forc't to return again, which they did secure, although through the enemies quarters, not a man being taken.[38]

On the same day, Fairfax increased the pressure on the town's Royalist occupiers by sending yet another letter into the town:

36 *Perfect Occurrences of Every Daie Journall,* Numb. 77, p.564.
37 *The Moderate Intelligencer,* Numb. 170, p.1408.
38 Carter, p.146.

Signifying his desire, that they should send out of the City all the women and children, letting them know that he hath a purpose to use all possible means by fire, sword, or other wayes to possesse himself thereof, but would have no one to suffer that doth not oppose him.[39]

Perhaps this tightening noose caused the thoughts of the besieged to turn towards a previously eschewed escape attempt into Suffolk, as on 23rd June they attempted to negotiate with the Suffolk forces who had secured or destroyed the river bridges over the river Stour to the north-east, which formed the county boundary with Essex. They were yet reluctant to cross the border, professing only to be interested in protecting Suffolk. The letter from the Colchester Royalists was a cautious hand of friendship, offering a 'Cordiall Reception' if the Suffolk men sent representatives to Colchester to negotiate; the response was crushing, however: they called Norwich's and Lucas's actions illegal, and saw them as 'enimies to the State, and to the peace of the kingdome', demanding that they remove themselves and their forces from Colchester.[40] The day after this exchange of letters the siege diary records that the Suffolk forces, as if to emphasise their point:

> advanced out of their County, & took up their Quarters upon Mile-end over against the North gate, being about 2500 Horse and Foot, leaving a guard at Cattaway, and Nayland, to secure those passes.

A newsbook report suggests that in fact they entrenched by the East Gate, and this is in accord with most other sources; it is more specific about numbers, suggesting 'two thousand foot, and five troops of Horse.'[41] The 'Suffolk' option, then, and any thought of making an escape through that county, was firmly off the table. Moreover, the addition of the Suffolk men to the lines of circumvallation brought complete encirclement of the town a significant step closer.

Fairfax, meanwhile, repeated his previous offer of surrender conditions, although excepting Norwich, Capel and Lucas; the primary sources do not explicitly record a response, but presumably the offer was rejected.

Alleged Royalist abuses and Parliament's retaliation

It is at this point in the siege, in late June, when most options for the Royalists other than relief or surrender were now closed, that reports appear in the London press accusing them of deeply unpleasant actions against their captives and activities in battle which broke generally accepted rules of engagement.

---

39   *The Perfect Weekly Account*, Numb. 14, no page numbers.
40   Both letters are printed in full, in *Perfect Occurrences of Every Daie Journall,* Numb. 78., pp.372-373.
41   *The Kingdomes Weekly Intelligencer*, Numb. 266, p.991.

Parliament was already aware that the Essex county committee was held under duress, and had already accused Norwich and Lucas of 'ways unusual to soldiers and men of honour', by allegedly forcing the committee members to write letters; now it received reports that the unfortunate men, who were still held captive in the town, had been quartered in a particular house in the path of the Parliamentarian artillery, effectively meaning they were human shields. A related accusation that the committee would be hauled from their beds during overnight alarms, and made to stand where they would be hit by any incoming artillery fire, must be regarded as dubious at best.[42] Carter emphatically denies that the committee were held this way:

> they being lodged there at our first comming to the Towne, not suspecting any such service, but as the best, and most convenient Inne, and after-wards the Towne being so full, would not admit any better conveniency for them.[43]

He adds that they were well fed, good food being allowed into the town for them, and they had also advised Fairfax of their location, that he might not aim his artillery too close.

Of other alleged breaking of accepted rules, the siege diary reports:

> Chewed and Poysoned Bullets [were] taken from severall of the Besieged. Affidavit made by those Souldiers of ye Besieged who brought them out of Colchester, that they were given out by the Lord Gorings [Norwich's] speciall Command. These Examinations were sent to ye Lord Goring, with this Message from Our Generall, That his men should expect no Quarter hereafter, if they used such Bullets.

Another newsbook speaks of 'chewed bullets cast in sand which was contrary to the law of armes'.[44] Musket balls might be 'chewed' or otherwise roughened in the hope that the broken edges would cause more damage going in, and perhaps yet more damage during extraction by a surgeon. Rolling them in dirt or sand would carry foreign bodies into a wound, and this is probably what the word 'poisoned' was being applied to at Colchester. A rolled bullet might also carry bacteria, particularly if it was dipped in a substance such as faeces or rotting flesh, but although the effect was long-observed in warfare by the 1640s, the bacterial cause was not yet understood. In response to Fairfax's accusation:

---

42   *The Moderate Intelligencer*, Numb. 181, p.1520.
43   Carter, p.158.
44   *The Kingdomes Weekly Intelligencer*, Numb. 266[b], p.999.

the three Generalls return Answer, that they deny any such practise, but for the rough cast pluggs they deny not the practise and excuse themselves, alleaging they were the best they could send them on the sudden.[45]

A few days after these first accusations, when an officer of Parliament's was shot during a sortie by musketeers led by Lisle:

the bullet is taken out, and we finde it poysoned, boyld in coppresse, our Souldiers hope to be revenged of them the next engagement for this poysoned bullet.[46]

In fact copperas – 'green vitriol', or ferrous sulphate, to use its formal chemical name – is a fairly innocuous iron salt, used anciently in inks and natural remedies and in the twenty-first century as a dietary supplement. An overdose can cause unpleasant side effects, but a small amount of it on a lead bullet would not be harmful; the lead bullet itself would be more likely to cause a problem. A bullet coated in copperas would look green, and if the one extracted from Parliament's officer on this occasion was intended primarily to alarm the recipient and his surgeon, then it was entirely successful. In early September *The Moderate Intelligencer* claimed that Lisle was executed because he 'directed the shooting of poysoned bullets', but neither Fairfax nor any of his officers on the day even mentioned the bullets, let alone named them as the reason for Lisle's death. The *Intelligencer* seems to have made an assumption based on Lisle leading the foot during the sortie where the harmless 'coppresse' bullet was found. Perhaps he felt he needed to offer his readers a distinct reason for Lisle's execution – just as Lucas's was generally given as his breach of previous parole – but nothing specific had been offered by Fairfax.[47]

Neither the poison accusations, nor the Royalist leaders' denials, can at this historical remove be confirmed. Moreover, individual musketeers may well have taken it upon themselves to 'poison' their musket balls without their officers' knowledge, so both Fairfax and Norwich could have been telling the truth. The consequence of the affair, however, was a further hardening in Fairfax's attitude towards the occupiers of Colchester. As a newsbook reported on 23rd June, Parliament's 'retaliation' for what it considered to be breaches of military protocol, was to round up the relatives of persons inside the town, and hold them as hostages:

Upon letters from Colchester League, that they in the Town put Sir Wil. Massum, and the rest with him, into an house against our Cannon mouth,

45   *Ibid.*
46   *The Moderate Intelligencer*, Numb. 173, p.1434.
47   *The Moderate Intelligencer*, Numb. 181, p.1518.

and their seising of Sir Harbottle Grimstons house plundering it, turning out his Lady, &c. Garisoning it, &c., The Commons passed Instructions concerning those who are to be sent for retaliation. The Lord Capels Son (a Child) is apprehended with others.[48]

Arthur Capel junior was then sixteen. Royalist newsbook *The Colchester Spie* alleged that his captors placed him in the path of the Royalist artillery, presumably just as the county committee had allegedly been used as human shields inside the town;[49] on this occasion the allegation is confirmed by *The Perfect Weekly Account*.[50] A few days later, *The Kingdomes Weekly Intelligencer* reported, the boy's mother petitioned on his behalf in the House of Lords, presumably asking for reassurance about his safety; the Lords concurred and sent a letter to Fairfax.[51]

Some accusations reached ridiculous heights. London pamphlet *Colchesters Teares*, an emotionally and religiously fevered piece published in late July which comes the closest to deliberate propaganda of all the papers published during the siege, made a particular effort. Amongst other things it alleged violent robbery against the town's inhabitants and numerous crimes against women, including an attempted rape at gunpoint and Sir Charles Lucas being interrupted by Norwich during an attempted assault, after which the woman ran off and told a neighbour 'shee could not have escaped his hands.'[52] The Parliament did not have a monopoly on alleging abuses however: in August *The Colchester Spie* was to claim that a fourteen-year-old boy sent out by Norwich with a message for the Scots was captured and tortured, his fingers first being burned 'almost to the bones' with lighted match, before he was hung upside down and then forced to sit over an increasingly large fire, screaming in pain, until he was 'black all over like an Ethiope'. 'In all probability', the *Spie* concluded, 'they have murthered him.' This may be the 'little ladde' noted by *The Perfect Weekly Account* in early July, who was reportedly returned to the town having 'given good intelligence on the strength of the town, and where their Ordinance and all their Ammunition is.'[53]

On Monday 26th June, the *Intelligencer* reports that the Royalists had:

marched forth, and possessed themselves of Sir Harbottle Grimstons house, and Bradfield Hall where they have placed two hundred Muskettiers,

48   *Perfect Occurrences of Every Daie Journall*, Numb. 78, p.371.
49   Numb. 1, no page numbers.
50   Numb. 15, no page numbers.
51   Numb. 266[b], p.998.
52   *Colchesters Teares*, pp.9-10.
53   *The Colchester Spie*, Numb. 1, no page numbers; the allegation is repeated in *Mercurius Elencticus* Numb. 3, pp.281-282. *The Perfect Weekly Account*, Numb. 16 (misnumbered as Numb. 15), 5th-12th July, no page numbers.

and two troops of Horse and have sent for Guns from Colchester to maintain them.[54]

The house being so near the siege lines, it is no wonder that *Perfect Occurrences of Every Daie Journall* promptly reports that Fairfax's council of war determined to reduce it.[55] Occupying the house was a hollow success for the Royalists, however:

the Towne is now blocked up round both by Land and Sea; That their batteries are finished, their Ordnance planted, which thunder against the Town with hot execution; And that in a short space his Excellence doth not doubt to give the Parliament a good account of the taking of it.[56]

All Fairfax and his New Model need do now, was wait. On Monday 26th a party of horse sallied out from the town but was beaten in again with the loss of '5. or 6. killed and taken'; on the 27th Fairfax burned four mills around the town, and on the morning of the 29th the Royalists fired Sir Harbottle Grimston's house, allegedly 'to retaliate for the milles',[57] although *The Kingdomes Weekly Intelligencer* suggests they were chased from the house by an artillery bombardment which made 'ruinous divisions' in it before the fire began, or was set.[58]

Meanwhile the county committee complained that:

they having yet received but one from the Parliament, to retaliate with, desire that more may be sent downe.[59]

Meanwhile, on 1st July, Fairfax offered Capel his unfortunate teenage son in exchange for Sir William Masham; Capel had turned down the offer, replying that:

he conceaved something in this offer to be inhumane, and that if all the Committee had been offered in exchange for him he should have disdained the motion, and that he joyed to see any of his (if no other way) yet by their sufferings to pay that duty which they owe the King, and the known Lawes of the Kingdome …[60]

---

54   Numb. 266 p.991.
55   Numb. 78, p.372.
56   *The Kingdomes Weekly Intelligencer*, Numb. 266 p.992.
57   Royalist sally, *Perfect Occurrences of Every Daie Journall*, Numb. 78, p.375; the burning of the mills, *ibid.*; the burning of the Grimston house, *Perfect Occurrences of Every Daie Journall*, Numb. 79, p.574.
58   Numb. 266[b], p.999.
59   30th June; *Perfect Occurrences of Every Daie Journall*, Numb. 79, p.574.
60   *The Kingdomes Weekly Intelligencer,* Numb. 266[b], p.999.

George Lisle, Charles Lucas, and the East Gate sortie

The focus of the siege now turned to the East Gate, where Carter takes up the account:

> About this time the enemy incroach't so neer upon us with their approaches, notwithstanding our daily sallies, and skirmishes with them on all parts, as that they fell down into East-street, and seized on the Mill on the river, and placed a strong guard there; which guard, (out of hopes to have fired all that part of the street betwixt them and the Town, because many of our men both quartered and guarded there also) set fire to a Tanners house and barn, with all the goods, leather and corn in it; the house being the next house to the inner-side over against them, and bringing downe two Drakes began to be something busie, and trouble-some to our guards …[61]

Presumably these activities were those reported by *Perfect Occurrences* on 3rd July, when:

> the Suffolke forces being joyned, they fell upon the Suburbs at East-gate street, and tooke the Turne-pike, where they had thoughts to have made a Breast-worke. And accordingly did.[62]

The Royalists held a council of war, and agreed upon 'a grand sally' in response:

> Sir Charls Lucas commanding in chief, marched in the head of the horse, and Sir George Lisle commanded the foot; the whole party consisted of five hundred foot, and two hundred horse, out of which a forlorn party being drawn out, they first marched towards the river, where the enemies guard was on both sides the street, and a Barricado crosse, from whence with their case shot from the Drakes, and small shot from the Barricadoe and guard-houses, they play'd very thick upon them, having no other passage over the river then a foot bridge; the end wherof reach'd within five foot of the enemies barricado.

Lisle, Lucas and their men were rushing down a corridor of shot and shrapnel; yet, Carter continues:

61 Carter, pp.149-150.
62 *Perfect Occurrences of Every Daie Journall*, Numb. 79, p.581.

as if it had been a sporting skirmish amongst tame souldiers at a generall muster, they regarded it not; but running on in a single file over the bridge, & some for hast through the river, mounted their barricado, and beat the enemy off in an instant …

Evidently their chosen time for the sortie was at low tide. According to the London newsbook account, the Suffolk men, completely surprised by the onslaught, retreated to their main guard. Lisle's soldiers overturned the drakes at the barricade – presumably the turnpike mentioned by the newsbook – pushing one of them into the river, but had no horse team to take them away. Instead the men charged straight at anyone still firing on them, clearing 'a great part of the street'. Having overtaken many of the besiegers they now turned back:

> then surrounding them, charged in upon them, who having neither possibility of reliefe, nor indeed of retreat or escape, yeelded upon Quarter.[63]

It is apparent that Carter's account does not tally with the illustrated version of the siege diary, which shows no buildings on the far side of the river, besides the water mill; whereas the action he describes clearly shows the Royalists crossing the bridge and fighting amongst houses on the other side, where they took a number of prisoners. Carter describes 'the whole street almost being full of Soldiers': the scene must have been extraordinary, a firefight and hand-to-hand melee involving perhaps a thousand men, if the besiegers were fielding the same numbers as Lisle. *The Moderate Intelligencer* believed Lisle had 1000 men on his own, but Carter's 500 must be taken as accurate, as he was there.[64]

Lisle's and Lucas's charge having now cleared the entire street:

> gave so great an Alarum to all their Leager, that they immediately rallyed together all the Foot and Horse on that side the River, and marched down the hill from behind the Windmill, on the top of another hill in a very full and orderly Body, onely they left their Colours and Pikes with a reserve behind the Windmill. But our Party having gained almost the top of the first hill, followed their charge so smartly upon them, that they soon forc'd them to a disorderly retreat …

The besiegers were 'distractedly disperst', Carter says, 'some from Houses out at Back-doores and windows, and others from Hedges in a great disorder.' Encouraged, the Royalists pressed on, beating them back beyond the windmill and also forced the reserve to retreat. Now, however, their horse made a stand:

---

63   Carter, p.151.
64   Numb. 173, p.1434.

one keeping the Colchester foot at bay while the rest of the cavalry tried to rally their own. Meanwhile some of Lisle's musketeers took to an insubstantial hedge to maintain their attack, but suddenly found themselves out of ammunition: the cavalry, which *The Intelligencer* says, was Colonel Whaley's, charged straight through the hedge, killing or taking most of the musketeers.

Now in retreat, Carter says, the Colchester men:

> faced about againe, and received their Charge with such an undaunted resort, they forced them againe to as speedy a retreat; and so marched easily off into the Towne againe, and in very good order.

He adds:

> In this action Sir George Lisle was once taken Prisoner, but immediately rescued; and in all we lost one Captaine, and one Lieutenant, and about 30 private Soldiers, which were taken at the broken hedge, but very few kill'd.[65]

The *Intelligencer* begs to differ, claiming:

> about 100 prisoners, most of them miserably wounded, the souldiers giving them a payment for their poysoned bullets. About 20 of them was slain upon the place, most of them Gent. as is conceived by their good aparrel and white skins … Some of the prisoners say a Col: was slain where their foot fell, their retreat was so hasty … One Col: Leile commanded their party …[66]

How the *Intelligencer* identified Lisle is a mystery, but presumably someone – Whaley, perhaps – recognised him. It is unfortunate that Carter did not record anything more about the circumstances of his brief captivity: it was the first occasion, as far as is presently known, that he had ever been taken prisoner. Two or three hundred besiegers were killed, Carter claims, and eighty or so prisoners brought into the town. It was after this sally that the musket ball supposedly 'boyld in coppresse' was discovered: at least one other newsbook besides *The Moderate Intelligencer* picks up on the claims, although it offers no more details and merely seems to be repeating the original hearsay.[67]

What the sally was supposed to achieve is not clear, other than causing a temporary disruption to the enemy's activities at the East Gate: although this would be

65   Carter, pp.153-154.
66   *The Moderate Intelligencer*, Numb. 173, p.1434.
67   *The Perfect Weekly Account*, Numb. 17, no page numbers.

in line with Capel's letter to Langdale explaining that they were tying up Fairfax for as long as they could. Besides, the alternative would have been to remain inside and do nothing, which would have sapped morale and been a tacit admission of defeat: something which nobody inside Colchester was yet prepared to openly voice.

Fairfax's long-awaited siege artillery arrived during the first few days of July, along with eight carts of ammunition from Windsor and Wallingford.[68] Now that the town was completely encircled, the frenetic action of the first month of the siege began to abate, and news reports became daily more focussed on the condition of those inside, and Fairfax now adopted a policy of refusing to allow anyone to leave the town, including women and children, unless they were 'well-affected'. Accordingly the wives of some of the Colchester Royalists were turned back towards the town, but some townswomen that were permitted to depart in early July reported that:

> there is great want of Bread in the town of Colchester; And that the horse have nothing to subsist on, which makes the Souldiers begin to murmure, and to consider of their hunger and hardships to come, when they shall have nothing to subsist on but their horse.[69]

They also alleged that when they complained to Norwich about the lack of food, he said 'they must not complaine till horse-flesh is 10d per pound but appeased by giving them monies.' The besieged were reported to have 200 barrels of powder and twenty pieces of artillery and, but little or no 'great shot' to fire from them: *The Kingdomes Weekly Intelligencer* reported that 'our Canon perpetually thunder against the Towne, who for want of great shott are silent, or very slow in their returnes.' Lack of shot may not have been the reason, however: when the town surrendered on 28th August, Carter reported that in fact 'many great shot' remained, being those Fairfax had himself shot into the town, so presumably there was some effort being made to collect and recycle them.[70] On 7th July the news-book noted that provisions inside the town were 'very scarce' and very expensive, and that the Royalist cavalry was expected to attempt an escape any time.[71]

Meanwhile Parliament had not given up trying to free the unfortunate county committee, who still suffered in the town along with everyone else: on 9th July the Commons voted to offer the captive John Ashburnham for Sir William Masham,

---

68   *The Kingdomes Weekly Intelligencer*, Numb. 266[b], p.1000.
69   Royalist wives, *Perfect Occurrences of Every Daie Journall*, Numb. 79, p.578; lack of bread, *The Kingdomes Weekly Intelligencer*, Numb. 267, pp.1004-1005.
70   Carter, p.190.
71   Royalist lack of great shot, Numb. 267, p.1008; scarce provisions, Numb. 267, p.1006.

the committee's leader, although the exchange did not occur for another three weeks.[72]

The Hythe, St Mary, St John's Abbey and the Gatehouse

On 11th July the *Intelligencer* reported the start of one of the most famous events of the siege: the bombardment of the bell tower of St Mary-at-the-Walls. Almost since the siege began, the Royalist fort next to the church had been raining shot on Fairfax's western siegeworks. Now the defenders had hauled a small brass saker into the church tower, to lengthen the cannon's range.[73] By the 8th, shot from Parliament's Essex Fort had 'beaten down the battlements', and a further report on the 10th boasted that the bombardment had also killed the Royalists' chief gunner, reputed to be 'one of the best Markes-men in England'. The *Intelligencer* claims that the attack:

> did such execution, that the beseigers had afterwards free liberty to continue the Fortification of their works on the Out-line.[74]

This may only have been temporary, however – perhaps in the immediate aftermath of the gunner's death – as the tower battery was maintained for several more days, and on the 11th the siege diary records a gunner and matrosse shot 'as they were battering St Maries steeple.'

On 12th July, with the assent of a council of war, Norwich dispersed a declaration in the fields outside the town, offering indemnity and payment of arrears to any man who joined the Royalists before 21st July. Whether anyone actually availed themselves of the offer, is not known. On the face of it, to genuinely expect deserters to come inside Colchester at this time would be laughable, but according to Carter not everyone out in the siege lines *was* an enemy: after the 'grand sally', he claims, many local men grew weary of their service in the trenches and were willing to pay ten shillings per week for someone else to take their place. By which means, Carter says:

> Many that came up from London and other places to have joyned with us, not being able to come into the towne, entred themselves in their Armes; by which meanes they might more advantageously come to us, if it had been our fortunes to march out into the Field.[75]

72   *CSP Domestic Series*, 1648-1649, p.179. The exchange was reported by *The Perfect Weekly Account*, Numb. 21, on 7th August.
73   Carter, p.162.
74   *The Kingdomes Weekly Intelligencer*, Numb. 267, pp.1007, 1008.
75   Carter, p.155.

Carter records that after the sally from the East Gate, the forces chased from that quarter soon returned, and began burning the suburbs on the far side of the river, hoping to dislodge the Royalist guards on the town side: the river prevented damage, however, and only hindered the besiegers. They also burned the windmills on the eastern side of the town, and bombarding one on the north side, supposing it was all the besieged had left. However, since being cut off from the rest of the mills a few weeks previously the Royalists had – as reported – been milling for themselves. According to Carter, a number of millstones had been found stacked at the Hythe for transportation, and had been carried back up into the town. He assumed that the besiegers had probably planted 'incendiaries' amongst the soldiers and planned to spark off a bread mutiny, but was confident that this would not happen, partly due to the new horse mills in the town, and partly because Henry Hastings had 'with diligent care' been organising the daily provision and distribution of food to the Commissaries. The town mayor had also been urged to set up mills for the populace, but had refused to comply despite 'dayly urgencies' from Hastings and Lucas: the inhabitants, 'not at all reflecting upon the duty of the Mayor and officers in the Town', now bypassed the mayor and brought their complaints directly to the army. Lucas, 'commisserating them as his own Towns-born people', was obliged to deliver them grain from the Royalists' stores, which, Carter lamented:

> proved afterwards so great an inconvenience to our selves, as that half that quantity would have supported us til we had obtained better conditions from the enemy.[76]

The *Intelligencer's* prediction of an attempted Royalist cavalry breakout was soon fulfilled. On 14th July a party of horse was reported to have met in the high street, and two days later, that:

> The last night the Enemy indeavoured to escape with their Horse at a Ford over a River, with some Foote neer the North-bridge, but so soon as our Scouts fired at them they run in againe.[77]

Meanwhile, Fairfax's present design was to finally take control of the Royalist strongholds in the south and south-east portion of the suburbs. On Thursday 13th a joint attempt was made on The Hythe, on the Lucases long-since ransacked home at St John's, and on the old abbey gatehouse. The Hythe fell immediately, the Royalist guard surrendering 'without so much opposition as the firing of one Musquet', says Carter, at the first approach of Colonel Whaley's forces. The next

76   Carter, pp.158-159.
77   *Perfect Occurrences of Every Daie Journall*, Numb. 81, p.591, 594.

morning Fairfax drew up his forces near St John's, where he set up two demi-cannons and fired 'three-score and odd great shot at St. Maries steeple', but ceased the attack after a sharp response from the tower which killed six or seven men. He breached the walls of St John's, however, says the siege diary, and forced all the Royalist soldiers there to retreat to the nearby gatehouse. The next morning, Friday 15th, Fairfax drew nearer to St John's, brought up eight artillery pieces, including the demi-cannons and began battering the gatehouse, inside of which were 100 musketeers.[78] A Parliamentarian eyewitness reported that:

> We discharged four pieces of Canon together, which much amazed the enemy in the works; and then discharged four more.[79]

Carter says:

> [The bombardment] beat one side of it to the ground, which falling into their worke (that was but a small halfe moone drawne from one side of the great House to the other,) anoyed them very much; then fired two or three Granadoes immediately with it, which buried many in the stones and dust, the rest not able to stand the shock; betaking themselves to their Swords, and the but end of their Muskets, disputed it very hard from one place to the other …[80]

The eyewitness:

> our Musquetiers fell on and storm'd the Gate-house, with Ladders and threw in hand Granado's: The Enemy opposed very stoutly for a while, and threw down several of the Ladders, but at last gave back, some held out their Handkerchiefes, others fired very fiercely, yet notwithstanding, our men gained the work, and part of the Gate-house & throwing in a hand Granado where there was some of the Enemy stood to their Arms, it hapned to light amongst their Magazine, consisting of about four barrels of powder, and blew up about forty of their men …

Carter claims that in fact, miraculously, most of the gatehouse guard fought their way clear and escaped through broken windows or holes in the damaged building. He put the Royalist death toll at only four, and prisoners at ten; the siege diary claims thirteen were pulled from under the rubble, and the eyewitness that his men spent the evening digging out body parts and that sixty Royalist prisoners

---

78   The Parliamentarian eyewitness in *Perfect Occurrences* claims that the prisoners admitted to 140.
79   *The Perfect Weekly Account*, Numb. 17, no page numbers.
80   Carter, pp.162-163.

had been taken. These last, he said, were 'put to the sword and destroyed', which the siege diary confirms.

Fairfax then possessed himself of St John's also, at which point occurred one of the grossest acts of the siege. Attempting to ransack the house, but finding nothing as it was already bare since an attack by mobs in 1642, the New Model soldiers found their way into the Lucas family vault at the adjacent church of St Giles. Here lay the coffins of Lucas's recently dead mother and sister: the soldiers raided the coffins for valuables, and strewed body parts around the vault. Writing in 1650, Carter is not coy about his disgust and despair:

> Is not the Common-wealth happy that must receive a reformation from such Saints? Who have these ten yeares been practising acts, absolutely monstrous to even nature it selfe: Beyond parallel, president, or politicall complotment of the most subtill Machavillian, or bloudy Tyrants in the world.[81]

As the survivors from the gatehouse retreated, the eyewitness said:

> The enemy was so enraged at this losse (having totally by this meanes shut themselves up within the walls, and not having any part of the Suburbs) that they set the Subburbs round the towne on fire, and at this present there is the saddest spectacle to be seen … there being now burning in a great Flame, house above a mile in length … by this we conceive that they are desperately bent, and will not onley destroy the Subburbs, but even burne also the town before they yield.

Another witness claimed that:

> the fire was so bright, 'that some of us being a mile distance had light almost to read a letter so far, and a terrible red duskie bloody Cloud seemed to hang over the Towne all night …

This appeared in the overwrought *Colchesters Teares*, but is one of its more credible claims.[82] *The Colchester Spie* asserts that Norwich, Capel and Lucas 'bound themselves by indenture to the inhabitants to make all good againe' and includes a full transcription of the document; although how genuine the story is, given the depths to which the siege had already plunged, is debatable.[83]

---

81   Carter, p.165.
82   *Colchesters Teares*, p.8.
83   Numb. 1, no page numbers.

As smoke wreathed Colchester on 16th July, Fairfax once more summoned the town, but Norwich and his officers allegedly answered that if any further such messages were delivered, they would hang the messenger.[84] *The Kingdomes Weekly Intelligencer* attributes their 'rash' response to being enouraged by news of the arrival of the Duke of York's ships in the Downes.[85] More likely, as David Appleby points out, they were angered by an arrow being shot into the town, offering the soldiers quarter and passes home if they delivered Norwich, Capel, Hastings, Lucas, Farr and Lisle to Fairfax.[86] Directly offering the common soldiers terms in this way was, as Appleby says, 'a contravention of military etiquette', but by this point in what had become a very brutal siege, such niceties were laughable.[87] The eyewitness to their refusal adds:

> Presently after our Trumpeter was returned they set an other street on fire, as if they had repented they had done so little evill the night before in burning many hundred houses.

Four hundred houses were reportedly burned.[88] Fairfax planned to start attacking the town walls, but intended first to send for all the women and children to leave. Some of the Royalists were also planning to leave, but not in full view of their enemy: powder and food now in scarce supply, Carter records, all bar 200 of the cavalry were now ordered to make a break for freedom. Accordingly, late at night on the 17th:

> the Horse were all drawne to a Rendevouz in the Castle yard late in the night, and a party of Foot with them for their assistance in forcing the Enemies line with Pioneers, to levell a way for them to let the Horse in, when the Foot should have forc't the Enemy from their line, which was supposed would easily have been performed …

The pioneers were to throw down cartloads of stones to help the cavalry cross the river; the plan quickly fell apart, however, as the noise alerted the enemy's guards, who 'laid privatly in Ambuscadoe on the other side of the River for their comming over …'[89] The pioneers, mostly townsmen, deserted, and the would-be escape force was forced to retreat. Although Carter says a second attempt was 'bootlesse', the new Leveller newsbook *The Moderate* suggests that this was in fact

84 *Perfect Occurrences of Every Daie Journall*, Numb. 81, p.594; identically reported in *The Kingdomes Weekly Intelligencer*, Numb. 269, p.1018.
85 Numb. 269[b], p.1029.
86 *Perfect Occurrences of Every Daie Journall*, Numb. 82, p.403.
87 Appleby, p.153.
88 *Perfect Occurrences of Every Daie Journall*, Numb. 81, p.596.
89 *Ibid.*

a second attempt, a party of 100 horse having attempted to leave earlier, before returning to try again with 200 foot. Colonel Rainsborough, who was on the alert for an escape, fired a single artillery piece to alert the entire leaguer, and the escape attempt was abandoned.[90]

Around 25th July, Carter says, Fairfax tightened the noose around the town even further, 'and now lay absolutely round us, so that we were soddainly begirt within a very little distance'; he then brought up two demi-cannon and two culverins and finished off the tower of St Mary's church, destroying the top portion and the saker lodged there.[91] An attempt by Colonel Rainsborough to burn more buildings, including another mill, was seen off, and the fire quenched.

On Sunday 30th Sir William Masham was finally released in exchange for John Ashburnham; whether the latter was actually sent into Colchester in exchange is not clear, but it seems unlikely, as he was not listed at the end of the siege.

Hunger: August 1648

Food stocks were now critically low, and the first reports of the Royalists eating horsemeat appeared in the London press in the third week of July.[92] A party which ventured out to cut green barley for the horses was attacked and two men mortally wounded. Water now also became increasingly scarce: besides Fairfax's soldiers taking lead from pipes and conduits, with which to make more ammunition, watercourses into the town were diverted away.[93] By 26th July, *The Moderate Intelligencer* reported, those leaving the town were reporting that 'they begin to eat horseflesh'.[94] Carter confirms that this was now occurring: every horse was brought to the castle yard, and a third part of every troop was given to the Commissary to be killed.[95] These horses may have included the 60 stolen by Colonel Whaley as they grazed under the town walls, 'which (it seems) were designed as much for food as service'; the town butcher, refusing to kill any more of them, was committed to Lucas's custody but fled the town.[96]

---

90 Numb. 2, p.9.
91 Carter, pp.154-155. Later stories associating the saker's fall with the origin of the nursery rhyme 'Humpty Dumpty' are almost certainly spurious: there is no proof of a connection, and numerous other suggestions have been put forward for the rhyme's origin.
92 For example, 21st July in *The Moderate Intelligencer*, Numb. 176, no page numbers; 21st July in *The Perfect Weekly Account*, Numb. 19, no page numbers.
93 *Perfect Occurrences of Every Daie Journall*, Numb. 82, p.403; *The Kingdomes Weekly Intelligencer*, Numb. 269[b], p.1031, 1033.
94 Numb. 175, no page numbers.
95 Carter, p.151.
96 Carter writes that in late August his Commissary's records showed that 730 horses had been killed for food and the meat distributed, besides those stolen out of stables by soldiers and killed, and others slaughtered for private tables, 'which I am confident made the number above eight hundred.' (pp.175-176).

On 31st July the London papers finally began to whisper of a Royalist surrender:

> From the siege at Colchester little this day only the Lord Gen. forces are in a good condition, very cheerefull and full of courage, the report goes they in the towne are inclined to a treaty, fearing that if reliefe faile, they also may faile of Quarter, when they have most need to seeke for it.[97]

Evidently the town's occupiers did not wish to go quietly, however: they were now expecting the worst, and preparing for it:

> Letters from Colchester doe advertise, that the Besieged are preparing for a storme, and have unpaved the streets, and digged therein many deep and cross Ditches to hinder the Advance and Intradoes of our horse; They have dismounted many of their owne Troopers, who are pleased to bee knowne by the name of Shavers. They have balls of Pitch, with which (being made liquid by fire) they mean to wash the heads and faces of those that shall approach them; In stead of a Rasor they have a long Sythe …[98]

The 'Shavers' made at least one sally from Botolph's gate on the south side of the city, briefly tricking the besiegers by holding up handkerchiefs as if surrendering; a short firefight ensued and they were beaten inside again.[99] Sallies continued intermittently around the city, and Fairfax crept closer, but gunpowder grew short inside the town, and rumours of surrender persisted. On the part of the newsbooks this was mostly wishful thinking, or stating the obvious: that the siege simply could not continue for much longer. Those inside the town were not unaware of the gossip, as Carter acknowledges: '[the enemy] hoped for, and expected, our dayly submission to a Treaty for rendition.' He denies reports that food had been delivered by sea, but admits that:

> we had no Horse-meat left in the Town, but what they first fought for, and brought in and sold.[100]

He adds:

> And now began Horse-flesh to be as precious to us as the choicest meat before, and Souldiers in generall, and all Officers and Gentlemen from the

---

97 *The Kingdomes Weekly Intelligencer*, Numb. 270, p.1032.
98 *The Kingdomes Weekly Intelligencer*, Numb. 271, p.1033.
99 *The Perfect Weekly Account*, Numb. 20, no page numbers; *Another great Fight On Sunday morning last …*
100 Carter, p.159.

Lords to the lowest degree or quality, eating nothing else, unlesse Cats and Doggs, which the enemy disgusted very much, expecting a daily rendition by us … It was so hansome a diet grown by this time amongst the Souldiers to eat such food, that we could hardly secure our Horses in the Stables, but every morning one Stable or other was rob'd, and our Horses knock'd o'th'head, and sold in the Shambles by the pound; nor was there in a short time a dog left, for it was the custome of the Souldier to reserve halfe his ammunition Loafe, and in a morning walke the streets, and if he discovered a Dog, to drop a peice of bread, and so drill him on, till within his reach, then with the but end of his musket knock his brains out, and away with him to his quarters; I have known there six shillings given for the side of a Dog, and yet but a small one neither.[101]

On Friday 4th August *The Perfect Weekly Account* reports that:

The Defendants in the towne are shortned of their former allowance, some of their Horseflesh which they powdred is taynted and about 8 Oxen, and some few sheepe which were very hardly preserved thus long, for the chief of the Commanders, are now killed, yet they have some Rye, Raisins, and other sustenance, but those which steal out of the town and come to us, say, they can hold out but a short time longer …[102]

The Kingdomes Weekly Intelligencer also reports on the same day that:

The allowance of bread is contracted from 14 ounces to 10 …[103]

Within a week the allowance was reported cut to seven.[104] The *Intelligencer* also reports bad food causing 'the Flux and other diseases', a claim repeated by *The Moderate Intelligencer* the same week. By the 9th, the latter reports:

their Wine and Raisins are near spent, so that the common souldiers get none, the souldiers hath a Rie loafe of ten ounces allowed for a day. Yesterday they killed 30 horses to powder up, some hors-flesh having been put up before, but not well, for it bred Maggots.[105]

---

101 *Ibid*, pp.160-161.
102 Numb. 21, no page numbers. 'Powdering' meant curing with gunpowder: one of its ingredients, saltpetre, had long been used as a curing agent.
103 Numb. 271, p.1031.
104 *Another Great Fight On Sunday Morning …*, p.2; *The Moderate Intelligencer*, Numb. 177, no page numbers.
105 Numb. 177, no page numbers.

Shortly afterwards, says *The Perfect Weekly Account*:

> The inhabitants of the town are in extream wants, & extremity forceth them to multiply their cries and petitions to their Leading Governors, they first killed their cats & eat them that they might not destroy the Rats and Mice, of which poor people after fed on …[106]

Even in late August, when the biting conditions inside Colchester could no longer be believably denied, the Royalist newsbooks were still keen to play down the deteriorating conditions widely reported by the Parliamentarian papers. *Pragmaticus* raised a sceptical eyebrow at one tale, that:

> his Excellencie sending in a Trumpet about exchange of Prisoners, the Trumpet was brought into a room, where the Earl of Norwich, the Lord Capell, Sir Charles Lucas, and six others were at dinner together upon a boil'd quarter of a Dog, and six Carrets: which is a likely matter the Trumpet should be admitted to see, is it not?[107]

Meanwhile, Carter says, Fairfax embarked on a campaign of disinformation designed to crush morale and split the men from their officers:

> false fires of strange improbable News of great victories over the Scots, long before they ever met with them … Lists of prisoners taken, never in arms … Then they sent private papers into the Town amongst the Souldiers by Women, incensing the Souldiers against their Officers, reproaching them with that odious name of Rebels (which they knew to whom more properly due) and men acting against the Peace of the Kingdome without Commission …

On the 11th, he adds:

> more Arrows were again shot into the Towne to entice the Souldiers by alluring charms, intermixt with as severe threats, to quit the service; intimating, That if they came not away before the next Monday (it being a Friday) that not a man which came after should have any quarter; Which Messages the Soldiers still resented so well, as that they resolved to answer it by the same Messengers, and took some of their own Arrowes annointing them with a T[urd], and wrapping the same in paper fastned

106 Numb. 23, no page numbers.
107 Numb. 21, no page numbers.

it to the heads of the Arrowes, and writ on the papers this superscription, *An Answer from Colchester August the 11th. 1648, as you may smell* …[108]

Initial negotiations

On 17th August, Carter records:

> having maintained and held it out in defence of a proud, succesfull, and imperious Enemy … still cherishing our resolutions with hopes of reliefe, and having yet no certaine intelligence of the state of affairs in the other parts of the Kingdom, nor reliefe approaching, and our stores very much wasted … by a Generall result of the Councell of Warre, His Excellency the Lord Norwich, the Lord Capell, and Sir Charles Lucas, signed Letters to the Lord Fairfax, to desire him to grant them twenty days respite, and a passe through his quarters, for them to send some Gentlemen to Sir Marmaduke Langdale, that they might receive a reall information of his condition, and if they found him as they had given him out, and not advancing towards us, and that in that time there was no hopes of reliefe, that then they would Treat for surrender.[109]

What nobody knew at this point, beseiged or beseiger, was that during the very hours they in Essex were disputing the desired Langdale message on 17th August, the Second Civil War was effectively being ended. After taking Berwick and receiving a commission from the Prince of Wales, Langdale had raised a substantial army of horse and foot to support the King, then marched across the country to meet Hamilton's Engager army on its way down from Scotland. On 17th August, poor cooperation between Langdale and the Scots forces had resulted in the combined Royalist army being split up: left on its own to face Cromwell at Preston, Langdale's English force was decisively crushed. Over the next two days Cromwell, Major General John Lambert, and Lieutenant General John Middleton, pursued and hunted down the Engager army, gradually tearing it apart. Langdale and the Scottish cavalry commanders initially escaped, but eventually all but two were captured.

Langdale's had been the very last English Royalist army in the field, and with that gone, the failure of a rising led by the 2nd Duke of Buckingham and the Earl of Holland on 5th July, most Welsh resistance finally wiped out by the surrender of starving and bombarded Pembroke Castle on 11th July, and relief of Colchester by sea impossible, there was no hope for Lisle, Lucas and their colleagues. Reportedly, Fairfax's response to the Royalist request to message Langdale, was that he believed

---

108 Carter, pp.165-166.
109 Carter, p.169.

he would be in the city much sooner than twenty days, and without terms:[110] at the time this may partly have been bravado, but it proved to be correct.

Fairfax also received a petition from the town mayor and aldermen, requesting that the inhabitants might be allowed to leave. Believing the petition had been 'wrung from' the inhabitants, Fairfax agreed they could leave only if the Royalists agreed to release the county committee first. As for rendering the town, he would only allow that:

> All such Officers and souldiers, under the degree of a Captain, (excepting all such who being Members of my Army, have since the 10 of May last deserted their Colours) shall have Passes, without injury offered them, to return to their respective homes, they engaging themselves never here-after to bear Arms against the Parliament.
> All Captains, and other superiour Officers, with Lords and Gentlemen, to submit to mercy.[111]

According to Carter, Fairfax ordered that any inhabitants who left the town in the meantime would be fired at; the private response from the officers inside was that they would 'maintaine and defend it to the last', presumably meaning until Fairfax stormed it and they were forced to make the ultimate last stand. However, a further survey of food an ammunition changed their minds, there being not enough bread for two days, or enough powder in the magazine to maintain a fight for two hours, if the town should be stormed. Thus, he says:

> a Councell of Warr was again summoned, where this want being consid-ered, it was agreed, That it was the best course to Treat with the Enemy in time; and by the Major part by voices it was carried; and Letters accord-ingly were drawn up, and Doctor Glyston a Phisician then living in the town employed in the Message.[112]

Their letter primarily objected to Fairfax's refusal to allow the inhabitants to leave:

> My Lord, We have received yours of the 20 of August, and for what concerns the Inhabitants of this Town, we find your Lordships Answer so apparently unreasonable, that we shall need no further justification of ourselves (in reference to our Commiseration of the Inhabitants) by the publication of your Letter: There being no relation between the businesse

110 *Perfect Occurrences of Every Daie Journall*, Numb. 86, p.419.
111 *The Moderate,* Numb. 6, no page numbers.
112 Carter, p.172.

of the Committee and the Townsmen, therefore our not yielding to that of the Committees inlargement, can be no justifiable impediment, why the other should not proceed … and therefore we are resolved of putting forth the Towns people accordingly …

They also pointed out that they did not ask Fairfax for terms, but for a treaty. Glyston returned the next morning with Fairfax's answer, and the numerous letters were reprinted in *The Moderate*:

My Lords, You were pleased to take advantage from the necessity of your own creating upon the miserable Inhabitants, to invite me into a Treaty, as much for your own, as the peoples concernment: They may hope, and may justly expect to share your provisions for Terms as you formerly theirs for subsistence: If not and by the Exercise of your cruelty upon them, they perish under your works, their blood will be required upon you and your souldiers, not doubting but our proceedings herein will be justifiable; which Resolution, by Gods assistance I shall endeavor to make good.

Meanwhile the mayor and aldermen told Fairfax that the Royalists had published an order that anyone in Colchester without provisions to last them twenty days was to depart the town the next day; he reiterated what Norwich had said about the townspeople's fate having nothing to do with the liberty of the committee, and again asked that the inhabitants be allowed to leave. Presumably the 'order' he mentioned concerned the original twenty day period which the Royalists desired, in order to contact Langdale, but whether it was issued before they received a response from Fairfax regarding this request, is not clear. Carter implies that the mayor's claim about the order is a lie, it being:

a very difficult thing, to have forc't so many people through a Sally Port, and dangerous to attempt, who of themselves were apt enough to a Mutiny, and as inhumane a policy (though policy is would have been) to have forced them from their own houses upon the swords of a most cruell and mercilesse Enemy.[113]

Fairfax responded that:

I have already offered conditions to a great part of the souldiers in the Towne better then … they could reasonably expect, and such as I shall not thinke my selfe obliged to make good … but for a Treatie (or ought that tends to delay,) I shall admit of none, except upon circumstances

---

113 Carter, pp.171-172.

necessary for the orderly performance of what is already offered, from such Considerations, as may be requisite for the saving the Towne from Plunder …

On 21st August, as the mayor and alderman had warned:

the Besieged being unable any longer to relieve the Inhabitants had turned five hundred Women and Children out of the towne, the Besiegers played with their Canon against them, but it they shot over their heads on purpose because they would not hurt them, but so importunate were their extreamities, and so sad their condition that rather then to returne to the Town; they adventured on the mercy of the Canon, and did run up to the very mouth of it, whereupon the Souldiers did threaten that they would stripp them, the feare and shame whereof caused the Women to goe back, and their sad Children with them, yet they could not be admitted into the towne againe, the Gates and all the avenues being made fast againe, where-upon they were inforced to take unto a Mill for protection, which caused such a relenting in the Hearts of his Excellencies Souldiers that they shot papers into Colchester, to let the besieged know that if they exposed the Wives and Children of the Inhabitants to such extreamities they would put them all to the sword as well Common Souldiers as Officers …[114]

According to *Perfect Occurrences* a horse was killed during the scramble, and three men who ran out from the town in an attempt to retrieve it, were killed. Carter offers a final summary of the stores available: scarce a cat or dog left uneaten in the town, although a few horses left; not enough corn for one more day's provision, having used every type of corn and bean available to make bread over the previous weeks. 'Our hopes,' he says, 'were now quite dissolved in absolute feare of unavoidable ruine.'[115]

An 'engagement' was now drawn up, to be signed by officers and gentlemen 'least there might be any mis-apprehension betwixt the Soldiers and Officers upon the putting any designe in execution.' In effect it was a promise that the officers and gentlemen would not make any underhand plans to shift for themselves and leave the infantry to their fate:

Wee whose names are here under written, doe in the presence of Almighty God, protest against all conditions that are or shall be sent from the Enemy, by which our libertyes may be infringed, and our Honours blemisht. And

114 *The Kingdomes Weekly Intelligencer*, Numb. 274, p.1060; there is a similar account in *Perfect Occurrences of Every Daie Journall*, Numb. 86, pp.423-424.
115 Carter, p.176.

we doe upon our honours solemnly engage our selves, not to desert one another, nor the Foot, till by Gods assistance we have forced our passage through all that shall oppose us, or to perish in the act, which we attest this three and twentieth of August, one thousand six hundred forty eight.

On Thursday 24th, Carter relates:

the Enemy sent in a paper Kite to the Towne, which hovering a good while over, that the Souldiers might take notice of it, at last they let drop in the midest of it, with many papers fixt to it, to the same purpose as those before shot in with the Arrowes, and with them a book also of the relation of a great Victory over the Scots, and their generall rout …[116]

An initial request for terms; a planned breakout, and a mutiny

The men in the town could have not a shred of doubt now, that they were finished. They knew there was no longer any point in Fairfax wasting men and resources to storm the town, as it could certainly, now, not hold out more than a couple more days. The siege was effectively over. Carter omits to say so, but the dates on the various sets of proposed surrender terms reprinted in the newsbooks reveal that it was at this point, on 24th August, that the Royalists first asked Fairfax for terms.

'My Lord,
Upon a Solemn debate of the Officers, here upon occasion of your former Letters of demanding the persons of all the Officers here above the quality of a Lieutenant to render themselves to mercy, it was resolved by them not to yeeld to the mercy of any other, but that of God alone. And that all meanes be on our part used for the avoiding of the effusion of more English blood, we have sent you inclosed the lowest conditions which in substance we can receive with honour, conceiving the like were never refused to any, farre lower reduced then we can yet yeeld our selves to be. But if there be any doubt in the forme of words, we will if you like of it, send one Gentleman or more, that by a conference with the like number appointed by you may clear all scruples, and agree of the time of performance.
Your Lordships Servants,
Norwich, Arthur Capell, Charles Lucas.
Colchester 24. Aug. 1648.

116 Carter, p.178.

1. That the Town and Castle of Colchester, and all the places of defence whatsoever in the same, with all the Ordinance, Arms, Ammunition and provisions of Warre, all Magazines and stores thereunto belonging (excepting what is allowed in the ensuing articles) shall be delivered to the Generall the Lord Fairfax, or whom he shall appoint without wilfull spoile or imbezzelment.

2. That the Earle of Norwich, Lord Capell, Sir Charles Lucas, the Lord Loughborow, and all the rest of the Officers, Gentlemen, and Souldiers both of Horse and Foot, shall march out of this Towne of Colchester, with his Horse and Arms a mile without the Towne, and then all to render up their Horses and Armes, excepting as followeth,

3. That the Earle of Norwich, the Lord Capell, Sir Charles Lucas, and the Lord Loughborow, shall march away from thence with all their Horses, Arms, and other Equipage particularly belonging to them,

4. That all other Generall Officers, Colonels, Lieutenant Colonels, Majors, and Captaines of Horse and Foot, Lieutenants and Cornets of Horse, and all Gentlemen of quality shall march away with two Horses a peece, and one Servant, themselves to march with their Armes, their servants with their Swords onely, and their Masters Baggage, and all other Officers to march with their sword only.

5. That all persons whatsoever included in these Articles shall have passes to go to their severall Countries and places of abode, and to be free from all violence and plunder in their march.

6. That all included in these Articles who shall desire it, shall have passes granted them freely to passe beyond the Seas within a month after their marching out, they onely ingaging themselves in the meane time to act nothing prejudiciall to the Parliament now sitting at Westminster.

7. That all private Souldiers shall be provided for in their passage for free-quarter in their march homewards lying but one night in a place. That convenient provision be made for all hurt and sicke souldiers who shall be left in Colchester, untill they be recovered, and then Passes to bee given unto them as before mentioned, according to their severall qualities.

8. That all the Inhabitants of the Towne of Colchester be free both in goods and persons, from any violence without distinction.

9. That all persons who have been taken prisoners on either side shall have the benefit of these Articles.[117]

117 *Perfect Occurrences of Every Daie Journall*, Numb. 87, pp.638-639.

Fairfax rejected the Articles out of hand, however:

> My Lords,
> When I looked upon your condition to be far better then now it is, I then offered such tearmes as was thought suitable to your condition, but you now being in a worse posture both in relation to your selves within, and in relation to any expectance of reliefe from without, it is not to be expected from me that your conditions should be better; wherefore I am still resolved not to grant any such termes as are now demanded by you.
>   Aug. 24. 1648.
>   Your Lordships Servant, Tho. Fairfax.

Early on Friday 25th, the Royalist council of war met again:

> Wherefore considering the condition we were so sadly plunged in, through the defeat of the Scots, the disloyalty of the whole Kingdom, and the want we were in of provision to subsist any longer, not having any hopes that we could possibly hold out two dayes longer, unlesse without bread, which we must do, or not at all; 'it was the finall result of the Councell of Warre, to draw out the whole party that night, to their Arms, both Horse and Foot, with what Ammunition was left, which was not much, and as many short Scaling Ladders as could be procured in the interim, and in the deadest time when we might be least expected, to set open two of the Gates, and march out and storm their Line, and so falling into their head quarters, beat up their whole Army, and relieve our selves, or force our march through all oppositions that they should endeavour to obstruct us with, or perish in the attempt; and if the private Souldiers should entertaine any suspicion that the Gentlemen and Officers, who had yet Horses, should seeke out their safety by flight, and leave them engaged, every man (excepting only the General and the Major General) to pistol his own horse in the head of them; Which design being agreed on, and secrecy enjoyned, and every one taken his orders according to his duty in it, the Councel broke up …[118]

The Moderate reveals that:

> they prepared poles and boards to lay over North bridge, which way they did intend to escape …[119]

---

118 Carter, pp.181-182.
119 Numb. 7, no page numbers.

An alarm in the afternoon opportunely called the common soldiers to the line without their 'Bag and Baggage':

> which was concluded generaly to be left behind; for if we gained our hoped victory we should command both them again, & our Enemies to boot; if we failed, we resolved to have no need of it.

The implication of Carter's words is that the officers and gentlemen, at least, had determined that if they failed to break the line then they would fight to the death. As soldiers they lived daily with the possibility of death, and were familiar with doing so, but this was an extraordinary situation with high odds of mortality: a last concerted attempt against an overwhelming enemy whom they knew was careless of their fate. Or perhaps rather, an enemy who now considered them merely stubborn obstacles to resolution of the affair, and for whose deaths, if they occurred, he would not feel responsible. It would seem perfectly normal, then, that those preparing to storm out to meet their potential demise might attempt to organise a few affairs, where that was possible inside a beleaguered town, or leave letters or instructions for their families with the abandoned baggage or secured inside their clothes. Perhaps many men in Colchester that evening did do all this, but it seems Lisle did not: for he asked to write a letter later on the day of his death, but was denied and had to be content with some verbal messages. Perhaps, on the 25th, he was superstitious and careful of routine, as many soldiers are, and thought that preparing anything 'in case' might tempt fate. Perhaps, with all the preparations for the sally, he being one of the commanders, he did not have time. Perhaps it was simply that, after soldiering for over ten years and going out upon so many dangerous sorties, he simply no longer stopped to dwell on consequences. Besides, he had his 'genius' to protect him. We cannot begin to know his thoughts towards nightfall on that Friday, but it seems he was not dwelling on his own mortality.

In any case, everyone's preparations, whatever they had been, were shortly of no matter, for the enterprise was called off at the last minute after a number of officers argued that it was better to wait until the next day because 'they should be in a far better readinesse'. That night, however, the entire plan fell apart. Carter relates that, as had been feared at the council of war:

> Some mutinous spirit had insinuated into the private Souldiers, that the Officers and the rest of the Gentlemen were resolved that night, or very sodenly to break away through the Leaguer, and escape, and leave them all engaged.[120]

The army fell into:

---

120 Carter, p.184.

a frenzy of desperate mutiny around the Line; in some places threatning to cast their Officers over the Line: So high a mutiny indeed it was grown before day, that it was rather likely to end in an immediate ruine to ourselves and Officers too, than a pacification …

Carter guessed there were also 'incendiaries' amongst the men who were placed there by the enemy, and they would do all they could to increase the damage. However, he adds:

Then the Lords, and Sir Charles Lucas, Sir William Compton, and Sir George Lisle, expressed themselves indeed in all the proceedings, men as active as honourable, and beyond expression in both; but never more than in the managing of this Businesse, the rest of the Officers as diligently bestirring themselves also as could be expected, and indeed to admiration, so that at the last they had wrought a little mildnesse amongst them, by endeavouring to give them all the satisfaction that could be in this their misapprehension.

Perhaps because, as suspected by Carter, there were spies in the Royalist camp, details of the furore in the town quickly made their way out across the siege lines. *The Moderate* reported that:

the Officers did give the souldiers Sack, burnt Claret, Raysons, and Pruens, new clothes and good words, but to joyn with them to break through …[121]

As to the other details of the mutiny, and perhaps proving that a spy with full knowledge of the situation was involved, *The Moderate* accords entirely with Carter: that the mutineers believed the officers were intending to abandon them. A council of war was called, to which the mutineers sent thirty or so representatives, who threatened to go and negotiate articles with Fairfax themselves, if the officers did not do it for them. Norwich tried to persuade the ringleaders that their fears were baseless, and that the officers themselves were willing to give themselves up to any punishment if it saved the common soldiery; this snuffed out the mutiny, but the intended plan for a final grand sally was beyond saving. The only remaining option was to send someone to treat with Fairfax, for which purpose Colonel Samuel Tuke was dispatched, 'with full power to accept of any conditions he could obtein.' It was Saturday 26th August.[122]

Tuke was sent with the following letter, which excused the lateness of the response to Fairfax's last offer:

121 Numb. 7, no page numbers.
122 Carter, p.188.

My Lord,

By reason of the late returne of M. Barnardiston last night, we could send you no answer of yours of August 25. till this morning; by your Letter we finde your resolutions to better our conditions formerly offered to us; wherefore to prevent the effusion of more blood, and out of the tender care we have of our common Souldiers, and inferiour Officers, presuming you will make good to all them (without exception) now bearing Armes in Colchester, the Conditions to have Passes, without injury offered them, to turne to their respective homes: we desire according to yours of the 23.[123] to treat with you about the Circumstances, necessary for the orderly performance of what hath been offered, and what may concerne the Towne; as also to explaine our meaning, in what concernes the conditions of the rest of us, in that of submitting to mercy: for which we have sent out Colonell Tuke to you, with M. Barnardiston, upon whose returne, we shall finally resolve what to doe.

Your Lordships servants, Norwich, Arthur Capel, Charles Lucas.
Colchester Aug. 26. 1648.[124]

The Moderate describes the scene in the siege lines:

This day about 12 of the clock, the Enemy sent out a Drum with Mr. Barnardiston, one of the Committee, and Colonell Tewk, one of their own party, desiring a Treaty upon what was offered formerly by his Excellency, viz. concerning the explanation of the words *to submit to mercy*, and concerning the inferiour Officers, souldiers, and Townsmen, his Excellency called a full Counsell of War, and upon Debate it was resolved, That in regard the inferiour Officers and souldiers had slipped their opportunity, that now they should only have fair Quarter, and no other conditions granted them: and it was further resolved, That a Treaty be admitted (provided that the Committee now under restraint, be so forthwith released) upon circumstances necessary for clearing an orderly performance of that which is now offered, viz. for the Lords, Gentlemen, Officers, field Officers, and Captains, to surrender to mercy, and to Treat with the Townsmen concerning the freeing the Town from plunder, which they must not expect to have granted unto them, without raising a considerable summe to content the souldiery for this long tedious siege, where they have taken so much pains, and undergone so hard duty in so wet a season.[125]

---

123 In fact it was that dated the 24th, beginning 'When I looked upon your condition …'
124 *Perfect Occurrences of Every Daie Journall*, Numb. 87, pp.639-640.
125 Numb. 7, no page numbers.

Tuke returned at around 8 p.m. that night, with Fairfax's response and the formal judgement of his council of war.[126]

My Lords,
As soon as I received your Letter, this day I called a full and generall Councell of War, upon advice with them, this inclosed is the Result; according to which I shall be ready to proceed: I remaine your servant, Thomas Fairfax.'

The Opinions and Results of the Councell of War, to his Excellency the Lord Fairfax upon, and in answer to the Letter from the Lord Norwich, Lord Capel, & Sir Charles Lucas, sent this day.

That the Generall (as was intimated in his letter of August 23) is not now obliged to the conditions of August 19, tendered to the Souldiery, but is since dis-ingaged, because they were not accepted within the time limited by the Papers sent in, viz. Thursday noone.

That being so dis-ingaged from the Conditions tendered, and the Councell of War in the Towne having since the Letter of August 23. refused any Treaty upon those conditions, and sent out a peremptory demand of other high termes, with a positive resolution not to accept of lesse, his Excellency is not now obliged (according to the Letter of August 23.) to admit a Treaty upon those former offers. That as he is not obliged, but dis-ingaged, so there is not (in respect to their condition or ours) the same reason now as then.

That the Souldiery and inferiour Officers (except as was excepted in the Letter of August 19) shall have free quarter upon the Surrender of the Towne, with themselves, their Horses, Armes, and other furniture of War, Provided, the Lords, Generall Officers, Field-Officers, and Captains, be rendered to Mercy.

That a Treaty be forthwith admitted (if desired) upon circumstances necessary for the clearing and orderly performance of that which is now offered; Provided, the Committee under restraint be forthwith released.

That for the saving of the Towne, as it hath been the Generalls care all along, and that which is a main Consideration for which he hath hitherto, and yet doth forbeare forcible entrance; so his Excellency hath no reason to let the favour he intends to the Townesmen in that particular, passe as gained for them upon Capitulation, by those who have beene the Authors of its suffering and destruction. But upon Treaty with Military persons for what concerns the Souldiery, his Excellency will also treat with such as the Townsmen shall intrust for what shall concerne the Towne.

---

126 The formal judgement echoes the account of *The Moderate*, but is included here as it helpfully dates the former letters of Fairfax's referred to.

At the Hieth August 26. 1648.'

Carter call the reduced terms '[an] insult over our miseries': the deal was now only 'fair quarter' for the common soldiers, and 'render upon mercy' for everyone else. The next morning the Council of War met again, but:

> there was no refuge, or remedy left, nor any thing to trust to, but what conditions the Enemy would give us; the [county] Committee was therefore immediately dispatched, and Col. Tuke with five other Officers sent forth again to the Enemy, to confirm and signe Articles for rendition, and manner of delivery. The Soldiers of the Enemies Army and ours being already mixt in many places of the Line, no fire given on either side, as if we had been absolute Prisoners, long ere any conclusion was made.

The next morning Tuke was sent back to Fairfax with several other officers – Sir William Compton, Sir Abraham Shipman, Colonel Edward Hammond, and Colonel William Ayliffe – to confirm and sign the Articles, and bring the details of handover. This was all to be put into effect the following morning, Monday 28th August:

> The severall Regiments to lay down their Arms at their severall Posts, and there to remain with their Officers under Captains, till they should be disposed of.
> The Lords, with the rest of the Officers, and Gentlemen to be by eight of the Clock in the morning at the Kings-head, and their Horses and Arms without any imbezilment, in Saint Maries Churchyard.
> All the Ordnance to be left on the platforms as they were planted; all the Ammunition of Powder, Match and Ball, to be left in the Magazen at the Town Hall.[127]

Carter notes that this was all:

> easily don, for there was but one barrell and a halfe of powder left; many great shot were indeed left, in the Lord Capels quarters, which the Enemy had shot into the Town, and the Souldiers gathering up, sold to him for six pence a Bullet. But many of our Horses were taken violently out of their Stables by the Souldiers of the Leaguer, who flockt into the Town before the Gates were opened, contrary to the Articles, and plundred every thing they could lay their hands on.

---

127 Carter, p.190.

Surrender

'And now,' says Carter, 'began the last sceene of this Tragedy.' On Monday 28th everything was completed according to the Articles, and at around 2 p.m. Fairfax entered the town, taking a tour of the defences and to show himself 'in triumph' to his soldiers out in the siegeworks. He then held a council of war in the town: during the meeting, it was decided by a show of hands, that some of the prisoners should be made example of.

Accordingly, says Clarendon, he requested a list of all their names. Then, Carter says, perhaps a couple of hours after Fairfax first entered the town:

> they sent Colonel Ewers to the Kings Head to visit, as we thought, the Lords and Gentlemen, but he brought a sentence of death in his heart, though not immediatly in his mouth, which easily discovered it selfe in his death-like countenance. Comming up into the Chamber, first saluted the Lords, and afterwards came to Sir Charls Lucas, and with a slighting gesture told him, That the Generall desired to speake with him at the Councell of War, with Sir George Lisle, Sir Bernard Gasquoine, and Colonell Farre if he were there, but he was not there; so Sir Charles Lucas as presaging what indeed did afterwards follow, took his solemn leave of the Lords and the rest of his fellow prisoners that were neer him, and calling Sir George Lisle (who was in discourse, and heard not what was spoke) and Sir Bernard Gasquoine went away with him, leaving the rest of the Gentlemen with sympathizing Souls, sighing prayers for them, for well they might imagine what evil was intended towards them.[128]

128 Clarendon, Book XI, 1840 vol. VI, p.96; Carter pp.192-193.

17

'Shoot me out of a cannon'

It is difficult to create a precise timeline of the events which took place at Colchester Castle in the early evening of 28th August 1648. Two coherent news-book accounts exist, from the Royalist *Mercurius Pragmaticus* and the Leveller paper *The Moderate*, which appear to be from eyewitnesses and were printed a few days later.[1] There is also an account from William Clarke, Secretary to the Council of the Army, who 'minuted' the occasion. His account is prefaced by a note from his son, which declares it as:

> An account of the death of Sir Charles Lucas &c., the originall of which, writt with my owne Fathers' hand, I gave Sir Thomas Clarges.[2]

Clarke's account comprises the conversations which took place between Lisle, Lucas, Sir Bernard Gascoyne, and their captors. Whilst it is the most direct primary eyewitness report and should in theory be taken as the definitive account by which to judge all others, unfortunately it does not – at least in its 1894 printed version – appear to be reliable. The conversations are incoherent, starting and stopping in odd places as if sections have been randomly moved around; whilst individual details closely match other eyewitness reports, the timelines do not. Furthermore, at least one section of speech has been wrongly attributed to Lucas instead of Lisle. In fairness to Clarke, it is likely that there were several conversations going on at once, and a number of random interjections occurred which Clarke recorded but could not insert in precisely the right place; another likely explanation, however, is that when Clarke's son gave his notes to Clarges, the pages were shuffled and

---

1 In fact there are two issues of *Pragmaticus* which include versions of Colchester: TT E.462[8], dated 29th August-5th September, and TT E.462[33], dated 5th-12th September. Both are numbered as issue 23. To distinguish them in this present work, E.462[33] is referred to Numb. 23[b]. It has a different masthead to that usually used by *Pragmaticus*, and may be a case of stolen identity by another publisher, but its news should not be discounted, as like *Pragmaticus* proper it appears to be firmly Royalist. It also contains several new details about the executions not found elsewhere.

2 Firth's version of Clarke's account can be found in *The Clarke Papers*, vol. II, pp.31-39.

they were filed incorrectly. Alternatively, this could have happened in an archival setting at any time between 1648 and when C. H. Firth edited the collection in the 1890s.

The events at the castle fall into three sections. First, the captives were taken to the castle from the King's Head, received the sacrament, and fell into an argument with Ireton over the legality of what was about to occur. Then they were taken to the castle yard, where more prayers took place and as custom dictated they were expected to offer their final thoughts to what appears to have been a large audience. Then came the executions.

Firth's edition of Clarke's account presents the events in a form similar to a play script, with intervening actions written in the manner of stage directions; this is the most obvious method, and was probably how Clarke wrote it up on the day. To preserve the conversations, and the immediacy of what happened, the account which follows is presented in the same way. It is not a straight rendering of Clarke, however. His shuffled notes have been split up into the individual sections of conversation which do form coherent blocks, and rearranged approximately according to the other eyewitness accounts; these contain many new details omitted by Clarke, which have been inserted in the appropriate place. Where the newsbooks are more explicit about what was said, their versions have been inserted instead: there is no reason why their eyewitnesses should be any less accurate than Clarke, as the same events were unfolding in front of everyone present, and in fact as he was writing at speed to get everything down, he may well have streamlined speech and omitted details in order to keep up. Gascoyne's speech in Clarke's version appears particularly disjointed, but apparently the Florentine's English pronunciation was terrible in any case, and it may be that Clarke did not have time to focus on much of what he said.[3] Clarendon, who must have encountered Gascoyne during the latter's sojourn in Paris with the exiled court in 1646-1647, and certainly would have met him at court after the Restoration, confirms that his English was basic.[4]

It must be stressed that the resulting account presented here is not intended as a definitive version of the order in which things happened, as the variance in the available sources, and the uncertainty of their reliability, makes that impossible to obtain. It is intended only as a fuller, and more accurate rendering of it than Clarke alone. Little of Carter's account is included: he was not an eyewitness to the executions as he was in the King's Head. Whilst the events were later related to him and the other officers by Norwich's chaplain, probably with other details inserted by Gascoyne, Lucas's adjutant, and Lisle's kinsman or servant, Carter only wrote up

---

3   Gascoyne's ODNB biographer, Roderick Clayton, presumably comes to his conclusion about his accent through study of his will and his extensive correspondence: at this period there was no fixed spelling and the majority of people wrote words as they thought they were pronounced. Thus, personal letters frequently give away regional or foreign accents.

4   Book XI, 1840 vol. VI, p.97.

his version two years later. The words and actions he attributes to Lisle and Lucas in particular are lifted straight from the 1648 newsbooks.[5]

Note: a superscript [C] indicates Clarke's text; [M] text from *The Moderate*; [P] text from *Mercurius Pragmaticus*; [S] text from 'Sir Charles Lucas His Last Speech'.[6] Firth includes a number of insertions in [square brackets]: presumably he found omissions or illegible text in Clarke's original. Insertions by the present author are in {curly brackets}.

'The Loyall Sacrifice'

Leaving the King's Head, Colonel Ewer escorted Lisle, Lucas and Gascoyne to Colchester Castle. Carter says it was 'nothing now but a Dungeon and the County Gaole': they were temporarily locked up there while arrangements were made for what was to follow. Ireton arrived to see them, and told them 'they must prepare themselves for death.' *The Moderate* tells us:

> his Excellency Commanded his Chaplain to administer comfort to their souls, and give them instructions to prepare for death; some of them desired to make an auricular Confession of all their sins, and desired absolution, which the Minister reproved them for, then they desired the Lord Gorings Chaplain, which was granted ...[7]

Carter relates that 'about an hower' after Lisle, Lucas and Gascoyne were escorted away by Colonel Ewer:

> came a Messenger from Sir Charls Lucas, to desire a Chaplaine to be immediately sent to him; which strook a dread sorrow into the hearts of all.[8]

The chaplain left for the castle accompanied by Lucas's adjutant William Hickes, and an unnamed kinsman or servant of Lisle's. Once there, *The Moderate* continues: Norwich's chaplain, it says:

> administered the Sacrament to them, and prayed with them a short time ...

---

5   Carter's account of the executions can be found at pp.194-200.
6   *The Moderate*, Numb. 8; *Mercurius Pragmaticus*, Numb. 33.
7   The request for auricular confession can only have come from Gascoyne, who as an Italian might be expected to be Catholic; indeed a subsequent account states that 'he had declared himself a Papist' (*A True and Exact Relation of the taking of Colchester ...*, p.3).
8   Carter, p.194.

Both Clarke and *The Moderate* record interjections from third parties during Lucas's argument with Ireton: it is possible that by this point the religious formalities were over, and the men had been taken outside. Meanwhile Colonels Whaley and Rainsborough had also arrived to witness the spectacle. When considering their responses in the following conversations, it is as well to bear in mind that all three Royalist men must have been in deep shock: they had not been expecting an execution, and now they were being given perhaps two or three hours to prepare for one. Lack of sleep over the previous few days, and lack of food during the previous weeks may also have affected their responses.

[C]**[Lucas]** Pray Gentlemen bee pleas'd to give a dyeing man leave to speak, I beseech you … I should very willingly hear, if you would please to satisfy my, by whom I am condemned, whether by my Lord Fairfax alone, or by a Councell of Warr; I beseech you to lett me know my judge.

[C]**[Ireton]** I may answer so far, as you were condemned by the Parliament, upon your own actions. [The war] wherein you have so voluntarily a second time engaged, hath rendred you in their judgement in generall your whole party deserving death, and your self is in some particular exception … Know, your self as all others that engage a second time against the Parliament are traitors and rebells, and they doe employ us as soldiers by authority from them to suppresse and destroy. Would you know our commission, it's that. Sir, you were here in armes, (the head), one of the heads of a great party; you have not yet had quarter given, not any of those gentlemen yonder, but by the Generall's demands of you, and by your commissioners consent to it, you were to render your selves att mercy; and for yourself you can't but know, because your commissioner came in to acquaint you with it, that by mercy it was meant to be free in the Generall's breast, without any obligation to the contrary, to put some of you to the sword, if he saw cause. Now as to any matter of judgement; neither the Generall nor any censure of the Councill hath pass'd in this businesse.

[C]**[Lucas]** Sir, it is a very nice point to take away a man's life, when there is a law in the Kingdome, which truely I must plead; and look to it [lest] my blood be upon you. I doe plead before you all the lawes of this Kingdome. I have fought with a commission from those who were my soveraignes, and from that commission I must justifie my action. For yeilding to mercy, wee must needs yeild to those in whose power we were then. I must starve or yeild. That yeilding of ours, all the world knows, was meer constraint.

[C]**[Ireton]** Wee take it for no other.

[C]**[Lucas]** If wee yeild ourselves unto you, if it be for our lives you should try us.

[C]**[Ireton]** If wee had taken it for any other then what you had voluntarily done upon confidence of the Generall's mercy.

[C]**[Lisle]** I am confident I did it upon that ground.

^C[**Ireton**] But now it is by constraint, and no otherwise. I did speak that that you may yet know there was no assurance of quarter given to any of you, and the Generall did expressly declare that he would be free to it.

^C[**Lisle**] Gentlemen, lay your hands seriously upon your breasts, you that were of the Council of Warr, and consider what it is to take away a man's life in this kind, that you may have nothing to rise against you hereafter.

^C[**Ireton**] Sir, wee have nothing more to add to that. But to what you said before: you know it is a certaine rule, that among armes the lawes are silent, and had not you by armes stopt the lawes of the land, you and other men might have had the justice of the lawes of the land; but you and others, by pretence of the lawes of the land, have stopt the current of judgement and law which wee had. When you are mett in armes there is no more reason for you to plead it then there hath been to many soldiers and officers of the Parliaments party, when they have mett some under your command, if they had pleaded the lawes of the land against them.

^M[**Lucas**] Was it ever known before that a man did suffer in cold blood in this kind?

^C[**Ensign**] May it please you Honour I will satisfy you –

^C[**Whaley**] Sir, shall I answer you for that. You have given us a president before, where there was Major Wanstead and about forty more, they submitted to mercy, and they hang'd up 14 of them. {Alternatively, ^M'doe you not remember that when we delivered up Froome (as I take it) to your selfe, upon faire quarter, you notwithstanding killed two of us with your owne hand, and hanged 14 in 40 more of us afterwards?'}

^C{**Interjection from two soldiers**} At St{inchcombe} he came in rageing, and swore a great oath, 'why should they have any more quarter, then wee had at Cannon-Froome.'

At this point *The Moderate* says that Lucas 'was silent, and could make no reply'. The incident Whaley referred to was genuine. It had occurred at Stinchcombe in Gloucestershire, in August 1645, when Lucas and Prince Rupert attacked a house where a party of Parliamentarians were sheltering; immediately they hanged a number of them, allegedly for no reason other than revenge. Lucas's alleged reference to Cannon Frome concerned an atrocity in June, where the Royalist garrison had been massacred by Scots; perhaps, in turn, in revenge for the massacre of Scots by the Royalists at the storming of Leicester in May.

Clarke's recording of Whaley's contribution to the conversation is fortunate: it explains a curious reference in the Royalist pamphlet *The Loyall Sacrifice* three months later, which states that when the council of war voted on whether to execute the men, Whaley:

is reported to have shewne himselfe more generously disposed, (notwith-standing that former disgust betwixt him and Sir George Lisle) in diss-wading the Generall from this inconsiderate Act …[9]

There is absolutely no evidence that Lisle and Whaley had ever met before Colchester, let alone that they had had some sort of altercation. As discussed else-where, they may have met briefly at Hampton Court, but any violent disagreement between them – both being well known on their respective sides – would surely have come to notice. Almost certainly the reference to Lisle is a mistake, and in fact the pamphlet was referring to Lucas. 'Disgust' would be an appropriate word for Whaley's feelings about the events at Stinchcombe in 1645, which judging by his and the soldiers' comments to Lucas about it, had left a very deep impression. Eventually Lucas answered them.

[C]**[Lucas]** If the Generall pleases, a man may be mercifull, and satisfy both his mercy, and the world besides, and justice. I doe here beseech the Generall that he will be pleased to look upon mee in that nature as I am in his power, that he will excuse mee with my life, if I can but obtaine the General's mercy and favour [to me] and these gentlemen; and if it be not, God's will be done, I must submit to it … [S]I have something which I would impart unto His Excellency, what I hope may give him such satisfaction, as may cause this bloody cloud to bee removed from over my head.

What knowledge Lucas possessed which he thought might save him, Lisle and Gascoyne is not known. Ireton was not interested in letting him take it to Fairfax, however.

[C]**[Ireton]** I have no more to say to you, nor is there any other judgement that wee have received from the Generall, but you being persons who being in armes and hostility against the Parliament, he may as justly kill and give no quarter to you as ever any was in this warr. He having given you no assurance of quarter nor any of you, has only determined to yourselves in particular, that you are not in the compasse of quarter. Tis no more then if the soldiers mett you and shot you.

[C]**[Lucas]** I am within the lawes of the Kingdome, for what I did is by commission, and quarter hath been given as the lawes of armes doth require elsewhere.

[C]**[Ireton]** Sir, you are better acquainted with the lawes of armes. Is any body bound to give quarter where it is ask'd?

[C]**[Lisle]** I have given many hundred men quarter.

[C]**[Ireton]** You being a traitor –

9   *The Loyall Sacrifice*, p.77.

[C]**[Lucas]** I am no traitor, but a true subject to my King, and the lawes of the Kingdome. Sir, you ought to prove mee one, before you condemne mee to be a traitor.

[C]**[Ireton]** Wee tell you what judgement you are concluded by, and that is by the judgement of the Parliament.

[P]**[Lucas]** Alas poore soules, how you deceive yourselves! But we that are conquered must be what you please to make us … [C] I can say no more. I shall only desire that my life may satisfy for all the rest of these gentlemen, and these gentlemen may goe free.

This lengthy argument perfectly exemplifies a central issue of both the Civil Wars: the question of authority. Ireton argued that Lucas had disobeyed Parliament, Lucas that he had a commission from the King. To Ireton, Lucas was a traitor; to Lucas, Ireton was a traitor. Both repeatedly reiterated their arguments, but ultimately the only winner would be the man able to physically force his own victory: in this case, Ireton.

At this point, Carter says, Lucas:

> desired time till the next morning, as to settle some things in this World, so especially to prepare and fit his Soul for another …

The request was denied; Lucas objected.

[P]**[Lucas]** Doe not think I wish this out of any desire to live, or escape that death I am doom'd to; for I scorne to take a life at your hands, but I have some addresses to make to God above, and also to some relations here below, if I might have but a little more time, but since it will not be, the will of God be done, and I am ready for Execution.

Carter continues:

> Sir George Lisle said very little, only in the like manner desired a little respite, that he might write to his Father and Mother; but was also denied.

According to *The Moderate*, Lucas was then told to 'prepare his soul for another world.' In Clarke's version he responded, 'Give mee leave to pray with these gentlemen'. *The Moderate* says he now entered into a private meeting, and Clarke that he retired with Lisle and Gascoyne. It is clear that they were outside in the castle yard.

[C]**[Lisle]** [To the minister] If you have the means to see his Majestie present my duty to him, he is my Prince and Master. Bid my parents and friends they should not afflict themselves. Truly I think it is a great deal of happinesse to mee [to die thus]. God might have taken mee away without such a sense of my sins. They know my genius would not let mee die upon any base thing; bid them blesse God, that I die so happy for the service of my country, as I believe I have, and have the honour of it.

In Firth's edition of Clarke's notes, this piece of speech and the exchange with Captain Packer which follows, are attributed to Sir Charles Lucas. However, it cannot be him: the speaker refers to his parents, and both of Lucas's parents were dead. Moreover, Lisle had been unable to write a letter to his parents himself, and it makes sense that he was forced to attempt a verbal message via a third party. The reference to 'my genius' seems to refer to a guardian spirit or angel: as noted elsewhere, Lisle had been incredibly lucky to survive the wars as long as he had, and it is understandable that he had come to believe that something or someone was watching over him. The speech is typically Lisle, referring to his duty to the King before anything else.

^C[**Lisle**] [To the officers] What is the death that is pleas'd to be assign'd to my self and these worthy gentlemen? doe you know by what means?
^C[**Captain Packer**] That which is most proper to soldiers, to be shot.
^C[**Lisle**] With all my heart, shoote mee out of a cannon when they please.

The conversation now returns to Lucas and Gascoyne, who are talking to Norwich's chaplain.

^C[**Lucas**] I confesse the great obligation our country owes to you, for your service to our Prince.
^C[**Gascoyne**] It is a very great consolation to mee for to die with such a companion. I did no man any hurt.
^C[**Lucas**] There may be something that I may vindicate my self in. In order to my duty, I came to this place in the Prince's service, but since I came hither, I am not guilty of wronging the least person the least soldier of this army. God knowes I never intended my owne particular in my life, and if God Almighty had pleas'd as for my sins I doe justly deserve death, but for this God Almighty is the best judge; yet I should have been very glad, that those people that made themselves my judges had been pleas'd to have allow'd me a longer time of repentance, for the best of us all hath not liv'd such a life but he does deserve a longer time of repentance then I have now.
^C[**Minister**] If it be true, it is as acceptable.
^C[**Lucas**] My sins are many, and Gods mercies are great that I doe expect. All those that have either kindnesse for the King, or so much conscience for themselves, I shall desire that they would be pleased to let me have their prayers. For what God hath bestow'd upon mee in this life, I praise him, and pray for his mercy upon mee after this life. I doe not professe my self a rhetorician att all. I doe

not know how it may be construed, but in the first place, I wish I could have liv'd longer, to have serv'd my Prince and my country, or at least [had] a larger time of repentance. But [since it] hath pleas'd …. to allow mee the means to receive the Sacrament, God make mee a worthy receiver, to my salvation, not my damnation; and so God blesse you all, and send you peace and happinesse in the Kingdome.

^c[**Gascoyne**] I would very faine take my leave of Sir Charles Lucas, for I care not how soon, when it shall please those God hath made my judges –

^c[**Lucas**] Farewell, Sir Bernard.

They embrace and kiss.

Gascoyne's reprieve does not seem to have come until after his colleagues were dead, but it only came about at all because, like Lisle, he wanted to write a letter. Clarendon, who as noted would have had ready access to Gascoyne and his recollections, says the Italian had:

only English enough to make himself understood, that he desired a pen and ink and paper, that he might write a letter to his prince the great duke, that his highness might know in what manner he lost his life, to the end his heirs might possess his estate. The officer that attended the execution thought fit to acquaint the general and the council, without which he durst no allow him pen and ink, which he thought he might reasonably demand: when they were informed of it, they thought it a matter worthy some consideration; they had chosen him out of the list for his quality, conceiving him to be an English gentleman, and preferred him for being a knight, that they might sacrifice three of that rank.[10]

Whether Gascoyne made this request inside the castle or out in the yard is uncertain, but it was probably the latter: whilst the man Lisle asked for pen and paper refused it outright, he whom Gascoyne asked decided to check with Fairfax. *The Moderate* states that Gascoyne actually did write his letter, but this seems unlikely: it would not make sense that he should be allowed to and Lisle not. Moreover, on this occasion Clarendon – who probably heard all this from Gascoyne, or perhaps Hickes – is undoubtedly the more reliable source. Clarendon records that Gascoyne's request and the hurrying of this request to Fairfax, delayed the proceedings at the castle.

This delay brought the news of this bloody resolution to the prisoners in the town; who were infinitely afflicted with it; and the Lord Capel

---

10 Book XI, 1840 vol. VI, p.97. Gascoyne, a Florentine, was personally close to the Medicis: his 'master' would have been Ferdinando II, the Grand Duke of Tuscany.

prevailed with an officer, or soldier, of their guard, to carry a letter, signed by the chief persons and officers, and in the name of the rest, to the general; in which they took notice of that judgement, and desired him 'either to forbear the execution of it, or that they might all, who were equally guilty with those three, undergo the same sentence with them.' The letter was delivered, but had no other effect than the sending to the officer to despatch his order, reserving the Italian to the last.

Only Clarendon offers this story, which again may have been insider information. Meanwhile, in the castle yard, everything was on hold, and the condemned men talked among themselves. The accuracy of the following passage requires scrutiny, however. The tone, and straightforward structure of the sentences beginning 'Come, my heart', and 'I will not say' sounds suspiciously like Lisle, rather than Lucas; furthermore, 'I do not apprehend death, but I can look him in the face now', which is attributed to Lucas, contradicts the subsequent speech – which is definitely Lucas – in which he says he had already 'often look't death in the face'. Whilst these attributions to Lucas are doubtful, there is presently no specific evidence available to justify changing them.

[c][**Lucas**] Come, my heart, I need not cheer you up, I know your chearfulnesse by my owne, but here is my amends, I die for my Prince, and you did not soe.

[c][**Gascoyne**] I thank God, I doe not fear death.

[c][**Lucas**] I will not say I do not apprehend death, but I can look him in the face now.

[c][**Gascoyne**] I wish to die, and repent of my sins.

[c][**Lucas**] You have God's word for it, if I may speak a divines part in it, [that] at what time [soever] a sinner does repent …

[c][**Minister**] Hee that repents truely and properly.

[c][**Gascoyne**] I could say so, wheras you repent: from the bottom of my heart I have not found so sorrowfull as it need to bee.

[c][**Lisle**] Better late than never. Though I don't believe in predestination, yet I believe it is God's will, and truly I should have thought myself a happy person, if I could live to have a larger time of repentance, and to see the King my master in his throne again, whom I beseech God to send all the happinesse which is due to so just, so good a man. I was bid to goe my way, say divers people; but truely I was confident my innocencie in this action would have rendred mee very clear from any such punishment, especially so suddenly.

[c][**Gascoyne**] My conscience is guilty of many things, but nothing in this way. I say that I have never in my life done any action which I will not acknowledge before all the world.

[c][**Lisle**] He will that his body remaine with my servant … I will beare it with as much patience as I can, I should take it for a very great favour done to my poor soul to have a little more time, I have deserve'd it as much as any enemy can doe.

The message must now have arrived from Fairfax, telling the presiding officer to get on with the executions and to at least dispatch the first two men: Lucas was now told that he was to be the first to die. *Pragmaticus* alleges that he told Ireton, Whaley and Rainsborough that:

> he had often look't death in the face both publique and private, and now they should see he was not afraid to die.

[C][**Lucas**] {To Lisle and Gascoyne} Gentlemen, I now die like a soldier, will you that these gentlemen shall looke upon mee?
They embrace and kiss.
[C][**Lucas**] Remember mee to all my friends.
[C][**Gascoyne**] I thank God I am no more troubled at it.

It was around 7 p.m., precisely sunset on that late August day in 1648, that Lucas walked out to a spot in the centre of the yard behind the castle.

[S][**Lucas**] Good people, I am now to pay that debt which wee all owe, every man must dye, that is most certaine, but how, or when is not knowne to any, It is my chance now, (although unhappily in blood) none of you know when it will be any of your turnes. As for my offence it is (you all know) for maintaining His Majesties Cause, which hath been according to my judgement, and I beleeve that I went the right way, And I am sure I was firme to that Cause I undertook. But seeing I must dye, and that there is no way to obtaine mercy, but that I must now finish my course in this way, to which I beseech Almighty God to assist me, to dye with comfort in my Saviour. I bequeath my soule into the hands of my Maker, God the Father, Son, and Holy Ghost, three Persons, and one God; Oh! doe thou my Lord God almighty (for my blessed Saviour the Lord Jesus sake) receive my soule to eternall glory. I have lived a Protestant and a Protestant here I dye, in the faith of the Church of England, that hath beene established so many yeares. As for my body, I doe desire you that it may be decently carried to my owne house, and that my friends may have liberty to interre it with my Ancestors, and set it in the vault of the Church where they were laide before me; And in the interim, that there bee no incivillity offered to my body here, when I am dead, and that my corps may remaine quiet without molestation when it is carried away. As for these Souldiers who stand ready to shoot me, I yeeld my life to their hands, and I pray God to forgive them, I do freely from my heart forgive them. {Alternatively, [C] Remember me to all my friends, and tell them that I have died in a good cause; if I have offended any, I desire forgiveness; I would have a decent buriall, and that I might be buried by my ancestours, and where they are. Their monuments are not only defac't, but their dead bodies remov'd. Let us from henceforth lye in quiet. I pray God forgive you all, I pray God forgive you, gentlemen. Farewell, I pray

God vengeance may not fall on you for it. When I shall [fall] lay mee downe decently.}

In the first few lines, Lucas seems to have been talking to acquaintances in the crowd. Undoubtedly, being a native of Colchester, there were many there, but we know of two in particular. *The Loyall Sacrifice*, written three months later, speaks of a male servant in the crowd, and *Mercurius Elencticus*, another Royalist newsbook, deploring the haste of the executions, rues the fact that Lucas had:

> not one minute … wherein to salute his sweet (but sorrowful) Lady with the last Lines of a Dying-man …[11]

Clarke records that Lucas asked 'leave to pray but a few words', and knelt for a moment; then he stood again. Someone went to pull down his cap, and he stopped them, saying 'Stay a little'; then, 'Now I have done.' Opening his doublet, he said 'Father, Sonne, and holy Ghost receive my soule!'; *Pragmaticus* claims he cried out 'now Rebells doe your worst!'

Then, Clarke says:

> six dragoones with fire locks discharg'd att him …

Carter:

> they immediatly fired at him and shot him in foure places, so that he was suddainly dead.

The Loyall Sacrifice records that:

> His sorrowful Servant, a sad spectator of his Death, was surprized with such passion for the losse of so deare a Master, as he earnestly besought those Executioners to dispatch him too: for life was to him a torment.

Whether this was Adjutant Hickes, is not clear; certainly Lucas's mistress's response was not recorded, and she is not mentioned anywhere else in the sources. Carter continues:

> Sir George Lisle his turne being next, (being before carried a little aside, that he might not see his Friend fall) was brought to the place to perform the conclusive part of this bloody scene.

---

11   *The Loyall Sacrifice*, pp.78-79; *Mercurius Elencticus*, Numb. 41.

According to *The Moderate*, Lisle now spoke to the crowd for the first time, saying:

> he hath acted only as a souldier, and to do his gracious King that service which all good subjects … ought to do.

This annoyed someone listening, who responded that Lisle:

> would improve that short time to the best advantage, there was but a moment between him & death and it was not the name of all the Kings of the world, or their Cause, would save his poor soul, and desired him to depend upon the mercies of the King of Kings, who was able to do him good, and save his soule by faith, and repentance in his Son Christ Jesus. And that he would be much comfort to those about him, to hear something of God from him.

The Moderate adds, of Lisle, 'This advise tooke little with him …'; however he briefly retreated to the wall to pray with Norwich's chaplain, then:

> come to the place of execution, and told the people, he was as willing to die, as they were to see his death, one answered, they were glad if God had prepared him for it.

At this point all the sources agree that Lisle knelt and kissed Lucas's body; however there is much variance in the details of what followed. *Pragmaticus*:

> Sir George Lisles turn was next, who beholding the dead body of his dearest Friend, fell upon it and kissed it, as if he meant to breath into it another soule; and … made a Funerall Oration over it, concerning the vertues in him, of which the Nation was not worthy …

November's *The Loyall Sacrifice* records a part of what Lisle said, which does not appear in any form elsewhere, and so probably came from a lost September newsbook:

> Often he would redouble these words: In how short a moment has a brave spirit expired! well; this priority was due to thee, but I shall not be long behind thee: my death which is now at hand, shall restore thee to me. This, with the assured hopes I have in Him that made me, shall make my translation cheerfull. My divorce from such a friend injoyned me to hasten to him. It is not death I fear, had I a thousand lives, I should willingly Sacrifice them all, to confirme my Loyalty.

The Moderate omits most of this, but includes and rephrases the last section in the third person: '[he said] if he had 1000 Lives more he would think them all too little to suffer for his Maiesty.' What *The Loyall Sacrifice* meant by Lisle 'redoubling' his words seems painfully clear: he was fighting to control his stammer. Despite the hostility of the situation, however – shock at imminent death, hunger, tiredness, a heckling crowd, Lucas lying dead but open-eyed in front of him[12] – he brazened it out. Naturally all the Royalist newsbooks were fulsome:

> he also was dispatched, as he stood in an heroick posture, courting grim death with a broad face and a greedy expectation.
>
> No Roman ever died more untroubled or dreadlesse of death …
>
> They both dyed with unutterable comfort and Courage: never Romane with more spirit, nor ever Christian with greater hope and confidence in his sufferings.[13]

Even Parliamentarian stalwart the *Kingdomes Weekly Intelligencer* says of Lisle that:

> without any sence of feare he seem'd to invite and welcome his approaching death.[14]

The Moderate Intelligencer was less impressed, claiming that 'after prayer by himselfe', Lisle:

> exprest a desire of speedy execution, more desperate then Romane.[15]

It is probably this comment which *Mercurius Elencticus*, writing a week later, countered with 'No Roman ever died more untroubled …'; however it is just possible the *Intelligencer* might be hinting at Lisle asking the firing squad to step closer, otherwise which incident only Clarendon, in the 1670s, takes notice of.

After kneeling by the body, *Pragmaticus* says, Lisle:

> stood up, and taking five peices of Gold out of his Pocket (which was all he had left) he gave one to his Executioners, and the other foure he sent to foure friends in London.

---

12   In a petition to Charles II in 1660, Adjutant Hickes wrote that after the shootings he had walked over to the bodies and closed Lucas's eyes; he also managed to burn his papers, 'which concerned the lives and fortunes of many persons of quality,' (*CSP Domestic Series*, 1660-1661, p.162).

13   *Mercurius Pragmaticus*, Numb. 23, no page numbers; *The Parliament Porter*, Numb. 2, p.8; *Mercurius Elencticus*, Numb. 41, p.332.

14   Numb. 275, p.1067.

15   Numb. 180, back page.

One newsbook claims that the money sent to his friends was in fact 'a 5s peece of gold broken in foure peeces': this is a very specific detail that no casual observer could discern from a watching crowd, which suggests it came from someone who knew him and was near him at the time. If true, breaking a piece of gold was not something that could be done on the spot, and indicates what at least partly occupied him since being locked up in the castle that afternoon.[16]

Clarke records that Lisle then turned to 'his Kinsman' and said 'Present my duty to my father'; Carter's version elaborates slightly, saying:

> he gave one of them to his Executioners, and the rest to a Gentleman then standing by (who formerly had been his servant) to deliver as his last Legacy to some friends in London, with some filial expressions of duty to his Father and Mother, and recommendations to some other friends.

Elencticus notes that the gold was handed to his acquaintance:

> not without speciall notice taken of their Names to whom he sent it, that they might be revenged on them also.

In this *Elencticus* appears to be accurate: Anthony Thelwall and two other men were arrested in London the next day, and two weeks later a fourth man, Thomas Foster, was investigated in London by the Committee for the Advance of Money, for allegedly holding funds belonging to Lisle.[17] Thelwall's arrest may be coincidence, but getting a message sixty miles from Colchester to London within twenty-four hours was perfectly possible: for weeks the London newsbooks had been printing siege information that was scarcely a day old. Thelwall was another unshakeable Royalist who knew Lisle well, and given the timings the odds are high that he was one of the friends to whom Lisle sent a farewell piece of gold. Whether he actually received it, however, or whether some agent of Parliament's intervened in the delivery, is another matter.[18] Sadly, the identity of Lisle's kinsman or 'former servant' is not known; or whether he played any part in the siege which later led to his own imprisonment.

As by now we would expect, Lisle was not going to go meekly. *Pragmaticus* describes how, despite the overwhelmingly hostile situation, he turned furiously on the crowd:

---

16 *Perfect Occurrences of Every Daie Journal*, Numb. 87. p.644. *Mercurius Elencticus* also states that it was a broken piece of gold, but *Elencticus* was published the week after, and may have been borrowing from *Perfect Occurrences*.

17 13th September; *Calendar of the Proceedings of the Committee for the Advance of Money*, Part II, p.948.

18 Why Thelwall was in London is not known, but it is likely that he participated in Owen's failed rebellion in Wales earlier in the year, and may have already been on Parliament's 'wanted' list.

Oh, how many do I see here about me, whose lives I have saved in hot blood; and now must mine be taken away in cold blood most barbarously! Sure, the like was never heard of among the Goths and Vandals, or the veryest Barbarians in the world in any age. But what dare not these Rebells and Traitors doe, that have imprisoned, and could willingly cut the throat of their King?

Carter, almost precisely echoing *The Loyall Sacrifice*, adds:

… For whose deliverance from His Enemies, and Peace to this unfortunate Nation, I dedicate my last prayers to Heaven. Now then Rebells and Traitors do your worst to me!

According to *Pragmaticus*, the last things Lisle said were 'a few Invocations upon the name of Jesus', and this is most likely to be the case; but it is Clarendon, in 1671, who provides another set of 'famous last words', for which Lisle has become famous, and which would entirely suit a final, scathing attack on his enemies. Where Clarendon found them is not known but they do not seem to have been copied from any surviving newsbook, and if genuine, may have been something he heard privately: the most obvious source would be Bernard Gascoyne.

[Lisle] looked those who were to execute him in the face; and thinking they stood at too great a distance, spake to them to come nearer; to which one of them said, 'I'll warrant you, sir, we'll hit you:' he answered smiling, 'Friends, I have been nearer you, when you have missed me.'[19]

The Kingdomes Weekly Intelligencer asserts that this was 'about halfe an houre' after Lucas's death, which if true means that it would now be getting dark; this would certainly explain why Lisle asked the dragoons to step closer.[20] Commanding such men was his speciality, and if anyone knew the effects of darkness and distance on a man's ability to hit a target in the correct place, it was him. He had also seen enough men terribly wounded by shot, to know he did not want to suffer the same way.

But, realistically, there was little chance they would miss. Clarendon adds:

Thereupon, they all fired upon him, and did their work home, so that he fell down dead of many wounds without speaking a word.

19   Book XI, 1840, vol. VI, p.98.
20   *Mercurius Civicus*, Numb. 275, p.1067.

18

Epilogue

… Each a Colosse of Honor was, and strid
Or'e Trophee's higher than a Pyramid.
Their Foes (more monstrous than what Affrick bred)
Insulted when these noble Victimes bled;
Whilst they were glad their Souls were Ushers made
To march in Glory 'fore the Royall Shade.
Malice thy work is done, While this sad Isle
New Seas surround for Lucas and for Lisle.'

Matthew Carter, 1650

Final indignities

According to the *Kingdomes Weekly Intelligencer* in 1661, it was the house of the Colchester town Recorder

> [to] which the Corps of those two Noble Knights were first brought, after they had been so basely murther'd and stripp'd; when the language of those Butchers was, Now make much of your great Friends.[1]

We only have the *Intelligencer*'s word for it that the bodies were looted, and its report was written at the height of public fervour following Charles II's restoration when an emotive story about the martyrdom of Lisle and Lucas would be perfectly in vogue. That is not to say that the story is untrue, however. In 1648 the Recorder was moderate Parliamentarian Sir Harbottle Grimston: it is unlikely that he was in the house at the time, as he was also a member of the Essex Committee which had been released from the town a few hours earlier. Who received the bodies, or found them, or reported their condition, is not known; however as the other Royalist officers were presently in custody and could not have seen them, it is likely that the

---

1   No. 24, 10th-17th June 1661. Not in the British Library collection.

details came from someone in the town who had, and the inhabitants had nothing to gain by making up such a story. Bodies were routinely stripped on the battle-field by soldiers and civilians alike, looking for loot and good quality clothing, but to permit it after a formal execution of two knights of the realm, subsequently dumping the bodies with sympathisers – which is what the *Intelligencer* seems to suggest was the case – stands out as a new low, particularly from someone as customarily sensitive to honour and to military formalities as Sir Thomas Fairfax. The *Intelligencer* does not say where the bodies were then buried, but presumably the location was well known as they were reburied in 1661.[2]

Evening, 28th August

For some hours Matthew Carter had been waiting in the King's Head with the peers and the rest of the senior officers. Eventually the chaplain, Hickes, and Gascoyne returned, and possibly Lisle's man; the chaplain told everyone what had happened. As night fell, Ireton, Whaley and Ewer came to the upper room in the King's Head. Saluting the lords, they told them:

> They were sent from the Generall, to them, and the rest of the Gentlemen, to tell them that now (for they supposed it was not unknown what had been done) he did give them an assurance of what before they held doubt-full: faire quarter as Prisoners of Warre.[3]

Clarendon states that Fairfax was there also, although this seems highly unlikely, as Carter was actually in the room at the time, and would certainly have mentioned him.[4] Capel gave the officers short shrift: refusing to thank them, he said:

> They should have given the Generall more thanks if he had saved the lives of those two Knights, whom they had already executed, then for the grant of their own; … that their conditions in relation to the service, and their owne yet alive, were alike, and all equally concern'd in the managing of that designe, and it was their desire to have run all one hazard …

Clarendon adds that:

2 Possibly they had been interred at St Giles all along, as John Lucas had put himself under Parliament's protection in 1648 and remained in favour, making an initial burial in the family vault perfectly possible (David Appleby, pers. comm. 21st March 2016). Moreover, for what it is worth, Lucas had himself requested that he be interred there.
3 Carter, pp.201-202.
4 Book XI, 1840 vol. 6, p.100.

there were two or three such sharp and bitter replies between him and Ireton, that cost him his life in few months after.

Again, however, Clarendon was not there, and it may be that he supposed that an argument must have happened, to justify blaming Ireton for Capel's execution in March. In fact it was a Parliamentary vote which decided Capel's fate, although how much influence Ireton may have had on that vote is a matter beyond the scope of this book. However, he and his colleagues were certainly 'displeased', Carter says: they left the room, and shortly afterwards the lords present and some other officers were separated and taken to a different house.

It is unclear what had happened to Colonel Farr: he had either escaped in the confusion of the surrender or found his way out of the King's Head later, presumably in the latter case, after the list of names had been sent to Fairfax. Carter notes that he:

> escaped also the judgement the other two underwent; but was afterwards taken, and sent with a guard, to his owne quarters, and there kept close prisoner till the remove of the rest.[5]

A London newsbook reported the next day that:

> Col. Farrer made an escape, but is since found in a ditch, I beleeve his turn will be next.[6]

Local man William Osborne, writing to his wife on the 29th, confirms that Farr was found 'in a kill in the town', a 'kill' being a riverbed or drainage channel.[7]

On 8th September the House of Commons received a letter from Colonel Whaley at Colchester, requesting that proceedings be initiated against renegade Parliamentarian officers, 'and especially against Lieutenant Colonell Farre.' Despite Parliament ordering that he should be 'left to his Excellence to suffer in the same manner', Farr avoided execution: allegedly by claiming he was acting under the orders of the Earl of Warwick, whereupon the trial was deferred in order not to offend Warwick, who was the Parliament's Admiral.[8] The case seems to have been dropped, and Farr was noted to be alive in 1665.[9]

5   Carter, p.202.
6   29th August; *Perfect Occurrences of Every Daie Journall*, Numb. 87, p.644. Repeated word for word in *Packets of Letters*, although Lisle is wrongly named as 'Sir Robert Lisle' (issue unnumbered, but last date in the letters is 29th August; TT E.461[29]).
7   Sir Henry Ellis (ed.), *Original Letters Illustrative of English History*, pp.272-273.
8   *Mercurius Elencticus*, Numb. 42, p.342.
9   Whaley's letter, JHC, 6, 1648-1651, p.10; p.1070; Parliament's order, *The Kingdomes Weekly Intelligencer*, Numb. 275, p.1070 and *The Moderate*, Numb. 8, p.53; Farr's survival, Newman, *Royalist Officers in*

From soldiers to martyrs

On 29th August Fairfax wrote a letter to the Earl of Manchester, Speaker of the House of Lords, to explain his actions:

> My Lord:
> I have herewith sent you the Articles, with the Explanations annexed, upon which it hath pleased God in his best time to deliver the Town of Colchester, and the enemy therein unto your hands without further bloudshed, saving that (for some satisfaction to Military Justice, and in part of avenge for the innocent bloud they have caused to be spilt, and the trouble, damage, and mischiefe they have brought upon the Towne, this Country, and the Kingdome) I have with the advice of a Counsell of Warre of the chiefe Officers both of the Country Forces and the Army, caused two of them who were rendred at mercy to be shot to death before any of them had Quarter assured them. The persons pitched upon for this example were, Sir Charles Lucas, and Sir George Lisle, in whose Military execution I hope your Lordships will not find cause to thinke your Honour or Justice prejudiced. As for the Lord Goring, Lord Capell, and the rest of the persons rendred to mercy, and now assured of Quarter; of whose names I have sent your Lordships a particular List. I doe hereby render to the Parliaments judgement for further publique Justice and Mercy to be used as you shall see cause …[10]

If he expected support, it was not forthcoming: a member stood up and said:

> Mr Speaker I for my part know (whatsoever is pretended otherwise in this Letter) that, neither Towne nor Country desired any severity toward those Gentlemen, nor doe they receive any content or satisfaction in it; and therefore I suppose it was wholly an Act of Revenge, and I feare out of a more private consideration, than publique.[11]

He was supported by a fellow MP who believed that:

> executing these 2. Knights now, was done on purpose to put an affront upon the Treaty, and to grieve and exasperate his Majesty.[12]

England and Wales, p.128.

10   *A Letter From his Excellency the Lord Fairfax … Concerning the Surrender of Colchester …*, p.1.

11   *Mercurius Pragmaticus*, Numb. 23, no page numbers.

12   The 'treaty' was the latest attempt at negotiated settlement between Parliament and the King; it had been forced on Westminster by the Scottish threat to declare war unless it reopened negotiations.

The Royalist newsbooks were having none of it, either. Fairfax was now 'that scorne of true Gallantry' and 'that matchlesse and bloody Traytor and Tyrant', Parliament 'the Mercilesse Juncto'; Lisle and Lucas were 'most Glorious and blessed martyres', an 'incomperable Paire of gallant soules', a 'maitchlesse paire of Worthies'. Their execution was 'savage murther', 'An act so unsouldierlike, unworthy and barbarous, that it will heap eternal Infamy on the heads of their brutish Executioners ...'[13] A shocking alternative version of the executions which appeared in two Royalist newsbooks – that Lucas was tied to a post and murdered by two soldiers, and Lisle pistolled in the head – can only have inflamed such emotions further.[14] The Royalist authors already thumbed their noses at the pursuing censors by prefacing each edition with pithy multi-verse poems critical of the Parliament; after the siege they held nothing back:

> ... What need they Lawes, whilst to their will,
> They can reduce all Parties :
> And rob, imprison, torture, kill,
> 'gainst whomsoe're their heart is?
> They slight all good the Treaty brings,
> Bid Fig for all offences,
> They weare the Sword; what need they Kings,
> When every Pimpe a Prince is?[15]

Courtesy of the newsbooks, public arguments about the legality of the killings were soon flying. Parliamentarians argued about the specifics of the rules of war, and what Fairfax had and had not offered to his captives; Royalists objected that the act was gratuitous, unnecessary and inhumane, particularly in respect of the haste with which the executions were conducted. As suggested earlier, an appropriate description for this fraught axis might be, 'the rules of war versus the rules of decency': the complete commander was expected to apply a balance of both, to ensure both justice and compassion. As the Royalist soldier Edmund Verney put it, in a letter of 20th September:

> Now let any person judge whither thiss answer and exposition of mercy did not implicitly promise lyfe to all, but it wass a high tyranny to bring thiss extreame into his power, for ass every gentleman and souldyer iss obliged to a punctuall observance of the trust committed to him by defending

13   *Mercurius Elencticus*, Numb. 41, pp.332-333; *Mercurius Pragmaticus, op. cit.*
14   *The Parliament Porter*, Numb. 1, p.3; *Mercurius Pragmaticus*, Numb. 23[b], no page numbers. *Pragmaticus* appeared the week after *The Parliament Porter*, and may have borrowed from it, although it omits the part about Lisle being pistolled. The alternative execution story contradicts all the eyewitness accounts of the events behind the castle, and appears to be nothing but lurid hearsay.
15   *Mercurius Elencticus*, Numb. 42, cover.

to hiss utmost all persons, townes, and forts under hiss command, soe there is a civill and honourable custome, and soe authenticke that it may not improperly be called a lawe, amongst souldyers to give noble and honourable conditions to theire enemy though in the greatest straight and necessity.[16]

At Colchester the Parliamentarians argued that the Royalists had either broken the rules of war or had misunderstood their application, whereas the Royalist objection was that Fairfax had not made any consideration towards decency, or what Verney called the 'civill and honourable custome'. Lucas reminded Ireton that:

I must starve or yeild. That yeilding of ours, all the world knows, was meer constraint.

In other words, he had physically no choice but to agree to whatever harsh surrender terms were offered: it was that or die of hunger, the implication being that Fairfax intended to shoot starving men who had submitted to him in the expectation of human compassion, if not forgiveness. Regarding quarter, Ireton's question 'Is any body bound to give quarter where it is ask'd?' and Lisle's response, 'I have given many hundred men quarter' exemplifies the conflict: the rules of war do not automatically require quarter, whereas decency expects that a man's life and health is wherever possible preserved. In this instance Ireton acknowledged only the one code; Lisle only the other.

Echoing Lucas's argument that his commission made his being in arms entirely lawful, *Elencticus* asked:

I would gladly know the offence of these Gentlemen. Was it for levying Forces to release the King from his base Imprisonment? They did but their Duty, and indeavoured no more but what … the generality of the Kingdome so much thirst after: and what the Lawes of the Land doe justifie them in. Was it to preserve their Religion, their Lawes, their Liberties? That's no more then at first the Rebells themselves pretended their Armies to be Raised for against the King. And if (for these ends) it was thought lawfull for them to Rebell against their King: Certainly it is much more lawfull for these men to resist their Fellow-Subjects that are about to destroy not onely our Religion, Lawes, and Liberties, but the King also and all such as adhere to him for the Preservation thereof.[17]

---

16 *Memoirs of the Verney Family*, 1892, vol. II, pp.338-339.
17 Numb. 41, 1648, p.333.

The broadest reasons offered for the executions were 'exemplary justice', and as *The Kingdomes Weekly Intelligencer* put it, to give 'some satisfaction to Revenge for the losse of so many lives during the siege …'[18] In a later vindication of his own conduct, not published until long after his death, Fairfax added that whilst the captive peers were turned over to the Houses of Parliament, whom he called 'proper judges in their case', Lisle and Lucas were 'mere soldiers of fortune, and falling into our hands by chance of war, were executed.'[19] This contradicts Clarendon's story that they and Gascoyne were picked purely because they were knights, and it is difficult to know who to believe: Clarendon had probably spoken to Gascoyne himself, and possibly other men who were present, whereas although Fairfax would of course know perfectly well why the men were chosen, he was writing a self-serving justification for his actions and would naturally say whatever he could to minimise their status.

Lucas was also accused of breaking his parole: having compounded after the First Civil War and exchanged letters with Fairfax and his secretary, to confirm that he had done so. When at Colchester Fairfax labelled him a parole-breaker, Lucas responded tartly that after compounding he had lived peaceably in London, until:

> there was a price set upon me by the Committee of Derby House, upon which I was constrained to retire myself into my own country, and to my native town, for refuge …[20]

Furthermore, *Mercurius Pragmaticus* claimed he knew of:

> certain Grudges boyling in the breast of the Generall against that noble Knight, because of a defeat which he gave him heretofore in the North …[21]

Fairfax's personal issues with Lucas, then, real or presumed, were the favoured reason of the Royalist newsbooks for the latter's execution. No accusations of parole-breaking are made against Lisle: this suggests that either he had avoided compounding and therefore had no parole to break, or that he was financially such a small fish that the Committee for Compounding had barely registered his presence and had not chased up his fine. There is not a hint of personal animosity with Fairfax or his primary officers either, besides the reference in *The Loyall Sacrifice* to a spat with Whaley, which as discussed elsewhere, was almost certainly

---

18   *The Perfect Weekly Account*, Numb. 25, no page numbers; *The Kingdomes Weekly Intelligencer*, Numb. 275, 1648, cover.

19   'Short Memorials of Thomas, Lord Fairfax'. Reprinted in *Select Tracts Relating to the Civil Wars in England*, vol. II. Lisle and Lucas, p.449.

20   Bell, vol. II, pp.56-57. Lucas was mistakenly thought to be fighting again in the north of England.

21   *Mercurius Pragmaticus*, Numb. 23, no page numbers.

a misprint for Whaley's deep dislike of Lucas over the Stinchcombe incident in 1645. As noted, *The Moderate Intelligencer* claimed that Lisle had 'directed the shooting of poysoned bullets', for which *The Perfect Weekly Account* informs us 'in other Countries no quarter is given',[22] but this was not brought up on the day of execution or in any official report afterwards, and was probably pure press conjecture.[23] One dedicated account of the surrender framed him as 'a great cause of burning of the houses about the Town, and a person bent to much mischief',[24] but *Pragmaticus* was quick to defend him:

> Sir George Lisle was accused only in generall Termes of being a person of much mischief, and of burning the Surburbs. But themselves began first (when they saw they could not take the Town by storm) to fall to fiering of Houses neare one of the Gates, which (as the wind stood) must have burnt the whole City, had it not been prevented by the industry of the Soldier[s]. Afterwards they fiered many places, but all in vaine. At length, having sheltred themselves under the Houses, and taken the Lord Lucas House, the severall Regiments not being otherwise able to make good and justifie their Line, were necessitated to burn the adjoyning Houses. In which busines, neither Sir Charles, nor Sir George gave any orders or consent: And it is cleare, Sir George Lisle was no Actor in it, because on that part of the Towne, where the Essex Foot lay (whereof he was Major-generall) few Houses were burnt.[25]

As for him being 'mischievous':

> he was no more than in his Actions as a Souldier: In which his gallantry was unparelleld, and would have merited from an honourable Enemy, a more honourable entertainment.

The Royalist pamphlet *The Loyall Sacrifice* claims he was also accused of 'debauch'd conversation', although where the author found this particular slur, is not clear. Undoubtedly much of the printed matter available in the weeks following Colchester did not survive to speak to us now, and there was probably far more circulating about Lisle and Lucas, both for them and against them, than we are able to study today.[26] What Laurence and Dorothy Lisle must have endured at this time is hard to imagine: not only losing their remaining son in the most

---

22   Numb. 16 (misnumbered as Numb. 17), 5th-12th July, no page numbers.

23   Numb. 181, p.1518.

24   *A True and Exact Relation Of the taking of Colchester,* p.3.

25   *Mercurius Pragmaticus, op. cit.*

26   p.62.

controversial circumstances, but doing so in the brutal battleground of the public eye. Although the language of Mary Lisle's petition to Charles II was carefully chosen to maximise sympathy for her plight, her claim that her parents died 'over-whelmed with greefe' is all too believable. *The Loyall Sacrifice is* scathing of the slights against Lisle as whole:

> such Objections (impertinences rather) as were produced against Sir George Lisle; but not till such time as he was dead: for then these impoysoned arrowes may be the safeliest shot, when these malitious Marks-men finde the Archer at whom they aim'd, disabled to returne his shot, or shaft upon them.[27]

Obviously the pamphlet is an overt pro-Royalist effort to defend Lisle and Lucas. Yet on the whole it is remarkably cool-headed and critically argumentative, rather than merely flaming those it opposes, and it offers some very good points. As it observes, the London press had little or nothing bad to say about Lisle when he was alive, but now he was dead they were willing to make any spurious claim against him that might sway readers' opinions of him. In fact, during the wars the worst – in fact, as far as is presently known, the *only* – negative thing they had ever found to say about him was that he used bad language during the storming of Leicester, and ironically the author of that slight, Marchamont Nedham, was now defending him in *Mercurius Pragmaticus*. Many other Royalist officers were seized upon in print for their behaviour, real or alleged, but never Lisle, and this despite his rank and therefore high visibility as a target for the London presses. There may have been mentions in newsbooks of 1642-1646 now lost, but much as the virtual absence of Lisle in Rupert's extensive correspondence tends to signal that they did not correspond, the lack of references to Lisle in the extensive body of surviving Parliamentarian newsprint tends to signal his absence in them, not his accidental loss from them.

Ultimately the London writers failed to besmirch his reputation: the quotes about Lisle's character and behaviour that are repeated and remembered today are not those from the Parliamentarian presses but those from *Pragmaticus*, *Elencticus*, *Melancholicus*, and *The Loyall Sacrifice*, repeated later by Restoration writers such as Heath, Lloyd, and Clarendon. These impressions of Lisle survive partly because the Royalist presses took up his cause at the time and proclaimed him a martyr, but partly also because the image they created of him and Lucas as loyal yet tragic heroes struck a chord with later generations of storytellers long after the Civil Wars. Naturally we would expect Royalist writers to sing Lisle's praises, however in Lisle's case they were not embroidering reality: as this biog-raphy has demonstrated, his personal reputation was unspotted, and the Royalist

---

27 p.61.

sources unanimously concur both consciously and unwittingly that he was a genial and compassionate man, universally liked and admired for both his affability and his military skills. Besides their weak efforts in 1648, the Parliamentarian sources made no conscious attempt to contradict this in print, and their silence about such a high-profile enemy unwittingly supports it. Even arch-politician Clarendon, who was not always kind to the King's officers when recalling them in his *History*, had nothing but the warmest praise for Lisle: and he offered it in his own words, rather than rehashing praise from earlier newsbooks. Whatever arguments might be offered for Lisle's military responsibility for particular events at Colchester, desperate supporting *ad hominems* such as his being 'debauched' or generally 'mischievous', or whatever other slights were pinned to him at the time, were never going to stick.

Fairfax spared Sir Bernard Gascoyne for fear of damaging relations with Tuscany, but perhaps he would have been wise to make the same political consideration domestically: his peremptory execution of Lisle and Lucas instantly gave the resurgent Royalist cause a pair of high-profile martyrs whose deaths would be remembered throughout the Interregnum and into the Restoration. In particular it is likely that Lisle's personal reputation amongst former officers and soldiers, as a much beloved and respected commander, would only have fuelled the determination of many of them to 'remember Colonel Lisle' and risk standing up again for their King. This was not the 'example' Fairfax had in mind when deciding to have Lisle shot. *Elencticus* proclaimed the knights as martyrs as early as the first week in September.[28] Their elevation to permanent hero-status was helped by a significant body of what could be termed 'martyr literature', which emerged over the following months: countless lengthy elegies and epitaphs dedicated to Lisle and Lucas, scattered throughout newsbooks and printed independently. In his account of the siege, G. F. Townsend includes a short selection of ballads written during it, but unfortunately does not source them.[29]

On 7th June 1661 Lucas's elder brother, John, was finally able to organise a formal funeral for the two knights in the Lucas family vault at St Giles's in Colchester; a full report appeared in *The Kingdomes Weekly Intelligencer*.[30] A large and elaborate procession conducted their remains to the church, each of the coffins carried 'upon six Pikes tied with match', and carried by four each of Lisle's and Lucas's own former officers. Although the *Intelligencer* named Lucas's officers, he did not name Lisle's, so it is not known whether they were officers from the first war, or the second, or a mix of both. The newsbook claims 'Ten thousand Gentlemen and Inhabitants' attended the occasion: this is probably an exaggeration – and as David Appleby points out, the entire population of Colchester was around 10,000 – but

---

28 Numb. 41, p.332.
29 G. F. Townsend, pp.132-138.
30 No. 24, 10th-17th June 1661. Not in the British Library collection.

it may be that large numbers of Royalists had arrived from elsewhere, perhaps London in particular, to swell the crowds. Although Lisle's parents were now dead, presumably Mary Lisle must have attended, and perhaps Elizabeth's family from Canterbury: one of the Holmans later permitted an engraver to take a copy of a portrait of George in their possession, and although that portrait is now lost, the engraving of it is the most copied and most ubiquitous image of Lisle which survives today.

After a sermon and narratives of the men's lives – the minister, a local man who knew Lucas well, also offered 'as much as he knew of Sir George Lisle' – the knights were interred.[31] A large black marble slab was laid over the tomb entrance, etched in stark capitals with the following epitaph:

> Under this marble ly the bodies of the two most valiant captains Sr Charles Lucas and Sr George Lisle knights, who for their eminent loyalty to their Soverain were on the 28 day of August 1648 by the command of Sr Thomas Fairfax, then generall of the Parliament Army, in cold bloud barbarously murderd.

At some point subsequently the 2nd Duke of Buckingham, who had married Fairfax's daughter, infamously asked King Charles to have the stone erased; John Lucas agreed, on the proviso that he would be permitted to replace it with another, saying that:

> Sir Charles Lucas and Sir George Lisle were barbarously murdered for their Loyalty to King Charles I, and that his son King Charles II ordered the memorial of their loyalty to be erased.[32]

Reportedly, the King ordered the existing words to be cut more deeply.

Today St Giles is deconsecrated and the building is owned by the Freemasons, who have honoured the memory of Lisle and Lucas – who still rest in the vault – by naming one of their lodges after them and maintaining an exhibition of memorabilia relating to the Lucases and the siege. The great marble slab has been moved safely to the wall of the former church, where it is on prominent display, and a smaller tile now marks the entrance to the tomb. Behind the castle a small obelisk marks the reputed spot where the executions took place; a local tradition recorded by Heath in 1665, held that after the executions no grass would ever grow on the spot where Lucas's body had fallen.[33]

---

31 As noted, they may in act have been interred there already, but removed temporarily for the ceremony.
32 Morant, vol. I, p.68.
33 Heath, p.139.

Other fates

John Rushworth, now employed as Fairfax's secretary, offers his impression of Colchester when Sir Thomas viewed the town immediately after its surrender:

> It was a sad spectacle to see so many fair Houses burnt to Ashes, and so many inhabitants made so sickly and weak with living upon Horses and Dogs. Many glad to eat the very Draught and Graines for preservation of life.[34]

Colchester took many years to recover, and adding insult to injury was forced to pay between £11,000 and £14,000 (depending on the report) in order to prevent the already ruined town being plundered utterly by Fairfax's soldiers.

After the executions, Carter says bitterly:

> The Lords, with the rest of the prisoners, were kept in the same places they were at first, till the Tuesday following, and then (that they might be disperst, as neare as possible to their absolute ruin) they first (by examining their servants) having gotten knowledge of each particular mans Country, transmitted them to severall prisons, as contrary and far distant from their own homes as they could contrive; the Lords with some of the Gentlemen to Windsor, and the rest to Oxford, Lynn in Norfolke, Warwick, Pendennis in Cornwall, & St. Michaells Mount, Arundell Castle in Southsex, Glocester, Hereford, Cardiff in Glamorganshire, and divers other places. What became of them since, is writ in the daily book of their several misfortunes.[35]

Carter is not fibbing: *The Moderate Intelligencer* records that whilst the captive Lords were to stay with the Army, the officers were to be sent:

> some to the Mount, some to Pendennis, some to Cardiff, Oxford, Arundell, and divers other strengths, but none beyond Trent, the common souldiers, prisoners, return not to London to their Masters to be ready for a new businesse, but will be convey'd West, in relation to Bristoll, and other Sea-towns, that they may passe to America, Venice, or as shall be appointed: the gentlemen not souldeirs are committed to the care of troopers and others, untill further order be taken …[36]

---

34 *A true Relation of the Surrendering of Colchester*; single page.
35 Carter, pp.204-205.
36 Numb. 181, p.1527.

Carter is very clear about the meaning of 'committed to the care of':

> [Fairfax] distributed to every Regiment a certaine number of Gentlemen that were prisoners, as slaves to the Gallyes, or to ransome themselves. The Officers whereof came to the pound (as the manner of grasiers is by their cattell) and cald them first out of that into another, and then drove them away for the market, to make the most of them; so most of them afterwards as they were able, and according to the civility of those they were distributed to, bought their liberties, and returned home; in which manner they disposed of the greatest part excepting those who in that designe were in principall command.[37]

Carter also claims that the private soldiers were penned up in Colchester's churches and Fairfax's men allowed to go in and pillage them for whatever they could take:

> so that in a very short time there was very few or none left with any cloathes on them, hardly shirts, and afterwards they having thus pillaged and stript them, some changing for their raggs, & some giving them nothing, they march't them away, in a day when it rained so violently, as (had we not had Gods engagement to the contrary) we might have feared a second deluge; how they disposed of them afterwards I know not, but there are divers in the Kingdom that will tell you how they marched them from place to place in the country, lodging them in Churches and such places till many of them starved, and divers that could not march by reason of their faintnesse, they pistold in the high waies, and some they sold … to be transported into foraine Countries from their wives and Children …'

Carter's assertion about the soldiers' fates would sound like exaggerated folklore if it were not made somewhat more credible by the twin claim in 1661 that Fairfax had allowed the looting of Lisle and Lucas's bodies; as to the selling and enslaving prisoners, again he is supported by the newsbooks: for example of the Scots prisoners captured at Preston, those found to have been pressed were sent home, but:

> 2. Those contracted for, to be sent by the London Merchants to Plantations. 3. Those that shall be contracted for Venice to be sent thither. And 4. The rest to be dispersed into severall Counties, and allowed 2.d. a peece a day till they shall be disposed on.'[38]

---

37   Carter, pp.202-203.
38   *Perfect Occurrences of Every Daies Journall*, Numb. 88, p.437.

The term 'contracted for', of course, simply meaning 'sold': such reports are a sobering testament to what England had become in 1648. Edmund Verney was scathing:

> the rebellion of England iss the most notorious of any that ever wass since the beginning of the world, soe certainly it iss prosecuted and justifyed with the most mercilesse inhumanity and barbarisme, otherwise what a time wass made choyce of to exercyse thiss cruelty, just when they had consented to a treaty, and would make all the kingdome believe they were wholly bent for peace and amity, theire actions would have given theire tongues the lye … We heare theire own party cry downe thiss act ass so Horrid and barbarous, that it is beleev'd they will proceede noe further in thiss bloudy manner. The sufferers have dyed with honour and glory, and the actors live in horror and infamy.[39]

The fates of the other principal actors in the uprisings of 1648 are well known: upon the vote of a speciall high court of justice set up in the House of Commons, Lord Capel, the Earl of Holland, and the Duke of Hamilton were condemned and then beheaded in front of Westminster Hall. Norwich was reprieved only upon the casting vote of the speaker; Sir John Owen, on trial for the Welsh uprising, was also granted a stay, and in May the two men were reprieved.

Sir Bernard Gascoyne was imprisoned at Windsor, then paroled, going abroad in January 1649; he returned at the Restoration and spent much of the remainder of his life around Charles II's court and fashionable London society. Although Anthony Wood claims he was murdered in 1682, in fact he died of natural causes in London in 1687.[40] Lisle's former captain, Robert Skerrow, was also held at Windsor where he scratched his name into the wall of his cell;[41] nothing is known of his release, but he claimed King's bounty in 1663 under William Ayliffe, who had been his last commander. Lisle's remaining senior officer, Major Edward Fowles, is lost to the historical record after Naseby, and unlike Skerrow did not claim bounty. Anthony Thelwall, as noted, survived until at least 1649, but thereafter disappears from view; Sir Richard Page was deeply involved in Royalist conspiracies in the 1650s, but was arrested in 1655 for debt matters, and seems to have died in a Paris prison. Sir Charles Lloyd joined the exiled court in France in 1654 and died suddenly in 1661. Sir Henry Bard turned diplomat for Charles II, and died in India in 1656. Henry Hastings, who was 'probably destined for trial by the high court of justice' for his part at Colchester, escaped from Windsor in January 1649 and

39 *Memoirs of the Verney Family*, 1892, vol. II, p.340.
40 Wood, *Life and Times*, vol. III, p.31.
41 Young, *Edgehill 1642*, p.215 and fn.

joined the Prince of Wales in the Netherlands;[42] a founder member of the Sealed Knot during the Interregnum, he died in London in 1667. Sir William Compton reportedly escaped from Windsor, and thus the clutches of the high court;[43] he and Ned Villiers were also Sealed Knot members, the former dying suddenly in 1663 aged only 38, the latter becoming Knight Marshall of the King's Household and dying in London in 1689. His niece Barbara, the only daughter of his late brother William Lord Grandison, famously became mistress to Charles II. The Villiers brothers' cousin, Colonel Henry Washington, last seen at Gravesend with Robert Legge in 1649, lived quietly through the Interregnum, and died in 1664. William Legge, who fled abroad as soon as Parliament allowed him to leave the country in 1649, turned down an earldom after the Restoration, and lived quietly in London in his old role as Master of the Armouries, and was also made Lieutenant of the Ordnance. He died in 1670. Of Prince Rupert, numerous biographers have traced his career through the Interregnum and Restoration, to his death in 1682.

Early in September 1648, on the Isle of Wight:

> His Maj. asked a Gentleman that wore a black Ribband, (which was here with him) who he mourned for, he answered Sir Charls Lucas, And being told of his death his Maj. wept, that tears trickled down his cheeks, and spak mournfull expressions for him.[44]

It is to be hoped that the King's sorrow was not for Lucas alone.

On 18th September a final set of negotiations began between Presbyterian and moderate MPs, and the King, at Newport on the Isle of Wight; in late November the long-sought after agreement was reached. It would come to nothing, however. On 10th November, Henry Ireton presented a Remonstrance to the Army Council calling for the King's trial, and a purge of Parliament; Fairfax and the Council rejected it, but Ireton stood his ground and demanded Parliament's dissolution. Cromwell, meanwhile, demanded that Charles be forced to accept the original Newport propositions in full. Other radicals continued to agitate, and on 2nd December the Army marched into London. Four days later the radicals engineered 'Pride's Purge': Colonel Thomas Pride prevented moderate MPs entering Parliament, and a number were arrested. The Commons immediately annulled the Treaty of Newport and reimposed the Vote of No Addresses.

On 28th December came the first reading of an ordinance to set up a court for the King's trial; after a second reading the ordinance was passed on 1st January 1649. On the 15th, recently released from custody and now waiting somewhere near

---

42   Martyn Bennett, ODNB.
43   *Mercurius Elencticus*, Numb. 42, p.342.
44   *Perfect Occurrences*, Numb. 88, p.440. Also reported in *The Kingdomes Weekly Intelligencer*, Numb. 276, p.1078; and *The Perfect Weekly Account*, Numb. 26, no page numbers.

London for a pass to go abroad, William Legge wrote to Prince Rupert in Holland. His handwriting, usually a beautiful cursive script, was shaky and disjointed.

> After my long imprisonment, I have the liberty to continue wthin 20 miles of London, until a pass be sent me to depart the Kingdom, and then goe, I must, if not sooner; we are heer in a most miserable condition, by the estate of my Gratious Master, who I fear will ear long perish in the hands of Murderers …[45]

Legge was correct to fear for his King. On 27th January Charles was declared to have made war on his own people, and was condemned to death. Three days later he was beheaded on a scaffold outside the Banqueting Hall in Westminster.

45 WSL, S. MS. 544.

19

Posterity

Whilst it is tempting to speculate about what might have been, had Lisle survived the Second Civil War, his actual fate – although in this biographer's opinion unnecessary and undeserved – seems darkly appropriate in both timing and manner. He spent the last six years of his life single-mindedly serving his King, to whom he was evidently devoted, and was executed for doing so, just five months before the King himself met his own executioner. Charles's Whitehall, in contrast to his father's – as a perusal of the notebooks of John Finet, Charles's Master of Ceremonies, will demonstrate – was orderly, sober, obsessive with details and correct chains of protocol; it well befitted his belief in the Divine Order. Lisle shared this observance of 'place', of correct social hierarchy, of the right way to do things. Laurence Lisle's positions in the Household, and Dorothy Ashby's connection to the Duke of Buckingham and the patronage he offered, meant that George was brought up close to both Stuart courts: by the 1640s he was thoroughly a product of Charles's, or at least the influence that it cast, and was unshakeably committed to him and to everything he stood for.

If we *were* to speculate, we might imagine Lisle after January 1649 transferring his allegiance to Charles II, and working covertly for a restoration. Whilst like Gerard, Lloyd, and many others he may have joined the exiled court abroad, Lisle appears to have been something of a homebody, preferring to remain on his own familiar London patch: thus he might well have stayed in England and joined or worked with the Sealed Knot, alongside members mostly very familiar to him – Henry Hastings, Sir William Compton, Ned Villiers, Sir Richard Willys, Colonel John Russell and John, Lord Belasyse – perhaps participating in the numerous risings the group engineered. Had he made it to 1660, undoubtedly his military record, and unswerving loyalty to the Crown would have fitted him for at least a baronetcy – had he accepted it – or elevation to some senior position at court, or perhaps to a post where he was far more valuable, and probably far more comfortable: in the Restoration military.

In November 1648, the cover of *The Loyall Sacrifice* portrayed a striking, even shocking image of Lisle and Lucas at Colchester: Lucas lying on the ground, peppered with bullet holes; Lisle standing by his dead colleague, and with a smile, tipping his hat to the firing squad about to impose the same punishment on him. 'Shoot Rebells', he says, in the seventeenth-century version of a speech bubble. Then underneath: 'Your shott, your shame; our fall, our fame.' Since then that image, or rather reimagined versions of it where Lisle is frequently kneeling by Lucas's body as per the original eyewitness accounts, has been repeatedly redrawn and reused as late as the nineteenth century. That frozen moment in time: a snapshot of a doomed man in his last moments, facing down his soon-to-be killers, with all its connotations of justice, injustice, love, loyalty, terror and defiant bravery in the face of death, seems to evoke fascination. Latter-day Royalist sympathisers obviously understand the images in their original context; yet perhaps, to the casual onlooker, the doomed man minus his original backstory might suggest other connections personal to the viewer. Lisle might become any beleaguered hero or villain, real or imagined. Or perhaps the courage he displays in that situation simply strikes a chord and becomes an inspiring example. At least five different versions of the scene exist besides the original, including an early one by an anonymous engraver, which despite being captioned *Execution of Sir Charles Lucas and Sir George Lisle at Colchester*, transfers the image into an eighteenth century military context, uniforms and all. In 1800 Benjamin Strutt (1754-1857) completed a painting with the same title and a similar composition, but depicting the execution on a smaller scale so as to include the looming side of the castle, and a stormy sky. It was later copied by the prolific engraver Francis Jukes. In the mid-1800s publisher J. & F. Tallis produced a new engraving of a popular scene entitled 'Cromwell Dissolving the Long Parliament', and included underneath a smaller depiction of 'Sir Charles Lucas & Sir George Lisle Shot', another variation on Lucas dead and Lisle waiting for death: this time Lisle stands in a heroic pose with a cloak draped over his shoulder, while musketeers take aim at him. In the 1880s William Barnes Wollen (1857-1936), a painter and sketcher of historical military scenes, focused once more on Lisle kneeling by Lucas's body, on this occasion looking accusingly at the firing squad. In the early twentieth century, Colchester artist Harry Becker composed a pensive painting, *Sir Charles Lucas and Sir George Lisle descending the Great Stair in Colchester Castle*, presumably intending them to be on their way to the castle yard, and their execution. Clearly Becker did some preliminary research, as both men look strikingly like the known portraits of them.[1]

Lisle's death has also provided writers with material. In 1817 his reputed comments to the firing squad were included in *The London Budget of Wit, Or, A Thousand Notable Jests*; in the same year, novelist William Godwin, husband of

---

1   *Oil painting of the execution of Sir Charles Lucas and Sir George Lisle at Colchester,* August 28th 1648. By Benjamin Strutt, about 1800 (COLEM: 122A); *Oil painting by Harry Becker of Sir Charles Lucas and Sir George Lisle descending the Great Stair in Colchester Castle.* 1900-20. (COLEM: 260A). Both paintings are in the collection of Colchester and Ipswich Museum Service.

the feminist writer Mary Wollstonecraft, wrote a historical trilogy which featured Lisle's son as a friend of the protagonist, and a widowed 'Lady Lisle' who had locked herself away from the world after her husband's execution.[2] Then came Charles Dickens and *A Child's History of England*, which included a line drawing of the usual execution scene – in this one Lisle kneels, touching the bullet holes in Lucas's coat – and revealed Dickens's Royalist sympathies by describing the 'cruel execution' of 'two grand Royalist generals, who had bravely defended Colchester under every disadvantage of famine and distress for nearly three months.'[3]

Whilst this continuing thread of remembrance has kept the horrors of Colchester fresh, it has sustained only the memory of Lisle's death, and not his life; given his known military career and reputation, his senior rank, and the circumstances of that death, it is surprising that in the 368 years since, no biographical work has been attempted. This book finally corrects the balance: bringing to public attention the full story of this most commendable 'Worthy Commander in the Warres.'

2   *Mandeville. A Tale of the Seventeenth Century in England*, vol. II, p.61.
3   *A Child's History of England*, 1883 edition, part four, p.328; line drawing between p.328 and 329.

Appendix I

Family Trees

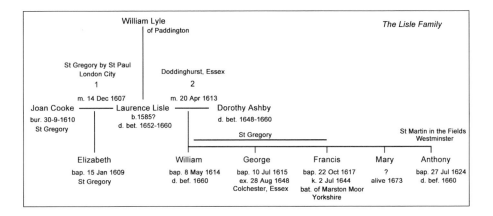

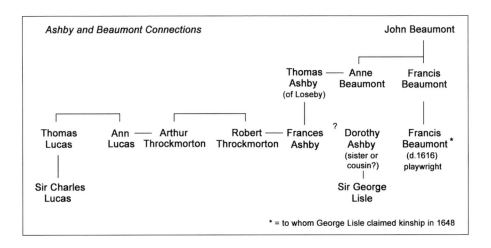

Appendix II

Images of Lisle

As of January 2016, three portraits of Lisle are known to be extant, and it appears that a fourth has been lost since the eighteenth century.

The 'Lace' Portrait, private collection
(see colour plate)
The frame states that the painter was William Dobson, but Sotheby's believe it to be Cornelius Johnson. Its provenance is unknown. Undated, but the style of lace on the falling band suggests late 1630s. The gorget, buffcoat and scarf indicate that the sitter has a military connection and this might confirm that Lisle fought on the Continent in the late 1630s. Certainly in this respect it is far too early to be a Dobson portrait, although coincidentally both Dobson and Lisle lived in St Martin's Lane, in Westminster, during the 1630s.

Castle Howard, North Yorkshire
(see colour plate)
'School of Anthony Van Dyke'. 28 × 24″. Bought by the 5th Earl of Carlisle from engraver Benjamin Vandergucht on 3rd June 1793, for 15 guineas. Lent to the South Kensington Exhibition in 1866. Undated.

According to Claydon House in Buckinghamshire, the home of the Verney family, an inventory of 1740 included a painting of 'Sir Geo Lyslle, killed at Colchester'.[1] In 1783, however, the family lost its fortune and many of the house contents were sold; given the timing, the Verneys' portrait of Lisle is the prime candidate to be that sold by the Vanderguchts to the Earl of Carlisle in 1793, and which is now at Castle Howard.

At the time of writing there *is* a picture at Claydon titled 'Called Sir George Lisle'; however, the portrait depicts a tall blonde man who is obviously not him.[2] Even the National Trust, who maintain the house, admit that:

---

1 *Claydon House Portraits. A Guide to the People in the Pictures.*
2 The picture is included in *Memoirs of the Verney Family*, 1892, vol. II, between p.340 and p.341.

426

'this portrait looks nothing like a contemporary engraving of Lisle, but does bear a resemblance to one of Richard Cromwell (1626-1712). There is though no known reason why a portrait of Oliver Cromwell's son should be at Royalist Claydon.

During the Verneys' disrupted domestic situation of the 1780s the identities of many sitters in the portrait collection were lost, and later family members were forced to use old family documents to put names to the canvasses still remaining in the house. If the Castle Howard painting was indeed that originally owned by the Verneys, presumably the Verney family had no record of its onward sale when they undertook their later art detective work, and so attributed the 1740 inventory reference to the wrong painting.

The Castle Howard portrait is clearly the origin for Lisle's miniature in the frontispiece of William Winstanleys *The Loyall Martyrology* in 1665; also for the miniature included in a similar set of engravings completed by Joseph Nutting (1660-1722), which was probably the frontispiece for a later reprint of Winstanley or for another book with similar subject matter.

The Durwards Hall Portrait – now in a private collection?
(see colour plate)
This painting first appeared in public on 10th July 1989 at Durwards Hall, Essex, where it was sold in a house sale as 'circle of Peter Lely' by Christie's of South Kensington. It was cleaned and restored, then re-attributed as 'Circle of John Michael Wright (1617-1694)' and sold again at Sotheby's in London on 11th July 1990. Its location is now unknown. The only pictures available are the colour plates in the Christie's and Sotheby's sale catalogues. No provenance is available, and the picture is undated. It is a three-quarter length painting depicting Lisle standing, in a sleeveless buffcoat, 'back and breast' armour and a red scarf with gold fringing; around the hair and head the painting looks indistinct and possibly unfinished or overpainted, and the clothing is undeniably 1660s. The sitter is certainly Lisle, but his hair is a different colour to that in the 'Lace' and Castle Howard portraits. Obviously with 1660s-style clothing it cannot have been painted from life: which means that either it was an unfinished portrait completed later, or an existing portrait of Lisle was used as a reference for the face. Possibly it was extensively overpainted, but the only known 'missing' painting is the Holman one (see below), and the sitter in that picture faced in the other direction. Although Wright used classical backgrounds with cliffs, trees, small battle scenes etc., so did William Dobson: if it was an incomplete painting from the 1640s it may well have been started or sketched out by Dobson and completed after the Restoration by Wright or his circle, but with 1660s clothing. Posthumous completion of paintings long after the subject's death is uncommon, but in the 1660s Lisle was famous as a 'Royalist martyr' and during the post-Restoration surge of Royalist sentiment

someone may well have commissioned a painting of him as an example of loyalty to the King and monarchy.

The fact that this painting emerged at a house near Colchester is significant. In 1902 Kelly's Directory of Essex stated that at the new Colchester town hall, 'the walls of the various rooms, the staircase and corridors are hung with a large assemblage of portraits, pictures and engravings; the former include portraits of royalist officers slain at the siege of Colchester …'.[3] Whilst Colchester and Ipswich Museum Service currently hold two later paintings portraying the Colchester executions,[4] they cannot confirm which other paintings may have been on display in 1902: therefore it is perfectly possible that the Durwards Hall portrait may have been one of them.

The Holman Portrait – presumed lost

This portrait is only known due to the several engravings made from it in the eighteenth century. It portrays Lisle in civilian clothing, but with a gorget and a small scarf, and probably dates from the late 1630s. Facially it bears a close resemblance to the Castle Howard and 'Lace' paintings.

The earliest engraving was created by Michael Vandergucht (d.1725), for the 1713 edition of Clarendon's *History of the Rebellion*.[5] The image states that is 'from an original painting' but gives no other detail. The second is a version by George Vertue (d.1756), who worked for some years under Vandergucht; the image appears in an unbound engraving published by an S. Austen in 1746, as part of 'The Set of Loyalists', a series depicting Royalists who suffered notable deaths.[6] It was placed in a double-oval with an engraving of Sir Charles Lucas, and an account of the executions at Colchester taken from Lloyd and Clarendon; unlike Vandergucht's version, the oval frames of both Vertue's images carry the names of the then owners of the originating portraits. That of Lucas is from a known Dobson painting, at that time 'in the Possession of Lord Biron', which rings absolutely true as John, Lord Byron, had been Lucas's brother-in-law and evidently the portrait was still in the Byron family many years later. The frame of Lisle's image says it was taken 'From a Painting in the Possession of Mrs Holman': which instantly verifies it as a genuine family portrait of Lisle, as his half-sister Elizabeth had married a William Holman in 1632. We can surmise that the Holman portrait – which presently must be presumed lost – had after the death of Lisle's parents or younger sister Mary been bequeathed to Elizabeth's family, and remained with them at least until Vandergucht engraved his copy from it in 1713. Whether Vandergucht's student Vertue used it at the same time for his version or went back to it later, is not

---

3   p.125.
4   The Strutt and Becker paintings, see chapter 18.
5   1713, vol. II, p.432.
6   In the collection at the NT Treasurer's House, North Yorkshire. 470 x 318 mm, paper.

Engraving of Lisle and Lucas for 'The Set of Loyalists', George Vertue for S. Austen (1746).

Engraving, creator uncertain, but evidently a reversal of Vertue's 1746 work. *The Universal Magazine* (1775).

Engraving, Michael Vandergucht, for Clarendon's *History of the Rebellion* (1713).

Engraving, John Grieg, for A *History and Description of the Ancient Town and Borough of Colchester, in Essex* (1825).

known, and what happened to it subsequently is a mystery. The purchase and sale of the Verney(?)/Castle Howard portrait by one of the Vanderguchts in the 1790s is probably just coincidence, as it is plainly not the Holman one.

The third engraving is a reversed version of Vertue's, created for the 'Universal Magazine' in 1775. The fourth, and apparently latest that exists, was created by John Grieg in 1825, for *A History and Description of the Ancient Town and Borough of Colchester, in Essex.*[7]

---

7   By Thomas Cromwell; vol. I, between p.152 and p.153.

Appendix III

Regiment Officers Under Bolle and Lisle

Listed at the highest rank obtained. The 'Indigent Officers' list of 1663, where former soldiers claimed bounty from King Charles II, lists four men under Colonel Bolle, and ten under Lisle. Some men are known only from other sources and did not claim in 1661.

COLONELS
Richard Bolle: 1590-1643; k. Alton, Dec 13th. Of Theddlethorpe, Lincs. Colonel August 1642–December 1643

George Lisle: 1615-1648; ex. Colchester, Aug 28th. Born City of London. Possible foreign service in 1637, known service in England in 1640. Began the war as a lieutenant colonel, mentioned at Edgehill by Bulstrode. Commissioned full colonel November 1644. Colonel of Bolle's regiment January 1644-June 1645, when regiment destroyed at Naseby.

LIEUTENANT COLONELS
Richard D'Ewes: 1615-1643; born Suffolk. Younger brother of political diarist Sir Simonds d'Ewes; died Reading, April 1643, of septicaemia after being injured in the thigh by a cannon shot. Buried St Mary's, Reading.

Edward Littleton: Captain with Cadiz expedition, 1625. Early officer under Bolle, so assumed to be from Staffordshire. Mortally wounded POW at Naseby, June 14th 1645; buried June 29th at Holy Sepulchre church, Northampton. Major of Wentworth's tercio at the storming of Bristol in 1643; major of Lisle's tercio at Naseby, possibly earlier. Worked his way up through the regiment from captain.

MAJORS
Nathaniel Moyle: Presence in regiment doubtful: only reference to Bolle's regiment is 'Deserter' pamphlet in December 1642. Later lieutenant colonel of Lunsford's regiment; k. at Bristol, July 1643.

Bevis Lloyd: Presence in regiment doubtful: only reference is a POW exchange petition in April 1644, after capture at Alton. Paperwork states he is in Bolle's regiment but probably an error: from Llanrhaedr, Denbigh, and cousin of Denbighshire colonel Anthony Thelwall; sought exchange after Alton with Thelwall's lieutenant colonel Urian Leigh, so almost certainly Thelwall's officer and not Bolle's.

Edward Fowles: Early officer under Bolle, so presently assumed to be from Staffordshire. Probably the 'Captain Fowler' on the Culham arms docket, May 1643. Commanded the regiment at Naseby when Lisle and Edward Littleton running the tercio. POW Naseby. Previously a captain. Did not claim King's bounty in 1663.

CAPTAINS

Richard Bagot: c.1619-1645; from Staffordshire. Captain under Bolle, left the regiment after Edgehill. Appointed governor of Lichfield April 1643; later colonel of own regiment. Died July 7th 1645, mortally wounded at Naseby.

Constable, Robert: 1645/46(?) Lisle signed a certificate to assist Constable obtain a 'poor knights place', probably at Windsor, where a scheme with this name was run. Presumed to be in Bolle's or Lisle's regiment, but might have a been a commanded man under either.

Thomas Corbett: Mentioned in 1663 by Richard Hill, his former Lieutenant. Corbett petitioned Prince Rupert in 1645(?) after being robbed and twice taken prisoner. Petition mentions Nantwich, where Lisle's regiment were not present, so Corbett was probably from the Shrewsbury Foot and only fought with Lisle at Naseby.

John Hanmer: Commissioned at York, Aug 8th 1642; absent by May 1643.

—— **Hawkred:** Captain under Bolle, mentioned on Culham arms docket, May 1643.

Rugely Littleton: POW Naseby 1645. Claimed from Stafford in 1663, under Lisle.

—— **Lloyd:** Mentioned on Culham arms docket, May 1643. Possibly Bevis Lloyd, but as noted, his tenure in the regiment is doubtful.

Thomas Pocklington: POW Naseby. Claimed from London & Westminster in 1663, under Bolle.

Robert Skerrow: Ensign in 1640; discharged from the army in December for being a Catholic. Lieutenant to Captain Throckmorton, 30th October 1642. Captain in May 1643, Culham arms docket. POW Naseby. Major to William Ayliffe at the siege of Colchester, 1648; imprisoned at Windsor afterwards. Claimed Kings bounty in 1663 under Ayliffe.

Thomas Smith: Mentioned in 1663 by James Robinson, his former Lieutenant; under Lisle.

John Taylor: Mentioned in 1663 by Edward Matthews, his former Ensign; under Lisle.

Thomas Throckmorton: Mentioned in Robert Skerrow's commission as his lieutenant on 30th October 1642. Gone from the regiment by May 1643. Like Skerrow, had been discharged from the army as a Papist in 1640.

John Tichbourne: Mentioned in 1663 by Henry Holman, his former Lieutenant; under Lisle.

—— **Walden:** Captain under Bolle in May 1643. Mentioned on Culham arms docket. Almost certainly Sir Lionel Walden (b.1620), who in 1679 claimed to have given Lisle some money in 1648.

Humphrey Whitgrave (or Whitgreave): POW Naseby. Claimed King's bounty from Essex in 1663, under Lisle.

Robert Moore: Captain of horse, claimed King's bounty in 1663 from Essex, under Lisle. Presumably under his command at Colchester in 1648, as Lisle did not command horse during the First Civil War.

LIEUTENANTS

—— **Carter:** POW Naseby, 1645.

William Heron: Claimed in 1663, London & Westminster list, under Bolle. Lieutenant to Major Bevis Lloyd, which suggests that in fact he may have been in Thelwall's regiment. If, like Lloyd, he was also captured at Alton and subsequently left the service, Bolle would be his last commander: hence the 1663 claim under him and not Thelwall.

Richard Hill: Claimed King's bounty 1663, from Worcester. Lieutenant to Captain Corbett, and so probably from the Shrewsbury Foot and only fighting under Lisle at Naseby.

Henry Holman: Claimed King's bounty from Worcester in 1663, under Lisle. Tichbourne's Company. May be a kinsman of Lisle's, as he had Holman in-laws, but as they were from Surrey and not Worcester, it may just be a coincidence of names.

Edward Norbury: Perhaps the same man who was lieutenant in Ireland 1641, William St. Leger's company. Claimed King's bounty from York in 1663, under Lisle, Skerrow's company.

John Roane: Arrested in Walsall, Staffordshire, 18th September 1642, whilst recruiting for Bolle. A man of the same name claimed King's bounty in London & Westminster in 1663, as a Captain-Lieutenant of Sir Edward Ford's Regiment of Horse.

James Robinson: Claimed King's bounty from London & Westminster in 1663, under Lisle. Smith's company.

ENSIGNS

Gilbert Crouch: Colonel's ensign under Lisle, mentioned on docket March 1643/44.

Edward Fowler: Bur. 12th August 1643, Yarnton Oxfordshire. Probably camp fever contracted at Culham.

William Graham: Claimed King's bounty from Cumberland in 1663, under Lisle.

John Hunt: Claimed King's bounty from Lincoln in 1663, under Bolle. Perhaps a kinsman of Bolle's, as his cousin married a Nathaniel Hunt.

James Littleton: POW Naseby, 1645. Claimed King's bounty from Stafford in 1663. Specifies Bolle's regiment, despite being with Lisle at Naseby.

Edward Matthews: Claimed King's bounty from Carmarthen, in 1663, under Lisle; Taylor's company.

—— **Turpin:** POW Naseby, 1645.

QUARTERMASTERS

Richard Cresswell: Claimed King's bounty at Stafford in 1663, under Lisle.

UNRANKED SOLDIERS

These private soldiers appear to be victims of the 'camp fever' outbreak in May 1643, which struck the Royalist army while it was quartered at Culham, Oxfordshire. The men were buried at the village of Yarnton, north-west of Oxford, which had been set aside as a hospital. Culham camp was broken up by mid June, when the regiments marched on towards Bristol.

William Berry (bur. Yarnton, 8th July 1643)
Benedict Bradly (bur. Yarnton, 15th June 1643)
John Breer (bur. Yarnton, 28th June 1643)
Ralph Deane (bur. Yarnton, 17th June 1643)
Richard Farmer (bur. Yarnton, 23rd June 1643)
Richard Gardiner (bur. Yarnton, 20th June 1643)
John Latimer (bur. Yarnton, 10th July 1643)
Walter Matthews (bur. Yarnton, 28th June 1643)
Richard Taylour (bur. Yarnton, 15th June 1643)
Thomas Taylour (bur. Yarnton, 20th June 1643)

References

Robert Skerrow's commission as lieutenant: British Library, Harley MS 6804 f.221.
Culham arms docket, 23rd May 1643: Roy, ROP part 2, p.238 (National Archives, WO 55/1661/3).
Culham camp burials: listed by Peter Young, *Edgehill 1642* (second edition), p.231.
Ensign Crouch docket, March 1644: National Archives, WO 55/1551/87.
Bevis Lloyd exchange letter, April 1644: British Library, Harley MS 6802 f.94.
Captain Thomas Corbett petition to Rupert (1645?): British Library, Add. MS 38848 f.14.
Captain Robert Constable certificate: Bodleian Library, Ashmole Mss 1132 f.147.
Indigent Officers: Civil War Officers Rewarded by Charles II, S. F. Jones (ed.), Tyger's Head Books, 2015.
Captain Walden money reference, 1679: Calendar of Treasury Books, vol. V part II, p.1288.

Appendix IV

Elegies and Epitaphs, 1648

The following elegies and epitaphs are a small selection of the many verses written about Lisle and Lucas in the weeks and months after the Colchester executions.

Mercurius Elencticus, 30th August-6th September[1]

Here lies interr'd a Lucas and a Lisle,
Both Knights, both Champions of this our wasted Isle:
Men whose Great spirits never could dispense
Or Cringe unto a State-Omnipotence.
Such whose firme hearts were never mov'd awrt
By tampering Traytors fraud, or Tyranny:
Whose Loyall breasts colud neve harbour feare
Nor yet Revenge: yet in Revenge were here
Both throwne by Fairfax, 'cause he came behind
Them both in Honour, Vertue, Body, Mind.
Because their Minds could not be Conquer'd, He
(Vile wretch!) fell on their fraile Mortality.
"Alas! what triumph or'e a clod of earth?
What Valour 'tis to stop a little Breath?
Yet these are all th' ingredients compound
This Tyrants Honour, that makes such a sound.
Curs'd Caitiffe! that in Blood hath writ thy shame
In such large Characters, as Fairfax's Name
Is odious to the world, and read so plaine,
The very Turkes usurp it in disdaine.
Could'st thou not exercise thy cruel Pawes
On lesse deserving Subjects? those Jack-dawes,
That sit and Caw distruction to the Land;

1   Numb. 41.

Deserve the justice of a Tyrant's hand:
Not these brave Heroes, who durst speake, and fight,
And Dye, to save their King and Countrey's Right.
   "Unhappy Fairfax! whose Revenge must Pay,
   "Thy soule at last, for this untimely Clay.
Rest happy soules! till Time shall raise your Dust,
And re unite it to fulfill your Trust.
Whilst this aspiring world shall Emulate
Your never-dying Vertues, Fame; and hate
Themselves to ashes, cause their actions could
Have no assurance of such sacred mold.
Sleep Blessed men! and, you whose Love they had
Whilst here they sojourn'd, grieve not but be glad
That no obscure disease did cut the thred
Of their bright Lives. Their precious Blood was shed
In publique by a Tyrant: And the Cause
They dyed in's just, and Noble, if heavens Lawes
Be Gospell; And 'twere pitty their great deeds
Should be forgot, or over-growne with weeds,
   In equall height of Honour both they Dy'd:
   Blesse God! who both at once hath Glorify'd.

Anon: 'An Elegie': 20th September
An Elegie
On the Death of
Sir Charles Lucas and Sir George Lisle[2]

Inspire me some prodigious Fury: all
The Muses are not enough Tragicall.
Hither you Leaguer Friends from your Black Tents;
Hell has but Three, Fairfax whole Regiments.

A Pompy's death, Caesar would chose t'enjoy,
His Butchers were an Eunuch and a Boy.
Cannibals thus War not to reduce, but chew,
As Mastiffs fight to worry, not subdue.
Lightning (heav'ns sword) blasts not, if not withstood,
Colchester's Bull deales tamely in cold Blood.

2   BL 669.f.13[20].

What plenteous harvests storming brought the Towne!
Each shaver Tarquin lopt his poppy downe,
All your shot, fire, steele, scarce murdred one,
Your Mercy only was destruction.
Poyson tooke in our certaine ruine is,
Serpents ne're sting, but when th'embrace, and kisse.
Scabbards stab'd most; no harm i'th' Cannons moat,
The onely murdring piece was Fairfax throat.

Quarter from Rebels, will dispatch or end;
The Devil's most pernitious, when our friend.
When you should Cure, you bleed us to our grave,
The booke does ne're condemne, but when't should save.
If the King scape by Rolfe, 'tis to be hurl'd
With Passe, and Pistoll, to another world.

Must ye be flesht? so soone faces about,
The Town's not starv'd, the famine is without:
They're guiltlesse sure must bid so soone dieu;
Or like the Devill, must you damne 'em too?
Horse-flesh is sober meat: Fairfax digests
Tigers and Wolves, and is himselfe turn'd Beast:
He keeps a Sessions, when he takes a Towne,
Councels of War are Juries, Buff Coats Gownds.
His Standards Gibbets are; he needs must fright,
His Physnomy's a funerall black and white.
Th'head quarters alwayes are at Tiburne; all
His power makes him but Hangman Generall.
Counter-march quickly all this Bloud: home, home
Lest we mistake the Devill for Black Tom.

This League murders more, then Marten could
Spawne (in a Holland's Leaguer) Bastard brood.
Must the Saints Feastivals be writ in Red?
Or are ye Gods with bloud and victim's fed?
Thus, and scarce thus, Turks Conquer, and embrew;
Turks are no Saints, yet Conquer more then toy.
If Executioners 'fore Reformers go,
Be Derrick henceforth Generalissimo.

Fairfax and Essex spell their Christian brands,
You'le find the same T. R. in all burnt hands.
Strange Parlies, which no Articles dispense,

But such as dispatcht Laud and Strafford hence.
If to Capitulate be such a thing,
And Treaties must end thus, God blesse the King.

Whilst Nol, and Tom dividedly doe awe,
The Land's bestrid wit th'Devils cloven paw.
In Lilly's dreames the King is still undone,
If so, these are his Lancashire Mocksuns.
For they will both be Kings; Fairfax i'th'dresse
Of the Black Prince, and Cromwell of Q. Besse.
Rossiter, Lambert, Ireton too must reigne,
England will suffer Heptarchy againe.

Come hallow'd quill, dropt from an Angels wing,
Inke from that Font: (we now of Christians sing)

An Ostridge plume with aquarfortis dres'd,
He that writes Lucas praise must steele digest:
His Epitaph, i'th' cripled Savoy stands,
Armelesse trunkes there shewes you his fatall hands:
All Hospitals his Monument conspire,
Ev'ry maim'd piece presents you him intire.
Thus his eternall fame shall last as long
As Rebels halt; or Royalists have tongue:
Search Marston-moore and in Yorkes Records seeke,
You'le find him writ in Stigmatiz'd Toms cheeke.

Such were his fierce Sallies, as some did doubt
Whether he rod, or had been discharg'd out:
Then at each sweep he made whole rankes to fall,
As if th' had duck't before a Cannon ball.
Some he o'retakes and joynts at knees; you'd sweare
Their legs had fled, and left the bodies there.
Now they must to't the Superstitious way,
Downe (saies his Morglay) Villaines kneel and pray.
He was the Townes best Wall; and O! to glutt
Revenge, this Royall Fort is made a Butt.

On Cut-throates, on, perfect your gamesome rites,
Forward and backward shoot, set up two whites;
Proceed, let not your lucky mischiefes slack;
Royalists mourne, but your soules were the black.

Lisle defies Quarter: now his friends bloud's spilt,
Your Charity's sin, your mercy will be guilt.
Great spirit, death's a Mistrisse in his eye
Or Nuptials; 'tis the same to kisse and dye.
His Grave's as welcome as his Quilt or Downe,
Would but his Ghost walke, 'twould nigh clear the Towne.
Holland's to him a Coate of Maile; what crowds
Did his thin Newbery shirt send to their shrowds?
They had not Braines to judge, nor heart to fight,
But ran and thought the Devill was turn'd white.
He vengance hurl'd like a pale dismall star,
Or th'milkie Genius of an innocent War.
No need of swords to have the Rebels sped;
He had soul enough to Lispe whole squadrons dead.

Farewell brave Twins of valour; may no spurne
Of Rebels foot light heavy on your Urne:
We shall wait upon your fate; this year
Starv'd Colchester will soone be every where.
Plenty and Lucas fled at once, this Isle
Together wants a Summer and a Lisle.

Your Graves are meritorious, Wharton lies
Still in his Sawpit, and will never rise.
Your Loyall hunger, and your leave Alarmes,
Was better then to feed Pyms loathsome swarmes.
Your glorious soules are free, whilst others have
A Conquerour who to his Gout's a slave.
Old Fairfax Corn's ill cut, there goes to wrack
Weather-wise Booker and an Almanack.

Their wounds are still i'th'legges, you know the spell
O'th' Greek, they were dipt too in Styx and Hell.
Rossiter's halfe dead; 'tis well he's so much man;
But geldings serve for th' worke Essex began.

Their Church is militant; and doth appeare
Triumphant too; for why? their heav'n is here.
Th' Army's the holy League; all for Saints go
Because their Murders make all others so.
May they be Angels too; and when they fall
Like Jacobs Angels upon ladders all.

Anon: 'Two Epitaphs': 23rd September
Two Epitaphs,
Occasioned by the Death of Sr Charles Lucas, and Sr George Lisle,
basely assassinated at Colchester[3]

'Mongst the black deeds of blacker Tom, this One
Be grav'n upon his Monumentall Stone;
Heere lyes a Fellow (Reader curse his Dust)
That kild a Worthy, of whom England must
A vouch he was not to be paralleld
For Loyalty, and Valour in the Field.
Had all things done by Fairfax been done well,
This Act had damn'd them all, and him to Hell.

Now we'le adjoyn brave Lucas Epitaph;
Here sweetly rests his Kings and Countries staffe:
Expect no Hattons Tombe to set him forth,
His owne Deeds are best Heralds of his Worth,
And long-defended Colchesters sad Story,
The never ending Volume of his glory.
The King has lost a Champion, and true Mirrour
Of Loyalty, the Parliament their Terrour:
Souldiers have lost a Leader to the Field,
And in Him only were ten thousands kild.
(No Hamilton, that Troupes rais'd not long since
To free his King, but sold both Troupes and Prince.)
His House has lost an Honour of their stemme,
Three Realmes a Chieftaine might have rescu'd them;
What has the Parliament and Fairfax won
By cutting his lives thred, 'fore 'twas out spun?
Taken a few dayes off: Alas whilst dayes
And Ages run, so long shall last his prayse.
And this dries every teare, cures every maime,
Charles shall live ever registred by Fame.

Tiberius hated Histories, because
He knew his owne foule deeds done 'gainst all Lawes
Should be recorded, and Truth telling Fame
Would speake his actions to the Actors shame:
Passion, and proper interest dimme our sight,

---

3   TT E.464[32].

And very few in their owne cause judge right.
Impartiall Censors are the after times,
And freely dare pronounce Crimes to be Crimes:
Who not abhors Wat Tiler and Jack Cade?
That such Com'otions here in London made:
(Base Levellers) who durst their Armies bring
By force to curbe, or take, or kill the King.
But let the Parliament prepare their eyes
From Lucas Ashes Lucasses shall rise;
Heroes, who like Elisha shall inherit
In double measure, Noble Lucas spirit:
Heroes, who to their King and Countrey true,
Shall quell them, and their Independent Crew.
Those Musketiers did unaware conspire
To this miraculous Birth, when they gave Fire,
And Noble Lucas fell a Victime downe
To Fairfax Rage, and Parliamentall Gowne:
So is the Phenix life, but then begunne,
When on the odorous Pile his life is done.
For who reflecting on this Worthies fate
Vowes not revenge 'gainst Fairfax and the State?
And who'le refuse in such a Cause to dy,
That frees his Nation from base Tyranny?
(Nay the long Asse-ear'd Cockneies vext with feares.
Might doe some good, could they prick up their eares.)
So Lucas undeserved Death shall bring
Much happinesse to'th Kingdome, and the King;
And Samson-like dead Lucas shall kill more
Preputiate Rebels then he did before

On Sir George Lisle

Lisle, had I knowne thee, I should praise thee more;
But now, as do's the Vulgar, I adore
Virtue by heare-say. May this be enough
To set thee forth, (more is superfluous stuffe)
In Worth, in Life, in Death, with Lucas share,
There never liv'd, nor dy'd a Worthier Paire:
And had not both of you so Matchless been,
You had not felt Fairfax Vindictive spleene.

George sweetly rest, sprout Lawrels from thy Dust,
Live ever with the world, and with the Just:

This Canzon with Apotheosde Patriots sing,
I dyed a Loyal Martyr for my King.

On the Death of both these Worthies

When Lisles and Lucas tragedy began,
They look'd not at base Iretons Message wan,
But as some Libian Lyon chast by Hounds,
(When force availes not) trotting on the grounds,
Disdaines to flye, and rearing without dread
His Crisp'd maine up, turnes oft about his head,
And viewes the following Curres, then sure to dye,
Acts his last Exit with much Majestie.
No otherwise our Cordelion Knights,
That had (undaunted) in so many fights
Look'd grim Death in the face, demand from whom,
The Parliament, or Fairfax came this doome?
'Tis answer'd, then the Raven stretcht his throate
When both the Houses made this bloody Vote,
That all who wag'd war for the Royal Cause
Should suffer death by their Draconick Lawes.

Our Cavaliers wel-knowing 'twas in vaine
To argue, where Pride, Will and Malice raign,
Not Reason, nor true Honour; first commend,
Their soules to God, then crowning their last end.
With justice of their Cause, yeeld to the guns
Of Fairfax, and his Earth-borne Myrmidons.
Ob. Some fooles object, that going to their graves
They call'd the Sainted Faction Traitrous knaves:
Resp. Did not great Casar stab'd, and falling downe,
Call Casca Raskall, then compose his Gowne?
Brave Soules, when to their ends they nearer be,
Are strangely rapt, and Truths more clearly see.

Anon: 'An Elegie': 28th September

An Elegie On the most [Barbarous, Unparallel'd, Unsouldiery,] Murder Committed at Colchester, upon the persons of the two most incomparable, Sir Charles Lucas, and Sir George Lisle[4]

Though all the Trophies Rebels can bring in,
Are but succesfull guilt, and prosperous sin:
And each defeat their savage heat can buy,
But outrage be, and high-way victory:
Though there be Juries due for all they've slaine,
And the just Bar each conquest must arraigne,
Though what they Charge, and vigorous Onset call,
Is down-right, Stand, Deliver, and that's all:
Though Forts reduc'd, and Holds suppres'd by awe,
Here's Storm [and] Siege, but Burglary i'th' Law:
And Colchester it self, in Truth's free scope,
Is no Towne Taken, but a Towne Broke ope:
That from the Booty gain'd, and wealthy prize,
Not their renowne, but their Indictments rise.
Whence they can naught but Tyburne Triumphs raise,
And Sessione-Laurell, where the Hemp's the Bayes:
Yet they had some Pretext, some Title still,
Though not to virtue, yet to generous ill:
And the next Age, by our Records, might say,
They went well on, though they mistook their way.
     So aged Rome ev'n in her out-lawes shines,
Some lustre gaines ev'n from her Cataline's.
But ours are sunke and falne, have stain'd their Name,
Things beneath Rebels, bashfull Annals shame.
Traytour! though the wild sound affrights beget,
Though it be Villaine deep, 'tis Manly yet:
And in the Herauldry of Crimes may find
Kin and Allyes 'mongst Sins of humane kind.
But this unpattern'd By-blow, base offence,
Must flie disclaim'd, and unaffianc'd hence.
Chain'd and immur'd in un-frequented Cell,
And live an Anchorite in Populous Hell.
     The stout Besieg'd, whom Force could ne're subdue,
Now long begirt with Foes, and Famine too,

4   TT E.465[1].

When the last drop lay gasping in the cruse,
And no accession-worne supplies renewes,
While clean, and unclean they alike imbarke,
Like the Creations shelter (once) the Arke,
When the exhausted Town defended hears,
'Bove the distresse of Troy, though not the years:
At last they doe subscribe, but leave this Fame,
They knew no Conquerour, till Hunger came:
So Tyre yeilds to th' Pellaean Youth at length,
The purchase of his patience, not his strength;
When now dis-abled, they for rescue come,
To private Shrines, to publique Altars some,
The Victor check'd their flight, and bade them know,
No Sanctuary saves like a just Foe.
But oh the difference 'twixt two Heathens gon,
'Twixt him of old, and Fairfax Macedon!
        In doubtfull conflict, where the equall day
Smiles fair on both sides, and gives neither sway,
Slaughter may prudence seem, and bloud allure,
Since 'tis not then to kill, but to secure.
But all contest laid by, and steele let go,
To cull, and slay! the Shambles vanquish so.
        A Coward's still unsafe; but honour knowes
No other Foe, but him that doth oppose.
Nor would this blasted act such field afford,
Were't the Escape or Heat of some Rash Sword,
The gastly monster might be then disguis'd,
And savage Murder found but Un-advis'd.
But this was Tame debate, and was let fall,
Thy coole result, deliberate Cannibal.
        Is this the Mercy? Are we pitied thus?
Had your Committee-Prisoners such from us?
We grant ten thousand such heap'd in one pile,
Can never poize a Lucas, or a Lile:
Yet be the diff'rence vast, the change is true,
And you are pay'd, if those be deare to you.
If Aesop's cock for Pearle would Barley get,
Who makes that change is nothing in his debt.
Persons and thing are as their Prizers deem,
Not rated from their Worth, but our Esteem.
With Indians Beads of Glasse 'bove Diamonds go,
The Traffick's just, because they count them so.
        Safe and untouch'd we sent your men in peace,

And must our Bloud requite for their Release?
We not expect Returns in our own way,
For then we must be Free as well as They.
Yet sure a full compleat discharge from thrall,
May for un-injur'd Bondage safely call.
      But since no danger in their Lives remains,
Since shackles scare not, and none awes in chains:
Nay since their Safety, is their Purchase now,
And equall Trade will men for men allow:
Since their comerce doth on a levell stand,
And all's but ware for ware at strictest hand;
Why then these crimson streames, this Sea of Bloud?
Is there no Head, no Spring derives this Floud?
Yes, a pale hoofe the Ruthlesse mountaine hit,
And rising thence, proclaim'd Revenge was it.
Revenge is she, that great incensed Pow'r,
Whose Altars humane sacrifice devour.
Revenge is Honour, Justice, Country, Laws;
Your selves at least should have conceal'd this clause.
Say, was that Scar receiv'd from Lucas hand,
(That which was once a Scar, but now a Brand)
Receiv'd in Fight, when what he then did give
Thy Cheek, had sped thy Heart, but He cry'd Live?
Was it a crime though could'st so not indure,
That Bloud must balsome it, and his Life cure?
Hast though complexion, lines, or ought to passe
For lesse then Vizour in they affrighted Glasse?
Then we might prize, not think the damage small,
But waile the losse of Lady Generall.
But in thy course, tough visage, home-spun face,
Wounds may imprint, and scar, but ne're disgrace.
      Yet know, who muse why Lisle and Lucas die,
They fall to Fairfax injur'd symetry.
        That beauteous feminine Buffe dispatch'd them hence,
        That featur'd Generall, He Her Excellence.
      But, there were friendship yet in destinie,
If those who kill, would but lend space to die:
Mark then how they are hudled to their fate,
How the next Sun would call their murder late:
To live till morne would seem a slow Reprieve;
To respite Death is almost to let live.
No, they are posted hence, and butcher'd go,
E're they can fansie you can murder so.

This tyranny alone belongs to you,
To slaughter Men, and expectations too.
On to the Tragick Amphitheater,
And see these Hero's in the Passive War,
Whose fortitude had deep this bottome laid,
The Valiant must affright, not be affraid.
E're this, your busie care sweats to digest,
Some that can ayme, and act the Villains best.
Can single out the eye, the braine, the heart.
(For Murder now is but their kind of Art)
Know each recesse, and all deaths secret maze,
Which path leads to Dispatch, which to Delaies.
With nice Dissectors they must enter Lists,
And Naked combate arm'd Anatomists.
When Force doth force, and Army Army meets,
Where wounds give wounds, & slaughter slaughter greets,
Blind Fortune fate in her own darknesse wraps,
Our falls are oft not Courage, but Mis-haps.
But here the guided ruine none can shun,
Keen death must on, and hath no track but one.
No Bullet roaves or wanders in the dark,
But unperplex'd designes one single Mark.
While they i'th' threatning storm undaunted rest,
And take th' whole peal of thunder on their Brest.
To Gideon's fleece alonge the Show'r did flie,
While the whole World was else untouch'd, and drie.
Thus peasants, England's Worthies veines doe broach,
Who were their Terrour once, now their Reproach,
Whom to Subdue, their Foes must first Betray,
Whom Fairfax durst assault no other way.
Whom Norwich, Capel, Loughborough, Compton, all
Must see aveng'd, or in that Justice fall.
Two of a matchlesse, yet a different heat,
A various mingled flame, where both defeat.

LUCAS, possess'd a stout Majestick fire,
Wound up to a just pitch, but yet no high'r.
Not shunning pride as he his worth not spi'd,
But making it his Worth to scorn all Pride.
Where Vigorous was Assisting: to be strong
Inabled not t'Inflict, but Shrowd from wrong.
Not sterne, yet fit to have instructed sway,
To make none Tremble, yet make all Obay.

LISLE,
Soft ev'n to tears, yet stout as Adamant:
So nature doth stiffe Rocks 'mongst Waters plant.
Gentle and Melting into Valiant came,
As supplest Oyle draines in and heightens Flame.
Slaine in his Friend, expiring in his groane;
Tender of all mens bloud, besides his owne.
     Both were so Peerlesse such, 'twas fit that they
Had not falne this, and yet this onely way.
         Vespasian thus when his renown was full,
         And could not adde to his throng'd Chronicle:
         Surpris'd, despises fate, and Rouzing, cries,
         The Valiant falls Erect, and Standing, dies.

'The Loyall Sacrifice': An Elegy, November
To the living Memories of those Two Heroick Knights,
Sir Charles Lucas, And Sir George Lisle[5]

Whose approved Valour Valour renown'd them living,
and impal'd them dying with Honour.

Brave Loyall pair, whose active worth was such,
No pen nor pencil can performe too much
To crowne your Mem'ries:-- this it was to gaine
Fame by your prowesse, though you mist you aime
At long-beleagred-famish'd Colchester;
Expecting aid that ne'ere approached there.
Your Noble thoughts did ever set their rest
On Princely ends, no private interest.
Your care was how to cure, and to restore
This Phrentick State to th' Wits it had before.
Your taske was how your Caesar might be showne,
Not in a Grate but on His Royall Throne.
You could not hugge the Time as many do,
Whose cringing garbe may worke their overthrow.
You scorn'd perfidious Juncto's, who doe make
Use of the State to nim away the Stake.
Your conscientious waies abjur'd such men
As with an end to Treaties, God knowes when:

---

5   TT E.1202[2].

And such sly spinning Rookes we have no doubt,
Who seeke noaght lesse then what they go about.
Your hearts were sweetly temp'red with pure zeale,
To your indeared Prince and Commonweale;
This made Death your advantage; and struck feares
I'th' bosomes of your Executioners
With such compassion, they could scarce forbeare
From rinsing their Death-Bullets with a teare.
Hear thou, imsulting Sena, whose desire
Is with fresh fuell to increase a fire
In this imbroiled State! Hear what a brand
Thy quenchless rage has brought upon this Land,
When Loyalty must suffer, and become
A Law-convicted person by thy doome!
When awfull fury must suppress the good,
Wrath censure worth, and guilt shed guiltlesse blood!
When just Allegeance must at Bar appear,
And stand condemn'd because a Cavaliere!
Who is he then values his vac'ing breath
At such a rate as not to court pale Death,
Rather then groane in this tyrannick Age,
Where Innocence's a Sacrifice to rage;
Where Mercy becomes Cruelty: And Shame
Hath lost both native colour and her Name?
O Gallant Loyall Souls, thrice blest be you
Who have pay'd Nature and your Caesars due!
From our State stalkers ye secured are,
And with a Land of Peace exchang'd your War.
The Lord of Hosts will on his Hoast bestow
This peacefull plot while Rebels march below.
For if Rebellion safely get a shore,
It is a passage never knowne before.

Their Anniversaries are intended to be continued; that the Actions of Loyall
Subjects may be to succeeding times, for living patterns, recommended.

Appendix V

'The Loyall Sacrifice': Extracts, November 1648

'The Loyall Sacrifice' was a pro-Royalist piece printed in November 1648, to rebut the accusations made against Lisle and Sir Charles Lucas at Colchester. It is a lengthy pamphlet; therefore, with no disrespect intended to Lucas, only the extracts pertinent to Lisle's character are included here. However it is well worth reading in full for what it says about Lucas, for its account of Colchester, and for its icy denunciations of those who adhered to Parliament. The pamphlet drew heavily on September newsbooks *Mercurius Pragmaticus* numbers 23 and 23[b].

[pp.61-65]
We will now briefly descend to such Objections (impertinences rather) as were produced and pressed against Sir George Lisle; but not till such time as he was dead: for then these impoysoned arrowes may be the safeliest shot, when these malitious Marks-men finde the Archer at whom they aim'd, disabled to returne his shot, or shaft upon them.

First then, to render Him his due Character; he was a Man, whose brave undaunted Spirit dignifi'd his Family, many stories high in the estimate of Fame. One, whom these Civill-wars had sufficiently experienc'd and inabled for any Field service. One, who to his higher honour, bestowed his approvedst endeavours in testimony of his Allegeance. For his yeares, he was an excellent distinguisher of Societies; using ever to consort with those most, where he hoped to be improved best. These rising, nay, ripening thoughts could not chuse but beget envy with such as were Foes to Loyalty. For mens abilities are generally eye-sores to their Enemies. Notwithstanding all this, so clear and unquestion'd did his carriage appeare, as he was accused onely in generall terme of being a person of much mischief, debauch'd conversation, and of burning the Suburbs. Calumnies all alike true. For his disposition, it was generous, pleasing, and naturally bounteous; full of valour, without ostentation; just and cheerful in his Commands, without a surly imperiousnesse. Infinitely belov'd and observed by his Souldiers; for so tender was he of their safety: as never to the houre of his death would he ingage them in that action; wherein he would not hazard his owne person. This might appear by his gallantry at the latter Fight at Newbury, where to animate his Souldiers, & beget in them an Emulation of valour, so bravely represented in their Commander; he marched before his men in his Shirt with his doublet put off, to the face of the Enemy. Where he perform'd such admirable service, as His Majesty took especiall observation of him. And for a pledge of his future favour, bestow'd upon him the honour of Knight-hood: with all other places wherein he was in his Commands imployed, & to his succeeding honour highly approv'd. Secondly, for his burning the Suburbs: his accusers were the principall Actors. For they began first (when they despair'd of taking the Town by Storme) to fall to firing of the Houses near one of the Gates, which (as the winde stood) must have burnt down the whole City, had it not been prevented by the assiduate care, and timely industry of the Souldiery. Afterwards (to continue their fury) they fiered many places, but all in vaine: being by the vigilancy of the Garrisons, no sooner fiered then quenched. At length, having sheltred them-selves under Houses, and taken the Lord Lucas House (now pitifully ruinated and defac'd) with many other about it, the severall Regiments being otherwise unable to make good and justifie their Lines, were necessitated to burne the adjoyning Houses. In which action, neither Sir Charles, nor Sir George gave any orders or consent. And to satisfie the jealousies of some touching this particular businesse, it is clear, Sir George Lisle was no Actor in it, because on that part of the Towne, where the Essex foot lay, (whereof he was Major-generall) few houses were burnt. As for his being mischievous (formerly objected, and fully answered) he was no more then in his Actions as a Souldier: In which his Gallantry was unparallel'd, and would have merited from an honourable Enemy, a more honourable enter-tainment then to be presented a sufferer in so tragicall a Story.

[pp.82-83]

> [Lucas] Being in a word, such a man of men, and Patterne of active Loyalty, as he was all, that Sir George Lisle, in a gallant emulation aimed to be; whom, as he dearly tendred, so he seriously imitated, and now in the end, nearly seconded; being reputed a most knowing and obliging Commander for the Infantry: and of such discipline and courage that he led them, as in a line upon any services, through the greatest danger and difficulty.

Appendix VI

Mary Lisle's Petition to Charles II, 1660

In November 1660 Mary Lisle presented the following petition to Charles II; it was the first of three that she would find herself forced to submit. The document can only be viewed on microfilm and appears to be damaged; some words are illegible:

> To the Kings Most Excellent Majestie
> The humble petition of Mary Lisle
>
> Sheweth
> That yor petrs ffather Lawrence Lisle deced was servant to yor late Royall ffather and for his Constant Loyalty had the value of 12 Thousand Pounds seized and taken Neerely from him.
>
> And to Compleate his misseries, had his two sonnes yor petrs brothers for there Cordiall & Faithfull service to yor late Royall father the one sleyne [at Yorke?] the other (namely Sr George : Lisle) murthered at Colchester.
>
> By the sad and sudeyne newes whereof yor petrs parents (overwhelmed with greefe) bothe dyed leaveing yor petr in a deplored Condicon without anie meanes of subsistence.
>
> She humbly prayeth that yor Matie will in Compassion of her sufferings (being the onely person of her ffamilly surviving the oppression of the late govermte) vouche safe to graunte unto yo:r petr a pattent for such a parte of the Impost of Twobacco and Twobacco pipes in Ireland as was formerly graunte to her said ffather by yor Majesties Grandfather by pattent or that yor Majestie will be pleased to provide a lively hood for her by which wayes and meanes as in yor Majesties wisdome shall thinke fitt.
>
> And yor petr shall ever pray &c.[1]

---

1   State Papers Domestic, Charles II. SP 29/22, f. 244. National Archives, Kew.

On 29th December the King received a report from the Treasurer:

> on the petition of Mary Lisle concerning the grant to her father Lawrence
> Lisle, 1621-2, Feb 8, of an imposition of 1s 6d per lb of tobacco and 2s for
> every grose of tobacco pipes imported into the Kingdom of Ireland for 21
> years at £21 per an, rent: which said imposition was reduced, 1636 Dec 13
> to 3d per lb, by the Deputy and Council for Ireland, who also put a stop on
> the said Lisle's collecting the said impost. Details the further proceedings
> herein and sufferings of Lisle.[2]

Charles agreed to grant a pension, and on 28th June 1661 wrote to the Lords
Justices in Ireland ordering them to pay Mary £2000 in four instalments in respect
of the Irish tobacco customs which Parliament had taken from Laurence in the
1630s.[3] Like so many of the restored King's petitioners, however, Mary had a fight
on her hands to get the money. Although Charles was frequently willing to make
such grants in principle, his coffers – so much abused during the Civil Wars and
the Interregnum – were unable to honour them. Evidently the response from
Ireland was precisely that: an objection that there was no money, as in January
1662 she petitioned again, asking for the £2000 and restating her case, adding that
she was 'the only survivor of her family, and in her is nothing but their miseries.'[4]

On 31st January and 18th February two successive warrants were submitted for
the £2000,[5] but evidently the Treasury could still not comply, for on 20th March
it passed:

> [a] Money warrant for £500 to Mary Lisle, sister of Sir George Lisle, who
> was murdered for his loyalty to the late King, in part of £2000 ordered her
> by the Privy Seal of Feb 24 last, as royal bounty in consideration of her
> afflicted condition.[6]

On 25th October she received another £500, but it was another three years
before even another £100 was granted, in December 1665.[7]

In 1667 Clarendon placed the blame for the country's financial woes directly at
Charles's door, and was scathing about Mary's case:

2   CTB 1660-1667, p.110.
3   Bodleian Library, MSS. Carte 42, f.302.
4   State Papers Domestic, Charles II. SP 9/210/140. National Archives, Kew; calendared *CSP Domestic Series*, 1661-1662, p.259.
5   *CSP Domestic Series*, 1661-1662, p.260, p.277.
6   CTB, 1660-1667, p.377.
7   *Ibid.*, p.443, p.699.

The King … had laboured to debase the morality of the country by an unblushing display of the grossest profligacy, and to ruin its finances by the wildest extravagance … who had permitted more than half a million of the public money to be diverted into the privy purse, on which a mistress drew at pleasure, while a part of the small grant which had been wrung from his ingratitude, for the aged sister of Sir George Lisle, shamefully remained unpaid …[8]

Clarendon's excoriating attack on Charles is not surprising, as he had been impeached due to the machinations of numerous political enemies – George Digby, for one – and had fled to France after the King refused to support him.

Three years later, in 1670 it appears that even the tiny £100 last promised to Mary had not actually have been paid as on 3rd March she petitioned Charles for a third time to receive a total of £900, the remainder of the sum granted nine years previously. She pleaded that:

whereas your petitioner is in great want and misery, her humble suite to your Majestie is, that you will bee graciously pleased to give order to the Lord Commissioners of your Majesty's Treasury for paying off the sayd sum of nine hundred pounds, for the reliefe of your poore petitioner, in her great distresse.[9]

Three more years passed. On 4th November 1673, Charles sent his Treasurer:

[A] Recommendation … of the petition of Mary Lisle, sister of Sir George Lisle, murdered for the sake and service of the late King, praying an order to the Lord Treasurer for payment of £900, the remainder of the £2000 granted her by a Privy Seal, his Majesty having a gracious sense of the great sufferings and eminent services of her father and brethren.[10]

This is the last time Mary appears in the records of the Treasury or the State Papers. It is not clear whether the money was paid, or if she simply gave up, or if she died and the case was finally closed. Where she had been living during the previous twelve years, who with, and who might have been supporting her, is presently a mystery.

---

8   *Life and Administration*, vol. II, pp.389-390.
9   *CSP Domestic Series*, 1670, p.99; *Life and Administration of Edward, First Earl of Clarendon*, vol. II, p.390.
10 *CSP Domestic Series*, 1673-1675, p.7.

Appendix VII

The Colchester Funeral, 1661

Account of the funeral of Sir George Lisle and Sir Charles Lucas, 7th June 1661. From London newsbook *The Kingdomes Weekly Intelligencer.*[1]

'And now we must give you some news from Colchester, of which we should have told you 12 years since, if the iniquity of the times had not forbid it; and that is of the funeral of those two most valiant and renowned Knights, Sir Charles Lucas, and Sir George Lisle, who you cannot forget were most savagely and cowardly shot to death in cool blood at Colchester, (Aug 28 1648) by order of those bloody wretches, Ireton, Whaley, Baxter and the rest, who afterwards arraign'd and murther'd our blessed Soveraign of ever glorious Memory.

Now the ancient Town of Colchester, desirous to manifest their abhorrency of this barbarous Fact, and the honour they bear to those famous Commanders, who laid down their lives in defence of it did most willingly joyn with the Neighbour Gentry in this Solemnity. Therefore on Fryday morning last, (June 7) Capt. Peeke and Capt. Lambe (two Captains of that Town's Trained Bands) caus'd their Drums to be beaten for their Companies to appear by one of the clock that afternoon: which they chearfully did, to the number of full 300 men, very completely arm'd; the Solemnity began at the Recorder's house, as well it might, not onely because the Recorder himself (John Shaw Esquire, a Member of this Parliament) took much worthy care to have it Honorably performed, but also in regard 'twas that very house, in which the Corps of those two Noble Knights were first brought, after they had been so basely murther'd and stripp'd; when the language of those Butchers was, *Now make much of your great Friends.*

Thence therefore were two coffins sent down, and about three in the afternoon the Trained Bands being come to the House, they marched in this manner: First Mr. Fromarteel, Captain Lambs Lieutenant, and after him the Musqueteers of both bands: Then Mr Cresfield, Capt. Peek's Lieutenant, after whom followed the Pikes of both bands: Then Mr. Flanner and Mr Emans the two Ensigns and then

---

1   No. 24, 10th-17th June 1661. Not in the British Library collection.

both the Captains in their several Funeral postures, (wherein Captain Tyrrel, and Captain Waghorn were willing Associats). Next these marched Mr Thurston who carried the gilt spurs upon a black staff; after him a gilt sword in a velvet scabbard, born by that loyal and valiant Capt. William Harris (an Officer under Sir Charles Lucas from the beginning of the War) the Gantlet carried by Mr Tho. Tulcot, the Helmet by Mr. Andrew Fromarteel; the breast by Mr John Robinson; and the back by Mr. John Merridale. Then Sir Charles Lucas his Eschutcheon was born by Mr, Tho. Ruse, and another for Sir George Lisle: Then two led Horses covered with mourning. After them two Trumpets, and then Mr. Laifield who preached the Funeral sermon (attended by two Clergy men, one on each hand) Then followed Sir Charles Lucas his Coffin carried upon six Pikes tied with match, born by Capt. Street, Mr. Mason, Mr. Wiggs, and Mr. Peter Soans in mourning; all of Sir Charles his own Regiment; and the Pall supported by six; *viz*, John Eldred sen. Hen. Ayloffe, Tho. Tulcot, Francis Nicholson, John Eldred junior, and George Sandford, all Esquires of good quality in that county, each of which were attended by an Officer bare-headed. Then followed three Clergy-men more, and after them Sir George Lisle's Coffin carried as the former upon pikes by four of his Officers in mourning, and his Pall born by six proper Gentlemen, *viz*. Mr. Thomas Beasen, Mr. Francis Wheeler, Mr. John Aylett, Mr. Mott of Stoake, Mr. Thomas Wyatt, and Captain Stephens; each of these also had a Town Officer bare-headed attending him. After these Coffins was born the great Mace of the Town cover'd with black Cypress: Then followed in their black Gowns , the Deputy-Mayor, and the Recorder (the Mayor himself being out of Town) Then all the Aldermen, with the Chamberlain, Town-Clerk, Assistants and Common-Counsel all in their Gowns, accompany'd with at least Ten thousand Gentlemen and Inhabitants of the Town and County, (had they been millions they had not been a man too many). In this manner they went through the chief streets of the Town to St Gyles's Church, where the Lord Lucas his Ancestors are interr'd. Being come to Church after Prayers Mr Laifield made a very learned and pious sermon, and then gave a Narrative of the Life and Death of Sir Charles Lucas, who was well known to him, and as much as he knew of Sir George Lisle, concluding with a commendation of the Magistrates and Inhabitants of Colchester for their Loyalty, and of the Town it self, which anciently had been a famous City. After Sermon the door of the Lord Lucas his Vault being open'd, the two Coffins were carried down, & the Gentlemen that bore the several pieces of Armor went into the Vault, the Drums beating a march until they all came out of the Vault, and then the Musquetiers gave three great Volleys with great acclamations, and then march'd back into the Town, where again they gave several Volleys, concluding the Ceremony with ringing of bells in all Churches of the Town.

Thus these two right-valiant Knights had all the Retribution that Colchester (we might say Essex) could pay unto them; though all their own Friends (be they twice Ten thousand) cannot honour them more then their Enemies did, when out of so many Commanders and persons of Honour as were lockt up in Colchester, the

Enemy excepted these two brave Knights, confessing thereby they were afraid to let them live; But know (when Ireton and others who butcher'd them basely in cold blood, are themselves found unworthy of a Grave, their loathsome carcasses being dragg'd and buried by the common-Hangman) these Noble Knights are revived again by this living Funeral, on the seventh of June, which was the very day that they first took Arms in the County of Essex.

Appendix VIII

James Heath:
A New Book of Loyal English Martyrs, 1665

In 1665 James Heath published a book containing short biographies of 'martyrs' who had died in the King's cause since the 1641. He drew heavily on *The Loyall Sacrifice*, and *Mercurius Pragmaticus*. Discussing Colchester, he focuses primarily on Lucas and the circumstances leading to the siege, and then to the siege itself, before finally mentioning Lisle. To assist the reader wishing to skip straight to that point, Lisle's name has been emphasised.

Sir Charles Lucas and Sir George Lisle shot to death at Colchester, by a Council of War, upon the Rendition of the same Town.[1]

These Gemini of Valour and Honour, as well as exact Loyalty, I could no well divide in this Martyrology, being so joyned in their deaths, honourable Burial, and Funerals, and being both of them so equally eminent in their Generation, for all true worth and Vertue.

Sr. Charles Lucas was descended of a very Ancient and Illustrious Family; he who knows not the name of Lucas, knows nothing of Gentility; but if this Noble Person had derived no Honour from his Ancestors, yet his own purchased Glory, and the Relative Merits of his two Famous Brethren, the Lord Lucas, and Sir Gervas, formerly Governour of Belvoyr Castle (in which three, Nature and Education had summ'd up a Perfection) will without any other Additaments, transmit him to Posterity as a worthy and English Heroe.

He was a Person assisted with a resolute Spirit, of an active disposition, and a sutable discretion to manage it; strict and severe in his Commands, without any pride or surliness, free in his Rewards to persons of Desert and Quality; in his Society, and with his Friends, he was affable, and pleasant; in his Charge serious

1   pp.126-140.

and vigilant; remiss in nothing that might any way improve or expedite his Dispatch in the Affairs of War, as he is well charactered by a good Pen.

We will therefore view him only in the Camp, in which he gloriously lived and died, excusing his Learning and other rare Endowments from the imputation of Crime, and lay all the Load of his miserable Fate, aggravated by the Name of an enemy to the Kingdom, upon his Loyal carriage, and magnanimity, abstracted from all other Considerations.

In the beginning of the Tumults and Preparations for War in Scotland, against their Native & pious Pr. he raised a Troop of Horse in London, and like an Expert and Resolute Commander, behaved himself in that uncertain Service, being a profest Enemy to the Insolencies and Rebellious Designs of that Nation.

That Broyl ceasing, through the great condescentions of the King, to the unreasonable Demands of that Kingdom, which kindled the Combustions in this, the King being necessitated to take up Arms, to defend his Person, and the Authority of the Laws against the like Rebellion at home, Sr. Charles readily engaged on his Soveraigns side against the pretended 2 Houses. The first place where he signally shewed his Valour in that just Cause (omitting Exploys of less concernment, as not to our purpose) was at Auburn Chase, and Newberry Field, where the first memorable Battel was fought; here Sr. Charles Lucas, with many other Gallant Gentlemen, behaved themselves with undaunted courage and Resolution, which so far engaged him in that dangerous Business, the fight being obstinately maintained, that he received some desperate wounds that fatal day; but the Blood he lost there, was but an Ernest or prognostick stillations & drops of that mass of Bloud which was afterwards to flow out with his Life, for the same Cause.

His next Appearance to the terror of his Enemies, his Valour having gained him a frighting name amongst them, was in his deserting of Cawood Castle, assaulted by the Parliaments Forces, whence with good conduct, and as true Courage, he forced his way through their Quarters, to such places as he thought convenient, and came at last in safety to York.

His Bravery in charging at Marston Moor, and enduring the Brunt of his Enemies, when the Fortune of that day declined on the kings side, as it then challenged the Praise of all men, so it deserves everlasting Remembrance.

His discreet and military Management of the Affairs at Newark, where he manifested himself an absolute Souldier, both in Discipline of war, and personal Action, to the great satisfaction of the Governour and Garrison, which alwaies consisted of Gallant and truly Noble Persons, merits a Record to serve and an Example to Future Times.

His brave and successful Attempt in his March from Berkly Castle, with part of his Regiment, betwixt Slymbridge and Beverston castle, upon Col. Masseys Garrisons, together with his incomparable Gallantry in the pursuit of his Design at Tedbury, was work for noble Imitation.

But all these Particulars signifie nothing to his Heroick Magnanimity in defence of the Town of Colchester, beleaguered by a potent and victorious Army; This was a the Corollary, the summing up of all his Atchievements in the times and circum-vallations of which place, we shall confine and circumscribe all his Glories.

After that the Parliament, by the success of their unlawful Arms had reduced the King, his Friends, Armies, Towns, and Forts into their power, it was hoped by all men, that now they would appear, what they had so long fallaciously pretended themselves, the Assertors of the publick Peace and Liberty, in order whereunto, no other Expedient was visible, then by complying with their reiterated Protestations of Loyal Obedience to the King, in a present and speedy Resumption of him to the Exercise of his Royal Authority, his Majesty having, and being willing to grant all that in Honor, Justice and Conscience could be expected from him: But contrary thereunto, they Voted to settle the Kingdom without him (as impossible, as to have day without the Light of the Sun, and so experimented in the dark Confusions that followed those Trayterous Resolves) which, so much discontented the Generality of the People, who were now, for the most part undeceived, of those principles which had been cunningly spread amongst them, of the Kings Averseness to hearken to his Parliaments, that after several fruitless Petitions for a Composure, and Treaty with the King, from several Counties, in the delivery whereof to the Houses, some of the Petitioners, as of Surry, were killed, and wounded, and sent home other-wise unanswered; they resolved to try another way, and have Recourse to Arms. Col. Langhorn, Powel, and Poyner rise in Wales, the Scots enter England; but that which most alarm'd the two Houses, was the Kentish Business, which lookt full of Terrour, the whole County unanimously declaring for a speedy Closure with the King, and has formed to that purpose, a very considerable Army, made up with a numerous Company of Volunteers, from London, under the command of the Earl of Norwich; against these therefore, General Fairfax was sent, with 6000 men, as requiring his Presence; who was valiantly opposed at Maidstone, by part of the Kentish Army, but they being not relieved by their Body at Rochester, were for the most part cut off, and the Town gained; whereupon, the Earl of Norwich, with 3000 men, marched hastily to Black heath, and from thence, ferryed and swam over the greatest part of his Army into Essex side, and quartered at Bow and Stratford.

Being there, he met with this Noble Heroe Sr. Charles Lucas, and other eminent Persons of Honour and Quality, as, the Lord Capel, Lord Loughborough, with a compleat Body of resolved men, with whom, after they had skirmished with some Parliament Horse at Mile-end, they marched to Chelmsford, where they seized the Committee; and thence, to Colchester, a Town defenceless, and inconsider-able, as was generally supposed, both by the Enemy, and the Adjacent Parts of the Countrey, either to receive by a provisional way of Relief any great Force into it, or by reason of the untenable Condition of it, to hold out any time, if they should venture to take up or stay there. Yet so constantly couragious, vigilant, and incred-ibly industrious, were these Loyally disposed Gentlemen, as this Town, which by reason of the in preparation of Necessaries, could not probably hold out against so potent and terrible an Enemy, the space of one Week; continued 3 Moneths, in a most resolute Defiance and resistance of a Victorious Army glutted with such variety of Conquests, and supplied with such fresh and continual Recruits, to accomplish those unjust Triumphs and Trophies, which they had begun to rear upon the Ruines of the whole Kingdom: But at length after many stout Endeavours, in Sallies, Eruptions, and perpetual Firings gallantly performed, the Loyal Garrison having eaten up all their Horses, the Dogs and Cats, and what-soever (though most reluctant to Nature, being sweetned with Prunes, and some other Fruit and Spice, whereof some store was found in the Town at their Coming) could afford them nourishment; was compelled to come to a Capitulation (though it was bravely resolved the night before, to attempt breaking through, which was not unfeasable) by which it was concluded, the Town should be surrendred upon these conditions, the Officers at Mercy, and the Souldiery upon Quarter for Life.

The Reason of these hard Conditions, and their standing out so long, which occasioned them, was threefold. The first was, That not only the County wherein they were besieged, but most of the Counties in England had engaged them-selves, that they would joyn with, and Assist them in the business; but all those Mountains of Promise came to nothing, an inconsiderable Party appearing about Saffron Walden, being routed by Major Sparrow. The Second, and which seemed more probable, was the hopes they had from London, a great many Persons of Quality, and known Royalists therein, having listed themselves under the Earl of Holland, who had with him in that Action, the Duke of Buckingham, the Earl of Peterborough, the Lord Francis Villers, and others; these appeared at Kingston, in a formidable manner, but were presently supprest by Sr. Michael Livesey, and the aforesaid Lord Francis, bringing up the Rear, was there killed, refusing the Quarter offered from Rebels, the Earl of Holland fled to St. Neats in Bedfordshire, where his Quarters were beaten up, by Col. Scroops Regiment of Horse, where Col. Dalbeir was slain; and himself taken Prisoner, and carried to Warwick castle. The third and chiefest Reason, which induced them to the continuance of the Siege, was their daily Expectation of the Advance of the Scotch Army, then entred England, and to whom were joyned a number of Gallant Persons, who had appeared for the King, throughout the War, Commanded by Sr. Marmaduke, now Lord Langdale. Over this Kirk-Army, Duke Hamilton was made General, a Person suspected of all hands, and of whom, and his success, his Majesty, it is said, very much desponded, when first he had notice of his Commanding in Chief. And so it fell out; for, at Preston in Lancashire, Lieut. Gen. Cromwel met with this Army, and with 11000 men, totally defeated them; so that Hamilton was forced to fly, and was taken by the Lord Grey of Grooby, at Uttoxeter, where, as Earl of Cambridge, he was after-wards for this business beheaded. But I venture not to Canonize him a Martyr.

Colchester being thus defeated of all hopes of Relief, rendred it self to the Victors, and 5 hours after the Surrender, according to a Decree of a Council of War, ensued the death of these to Noble Persons, being destined by them to be shot in a military Execution. The only Reason why they were picked out from amongst the rest, was nothing else, but their superlative Courage, and their fixedness of Duty towards the King, in whose Cause and Defence, they assured themselves, they would never be wanting, as long as their Breath would last, were the Difficulties and Dangers of doing it, never so great, and so many. An Honourable Enemy would have scorned so unwarrantable and impotent revenge, and for which, the names of some Persons will stink for ever.

But never was the Message of Death entertained by any with more Magnanimity, and undaunted Resolution and Bravery of mind, both the Roman, and Christian confidence striving to Excellency in this harsh Encounter with an unexpected Death: Sr. Charles was the first by designation, to be sacrificed to their Cruelty, who having retired himself a while, to offer up his last Prayers to God, commending his Soul into his hands, presented himself to his Executioners, and tearing open his Doublet, exposed his naked Breast, saying aloud, *Now Rebels, do your worst*; and so by their murdering Bullets was dispatched in the place.

Sr. George Lisle was appointed to be next in this Tragedy, of whom, take this brief Account: He was extracted from a Gentile Family in Surrey, and from the beginning of the Troubles, had strenuously and couragiously assisted the King: the most remarkable place (saving this of his Death) where his great Spirit, and military experience, most manifested it self, was at the second Newberry Battel, where he made good his ground, being Col. of a Regiment of Foot, against several Charges both of Horse and Foot, of the Enemy, who did all they could, to drive him from some Advantages, which, could they have obtained by subduing that handful of men, might have facilitated their way to Victory. This he sustained, with an Invincible Resolution, animating his Souldiers, and leading them on without any Supplies or Reserves, several times, and for the more Encouragement, took off his own Doublet, and charged in his Shirt, bidding them, come on once more for the King, then for the Prince, then for the Duke, till such time as night came, and quitted him from his hot Service and Enemies together. This noble Action was taken notice of by the K., & acknowledged so at Court, which rendred him deservedly famous among the Swordsmen of his own party, and as dreadful to the other, so that having him in their hands, by this Surrender, they resolved, to be thus cowardly and basely rid of him.

It being, as was said before, his turn to die; seeing and beholding that sad Spectacle, the dead Body of his dearest Friend, he fell upon it, kissed it, as if he meant to breath into it another Soul; and with a free and full, yet true Relation of his Vertues, and Endowments, he did often repeat these words In how short a moment has a rare Spirit expired! well, this Priority was due to thee, but I shall not be long behind thee, my Death which is now at hand, shall restore thee to me.

After this, standing up, and taking five Pieces of Gold out of his Pocket, he gave one to his Executioners, and the other four he sent to four Friends in London, and then addressing himself to the standers by, he said, Oh, how many do I see here about me, whose Lives I have saved in hot bloud, and now must mine be taken away most barbarously in could bloud! Sure the like was never heard of among the Goths and Vandals, or the very Barbarians, in any Age. After which words, some short Ejaculations, and some few Invocations upon the name of Jesus, as he stood in an unconquerable Resolution of mind, and in an Heroick Posture, he was also dispatched by the same hands.

Thus these 2 stars of the first Magnitude, for valorous Loyalty, were put out and extinguished, by the malice of their Enemies; but though they shine not here, in that splendor, which their desired Lives would have appeared in, yet they shine in a full Lustre, in that Region of Glory, whither the Violence of their Enemies transplanted them.

Most certain it is, that upon the Ground where Sr. Charles Lucas fell when he was shot, there hath grown no grass, where the Print of his Body was, it remaining still bare, though it be green round about; an indignation of the unreasonable, unjust, and cruel usage of so brave a person; and if the Earth be punished, that groan'd at their untimely end, how much more heavy will their punishment be, that contrived, and rejoyced at it?

Since the Restitution of his Majesty, the corps of these Worthies have been taken up, and with all due Magnificence, attended by the Gentry thereabouts, and the Mayor, and other principal persons of Colchester, interred in the Repositories of the Right Honourable Family of the Lucas's, with a Funeral Oration, and other requisite Solemnities, the deserved Honour to their precious memory.

Appendix IX

David Lloyd: *Memoires ...*, 1668

In 1668 David Lloyd compiled a book similar to Heath's, and this time included an individual entry for Lisle. Lloyd primarily drew on *The Loyall Sacrifice*.[1]

The life and death of Sir George Lisle[2]

Sir George Lisle, an honest Bookseller's Son (great streams run sometimes from muddy Springs) that having Trailed a Pike in the Low Countries, by keeping good Society and improving Company, Ever (as he would say) consorting with those most by whom he might accomplish himself best. By generous pleasing and naturally bounteous disposition; by his great skill (above his years) gained by observation in the modern and ancient Militia, excelling in the Command of Foot, as (a) Sir Charles Lucas did that of Horse: By the great sense he had of Honor and Justice, was admitted into Inferior Commands in England, where his Valor without Ostentation, his Just and Chearful Commands, without a Surly Imperiousness, rendred him so infinitely beloved and observed by his Souldiers, that with his Discipline and Courage, he led as in a Line, upon any services through the greatest danger and difficulty, that he was preferred to a Superior, in which capacity he had one quality of an obliging and knowing Commander, that never to the hour of his death would he Engage his Souldiers in that Action, wherein he would not hazard his own person, as at the last Newbery Fight (before his Majesties face, who then Knighted him for it) leading his men in his (b) Shirt, both that they might see his Valor, and (it being Night) discern his Person from whom they were to receive direction and courage at Brambdean-heath, where he gained and kept an advantageous Hill against all Wallers Army, at the first Newbery Fight, where he

---

1   The book's full, and forbiddingly long, title, is *Memoires of the Lives, Actions, Sufferings & Deaths of those Noble, Reverend and Excellent Personages, That Suffered By Death, Sequestration, Decimation, or Otherwise, For the Protestant Religion, And the great Principle thereof, Allegiance To their Soveraigne, In our late Intestine Wars, From the Year 1637, to the Year 1660, and from thence continued to 1666. With the Life and Martyrdom of King Charles I.*

2   Lloyd, pp.478-479.

Commanded the Forelorn-hope; at Nazeby, where he and the Lord Bard led the left-hand Tertia of Foot; and at the two Garrisons he held with the last, surrendring them with Oxford. He was approved and admired for his Judgement, Direction, Dispatches and Chearfulness, Virtues that had special influence upon every common Souldier; especially in his three great Charges (in each whereof he came to the Butt-end of the Musquet) for the first whereof, his Word was The Crown; for the second, Prince Charles; and for the third, The Duke of York; resolving to have gone over all his Majesties Children, as long as he had a Man to fight for them, or there was a Rebel to fight against them. Being in most of the Sallies in Colchester, and having three times scowred the Leaguer, with so much hazard, that he was twice taken Prisoner, but rescued he was to second Sir Charles Lucas, as he always desired to imitate him; saying over his Corps, *How soon is a brave spirit expired? we shall be together presently.* Dispatching some Tokens to his friends in London, and expostulating with them that (c) his life should be taken away in cold-bloud, when he had saved so many of theirs in hot, and praying for his Majesty and the Kingdom, he entertained grim death with a sprightly countenance, and heroick posture; saying, *Now then Rebels and Traytors do your worst.*

It will be Embalming enough to these deserving persons, that King Charles the First, upon the news of their death, wept. Monument enough, that the very Parliament was amazed at it. Epitaph enough, that a grat Man, and a great Traveller too protested, *That he saw many dye, but never with any more Souldier or Christian-like resolution.*

Margin notes:
a)   Esteemed the best in Europe
b)   Whereupon they reported in London, that they saw a white witch run up and down in his Majesties Army
c)   What a Christian note did he leave in Mr. Dolmans house near Newbery, that the poor, wounded, helpless men should be cared for.

Bibliography

17th Century Sources
Primary/Contemporary Sources (Anonymous)

A collection of all the publicke orders, ordinances, and declarations of both houses of Parliament from the ninth of March, 1642 untill December, 1646 together with severall of His Majesties proclamations and other papers printed at Oxford. London, 1646. TT E.1058[1] / Wing (2nd edn.) E878.

A Copie of a Letter of the taking of Leicester On Wednesday the 18th of June, 1645. London, June 1645. TT E.288[42].

A Diary of the Siege of Colchester by the Forces under the Command of his Excellency the Lord Generall Fairfax. BL 669.f.13[6]. Single sheet. Also Wing D1378A (an alternative version with a map of the siegeworks).

A Great Over-throw: Given to Sir Ralph Hopton's whole Army by Sir William Waller neere Farnham, with onely six Troope of Horse, and some Foote … London, 30th November 1643. TT E.77[14].

A Great Victory Obtained By His Excellencie The Lord Generall Fairfax Neer The Island of Mersey …, London, June 1648. TT E.449[20].

A happy defeat given to the King's forces neere Tipton Green in Staffordshire … London. TT E.51[12].

A Letter from Kent on the Rising at Rochester. London, May 1648. TT E.443[26].

A Letter from Sandwich in Kent. Included in *The Declaration And Propositions of the Navie.* London, June 1648. TT E445[32].

A list of the colonels as also of the severall counties out of which they are to raise their men … London, 1640. STC 19616.

A List of the Field Officers chosen and appointed for the Irish Expedition, by the Committee at Guild-hall London, for the Regiments of 5000. foot and 500. horse. British Library, 669.f.6.31.

A more Exact Relation of The Siege laid to the Town of Leicester: How it was maintained, and how lost, and what Quarter was given by the Kings Forces. London, June 1645. TT E.287[6].

A Most True Relation of the Present State of His Majesties Army … London, 3rd December 1642. TT E.244[2]. Generally referred to as '*Deserter*'.

A Narration of The Great Victory, (Through Gods Providence) Obtained by the Parliaments Forces Under Sir William Waller, At Alton in Surrey the 13. of this instant December, 1643. London, 16th December 1643. TT E.78[22].

A Narration of the Siege and taking of The Town of Leicester The last of May, 1645. by the Kings Forces. London, June 1645. TT E.289[6].

A Narrative of the Great Victory Obtained by the Lord Generall in Kent … London, 1648. TT E.446[10].

A Particular Relation of the Action before Cyrencester (or Cycester) in Glocester shire. Taken in on Candlemas day 1642 … [i.e. 1643] Oxford? 1643. Wing P597.

A perfect Relation of the taking of Leicester: With the severall marches of the Kings Army since the taking thereof … London, June 1645. TT E.288[4].

A Proclamation declaring His Majesties grace to his Subjects, touching matters complained of, as publique greevances. London, 10th July 1621. STC (2nd ed.) 8667.

A Proclamation for apprehending and punishing of Souldiers prested for His Majesties Service, who shall depart from their Commanders, or shall be Mutinous, or otherwise disorderly in their passage to the North. STC (2nd edn.) 9161.

A Relation Made in the House of Commons, by Col: Nathaniel Fiennes, Concerning The Surrender of the City and Castle of Bristoll, August 5. 1643. Together with the Transcripts and Extracts of certain Letters, wherein his care for the preservation of the City doth appear. London, August 1643. TT E.64[12].

A True and Exact Relation of the taking of Colchester, Sent in a Letter From an Officer of the Army, (who was present during the siege in that service,) to a Member of the House of Commons. London, 1648. TT E.461[24].

A true relacon of the Earle of Denbigh his proceedings after he had received his Commission from both houses of Parliament to command as Generall of all the forces raised or to be raised in the countyes of Warwick Worcester Stafford and Salop with the cittyes and countyes of Coventry and Leichfeild and parts adioned in the yeare 1644. Unpublished MS. Warwick Record Office, CR 2017/R8.

A True Relation Of a Victory obtained over the Kings Forces, by the Army of Sir Thomas Fairfax: Being Fought betweene Harborough, And Nasiby, On Saturday June 14. 1645. TT E.288[22].

A true Relation of my Lord Ogle's Engagements before the battle of Edgehill and after, BL Add MS 27402, f.82.

A True Relation Of a Great and Happy Victory. Which it hath pleased God to give to His Excellency the Earle of Essex, and his Forces, over the Kings Army, as it was brought to both Houses of Parliament, by the Lord Wharton, and Mr. Stroud, a Member of the House of Commons on Wednesday in the Afternoone, Octob. 26. 1642. London, 27th October 1642. Wing T2878.

A True Relation of the Late Battell Neere Newbury … London, 26th September 1643. TT E.69[2].

A True Relation of the Late Expedition of His Excellency, Robert Earle of Essex, for the Relief of Gloucester. With the Description of the Fight at Newbury. Reprinted in John Washbourne's *Bibliotheca Gloucestrensis,* pp.233-249

(1825). Generally considered to be the official Parliamentarian account of the First Battle of Newbury.

A True Relation Of the taking of Mountjoy in the County of Tyrone, By Collonell Clotworthy … London, 4th August 1642. TT E.108[47].

An Elegie On the Death of Sir Charles Lucas and Sir George Lisle, 1648. BL 669.f.13[20].

An Exact Relation of Prince Rupert His marching out of Bristoll, the 11. of this instant Septemb. 1645. according to the Articles of agreement made betweene him and the Right Honourable, Sir Thomas Fairfax. London, 18th September 1645. TT E.302[3].

An Order Of The Lords and Commons For the Restraint of Passage from Oxford, or any other parts of the Kings Army to London … London, 18th October 1643. Wing E1713.

Another great Fight On Sunday morning last between the Shavers of Colchester, and the Parliaments Forces …, London, August 1648. TT E.457[15].

Bloudy Newes from Kent. Being A Relation of the great fight at Rochester and Maidstone, betwixt the Parliaments Army under the comand of the Lord Generall Fairfax, and the Kentish Forces commanded by Generall Hales. London, 1648. TT E.445[36].

Colchesters Teares: Affecting and Afflicting City and Country, Dropping From the sad face of a new Warr, threatning to bury in her own Ashes that wofull Town. London, July 1648.

His Highnesse Prince Ruperts Late Beating Up The Rebels Quarters At Post-comb & Chinner in Oxford shire. And his Victory in Chalgrove Feild, on Sunday morning June 18. 1643. Oxford, 1643. Wing H2076B.

Prince Rupert's Diary. Anonymous. Written after 1662. Benett Family of Pythouse, Tisbury. Wiltshire and Swindon Archives, reference 413/444. Note, the archives hold only photocopies of these documents, the originals having been withdrawn by the owner. An abridged version edited by C. H. Firth, containing just the dates of movement and a very few original marginal notes, was printed in the *English Historical Review* vol. 13, issue 52, Oct 1898 (pp.729-741). Peter Young includes in full the section pertinent to Edgehill, in his *Edgehill 1642* (pp.273-275).

Remarkable Passages from Nottingham Lichfield, Leicester, and Cambridge … A Letter from a Gentleman neere Nottingham, to a friend in London. 1st September 1642. BL 669.f.6[75].

VI [Six] Severall Victories Obtained By Major-Generall Browne, Lieutenant-Generall Cromwell, and Col. Fines, Against the Kings Forces neere Oxford … London, 1645. Wing S2814B.

The Accusation Given by His Maiestie Against the Lord Wilmot: Together With the Lord Wilmots Declaration of his innocency. Also A Petition of the Officers of the old Horse to his Maiesty, in behalfe of the Lord Wilmot: With his Maiesties Answer thereunto. London, 30th August 1644. TT E.7[27].

The Copie of A Letter From The Lord Generall his Quarters. Certifying, How the Lord Generals Horse brake through the Kings Army; and how Major Generall Skippon fought like a Lion, and gained better conditions from the Enemy then was expected; the Kings Forces having before intended to put all our Foot to the Sword. London, September 1644. TT E.8[22].

The humble Petition of the Knights, Gentry, Clergy, and Commonalty of the County of Kent … 11th May 1648. TT E.441[25].

The joynt Declaration of the severall Counties of Kent, Essex, Middlesex, Surrey, unto The Souldiers of the Army, now under the Command of the Lord Fairfax. BL 669.f.12[35].

The Letters From His Maiesty, and from the Officers of His Majesties Army, To The Earle of Essex at Lestithen, Inviting him to Peace, and his refusall thereof. Oxford, 1644. TT E.8[26].

The Loyall Sacrifice: Presented in the Lives and Deaths of those two Eminent-Heroick Patternes, For Valour, Discipline, and Fidelity; The generally beloved and bemoaned, Sir Charles Lucas, And Sir George Lisle, Knights … London(?), November 1648. TT E.1202[2].

The third Intelligence From Reading. Dated from His Excellency His Quarters Before Reading, April 26. at night. London, 28th April 1643. TT E.99[29].

Three Letters, From the Right Honourable Sir Thomas Fairfax, Lieut. Gen. Crumwell, and the Committee residing in the Army. Wherein All the Particulars of the Great Victory obtained by our Forces against his Majesties, is fully related, fought the 14 of June, 1645. London, 17th June 1645. TT E.288[27].

Primary / Contemporary Sources (Known Author)

Archer, Elias. *A True Relation of the Marchings of the Red Trained Bands of Westminster, the Green Auxiliaries of London, and the Yellow Auxiliaries of the Tower Hamlets, under the command of Sir William Waller, from Munday the 16. of Octob. to Wednesday the 20. of Decemb. 1643.* London: 1643. Wing A3605B.

Archer, Elias. *A Fuller Relation of the Great Victory obtained (through Gods Providence) at Alsford, on Friday the 28. March, 1644. By the Parliaments Forces, under the Command of Sir William Waller* … London: 1644. TT E.40[1].

Archer, Thomas. *Ravens Almanack – foretelling of a Plague, Famine, and Civille Warre that shall happen this present yeare 1609.* London, 1609. STC (2nd edn.) 6519.4.

Belasyse, John. 'A Brief Relation of the Life and Memoirs of John, Lord Belasyse, written and collected by his Secretary, Joshua Moone.' In *Calendar of the Manuscripts of the Marquess of Ormonde, K. P. Preserved at Kilkenny Castle.* New Series, Vol. II. London: His Majesty's Stationery Office, 1908.

Birch, John. *Military Memoir of Colonel John Birch, Sometime Governor of Hereford in the Civil War Between Charles I. and the Parliament.* London: Camden Society, 1873.

Bulstrode, Sir Richard. *Memoirs and Reflections upon the Reign and Government of K. Charles the IId.* London, 1720.

Byron, (John) Lord. An account of the first battle of Newbury, written after the Restoration, in a letter to the Earl of Clarendon. Add MS 1738, Clarendon State Papers, Bodleian Library.

Campion, Thomas. *The Description of a Maske: presented in the Banqueting Roome at Whitehall … at the Mariage of the … Earle of Somerset and … the Lady Frances Howard.* London, 1614. STC (2nd edn.) 4539.

Carter, Matthew. *A Most True And exact Relation Of That as Honourable as unfortunate Expedition of Kent, Essex, and Colchester. By M. C. A Loyall Actor in that Engagement, Anno Dom. 1648.* 1650. Wing C662.

Chapman, George. *Andromeda Liberata. Or The Nuptials Of Perseus and Andromeda.* London, 1614. STC 4694.

Chapman, George. *A Free And Offenceles Justification, Of A Lately Publisht and most maliciously misinterpreted Poeme: Entituled Andromeda Liberata.* London, 1614. STC 4977.

King Charles I. *By the King. A Proclamation declaring His Majesties grace to his Subjects, touching matters complained of, as publique greevances.* STC II 8667. London, 1621.

Clarendon, 1st Earl of (Edward Hyde). *History of the Rebellion and Civil Wars in England. A New Edition, from the Original Manuscript.* Seven volumes. Oxford: Oxford University Press, 1840.

Codrington, Robert. *The Life and Death, of the Illustrious Robert Earle of Essex, &c …* London: 1646. TT E.358[7].

Coe, Richard. *An Exact Dyarie, or a briefe Relation Of the Progresse of Sir William Wallers Army since the joyning of the London Auxiliaries with his Forces: which was the twelfth day of May 1644, untill their returne homeward on thursday the 11 of July following. Relating the perticulars of every Skirmish Battle and March dureing the said time.* London, 19th July 1644.

Corbet, John. *An Historical Relation of the Military Government of Gloucester,* 1647. Included in Washbourne's *Bibliotheca Gloucestrensis,* 1825 (pp.1-152).

Corbet, William. *The Copy of a Letter from his Majesties Court at Hampton Court.* Included with *Propositions Agreed upon By Both Houses of Parliament. To be sent to the Kings Majesty, for Peace, And for setling of the Church and Kingdome, that His Majesty may come to London, and sit with his Parliament.* London, 1647. TT E.404[36].

Corderoy, Jeremy. *A Warning For Worldlings, Or a comfort to the godly, and a terror to the wicked.* London, 1608. STC (2nd edn.) 5757.

D'Ewes, Sir Simonds. *The Autobiography and Correspondence of Sir Simonds D'Ewes, Bart., During the Reigns of James I. and Charles I.* Ed. James Orchard Halliwell. Two volumes. London: Richard Bentley, 1845.

De Gomme, Bernard (attributed). *The Storm of Bristol. De Gomme's Account.* Stephen Ede-Borrett (ed.). Leeds: Raider Games, 1988. From the contemporary account, *Bristoll taken, by Prince Rupert: Julye 26, 1643…*

Digby, Lord George (attributed). *A True and Impartiall Relation of the Battaile betwixt, His Maiesties Army, and that of the Rebells neare Newbery in Berkshire, Sept. 20. 1643.* Oxford: September 1643. TT E.69[10].

Dugdale, Sir William. *The Life, Diary, and Correspondence of Sir William Dugdale.* William Hamper (ed.). London: Harding, Lepard, and Co., 1827.

Ellis, Thomas. *An Exact and Full Relation of the last fight between the Kings Forces and Sir William Waller. Sent in a Letter from an Officer in the Army to his friend in London.* London: July 5 1644, TT E.53[18].

Fairfax, Sir Thomas. *A Letter From his Excellency the Lord Fairfax Generall of the Parliaments Forces: Concerning the Surrender of Colchester, The Grounds and Reasons of putting to death Sir Charles Lucas and Sir George Lysle; with the Articles and Explanation of the same.* London, 2nd September 1648. TT E.461[35].

Fairfax, Sir Thomas. *Short Memorials of Thomas, Lord Fairfax. Written by Himself.* London, 1699. Included in Maseres, Francis. *Select Tracts Relating to the Civil Wars in England, In the Reign of King Charles the First.* Two volumes. London, 1815.

Foster, Henry. *A true and exact Relation of the Marchings of the Two Regiments of the Trained Bands of the City of London, Being the Red & blew Regiments, As also, Of the three Regiments of the Auxiliary forces, the Blew, Red, and Orange, who marched forth for the reliefe of the City of Glocester from August 23. to Sept. 28.* London: 1643. Wing F1625A.

Glanville, John. *The Voyage to Cadiz in 1625. Being A Journal Written by John Glanville.* Rev. Alexander B. Grosart (ed.). Camden Society: 1883.

Goodman, Godfrey. *The Court of King James the First.* Two volumes. Ed. J. S. Brewer. London: Bentley, 1839.

Gwynne, John. *Military Memoirs of the Great Civil War. Being the Military Memoirs of John Gwynne; and an Account of the Earl of Glencairn's Expedition, as General of His Majesty's Forces, in the Highlands of Scotland, in the Years 1653 & 1654.* Edinburgh: Archibald Constable and Co., 1822.

'H. T.' *A Glorious Victorie Obtained by Sir William Waller, and Sir William Balfoure, against the Lord Hoptons Forces, neere Alsford, on Fryday last March 29.* London: printed 1st April 1644. Wing G871.

Harley, Captain Robert. Letter to his brother, Colonel Edward Harley, 12th April 1643. HMC Portland MSS, vol. 3, pp.106-110. Quoted by John Adair in *Cheriton 1644. The Campaign and the Battle,* p.127.

Harsnet, Samuel. *A Full Relation Of The Defeat given, and Victory obtained upon Saturday last, by our Forces at Abbington …* TT E.24[14].

Heath, James. *A New Book of Loyal English Martyrs and Confessors*. London: 1668.

Heath, James. *A Chronicle of the Late Intestine War in the Three Kingdoms of England, Scotland and Ireland*. Second edition. London: 1675. Wing H1321.

Helaw, Edward. *A Letter from Hampton-Court, of the manner of His Majesties departure*. Included in *The Kings Majesties Most Gratious Message in Foure Letters*. London, November 1647. TT E414[10].

Henny, Patrick. *The Husbande. A Poeme expressed In a Compleat Man*. London, 1614. STC (2nd edn.) 14008.

Heselrige, Sir Arthur. His speech to the House of Commons on 3rd April 1644, from a shorthand transcript by Walter Yonge. BL Add MS 18779, f.87.

Hexham, Henry. *A True and Briefe Relation of The Famous Siege of Breda: Besieged, and Taken In …* The Hague: 1637.

Hopton, Sir Ralph. *Bellum Civile. Hopton's Narrative of his Campaign in the West (1642-1644) and Other Papers*. Ed. Charles E. H. Chadwyck Healey. London: Somerset Record Society, 1902.

Jones, Captain John. *A Letter from Captain Jones being a relation of the proceedings of Sir William Waller's Armie*. 2nd April 1644. TT E.40[12].

Laud, William. *The Works of the Most Reverend Father in God, William Laud, D.D. Sometime Lord Archbishop of Canterbury*. Vol. VII: *Letters*. Oxford: John Henry Parker, 1860.

Lithgow, William. *The Present Surveigh Of London And England's State …* London: 1643. Wing L2543.

Lloyd, David. *Memoires of the Lives, Actions, Sufferings & Deaths of those Noble, Reverend, and Excellent Personages, that Suffered by Death, Sequestration, Decimation, or otherwise, for the Protestant Religion, And the great Principle thereof, Allegiance to their Soveraigne, in our late Intestine Wars …* London: 1668.

Lucas, Sir Charles. *Sir Charles Lucas His Last Speech At the place of Execution, where hee was shot to Death*. London, September 1648. TT E.462[20].

Ludlow, Edmund. *Memoirs of Edmund Ludlow Esq; …* Two volumes. Bern: 1698

Luke, Sir Samuel. *Journal of Sir Samuel Luke*. Three volumes. Oxford Record Society, 1950. I. G. Philip (ed.).

Luke, Sir Samuel. *The Letter Books of Sir Samuel Luke, 1644-45*. Bedfordshire Historical Record Society, vol. XLII. London: Her Majesty's Stationery Office, 1963. H. G. Tibbutt (ed.).

Morrillon, Claude. *The Funeral Pompe and Obsequies of … King Henry IV of France*. A translation from French. London, 1610. STC (2nd edn.) 13136.

Ormonde, Marquess of. *The Manuscripts of the Marquis of Ormonde, Preserved At The Castle, Kilkenny*. Vol. I. Historical Manuscripts Commission. London: Eyre and Spottiswoode, 1895.

Overbury, Sir Thomas. *Sir Thomas Overbury his observations in his travailes upon the state of the Xvii. Provinces as they stood anno Dom. 1609*. London, 1609. (STC (2nd edn.) 18903).

Overbury, Sir Thomas. *A Wife. Now The Widdow of Sir Tho: Overburye … Fourth impression.* London, 1614. STC 18906.

Parliament. *An Ordinance of the Lords and Commons Assembled in Parliament, For Putting Malignants and Papists out of the Cities of London, Westminster, late Lines of Communication, and twenty miles distant.* London, May 1648. TT E.443[36].

Prince Rupert. *A Declaration Of His Highnesse Prince Rupert.* November(?) 1645. TT E.308[32].

Rushworth, John (attributed). *The Copie of a Letter sent from a Gentleman of publike employment in the late service neere Knaseby.* Included in *An Ordinance of the Lords and Commons … For next Thursday to be a day of Thanksgiving …* London, 17th June 1645. TT E.288[26].

Rushworth, John. *A true Relation of the Surrendring of Colchester to his Excellency the Lord Generall Fairfax. As it was sent in a Letter to the Honourable William Lenthall, Esquire, Speaker of the Honourable House of Commons.* London, 28th August 1648. , British Library 669.f.13[7].

Rushworth, John. *Historical Collections. The Second Part, Containing the Principal Matters Which happened from the Dissolution of the Parliament, On the 10th of March, 4. Car. I. 1628/9. Until the Summoning of another Parliament, which met at Westminster, April 13. 1640.* London: 1686.

Rushworth, John. *Historical Collections. The Third Part; In Two Volumes. Containing the Principal Matters Which happened from the Meeting of the Parliament, November the 3d. 1640. To the End of the Year 1644.* London: 1691.

Rushworth, John. *Historical Collections. The Fourth Part (Volume 6).* London: 1722. Viewed via British History Online.

Slingsby, Sir Henry. *The Diary of Sir Henry Slingsby, of Scriven, Bart.* Rev. Daniel Parsons (ed.). London: Longman, Rees, Orme, Brown, Green, and Longman, 1836.

Slingsby, Colonel Walter. *Colonel Slingsby's relation of the movement from Crewkerne to Lansdown, and after of the taking of Bristol.* Bodleian Library, Clarendon MSS., vol. 23, No. 1738 (3). Reprinted in Hopton's *Bellum Civile*, Somerset Record Society, 1903 (pp.90-94).

Slingsby, Colonel Walter. *Colonel Slingsby's Relation of the Battle of Alresford.* Bodleian Library, Clarendon MSS., vol. 23, No. 1738 (7). Reprinted in Hopton's *Bellum Civile*, Somerset Record Society, 1903 (pp.99-103).

Sprigge, Joshua. *Anglia Rediviva; Englands Recovery: Being the History Of the Motions, Actions, and Successes of the Army under the Immediate Conduct of His Excellency Sr. Thomas Fairfax, Kt. Captain-General Of all the Parliaments Forces in England.* London, 1647.

Symonds, Richard. A notebook mostly comprising sketches of regimental colours, and a few military notes. Harley MS 986, British Library.

Symonds, Richard. *A Diarye Of the marches and moovings of his Maties Royall Army, beginning April 10, 1644, ymediately after ye Battayle at Alresford, wch.*

was 29 of March, 1644, ending with ye ruine of two great armyes commanded by Robt. Devereux, late Earle of Essex, and Sr. Wm. Waller. British Library, Harley MS 17062. Published by the Camden Society as *Diary of the Marches of the Royal Army during the Civil War* (Charles Edward Long, ed.). London: 1859.

Tuvill, Daniel. *The Dove and the Serpent*. London, 1614. STC 24394.

Walker, Sir Edward. *Historical Discourses, Upon Severall Occasions …* London: 1705.

Walkley, Thomas. *A New Catalogue Of the Dukes, Marquesses, Earls, Viscounts, Barons …*, London, 1657. TT E.1602[3].

Warburton, Eliot. *Memoirs of Prince Rupert, and the Cavaliers. Including their Private Correspondence*. Three volumes. London: Richard Bentley, 1849.

Washbourne, John (ed.). *Bibliotheca Gloucestrensis: A Collection of Scarce and Curious Tracts, Relating to the County and City of Gloucester; Illustrative of, and Published During the Civil War*. Gloucester: printed for the editor, 1825.

Whalley, Edward. *A Letter Sent from Col: Whaley, Being Commanded by the King to declare his Majesties great dislike of a late Pamphlet scandalous to his Majesty …* London, August 1647. TT E.405[4].

Whitelocke, Bulstrode. *Memorials of the English Affairs: Or, An Account Of What Passed from the beginning of the Reign of King Charles the First, to King Charles the Second His Happy Restauration*. London: 1682 Wing W1986.

Wood, Anthony. *The Life and Times of Anthony Wood, antiquary, of Oxford, 1632-1695, described by Himself. Collected from His Diaries and Other Papers by Andrew Clark, M.A.* Three volumes. Oxford: Oxford Historical Society, 1891-1892.

Newsbooks

Note: 'TT' = Thomason Tracts, British Library

A Continuation of Certaine Speciall and Remarkable Passages:
Number 14, 28th March-4th April 1644 (TT E.40[22])
Number 16, 24th-28th October 1644 (TT E.124[27])
A Diary, or an Exact Journall:
No. 25, 24th-31st October 1644 (TT E.15[2])
No. 55, 29th May-5th June 1645 (TT E.286[27])
No. 57, 12th-18th June 1645 (TT E.288[34])
A Perfect Diurnall:
Numb. 35, 25th Mar-1st April 1644 (TT E.252[26])
Numb. 47, 17th-24th June 1644 (TT E.252[47])
Numb. 58, 2nd-9th September 1644 (TT E.254[29])
Numb. 97, 2nd-9th June 1645 (TT E.262[4])
Numb. 116, 13th-20th October 1645 (TT E.266[5])

An exact and True Diurnall of the Proceedings in Parliament:
   Unnumbered, 8th-15th August 1642 (TT E.202[38])
   Unnumbered, 22nd-29th August 1642 (TT E.202[39])
Britaines Remembrancer, Numb. 3, 26th Mar-2nd April 1644 (TT E.40[11]) *Certain Informations, From severall parts of the Kingdome … Numb.* 21 (TT E.105[27])
Mercurius Aulicus:
   Week 1, 1st-7th January 1643 (TT E.244[30])
   Week 15, 9th-15th April 1643 (TT E.99[22])
   Week 16, 16th-22nd April 1643 (TT E.100[18])
   Week 50, 10th-16th December 1643 (TT E.79[19])
   Week 13, 24th-30th March 1644 (TT E.42[26])
   Week 14, 31st March-6th April 1644 (TT E.43[18])
   Week 24, 9th-15th June 1644 (TT E.53[5])
   Week 25, 15th-22nd June 1644 (TT E.54[5])
   Week 26, 23rd-29th June 1644 (TT E.2[6])
   Week 36, 1st-7th September 1644 (TT E.10[20])
   Week 38, 17th-23rd September 1644 (TT E.69[18])
   Week 42, 13th-19th October 1644 (TT E.16[24])
   Week 44, 27th October-2nd November 1644 (TT E.18[11])
   Week 46, 10th-19th November 1644 (TT E.22[5])
   Unnumbered, 5th-12th January 1645 (TT E.27[7])
   Unnumbered, 20th-27th April 1645 (TT E.284[20])
   Unnumbered, 27th April-4th May 1645 (TT E.284[20])
   Unnumbered, 4th-11th May 1645 (TT E.286[17])
Mercurius Britanicus:
   Numb. 6, 26th September-3rd October 1643 (TT E.69[19])
   Numb. 87, 16th-23rd June 1645 (TT E.288[49])
   Numb. 101, 13th-20th October 1645 (TT E.305[12])
Mercurius Civicus:
   Numb. 19, 28th September-6th October 1643 (TT E.70[3])
   Numb. 20, 5th-12th October 1643 (TT E.70[19])
   Numb. 30, 14th-21st December 1643 (TT E.79[3])
   Numb. 31, 21st-28th December 1643 (TT E.79[18])
   Numb. 41, 29th February-7th March 1644 (TT E.36[2])
   Numb. 43, 14th-21st March 1644 (TT E.38[14])
   Numb. 54, 30th May-6th June 1644 (TT E.50[18])
   Numb. 56, 13th-20th June 1644 (TT E.51[16])
   Numb. 69, 11th-19th September 1644 (TT E.9[7])
   Numb. 72, 3rd-10th October 1644 (TT E.12[11])
   Numb. 79, 21st-28th November 1644 (TT E.19[4])
   Numb. 106, 29th May-5th June 1645 (TT E.286[28])
   Numb. 108, 12th-18th June 1645 (TT E.288[35])
   Numb. 109, 18th-25th June 1645 (TT E289[10])

Mercurius Elencticus:

    Numb. 36 (misprinted as Numb. 3), 26th July-2nd August 1648 (TT E.456[19])

    Numb. 41, 30th August-6th September 1648 (TT E.462[17])

    Numb. 42, 6th-13th September 1648 (TT E.463[6])

Mercurius Melancholicus, Numb. 8, 16th-23rd October 1647 (TT E.411[18])

Mercurius Morbicus, Numb. 1,2,3, November 1647 (TT E.407[30])

Mercurius Pragmaticus:

    Numb. 3, 28th September-6th October 1647 (TT E.401[4])

    Numb. 23, 29th August-5th September 1648 (TT E.462[8])

    Numb. 23[b], 5th-12th September 1648 (TT E.462[33])

Mercurius Veridicus:

    No. 10, 28th March-4th April 1644 (TT E.40[17])

    No. 3, 26th April-3rd May 1645 (TT E.281[11])

    No. 8, 31st May-7th June 1645 (TT E.286[32])

Packets of Letters, issue unnumbered, ending 29th August 1648 (TT E.461[29])

Perfect Occurrences of Every Daie Journall

    Numb. 46, 12th-19th November 1647 (TT E.520[6])

    Numb. 52, 24th-31st December 1647 (TT E.520[20])

    Numb. 76, 9th-16th June 1648 (TT E.522[40])

    Numb. 77, 16th-23rd June 1648 (TT E.522]42)

    Numb. 78, 23rd-30th June 1648 (TT E.522[45])

    Numb. 79, 30th June-7th July 1648 (TT E.525[2])

    Numb. 81, 14th-21st July 1648 (TT E.525[7])

    Numb. 82, 21st-28th July 1648 (TT E.525[9])

    Numb. 86, 18th-25th August 1648 (TT E.525[20])

    Numb. 87, 25th August-1st September 1648 (TT E.526[1])

    Numb. 88, 1st-8th September 1648 (TT E.526[3])

Perfect Occurrences of Parliament:

    No. 26, 14th-21st June 1644 (TT E.252[46])

    No. 28, 28th June-5th July 1644 (TT E.252[51])

    The 19th Week 19, 2nd-9th May 1645 (TT E.260[33])

    The 23rd Week, 30th May-6th June 1645 (TT E.262[3])

    The 25th Week, 13th-20th June 1645 (TT E.262[10])

Perfect Passages:

    Numb. 2, 23rd-29th October 1644 (TT E.14[14])

    Numb. 4, 6th-13th November 1644 (TT E.17[1])

    Numb. 32, 28th May-4th June 1645 (TT E.262[2])

    Numb. 34, 11th-18th June 1645 (TT E.262[9])

The Colchester Spie, Numb. 1, August 1648 (TT E.458[4])

The Kingdomes Weekly Intelligencer:

    Numb. 36, 12th-19th December 1643 (TT E.78[24])

    Numb. 50, 10th-16th April 1644 (TT. E.42[28])

Numb. 97, 22nd-29th April 1645 (TT E.279[11])
Numb. 104, 10th-17th June 1645 (TT E.288[31])
Numb. 105, 17th-24th June 1645 (TT E.289[3])
Numb. 154, 23rd-30th June 1645 (TT E.342[6])
Numb. 227, 14th-21st September 1647 (TT E.407[35])
Numb. 263, 30th May-6th June 1648 (TT E.446[11])
Numb. 264, 6th-13th June 1648 (TT E.447[10])
Numb. 265, 13th-20th June 1648 (TT E.448[20])
Numb. 266, 20th-27th June 1648 (TT E.449[45])
Numb. 266[b], 27th June-4th July 1648 (TT E.451[2])
Numb. 267, 4th-11th July 1648 (TT E.452[6])
Numb. 269, 18th-25th July 1648 (TT E.454[5])
Numb. 270, 25th July-1st August 1648 (TT E.456[8])
Numb. 271, 1st-8th August 1648 (TT E.457[16])
Numb. 275, 29th August-5th September 1648 (TT E.462[10])
The Kingdomes Weekly Post, week ending 28th November 1645 (TT E.310[11])
The London Post, no. 1, 6th August 1644 (TT E.4[16])
The Moderate:
Numb. 2, 18th-25th July 1648 (TT E.454[2])
Numb. 6, 15th-22nd August 1648 (TT E.460[18])
Numb. 8, 29th August-5th September 1648 (TT E.462[11])
The Moderate Intelligencer:
Numb. 68, 18th-25th June 1645 (TT E.341[16])
Numb. 139, 11th-18th November 1647 (TT E.416[8])
Numb. 166, 18th-25th May 1648 (TT E.444[9])
Numb. 170, 15th-22nd June, 1648 (TT E.449[13])
Numb. 173, 6th-13th July 1648 (TT E.452[28])
Numb. 175, 20th-27th July 1648 (TT E.454[16])
Numb. 177, 3rd-10th August 1648 (TT E.457[33])
Numb. 180, 24th-31st August 1648 (TT E.461[22])
Numb. 181, 31st August-7th September 1648 (TT E.462[18])
The Parliament Porter:
Numb. 1, 28th August-4th September 1648 (TT E.462[3])
Numb. 2, 4th-11th September 1648 (TT E.462[26])
The Parliament Scout:
Numb. 25, 8th-15th December 1643 (TT E.78[19])
Numb. 71, 24th-31st October 1644 (TT E.15[3])
The Perfect Weekly Account:
Numb. 14, 14th-21st June 1648 (TT E.449[12])
Numb. 15, 21st-28th June 1648 (TT E.450[3])
Numb. 16 (misnumbered as Numb. 17), 5th-12th July 1648 (TT E.452[11])
Numb. 19, 19th-25th July 1648 (TT E.454[3])
Numb. 20, 26th July-1st August 1648 (TT E.456[20])

Numb. 21, 2nd-9th August 1648 (TT E.457[24])

Numb. 23, 16th-23rd August 1648 (TT E.460[27])

Numb. 25, 30th August-6th September 1648 (TT E.462[13])

The Scottish Dove, No. 85, 30th May-6th June 1645 (TT E.286[30])

The Spie, no. 19, 30th May-6th June 1644 (TT E.50[19])

The True Informer:

Numb. 28, 30th March-6th April 1644 (TT E.40[28])

Numb. 51, 19th-26th October 1644 (TT E.14[6])

Numb. 7, week ending 7th June 1645 (TT E.286[33])

Numb. 9, week ending 21st June 1645 (TT E.288[46])

The Weekly Account:

Numb. 16, 20th December 1643 (TT E.78[29])

Num. 31, 27th March-3rd April 1644 (TT E.40[16])

The XXII Week, 28th May-4th June 1645 (TT E.286[24])

Collections of Government Papers

Acts of the Privy Council of England 1629 May-1630 May. Monger, R. F. and Penfold, P. A. (eds.). London: Her Majesty's Stationery Office, 1960.

Acts of the Privy Council of England 1630 June-1631 June. Penfold, P. A. (ed.). London: Her Majesty's Stationery Office, 1964.

Calendar of State Papers, Domestic Series, of the Reign of James I. 1611-1618, Preserved the State Paper Department of Her Majesty's Public Record Office. Green, Mary Anne Everett (ed.). London: Her Majesty's Stationery Office, 1858. Reprinted Liechtenstein: Kraus Reprint Ltd., 1967.

Calendar of State Papers, Domestic Series, of the Reign of James I. 1619-1623, Preserved in the State Paper Department of Her Majesty's Public Record Office. Green, Mary Anne Everett (ed.). London: Her Majesty's Stationery Office, 1858. Reprinted Liechtenstein: Kraus Reprint Ltd., 1967.

Calendar of State Papers, Domestic Series, of the Reign of Charles I. 1627-1628, Preserved in the State Paper Department of Her Majesty's Public Record Office. Bruce, John (ed.). London: Longman, Brown, Green, Longman's, & Roberts, 1858.

Calendar of State Papers, Domestic Series, of the Reign of Charles I. 1637-1638. Preserved in Her Majesty's Public Record Office. Bruce, John (ed.). London: Longmans, Green, & Co., 1869.

Calendar of State Papers, Domestic Series, of the Reign of Charles I. 1640-1641. Preserved in Her Majesty's Public Record Office. Hamilton, William Douglas (ed.). London: Longmans & Co., 1882.

Calendar of State Papers, Domestic Series, of the Reign of Charles I. 1644. Preserved in Her Majesty's Public Record Office. Hamilton, William Douglas (ed.). London: Longmans & Co., 1888.

Calendar of State Papers, Domestic Series, of the Reign of Charles I. 1644-1645. Preserved in Her Majesty's Public Record Office. Hamilton, William Douglas (ed.). London: Longmans & Co., 1890.

Calendar of State Papers, Domestic Series, of the Reign of Charles I. 1645-1647. Preserved in Her Majesty's Public Record Office. Hamilton, William Douglas (ed.). London: Eyre and Spottiswoode, 1891.

Calendar of State Papers, Domestic Series, of the Reign of Charles I. 1648-1649 (including undated Petitions, etc.) Preserved in Her Majesty's Public Record Office. Hamilton, William Douglas (ed.). London: Eyre and Spottiswoode, 1893.

Calendar of State Papers, Domestic Series, of the Reign of Charles II. 1661-1662, Preserved in the State Paper Department of Her Majesty's Public Record Office. Green, Mary Anne Everett (ed.). London: Longman, Green, Longman, & Roberts, 1861.

Calendar of State Papers, Domestic Series, of the Reign of Charles II. 1670. With Addenda 1660-70. Green, Mary Anne Everett (ed.). London: Her Majesty's Stationery Office, 1895.

Calendar of State Papers, Domestic Series, of the Reign of Charles II. 1673-1675. Blackburne Daniel, F. H. (ed.). London: His Majesty's Stationery Office, 1904.

Calendar of State Papers, Colonial Series, 1574-1660, Preserved in the State Paper Department of Her Majesty's Public Record Office. Sainsbury, W. Noël (ed.). London: Longman, Green, Longman & Roberts. 1860.

Calendar of the State Papers Relating to Ireland, of the Reign of James I. 1615-1625. Russell, the Rev. Charles W. and Prendergast, John P. (eds.). London: Longman & Co., 1880.

Calendar of the State Papers Relating to Ireland, of the Reign of Charles I. 1633-1647. Preserved in the Public Record Office. Mahaffy, Robert Pentland (ed.). London: His Majesty's Stationery Office, 1901.

Calendar of the Clarendon State Papers Preserved in the Bodleian Library. Ogle, the Rev. O., and Bliss, W. H. (eds.). Oxford: The Clarendon Press, 1872.

Calendar of the Proceedings of the Committee for the Advance of Money, 1642-1656, Preserved in the State Paper Department of Her Majesty's Public Record Office. Parts I, II, and III. Mary Anne Everett Green, (ed.). London: Eyre and Spottiswoode, 1888. Note: up to August 1645.

Calendar of the Proceedings of the Committee for the Advance of Money, 1642-1656, Preserved in the State Paper Department of Her Majesty's Public Record Office. Part II [only]. Mary Anne Everett Green, (ed.). London: Eyre and Spottiswoode, 1888.

Calendar of Treasury Books, 1660-1667. Vol. 1. Preserved in the Public Record Office. William A. Shaw, (ed.). London: His Majesty's Stationery Office, 1904.

Calendar of Treasury Books, 1676-1679. Vol. V, part 2. Preserved in the Public Record Office. William A. Shaw, (ed.). London: His Majesty's Stationery Office, 1911.

Docquets of Letters Patent and Other Instruments Passed Under the Great Seal of King Charles I. at Oxford, in the Years 1642, 1643, 1644, 1645, and 1646: Ed.

from Original Books in the Ashmolean Museum, and in the Office of the Clerk of the Patents. W. H. Black. (ed.). Record Commission, 1837.

Index to Acts of Administration in the Prerogative Court of Canterbury 1609–1619. British Record Society: London? 1967.

Middlesex county records: Volume 3: 1625-67 (1888). John Cordy Jeaffreson (ed.)

The Royalist Ordnance Papers. Two volumes. The Oxfordshire Record Society, 1964. Ian Roy (ed.). References marked 'WO' refer to papers now in the National Archives at Kew, those marked 'Rawl. MS. D. 395' to papers in the Bodleian Library, Oxford.

Later Commentaries and Analysis

'A Friend to Rational Mirth'. *The London Budget of Wit, Or A Thousand Notable Jests.* London: Walker and Edwards, 1817.

Adair, John. *Roundhead General. A Military Biography of Sir William Waller.* London: Macdonald, 1969.

Adair, John. *Cheriton 1644. The Campaign and the Battle.* Kineton: The Roundwood Press, 1973.

Andriette, Eugene A. *Devon and Exeter in the Civil War.* Newton Abbot: David & Charles, 1971.

Appleby, David. *Our Fall Our Fame. The Life and Times of Sir Charles Lucas.* Newtown: Jacobus Publications, 1996.

Arber, E. (ed.). *A transcript of the registers of the Company of Stationers of London, 1554–1640.* 5 volumes. London: Stationers' Company, 1875.

Ashton, Robert. *Counter Revolution. The Second Civil War and its Origins.* New Haven and London: Yale University Press, 2004.

Barratt, John. 'A Cure for the Scots', *English Civil War Times* #54, January 1988. Partizan Press.

Barrès-Baker, M. C. *The Siege of Reading, April 1643. The Failure of the Earl of Essex's 1643 Spring Offensive.* Ottawa: eBooksLib, 2004.

Beck, Theodore. 'Anthony Sayer, Gentleman, The Truth at Last'. Prestonian Lecture for 1975. *The Collected 'Prestonian Lectures' 1975-1987.* Volume 3. London: Lewis Masonic, 1988.

Bell, Robert (ed.). *Memorials of the Civil War: Comprising the Correspondence of the Fairfax Family with the Most Distinguished Personages Engaged in that Memorable Contest.* Two volumes. London: Richard Bentley, 1849.

Bond, W. G. *The Wanderings of Charles I.* Birmingham: Cornish Brothers Ltd, 1927.

Bray, William. *Memoirs of John Evelyn, Esq. F.R.S. … To which is subjoined The Private Correspondence between King Charles I. and Sir Edward Nicholas.* Five volumes. London: Henry Colburn, 1827.

Bruce, John (ed.). *Charles I in 1646. Letters of King Charles the First to Queen Henrietta Maria.* London: Camden Society, 1856.

Burne, Alfred H. and Young, Peter. *The Great Civil War. A Military History of the First Civil War 1642-1646*. The Windrush Press: Moreton-in-Marsh, 1988 (reprint). Originally published by Eyre & Spottiswoode, 1959.

Cammell, C. R. *The Great Duke of Buckingham*. London: Collins, 1939.

Carlton, Charles. *Charles I. The Personal Monarch*. London: Routledge & Kegan Paul plc, 1983.

Christie's South Kensington (auction catalogue). *Durwards Hall, Kelvedon, Essex. Monday 10 and Tuesday 11 July 1989*.

Coward, B. *The Stuart Age. England 1603-1714*. Second edition. London: Longman, 1994.

Cromwell, Thomas. *A History and Description of the Ancient Town and Borough of Colchester, in Essex*. Two volumes. London: Robert Jennings, 1825.

Dickens, Charles. *A Child's History of England*. Four parts. New York: J. W. Lovell Company, 1883.

Dixon, John. *The Unfortunate Battaile of Alresforde. Being an Account of the Campaign and Battle of Cheriton, March 29th 1644*. Nottingham: Partizan Press, 2012.

Dore, R. N. 'Dee and Mersey in the Civil War', *Transactions of the Historic Society of Lancashire and Cheshire*, 1986.

Ede-Borrett, Stephen. 'The Signatories to the Letter to the Earl of Essex', *Arquebusier – The Journal of the Pike & Shot Society*, vol. XXIII, no. 5.

Ede-Borrett, Stephen. *Lostwithiel 1644. The Campaign and the Battles*. Farnham: The Pike and Shot Society, 2004.

Ellis, Sir Henry (ed.). *Original Letters, Illustrative of English History*. Third Series. Vol. IV. London: Richard Bentley 1846.

Emberton, Wilf. *Love Loyalty. The Close and Perilous Siege of Basing House 1643-1645*. Basingstoke: published by the author, 1972.

English Heritage. *English Heritage Battlefield Report: Cheriton 1644*. 1995.

Ferguson, W. Craig. *The Loan Book of the Stationers' Company – With a List of Transactions, 1592-1692*. Occasional Papers of the Bibliographical Society, Number 4. London: Bibliographical Society, 1989.

Firth, C. H. (ed.) *The Clarke Papers. Selections from the Papers of William Clarke*. Four volumes. London: Camden Society, 1891-1901.

Firth, C. H. and Rait, R. S. (eds.) *Acts and Ordinances of the Interregnum, 1642-1660*. London: His Majesty's Stationery Office, 1911.

Fissel, Mark Charles. *The Bishops' Wars. Charles I's campaigns against Scotland 1638-1640*. London: Cambridge University Press, 1994.

Foard, Glenn. *Naseby: The Decisive Campaign*. 2nd edition. Barnsley: Pen & Sword Military, 2004.

Frank, Joseph. *The Beginnings of the English Newspaper 1620-1660*. Cambridge, Mass.: Harvard University Press, 1961.

Fraser, Antonia. *King James VI of Scotland, I of England*. London: Weidenfeld & Nicolson, 1994. Reprinted 1994.

Fullerton, A. & Co. *The Parliamentary Gazetteer of England and Wales*. Twelve volumes. Edinburgh: A. Fullarton & Co., 1851. No editor acknowledged.

Gardiner, S. R. *History of the Great Civil War 1642-1649*. Four volumes. London: The Windrush Press, 1987. Originally published by Longmans, Green & Co., London, 1889.

Godwin, Rev. G. N. *The Civil War in Hampshire (1642-45). And the Story of Basing House*. Southampton: Henry March Gilbert and Son, and London: John and Edward Bumpus Ltd., 1904.

Godwin, William. *Mandeville. A Tale of the Seventeenth Century in England*. Three volumes. Edinburgh: Archibald Constable and Co., 1817.

Goodrich, Rev. P. J. *Great Faringdon, Past And Present*. Oxford: published privately, 1928.

Hartmann, Cyril Hughes. *Faringdon in the Civil War*. Pamphlet. Printed for the author, 1964.

Hollings, John F. *The History of Leicester During the Great Civil War; A Lecture, Delivered to the Members of the Leicester Mechanics Institute, November 4, 1839*. Leicester: 1840.

Hopper, Andrew. *Turncoats & Renegades. Changing Sides during the English Civil Wars*. Oxford: Oxford University Press, 2012.

Jackson, W. A. (ed.). *Records of the Courts of the Stationer's Company, 1602–1640*. London: Bibliographical Society, 1957.

Kelly's Directories Limited. *Kelly's Directory of Essex 1902*. London, 1902.

Kitson, Frank. *Prince Rupert. Portrait of a Soldier*. London: Constable, 1996.

Lockyer, R. *The Early Stuarts: A Political History of England*. Second edition. London: Longman, 1998.

Macray, Rev. William Dunn (ed.). *Letters and Papers of Patrick Ruthven, Earl of Forth and Brentford, and of his Family: A.D. 1616 – A.D. 1662. With an Appendix of Papers Relating to Sir John Urry*. London: J. B. Nichols and Sons, 1868.

Malone Society. *Dramatic Records: The Lord Chamberlain's Office*.

Marix Evans, Martin; Burton, Peter; Westaway, Michael. *Naseby; English Civil War – June 1645*. Barnsley: Pen & Sword Books Ltd., 2002.

Marix Evans, Martin. *Naseby 1645. The triumph of the New Model Army*. Osprey 'Campaign' series no. 185. Oxford: Osprey Publishing, 2007.

McKenzie, D. F. *Stationers' Apprentices 1605-1640*. Charlottesville (Virginia), 1961.

McKerrow, R. B. (ed.). *A dictionary of printers and booksellers in England, Scotland and Ireland, and of foreign printers of English books 1557-1640*. London: Bibliographical Society, 1910.

Money, Walter. *The First and Second Battles of Newbury and the Siege of Donnington Castle During the Civil War, A.D. 1643-6*. Second edition. London: Simpkin, Marshall, And Co.; Newbury: W. J. Blacket: 1884.

Morant, Rev. Philip. *The history and antiquities of the county of Essex*. Two volumes. London: Osborne, Whiston, Baker, Davis, Reymers, White, 1768.

The National Trust. *Claydon House Portraits. A Guide to the People in the Pictures.* High Wycombe: The National Trust, 1999.

Newman, P. R. *Royalist Officers in England and Wales, 1642-1660. A Biographical Dictionary.* New York & London: Garland, 1981.

Newman, P. R. *The Old Service. Royalist regimental colonels and the Civil War, 1642-46.* Manchester University Press: Manchester, 1993.

Nugent, Lord George. *Some Memorials of John Hampden, His Party, And His Times.* Two volumes. Second edition. London: John Murray, 1832.

Peachey, Stuart. *The Battle of Powick Bridge 1642.* Bristol: Stuart Press, 1993.

Peacock, Edward. *The Army Lists of the Roundheads and Cavaliers, Containing the Names of the Officers in the Royal and Parliamentary Armies of 1642.* London: Chatto & Windus, 1874.

Petrie, Sir Charles. *King Charles, Prince Rupert, and the Civil War. From Original Letters.* London: Purnell book Services, Limited, 1974.

Reid, Stuart. *Officers and Regiments of the Royalist Army.* Five volumes. Leigh-on-Sea: Partizan Press, 1985.

Reid, Stuart. *All The King's Armies.* Staplehurst: Spellmount Limited, 1998.

Richards, Dr. Jeff. *The Siege and Storming of Leicester – May 1645.* London: New Millennium, 2000.

Roberts, Keith and Tincey, John. *Edgehill 1642. First Battle of the English Civil War.* Osprey Campaign Series. Oxford: Osprey Publishing Ltd., 2001.

Roberts, Keith. *First Newbury 1643. The Turning Point.* Osprey Campaign Series. Oxford: Osprey Publishing Ltd., 2003.

Scott, Christopher L. *The Battles of Newbury. Crossroads of the English Civil War.* Barnsley: Pen & Sword Military, 2008.

Scott, Eva. *Prince Rupert Palatine.* London: G. P. Putnam & Sons; New York: A. Constable & Co, 1899.

Smith, David L. *The Stuart Parliaments 1603-1689.* London: Arnold, 1999.

Snow, Vernon F. *Essex the Rebel.* Lincoln, Nebraska USA: University of Nebraska Press, 1970.

Somerset, Anne. *Unnatural Murder – Poison at the Court of James I.* London: Phoenix, 1998.

Sotheby's (auction catalogue). *British Paintings 1500-1850. London. Wednesday 11th July 1990.*

Thomas, K. *Religion and the Decline of Magic.* London: Penguin 1991.

Thomson, Katherine Byerly. *The Life and Times of George Villiers, Duke of Buckingham.* Three volumes. London: Hurst and Blackett, 1860.

Townsend, Dorothea. *George Digby 2nd Earl of Bristol.* London: T. Fisher Unwin Ltd., 1924.

Townsend, George Fyler. *The Siege of Colchester; or, An event of the Civil War, A.D. 1648.* London: Society for Promoting Christian Knowledge, 1874.

Toynbee, Margaret & Young, Peter. *Cropredy Bridge, 1644. The Campaign & the Battle.* Kineton: The Roundwood Press, 1970.

Toynbee, Margaret & Young, Peter. *Strangers in Oxford. A Side Light on the First Civil War 1642-1646*. Phillimore: Chichester, 1973.

Tucker, Norman. *Royalist Officers of North Wales 1642-1660. A Provisional List*. Published by the author, 1961.

Varley, Frederick John. *The Siege of Oxford. An Account of Oxford during the Civil War, 1642-1646*. London: Oxford University Press, 1932.

Verney, Frances Parthenope. *Memoirs of the Verney Family During the Civil War*. Two volumes. London: Longmans, Green, and Co., 1892.

Wanklyn, Malcolm. *Decisive Battles of the English Civil War*. Revised edition. Barnsley: Pen & Sword Military, 2014.

Warburton, Eliot. *Memoirs of Prince Rupert, And The Cavaliers. Including their Private Correspondence*. Three volumes. London: Richard Bentley, 1849.

Wing, William. *Annals of Bletchingdon, in the County of Oxford*. 'Reprinted from the Oxford Chronicle, 1872'.

Young, Peter and Holmes, Richard. *The English Civil War. A Military History of the Three Civil Wars 1642-1651*. Ware: Wordsworth Editions, 2000. First published by Eyre Methuen, 1974.

Young, Peter. *Naseby 1645. The Campaign and the Battle*. London: Century Publishing Co. Ltd., 1985.

Young, Peter. *Edgehill 1642. The Campaign and the Battle*. Second edition. Moreton-in-Marsh: The Windrush Press, 1995. First published by The Roundwood Press, 1967.

Young, Peter. *Marston Moor 1644. The Campaign and the Battle*. Moreton-in-Marsh: The Windrush Press, 1998. First published by The Roundwood Press, 1970.

Zaslaw, Neal. "An 'English Orpheus and Euridice' of 1697", *Musical Times* vol. 118 no. 1616 (Oct. 1977), pp.805-808.

Web Resources, and printed sources accessed online

British History Online
    Includes Journal of the House of Commons: volumes 2 (1640-1643); 3 (1643-1644); 4 (1644-1646); 6 (1648-1651); Journal of the House of Lords: volumes 4 (1629-1642); 5 (1642-1643); 6 (1643) <http://www.british-history.ac.uk>

Dace, Richard. *'Who lieth here?' Sir Marmaduke Rawdon (1582-1646)*
    <http://richarddace.website/pdf/rawdon.pdf>

The History of Parliament
    <http://www.historyofparliamentonline.org>

The Oxford Dictionary of National Biography ('ODNB')
    <www.oxforddnb.com> (requires subscription)

UK Battlefields Resource Centre. Created by the Battlefields Trust
    <http://www.battlefieldstrust.com/resource-centre/index.asp>

University of Leicester, Special Collections Online
    <http://specialcollections.le.ac.uk>

Index

INDEX OF PEOPLE

INDEX OF PLACES

INDEX OF GENERAL & MISCELLANEOUS TERMS

INDEX OF NEWSBOOKS

INDEX OF OTHER CONTEMPORARY PRINTED DOCUMENTS

INDEX OF STATIONERS' SHOPS

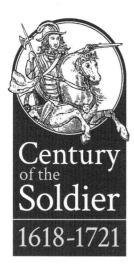

The Century of the Soldier series – Warfare c 1618-1721

www.helion.co.uk/centuryofthesoldier

'This is the Century of the Soldier', Falvio Testir, Poet, 1641

The 'Century of the Soldier' series will cover the period of military history c. 1618–1721, the 'golden era' of Pike and Shot warfare. This time frame has been seen by many historians as a period of not only great social change, but of fundamental developments within military matters. This is the period of the 'military revolution', the development of standing armies, the widespread introduction of black powder weapons and a greater professionalism within the culture of military personnel.

The series will examine the period in a greater degree of detail than has hitherto been attempted, and has a very wide brief, with the intention of covering all aspects of the period from the battles, campaigns, logistics and tactics, to the personalities, armies, uniforms and equipment.

Submissions

The publishers would be pleased to receive submissions for this series. Please contact us via email (info@helion.co.uk), or in writing to Helion & Company Limited, 26 Willow Road, Solihull, West Midlands, B91 1UE.

Titles

Books within the series are published in two formats: 'Falconets' are paperbacks, page size 248mm × 180mm, with high visual content including colour plates; 'Culverins' are hardback monographs, page size 234mm × 156mm. Books marked with * in the list above are Falconets, all others are Culverins.